Jacks, Knaves and Vagabonds

Crime, Law, and Order in Tudor England

Gregory J Durston

≋ WATERSIDE PRESS

Jacks, Knaves and Vagabonds: Crime, Law, and Order in Tudor England
Gregory J Durston

ISBN 978-1-909976-76-4 (Paperback)
ISBN 978-1-910979-93-8 (Epub ebook)
ISBN 978-1-910979-94-5 (Adobe ebook)

Cover design © 2020 Waterside Press.

Printed and bound by Severn, Gloucester, UK.

Main UK distributor Gardners Books, 1 Whittle Drive, Eastbourne, East Sussex, BN23 6QH. Tel: +44 (0)1323 521777; sales@gardners.com; www.gardners.com

North American distribution Ingram Book Company, One Ingram Blvd, La Vergne, TN 37086, USA. Tel: (+1) 615 793 5000; inquiry@ingramcontent.com

Cataloguing-In-Publication Data A catalogue record for this book can be obtained from the British Library.

Ebook *Jacks, Knaves and Vagabonds: Crime, Law, and Order in Tudor England* is available as an ebook including via library models.

Published 2020 by
Waterside Press Ltd.
Sherfield Gables, Sherfield on Loddon,
Hook, Hampshire, RG27 0JG.

Online catalogue WatersidePress.co.uk

Table of Contents

Copyright and publication details   *ii*

About the author   *v*

Acknowledgements   *vi*

PART 1: PRELIMINARY MATTERS 7

1   Introduction..8
2   Setting the Scene...21
3   The Quest for Order..52

PART 2: THE CRIMINAL JUSTICE SYSTEM 69

4   Policing...70
5   The Justices of the Peace... 100
6   The Coroner and his Inquest.. 139
7   Entering the Criminal justice System.................................. 170

PART 3: PROSECUTION, THE COURTS, TRIAL, AND PUNISHMENT 223

8   Methods of Prosecution for Felony....................................224
9   The Criminal Courts..258
10 Lesser Courts... 313
11 Trial on Indictment... 331
12 Punishment...396

PART 4: AVOIDING THE DEATH-FOR-FELONY RULE......431

13 Sanctuary and Abjuration 432
14 Down-valuing and Lesser Verdicts 466
15 Benefit of Clergy, Pregnancy, and Pardons 477

PART 5: CRIME 547

16	**Homicide and Violence**	548
17	**Infanticide and Abortion**	597
18	**Sexual Offences**	635
19	**Property Crime**	655
20	**General Conclusion**	683

Frequently Used Acronyms *688*

Bibliography *689*

Index *720*

About the author

Gregory J Durston is a barrister-at-law who has taught in Law Schools in England and Japan. He was for many years Reader in Law at Kingston University, Surrey and is currently an adjunct professor at Southern Cross University School of Law and Justice, New South Wales, Australia. He is the author, among other works, of *Whores and Highwaymen: Crime and Justice in the Eighteenth-Century Metropolis* (2012); *Fields, Fens and Felonies: Crime and Justice in Eighteenth-Century East Anglia* (2016); and *Crimen Exceptum: The English Witch Prosecution in Context* (2019)(all published by Waterside Press).

Acknowledgements

I would like to acknowledge the assistance provided by the staff of Kingston University Library, Southern Cross University Library, the British Library, and Lincoln's Inn Library. Additionally, I would like to thank archivists at the National Archives in Kew, the Surrey History Centre in Woking, the Essex Record Office in Chelmsford, and the Norfolk Record Office in Norwich, along with those of numerous other counties and institutions who have been generous with their time in helping me, and whose collections are cited in the footnotes. On a personal basis, I would like to thank Rhoda Koenig, Crystal Hollis, and Judge Nicholas Philpot, along with Professors Shannon McSheffrey, Louis Knafla, Randolf Roth, Sara Butler, and Krista Kesselring for their very considerable assistance.

Gregory Durston
London
June 2020

PART I
PRELIMINARY MATTERS

CHAPTER 1

Introduction

Parameters

This book examines crime and the criminal justice system in England between 1485, when Henry VII won the Battle of Bosworth and the English Crown, and the death of Elizabeth I in 1603, which brought the Tudor era to a close. Of course, attempting to establish a general identity for well over a century of history, one that witnessed enormous social, religious, political, economic, and (most important for present purposes) legal changes, both in England and throughout the rest of Europe is problematic. In many ways, Henry VII was the last medieval king of England rather than its first early modern monarch. His reign was untouched by the Reformation, although its latter years saw the impact of Renaissance humanism. By contrast, Queen Elizabeth was the monarch of a nominally Protestant and increasingly centralised and administered country, one that had passed through decades of religious strife and upheaval.

The early Tudor era had numerous continuities with its medieval past. Unfortunately, because 1485 is traditionally taken as the end of the latter period in England, there is a tendency to focus on what came after, rather than what had gone before, although the fifteenth century inheritance was vital. This affected not only systems of law and government but also social trends. Marjorie McIntosh has noted that many of the cities, towns, and villages that reported large numbers of behavioural offences during the late fifteenth century were also disproportionately likely to be receptive to Protestantism in the years between 1530 and 1560, and to a significant Puritan presence (with its attendant antipathy for disorder) in the later Elizabethan period.[1]

McIntosh makes a good case for seeing the years from the Black Death of 1348 (the traditional end of the "high" medieval era) to the close of the sixteenth century as a suitable period for study in its own right. In the realm of criminal procedure alone, these years saw three vital and possibly connected developments: justices of the peace started to investigate and process serious criminal matters; the grand jury (largely) finished its metamorphosis from active presenter of felonies to passive indicter of such crimes; and trial jurors began to receive the bulk of evidence at the hearing itself, rather than deciding cases on their own out-of-court knowledge.[2]

Tudor criminal law was a pervasive instrument that was used to address a wide range of social evils and problems. To keep the subject within reasonable bounds, this book is primarily about what might, very loosely, be termed "conventional" crime, something that would be recognised as such by a modern reader, rather than, for example, political or religious offences, such as treason, sedition, heresy, recusancy, and witchcraft. This was not a distinction that contemporary observers would necessarily have made. Policing the Reformation was one of the functions of the justice system. Nevertheless, the 275 or so Protestants who, like Edmund and Katherine Allen at Maidstone in 1557, were burned at the stake (the punishment for heresy after 1401) during the reign of Queen Mary, or the Jesuit priests, such as Edmund Campion, who were hanged, drawn, and quartered for treason during the Elizabethan period, are not the primary subject of this work, and will be referred to only in passing.[3] Similarly, the growing number of people (mainly women) accused of malefic witchcraft during the Elizabethan period and, at a much less serious level, the many ministers of religion who appeared in court because of disturbances occasioned by their churchmanship, such as Martin

---

1. Marjorie McIntosh, *Controlling Misbehavior in England, 1370–1600* (Cambridge: Cambridge University Press, 1998), pp. 210–211.
2. Thomas A. Green, *Verdict According to Conscience: Perspectives on the English Criminal Trial Jury, 1200–1800* (Chicago: University of Chicago Press, 1985), p. 114.
3. Michael Zell (ed.), *Early Modern Kent, 1540–1640* (Woodbridge: Boydell Press, 2000), p. 243.

Clipsam, who celebrated communion "after the popishe manner", are largely beyond its remit.[4]

In like manner, the dozens (if not hundreds) executed after Kett's East Anglian Rebellion of 1549, the more than 500 men of the "meaner sort" who were hanged on hastily erected gallows after the 1569 Rebellion (many of them convicted under martial law), when Queen Elizabeth refused to pardon lower-class rebels who had surrendered, or the thousands more who were executed after the numerous other Tudor uprisings, are not the focus of this study, although they, too, will sometimes be mentioned.[5]

Nor is this book primarily concerned with what might be termed regulatory or administrative offences, such as a failure to maintain bridges, highways, gaols, and asylums, even though the boundaries between judicial and administrative action were much less clearly drawn during the sixteenth century than is the case today. In the absence of effective local government of a modern type, quarter sessions and, to a lesser extent, the assizes, would receive presentments that identified a specific problem and led to indictments against those who, it was thought, ought to remedy it or be punished for having failed to prevent it. As a result, a "respectable" yeoman who had failed to pay his share of the cost of road repairs might find himself being prosecuted in the same list as a common pickpocket.[6]

For example, and fairly typically, at the Epiphany Quarter Sessions for Essex in 1571, and among several cases of petty theft, the Hundred (an administrative district) of Ongar and Harlow presented Bryan Darcy for allowing the mill-bridge at Machen to fall into disrepair, as it was his responsibility as Lord of the Manor of Benton. Additionally, the residents of Shelley were presented for failing to maintain the highway in two places within their parish.[7] Such actions were important; if no person or place could be charged with the relevant repairs, as was the

---

4. J. S. Cockburn (ed.), *Calendar of Assizes Records. Essex Indictments: Elizabeth I* (London: HMSO, 1978), p. 375.

5. K. Kesselring, *The Northern Rebellion of 1569: Faith, Politics and Protest in Elizabethan England* (Basingstoke: Palgrave Macmillan, 2007), p.vii and p. 185.

6. E. W. Ives, *The Common Lawyers of Pre-Reformation England: Thomas Kebell: A Case Study* (Cambridge: Cambridge University Press, 2008), p. 9.

7. ERO Q/SR 38/5.

case with the decaying Wye Bridge in Kent in 1602, the expense would eventually have to be borne by the county.[8] Nevertheless, these derelictions were not truly "crimes".

Many moral offences are also outside the remit of this book. Contemporary writers may, ostensibly, have considered adultery and theft to be equally grave violations of the norm, but they also recognised that offenders could not be executed for the former, and that it was usually the concern of ecclesiastical forums rather than secular courts. It was a matter of great seriousness, but in a slightly different way from the commission of property crimes.[9]

Instead, most of the crimes considered in this book are — or, like sodomy, were until very recently — viewed as mainstream criminal offences, even if their treatment was then radically different. Legally they were divided into two main classes: felonies and misdemeanours. The former, the primary focus of this book, were serious crimes (from an early modern perspective) for which, at least in theory, a death sentence would be imposed, and possessions forfeited, although they included some decidedly modest (to modern eyes) property offences. The Tudor era saw significant statutory additions being made to the short list of longstanding common law felonies (rape, robbery, larceny, etc.) inherited from the medieval period.[10] Such diverse offences as, inter alia, military desertion, buggery, witchcraft, holding prisoners for ransom, destroying Norfolk dikes, and knowingly receiving a Catholic seminary priest joined their ranks.[11] Even so, despite these additions, the vast majority of prosecuted felonies involved a violation of at least one of the Ten Commandments and had been common law crimes for centuries.

Misdemeanours, which were also sometimes referred to by their older name as "trespasses", were a large and diverse set of minor offences for

---

8. Louis A. Knafla, *Kent at Law 1602: The County Jurisdiction: Assizes and Sessions of the Peace* (London: Stationery Office Books, 1995), p. 39.
9. J. R. D. Falconer, "'Mony Utheris Divars Odious Crymes': Women, Petty Crime and Power in Later Sixteenth Century Aberdeen", *Crimes and Misdemeanours: Deviance and the Law in Historical Perspective*, Vol. 4, No. 1, p. 10.
10. B. A. Hanawalt, "Fur Collar Crime: The Pattern of Crime among the Fourteenth century English Nobility", *Journal of Social History*, Vol. 8, No. 4, p. 2.
11. Francis Bacon, *Cases of Treason* (London: John More, 1641), p. 8; K. J. Kesselring, *Mercy and Authority in the Tudor State* (New York: Cambridge University Press, 2003), p. 39.

which death and post-conviction forfeiture of property could never be imposed. They included what appear to modern eyes to be very mild "crimes", such as those alleged against the Reverend Patrick Fearne in 1591. The obstreperous rector of Sandon was indicted at the Essex Quarter Sessions as a common "objurgator" (quarreller) and "barrator" (one who stirred up discord) in his church and parish. He was convicted and fined 3s 4d on the first count and 1s 8d on the second.[12] However, misdemeanours also extended to most non-lethal assaults, however serious, including some offences that would be considered attempted murder in the modern era.

As with felonies, numerous statutory misdemeanours were added to existing common law trespasses during the era. These included such offences as the abduction of heiresses who were under 16 years-of-age, damage to standing crops, fence breaking, swearing, profanation of the Sabbath, alehouse nuisances, drunkenness, perjury, and the misdeeds of officeholders. By the start of the seventeenth century, such crimes often dominated the judicial duties of JPs.[13] Far more defendants came before the courts for misdemeanours than for felonies, and they were drawn from a wider range of social backgrounds. These crimes did not normally have the same moral stigma as felonies.

A third class of crime, high treason, was political in nature and would be outside the remit of this book were it not that, for arcane historical reasons, and as a result of a statute of 1416 supplementing the Great Treason Act of 1351, treason included various coining offences, such as "clipping" slivers of gold or silver currency with pincers, as well as straightforward counterfeiting (a much more skilled task, usually employing precious-metal alloys).[14] The precise parameters of this crime fluctuated during the sixteenth century. Nevertheless, and as a result, at the assizes held at Chelmsford in March 1578, George Chopin, a High Roding labourer, who had made a modest amount of counterfeit shillings and sixpences, was indicted for, and pleaded guilty to, treason.[15]

---

12. ERO Q/SR 34/23,24.
13. G. C. F. Forster, *The East Riding Justices of the Peace in the Seventeenth Century* (Micklegate: East Yorkshire Local History Society, 1973), p. 15.
14. John Bellamy, *The Tudor Law of Treason: An Introduction* (Abingdon: Routledge, 2013), p. 12.
15. ERO T/A 418/29/76.

Sources of Information

Court Records

Unfortunately, unlike the Roman law countries on the Continent, which used and preserved extensive parchment and paper records, including witness depositions, the English system of criminal law produced relatively few written records, while those that were drawn up often contained quite limited information. Frequently they were just brief summaries of charges, verdicts, and sentences, perhaps supplemented by a mention of bail status and any ancillary orders. Even assize indictments omit a great deal of information that is of vital interest to historians, such as the perpetrator's motive in cases where it is not obvious from the crime. Furthermore, many of the English records that were created prior to a hearing, such as magistrates' examinations (potentially one of the most extensive sources of information) and those bills of indictment that were found *ignoramus*, were destroyed fairly quickly afterwards. (Rejected bills of indictment were supposed to be ripped up in the presence of the defendant.) In addition, many of the formal documents produced at trial have since been lost. There is a particular dearth of records for the first half of the Tudor era, and, though present in significantly greater numbers in the second half, they are still relatively scarce, even for the highest provincial jury court, the assizes. These were not permanent forums, and so lacked both continuity and a fixed base to store records. The assize clerks probably kept many of them in their homes between circuits, a practice that helps explain their poor rate of survival. Records were also discarded in later centuries, if only to save space: there are no records at all for the large Midland Circuit before 1818.

Tudor assize records do not survive in significant numbers, anywhere in the country for the years prior to 1559; after that date they exist in large numbers only for the Home Circuit in south-eastern England, and a significant number of even these files are missing.[16] However, a few random Home Circuit Assizes papers from earlier in the Tudor era, or from other circuits, have survived. For example, those pertaining to

---

16. J. S. Cockburn (ed.), *Western Circuit Assize Orders, 1629–48: A Calendar* (London: Royal Historical Society, 2012), p. xi.

the Surrey gaol delivery held at Southwark by Sir John More (father of Thomas) and Thomas Inglefeld on 14 and 15 February 1530, including lists of Surrey coroners, justices of the peace, and bailiffs, as well as calendars of prisoners and indictments, lists of jurors, and recognisances for the appearance of the accused, still exist.[17] Furthermore, the palatinate of Cheshire (the county was then a substantially autonomous area) and its biannual Court of Great Sessions held at Chester, the county equivalent of the assizes after 1536, also enjoy somewhat better record survival than most of the circuits; this helps fill some of the gaps, even if the county was not always typical of the rest of the country.[18] Some records for Middlesex cases conducted at the Old Bailey, the equivalent court to the assizes for that county and the City of London, also predate those available for the Home Circuit by a decade. (London indictments for the court do not survive before 1605).[19]

Tudor quarter and borough sessions records are even scarcer than those for the assizes. The former, in particular, are notably lacking prior to 1549. The Elizabethan JP William Lambarde expressed concern about their poor preservation, even at the time, noting that many were left in the custody of the clerk of the peace, and when he died "are hardly recovered, and that, piecemeal, from his widow, servants, or executors, who, at their pleasure, may embezzle, misuse, or conceal what they will".[20]

No quarter sessions rolls at all exist from the reign of Henry VII.[21] Norfolk has the earliest surviving shire quarter sessions records in England, with those held from May 1532 to April 1533 available, covering sessions at Norwich, King's (then Bishop's) Lynn, Little Walsingham, and Swaffham. These include indictments by the grand jury and presentations by head constables, along with memoranda of the swearing-in of grand, county, and hundred juries, and the appointment of chief

---

17. SHC LM/961/1–16.
18. J. A. Sharpe and J. R. Dickinson, "Revisiting the 'Violence We Have Lost': Homicide in Seventeenth century Cheshire", *The English Historical Review*, Vol. 131, No. 549, pp. 293–294.
19. Sir John Baker, *The Oxford History of the Laws of England: 1483–1558* (Oxford: Oxford University Press, 2003) pp. 286–287.
20. John Lister (ed.), *West Riding Sessions Rolls, 1597/8–1602* (Cambridge: Cambridge University Press, 2013), p. vii.
21. J. R. Lander, *English Justices of the Peace 1461–1509* (London: Alan Sutton, 1989), p. 19.

(high) constables.[22] A few quarter sessions records for the urban (and so not typical) County of Norwich survive from earlier in the sixteenth century. Otherwise, only sporadic and isolated records can normally be found for Norfolk until the middle of the century. Similarly, although the Essex Quarter Sessions records are among the most complete for an English county, they only date from about 1555. More typically, those for Hampshire provide intermittent coverage from the late 1560s onwards, while in neighbouring Surrey they are totally missing until well into the seventeenth century, most not surviving from before 1659.

The paucity of early Tudor legal records, in particular, sometimes even by comparison to their fifteenth century counterparts before about 1460, has encouraged medieval studies in this area to finish at, or prior to, 1485, while those dealing with the early modern era often begin in 1558, with the advent of Queen Elizabeth, leaving the majority of the Tudor era neglected.[23] This dearth of records also places firm limits on the ability of modern scholars to quantify crimes and punishments, something that is compounded by the plethora of often overlapping criminal jurisdictions during the period, and the uncertainty of demographic knowledge. As has long been observed, it is pointless to apply statistical procedures to randomly captured data.[24]

Tracts, Notebooks, Chapbooks, Letters, and Monographs

Of course, formal court records are not the only sources of information available. There are several major legal tracts from the Tudor era or just after it. Foremost amongst them is that of the long-lived Ferdinando Pulton (1536–1618). Although he did not produce his magnum opus on criminal law, *De pace Regis et regni,* until 1609, he had been active in legal scholarship for decades, and was shaped by the late Tudor experience.

Contemporary notebooks compiled by those involved in the legal process also provide valuable assistance. For example, Sir John Spelman (c.1495–1546) was a member of Gray's Inn, a serjeant-at-law, and,

---

22. NRO C/S 3/1.
23. William B. Robison, "Murder at Crowhurst: A Case Study in Early Tudor Law Enforcement", *Criminal Justice History*, Vol. 9, p. 31.
24. J. B. Post, "Crime in Later Medieval England: Some Historiographical Limitations", *Continuity and Change*, Vol. 2, No. 2, pp. 211–224.

eventually, a judge of the Court of King's Bench. He witnessed numerous legal changes during his life and kept notebooks for much of that time. Similarly, Sir John Port (c.1472–1540), a member of the Middle Temple, who was made solicitor general to Henry VIII and later appointed a justice in the King's Bench, kept a notebook of varying degrees of thoroughness for many years from 1494, although its detail deteriorated after 1509, as his duties increased.

Lower down the judicial pyramid, the letters and notebooks of a number of active Tudor JPs have also survived. For example, much of the correspondence (official and private) of the More family, who were resident at Loseley Park in Surrey during the sixteenth century, has been preserved. The Mores were prominent gentry in the county for much of the era and held most local offices of significance, being particularly noteworthy as JPs but also serving as sheriffs and deputy lieutenants at various times. Sir William More (1520–1600), in particular, was heavily absorbed with the local administration of Elizabethan Surrey, and has left an invaluable archival record of his activities as a magistrate. Although outside the timeframe of this book, the legally trained Bostock Fuller, another prominent Surrey JP, kept a valuable notebook of his work from 1608 to 1622. Similarly, William Lambarde, a very active JP in his native Kent as well as a lawyer and legal author, kept an important record of his work in the 1580s.

By the latter decades of the sixteenth century, chapbooks — pamphlets detailing notorious crimes, especially murder and witchcraft — also provide valuable information about the justice system. They normally contained up to 16 quarto size pages (many were smaller and some longer), and began to be published during the early 1560s; their number increased significantly after about 1580. (Prior to this time, England had lacked the level of popular literacy and commercial printing infrastructure required to create and satisfy a demand for such mass-produced literature.) The author would often sell his text to a printer, who covered the cost of producing the work (usually on fairly poor-quality paper) and getting it to market, and kept any profits. The chapbooks were sold in shops, especially those in the bookselling district near St Paul's Churchyard, in London, or by travelling peddlers and chapmen, who bought them at wholesale prices from the printer and sold them in markets and taverns. They would usually retail for between a halfpenny and sixpence (depending on size and topicality), perhaps averaging two to three pence a copy.[25]

The authors of such "true" accounts of crime were often not particularly reliable reporters, frequently embellishing or even fabricating facts to fill in gaps, for literary or dramatic effect, or to make a moralising point. Comparison of two versions of the murder of a young boy named Anthony James, both published in 1606 (just after the Tudor era), show some of their limitations. The pamphlets, although often in agreement, contain a considerable amount of contradictory information, and appear to have been written for very different audiences.[26]

However, because chapbooks were sold as truthful accounts of crimes, they had to be at least vaguely plausible to their readers. As a result, when they discuss the criminal justice system in general terms they are fairly accurate; they are also an invaluable source of evidence for popular attitudes towards crime (which such publications helped shape), even if the facts of a specific case are often less reliable.

Even so, the lack of readily available sources can lead modern academics to ascribing disproportionate attention to the preserved views of a limited number of observers. The shortage of sources means that there is a particular danger that a quite localised situation might be taken as being typical of the wider nation. For example, it might be assumed that because some late Tudor parishes struggled to find men of reasonable quality to serve as constables, they all did (clearly not the case), or that because a few quarter sessions were still regularly dealing with very serious capital felonies at the end of the era, they all were (again, not the case). There is also a temptation to extrapolate what went on in the early decades of the Tudor period from the much better-recorded Elizabethan

---

25.   Ken MacMillan, "True Crime Reporting in Early Modern England", in Nicole Rafter and Michelle Brown (eds.), *The Oxford Encyclopedia of Crime, Media, and Popular Culture, Vol. 3* (Oxford: Oxford University Press, 2018), pp. 482–500.

26.   Ken MacMillan and Melissa Glass, "Murder and Mutilation in Early-Stuart England: A Case Study in Crime Reporting", *Journal of the Canadian Historical Association*, vol. 27, no. 2, pp. 88–89.

years, although the short reign of Queen Mary saw significant legal change, or even from the sometimes better-recorded late medieval era.

Lack of Standardisation

Writing on the Tudor criminal justice system as a whole is inherently difficult because of the acute lack of standardisation, especially (but not solely) in the first 75 years of the period, something that requires numerous qualifications to be made to most generalisations. In the late 1400s, much criminal procedure was still regulated by local custom and tradition, while regional government took a wide variety of institutional forms, reflecting historical, geographical, topographical, social, and economic differences within the wider country. The personal views of JPs and judges on law and procedure also differed greatly, and might affect practice at all stages of the criminal justice process. Even so, the advent of printed law books in the Tudor era encouraged much greater consistency of practice across the country.

The Impact of Printing

Until well into the fourteenth century, rote memorising had characterised much legal training. Because handwritten collections of statutes for reference did not circulate before about 1350, even royal judges had to internalise them.[27] During the fifteenth century, lawyers still based much of their knowledge and understanding of the law on what was often called the "common learning" or "our learning". This was a set of assumptions about the law held by most lawyers, much of which was acquired by participation in the formal learning exercises held at the Inns of Court or through a process of socialisation in the course of their communal activities.[28] This would gradually change after William Caxton introduced the printing press to England in 1476, some three years after he had produced the first printed book in English in Bruges.

---

27. Sara M. Butler, *Forensic Medicine and Death Investigation in Medieval England* (New York: Routledge, 2015), p. 34.
28. Ian Williams, "'He Creditted More the Printed Booke': Common Lawyers' Receptivity to Print, c.1550–1640", *Law and History Review*, Vol. 28, No. 1, p. 42.

The first printed law book in England, *Tenores Novelli*, was published in London in 1481 by John Lettou (a Lithuanian) and William de Machlinia (originally from Flanders). For the next five years they published volumes of statutes and yearbooks, although there was then a hiatus for a few years before Richard Pynson set up his printing shop in 1490 and focussed much of his energy on legal publication.[29] Such books quickly became popular. For example, *The boke of Justyces of peas*, a short anonymous work printed in London in 1506, went through 32 editions, under various titles and authors, during the sixteenth century. (Unfortunately, it was not properly updated, quickly becoming obsolete.)[30] Many other legal works followed that touched on criminal matters (whether substantive law or procedure), such as the judge Sir Anthony Fitzherbert's collection of cases drawn from yearbooks entitled *La Graunde Abridgement*, which was first published in 1514.

The introduction of the printing press had enormous ramifications for the English legal system. Although much less expensive and much more quickly produced than hand-copied manuscripts, printed books were still costly. Suitable paper was expensive and had to be imported from France and the Low Countries for much of the period, as did the type from which the books were printed. As a result, it was not economic to print short editions, and most books ran to about 500 copies. This had major consequences. The printed book solved the previously intractable problem of keeping the country up to date with the increasing volumes of new legislation emanating from London, especially in its remoter parts. For example, English printers published the laws passed by the only Parliament during the reign of Richard III just two years after it had sat.[31]

More generally, printed material helped address the acute lack of standardisation in Tudor England. This was appreciated even at the time. In a preface to his unpublished work on manorial law, the unsuccessful legal author William Barlee (1538–1610), a provincial lawyer from Essex, stressed that it would help smooth differences, reduce error, and promote

---

29. David John Harvey, *The Law Emprynted and Englysshed: The Printing Press as an Agent of Change in Law and Legal Culture, 1475–1642* (London: Hart, 2015), p. 22 and p. 92.
30. S. B. Chrimes, *Henry VII* (New Haven: Yale University Press, 1999), p. 167.
31. Henry N. Ess III, "The Sixteenth Century English Lawyer's Library", Talk delivered at the Association of the Bar of the City of New York, 28 November, 1978.

justice in the country by providing an impartial source of reference for the wider nation.[32] Similarly, William Lambarde's *Eirenarcha* of 1581 was partly motivated by the author's own service as a JP and his realisation that there was a dearth of standardised procedures regulating the office.[33]

---

32. Richard J. Ross, "Commoning of the Common Law: The Renaissance Debate over Printing English Law, 1520–1640", *University of Pennsylvania Law Review*, Vol. 146, No. 2, pp. 333–334.

33. R. J. Terill, "William Lambarde: Elizabethan Humanist and Legal Historian", *The Journal of Legal History*, Vol. 6, Issue 2 (1985), pp. 157–176.

CHAPTER 2

Setting the Scene

Introduction

A considerable number of factors — social, legal, and economic — shaped the development of the Tudor criminal justice system. Some of them warrant special consideration, as they make it easier to understand that system and the way in which it changed during the course of the sixteenth century.

Inefficiency of the Late Medieval Justice System

The late medieval criminal justice system inherited by the Tudor regime in 1485 was grossly inefficient and ineffective by modern standards. JPs, coroners, sheriffs, and the royal (rather than manorial) courts were often highly erratic and frequently partisan or vulnerable to outside influence when making decisions, a problem that survived into the early Tudor period. Corruption was widespread. John Hussey (1466–1536), Chief Butler of England from 1521 until his execution following the Pilgrimage of Grace rebellion, provides a telling (if extreme) example. He was made a JP for Lincolnshire in the 1490s and appointed high sheriff of the same county for the year from 1493 to 1494. While sheriff he released a prisoner at the Lincoln Assizes in exchange for a cash payment of £5 and two geldings. When one of his former servants was implicated in a robbery, Hussey had him released for want of evidence. He also had a mercer arrested on the word of a thief, and then appears to have confiscated the detained man's spices for personal use. Some of his fellow JPs claimed that he practised extortion, maintained murderers and other felons, intimidated potential prosecutors at quarter sessions, and packed a coroner's inquest into a violent death with his own servants. He was even forced to obtain a pardon for murder, but still made a judge in 1526.[34]

As a result of a combination of corruption, intimidation, and simple inefficiency, the attrition rate between the commission of a serious crime and the conviction and (even more so) punishment of its perpetrator was enormous. Huge numbers of even the gravest offences failed to come into the system at all, quickly dropped out of it if they did, or produced acquittals at trial, for a variety of reasons. As an extreme example, research suggests that when the (then still mobile) Court of King's Bench visited Lincoln in 1396 and determined all the outstanding peace court cases, some 255 felons were summoned. Of these only 54 appeared, the remainder presumably being outlawed. Of those who did appear, 42 were acquitted after trial, while eleven cases produced pardons and were released. Nobody appears to have been convicted.[35]

On another assessment, in late-thirteenth and early-fourteenth century London, only 104 men and women out of almost 1,000 described as killers were ultimately convicted and either hanged or died in prison while awaiting punishment. By contrast, 750 of those informally accused of a homicide offence escaped arrest, while a further 112 were acquitted or pardoned at trial.[36] At about the same time, more than half of those suspected of homicide in many parts of provincial England did not appear at court for their hearings and were simply outlawed, while the great majority of those who stood trial, whether by indictment or appeal, were not convicted, let alone executed. For example, in fifteenth century Northamptonshire only about a third of those identified as having perpetrated homicides in coroners' inquests appeared for trial, and most of them were acquitted.[37]

---

34. Steven Gunn, *Henry VII's New Men and the Making of Tudor England* (Oxford: Oxford University Press, 2016), p. 176.

35. Kathleen E. Garay, "Women and Crime in Later Mediaeval England: An Examination of the Evidence of the Courts of Gaol Delivery, 1388 to 1409", *Florilegium*, Vol. 1, p. 101.

36. Henry Summerson, "Peacekeepers and Lawbreakers in London, 1276–1321", in Janet Burton, Philipp Schofield, and Bjorn Weiler (eds.), *Thirteenth Century England, Vol. XII: Proceedings of the Gregynog Conference, 2007* (Woodbridge, Suffolk: Boydell & Brewer, 2009), pp. 107–122.

37. James Sharpe, *A Fiery & Furious People: A History of Violence in England* (London: Random House, 2016), p. 52.

The late medieval process for bringing suspected felons to trial (whether on indictment or by appeal) was particularly inefficient. In theory, the procedure required that a writ of *capias* or arrest be issued twice, after which the accused, if he had not voluntarily surrendered, was summoned four times to the county court, a failure to appear eventually resulting in outlawry. The whole cumbersome process could take a year or more. Thus, in April and May 1507, Thomas Moles and John Heath were found by inquests to have committed homicides. Both were outlawed at Chichester on 1 June 1508.[38] In the twelfth and thirteenth centuries outlawry had been a fearful sanction, allowing the summary execution of any outlaw found at liberty and the seizure of his property. By the early fifteenth century, its effects had become attenuated by overuse; those being outlawed often suffered little real inconvenience and few consequences, something that undermined the summoning process. As a result, only between 30 per cent and 50 per cent of those indicted actually attended their trials.[39]

As some of the above evidence suggests, even if crimes did come for trial the results were often benign for the accused. The medieval conviction rate for all types of felony indictment was consistently low. In the early fourteenth century, the counties of Norfolk, Yorkshire, Essex, Somerset, and Herefordshire, taken together, produce an average rate of just 23 per cent.[40] Even more modestly, in Warwickshire, during the 20 years after 1377, 231 people were indicted for felony, of whom the fates of 169 are known. It seems that just 13 (about seven per cent) were convicted and hanged.[41] More generally, a conviction rate of about 20 per cent seems to have been typical between the reigns of Edward I and Henry VI, and, provided it did not extend to treason cases, does not

38.   R. F. Hunnisett, *Sussex Coroners' Inquests 1485–1558* (Lewes: Sussex Record Society, 1985), pp. 5–6.
39.   Edward Powell, *Kingship, Law, and Society: Criminal Justice in the Reign of Henry V* (Oxford: Oxford University Press, 1989), pp. 75–77.
40.   Barbara A. Hanawalt, "'Good Governance' in the Medieval and Early Modern Context", *Journal of British Studies*, Vol. 37, No. 3, pp. 246–257.
41.   J. A. Sharpe, *Judicial Punishment* (London: Faber & Faber, 1990), p. 28.

appear to have occasioned the Crown significant concern. This was still the case when Henry VII came to the throne.[42]

The Death-for-Felony Rule

A fundamental issue facing the Tudor criminal justice system was the draconian and unvariegated nature of the punishment allotted for any serious crime, the death-for-felony rule, which it inherited from the medieval era. This was unusual in a European context. The rule had been established by the early 1200s and had only one significant modification during the remainder of the medieval period. A case in which a thief was executed for stealing just four pence worth of goods, and several others like it, occasioned concern during the thirteenth century, and prompted the introduction of a statute in 1279 by which 12 pence or more was made the measure of a man's life.[43] (Some contemporary legal observers thought that it was 13 pence or more.) This produced the crime of "petty theft", the stealing of cash or goods worth less than a shilling and, quite uniquely, a non-capital felony, for which whipping was the most common punishment.

In practice, and whatever the theory, such small crimes were rarely prosecuted before royal courts during the medieval period, greatly reducing the significance of the one shilling rule. The average value of goods stolen by those tried at gaol delivery in the 1300s was more than £3 (a symptom of the general marginalisation of royal justice).[44] However, it was far lower by the Tudor era (an indication of increasing efficiency). Furthermore, inflation had eroded the value of a shilling, a process that accelerated quickly during the 1500s. By the latter part of the century, a London labourer might earn that sum in a day. Unavailing attempts were made to raise the bar at which ordinary theft became capital. In 1593 a bill that would have effected this ultimately failed to go through

42. J. G. Bellamy, *The Criminal Trial in Later Medieval England* (Stroud: Sutton Publishing, 1998), p. 14.
43. Sean McGlynn, "Violence and the Law in Medieval England", *History Today*, Vol. 58, Issue 4, pp. 53–59.
44. Hanawalt, "Fur Collar Crime", p. 4.

Parliament; during the debate, one MP suggested that, when 12 pence was chosen, it was worth the equivalent of 3s 4d in 1590s' money.[45]

At the start of the Tudor period, almost everyone accused of a felony other than petty theft, whether statutory or common law faced the prospect of death if convicted. Approximately 80 per cent of all executions in late medieval England were for non-violent crimes.[46] Even then, the breadth of offences for which death by hanging was the set punishment, which ranged from relatively small instances of theft to the most brutal murders, appeared unjust to many observers. It did not allow for differentiation according to the seriousness of an offence and the personal circumstances of the accused.[47] This was not just an elite viewpoint; many "ordinary" people shared it. In a letter to the bailiffs of Elizabethan Colchester, discussing a case of theft committed by his discharged apprentice, Albon Clark urged that the youth should not be hanged, but receive some lighter disposal instead.[48]

The effects of the death-for-felony rule had been greatly attenuated before the Tudor era by the grossly inefficient nature of the late medieval criminal justice system (see above) and the correspondingly modest total of capital convictions that it produced. This changed quickly after the early decades of the sixteenth century, making the rule increasingly problematic. Many observers, like Robert Parsons, lamented to see so many people executed in England, and contrasted it with the much lower totals found in most other major European countries.[49] It was also widely thought that such harsh punishments were ineffectual. In the 1570s John Florio (c.1553–1625), the English-born son of an Italian Protestant refugee, spoke for many when noting that there were always numerous criminals at work in England, especially London, although "dayly ther is a great number hanged".[50]

---

45. Kesselring, K. J., *Mercy and Authority*, p. 107.
46. McGlynn, "Violence and the Law", pp. 53–59.
47. Thomas Starkey, *A Dialogue Between Reginald Pole and Thomas Lupset*, Kathleen M. Burton (ed.), (London: Chatto & Windus, 1948), p. 114 and p. 177.
48. ERO D/Y 2/7/43.
49. Robert Parsons (ed.), *The Jesuit's memorial for the intended reformation of England under their first popish prince published from the copy that was presented to the late King James II* (London, 1690), p. 254.
50. John Florio, *Florio his Firste Fruites: which yeelde familiar speech, merie Prouerbes, wittie sentences, and golden sayings* (London, 1578), p. 16.

Nevertheless, if the death-for-felony rule had been applied strictly, far more people would have been hanged than was actually the case—too many, even by the standards of an age that was not noted for its squeamishness. This encouraged the emergence or enhancement of stratagems to reduce its impact.

Circumventing the Death-for-Felony Rule

A variety of mechanisms, such as the use of sanctuary, abjuration, complainant and jury down-valuing, benefit of clergy, pleas of pregnancy, and Crown pardons, were used to reduce the toll in a way that had not been necessary in the early fifteenth century, even though almost all these privileges and stratagems existed or could have been employed at that time.[51] All but the first two survived to the end of the Tudor period and beyond.

A selection of cases from the gaol calendar for one sitting of the Cheshire Great Sessions (the palatinate county equivalent of the assizes), held just after the Tudor era in 1607, is indicative of their operation. Thus, although Richard Bradford was found guilty of murder and sentenced to death, he was given a temporary reprieve from hanging so as to be able to petition the Crown for a pardon. Raphe Darlington, who was convicted of grand larceny (the theft of oxen), successfully claimed benefit of clergy and was released. Elena Winstanley, although found guilty of several felonies, avoided immediate execution by successfully claiming to be pregnant. Daniel Casman, accused of stealing a large quantity of cheese, and James Hopwood, indicted for the theft of several hats (both cases of capital grand larceny), were merely found guilty to the value of ten pence by their Cheshire juries (i.e. non-capital petty theft).[52]

Moving county, John Skerne, a carpenter and labourer from Essex, had a variety of experiences within the criminal justice system before his final, fatal encounter. At the Essex Assizes in March 1588, he was tried on two counts of poultry theft. One, the theft of 15 hens, was indicted as

---

51. Shannon McSheffrey, *Seeking Sanctuary: Crime, Mercy, and Politics in English Courts, 1400–1550* (Oxford: Oxford University Press, 2017), p. 17.
52. TNA CHES 24/109/1, Reproduced by Sharon Howard http://www.earlymodernweb.org.uk/waleslaw/prisoners.htm

grand larceny, the birds being valued at their real worth of ten shillings by the victim. However, in the second, the (different) victim down-valued 12 geese to a ludicrous six pence, making the crime a case of petty theft. Satisfied that justice had been served, a jury acquitted him of the former count after he pleaded guilty to the latter (non-capital) offence, for which he was duly whipped. Skerne appears to have been back at the same forum in July 1590, when he was convicted of grand larceny after breaking into a house, and also pleaded guilty to another count of theft. On this occasion he successfully pleaded benefit of clergy and walked free from court. In his next encounter, in March 1591, Skerne refused to enter a plea ("stood mute"), when accused of grand larceny from a house, during which cash and valuables of more than £50 had been taken, and was remanded in custody; presumably, this was done so that he could be pressed to death under the *peine forte et dure* (see *Chapter 11*). It seems that the threat of this procedure prompted a change of heart, as he was indicted for the same crime at the ensuing July assizes, where it was also noted that he had had his clergy before. However, it seems that on this occasion he was acquitted, as at the March assizes for the county in 1592 he was finally capitally convicted of stealing £4 in cash from Anthony Baker in December 1591, and so sentenced to death.[53]

Defendants could even choose and combine such privileges to serve their needs. Richard Sandy was arrested in Kensington on 13 May, 1510, on suspicion of horse theft, but then escaped to sanctuary in the local St Mary's church and shortly afterwards abjured, after admitting several other serious robberies to the coroner. However, he was found at large, having failed to depart the realm, and then claimed benefit of clergy when convicted. Unfortunately, it transpired that he had already made such a claim five years earlier, so that he was sentenced to death.[54] The expedients used to circumvent the death-for-felony rule are considered in more detail in *Chapters 14* and *15*.

---

53. Cockburn, *Calendar of Assize Records. Essex Indictments: Elizabeth I*, p. 378.
54. McSheffrey, Shannon, "Sanctuary Seekers in England, 1380–1557" (online companion to *Seeking Sanctuary*).

English Exceptionalism

In many respects, Tudor England was similar to most other sixteenth century Western European states. Many of the same social, administrative, religious, and cultural changes that can be identified on the Continent occurred in England. Sometimes, as with the *de jure* or *de facto* criminalisation of witchcraft, buggery, and neonaticide, this was a slightly belated echo of wider developments in the rest of Europe; frequently, it occurred in a somewhat modified form, as might be expected in an island nation.

However, in its laws, especially its criminal justice system, and the way in which the wider country was administered, England was markedly different from almost all the major countries on the Continent. Even at the time, this was widely appreciated by informed observers, whether native or foreign, and whether they praised or deprecated the fact.

Tudor England had a unique system of common law, not having participated in the Reception of Roman (Civil) Law that took place in most continental nations during the late medieval period, which had replaced earlier, highly localised, indigenous legal systems. As a Venetian envoy observed in 1500, "They reject the Caesarean code of laws and adopt those given to them by their own kings". Very few English lawyers of the era wished to adopt Roman law. Even the Jesuit Robert Parsons thought that it would be troublesome, inconvenient, and possibly dangerous to replace common law, given that it had (supposedly) lasted for more than 500 years. However, Parsons also felt that it was a flawed system, brought in hurriedly by William the Conqueror to keep down the native English, and had survived even though the French descendants of the Normans had "long ago, in their own Country, forsaken them, and betaken themselves to the Government of the Civil Law".[55] Most Englishmen had a rather higher opinion than Parsons of their national legal peculiarity.

When it came to administration, Tudor England was also different from its major European counterparts, being run largely by unpaid amateurs. One reason for this was the relative poverty of its Crown; another was its political and legal history. To an extent, the two were linked.

---

55. Parsons, *The Jesuit's Memorial*, p. 248.

Unlike salaried officials, unpaid juries that would present and try felons from their own knowledge did not strain the royal purse.[56] Similarly, as a punishment, the death penalty was cheap and did not require long-term administration. Even in the early modern period, England's lack of a professional bureaucracy was no longer typical of most large states in Western Europe. By the early seventeenth century France had between 40,000 and 50,000 salaried royal officials administering central and local government. By contrast, late Tudor England paid salaries to about 1,200 men. Even allowing for the very substantial difference in size between the two countries (France had three times as many subjects), the divergence was striking.[57]

This situation had not developed without resistance; some observers, such as Sir Geoffrey le Scrope (1285–1340), Chief Justice of the King's Bench, had expressed serious reservations about handing over local administration to the county gentry in the form of the amateur justices of the peace rather than establishing a professional bureaucracy. Until the early decades of the fourteenth century, the Crown had sought the professionalisation of the sheriff's office, something that might, at least, have produced a body of experienced long-term career officials, subservient to the interests of central government. Instead, the office became one for locally resident gentlemen, selected for just a year of unpaid service.[58]

Of course, this process should not be exaggerated; even unpaid officials often had (modestly) paid assistants. For example, the sheriff had an under-sheriff and bailiffs, and the clerk of the peace assisted JPs at quarter sessions.[59] Nevertheless, such men were few in number. In sixteenth century France, as in England, private individuals could bring criminal prosecutions, and bear the attendant cost. However, in France, if a crown attorney, the *procureur du roi*, became aware of a serious crime,

---

56.   Stephen C. Yeazell, "The New Jury and the Ancient Jury Conflict", *University of Chicago Legal Forum*, Vol. 1990, Issue 1, p. 89.

57.   John Morrill (ed.), *The Oxford Illustrated History of Tudor & Stuart Britain* (Oxford: Clarendon Press, 1996), p. 44.

58.   Lander, *English Justices*, p. 108 and p. 162.

59.   Penry Williams, *The Later Tudors: England 1547–1603* (Oxford: Oxford University Press, 1983), p. 154.

he could lodge a complaint in the King's name on his own initiative, in which case prosecution costs were borne by the state.[60]

In England the heavy reliance at all levels on unpaid officeholders and functionaries, whether sheriffs or JPs, grand and petty jurymen, high and petty constables, or churchwardens, meant that the country was dependent on the active cooperation, rather than merely the passive acquiescence, of a substantial minority of the governed for its criminal justice system to operate properly. In turn, this required that such people ascribe at least a modicum of legitimacy to that system. If it became too harsh, if it lost popular support, it would become difficult or impossible to administer effectively.

Furthermore, certain procedures, such as administering torture to criminal suspects, were not practicable in the absence of a significant number of government officials who were employed and trained to carry them out and to record any results obtained. It has also been suggested that the participatory nature of the English criminal justice system, whether at the policing or trial stage, encouraged transparency and discouraged secret interrogation. By contrast, where such participation was weak and poorly developed (as was the case in Scotland), such practices were more likely to occur.[61]

The Rule of Law

It might appear slightly strange to discuss the rule of law in the context of Tudor England. Nevertheless, the concept — if not the phrase itself — had some currency, albeit usually manifest as a belief in what were termed the "rights and liberties" of Englishmen. Even late medieval people recognised tyranny and the way in which it differed from lawful government. There was a widespread feeling that a true king was distinguishable from a Herod-like tyrant by his observance of law and

---

60. Jonathan L. Pearl, *The Crime of Crimes: Demonology and Politics in France, 1560–1620* (Waterloo, Canada: Wilfrid Laurier University Press, 1999), p. 33.

61. Rab Houston, *Law and Literature in Scotland, c.1450–1707*, in Lorna Hutson (ed.), *The Oxford Handbook of English Law and Literature, 1500–1700* (Oxford: Oxford University Press, 2017), p. 683.

custom.[62] Significantly, the Kentish rebels during Jack Cade's Rebellion of 1450 expressly complained that some royal advisers were saying that the king was above the law, so that he could breach it whenever he wished, even though preserving the law was a fundamental part of his coronation oath.[63]

More than a century later, in the 1560s, Sir Thomas Smith thought that punishing jurors for returning verdicts that did not find favour with the Crown was widely seen as "tyrannical, and contrarie to the libertie and custome of the realme of England". Legal treatises spoke of the king's obligation to ensure justice for all his subjects, and of the necessary participation of those subjects in the machinery of the law. In *Richard III* and *Macbeth*, Shakespeare accepted that, in very extreme circumstances, there was a right to rebel against tyrannical, wicked, and murderous monarchs. (His work suggests that this would not necessarily be the case with simply abusive kings, as rebellion occasioned great disorder and suffering.)[64]

Whatever the reality, which was often very different, royal courts were supposed to dispense law equitably, unsullied by favouritism. During the fifteenth century, the Mayor of Bristol swore, as part of his oath of office, not merely to chastise evildoers in his city, but also to "do every man right, as wel as to the poor as to the riche".[65] Early in his reign, even Cardinal Wolsey assured Henry VIII that the criminal law was everywhere being "indifferently administered without leaning of any manner".[66] That this was desirable was also a given with ordinary people. For example, in 1611 William Adams, an English mariner who had been shipwrecked on the coast of Japan towards the close of the sixteenth century, noted approvingly that, in his adopted land, "justice is severely executed upon the traunsgressor of the lawe without partiallety". Tudor lawyers tended

62. Stephen Cooper and Ashley Cooper, "Putting Richard III on Trial", *History Today*, Vol. 63, Issue 11, pp. 35–40.
63. Anthony Musson and Edward Powell, *Crime, Law and Society in the Later Middle Ages* (Manchester: Manchester University Press, 2009), p. 62.
64. Theodor Meron, "Crimes and Accountability in Shakespeare", *American Journal of International Law*, Vol. 92, Issue 1, p. 5.
65. Pat McCune, "Justice, Mercy, and Late Medieval Governance", *Michigan Law Review*, Vol. 89, 1991, p. 1661.
66. Kenneth Pickthorn, *Early Tudor Government* (Cambridge: Cambridge University Press, 1934), p. 18.

to idealise the rule of law as a system of authority before which all men were, very roughly, equal.

The notion that law was necessary for the maintenance of society in general was widespread. Most paid lip service to Sir Edward Coke's declaration at the Norwich Assizes in 1606 that if justice were withheld "the poorer sort are those that smart for it".[67] Fairly typically, in *An Oration in Commendation of the Laws,* a manuscript treatise written in the 1540s, the Court of Chancery official John Hales wrote that if law was lost, love, shame, honesty, truth, faith, and virtue would disappear, to be replaced by "deceipte, crafte, subtiltie, periurye, malice, envie, discorde, debate, murder, manslaughter, tyrannye, sedition, Burnyng of houses, pullinge downe of Cyties and townes, ravishing of virgins, violation of widowes".[68]

All government in Tudor society, whether royal, ecclesiastical, or seigneurial, was channelled through legal forms.[69] Despite the short-lived Statute of Proclamations of 1539, Tudor England was a limited monarchy in which the King effectively ruled through Parliament and the courts. As a result, even the Crown's most serious opponents were dispatched by means of formal trials. When an officer of state who had offended the monarch was executed as a traitor, as was the case with Thomas More in 1535, the procedural niceties of a formal charge alleging an offence that was known to law, followed by public trial, and an opportunity for the defendant to present his case (even if hopeless), were observed.[70] It was a major criticism of Richard III that this had not always happened during his brief reign. For example, in 1483 there does not seem to have been any legal process before the execution of William Hastings, and very little before the executions of Earl Rivers, Sir Richard Grey, and Sir Thomas Vaughan.

---

67. Christopher W. Brooks, *Lawyers, Litigation and English Society Since 1450* (London: Hambledon, 1998), p. 24.
68. Christopher W. Brooks, "The Place of Magna Carta and the Ancient Constitution in Sixteenth century English Legal Thought", in Ellis Sandoz (ed.), *The Roots of Liberty: Magna Carta, Ancient Constitution, and the Anglo-American Tradition of Rule of Law* (Indianapolis: Liberty Fund, 2008), pp. 75–114.
69. Martin Ingram, *Church Courts, Sex and Marriage in England, 1570–1640* (Cambridge: Cambridge University Press, 1987), p. 27.
70. Narasingha P. Sil, "'My Bitter Comedie': The Treason Trial of Sir Nicholas Throckmorton and the Rule of Law in Tudor England", in Christopher Ocker et al. (eds.), *Politics and Reformations: Communities, Polities, Nations and Empires* (Leiden: Brill, 2007), pp. 381–406.

By contrast, in 1532 even the royal judges advised Henry VIII that he could not deal with his subjects contrary to law by, for example, imprisoning or otherwise punishing them without trial. The demise of Elizabeth Barton, the "Holy Maid of Kent", in 1534 is illustrative of such attitudes. Barton was a visionary (possibly manipulated by others) who publicly prophesied that Henry VIII would lose his throne, and perhaps, his life, if he proceeded with his divorce from Catherine of Aragon. Unsurprisingly, the king was keen to have her indicted for treason. However, the judiciary resisted, on the ground that her prophecy had been both conditional ("if") and not a conspiracy, as she had spoken it openly to Henry's face. A three-day conference of senior judges and high-level courtiers was held in which, despite very considerable pressure, the judiciary remained firm that Barton's behaviour did not constitute treason as the law stood. As a result, the only charge available was sedition. Unsatisfied with this, the King ultimately ensured that Barton was dealt with by a parliamentary act of attainder (rather than common law trial), being declared guilty of treason by statute and executed, as were those closely connected to her.[71]

Of course, Tudor treason trials were heavily stacked against defendants. If the Crown wished to take away men's lives, it could easily do so with a "show of Justice".[72] The Duke of Buckingham had almost no prospect of acquittal at his treason trial in 1521, not least because Henry VIII had selected the peers who would sit on his jury, all of whom were dependent on preserving good relations with the Crown. Nevertheless, the trial was conducted according to well-established procedures, and Buckingham allowed all the customary rights granted to a defendant.[73] As this suggests, trials were never entirely arbitrary affairs. For example, in a case from 1534 the judiciary laid down the rule that a judge could not communicate with jurors in the absence of the accused.[74]

---

71. William R. Stacy, "Richard Roose and the Use of Parliamentary Attainder in the Reign of Henry VIII", *The Historical Journal*, Vol. 29, No. 1, pp. 6–7.
72. Martin Aray, *The Discoverie and Confutation of a Tragical Fiction, Devysed and Played by Edward Squyor, yeoman soldier, hanged at Tyburne the 23. November, 1598* (London, 1599), p. 14.
73. Barbara Harris, "The Trial of the Third Duke of Buckingham-A Revisionist View", *The American Journal of Legal History*, Vol. 20, Issue 1 (1976), p. 26.
74. John Baker, "Human Rights and the Rule of Law in Renaissance England", *Northwestern Journal of International Human Rights*, Vol. 2, Issue 1, article 3, https://scholarlycommons.law.northwestern.edu/njihr/vol2/iss1/3

On a very local basis, the career of James Morris, a senior barrister of the Middle Temple, an Elizabethan burgess for Colchester, and also clerk of that borough provides a low-level illustration of such attitudes. He was committed to what might be termed the rule of law in the town. In his correspondence with its officers, he always advised them that the letter of the law must be upheld, even if it was inconvenient and led to extremely suspicious people being released. Although a passionate Puritan, he also applied his legal scrupulousness to local Catholics accused of sedition, resisting pressure to prosecute a man that he himself had described as a "notable papist and a lewd and busy fellowe". Even so, Morris opined that this man's behaviour was not "so offensyve to the Lawes of this realm as that by ordinary way of Justice he may be endited".[75]

The ongoing concern occasioned by the original Bridewell prison, established in 1553, is also indicative of the prevalence of such attitudes. (It gave its name to a new class of national prison used to punish low-level offences, though these lacked the powers of the original.) It was a novel and unique institution that could police, prosecute, and punish vice and disorder without reference to an external authority, such as a justice of the peace. Furthermore, its court sat without a jury, all deliberations being left to the governors. However, these features, and its dubious legal basis, troubled the authorities for many years after its establishment. Some observers, such as Sir Francis Bacon, thought that it violated the rights set out in Magna Carta. In 1577 the Recorder of London was asked to go through its original charter to identify precisely what the governors could do by dint of the letters patent granted by King Edward VI. A list of their powers was put together in 1579. In the same year, the Bridewell's governors were ordered to draft a bill to be sent to Parliament to put them on a statutory footing (it did not reach a first reading). In 1600 the governors put a series of questions to Lord Chief Justice John Popham, hoping to tidy up their institution's jurisdictional problems. For example, they asked whether they could sign warrants to authorise the search of suspected places in the metropolitan area.[76]

---

75. Joel B. Samaha, "Hanging for Felony: The Rule of Law in Elizabethan Colchester", *The Historical Journal*, Vol. 21, Issue 4, pp. 773–775.
76. Paul Griffiths, "Contesting London Bridewell, 1576–1580", *Journal of British Studies*, Vol. 42, Issue 3, p. 287.

Practical Reality

Of course, the reality of the country's justice system was often very different to the theory. As Pulton noted, there was little dispute that the king should choose as judges men who were wise, God-fearing, and truthful, who would not part from the path of justice for personal gain or advantage, and who would "denie justice to none". Even so, corruption amongst the judiciary was fairly widespread, especially at the start of the Tudor era. Indeed, it was often not identified as such. Many judges (some of whom were not very well paid) would accept retainers from the nobility and gifts from suitors.[77] This continued to the end of that era, if in a markedly less blatant fashion than at its start. William Lambarde (1536–1601), a qualified barrister and Kentish JP who maintained close connections with his Inn of Court, and so was well-equipped to make an accurate assessment (unlike many lay moralists and clerics), condemned the private solicitation of judges and judicial favoring of barristers, something that suggests that the rule of law frequently bent under the pressures of patronage.[78]

Clearly, even late in the period, at least some ordinary people thought that senior members of the judiciary who were involved in the criminal process were susceptible to bribery. When examined in October 1587, Thomas Robiant of Good Easter, in Essex, said that shortly before the Lent Assizes that same year, when a local man and his daughter had been due to stand trial for various felonies, he had been given a gold piece worth ten shillings to give to Baron Clarke, a judge on the Home Circuit from 1587 to 1593, who would preside over the hearing. This was to ensure that he would show "favour" to the accused. (Robiant kept the coin, and did not offer it to the judge.)[79] Of course, many criminal defendants were far too poor to offer worthwhile bribes.

Perhaps more commonly, rich and powerful men could influence the judicial process. This was blatant at the start of the Tudor era, declined

---

77. J. G. Bellamy, *The Criminal Trial in Later Medieval England: Felony Before the Courts from Edward I to the Sixteenth Century* (Buffalo: University of Toronto Press, 1998), p. 10.
78. Wilfrid Prest, "William Lambarde, Elizabethan Law Reform, and Early Stuart Politics", *Journal of British Studies*, Vol. 34, No. 4, pp. 464–480.
79. ERO Q/SR 102/73.

during the sixteenth century, but can still readily be identified at its close. For example, in July 1569 Francis Walsingham wrote to William More, asking that the bearer, Walsingham's wife's cousin, who had admitted his "mistake" and promised amendment in his life, be excused from personal appearance at the next Surrey Assizes. (Walsingham noted that he was a young man and this was his first offence, one that did not deserve "so sharp a punishment as open discredit in an open assembly".)[80] In 1590 Joan Hussie, whose husband, John, had been fatally stabbed by a wealthy man in London, complained about the lack of progress in the investigation: "By reason of the wealth and countenance of the offendor no triall of the fact according to justice could hitherto be had with expedicion".[81] Ordinary people had no illusions that the criminal justice system was always impartial in practice. Typically, in 1560 a fishmonger observed that at London's Bridewell prison, "beggarly harlots are ponysshed and the riche eskape."[82] Nevertheless, even the public paying of lip service to the notion of equality before the law placed some restraints on the system.

Population Increase and Poverty

England had taken a long time to recover from the demographic reverses occasioned by famine in the 1310s (part of the Continent-wide Great Famine) and, much more significantly, the Black Death of 1348. In 1450 there were only about two million people in the country. This number increased quite slowly, by well under half a million, during the ensuing 70 years, so that in 1500 a visiting Venetian could still observe that the modest population of the country did not bear any relationship to its fertility.[83] It also meant that wages were relatively high, and there was no shortage of land. However, after about 1520, growth accelerated swiftly, so that the number of Englishmen increased from about 2.4 million to approximately 3.5 million during the 60 years to 1580, despite the

---

80. SHC LM/COR/3/99.
81. Douglas Walthew Rice, *The Life and Achievements of Sir John Popham, 1531–1607* (Vancouver: Fairleigh Dickinson University Press, 2005), p. 98.
82. Griffiths, "Bridewell", p. 287.
83. Anon, *A Relation, or Rather a True Account, of the Island of England…About the Year 1500*, Charlotte Augusta Sneyd (trans.), (London: Camden Society, 1847), p. 31.

influenza epidemics of 1556 and 1559 that killed about 200,000 people.[84] By 1580 the military author Robert Hitchcock thought that England was "very populos".[85] The population had reached as high as four million by 1600 (still probably very slightly less than it had been in 1300), and was set to rise further.

Although population increase was an international phenomenon during the sixteenth century, it was particularly marked in England, as contemporary observers appreciated. When, in July 1596, it was ordered that impoverished "Blackamoors" be removed from the realm, it was also noted that there was no need for extra people in a country that had already seen one of the largest increases in the number of its inhabitants to be found in Europe.[86]

Some of the burgeoning population was decanted into the expanding urban centres, particularly London, which grew from approximately 60,000 inhabitants in 1525 to about 215,000 in 1601. Provincial towns and cities also saw significant expansion, if not on anything like the same scale. However, they were too small to absorb the requisite numbers. Although Exeter was effectively the regional capital of the southwest, it had only about 10,000 inhabitants in the 1550s (enough to place it firmly in the top eight English provincial cities). To consider a selection of important Kentish towns in 1572, Maidstone (the county town) had only 2,267 inhabitants, Cranbrook 2,415, and Sevenoaks just 1,027.[87]

This increase engendered numerous social and economic pressures. Although the English economy grew and diversified in the century after 1500, its expansion could not keep pace with the near doubling in population over the same period. As a result, by the late sixteenth century, the country could not provide ready employment for all those who were willing and able to work. Even for those in employment, inflation often outstripped any increase in wages. From 1545 to 1557, in particular, the prices for consumables soared due to a combination of successive

84. Gunn, Steven and Tomasz Gromelski, "For Whom the Eell Tolls: Accidental Deaths in Tudor England", *The Lancet*, Vol. 380, Issue 9849, pp. 1222–1223.

85. Robert Hitchcock, *A pollitique platt for the honour of the Prince, the greate profite of the publique state, relief of the poore, preseruation of the riche, reformation of roges and idle persones, and the wealthe of thousandes that knowes not howe to liue*, London, 1580, pp. 1–52.

86. G. B. Harrison, *A Second Elizabethan Journal* (London: Routledge, 1974), p. 109.

87. Zell, *Early Modern Kent*, pp. 7–38 and p. 174.

debasements of the coinage and deficient harvests.[88] The latter were partly caused by the onset of the Little Ice Age, a period of sustained poor weather caused by climate change. As a result, prices, which had been relatively stable in the fifteenth century, had trebled by the 1570s, with foodstuffs being particularly badly affected, at a time when ordinary people spent the majority of their income on sustenance. By 1600, wages for labourers in some (not all) parts of the country may have been, in real terms, as little as half what they had been a century earlier.[89]

Poverty in England may not have matched the desperate levels reached in some of its continental counterparts, but it was, nonetheless, a highly disturbing phenomenon. By the end of the Tudor era, a substantially larger percentage of the population was living in poverty than had been the case 50 years earlier. Unfortunately, even as hardship was increasing, the Reformation of the 1530s removed many traditional forms of assistance from the most vulnerable. Although their extent can be exaggerated, many of the charities operated by the Catholic Church, whether sheltered housing for the infirm, alms for the poor, or accommodation for travellers, were lost abruptly and not replaced (by poor law and private charity) for some years. For example, when John Leland visited Winchester in 1542, he noted, "There was a hospital for the poor just outside King's Gate which was maintained by the monks of St Swithun, but it has been suppressed". There was also the ongoing phenomenon of enclosure, which deprived the poorest people of access to traditional grazing on common lands, even if it promoted agricultural efficiency. When all these factors were combined with a major shock to the system, such as bad harvests, crisis conditions could quickly develop.

A Mobile Society

A combination of demographic change and an over-supply of labour greatly increased the number of the "poorer sorte" who were on the roads. This was not a new phenomenon in 1485. Increased public concern

---

88. W. G. Hoskins, "Harvest Fluctuations and English Economic History, 1480–1619", *The Agricultural History Review*, Vol. 12, No. 1, p. 28.
89. G. R. Elton, *Reform and Reformation: England 1509–1558* (London: Edward Arnold, 1977), pp. 2–3.

about transients can be identified throughout Europe from the late 1300s onwards. In turn, this development has been linked to the impact of the Black Death, which arrived in 1348, a phenomenon that quickly eroded social stability. By the late 1380s, the geographic origins of the notorious horse thief and highwayman William Rose's various accomplices in crime were extraordinarily varied. There were men from Oxford, Berkshire, Buckingham, Southampton, Warwick, Gloucester, Hertford, Wiltshire, Bedford, Leicester, Essex, Monmouth, Cambridge, Nottingham, Chester, and even one from Ireland. Rose himself admitted to committing crimes in most of these counties, along with several others, such as Norfolk, Suffolk, and Hampshire.[90]

However, although medieval in origin, the problem of transients, and the crime that was associated with them, was to become much more serious during the Tudor era, as the effects of population increase and economic hardship took hold. Their ranks and visibility were further swollen by large numbers of casually discharged retainers (early in the era) and disbanded soldiers and sailors (throughout the period), along with the arrival of gypsies from abroad.

Discharged Servicemen

Many servicemen, often still in possession of their weapons, were released at the end of the various wars and conflicts of the period. Some had originally been taken from the country's gaols in lieu of punishment, or as a condition of reprieve from execution; others had been forcibly recruited because they were vagrants. For example, in 1597 the Privy Council, sitting at Greenwich, wrote to the deputy lieutenants of Surrey, asking that they send 50 able-bodied "masterless men" to the Bridewell to be shipped to Picardy "to fill up the bands therein". (They were later warned that the selected men should not be sent over in "naked and ragged sorts", so the county had to provide them with basic apparel.)[91] In the same year, and as part of the same effort, the constables of Halstead, in Essex,

---

90.   J. B. Post, "The Evidential Value of Approvers' Appeals: The Case of William Rose, 1389", *Law and History Review*, Vol. 3, Issue 1, pp. 91–100.

91.   SHC 6729/4/114.

were ordered to press idle men for the queen's service. In response, one of those selected, a man named Thomas Keape, who had been living in the town in a disorderly manner for the previous eight weeks, "did rayle of the constables with approbrious words".[92]

Many soldiers, if they served abroad, were discharged at the port where they returned from the Continent, sometimes without the means to reach their homes. For example, in 1580, when Sir Robert Ryche directed JPs to license Richard Asheley and John Edward to undertake a journey of three weeks' duration from the coast to Gloucester (where they claimed to have friends who would help them), with permission to beg on the way, he noted that they were "souldiers lately come out of Flanders, poor men and haveinge not wherewith to sustaine there want".[93]

Such men were a particular problem in and around the metropolitan area. In 1589 500 of them threatened to ransack Bartholomew Fair in London; 2,000 members of the city militia had to be called out to deal with the threat.[94] In the spring of 1590, a substantial group of "rogues" who had been rounded up in Essex turned out to be largely made up of former soldiers. They were committed to the county house of correction, but not intimidated by the process, even threatening that they would "kyll hym that whypped them".[95]

Ultimately, these problems contributed to the Elizabethan appointment of provost marshals and the introduction of a system of passports whereby veterans were authorised to journey home via a designated route, and within a certain period of time, and also granted a sum of money on discharge at a port to fund their journey. (Unfortunately, seeing potential advantage, many ordinary vagabonds then claimed to be ex-soldiers.)[96]

Gypsies

Few Tudor social problems were entirely novel, but gypsies were one of them. They first arrived in England at the beginning of the sixteenth

---

92. ERO Q/SR 94/29.
93. ERO Q/SR 76/24.
94. John F. Pound, *Poverty and Vagrancy in Tudor England* (London: Routledge, 1986), p. 3.
95. ERO Q/SR 113/39.
96. Pound, *Poverty and Vagrancy*, p. 3.

century in a late stage of the Romani migration from India that had reached Eastern Europe in the century after the Black Death. Initially, many gypsies travelled about the country making a living as entertainers, singers, and fortune tellers, capitalising on the novelty of their dark skins, exotic dress, and esoteric language. However, although their numbers probably never exceeded the very low thousands during the sixteenth century, public curiosity gradually gave way to alarm. Gypsies swiftly became associated with idleness, immorality, crime, and disorder.[97] It was widely thought that they "deceived the people for their money; and also have committed many heinous felonies and robberies". Thomas Cromwell and Parliament attempted to deal with the problem by formally banishing these "outlandish people" from the country (22 Henry VIII, c. 10) in what was the first of four Tudor gypsy statutes. Under this act, "Egyptians" were to be shipped abroad by the first available sailing. If they did not leave within 16 days they were to face imprisonment and forcible expulsion, with their goods and chattels being confiscated by the state. However, the gypsies proved uncooperative, so that Cromwell complained they "do yet linger here within this realm". Most failed to depart and few were punished.

Subsequent Tudor monarchs attempted to address the problem in similar terms, with an equal lack of success. Queen Mary passed the Egyptians Act 1554 (1 & 2 Philip & Mary, c. 4), which complained that gypsies were still plying their "devlish and naughty practices and devices". However, the new statute allowed them to escape prosecution if they abandoned their "idle and ungodly life and company". An Elizabethan Act of 1563 also criminalised "Egyptians", forbidding their entry, ordering their expulsion, and even making them liable to the death penalty in some situations. It was made illegal for Englishmen to associate with gypsies in certain circumstances. In July 1566 six men were tried (and acquitted) at the Essex Assizes for consorting with "about 40 persons called 'Egyptians'".[98] Less fortunately, in July 1569 David and Nicholas

---

97.   David Cressy, "Trouble With Gypsies In Early Modern England", *The Historical Journal*, Vol. 59, Issue 1, p. 49.
98.   Cockburn, *Calendar of Assize Records. Essex Indictments: Elizabeth I*, p. 47.

Fawe were convicted at the Kent Assizes for consorting with "Egyptians" and sentenced to death.[99]

Nevertheless, the evidence, fragmentary as it is, suggests that gypsies could travel around England with relatively little risk, despite the draconian legislation. In 1559 it was claimed that a group of gypsies being prosecuted at the Dorchester Assizes had originally entered the country from Scotland before moving south.[100] Interceptions and arrests, let alone convictions, were rare. They often travelled in groups of a dozen or so, and seldom more than 30 or 40 people, although temporary companies of over 100 were not unknown. They would travel on foot or with small strings of horses, often following markets and fairs.[101] Some apparently proved adept at acquiring or manufacturing forged papers, giving them a measure of protection from JPs.[102]

However, distinguishing true gypsies from ordinary vagabonds (who heavily outnumbered them) sometimes proved difficult, and there was a growing tendency to conflate the two as the century advanced. For example, in March 1569 Sir Henry Weston, the High Sheriff of Surrey, sent the JP William More a copy of a letter from the Privy Council. The queen was apparently concerned by the problems being occasioned by the "universal negligent and wilful permission of vagabonds and sundry beggars commonly called rogues and in some parts Egyptians".[103] Further complicating matters, some ordinary rogues may have associated with, and even claimed to be, gypsies. In 1594 William Standley and four other men, apparently calling themselves gypsies, were seen in the company of vagabonds "commonly called Egipcians" over a period of a month. Three of them were subsequently sentenced to death.[104] In *The Art of Juggling*

99.   J. S. Cockburn (ed.), *Calendar of Assize Records. Kent Indictments: Elizabeth I* (London: HMSO, 1979), p. 88.
100. Robert Lemon (ed.), *Calendar of State Papers Domestic: Edward VI, Mary and Elizabeth* (London: HMSO, 1856), pp. 138–140.
101. Harrison, *A Second Elizabethan Journal*, p. 137.
102. Cressy, "Trouble With Gypsies", p. 61.
103. SHC 6729/11/52.
104. John Cordy Jeaffreson (ed.), *Middlesex County Records: Vol. 1, 1550–1603* (London: Middlesex County Record Society, 1886), pp. 219–225.

of 1612, Samuel Rid claimed that "many of our English loiterers joined with them [gypsies], and in time learned their craft and cozening".[105]

A combination of the mobile poor occasioned by population growth and lack of work, combined with the presence of military veterans and gypsies, meant that an unprecedented number of rootless people moved about the country. Such itinerants were often called rogues, vagabonds, or masterless men.

Rogues and Vagabonds

Rogues and vagabonds were disproportionately, but not solely, itinerant able-bodied males who, for whatever reason, had left or were absent from their home parishes and were thought to make their livings from a combination of begging, other forms of charity, casual work, and opportunistic recourse to crime. They appeared to be a worsening problem as the sixteenth century advanced. In 1596 Edmund Hext complained about the "infinite numbers of the wicked wandering idle people of the land".[106]

Although vagrancy was a problem throughout the country, it was a particularly serious one in and around the metropolitan area. Indicative of this, in the late 1570s the Privy Council wrote to the Surrey JPs complaining that vagabonds plagued the highways within 30 miles of London.[107] The villages bordering London experienced some of the most acute problems in this regard. In response, local forums attempted to limit their impact on the wider society. For example, in 1567 the Ruckholt Leet Court in Essex ordered that no-one, other than friends or relations, should take in vagrant women for more than 24 hours.[108] In the early seventeenth century, Surrey JPs attempted to curb unauthorised cottages in the west of their county; these had increased greatly, despite Elizabethan legislation against such illicit building. It was thought that these cottages often harboured "rogues" and burdened parishes with needy

---

105. Carol Mejia LaPerle, "An Unlawful Race: Shakespeare's Cleopatra and the Crimes of Early Modern Gypsies", *Shakespeare*, Vol. 13, No. 3, p. 229.
106. Newton Key and Robert Bucholz (eds.), *Sources and Debates in English History, 1485–1714* (Hoboken: Wiley-Blackwell, 2009), pp. 128–129.
107. SHC 6729/11/56.
108. D. A. Crowley, *Frankpledge and Leet Jurisdiction in Later Medieval Essex*, University of Sheffield PhD. thesis, 1971, p. 13.

people requiring poor relief. (As always, greedy landowners encouraged the problem by selling off small parcels of land for development).[109]

A specific example of the lives of such vagabonds is the career of Thomas Lynwood. In 1576 Edward Barrett, an Essex JP, examined Lynwood, who had been brought before him by the constables of West Thurrock. Lynwood was originally from Wootton, in Bedfordshire, where he had been married for 17 years and fathered three children. Just after Whitsun 1575, he had abandoned them, along with his hometown, for reasons that are unclear. Since then he had drifted around London, Gravesend in Kent, and Thurrock in Essex, associating with different men as he did so, doing short-term work when he could find it, but not being in regular service to a master or having a proper dwelling place. He had eventually taken-up with a widow and beggar named Agnes, pretending to be married to her, and living a "beastly and filthie life".[110]

Many vagabonds travelled much greater distances than Lynwood. In 1573 Philip Dyer, a labourer from Bristol, was apprehended as a vagabond at Malden, in Essex. He had been in the county for some time, carrying a false pass from his native city, with a counterfeit Bristol seal authorising him to beg. He was sentenced at Chelmsford Assizes to the pillory.[111] Early the following year, John Harte appeared at the Essex Quarter Sessions as a vagabond. An Irishman, he had been travelling round Kent and East Anglia for several months, carrying a forged testimonial.[112]

The presence of vagrants was thought to encourage much more serious offences than minor pilfering and begging. The 1572 Vagrancy statute complained that every part of England and Wales was by "rogues, vagabonds and sturdy beggars exceedingly pestered, by means whereof daily happeneth in the same realm horrible murders, thefts and other great outrages". According to the Kentish JP, William Lambarde, idle vagabonds were the "very seede of robbers and theeves".[113] Robert Hitchcock feared that they readily acquainted themselves with those who lived by

---

109. SHC 6729/11/75.
110. ERO Q/SR 58/56/57.
111. ERO T/A 418/21/41.
112. ERO Q/SR 47/17.
113. W. Lambarde, *A Perambulation of Kent* (London, 1576), p. 19.

"dicing, cosening, picking or cutting of purses: or … plain robbing by the wayside".[114]

More specifically, in July 1590, Sir John Smythe wrote to the keeper of the county gaol in Colchester, noting that two men had been convicted and punished as rogues at an earlier quarter sessions held at Blythburgh, in Suffolk, and then directed to return to their home parishes in Devonshire and Hampshire. However, they had not done this, but had "bene founde still roguinge like vacabondes and taken with two stollen pigges about them which they stoole at Malden".[115] Such transients were, almost by definition, not susceptible to the traditional informal forms of social control that were premised on a relatively static society.

This was certainly not a uniquely English problem. A concern about vagrancy and its link to crime was widespread in sixteenth century Europe. For example, Spaniards often complained about the hordes of vagabonds that infested their towns and countryside, allegedly committing all sorts of offences on a regular basis.[116]

Social Resentment

Poverty engendered widespread resentment among the poor, particularly during times of dearth, and, unsurprisingly, much of this was directed against the "political nation" — that is, the rich. Very occasionally, this produced open revolt. Kett's East Anglian Rebellion of 1549, which was sparked by resentment over rights to common land and grazing, was notable for the absence of gentlemen who openly took the side of the rebels, although a number of substantial yeomen, including Robert Kett himself, provided much of the leadership. There was clearly an element of anti-gentry feeling in the rising.[117] To an extent, it was the last peasants' revolt in England, even if many of its more prominent supporters were not drawn from that class.

114. Hitchcock, *A pollitique platt*, pp. 1–20.
115. ERO Q/SR 113/38.
116. Ruth Pike, "Crime and Criminals in Sixteenth century Seville", *The Sixteenth Century Journal*, Vol. 6, No. 1, p. 3.
117. Jane Whittle, "Lords and Tenants in Kett's Rebellion 1549", *Past & Present*, No. 207, Issue 1, pp. 3–52.

At the end of the era, the straitened 1590s produced fresh popular outbursts. In June 1595 around 1,000 apprentices took part in a riot on Tower Hill, in London, protesting the acute scarcity and cost of food, the greed of wealthy citizens, and the mistreatment of colleagues who had been punished harshly for smaller demonstrations earlier in the same month. It was the largest disturbance there in nearly 80 years (since the Evil May Day riot of 1517), and was notable for its direct criticism of the City elite. Five of the rioters were subsequently convicted of treason and hanged, drawn, and quartered on Tower Hill.[118]

The following year, the Somerset JP Edmund Hext, writing to Lord Burghley, warned that widespread dearth was prompting poor people to hold nobles and gentlemen in contempt.[119] Just two months afterwards, the doomed and small-scale Oxfordshire Rising manifested acute social resentment. It followed an abortive visit to Lord Norris, the local lord lieutenant, to complain about enclosure and grain prices. A tiny band of impoverished men, having threatened to "knocke downe gentlemen", planned to throw down enclosures, seize weapons from Norris, and kill several local landowners before marching on London, hoping to attract others to their cause on the way. A carpenter named Bartholomew Steer, who declared that he was prepared to die rather than "live like a slave", became their leader. The rising did not progress very far beyond the planning stage before collapsing. Several men were subsequently arrested, and a year later two of them were hanged, drawn, and quartered for treason.[120]

More commonly, and throughout the era, a vein of plebeian speech rejected conventional notions of hierarchy, deference, and respect for authority, often in fairly crude terms, despite the risk of being prosecuted for sedition or even treason. For example, in June 1566 Edward White, a Colchester wool-weaver, was heard warning that "the commons wyl ryse". He was subsequently convicted at the Essex Assizes of uttering seditious words.[121] In July 1591 John Feltwell, a labourer from Great Wenden in

---

118. Anon, *A students lamentation that hath sometime been in London an Apprentice for the rebellious tumults lately in the citie hapning: for which fiue suffred death on Thursday the 24. of Iuly last* (London, 1595), pp. 1–10.
119. Key and Bucholz, *Sources and Debates*, pp. 128–129.
120. John Walter, *Crowds and Popular Politics in Early Modern England* (Manchester: Manchester University Press, 2010), p. 81 and p. 211.
121. Cockburn, *Calendar of Assize Records. Essex Indictments: Elizabeth I*, p. 51.

the same county, was convicted at the same forum of an identical crime after declaring that the "gentlemen and farmers would hold together one with another so that poor men could get nothing among them". He was sentenced to stand in the pillory for two hours.[122]

Such popular resentment, which would have been shared by many of the natural "recipients" of the era's criminal justice system, placed constraints on those who controlled that system. The criminal law was made largely in the centre, and enforced in the localities, by the social elite, and primarily reflected their interests. However, the Crown, judiciary, and JPs knew that there were de facto limitations on what they could do if they did not wish to risk disorder.

Magnate Violence

Henry VII inherited a decentralised land in which there was little pretence that the Crown enjoyed a monopoly of even vaguely legitimate violence (something that Max Weber considered the hallmark of the modern state). The willingness of members of the upper orders, whether aristocracy or gentry, to pursue personal quarrels and disputes by force (especially but not solely those involving property), and their frequent de facto immunity from the reach of the criminal law when they did so, posed a major challenge for the new Tudor state. Historians have sometimes criticised late medieval English government for its failure to curb the apparently corrupting power of great Border families, such as the Percys and Nevilles, although the need to ensure protection from both Scotland and local reivers meant that there were few ready alternatives to allowing them a privileged position. However, magnates were subverting royal justice in many other regions of fifteenth century England, with far less obvious justification.[123]

For example, in 1455 Nicholas Radford, a prominent and active Devon JP, who was also the Recorder of Exeter, was robbed in his own house, abducted, and murdered nearby by a group of heavily armed men led

---

122. *Ibid*, p. 373.
123. Cynthia Neville, "Border Law in Late Medieval England", *The Journal of Legal History*, Vol. 9, No. 3, p. 352.

by the well-connected Sir Thomas Courtney. It was a brutal killing, with the dead man's body being desecrated. Even so, Courtney was pardoned within a year.[124] Such incidents continued during the early Tudor era, if with decreasing frequency. In the 1560s Sir Thomas Smith could still deplore the social disorder occasioned by powerful noblemen who "made their force their Law, banding themselves together with tenants and servants to do or revenge injury against one another". Such men intimidated or otherwise prevented those involved in the ordinary court and justice system from intervening. For example, in September 1533 Thomas Leigh wrote to Thomas Cromwell, informing him that a kinsman named John Bardsey had been savagely murdered and mutilated at Furness, in Lancashire. He claimed that the Prior of Conisheved and a man named William Lancaster had been behind the attack. Leigh's cousin had informed Anthony Fitzherbert, a judge of the common pleas and noted legal author, about the whole affair, at the Lancaster Assizes. Even so, no indictment had been put in. He asked that, as the matter was "colorably borne [evidenced] by divers gentlemen, I beg you to provide a remedy".[125]

It was not only aristocrats who became involved in such activity. Ordinary members of the gentry also used physical force to advance their interests, even fairly late in the period and close to London. In August 1574 an armed mob of about 60 men, led by Thomas Kelsey, attacked the servants and cattle of the Surrey JP Sir Edward Bray at his home in Shere. Bray subsequently complained to Sir Thomas Browne about this "riot". He asked that the county's high sheriff be instructed to call special quarter sessions to try the matter.[126] Kelsey and 19 other men, including a butcher, a carpenter, and a number of colliers, were duly prosecuted for the matter at sessions held at Guildford at the end of the same month, William More being one of the justices present. However, the grand jury threw out their indictments, so the matter did not come for trial.[127] A few weeks later, the High Sheriff for Surrey and two county JPs made a

---

124. Musson and Powell, *Crime, Law and Society*, pp. 87–89.
125. James Gairdner (ed.), *Letters and Papers, Foreign and Domestic, Henry VIII, Vol. 6, 1533* (London: HMSO, 1882), pp. 466–477.
126. SHC LM/COR/3/163.
127. SHC LM/971.

report on the incident to the Privy Council.[128] The case rumbled on for some time afterwards. Bray had long been crippled by financial problems. In about 1569 one of his creditors, Robert Lloyd, sued him in the Court of Requests. In November 1577, he was a debtor in the Queen's Bench Prison. It is likely that it was this type of problem that lay behind the attack of 1574, and which, along with local influence, explains the grand jury's decision not to indict the matter.

The Military Revolution

Innovations in military technology, training, and tactics in the post-medieval era meant that war became increasingly costly in real terms, even as European states became militarily more competitive. This required a significant growth in government revenue, as the income from Crown lands and customs dues, the traditional source of funding, were no longer sufficient. This became a regular issue during the sixteenth century, especially as Henry VIII abandoned his father's caution about conducting expensive foreign military ventures. For example, Thomas Wolsey's famous Amicable Grant was an attempt to finance Henry VIII's French wars; however, it prompted major uprisings on the Suffolk-Essex border in 1525 that required the personal intervention of the Dukes of Norfolk and Suffolk.[129] More than 60 years later, Queen Elizabeth's need to raise money and armies for war in Ireland and against Spain in the Netherlands meant that JPs regularly had to oversee unpopular local taxation. At the height of the Nine Years' War (1594–1603) with the Irish earls, some 18,000 soldiers were serving in Ulster or other parts of Ireland.

By the sixteenth century, the English Crown had started to monopolise possession of certain types of weapon, such as heavy siege artillery; it also restricted the arsenals that magnates could possess, and reduced the state's reliance on devolved military weapon-holding by building up its own stocks. For example, by the mid-sixteenth century, the Crown had access to a store of 20,000 pikes and 6,500 firearms, much of it held in

---

128. SHC LM/971.
129. J. F. Pound, "Rebellion and Poverty In Early Sixteenth Century Suffolk: The 1525 Uprising Against The Amicable Grant", *Proceedings of the Suffolk Institute of Archaeology and History*, Vol. 39, p. 317.

the Tower of London.[130] It had also funded a series of expensive coastal forts, built from 1538 to 1547 and designed to mount the increasingly powerful cannon of the period. Furthermore, the Crown launched a prolonged campaign against "retaining", the keeping of private armies by magnates, especially outside the border country of Scotland (where the demands of national security slowed the process), and increasingly made its own provision for military defence and expeditionary forces.

In the long-term, these pressures encouraged the growth of the "fiscal state", one that could monopolise tax collection and gather a large amount of revenue efficiently. This required standardised and properly enforced judicial procedures.[131] It also favoured "ordered" countries, with powerful and centrally focussed governments, strong administrative structures and tractable populations. In England government revenue in the second half of the sixteenth century was twice what it had been in the first.[132]

Contemporary Explanations for Crime

According to what might be termed the traditional early modern English (and European) analysis, crime was rooted in human wickedness. It worked on vice and weakness, and could often be attributed to the malice of the devil, who tricked humans into offending. Satan could exploit the smallest opening, so that apparently minor sins might quickly snowball into the most heinous crimes: "For sloth is linked with drunkenness, drunkenness with fornication and adultery, and adultery with murder".[133]

Pride and vanity were thought to be particularly dangerous, and fear of these vices was in part responsible for the sumptuary legislation that reached its apex during the reign of Henry VIII. (It was largely abandoned

---

130. Matthew Lockwood, *The Conquest of Death: Violence and the Birth of the Modern English State* (New Haven: Yale University Press, 2017), p. 64.
131. Noel D. Johnson and Mark Koyama, "Taxes, Lawyers, and the Decline of Witch Trials in France", *The Journal of Law and Economics*, Vol. 57, No. 1, p. 86.
132. K. Kivanç Karaman and Şevket Pamuk, "Different Paths to the Modern State in Europe: The Interaction Between Warfare, Economic Structure, and Political Regime", *American Political Science Review*, Vol. 107, No. 3, pp. 603–626.
133. Anon, *The Unnatural Father, or, A Cruell Murther, Committed by one John Rowse, of the Towne of Ewell* (London, 1621), sig C5.

in 1604.) In 1510, just after the start of his reign, Parliament passed "An Act against wearing of costly Apparrell" (1 Henry VIII c. 14), repealing earlier statutes of a similar nature. It prohibited, inter alia, the wearing of sables by those below the rank of earl, and banned foreign furs from those under the degree of gentleman. As with earlier statutes, the normal punishment was forfeiture of the garments, although labourers wearing hose above the price of ten pence a yard did so "upon payne of imprisonment in the Stokkys by thre days". Although in practice this helped maintain hierarchy in an increasingly mobile society (socially as well as geographically), its publicly expressed rationale was crime prevention, on the basis that wearing inappropriate and expensive clothing encouraged people to "robbe and to doo extorcon and other unlawfull Dedes to maynteyne therby ther costeley arrey".[134]

However, even at the time, many observers were well aware that economic factors were an important cause of crime and that much crime occurred against a backdrop of acute poverty. Even such a narrow interpreter of the law as Chief Justice of the King's Bench Sir John Fortescue, writing in the 1460s, had understood, and sympathised with, the temptations faced by the indigent when exposed to a man "havynge rychesse, wich mey be taken ffrom hym be myght".[135] Many commentators, such as Thomas More, thought that it would be much better to make provision for all subjects to earn a living than to leave them to be driven by indigence to steal and so run the risk of execution.[136]

134. Ruthann Robson, "Beyond Sumptuary: Constitutionalism, Clothes, and Bodies in Anglo-American Law, 1215–1789", *British Journal of American Legal Studies*, Vol. 2, No. 2, p. 481.
135. John Fortescue, *The Governance of England* (Oxford: Clarendon Press, 1885), pp. 141–2.
136. Thomas More, *Utopia* (Ware: Wordsworth Classics, 1997), p. 31.

CHAPTER 3

The Quest for Order

Introduction

Faced with the pressing challenges and demands identified in *Chapter 2*, whether from rootless vagabonds, violent magnates, or the need to raise revenue efficiently, the Tudor polity experienced mounting concern about crime, especially after the accession of Henry VIII to the throne in 1509. By 1561 the Privy Council could lament that across England many "shameful murders, burglaries and robberies are daily committed".[137] In 1595, near the end of the era, a pamphlet went further, and complained that the "most horrible and abhominable practises yeerly, monthly, nay howrely are used and practiced".[138]

Whether deviant behaviour really was increasing is another matter. There probably were times when general levels of order did deteriorate, such as the 1590s, when quite acute dearth may have encouraged an increase in crime, but these were not typical of the entire period. After the early 1560s, the advent of mass-produced popular chapbooks that dwelt on heinous and gruesome offences, combined with an expansion in literacy, may also have increased popular anxiety about crime, at least to some degree.

Perhaps more important, there were new expectations for order. Levels of crime that were previously considered normal were no longer deemed acceptable. The process of state formation required a more ordered society. It meant that the decentralised and often laissez-faire approach to law enforcement of the medieval era was no longer viable. As a result, magnate immunity to the criminal law had to be addressed, while the

---

137. SHC 6729/10/22.
138. T. I., *World of Wonders, a Masse of Murthers, a Covie of Cosenages* (London, 1595), pp. 1–10.

large number of poor transients who moved about the country had to be controlled. This required what contemporary observers termed an "increase in governance". The change was especially evident after the early years of the sixteenth century, although it set in before the historian Geoffrey Elton's "revolution in government" of the 1530s. Its arrival was marked by a plethora of interventionist legislation and the active enforcement of older rules.

In one instance, an act of 1541 (33 Hen. 8, c. 6) limited legal possession of handguns and crossbows to those with incomes exceeding £100 a year (longbow and long-gun possession was not restricted). These weapons were seen as inherently associated with crime, being responsible for numerous "shameful murders, robberies, felonies, riot and rout", particularly highway robbery. Those who violated the statute would be liable to a £10 fine. In 1548 a little-enforced Edwardian statute required those who "shoot guns" to register with their local JP. More generally, there was a growing desire for what might be termed the amendment of popular manners.

The Amendment of Manners

Although this was to be a particular preoccupation of Elizabethan Puritans, its roots were far older, and it extended very much further than the more pronounced forms of reformed religion. It long preceded the Reformation, being traceable to at least the Yorkist kings.[139] For a very specific, and low-level, example, in 1515 the presentment jurors of the Colchester law hundred noted that a local miller, Robert Milles, had kept a whore, contrary to God's law and "in evil example to others".[140]

The Catholic Queen Mary encouraged moral reform, just as the Protestant Edward VI had. Thus in February 1557 an order in the name of King Philip and Queen Mary, signed by the queen, and sent to the JPs of Surrey, required that every parish should have an honest and substantial man (who was also a reliable Catholic) "secretly instructed" to report on

---

139. Norman L. Jones and Daniel Woolf (eds.), *Local Identities in Late Medieval and Early Modern England* (Basingstoke: Palgrave Macmillan, 2007), p. 158.

140. Laquita M. Higgs, *Godliness and Governance in Tudor Colchester* (Ann Arbor: University of Michigan Press, 1998), p. 252.

the inhabitants' behaviour. Obviously, this included a focus on heresy; however, it went much further, and covered other forms of disorder, such as the presence of idle men and vagabonds. In the same month the joint monarchs required the Surrey JPs to meet and take measures for the "conservation of quietness and good order", including action against unlawful games and failings in the imposition of the hue and cry.[141]

The notion of reforming popular manners extended to a myriad of different forms of misbehaviour, including tippling and drunkenness, swearing, pilfering, gambling with cards and dice, playing football and other violent or boisterous games and sports, and various forms of sexual misconduct, such as fornication, adultery, and prostitution.[142] It was feared that such conduct encouraged disorder, disruption, idleness, dependence on charity, and bastardy.

For example, although football, an unregulated and potentially violent game, had been frowned upon, and periodically forbidden, since the late medieval period, the Tudor era saw enhanced (if unavailing) efforts to enforce this legislation. Thus, at the Essex Quarter Sessions in February 1562, 13 men from Good Easter were indicted for unlawfully playing football in the village. Each man was fined 12d.[143] The disorder that often arose in alehouses, which was thought to be especially prevalent amongst the "inferior sorte of people" was another particular focus of reformers. Attempts were made to control the licensing of such establishments, along with the strength of the beer they served—the relatively new hop-based beverage was normally stronger than traditional ale—and to crack down on the gambling often found within them. For example, in 1582 Thomas Keyes of Goldhanger was indicted at the Essex Quarter Sessions for keeping an alehouse in which there was much "playing at dyse and drynkynge exsessyvely". He was charged at the same court the following year for allowing unlawful games in his tavern, while two of his customers were also prosecuted for playing cards in the same establishment; they were each fined 6s 8d.[144]

---

141. SHC 6729/10/17.
142. Martin Ingram, *Carnal Knowledge: Regulating Sex in England, 1470–1600* (Cambridge: Cambridge University Press, 2017), pp. 14–16.
143. ERO Q/SR 5/9.
144. ERO Q/SR 80/63 and Q/SR 85/30.

Progress was slow, as even some clerics resisted the erosion of traditional recreations. In May 1585 Thomas Cooper, the Bishop of Winchester, wrote to all clergymen, constables, and churchwardens within his diocese deploring the "heathenish and ungodly custom" of holding church ales, May games, and Morris dances on Sundays to support the repair of church fabric. This was, apparently, still widespread in the diocese, despite Protestant reform. He asked that anyone found drinking, dancing, and gambling on the Sabbath and other days of prayer should be bound over to appear before the JPs at quarter sessions.[145]

Increased Surveillance

The search for order in an increasingly mobile world also spawned the rise of what has been termed (with considerable exaggeration) a "surveillance state", manifest in various measures aimed at keeping the authorities apprised of what was going on in the lower reaches of society. For example, the keeping of parish registers was made compulsory in 1538, when Thomas Cromwell declared that clergymen should keep a record of every wedding, christening, and burial that took place in their livings.[146] Licences allowing begging and travelling, for specific individuals in particular circumstances, were also introduced.

Unfortunately, forged documents were endemic, and difficult to challenge in an era of limited communication, greatly limiting the effectiveness of the law. For example, in December 1581 Edward Symson was detained by the constable of Terling, in Essex, and taken before Anthony Maxey, a local JP, for examination. Symson claimed that there were at least two expert counterfeiters at work in the county. One of them, Davy Bennett, could produce a variety of "counterfeite pasportes". Typically, they might identify someone as a soldier travelling home from Berwick-upon-Tweed after disbandment. Bennett could apparently counterfeit the seal of any magistrate in his county from sight, and carried a small bag of them around with him.[147] Such documents were not expensive. In the

---

145. SHC LM/COR/3/377.
146. Edward Higgs, *Identifying the English: A History of Personal Identification 1500 to the Present* (London: Continuum, 2011), p. 75.
147. ERO Q/SR 79/92.

summer of 1590, Sir Henry Graye examined a group of men who were travelling through Essex under false names and documentation. One of them, Thomas Hastings, had travelled around Leicestershire, Kent, and East Anglia using a forged passport for which he had paid a shilling.[148] Two years later, John Ive, an Essex JP, questioned Robert Buck, a sawyer from Dedham, as to who had made his counterfeit passport. Ostensibly, it had been issued in the names of the minister of Dedham, his master (who had supposedly authorised him to leave his employment), and local constables, complete with formal seals. Buck revealed that Thomas Elmes, a disabled tailor from the same town, had forged the document for the modest sum of 2d. Elmes subsequently confirmed the allegation.[149]

Increasing Efficiency of the Criminal Justice System

Although, by modern standards, the Tudor criminal justice system was still extremely inefficient, after the early years of Henry VIII's reign it became much more effective. This became increasingly apparent during the remainder of the sixteenth century, particularly following the Marian reforms of the 1550s. Both the rate of prosecution of those who committed serious crimes and their conviction rate at trial grew significantly.[150] One explanation lies in the greater attempts by central government to deal with failings in the common law courts and among its officials, not least by its use of the Court of Star Chamber.

Star Chamber

Star Chamber was the judicial arm of the King's Council, from which it had emerged during the late medieval period, although it did not become fully separate until about 1540. It was founded on the use of the monarch's prerogative, and gradually became a separate court in the years after 1485, receiving a major boost as a result of the Act *Pro Camera Stellata* of 1487, and again after the accession of Henry VIII in 1509.

---

148. ERO Q/SR 113/39.
149. ERO Q/SR 120/46.
150. J. G. Bellamy, *The Criminal Trial in Later Medieval England* (Toronto: University of Toronto Press, 1998), p. 14.

Star Chamber judicial business expanded particularly rapidly during the chancellorship of Thomas Wolsey (1515–1529), who placed the court on a more organized, resourced, and efficient basis, and who was a self-professed opponent of disorder, inefficiency, and corruption in the wider criminal justice system. By the 1530s the court was dealing with about 150 cases a year, but this had quadrupled by 1600. To a significant extent, it became a criminal court of equity, supplementing the common law criminal process, although in its early decades it also dealt with some civil matters (a practice that was largely abandoned during the reign of Queen Elizabeth).[151]

Star Chamber judges (it had a collegial bench) were normally drawn from senior royal/privy councillors, such as the Lord Chancellor, the Lord Treasurer, and the Lord Privy Seal, along with the judiciary of the common law courts, particularly the chief justices of the King's Bench and Common Pleas, supplemented by puisne judges from the same forums. An Act in 1529 slightly modified its composition, its main effect being to add the Lord President of the Council to the court's bench.[152]

Proceedings in a Star Chamber case began by the plaintiff issuing a petition, addressed to the King or Lord Chancellor (who presided over the court), setting forth his grievance and asking for a remedy. It was relatively easy to make a Star Chamber matter of most criminal justice problems, if only by claiming that local influence was preventing the normal system from operating properly. Although it did not use a jury, the Star Chamber was not an informal summary court. It employed written pleadings and interrogations of the defendant and witnesses in a quasi-inquisitorial procedure.[153] Only a minority of the cases submitted ultimately produced a public trial. Where this did occur, the parties would be summoned by subpoena to appear before the judges in London. By the Elizabethan period, the Star Chamber would often meet two mornings a week.

---

151. John H. Langbein et al., *History of the Common Law: The Development of Anglo-American Legal Institutions* (New York: Aspen Publishers, 2009), pp. 560–561.

152. F. W. Brooks, *Yorkshire and the Star Chamber* (Micklegate: East Yorkshire Local History Society, 1954), p. 21.

153. Thomas G. Barnes, "Star Chamber Mythology", *American Journal of Legal History*, Vol. 5, No. 1, pp. 2–9.

However, despite the eminence of its judges, the Star Chamber had what was essentially a misdemeanour jurisdiction, so that it could not touch life or limb, although it occasionally mutilated those convicted before it by ordering that their ears be cut off or their nostrils slit. More commonly, it subjected those found guilty to public humiliation by requiring them to wear papers setting out their offence while standing in the pillory, or even when riding at a horse's "tail". Even so, the vast majority of its sentences involved fines or imprisonment, the latter usually for just a few months and often in the Fleet Prison.

Many Star Chamber cases concerned longstanding allegations of serious crimes that had not previously been prosecuted because of a failure in the criminal justice system where they arose, especially at the assizes and quarter sessions. As a result, the forum played an important role in establishing the rule of law during the early 1500s. The court received, inter alia, numerous allegations of public disorder, riot, forcible entry, arson, and assault that had originated in private disputes about property rights. For example, in about 1554, Roger Poole petitioned for John Sawen and a group of men from Blastford Hill, in Essex, to be called before the Star Chamber to answer his complaint that they had forcibly entered his estate.[154]

These issues could be complicated, and establishing the truth was sometimes difficult. In 1534 a bitter dispute over the ownership of property at Shipbourne, in Kent, resulted in a justice of the peace, Sir Richard Clement, being sent to the Fleet. Sir John Crosse had asked the magistrate to expel one Robert Brenner from the premises at Shipbourne, alleging that he had entered illegally. Sir Richard then raised almost 200 men locally and managed to re-enter the property and eject Brenner's men. However, Brenner complained to the Star Chamber, which concluded that he had been expelled unlawfully, leading to Sir Richard's (temporary) incarceration.[155]

The Star Chamber also played a major role in dealing with institutional failings and corruption in the criminal justice system. The preamble to the

---

154. ERO D/P. 220/25/52.
155. Malcolm Mercer, "Sir Richard Clement, Ightham Mote and Local Disorder in the Early Tudor Period", *Archaeologia Cantiana*, Vol. 115, p. 155.

1487 Act, which had set out the evils it was intended to remedy, included, inter alia, the "untrue demeanings of sheriffs in making of panels and other untrue returns, by taking of money by juries". Together, these failings could mean that the "laws of the land in execution have little effect, [leading] to the increase of murders [and] robberies".[156] Hans Symonds, a German merchant who visited York with a female companion, may have been on the receiving end of just such corrupt practices. The pair were unjustly arrested and brought before the city sheriffs on a charge of felony. They accused Symonds of running away with a man's wife or servant and his goods, and seized his purse, which contained cash and jewels worth more than £70, before committing him to gaol. Subsequently, they tried to bribe the woman to implicate him and then tried to extort money to release the pair. The couple were eventually released, but a significant part of their seized property was not returned. Hans took up his case in the Star Chamber.[157]

Similarly, in either 1514 or 1526, Robert Bolton petitioned the Star Chamber asking that Raufe Shirley (this appears to mean his son Richard Shirley), the High Sheriff of Sussex, be ordered to return his goods, which were worth £20. Bolton had gone down from Cambridge University with his "arayment and stuff" and decided to visit Sussex with a view to taking a farm there. The sheriff had arrested him, "supposing him to be a felon and to have stolen his said arrayment". Shirley had then taken Bolton to his estate at Wiston and held him for five weeks until having him indicted for felony, of which he was acquitted (unsurprisingly, given the absence of a victim).[158]

It was not just the failings of high sheriffs that came before the court. Juries (dealt with elsewhere) and justices of the peace also featured regularly in the allegations made to the Star Chamber. For example, in 1538 an incident involving several Devon JPs led to Attorney General Sir John Baker's bringing a bill of complaint in the court. It was alleged that the justices were guilty of concealing a serious robbery committed by two

---

156. Ryan Patrick Alford, "The Star Chamber and the Regulation of the Legal Profession 1570–1640", *American Journal of Legal History*, Vol. 51, No. 4, p. 648.
157. Brooks, *Yorkshire and the Star Chamber*, p. 6 and p. 22.
158. Percy D. Mundy (ed.), *Abstracts of Star Chamber Proceedings Relating to the County of Sussex, Henry VII to Philip and Mary* (Lewes: Sussex Record Society, 1913), p. 45.

nephews of Andrew Hillersden (one of the magistrates involved). Their case had been heard at the October quarter sessions, but produced no convictions, and little effort appears to have been made to apprehend other accomplices to the crime. More generally, John Hull, an Exeter lawyer, claimed that Hillersden and others had accepted payment to save other thieves and murderers, so that local justice had been perverted. Although Sir George Carew, the High Sheriff for Devon, had not attended the relevant sessions because of an outbreak of plague in the area, he promised to take a more active supervisory role in future. (The JPs involved maintained their innocence.)[159]

At an even more elevated level, in January 1525 Lord Dacre was summoned before Cardinal Wolsey and members of the council in the Star Chamber for an investigation into how he had discharged his law-enforcement duties on the Scottish Border. He admitted, amongst other transgressions, to "remysnes & negligens" in punishing thieves, and even being familiar with those he knew to have committed serious felonies. He was committed to the Fleet Prison, although released in September that year to help negotiate an extension of the truce with Scotland. He compounded for his maladministration of justice with a payment of 1,500 marks (about £1,000), and was dismissed from all three Lord Warden of the Marches offices and various northern commissions of the peace. He also entered into heavy recognisances for his future good conduct, and promised to do his best to bring to justice all thieves, murderers, and outlaws with whom he had had dealings. (In the event, he died after falling from his horse at the end of October.) Cases like these meant that the Star Chamber made a major contribution to improving the quality and consistency of the English criminal justice system during the Tudor era.[160]

159. Mary L. Robertson, "'The Art of the Possible': Thomas Cromwell's Management of West Country Government", *The Historical Journal*, Vol. 32, No. 4, p. 800.
160. Steven G. Ellis, "A Border Baron and the Tudor State: The Rise and Fall of Lord Dacre of the North", *The Historical Journal*, Vol. 35, No. 2, pp. 266–267.

Controlling Magnates

The Star Chamber also provided a powerful forum to deal with the dis-order (see *Chapter 2*) produced by locally powerful "noble men" who could not otherwise be controlled by "meane Gentlemen".[161] For example, in the late 1510s, what has been described as a "judicial offensive" took place in the court against important members of the Cheshire gentry who had committed serious crimes in their county. (Few cases from the area had reached the court in previous decades.) Thus, in November 1518 Sir William Brereton was fined for his involvement in the murder of Lawrence Swettenham while they were playing bowls at Brereton Green, some two years earlier.[162]

However, sometimes, even the Star Chamber was not up to this task, and the Privy Council had to have recourse to alternative methods of adjudication to deal with magnate quarrels. For example, in 1580 the Earl of Oxford fathered an illegitimate child by a gentlewoman who was under the protection of Sir Thomas Knyvett, engendering a feud between the two men. This included an assassination attempt on Knyvett and several armed affrays between their retainers and servants in the streets of London, in which four men were killed and three more seriously wounded. Even so, the courtiers responsible were too powerful to be indicted. Ultimately, the Privy Council pacified the situation in other ways.[163]

Similarly, in 1589, following "mutual provocations", Sir Thomas Langton and 80 of his men besieged Sir Thomas Houghton and 30 of his followers at Lea Hall, in Lancashire, after the latter had seized some of the former's cattle. When they finally broke in, they killed Houghton and at least one of his men.[164] Langton, who was wounded in the confrontation, was subsequently arrested. The government established a special commission to investigate this case of inter-gentry feuding, but only three of the

---

161. Thomas Smith, *De Republica Anglorum* (London, 1583), pp. 125–126; Alford, "The Star Chamber", p. 647.
162. Tim Thornton, *Cheshire and the Tudor State, 1480–1560* (London: Royal Historical Society, 2000), p. 111 and pp. 189–192.
163. Lawrence Stone, *The Crisis of the Aristocracy, 1558–1641* (Oxford: Clarendon Press, 1964), p. 168.
164. Keith Wrightson, *English Society 1580–1680* (New Brunswick, New Jersey: Rutgers University Press, 2003), p. 168.

appointed jurors turned up. The rest were too intimidated by the local power of those responsible, so that no formal presentment was ever made, and Langton and his accomplices were never tried, despite the queen's expressing concern that the perpetrators had escaped without punishment.[165] Eventually, after two years had passed, Lord Derby interceded with Lord Burghley, asking that further proceedings be abandoned in what had been the "most dangerous quarrel betwixt the gentlemen that any county of her Majesty's hath this many years contained".[166] Again, the Privy Council had to deal with it using alternative means. Langton was released, but transferred the Manor of Walton to Thomas' son Sir Richard Houghton in compensation.[167]

Nevertheless, despite such cases, and largely as a result of pressure from both the Star Chamber and the Privy Council, upper-class violence and de facto immunity from the criminal law was on a firmly downward trend long before the end of the Tudor era, although it would linger well into the seventeenth century and beyond. Pacification became increasingly marked. This can be seen in the construction of gentlemen's houses. In the early sixteenth century, although very far from being castles, they sometimes incorporated a modest amount of defensive features, such as windowless outer walls, even if they were far from the Scottish border. These disappeared after the mid-century, except for ornamental purposes.

Vagabond Legislation

Although there had been laws against vagabonds since the fourteenth century, a great many more were enacted in Tudor times — unsurprisingly, given the unprecedented numbers of apparently threatening transients on the roads (see *Chapter 2*). Henry VII's laws on the subject did not distinguish between sturdy rogues and genuinely and unavoidably needy men, the "impotent poor", who could not work. Even so, the Vagabonds and Beggars Act of 1494 was fairly mild; it merely provided that

---

165. E. A. J. Honigmann, *Shakespeare: The "Lost Years"* (Manchester: Manchester University Press, 2013), p. 13.

166. William Farrer and J Brownbill (eds.), *A History of the County of Lancaster: Vol. 6* (London: Victoria County History, 1911), pp. 289–300.

167. Lawrence Stone, *The Crisis of the Aristocracy*, p. 168.

"vagabonds, idle and suspected persons shall be set in the stocks for three days and three nights and have none other sustenance but bread and water and then shall be put out of Town". Similar legislation was passed in 1504, again without defining and distinguishing the impotent poor from the rest.[168]

This changed in 1530, when a new statute (22 Henry VIII c. 12) set out "how aged, poor and impotent Persons, compelled to live by Alms, shall be ordered; and how Vagabonds and Beggars shall be punished". Under this, more draconian Act, vagabonds were not merely to be placed in the stocks but whipped. They were then to be forced to return to the parish where they had been born or where they had lived for the previous three years. However, the Act also provided that "impotent" beggars, those genuinely unable to work due to age or infirmity, could be officially licensed to beg by JPs, making it the first English poor law to provide (limited) relief for the indigent. Unfortunately, Edward VI, or those around him, thought that the "slake execution of the lawes" on vagabondage, which was allegedly due to bribery or "foolish pitey", was not dealing with the problem. A ferociously draconian law of 1547 (1 Edw. VI c. 3) provided that able-bodied vagabonds could be enslaved for two years, fed on bread and water, and beaten if necessary to force them to work. This statute does not seem to have been employed, and was swiftly repealed by an act of 1549, which noted that its predecessor had been too severe to be enforced (the "extremitie of some [of the laws] have byn occation that they have not ben putt in use").[169] It also reinstated the provisions of the 1530 Act, so that whipping once again became the punishment for sturdy vagabonds.

However, concern about rogues did not abate, not least because their numbers increased with the population. In March 1569, Sir Henry Weston, the High Sheriff of Surrey, sent the JP William More a copy of a letter he had received from the Privy Council. The queen was apparently concerned by the problems being occasioned by the "universal

---

168. Neil L. Kunze, "The Origins of Modern Social Legislation: The Henrician Poor Law of 1536", *Albion: A Quarterly Journal Concerned with British Studies*, Vol. 3, No. 1, pp. 9–20.
169. C. S. L. Davies, "Slavery and Protector Somerset: The Vagrancy Act of 1547", *The Economic History Review*, New Series, Vol. 19, Issue 3, p. 533.

negligent and wilful permission of vagabonds".[170] This prompted fresh legislation. The 1572 Act (14 Eliz. I c. 5) was the harshest statute passed for the "Punysshement of Vacabondes" during the Tudor era apart from the generally ignored 1547 Act. It stipulated that a whipping would be imposed for a first offence, and a severe whipping accompanied by boring through the gristle of the right ear with a hot iron an inch in diameter for a second; those convicted of a third offence were to be deemed felons and executed. It appears that even the most severe provisions of the 1572 Act were sometimes enforced, especially in and around London. At the Middlesex Sessions between 1572 and 1575 it seems that 44 vagabonds were sentenced to branding, eight to service, and five to execution.[171] More specifically, at the Old Bailey in March 1575, Thomas Maynerde, Oswald Thompson, and John Barres were sentenced to be flogged severely and bored with a hot iron "per le gristle dextre auricule" after being convicted under the statute, being over 18 years-of-age, fit for labour, but masterless and without any lawful means of livelihood. Despite this punishment, and perhaps indicative of its ineffectiveness, they were arrested again in June of the same year, wandering as vagrants in Middlesex. Such repeat offending meant that each was to be "deemed a felon". Pleading guilty, the three incorrigible men were sentenced to death.[172] As a result of this legislation, by the latter decades of the Tudor era it could be observed that such transients were "hated, whipped, almoste sterved, poore and naked, imprisoned and in daunger daiely to be marked with a burnyng Iron for a Roge, and to be hanged for a Vacabounde".[173]

Nevertheless, no amount of penal legislation seemed to solve the problem. Like the Royal Council before it, the Privy Council frequently attributed this to the failure of mayors, JPs, and constables to enforce the law properly. In the late 1570s, the Privy Council wrote to the Surrey JPs complaining that magistrates had been remiss in dealing with this growing problem, and ordering them to arrest and punish vagabonds. They were also to ensure that a watch was kept twice a week, between 4 pm and 8 am, to look out for them. The constables, who were also

170. SHC 6729/11/52.
171. Pound, *Poverty and Vagrancy*, p. 45.
172. Jeaffreson, *Middlesex County Records: Vol. 1, 1550–1603*, pp. 90–96.
173. Hitchcock, *A pollitique platt*, pp. 1–52.

deemed to have been negligent, were ordered to provide bonds to "carefully visit the places within their charge for the apprehending of the said vagabonds".[174]

Vagrancy was primarily a crime of status rather than specific conduct, although some forms of the latter were taken as indicative of the former. In about 1569 rules touching wandering rogues sent to Surrey JPs suggested that men deserting their illegitimate children, parents leaving their children to be supported by the parish, and those using infants who were not their own to assist in their begging could all be treated as vagabonds.[175] Under the 1572 Vagabonds Act, anyone could be deemed a vagrant if caught "begging in any part of this realm, or taken vagrant wandering and misordering themselves". Nevertheless, there was always a danger that poor but legitimate travellers would be mistakenly arrested as vagrants. Lord Morley, an Essex JP, alluded to this in 1578 during a heated argument with an officious colleague. Morley noted that JPs of the latter's stamp would "take up poor travelling men" as vagabonds. Such men were too far from home to have anyone to vouch for them, so that they would be sent to gaol, and even bored in the ear, although entirely honest.[176]

The establishment of the London Bridewell in 1553 (it opened two years later but was not favoured by Queen Mary) constituted one of the most drastic initiatives to deal with vagrancy in the metropolitan area. It was handed sweeping police powers under its charter, allowing its beadles to "searche, enquyre, and seke owt" vagabonds, prostitutes, and beggars. Within a few days of arrival at the prison, those arrested were put on trial, and if convicted dealt with "as shall seem good". Frequently this was by a mixture of incarceration, hard labour, and flogging. The Bridewell governors ("men of much worship and wisdom") presided over the court without a jury, often sitting twice a week, so that it dealt with many hundreds of people a year.

Nevertheless, despite such legislation and extraordinary initiatives, a general realisation that crime flourished where there was indigence meant

---

174. SHC 6729/11/56.
175. SHC 6729/11/54.
176. Joel Samaha, *Law and Order in Historical Perspective: The Case of Elizabethan Essex* (New York: Academic Press, 1974), p. 68.

that there was also widespread acceptance that a purely penal response was not enough to control crime. It was necessary to make some provision for the poor, especially the impotent members of society, if only to ensure social stability, an absence of which would otherwise threaten the "wise and wealthie".[177] A variety of mechanisms were used in an attempt to achieve this difficult aim.

Provision for the Poor

Most important, the Tudor era saw the emergence of a basic system of poor relief. The famous Elizabethan Poor Law of 1598, which was slightly modified in 1601, codified earlier statutes and, in theory, extended throughout the country what was already long-established "best practice" in much (but very far from all) of England. These practices had, over the past two generations, replaced pre-Reformation models of assistance. They required that parishes provide a basic allowance of food, shelter, and clothing for their genuinely needy (and legal) residents, financed by taxing their better-off counterparts. Much discretion was left to individual parish officials as to how the poor relief should be administered, such as whether it would be granted in cash or kind.[178] Poor but "respectable" working men who had been locally resident for years (often since birth), before becoming obviously ill or infirm, might be confident of some assistance. Idle or vagrant individuals who were newly arrived in a parish before claiming to have fallen sick or otherwise becoming indigent would get short shrift.

Almost "ideal typical" examples of the former (deserving) category can be seen in a petition from some of the inhabitants of Marks Tey, in Essex, to their county JPs concerning Daniel George, a homeless and partly blind labourer who was married to a lame woman, asking that he be allowed to build a cottage in the town. The petition noted that the couple had lived in Marks Tey for many years, had no residential rights elsewhere, behaved honestly, and had always worked, as far as their

---

177. Hitchcock, *A pollitique platt*, pp. 1–52.
178. Marjorie K. McIntosh, "Poverty, Charity, and Coercion in Elizabethan England", *The Journal of Interdisciplinary History*, Vol. 35, No. 3, pp. 457–479.

physical impediments allowed. If not permitted to build a cottage they would be likely to "lie in the stretes or ells go wandringe abroade as idle people to there further peril". Permission was duly granted.[179]

At the same time, attempts were made to control the price of food, especially staples. At the start of the Tudor period, there were several longstanding common law offences, such as engrossing, forestalling, and regrating (all to do with bulk purchase with the intent of resale) that were intended to prevent speculation in grain and other foodstuffs. The terms were sometimes used together indiscriminately, with overlapping meanings, although (in theory) they were distinct crimes. For example, strictly speaking, forestalling meant buying up foodstuffs, especially flour, before it reached the market and then inflating its price prior to resale. Even so, by the middle of the sixteenth century, these common law powers were felt to be inadequate. As a result, they were reinforced by an "Act against Regrators, Forestallers and Ingrossers" in 1552 (5&6 Edward VI c. 12). Initially lax enforcement of the legislation by JPs and local officials led to warnings being sent to high sheriffs urging their proper application, the lack of which allegedly occasioned the "number of enormities grown in our commonwealth".[180] However, the 1552 statute itself was quickly thought to be lacking, and so was supplemented in 1562 by a further Act (5 Elizabeth I, c. 12), tightening up the regulation of "badgers"—dealers who purchased foodstuffs in one place and carried them to another for resale. Under this statute, licensed badgers had to have been resident householders in the county in which they operated for three years, and to be at least 30 years-of-age. In addition, they had to hold a licence granted by a bench of at least three justices, one being of the quorum (a special group of senior JPs), sitting at quarter sessions, permitting them to buy grain outside a market for resale. Such a licence could be granted for no more than a year at a time. Those who lacked this documentation, could be prosecuted, as occurred at the Essex Quarter Sessions held at Easter in 1572, when Thomas Radley was accused of buying, transporting, and selling divers kinds of grain without a licence.

---

179. ERO Q/SR 115/61.
180. R. W. Heinze, *The Proclamations of Tudor Kings* (Cambridge: Cambridge University Press, 2008), p. 239.

The authorities took these provisions seriously, especially during hard times, such as those experienced towards the end of the century. Surrey provides a number of illustrations. For example, in June 1573 a circular letter from the council to its sheriff and justices of the peace ordered them to reduce the price of corn, and to take measures to prevent the forestalling of grain, such as limiting the number of licensed badgers.[181] In August 1596, the Privy Council, meeting at Greenwich, wrote to the county sheriff and JPs commanding them to enforce orders intended to prevent the then acute "dearth of grain". In particular, they were to prevent "greedy" buyers purchasing large stores of corn directly from farmers' houses, rather than in the open market. Those who held substantial supplies of corn were to be required to sell a proportion each week in local markets at the prices that had prevailed a few months earlier. JPs were to attend markets close to their houses to regulate prices and ensure that affordable corn was distributed, "specially to the poorer sort". Traders who refused to obey these orders were to be imprisoned without bail. JPs who themselves held large stocks of grain were to be treated in the same way as other men.[182]

Two months later, in October 1596, the Privy Council wrote to the high sheriff and justices of the peace of Surrey, reiterating the need to ensure markets were well-stocked with reasonably priced corn and requiring them to prevent the unnecessary export of grain or its use in making alcohol. Superfluous alehouses were to be closed, and those remaining were to sell only weak beer (which used less grain).[183] In August 1597 an order from the Privy Council to the sheriff and JPs of Surrey reiterated the rules against the forestalling of corn, butter, and cheese by "wicked" people who, it was claimed, were behaving like wolves and cormorants.[184] In July 1601 another letter from the same source to the Surrey JPs went further, and complained that people were secretly buying up rabbits, pigeons, partridges, and pheasants to sell in London at inflated prices.[185]

---

181. ERO Q/SR 39/114, ERO LM/1012/1 and LM/1012/1.
182. SHC 6729/13/86.
183. SHC LM/COR/3/561.
184. ERO LM/1016/2.
185. SHC 6729/11/16.

PART II
THE CRIMINAL JUSTICE SYSTEM

CHAPTER 4

Policing

Introduction

Law enforcement officers provided many offenders with their first contact with the Tudor criminal justice system. The three main categories of officer were made up of high constables, petty constables, and watchmen, although a few more specialised positions were sometimes found in towns. All three were normally held by part-time, unsalaried (if not always unpaid), temporarily appointed amateurs, recruited locally, and based in their homes (rather like the era's JPs). Such amateurism, although not unique to England, was not found everywhere in Europe at this time. For example, during the fifteenth century, police officers or *birri* in Italian cities, such as Bologna, whether patrolmen, searjeants, or constables, were often paid outsiders employed on short-term contracts of about six months' duration. Frequently, these men would move from city to city, exercising their unpopular trade as they did so.[1]

In England amateurism and localism meant that, throughout the Tudor era, routine policing resources were extremely limited, placing numerous constraints on how officers carried out their duties, and on their ability to implement directives from higher authorities. A selection of late Elizabethan cases from Essex and Surrey is indicative of these limitations. For example, in 1595 Sir Edmund Huddleston wrote to his fellow Essex JPs noting that, two years earlier, the constables of Halstead had complained to him about one Hercules Turner's "lewd" behaviour, as he was disturbing the peace of their town and abusing its nocturnal watch. Finding the matter proved to his satisfaction, Huddleston thought

---

1.   Trevor Dean, "Police Forces in Late Medieval Italy: Bologna, 1340–1480", *Journal of Social History*, Vol. 44, Issue 2 (2019), pp. 151–172, p. 151.

it proper, if only "for example sake", to sentence Turner to a spell in the stocks. Unfortunately, Turner was rescued from the apparatus by friends and then behaved in an outrageous manner, threatening the town's peace officers and its respectable residents. He ignored the constables' orders and those contained in the JP's original warrant, before escaping. Not content with this, he sued the town's constables in the Court of Excheq-uer for false imprisonment — allegedly merely to harass them — before abandoning and then restarting the action. Subsequently, he returned to Halstead and issued fresh threats to its constables and other local people. Sir Edmund merely bound Turner over to appear at quarter sessions to answer for his behaviour.[2]

Five years earlier, in the spring of 1590, a group of rogues had been committed to the Essex House of Correction. The night after they were sentenced, they were watched continuously to prevent escape, but "would not rise in the morning until their breakfast was ready, which they had and were conveyed to the next parish being but a mile distance". Once there they announced that they would not leave until they had their din-ners unless the constable would arrange for them to be carried in carts. They continued with this obstructionism until they reached the prison.[3]

Any active resistance to the orders issued by JPs and carried out by peace officers could occasion difficulties. For example, in 1567 two Suf-folk millers and a cleric assaulted Anthony Carter and Thomas Dereman, a pair of Essex constables who were trying to arrest them pursuant to a warrant issued by Sir William Cordall. The trio then escaped.[4] In June 1589, Thomas Glascocke of Wethersfield appeared at quarter sessions for similar recalcitrance. He had been arrested by one of the local consta-bles, and ordered to appear before a county JP after being accused of a misdemeanour. He simply abused the officer and "verye contemptuously refused to obey the sayd Justice his Warrante and threathynd to shote at the sayd Constable for charging him to goe with him".[5]

Even more seriously, already detained individuals were regularly "res-cued" from the hands of constables or watchmen by mobs. Thus, in

---

2.   ERO Q/SR 131/33.
3.   ERO Q/SR 113/39.
4.   ERO Q/SR 23/39.
5.   ERO Q/SR 102/36.

1568, when two Southwark constables arrested Peter Byrcherley, a petty chapman, they were assaulted by a small group of men, and Byrcherley was taken from their custody.[6] A similar event occurred in the summer of 1583, after Robert Stowe, a well-to-do Colchester man attacked John Eve with his sword and severely wounded him. Stowe fled immediately afterwards, and a hue and cry was raised in pursuit, which led to two constables' arresting him. However, before he could be produced before a magistrate, four of Stowe's servants, armed with a pike, swords, daggers and other weapons, assaulted the two officers, and rescued their master.[7]

High Constables

One or two high constables (sometimes called "chief constables") were appointed to act as the supervisory police authority for each hundred. In the North and some other former parts of the Danelaw (parts where Danish law had sometimes prevailed between the ninth and eleventh centuries), these areas were sometimes referred to as wapentakes. Many, however, were larger than southern hundreds. For example, there were over 30 hundreds in Norfolk and more than 20 in Suffolk, so that there were dozens of high constables in these counties. However, in the East Riding of Yorkshire, there were just six wapentakes: Howden, Holderness, Ouse, Buckrose, Dickering and Harthill.[8]

The position of high constable dated back to 1285. Its holders normally had responsibility for maintaining the urban watch in towns, organizing the removal of vagrants, and, most important, acting as a conduit between JPs and parish (petty) constables while allowing the latter to legally operate outside their immediate jurisdictions (when necessary). They would also report to quarter sessions and assizes about local abuses and grievances.

During the Tudor era, most high constables were drawn from the ranks of very minor gentlemen or prosperous yeomen; some of them used both

---

6.   J. S. Cockburn (ed.), *Calendar of Assize Records. Surrey Indictments: Elizabeth I* (London: HMSO, 1980), p. 71.
7.   ERO Q/SR 86/46.
8.   G.C.F. Forster, *The East Riding Justices of the Peace in the Seventeenth Century* (Micklegate: East Yorkshire Local History Society, 1973), p. 9.

social titles on different occasions in their daily lives. A marked difference between high and petty constables lay in the way they were appointed and removed — the former by JPs sitting at quarter sessions, the latter by the local community.[9] (Nevertheless, JPs could fine, or threaten to fine, both high and petty constables for negligence or other failures in office).

The office of high constable could be onerous, and the JPs' choice was not always welcome. At the West Riding Quarter Sessions held at Doncaster in 1598, John Savile was discharged from office in the Wapentake of Strafforth, in view of his age and previous good service. The JPs then appointed Robert Mote, who was present in court, and considered a fit and proper man for the position, as his replacement. Unfortunately, Mote was not impressed by their decision and "obstinately and in contemptuousse maner without shewing any just cause refuseth both to be sworne and also to execute the same place & c".[10] He would eventually have faced punishment for such recalcitrance.

There was no statutorily limited term for the high constables' service, and they usually were in position for considerably more than a year. Nevertheless, some counties, especially in the latter decades of the Tudor era, restricted their time in office.[11] For example, in Yorkshire, by the end of the sixteenth century, it was often limited to three years. Similarly, in April 1566 John Bowyer wrote to the Surrey JPs, supporting the application of Richard Ingham to be discharged as High Constable of the Hundred of Brixton. When appointed, Ingham had secured the agreement of the JPs of the division that high constables should serve for only two or three years rather than for life, the unpopular previous practice.[12] In parts of seventeenth century Yorkshire, JPs required the outgoing high constable to explain the duties to his successor, and the two men then served together until the next sessions (i.e. three months), when the former presented his accounts to the JPs for audit.[13] This may already have occurred in the Tudor years.

9. Joan Kent, "The English Village Constable, 1580–1642: The Nature and Dilemmas of the Office", *Journal of British Studies*, Vol. 20, Issue 2 (Spring 1981), pp. 26–49, p. 34.
10. Lister, John, *West Riding Sessions Rolls,* p. 98.
11. Bacon, Francis, *Cases of Treason*, p. 25.
12. SHC 6729/11/51.
13. Forster, *East Riding Justices,* p. 39.

Those who proved unsatisfactory might be discharged prematurely. In 1578 Elizabeth Clinton, the Countess of Lincoln, wrote to Sir William More, a Surrey JP, on behalf of her neighbours in the Hundred of Woking. They were angry with their high constable and wanted him replaced.[14] By contrast, some years later, in July 1583, Elizabeth's husband, Edward, the Earl of Lincoln, wrote to Sir William and other JPs noting that James Sutton of Cobham was honest and fit to be High Constable of Elmbridge, and urging that he should be sworn in at the forthcoming Surrey Quarter Sessions at Guildford.[15]

High constables needed some physical vigour, not least because of the travel that the position entailed, explaining why John Savile (see above) might be discharged "in respecte of his age". In 1592 Laurence Swettenham of Somerford, in Cheshire, who had served satisfactorily for many years as one of the high constables for the hundred of Macclesfield, was in even worse shape. He petitioned the county quarter sessions to be replaced because he had become "verey aged, corpulent, greived with sicknes and other infirmities and not able to travell neither on horse-backe nor on foote for the full execucion of the said office".[16] The position could also be time-consuming. In 1577 Lord Howard wrote to the Surrey JPs asking that they discharge one Johnson, a gentleman in his employment, from being high constable of the Hundred of Tandridge, and find a replacement. Apparently, Johnson was heavily involved (with his master) in working on the queen's affairs. More generally, Lord Howard considered that noblemen's servants were not the most appropriate choice for such positions.[17]

High constables did not normally carry out low-level face-to-face policing, which was the role of the ordinary "petty" or parish constables. Nevertheless, there were regular exceptions. In January 1591 three men from Stowe were accused of assaulting Richard Gosling, one of the chief constables of the Dengie Hundred in Essex. It was claimed that they had hit him on the head with a pitchfork, so that blood was drawn, although

---

14. SHC 6729/9/137.
15. SHC 6729/9/154.
16. Sharon Howard (ed.), *Petitions to the Cheshire Quarter Sessions*, *British History Online* http://www.british-history.ac.uk/petitions/cheshire/1590s [accessed 1 October 2019].
17. SHC 6729/9/38 and 137.

Gosling had advised them of his official status and required them to keep the peace.[18] In 1586 a gentleman and two yeomen who assaulted William Lyn, another Essex chief constable, punching him with their fists while he was in the execution of his duty, were each fined 12 pence.[19]

One of the most important aspects of a high constable's authority was his power to order petty constables to work together, outside their own parishes (usually the legal limit of the latter's power without higher authorisation) but within the former's hundred. He might also supervise them when they did so. High constables would often do this in response to directives from JPs. For example, in October 1593 justices at Sussex Quarter Sessions ordered them to organize searches and watches to apprehend Edward Strudwick and three other men who were thought to be behind a rash of robberies and burglaries near the border with Surrey. (They also liaised with their Surrey counterparts about the problem.)[20] This seems to have been successful, as the following month a letter from the Privy Council at Windsor to a group of Surrey JPs commended them for apprehending the gang of "notorious thieves", including Strudwick, the "chief ringleader of the rest".[21] (A relative, Robert Strudwick, may have escaped the net, as in December that year George Paulet wrote to Sir William More informing him that he would order his arrest if he were found.)[22]

High constables might also become involved in disciplining petty constables. At the Essex Quarter Sessions in 1585, John Hasteler and Benjamin King, two Essex high constables, indicted Thomas Owghan, who had been a petty constable at Burnham, for misconduct in office. Owghan had refused their command to arrest a vagrant, on the basis that he had no warrant to do so (although this was unnecessary), and, when the vagrant was eventually placed in the stocks, had repeatedly released him on his own initiative. Local feelings were mixed about this: "Many

---

18.   ERO Q/SR 116/24.
19.   ERO Q/SR 26/3.
20.   SHC LM/1030/1.
21.   SHC 6729/11/33.
22.   SHC LM/COR/3/525.

honest persons seemed offended, beinge then present, and some others, of light sorte, scoffed at the matter".[23]

Petty Constables

Petty or parish constables numbered in the thousands, and conducted the vast majority of face-to-face policing in Tudor England. The traditional English system of crime control during the high medieval period had revolved around a system of communal policing known as frankpledge, which was based on joint suretyship. Originating in Anglo-Saxon times, it was heavily reformed under King Canute (1016–1035) and in ensuing years. Under this system, males who were over twelve years-of-age, drawn from groups (tythings) of ten or more households (clerics and high-status laymen excepted), and headed by tythingmen, entered into mutual obligations and responsibilities for each other's conduct. If a member of a tything broke the law, the others had to take responsibility for reporting the crime and producing him for trial.[24]

However, such a system required a largely static society to be effective. Largescale or serious offending was difficult in small communities, where people were well apprised of their neighbours' affairs. (Both the jury of presentment and the self-informing trial jury were also by-products of this form of society.)[25] It became increasingly anachronistic during the late medieval period as population mobility grew rapidly, particularly after the Black Death. Tythings broke down, were hollowed out, or lumped together indiscriminately. The deficiencies of the system meant that it was gradually supplemented, and then effectively superseded, during the fourteenth and fifteenth centuries, by part-time village officers or constables with a special personal responsibility for general law enforcement. To some extent, these officers had grown out of the particular responsibility held by tythingmen, who were their lineal thirteenth century predecessors. (By the sixteenth century, "view of frankpledge" had come

---

23.   ERO Q/SR 94/15a.
24.   D. A. Crowley, "The Later History of Frankpledge", *Bulletin of the Institute of Historical Research*, 1975, Vol. 48, No. 117, pp. 1–15, p. 1.
25.   Green, T. A., *Verdict According to Conscience*, p. 114.

to mean an appearance before a leet court with reference to some form of criminal activity or disorder.)

Although constables were being appointed during the fourteenth century in some parts of England, many manors and parishes only introduced such officers after 1400. For example, it appears that the office was introduced at Kirtlington, in Oxfordshire, as late as the years between 1470 and 1509. Constables were not always known as such. In Kent, they were often termed borsholders, while in other places they were called tythingmen or headboroughs.[26]

Petty constables were local, part-time, untrained, temporarily appointed, law-enforcement and general-purpose officials. Although they were normally unsalaried, they were usually able to recover expenses and to obtain a modest degree of remuneration by charging fees for specific tasks relating to the administration of justice. For example, in 1598 the West Riding Quarter Sessions ordered that the constable of Sowerby be reimbursed for securing a suspect for ten days in his own home prior to the man's hearing before the court.[27]

During the late medieval and Tudor period, the position of the constables was transformed by legislation. Their duties included, inter alia, apprehending criminals, serving summonses, dealing with disturbances, enforcing arrest and search warrants, preserving the peace and preventing disorder, as well as conducting a multitude of other administrative duties, including raising some local taxes and rates and implementing social legislation.

Appointment as Petty Constable

There was little dispute as to what sort of man should be chosen to be a constable. He ought to be "fit for his ability of body and estate". Obviously, this excluded old or sick individuals. In 1598, 24 men from the Cranbrook Hundred in Kent were indicted at assizes for contempt because they had elected one William Sheafe as a constable, despite his

---

26.   Smith, Thomas, *De Republica Anglorum*, p. 109.
27.   Lister, *West Riding Sessions Rolls, 1597/8–1602*, p. 75.

being an "infirm man incapable of discharging the office".[28] It also precluded the employment of men who were not local, and (in theory) of "poor needy" individuals who were dependent entirely on their labour, and so without a modicum of personal independence or the time to carry out what could be an onerous duty.

At the start of the Tudor era, the appointment of parish constables was largely a matter for manorial forums, particularly courts leet (the "view of frankpledge"), and this remained the case in many parts of the country throughout the sixteenth century and beyond, surviving in a few places until being formally abolished in 1842. For example, in the West Riding of Yorkshire, constables were appointed in manorial leets and wapentake courts, so ensuring the continuing importance of these forums in local administration.[29] More specifically, in April 1560 William Ridley and John Heath were elected as constables at the Surrey manor of Limpsfield's view of frankpledge.[30]

Such courts employed diverse systems in selecting their officers. In some cases, designated officials, such as the lord of the manor, its steward, or even a selection of the manor's "better" inhabitants might make the initial decision, even if the court had to approve their final choice. In a few places, the incumbent constable suggested several possible successors, and the new officer was chosen from among them. Other constables were chosen automatically in rotation by house row: the best qualified (by age, health, etc.) owner or tenant living next to a person currently serving in the office would be required to replace him when the latter's time was over. This appears to have been the most common system in Lancashire in the following century, and was presumably employed for at least some of the Tudor period.[31]

However, during the later sixteenth century, as the role of parishes as units of local administration increased, and that of manorial courts

---

28.   Clive Emsley, *The English Police: A Political and Social History* (Abingdon: Routledge, 2014), p. 11.
29.   John L. Cruickshank, "Courts Leet, Constables and the Township Structure in the West Riding, 1540–1842", *Northern History*, Vol. 54, Issue 1 (2017), pp. 59–78.
30.   SHC 2186/1/15.
31.   Walter J. King, "Leet Jurors and the Search for Law and Order in Seventeenth century England: 'Galling Persecution' or Reasonable Justice?", *Histoire sociale/Social History*, Vol. 13, No. 26, p. 310.

waned, the election of constables was often relinquished to the parochial vestry (although, very strictly speaking, the constable was not a parish officer). Local JPs might call such a meeting for the specific purpose of selecting a constable. In other instances, the constable appears to have been nominated by a vestry but formally confirmed in office by the leet. The wording of the Poor Law Act of 1602 suggests that vestry involvement had become fairly common by the end of the Tudor period, if only because many communities no longer possessed properly functioning leets. Nevertheless, in other places, such as Stock, in Essex, leets appointed constables throughout the Tudor period without any vestry involvement.[32]

JPs also had a role in the process, punishing some of those who refused to accept a leet's decision to appoint them, swearing in new officers, and helping to replace men who were suddenly indisposed or deemed to be unsuitable. Thus, in the first decade of the seventeenth century, the Briston Manorial Court Leet in North Norfolk selected John Colffer to serve as its constable "by general consent". However, Colffer "utterly refused to bear such office", and walked out of the meeting. The leet petitioned Sir Nathaniel Bacon, the local JP, to force him to take up the position.[33] Nevertheless, and vitally, although constables were primarily responsible to the JPs, their initial appointment normally remained a local process (whether it was done by leet or vestry) throughout the Tudor era. Unlike the position of high constable, it was not something for magistrates to decide.[34]

In the sixteenth century, one or two constables were normally chosen for each parish. Larger towns might appoint more men, though these were often attached to specific wards. In Essex, both Colchester and Maldon were divided into four wards, each of which elected two constables, for a total of about eight officers for each town. Chelmsford, which had a population of about 2,500 during the 1580s, selected seven constables. Officers were nearly always appointed for just one or, at most, two years at a time. Between 1613 and 1620 the vestry minutes

32. Ann Catherine Robey, *The Village of Stock, Essex, 1550–1610: A Social And Economic Survey*, London School of Economics and Political Science, PhD thesis, 1991, p. 202.

33. Herbert Washington Saunders (ed.), *The Official Papers of Sir Nathaniel Bacon of Stiffkey, Norfolk, as Justice of the Peace, 1580–1620* (London: Camden Society, 1915), p. 50.

34. Kent, "The English Village Constable", pp. 26–49, p. 34.

for the small but wealthy parish of St Mary Colechurch in the City of London show the vast majority of its two parish constables serving for just a year, with a small number doing two years.[35] Frequently, if a village had two constables, their appointment would be timed to allow an overlap of responsibility, if only to ensure continuity of experience. For example, Stock always appointed two men, who were elected by the leet jury at Easter for a two-year term. A newly appointed man usually served alongside one who had already been in office for a year, so that the first year constituted a form of apprenticeship, with the previous year's constable mentoring the less experienced man.[36]

Even so, constables might serve for significantly longer than two years *if* they were willing to do so. According to Sir Thomas Smith, writing in the 1560s, rural constables might be re-elected, when their time was up, so that they sometimes kept the office for up to four years, gaining a significant degree of experience in the process. Some served even longer, although very few matched John Andrews, who was constable for Kirklington in Oxfordshire for 17 years, without a break, from 1519 until 1536. Why he should have been willing to take on the position for such a long time is not readily apparent, especially as he was a relatively prosperous individual. However, presumably there was prestige, local power, indirect reward, or even enjoyment in it.[37]

On a fictional basis, Elbow, the constable in Shakespeare's *Measure for Measure* (1603), served more than seven years, but as a paid substitute for the more prosperous men initially selected for the office in his ward: "As they are chosen, they are glad to choose me for them; I do it for some piece of money" (Act II, Scene 1). Although the play is set in Vienna, this probably reflects what was not an uncommon practice in parts of London, although very far from being universal (as it nearly was by the eighteenth century). Hiring a substitute was normally cheaper than paying the fine for refusal to serve.

---

35. St Mary Colechurch Vestry Minutes 1612–1700, LMA P69/MRY8/B/001/MS00064.
36. Robey, *The Village Of Stock, Essex*, pp. 202–206.
37. Matthew Griffiths, "Kirtlington Manor Court, 1500–1650", *Oxoniensa*, v. 45 (1980), pp. 260–283, p. 269.

Performance in Office

The public image of the Tudor constable has suffered badly from Shakespeare's portrayals and those of other dramatists of the period. Along with Elbow, Dull in *Love's Labour's Lost* and Dogberry in *Much Ado About Nothing* were depicted as bumbling, dim, and naive men who were often unsure what their positions entailed, although sometimes fairly effective despite these limitations.[38] Certainly, real individuals of their stamp can be identified, explaining why the office was satirised. Ignorant, stupid, incompetent, and lazy constables can readily be found in the historical record. The Kent JP William Lambarde complained about their frequent indolence and ineffectiveness, even producing a handbook, *The Duties of Constables*, to better instruct them in their work.

A litany of prosecutions of constables for failings in office, the main (and almost only) way to penalise poor performance, bears witness to their faults. Such prosecutions were often conducted in local leet courts. However, during the last decades of the sixteenth century this disciplinary function was increasingly taken over by JPs sitting at quarter sessions, and even by judges at assizes. For example, in 1556 William Steven and John Sakes, two Alresford constables, were each fined 3s 4d at the Essex Quarter Sessions for allowing Richard Harding, a suspected felon, to escape after a county JP placed him in their custody for conveyance to Colchester Gaol.[39] In the summer of 1602, William Browne, an Audley End tailor and also the local constable, was bound over to appear at the following Essex Quarter Sessions for refusing to execute various arrest warrants or to implement the hue and cry.[40] At about the same time, and in the same county, Edward Tynge, one of the constables of Stanford Rivers, was prosecuted for allowing three vagrants to go unpunished and for letting three suspected felons go after they had been committed to his custody.[41]

---

38.   Hugh C. Evans, "Comic Constables—Fictional and Historical", *Shakespeare Quarterly*, Vol. 20, No. 4, p. 427.
39.   ERO Q/SR 2/4.
40.   ERO Q/SR 159/63.
41.   ERO Q/SR 159/105,106.

To consider the higher forum, at the Hertfordshire Assizes in 1576, John Cawdwell and Nicholas Bayes, two constables from Baldock, were acquitted after being accused of negligently allowing a thief to escape while on the way to the same prison. (That the thief was eventually recaptured, tried, and acquitted may have influenced the jury's verdict.) Some 20 years later, George Blackwell, a Bushey constable, was indicted at the same forum for negligently allowing the escape of Thomas Spencer the previous September, after a local JP had committed him to his custody for delivery to Hertford Gaol. He pleaded guilty and placed himself at the queen's mercy.[42] Moving county, at the Surrey Assizes held in February 1588, John Ricketts, the constable of Ewell, was indicted for allowing the escape of an innkeeper after arresting him pursuant to a warrant issued by a local JP. He pleaded guilty and was fined.[43]

By contrast, a few prosecutions involved officers who had exaggerated notions of their own power or who had been overly aggressive in the performance of their duties. For example, Robert Ryce, one of the constables of Belchamp Walter, in Essex, was indicted at the county quarter sessions for assaulting a gentleman named Edward Coo late one evening, and striking him with a pitchfork, allegedly "intending to kill and murder him, so that he greatly despaired of his life".[44]

Inevitably, the constables' power and interaction with the public afforded considerable opportunities for petty corruption, something that also led to occasional prosecutions, although most cases probably went unnoticed. For example, at the Michaelmas Quarter Sessions for Essex in 1576, Libeus Ebbes, the constable for Mountnessing, was indicted for misconduct in office. He had been ordered by local high constables to summon 24 men to "petty sessions" at Chelmsford to enquire into offences against the statute of labourers. However, he then received six pence each from two of the men to discharge them from appearing.[45]

---

42. J. S. Cockburn (ed.), *Calendar of Assize Records: Hertfordshire Indictments, Elizabeth I* (London: HMSO, 1975), p. 79 and p. 119.
43. Cockburn, *Calendar of Assize Records. Surrey Indictments: Elizabeth I*, pp. 317–318.
44. ERO Q/SR 134/40.
45. ERO Q/SR 59/2.

Hazards

The constable's position could be physically dangerous, something that helps to explain the reluctance of some men to serve and the frequent circumspection found amongst officers when carrying out their duties. Many were assaulted while on duty. Even when offences were proved, whether at leet, quarter sessions, or assizes, the courts often took a fairly lenient approach to sentencing those who had committed such crimes, and imposed a modest fine, just as they usually did with any other type of assault, rather than passing an exemplary punishment. For example, Christopher Sydaye was fined only a shilling at the Essex Quarter Sessions for his attack on a constable in 1575 (see below).[46] In September 1583 Nicholas Jackson of Hatfield Broadoak assaulted Barnaby Fenner, one of the local constables, and was fined just 2s 6d.[47] The upper orders might (sometimes) expect to pay slightly more. In April 1572 Peter Jerome, a gentleman from Woodham Mortimer, was fined 6s 8d for assaulting William Coke while in the execution of his office, striking him with a dagger so that he drew blood.[48]

Some officers received life-threatening injuries while on duty. At the Essex Quarter Sessions in 1586, John Lidgett was prosecuted for assaulting Edward Lowe and William Ferne, the constables for Waltham. Lowe was apparently so badly hit with an "edge byll" that he initially despaired of his life.[49] A few officers were even killed. For example, one summer night in 1554 a Westminster baker stabbed Robert Hill, a local constable, to death with a dagger, whilst the latter was watching a house because of its "disorderly rule". (Presumably the baker was a patron.)[50] In July 1555 a man wielding a pikestaff murdered Nicholas Maryett, the constable of Winkburn, in Nottinghamshire, in the village high street.[51]

If a police task appeared potentially dangerous, constables might seek the assistance of other able-bodied villagers to help enforce the law. For

---

46. ERO Q/SR 53/31.
47. ERO Q/SR 86/39.
48. ERO D/DCe C9.
49. ERO Q/SR 96/50.
50. Jeaffreson, *Middlesex County Records: Vol. 1, 1550–1603*, pp. 17–21.
51. R. F. Hunnisett (ed.), *Calendar of Nottinghamshire Coroners' Inquests, 1485–1558* (Nottingham: Derry and Sons, 1969), p. 150.

example, in the early 1530s a Waltham Forest official, living in Theydon Bois, was told that the local prior had required him to take possession of a farm (presumably owned by the abbey), forcibly if necessary, and exclude the then occupant. He was advised to take the constable of the town and three or four local men to do this.[52] In November 1598. Daniel Hewett, one of the constables of Great Bentley, sought to enforce an arrest warrant issued by two Essex JPs against two men. One of the latter was armed with a sword. Perhaps in light of this, Hewett brought along a villager named Edward Parven to help him carry out this duty. (Unfortunately, one of the men hit Parven on the head with a stick.)[53]

In an emergency, constables could also demand assistance from bystanders. In 1596 the Manchester Court Leet reiterated the requirement that "every inhabitant within this town shall be ready at the constables' commandment, either day or night, to aid the constables in her majesty's service".[54] Nevertheless, although failing to provide assistance when requested was a common law offence, such help was not always forthcoming.

Reluctance to Serve

Perhaps unsurprisingly, given that the position was often onerous, sometimes hazardous, and did not carry enormous prestige, there was sometimes opposition to being appointed as a constable. This was not a new phenomenon in Tudor England; it can be identified in the late medieval period. For example, in 1423 two men refused to assume their duties after being selected in Winchester; one was fined 40 shillings, the other 100 shillings (half of which would be respited if they accepted the position).[55] By the Tudor era it is apparent that there could be considerable resistance to appointment, especially amongst the more well-to-do members of the community. Some men, such as John Solly of Stourmarsh in 1602, had to be forced to serve as constables by court order, having

---

52.   ERO D/DCe C9.
53.   ERO Q/SR 144/34.
54.   John Harland (ed.), *Continuation of the Court Leet Records of the Manor of Manchester AD 1586–1602* (Manchester: Chetham Society, 1865), p. 44.
55.   W. H. B. Bird (ed.), *The Black Book of Winchester* (Winchester: Wykeham Press, 1925), p. 118.

initially refused to do so.[56] Others were fined heavily after persisting in their recalcitrance or occasionally were allowed to pay for a substitute to serve in their place (see above).

As a result of these developments, by the middle of the sixteenth century there were regular complaints that the position was often being given to what Sir Thomas Smith termed "men of small favor and abilitie" who were devoid of experience, knowledge, or authority. He claimed that there had been a noticeable decline in the quality and reputation of constables over the previous decade or so, and that officers were often being drawn from what he termed the "fourth sort" of men — that is, base people who traditionally had little say in the commonwealth. Many were, allegedly, day labourers, poor husbandmen, and landless craftsmen.[57] Perhaps indicative of the presence of such lower-quality officers, in 1613 a Sussex grand jury lamented: "Our Constables in most part are honest men but of meane estate and fewe of them knowe what belongeth to the office".[58]

Even worse, some were not of good moral character. At the start of 1591, John Perry, a constable in Stanford-le-Hope, in Essex, was indicted for having kept a tippling-house without a licence for the previous three years, and also for holding unlawful games in his establishment.[59] (Ideally, it was thought, even those involved in the legal sale of alcohol should not become constables.) In 1604 the JP Sir William Ayloff examined five men about John Lufkin's behaviour in Layer Marney, the Essex village where Lufkin was constable. It was claimed that he frequented a local alehouse, often for many hours on end, and drank to excess. On one occasion he allegedly urinated into a mug and then proffered it to unwitting patrons as beer. As a disappointed man who had drunk some of the urine noted, "It was a shame for yowe Goodman Lufkin being constable to offer this".[60] (However, in 1605 at least one of the complainants was among a group of men fined for assaulting Lufkin).[61]

---

56. Louis A. Knafla, *Kent at Law, 1602. The County Jurisdiction: Assizes and Sessions of the Peace* (London: HMSO, 1994), p. 42.
57. Smith, *De Republica Anglorum*, pp. 76–77 and p. 109.
58. Clive Emsley, *The English Police*, p. 10.
59. ERO Q/SR 115/53.
60. ERO Q/SR 170/3.
61. ERO Q/SR 171/52.

Nevertheless, it is quite important not to generalise from such cases, opinions, and anecdotal accounts. Much evidence also reveals numerous efficient constables from good backgrounds, diligently conducting their duties within their villages, and discharging the (often) heavy demands of their position in a satisfactory manner. Although there were frequent localised problems in recruitment, the majority of Tudor constables, even late in the era, were not drawn from the "meaner sort". Certainly almost no gentlemen (even broadly construed) served in the office. This had always been the case. As Thomas Powell (1572–1635) noted in his handbook *Tom of All Trades*, it was not a suitable position for men aspiring to that status. However, officers were frequently chosen from the more substantial yeomen in a parish, or, if there were not sufficient men of this type, from husbandmen and lesser craftsmen; only rarely did they come from the most impoverished inhabitants.

For example, well-to-do men normally held the position in sixteenth century Kirtlington. John Andrews, a major freeholder and farmer, as well as a longstanding constable (see above) was assessed as having £30 in lands in the lay subsidy (a form of tax) of 1523, when he was even described as a gentleman, although in his own will (proved in 1542) he more realistically termed himself a yeoman.[62] Similarly, the Tudor constables of Wigston Magna, in Leicestershire, were apparently drawn from the leading yeomen, husbandmen, and craftsmen of the village; the office was not given to cottagers or simple householders.[63] In Elizabethan Pattingham, in Staffordshire, most of the constables were at least middling size farmers, by the standards of the community, with others being craftsmen or tradesmen. The same men often filled other local offices, including that of churchwarden, a position that is sometimes assumed to have been inherently more desirable and prestigious than the constableship. It was not until well into the seventeenth century that Pattingham saw those selected as constables challenging their appointments on a regular basis, or trying to procure substitutes.[64]

---

62. Griffiths, "Kirtlington Manor Court", pp. 269–270.
63. W. G. Hoskins, *The Midland Peasant* (London: Macmillan, 1957), p. 208.
64. Kent, *"The English Village Constable"*, pp. 27–30 and p. 43.

Similarly, evidence from Stock, in Essex, suggests that during the second half of the sixteenth century most of the constables appointed by the local leet were of yeoman status or, at the very least, the better sort of husbandman or craftsman. Between 1556 and 1602, of the 39 known constables appointed in the village, only four men fell outside these categories, while 22 were drawn from the former group (yeomen) and 13 the latter. Furthermore, there is almost no evidence that any man appointed as constable refused to serve, and they were not so socially intimidated that they were afraid of presenting local gentlemen at their leet.[65]

Even in a fairly affluent part of Jacobean London, St Mary Colechurch, between 1613 and 1620, several of those who had been constables, such as John Slater, also served as churchwardens, while only three men paid a fine to avoid the office, one of them (Rowland Heylin) apparently after starting in the position and finding it too onerous.[66]

Reactive and Proactive

Much of a constable's work was carried out in response to orders from JPs and high constables. In their capacity as executive officers for local magistrates, constables would transmit summonses, enforce arrest and search warrants, and escort prisoners to gaol. At other times they might raise the hue and cry in response to requests from travellers who had been robbed or other crime victims. However, the purely reactive nature of the constable's office can also be exaggerated. They may not normally have been on duty for set periods, but if an affray or serious disturbance suddenly broke out, local officers were required to act promptly, on their own initiative, to suppress it and keep the peace, without waiting for instructions.

For example, in 1575 Christopher Sydaye of Great Horkesley, in Essex, assaulted two men from the same village. John Smith, the local constable, swiftly arrived to deal with the disturbance and was himself attacked.[67] Inevitably, mistakes were sometimes made in these situations. In 1569 a

---

65. Robey, *The Village Of Stock, Essex*, pp. 202–206.
66. St Mary Colechurch Vestry Minutes 1612–1700, LMA P69/MRY8/B/001/MS00064.
67. ERO Q/SR 53/31.

bystander named George Strond made valiant efforts to keep the peace between two armed men who were set on fighting in his Essex village. He "beat downe both their weapons or elles one of them had killed an other". Unfortunately, at this point the local constable arrived and appears to have identified the peacemaker as the cause of the disturbance, seizing Strond and putting him in the stocks.[68]

Many constables would also take it upon themselves to investigate and, if necessary, report to the authorities anything untoward or unusual that occurred in their parishes. For instance, shortly before Christmas 1537, in Bildeston, in Suffolk, Philip Witherick's lodger, a tailor named Ambrose Letyce, suddenly disappeared, leaving his tools behind. Gossip started to circulate in the village, suggesting that Witherick had murdered Letye in a dispute over rent, and then disposed of his body. A few days later, the two local constables, becoming concerned about the missing man's abandoned gear, and presumably aware of the rumours, reported the matter to a local JP, John Spring of Lavenham. Spring told them that if Letyce had not returned by Christmas, they should bring Witherick before him for questioning, which they duly did on 26 December.[69]

Given the association of transients with both crime and the abuse of charity, it is unsurprising that constables (like watchmen) would be alert to suspicious strangers who arrived in their areas. They would often question them (on their own initiative) about their origins, what they were doing, where they were going, and about any valuable goods, animals, or large amounts of cash found in their possession, especially if these seemed out of keeping with their socio-economic status. Indicative of this practice, at the end of the Tudor period, the barrister John Manningham, recounting a fairy tale, observed that two talking animals "began to be very inquisitive, like a couple of constables, to know whence he came and what his name might be".[70] Thus, and for example, in December 1581 Edward Symson was detained by the constable of Terling, in Essex, and eventually taken before Anthony Maxey, a local JP, who examined

---

68.   ERO Q/SR 30/1.
69.   John Bellamy, *Strange, Inhuman Deaths: Murder in Tudor England* (Cheltenham: The History Press, 2005), pp. 94–95.
70.   John Manningham, *Diary of John Manningham, of the Middle Temple, and of Bradbourne, Kent, Barrister-at-Law, 1602–1603* (London: J. B. Nichols and Sons, 1868), p. 46.

him about the items found in his possession. He provided the magistrate with a slightly unsatisfactory explanation.[71]

Tensions of the Office

By the sixteenth century, a series of statutes stretching back into the medieval period meant that constables had become servants of the state and its higher officials rather than being purely answerable to their original masters, the view of frankpledge (effectively their local communities).[72] Amongst the representatives of the Crown that constables were sworn to serve were a county's: lord lieutenant, high sheriff, high constables, and coroners. Most importantly of all, they were, in practice, the executive assistants for its JPs.[73] In Sir Thomas Smith's words, they acted as "executors of the commaundement of the Justices of peace".

The gradual transformation of the constable into a royal official was reflected in changes to the content and administration of his oath of office, which became progressively longer and was eventually taken before a JP. As a result, the constable was the lowest rung in a hierarchy of authority that stretched up to the monarch, and could be punished for any failure in office by those above him. Indicative of this, after the Northern Rebellion in 1569, Queen Elizabeth asked that her agents pursue village constables who had supported the rising with special vigour. Some of them were executed under martial law.[74]

However, and vitally, petty constables were still selected on a local basis, rather than being appointed by the Crown or its representatives, unlike JPs and high constables, and had to represent the interests of their parish to their superiors. Most served only a year or two, after which they would return to being ordinary villagers for the rest of their lives. Ties of kinship and friendship, as well as a fear of making enemies, bound

---

71. ERO Q/SR 79/92.
72. Marjorie McIntosh, *A Community Transformed: The Manor and Liberty of Havering-atte-Bower, 1500–1620* (Cambridge: Cambridge University Press, 2009), p. 317.
73. Michael J. Braddick, *State Formation in Early Modern England, C.1550–1700* (Cambridge: Cambridge University Press, 2000), p. 33.
74. Kesselring, *Mercy and Authority*, p. 185.

them to their neighbours. These would last long after they handed over their position to someone else.[75]

The need to consider both town and Crown created an inherent tension in the office. It meant balancing the demands of central government, as manifest in the orders of magistrates, against the needs of fellow villagers. An over-enthusiastic willingness to follow the former might make enemies amongst the latter; however, a failure to carry out such directives could lead to official punishment. These conflicting pressures required officers to navigate a difficult path during their time in office, one that often meant vigorously enforcing measures for which there was widespread community support, while doing the bare minimum with regard to those that were acutely unpopular, or even turning a discreet blind eye.

Inevitably, some men failed to square this circle in an entirely satisfactory manner. For example, and perhaps unsurprisingly, in 1598 the West Riding Quarter Sessions ordered that William Rayner, the constable of Tonge, be fined 20 shillings for failing to execute a warrant to arrest his own brother and then produce him for examination before Sir John Savile, a county JP. At the same sessions, they ordered that sureties be brought against William Ramscarr, the constable of Wentbridge, to ensure his appearance before them for failing to arrest a group of suspicious people who regularly frequented a local inn of bad reputation. It was said that his inaction was founded on his personal relationship with the innkeeper, or "in respecte of some favour which he specially caryeth towarde the said Dicconson".[76]

In 1589 Margaret Clark, a serving maid in a yeoman's house in High Leigh, in Cheshire, was "beaten verye cruellye" by her master's son, Thomas Wilkinson. Eventually, and with the agreement of her employer, she went to a JP and obtained a warrant against Wilkinson to keep the peace. She then sought out one of the two Leigh constables, to whom the warrant was directed, to serve it. This man, Thomas Stelfox, pretended not to be at home when she turned up at his door. Clark next approached the other parish constable, Richard Prince, who went with her to Wilkinson's house, but then refused to serve the warrant on him.

---

75. Kent, "The English Village Constable", p. 38.
76. Lister, *West Riding Sessions Rolls, 1597/8–1602*, p. 119 and p. 121.

Even worse, he not only did nothing when Wilkinson brandished a sword in Clark's face but said that in his (Wilkinson's) place he would beat her every day. Clark then sought out another JP, although pursued on the way by Wilkinson, and asked that "some faythfull bayliffe or officer" be required by the magistrate to serve the warrant.[77]

Such tensions may also explain why, in September 1585, Arthur Harris (c.1530–1597), an Essex JP from Creeksea, wrote to Sir Thomas Mildmay and the other county JPs sitting at quarter sessions, complaining about the arrogant behaviour of a petty constable. A blacksmith named Burnham had been set in the stocks by order of the high constables. However, the local constable had set him free on his own initiative. Harris claimed that this particular constable always behaved "rather after a malytiouse pryvate humour then according to equytie".[78]

The Watch

Watchmen formed an extra tier of policing in urban areas during the hours of darkness. They were separate from the constables, under whose authority they served. Watchmen were also supposed to provide military protection from external threats in time of war or internecine conflict, although this role became less important as the Tudor period advanced and society became more settled. Even so, in January 1554, during Sir Thomas Wyatt's rebellion, the Earl of Arundel wrote to the Mayor of Guildford, reminding him to ensure that its inhabitants kept good watch to protect the borough.[79]

The urban watch's roots lay deep in the medieval period. In 1242 an ordinance had required that a night watch be kept from dusk to dawn in every town during the warmer months between Ascension Day and Michaelmas, although it was probably building on already well-established practice in many places. This was reiterated and consolidated by the Statute of Winchester of 1285 (13 Edw. I, St. 2), that remained in force throughout the Tudor era. In practice there was some variation in

---

77.   Howard, *Petitions to the Cheshire Quarter Sessions.*
78.   ERO Q/SR 94/15.
79.   SHC BR/OC/5/2.

dates and timings as to when the watch operated. Some towns voluntarily kept the watch from as early as Easter, while it was common practice for watchmen to go on duty from late evening until the small hours, rather than to serve the entire night.

The 1285 Act ordered towns and boroughs to provide watches of between four and a dozen men. Thus the City of London was divided into 24 wards, each with its own small watch. In many cases, the wards into which other large towns and cities were divided also provided the basis for their allocation of watch responsibility. However, watchmen could be found operating in quite modest urban areas (villages by modern standards), if only on an intermittent basis. For example, at the Michaelmas Quarter Sessions for Essex in 1592, John Parker and Thomas Smyth, the constables for Earls Colne, were prosecuted for not appointing any of the inhabitants of their tiny town to conduct a watch from sunset to sunrise, as required by the statute.[80]

In theory, almost all able bodied townsmen were obliged to take turns as watchmen, as an unpaid civic duty. A failure to do so could result in prosecution. For example, in September 1600 Henry Edlyn of St Stephen's Alley in Westminster was indicted for refusing to keep watches in the same alley.[81] In this regard, Exeter was probably fairly typical of larger provincial conurbations during the Elizabethan period. Watchmen there were householders who were required to keep watch at night by rota, whether in person or, alternatively, by "appoint[ing] some meet and convenient persons in their place". The latter would usually be paid substitutes.[82] The use of substitutes was already well established by then. Although the arrangements for the Southampton watch are not available before 1522, substitutions were being allowed by this time, provided that no "foreigners" (who were distrusted) were employed. The use of such stand-ins would become increasingly common over the next 200 years until, during the early eighteenth century, the duty to serve personally

---

80.   ERO Q/SR 122/29.

81.   Jeaffreson, *Middlesex County Records: Vol. 1, 1550–1603*, pp. 257–266.

82.   John Hooker, *A pamphlet of the offices, and duties of euerie particular sworne officer, of the citie of Excester: collected by Iohn Vowell alias Hoker, Gentleman & chamberlaine of the same* (Exeter, 1584), pp. 1–40.

was normally replaced by a parish levy from which paid watchmen could be funded.

The employment of substitutes by those with money to do so is unsurprising. Service on the watch could be fatiguing for men who would have to be at work the following day, while it was also very tedious and occasionally dangerous. In April 1578 three "poor" watchmen from the parish of St Bride's, Fleet Street, petitioned the Lord Mayor and aldermen of London for relief for themselves and their families. They had been called out one Thursday night to deal with a disturbance and were so badly wounded that they thought it likely that they would be permanently crippled.[83] Similarly, in 1617, in Worcestershire, Francis Hughes, who was serving a turn on the watch as a householder, was attacked so viciously, being knocked down and beaten with a staff, that his ability to maintain his family was affected.[84] Funding a substitute was also significantly cheaper than paying the fines set out for those who simply ignored their duty and failed to appear. These were certainly not new in the Tudor era. In 1299 the Winchester city court fined three men "for refusing to take the great horn for the watch".[85]

The methods used to organize, equip, and deploy the watch varied from place-to-place and over time. For example, in 1450, a few decades before the start of the Tudor era, the Coventry Leet ordered that 40 upright and healthy men serve each night in the city watch, from 9 pm until the ringing of the day bell in the early morning. They were to be equipped with jacks (padded doublets) and sallets (helmets), and armed with poleaxes or glaives (a form of spear) and similar weapons.[86] The more peaceful society that developed in England more than a century later allowed a slightly less martial watch.

Watchmen in Elizabethan Exeter were fewer in number than their predecessors in Coventry, and merely "sufficientlie armed with harnesse and weapon". (A short pike, or even a wooden staff, was often used by

83. Mary Anne Everett Green (ed.), *Calendar of State Papers Domestic: Elizabeth, Addenda, 1566–79* (London: HMSO, 1871), pp. 538–543.
84. Brodie Waddell (ed.), *Petitions to the Worcestershire Quarter Sessions*, British History Online http://www.british-history.ac.uk/petitions/worcs-quarter-sessions/1617 [accessed 1 October 2019].
85. J. S. Furley, *Town Life in the Fourteenth Century* (Winchester, 1946), p. 147.
86. Mary Dormer Harris (ed.), *The Coventry Leet Book or Mayor's Register* (London, Routledge, 1907), pp. 253–254.

the late Tudor period.) They were supposed to assemble at the Guildhall before going on duty after dark, where they would be sworn in, reminded of their standing orders, and receive their "watchword" for the night, which would be exchanged with fellow watchmen in the dark for mutual identification. They would then make fast the city gates and go on duty, which would, in theory, require that they "all night be watchfull and walking abroad in their divisions". While doing so they would ensure that everything was "quiet and in good order". In particular, they would investigate unsecured premises, any lights on in houses, and possible fires. They would challenge any drunkards, nightwalkers, strangers, vagrants, or other suspicious people that they came across, escorting them to their lodgings or securing them overnight, as necessary, and then producing anyone they had detained before a magistrate (often the mayor) the following morning.[87] For example, when John Hamonde appeared in Billericay at 11 pm one night in 1572, he was challenged by a watchman, and then escorted to his master's house, where he had been residing before going to Hornchurch to visit his father.[88] Many watchmen would also keep an eye on local alehouses.

The typical challenges issued to nightwalkers, albeit in a very small urban environment, are illustrated by a case from Essex in 1599. One night in May, at about 11 pm, watchmen at Booking met two individuals named Capell and Freeman who were carrying beer from an alehouse. They ordered the men to stop in the queen's name and to tell them where they were taking the alcohol. At this, the two men "brangled" with the watch, who called on a nearby resident for help. Unfortunately, this man not only refused to assist them, he actively encouraged Capell and Freeman to resist the watchmen. (He was later fined.)[89]

The absence of any major source of artificial light, other than a candle-powered lantern, could occasion difficulties, and explains the need for a nocturnal watchword. Darkness produced tragedy in 1572, when three labourers were appointed to keep watch in Goring, in Sussex. They went to their stations separately, but stumbled into each other late in the

---

87. Hooker, *A pamphlet of the offices, and duties*, pp. 1–40.
88. ERO Q/SR 41/4.
89. ERO Q/SR 146/15.

night and, oblivious of each other's identities, and thinking that they had encountered nefarious individuals, fought, so that one of them was killed.

In practice, many corporations, especially those in the smaller boroughs, would make the most modest provision that they could when it came to watchmen, and, given the nature of the work, the men appointed would often do the minimum possible. As one of Shakespeare's watchmen in *Much Ado About Nothing* declares: "Let us go sit here upon the church-bench till two, and then all to bed". Thomas Dekker was just as critical. In *The Seven Deadly Sins of London*, he claimed that not only did watchmen sleep while on duty, but they would snore so loudly that to "Night walkers (whose wittes are up late) it serves as a Watch-word to keepe out of reach of their browne Bille". Lord Burghley was equally unimpressed, as a result of personal experience. In a letter sent to Sir Francis Walsingham in August 1586, shortly before the trial of Mary, Queen of Scots, when security in the country was in a heightened state, he reported on their performance. As Burghley travelled towards London in a coach, he noticed clusters of men, up to a dozen strong, standing around in the small towns he passed, and eventually realised that they were watchmen. He approached a group at Enfield, and learned that they were looking for three young men, though the only intelligence they had to identify them was that one of the trio had a hooked nose. He asked to see the constable under whose instructions they were operating, and unavailingly pointed out that the watchmen were standing so openly in groups that "no suspected person will come neare them; and if they be no better instructed but to fynd 3 persons by one of them havyng a hooked nose, they may miss therof".[90]

However, and as with the constables, although there was a significant element of truth to these portrayals, they do not tell the entire story. Nocturnal surveillance by watchmen could have an important inhibiting effect on potential offenders. It could also secure vital intelligence. This can be seen in the murder of Robert Greenoll, a young Warwickshire merchant, in 1583. One Thomas Smith resented Greenoll's success and popularity. He lured him into his house for drinks on New Year's

---

90.   Evans, "Comic Constables", pp. 427–433.

Eve, then bludgeoned and stabbed him to death and buried his body in the cellar, where he had dug a shallow grave in readiness. However, and disastrously, he then went to Greenoll's shop and burgled it, calling out to the night watchmen as he went by. Unfortunately, the watchmen remembered this the next morning, when it was discovered that the shop had been ransacked. Smith was investigated, his cellar searched, and the body found.[91]

An interesting illustration of the trials and tribulations faced by watchmen, the popular suspicions and resentment that they engendered, but also of a degree of diligence on their part, and the way in which policing was often negotiated, can be seen in a case that occurred in Essex during the summer of 1586. John Wayland, John Seale, and two other watchmen for the parishes of Fordham and Aldham were on duty at about midnight. Unusually, they saw lights in the home of one William Hills. They went to investigate (a common practice in such situations), but not hearing any suspicious noises from the premises resumed walking the streets. Hills then came out and accused Wayland of having "evesdropped his house". He went back inside and returned with Joshua Newton. The two men, armed with a bill and pitchfork, then threatened the watchmen, and demanded that they leave the parish, claiming that they had been "scullkynge aboute ye backe sydes of the howses to steale poultrye". The officers refused to go, as they had been ordered to watch there. A heated confrontation ensued, with weapons being brandished. The shouting woke up neighbours, and the local constable was forced to get out of bed to deal with the situation. He advised the watchmen to withdraw for fear of further trouble, which they did with great reluctance.[92] At the Michaelmas Quarter Sessions for Essex that year, Hills and Newton were indicted for assaulting and beating Wayland and Seale while uttering threats and abuse, but were acquitted.[93]

---

91. Black, Jennifer (2013) "Religion and the Maintenance of Hierarchy in Murder Pamphlets in Renaissance England", *Constructing the Past*, Vol. 14, Issue 1: http://digitalcommons.iwu. edu/constructing/vol14/iss1/3; Anon, *A briefe discourse of two most cruell and bloudie murthers, committed bothe in Worcestershire, and bothe happening unhappily in the yeare 1583* (London: 1583), pp. 1–10.
92. ERO Q/SR 98/77.
93. ERO Q/SR 98/37.

JPs and Policing

Although justices of the peace authorised and ordered much action by petty constables, and carried out some detective work, they occasionally became directly involved in supervising ordinary policing operations. For example, in May 1568 the Privy Council in Westminster wrote to William More, a Surrey JP, requiring him to go with another justice to one Henry Owen's house in Wotton. Owen was suspected of coining and of detaining his wife in their home for an evil purpose. The magistrates were ordered to arrest Owen and free his spouse, and then send both to the Privy Council for investigation.[94] Nevertheless, this was comparatively unusual.

More important, the JPs' ability to force obstreperous or threatening members of the community to enter into recognisances to keep the peace and be of good behaviour, whether generally or towards specific named individuals, served a vital policing function in Tudor England. They helped to defuse interpersonal disputes before these produced serious violence, and could be ordered by JPs both in and out of sessions. Frequently they were combined with an order to appear at quarter sessions, giving the complainant a chance to indict the recipient for a substantive offence if this was deemed necessary. In practice, this was often not done, if there had been no further problems. In these circumstances, the recognisance would normally be discharged when the person who had been bound over appeared at the sessions and paid a small fee; he would then be released.

This procedure was inherited from, and regularly used during, the late medieval period.[95] Thus, in 1469 Thomas Chaplin and Daniel Digby entered into recognisances to ensure that the latter's wife, Rose, keep the peace towards Katherine Dodd in Halstead and attend the Essex Quarter Sessions.[96] It was employed throughout the Tudor era. For example, in 1526 Francis Badely and Robert Piper from Walthamstow were bound over to keep the peace towards John Dickenson and to appear at the

---

94.   SHC 6729/11/12.
95.   ERO D/B 5 Sb1/2.
96.   ERO Q/SR 342/61.

following Essex General Sessions.[97] In the same county, in April 1582, William Deane noted that Alice Wafforde, a widow from Wethersfield, had sworn before him that she was in fear of two local men, a father and son, both named Thomas Cranford. He ordered that the constables of Wethersfield bring the men before a JP so that they might find sureties to keep the peace.[98] These were often quite modest. In December 1601 Henry Bond, a Kentish shoemaker, was bound over to be of good behaviour in the sum of just £5 prior to appearing at the Maidstone Quarter Sessions.[99]

This power was also used to deal with domestic and familial disputes. In February 1566 George Nicholls, an Essex JP, ordered Peter Allam to appear at the next quarter sessions at Chelmsford and, in the meantime, to keep the peace towards his brother.[100] Not infrequently, both parties were bound over in mutual recognisances. For example, in 1568 Kenelm Throckmorton, another Essex JP, took recognisances from Thomas Halydaye, the vicar of Thaxted, to keep the peace towards a local gentleman named Thomas Patteshall, who, in his turn, was bound over to keep the peace towards the cleric. Patteshall claimed that he feared being attacked and having his house burned down by Halydaye.[101]

In 1602, in Lincolnshire, after the Reverend William Storre was publicly threatened with serious violence by Francis Cartwright, he immediately went to "some Justices neere adjoyning: [where he] acquainted them with these proceedings, & desired the good behaviour against the said Cartwright". However, and perhaps because of the latter's social status, these JPs doubted whether they could bind him over to be of good behaviour towards Storre specifically, but were willing to adopt the less drastic option of binding him over to keep the peace generally, so they offered him "for his present safegard the peace, and the other at the next quarter sessions, if occasion so required".[102]

---

97.   ERO D/B 5 Sb1/3.
98.   ERO Q/SR 80/38, 55.
99.   Knafla, *Kent at Law 1602*, p. 226.
100. ERO Q/SR 18/48.
101. ERO Q/SR 26/45, 46.
102. Anon, *The manner of the cruell outragious murther of William Storre Mast. of Art, minister, and preacher at Market Raisin in the county of Lincolne committed by Francis Cartwright one of his parishioners, the 30. day of August anno. 1602* (Oxford: Joseph Barnes, 1603), pp. 1–20.

A failure to enter into a recognisance when required to do so by a JP would lead to committal to prison. Thus, in 1586 Sir Thomas Gawdey directed the constables of Stock to bring the Reverend William Pynder before a county justice to be bound over for good behaviour and to appear at the next general gaol delivery. He ordered that, if the cleric refused to enter into such an undertaking, he was to be committed to Colchester Gaol until he changed his mind.[103] In 1604 Humphrey Mildmay wrote to his fellow Essex JPs complaining that the constables in Danbury had ignored a *mittimus* that he had issued, committing an elderly widow, Denise Clarke, to prison for refusing to provide sureties for keeping the peace towards her neighbours, in light of "her bad toonge and malitious minde".[104]

The sums pledged were usually fairly small, but marginal members of society might struggle to provide them. In March 1585, Sir John Smythe committed William Stephens to gaol, after Stephens had appeared before him on numerous occasions, following complaints about the commission of various acts of disorder. Smythe had required Stephens to enter sureties for his good behaviour, and, as he was not able to do so, committed him to prison.[105]

---

103. ERO Q/SR 96/57.
104. ERO Q/SR 166/149.
105. ERO Q/SR 92/4.

CHAPTER 5

The Justices of the Peace

Introduction

The Tudor criminal justice system revolved around the country's justices of the peace (JPs), who decided questions relating to arrest, examination of suspects, committal for trial, choice of forum, bail, and case management, and sometimes even conducted basic detective work in serious crimes. As a result, they warrant special scrutiny. Although Richard I had appointed "Keepers of the Peace" in 1195 to preserve order in unruly areas, the JP's office more properly originated in a statute from 1327, which provided for the appointment of "good and lawful men" by commission from the Crown to help maintain public order in their counties. A stream of legislation during the reign of Edward III (1327–1377) expanded their powers, something that may have been accelerated by a need to deal with the social consequences of the Black Death.[106] A statute passed in 1361 first referred to them as "justices of the peace", a title that eventually stuck. They were almost universal in England, but not appointed in Cheshire until 1536, because of its highly singular history as a county palatine.

By the start of the Tudor era, the JPs had largely superseded both coroners (considered in *Chapter 6*) and high sheriffs as the most important government officers in the localities. (The lord lieutenant and his deputies were not introduced until the 1540s and were primarily involved with county military and militia arrangements). Nevertheless, the sheriff warrants some further consideration, not least because he was usually drawn from the ranks of serving JPs.

---

106. Langbein, *History of the Common Law*, p. 230.

The Tudor Shrievalty

The high sheriff's position dated from Saxon times. It had lost much of its power during the late medieval period; for example, the sheriff's biannual "tourn" (an inspection of the hundreds) could not hear indictments after 1461. Even so, in 1485 the sheriff still had significant influence over how justice was administered in his county. Although this waned over ensuing decades, he remained loosely responsible for, inter alia, the county gaol and gallows, the conduct of executions, empanelling juries, logistical arrangements for assizes, and (in practice) transmitting information to central government throughout the Tudor era. In 1603 the shrievalty was still confined to prominent gentlemen, appointed annually by the Crown, usually from the ranks of serving JPs. It was an expensive, time-consuming, and burdensome position, as Sir Piers Edgecumbe of Cornwall complained in 1535, when asking Thomas Cromwell (who took a personal interest in appointing high sheriffs) to be excused from having to travel to London to account to the Exchequer for his year in service (1533–1534). Edgecumbe claimed that he had not wanted the position when appointed and was already 40 marks (more than £26) out of pocket because of it. By the start of the seventeenth century it was an honour that some gentlemen preferred to avoid altogether if possible, not least because inflation and reduced county revenues had made it even more of a financial burden. In 1535, when Cromwell asked Sir Nicholas Wadham if he would be willing to serve a second consecutive term as High Sheriff of Somerset, the latter politely declined the offer.[107]

High sheriffs usually returned to their county commission after their year in office, although a few would serve again during the course of their lives.[108] (Sir Alexander Radcliffe was thrice high sheriff for Lancashire, in 1524, 1529, and 1539.) Of the 55 Devonshire JPs in 1592, some 28 were at one time or another high sheriffs for their county.[109] Nevertheless, as this suggests, at any one time there was only one sheriff (and some positions were shared with other counties), but numerous justices of the peace.

---

107. Mary L. Robertson, "'The Art of the Possible,'" *The Historical Journal*, pp. 806–807.
108. Forster, *East Riding Justices*, p. 7.
109. Edward Potts Cheyney, *European Background of American History: 1300–1600* (New York: Harper & Brothers, 1904), p. 277.

JPs and Central Government

The rise of the JPs meant that central authority, manifest in legislation and directives made in Westminster, could be exercised through regional elites who were answerable to the monarch. For example, during the 1530s Thomas Cromwell kept in close contact with a group of powerful resident JPs in the West Country, as well as maintaining connections with many of their less elevated colleagues (up to 40 per cent communicated with him at some point in their working lives). The former would travel between their own counties and the court, promoting central influence and control.[110] Presumably a similar situation pertained in other English regions. More prominent magistrates were also tied directly to the centre as MPs in Parliament. For example, the 55 JPs in the Devonshire Commission in 1592 produced six men who sat in the House of Commons at some point, and many counties had an even higher proportion of parliamentarians on their bench. Indicative of the importance of central control, JPs might receive orders, exhortations, and other communications directly from the Privy Council.[111] This was especially common for those resident near London, in counties such as Surrey, but extended to all parts of the country, Privy Council letters becoming the most common means for asserting central direction in local affairs.[112]

For example, in September 1578 the Privy Council wrote to the sheriff and justices of the peace of Surrey, claiming that Catholic priests were going about the country disguised as artisans, saying mass, and subverting people from their allegiance to the queen. The JPs were ordered to search out and arrest them. More mundanely, but more relevantly for this book, in December 1589, Lord Howard wrote (from the Court) to Sir William More in Surrey, asking him to arrest and question men who had hunted illegally in Woking Park and wounded and tied up the keepers there.[113] At other times, government pressure on JPs was brought to bear indirectly, by visiting assize judges and courtiers.

The Tudor era saw a constant increase in the justices' ostensible responsibilities, both when it came to conducting the business of local

---

110. Robertson, "'The Art of the Possible,'" p. 800.
111. Forster, *East Riding Justices*, p. 10.
112. Robertson, "'The Art of the Possible,'" p. 815.
113. SHC 2/407/MSLb.220 and SHC 6729/9/48.

government and when acting as royal judges or magistrates. The Parliaments of Henry VII alone passed 21 statutes adding to or regulating their work.[114] On one assessment, by the end of the sixteenth century, 309 statutes placed duties on JPs, and 176 of these had been passed since the accession of the Tudors in 1485.[115] By then, they were charged with dealing with issues pertaining to, among others, religion, industry, relations between masters and workers, the fabric of roads and bridges, and the relief of poverty and distress. Thus, under an Act of 1556, alehouse and innkeepers had to be licensed by JPs, while in 1562 they were empowered by statute to fix maximum wage rates. These new administrative duties distinguished the JPs of 1600 from those of 1500 just as much as their enhanced responsibility for law and order.

The JPs' primary judicial function was to preside over quarter sessions, where, working with a jury, they would "determyne felonies and trespasses committed and done agaynste the peace, and doo reasonable punyshement, accordying to lawe and reason".[116] Additionally, they were required to attend assizes, albeit in a more advisory and ceremonial capacity. However, and just as important, they also conducted much interlocutory and investigative criminal work "out of sessions" — examining witnesses and suspects, committing matters for trial, granting bail, etc.

Backgrounds

Despite their importance, Tudor JPs were largely untrained, part-time amateurs who were usually appointed from the ranks of significant landowners in each county, supplemented by a small but disproportionately important number of locally-based professional lawyers. In theory, under a statute from 1439, most had to live in the counties where they were members of the local commission. Only lords, judges, and stewards of the Duchy of Lancaster were permitted to be non-resident JPs, although this provision was often being ignored by the latter decades of the fifteenth century. The statute also required that they have an income of at least

---

114. Lander, J. R., *English Justices of the Peace*, p. 7.
115. Forster, *East Riding Justices*, p. 15.
116. Anon, *The Boke for a Justyce of Peace* (London: Thomas Berthel, 1534), p. 1.

£20 a year from their lands, unless they were barristers/apprentices-at-law or serjeants-at-law who had been appointed to the commission to provide legal expertise in the absence of wealthier lawyers.[117] If any non-lawyer was made a JP and could not meet the property requirement, he would not only be put out of the commission but might also be fined £20 if he failed to inform the chancellor within a month of appointment of his impecunious status, or if he were to sit in sessions, issue a warrant or conduct other official business by dint of his membership of the commission.

The relatively small £20 qualification had been set with a view to excluding those whose poverty made them "covetous and contemptible" and who sought the office for profit.[118] Most, but not quite all, English county JPs had much greater incomes than the requisite minimum, and borough magistrates (see below) did not have to meet the £20 property requirement. The amount was much more modest (just £10) for JPs from Wales after the office was extended to the principality during the reign of Henry VIII. This was necessary: in March 1536, Roland Lee, the Bishop of Coventry and Lichfield, had written to Thomas Cromwell, after learning that the King planned to introduce JPs, noting that there were "very few Welsh in Wales above Brecknock who have 10*l*. land"[119] However, small though it was, the property requirement still created problems in the far north of England, especially during the early Tudor period. The relative poverty of members of the Border gentry (like that of their Welsh counterparts), whose estates were often valued at less than £10 a year, rendered many of them ineligible for service.[120]

More typically, a sample of a large number of Kentish justices in the latter years of the reign of Henry VIII would suggest that the average magistrate in this southeastern county held almost £90 per annum in lands, although one had as little as £30 per annum and three others about

117. P. R. Glazebrook (ed.), *The Boke of Justices of Peas, 1506* (Devizes: Professional Books, 1991), p. Aii.
118. William Lambarde, *Eirenarcha* (London: Thomas Wright, 1599, pp. 30–31.
119. James Gairdner (ed.), *Letters and Papers, Foreign and Domestic, Henry VIII, Vol. 10, January–June 1536* (London: HMSO, 1887), pp. 182–195.
120. Claire Etty, *Tudor Revolution?: Royal Control of the Anglo-Scottish Border, 1483–1530*, Durham University, PhD thesis, 2005, p. 118.

£50 (several, though, had much more than the average).[121] The situation was broadly the same in Sussex during the 1520s, where JPs averaged £100 a year in lands.[122]

Like some of his late medieval predecessors, Henry VII selected a significant part of his county JPs from the second tier of local land-owners — the major gentry, rather than noblemen — if only to limit the power of great magnates. Nevertheless, throughout the Tudor era, the magistracy reflected a broad spectrum of the upper ranks of English society, and commissions of the peace always included an admixture of local aristocrats. In 1600 the Wiltshire commission consisted of 52 men, of whom two were national statesmen appointed on an honorary basis and four were judges, appointed because of their positions (see below). Even so, the remaining 46 "local" men included two earls and five barons, as well as the Bishop of Salisbury and his chancellor. However, the great majority, some 37 justices, were simply country gentlemen, even if several were knights.[123]

There were a few local variations to this general pattern. For example, although the London-influenced county of Middlesex had its own commission of the peace, like any other shire, it was unusual for the presence among its ranks of a significant number of City merchants and professional lawyers who had a residence in the county. Furthermore, by the late 1580s, and unlike many other parts of the country, most men who met the £20 a year property requirement, and who actively sought admission, would be appointed, unless suspected of recusancy or thought to be unsuitable for some other reason. In part this reflected the differing nature of wealth in Middlesex, but it was also indicative of the emerging problems attendant on dealing with the high level of crime found in and around London, something that, a century later, would produce Middlesex's notorious "trading justices".[124]

---

121. Zell, "Early Tudor JPs at Work", *Archaeologia Cantiana*, Vol. 93 (1977), p. 129.
122. Julian Cornwall, "The Early Tudor Gentry", *The Economic History Review*, Vol. 17, No. 3, 1965, p. 467.
123. R. B. Pugh and Elizabeth Crittall (eds.), *A History of the County of Wiltshire: Vol. 5* (London: Victoria County History, 1957), pp. 80–110.
124. P. S. King, *The Middlesex Justices 1590–1640: The Commissions of the Peace, Oyer and Terminer and Gaol Delivery for Middlesex*, Durham University, Masters thesis, 1972, p. 40.

Honorary Appointments

In each commission about ten to 20 per cent of JPs were appointed "for honour's sake", because of their official status in the nation or their social pre-eminence in the county. They made up what modern historians sometimes term the commission's "dignitary group".[125] Traditionally, major statesmen, such as the lord chancellor, were included in most (if not all) commissions of the peace in England, even though they were not local residents.[126] Thus in 1539 the Devonshire Commission listed 12 ex-officio appointments: Sir Thomas Audley; the Duke of Norfolk; the Duke of Suffolk; Thomas Cromwell; the Marquess of Dorset; the Earl of Southampton; the Bishop of Exeter; John, Lord Russell; John, Lord Zouche; Edmund, Lord Braye; Sir Richard Lyster; and Sir Thomas Willoughby.[127] In like manner, and among several other similar men, in 1562 the Wiltshire Commission included Sir Nicholas Bacon, the lord keeper, the Marquess of Winchester, the lord treasurer, and the Earl of Arundel, who was the lord steward.[128]

Henry VII sometimes made use of talented ministers with legal, political, and financial skills to enforce his government as locally-appointed and active JPs during times of crisis. Such men might be named to commissions, in counties near where they had land or employment, and attend local quarter sessions. Some would focus their involvement on cases that required careful handling or a show of conciliar authority, such as murders involving prominent individuals. For example, Edmund Dudley, effectively the financial agent for the King, was very active on the Sussex Commission in the mid-to-late 1490s.[129] However, such local activism by major statesmen was not typical of the Tudor era as a whole.

Important local aristocrats might also be appointed in a largely (if not purely) honorary sense, able to serve, but only rarely doing so. Judges who regularly covered the relevant county's assizes would also be appointed

---

125. D. J. Wilkinson, "The Commission of the Peace in Lancashire, 1603–1642", *Transactions of the Historic Society of Lancashire and Cheshire*, Vol. 132 (1982), p. 43.
126. Smith, *De Republica Anglorum*, London, p. 103.
127. Rebecca J. Zmarzly, *Justices of the Peace in Mid-Tudor Devon Circa 1538–1570*, Texas State University at San Marcos, MA thesis, p. 26.
128. Joel Hurstfield, *Freedom, Corruption, and Government in Elizabethan England* (London: Jonathan Cape, 1973), p. 252.
129. Gunn, *Henry VII's New Men*, pp. 55–57.

as a matter of course, although some of these men did sit at quarter sessions on a fairly regular basis (see below).

Clerical JPs

After the 1420s, bishops began to be appointed as JPs, and from the 1460s onwards several abbots and priors joined them. Initially, clerical JPs were confined to the Home Counties and the South West, but by the 1520s they could be found across the South, in the Midlands, and even in Yorkshire and Northumberland.[130] This practice survived the Reformation, although abbots and priors did not. Typically, Henry VIII appointed John Veysey, the Bishop of Exeter, and the highest-ranking clergyman in the South West of England, to the Devonshire bench.[131] During the sixteenth century, most commissions had a cleric, and the senior JP in a county was often a bishop. For example, in Surrey, during the 1570s, it was John Whitgift, who eventually became Archbishop of Canterbury. Some of these men were relatively active magistrates, rather than being purely honorary appointments. For example, John Walton, the Bishop of Exeter from 1578 to 1593, appeared regularly in the lists of those present at Devonshire Quarter Sessions, and, as his name was normally placed first, may sometimes have had a presiding role.[132] Some even engaged in out-of-sessions work.

Nevertheless, although there was a modest expansion in clerical JPs in the years after 1590, lower-ranking clergymen did not normally become magistrates during the Tudor era (unlike the situation found in the later eighteenth century), and the number of clerical JPs was always very small. In 1590 clergymen held just 95 places on various English commissions, and bishops held 78 of these; the Bishop of St Asaph alone had 13. Other

---

130. Martin Heale, *The Abbots and Priors of Late Medieval and Reformation England* (Oxford: Oxford University Press, 2016), p. 211.
131. Zmarzly, *Justices of the Peace*, p. 55.
132. Alexander Henry Abercromby Hamilton, *Quarter Sessions from Queen Elizabeth to Queen Anne: Illustrations of Local Government and History, Drawn from Original Records* (London: Sampson Low, 1878), p. 351.

clergymen (mainly deans) held just 17, a figure that increased to 19 in 1596, and 29 in 1604.[133]

Even so, the great majority of JPs were members of the gentry, rather than dignitaries or clergymen, and were chosen in the hope that they would make an active contribution to the criminal justice system. Therefore, their selection and appointment must be considered.

Selection and Appointment

The Lord Chancellor was responsible for appointing JPs, although the Chancellor of the Duchy of Lancaster was responsible for those in the Lancashire Commission.[134] Their decisions were largely based on advice to the Crown from visiting assizes judges, who acted as conduits for provincial opinion in this regard. The judiciary also made personal assessments of likely men while on circuit, this being an aspect of their official work. For example, in June 1592 John Popham, the Attorney General, and William Peryam, a judge of the Common Pleas, recommended that six new men (three of them lawyers) be appointed as JPs on the Norfolk Circuit, where they sat as judges. In the 1560s, Elizabeth's principal minister, William Cecil, Lord Burghley, was noted for the meticulous records he kept on members the of county gentry, identifying their suitability for appointment as JPs based on information supplied by judges after they returned from their circuits.

However, central government also received information about the suitability of prospective magistrates from other sources, such as peers, heralds' visitations, and bishops.[135] For example, the Earl of Derby and the Bishop of Chester were always influential in deciding who should become justices in Lancashire.[136] Clerics were especially important when providing information on questions of spiritual allegiance after the Reformation. In 1564 the Privy Council sent a questionnaire to every bishop

---

133. Christopher Haigh and Alison Wall, "Clergy JPs in England and Wales, 1590–1640", *The Historical Journal*, Vol. 47, No. 2, p. 235.
134. Wilkinson, "The Commission of the Peace in Lancashire", p. 41.
135. Lander, *English Justices of the Peace*, p. 157.
136. Wilkinson, "The Commission of the Peace in Lancashire", p. 51.

about the religious attitudes of current and potential JPs, something that was repeated in 1587.[137]

Backgrounds

Some prominent county families provided generations of JPs during the fifteenth and sixteenth centuries. Among them were the Wakes in Northamptonshire, the Lygons in Worcestershire, the Tailboys in Lincolnshire, and the Brockets in Hertfordshire.[138] Further south, the Gaynesfords had resided at Crowhurst in Surrey since 1338, and by the early sixteenth century had produced several generations that served the county as JPs (and sheriffs).[139] Other families produced just one magistrate and then disappeared from the records in what was a socially fairly mobile world. Nevertheless, by the Elizabethan period important families often had several members on the bench at the same time; sons were recruited to the bench while their fathers were still in office, if only to give continuity of service.[140]

Although the possession of genteel status was normally a prerequisite for appointment to a county commission, it was not remotely sufficient, on its own, to guarantee membership of the magistracy. Even after the major sixteenth century expansion in the number of JPs, there were far more gentlemen than justices of the peace. For example, there were about 80 resident adult men of gentry-status in Buckinghamshire during the 1520s, but only ten to 15 of them were JPs. At about the same time, there were almost 200 gentlemen in Suffolk, just 18 of whom were justices.[141]

Of course, not all English gentlemen had the same status. For much of the medieval period, JPs had not necessarily been drawn from the richest and most prominent gentry families in their counties. This changed in the late fifteenth century, after which most locally-resident justices

---

137. Alison Wall, "'The Greatest Disgrace': The Making and Unmaking of JPs in Elizabethan and Jacobean England", *English Historical Review*, Vol. 119, Issue 481, p. 313 and p. 318.
138. Lander, *English Justices of the Peace*, p. 80.
139. W. B. Robison, "Murder at Crowhurst: A Case Study in Early Tudor Law Enforcement", *Criminal Justice History*, 1988, Vol. 9, pp. 33–34.
140. Zell, "Kent's Elizabethan JPs at Work", Vol. 119, *Archaeologia Cantiana*, pp. 1–44, p. 4, and p. 10.
141. Cornwall, "The Early Tudor Gentry", pp. 468–469.

were drawn from leading members of what has been termed the county rather than the parish gentry.[142] Traditionally, the provincial gentry of Tudor England were divided between these two main groups, although the distinctions were often vague and uncertain. (Some individuals were described as both esquires and gentlemen in different legal surveys, while others became knights later in their lives.)[143] Nevertheless, in Lancashire baronets, knights, and esquires, rather than "mere gentlemen", were predominant on the county commission, as they were in Essex, Yorkshire, and most other English counties.[144]

Furthermore, whatever their social status some members of the gentry were considered too young, and others too old, to be put on their local commissions as active JPs. The age of newly appointed magistrates varied greatly, ranging from those who were barely (legal) adults (although this was unusual) to men in their early sixties (also rare). Most were in their thirties or forties when they first became JPs, although Sir John Oglander, appointed to the Hampshire Commission at the age of 22 in 1607, was "aschamed to sitt on ye Bench, as not havinge any hayre on my face, and less wit". There was also considerable regional variation in this regard. In the first half of the seventeenth century, the average age on first appointment in Sussex was 45, a decade older than it was in Lancashire.[145]

Other gentlemen were too infirm to be made JPs, although this did not necessarily lead to exclusion from the bench if their condition set in after appointment. Richard Thimbleby was on the Commission for the Parts of Lindsey (one of the three Divisions of Lincolnshire) from 1486 to 1509, even though, for the last 20 years of this period, he was normally exempted from attending assizes and quarter sessions because of "trustworthy testimony" that he suffered from internal ulcers occasioned by a riding accident. This meant that he was "unable to go on horseback without endangering his life".

---

142. Norma Landau, "The Changing Persona of the Justices and their Quarter Sessions" in L. Hutson (ed.), *The Oxford Handbook of English Law and Literature, 1500–1700* (Oxford: Oxford University Press, 2017), p. 242.
143. Cornwall, "The Early Tudor Gentry", p. 468.
144. Wilkinson, "The Commission of the Peace in Lancashire", p. 43.
145. Wilkinson, "The Commission of the Peace in Lancashire", p. 52.

However, even important gentlemen of appropriate age and in good health sometimes had to lobby hard to become JPs in areas where there were numerous candidates for the position. Robert Dormer (1485–1552) of Wing, in Buckinghamshire, was one of the richest landowners in the county, but was not made a justice until 1536, when he was 50-years-old.[146]

Qualities

Ideally, those selected as JPs would be personally suitable, as well as being wealthy and locally influential.[147] In 1506 it was noted that "well disposed men & lawfull that ben not meyntenours of quarrelles sholde be Justyces off the peas".[148] In similar terms, some 28 years later, it was suggested that the Lord Chancellor should appoint "good men and laufull, that ben no maynteiners of yuell".[149] From the perspective of central government, certain other qualities were also desirable. Among them were native ability and a willingness to implement government initiatives. Thus, in May 1528 the influential Sir Henry Guildford wrote to Cardinal Wolsey, suggesting John Crowmer for the Kentish Commission; Crowmer was, he said, a "wise man of good order and always ready to accomplish such commandments as cometh from the King's highness and your grace".[150]

The career of the very conscientious early Tudor JP Sir John Gaynesford is indicative of those of the "better sort" of magistrate. He was admitted to Lincoln's Inn as a student in 1485, when he was probably about 19, and would have gained some knowledge of the law before inheriting Crowhurst Manor, in Surrey, in 1491. In early 1500 he was appointed to the county commission of the peace, where he remained until his death in 1540, attending quarter sessions regularly, working hard at out-of-sessions business, and frequently liaising with the Privy Council. He was the (combined) Sheriff of Surrey and Sussex in 1500 to 1501 and again in 1517 to 1518.[151]

---

146. Cornwall, "The Early Tudor Gentry", p. 468.
147. Alison Wall, "'The Greatest Disgrace': The Making and Unmaking of JPs in Elizabethan and Jacobean England", *English Historical Review*, Vol. 119, Issue 481, p. 313 and p. 318.
148. Glazebrook, *The Boke of Justices of Peas*, p. Aii.
149. Anon, *The Boke for a Justyce of Peace*, p. 1.
150. Zell, "Early Tudor JPs at Work", p. 126.
151. Robison, "Murder at Crowhurst", pp. 33–34.

Nevertheless, whatever the ideal, reality was often rather different. Despite the formalities of appointment, selection was primarily a local process, and so vulnerable to factionalism and vested interests. Many of those appointed were not men of sterling character, even if they were rich and locally powerful individuals who could not be ignored, while others were men of limited ability. The regular denunciations of the quality of magistrates by statesmen such as William Cecil, even late in the Tudor era, suggest that central government was not, in practice, in full control of their appointment and dismissal, and that there was not a vast pool of suitably qualified and locally acceptable men waiting to supply ready alternatives.[152]

Simple family pride and local esteem had rarely been the sole motivation behind desire for membership of the commission of the peace. In the late 1400s a need for self-preservation and the ability to manipulate legal forms and institutions, in a frequently violent world that was often characterised by legal chicanery, was always present, and this did not fully change over the ensuing century.[153] In 1565 Lord Keeper Bacon opined that many JPs were not concerned with preserving the "common goode" of their counties. Some were not merely indolent (see below), but sought the position to advance their personal interests by "overthrowinge an enemy or maynteyning a frende". In 1602 Lord Keeper Egerton complained that others were busybodies, actively cultivating dissension among their inferiors to gain a reputation for action with their neighbours, and so sitting "high on the Bench in the Quarter-Sessions".[154]

Active Misconduct

There were fairly regular allegations of active misconduct by JPs. This is, perhaps, unsurprising, as some already had a poor record prior to appointment, especially in the early Tudor period. For example, in February 1512 John Raynsford and several other men were indicted for murdering John Burges of East Greenwich the previous month. Raynsford, a member

---

152. Felicity Heal and Clive Holmes, *The Gentry in England and Wales, 1500–1700* (Basingstoke: Palgrave, 1994), p. 170.
153. Lander, *English Justices of the Peace*, p. 160.
154. Heal and Holmes, *The Gentry in England and Wales*, p. 168.

of a very prominent family of Essex gentry who were well connected at Court, took sanctuary at St John's Abbey in Colchester. Perhaps unsurprisingly, he was pardoned of all felonies in July 1513. More notably, in 1523 he was knighted and became a JP for Essex, an office he was to hold until his death in 1559 (the years from 1530 to 1536 apart).[155] He was also appointed (combined) High Sheriff of Essex and Hertfordshire for the year from 1537 to 1538.

Misconduct in office was certainly not a new phenomenon in the Tudor era. In the fifteenth century, JPs often took fees and retainers from local landowners and religious houses, albeit that these can partly be explained by the general need to encourage active magistrates to give up their time to the administration of justice.[156] (This became much less common after about 1500.) Nevertheless, it is apparent that, in return for their support, the late medieval Crown was prepared to tolerate a considerable degree of lawless behaviour amongst the country's JPs. For example, Sir Gilbert Debenham (c.1404–1481) of Little Wenham was on the Suffolk Commission for many years until 1475, although his life was characterised by riot, bribery, smuggling, corruption, and intimidation. Thomas Tethewy (1425–1485), a JP and coroner for Cornwall, was accused of attempted murder.[157]

Allegations of misconduct by JPs continued to be made on a regular basis throughout the Tudor era, even if the average gravity of the problems declined. For example, in about 1566 the Surrey JP William More wrote to his recently appointed fellow magistrate Richard Bydon, informing him that the wife of a man from Witley had alleged that Bydon had offered to restore cattle and land he had seized "if that you might have filthily used her". (Bydon vigorously rejected the allegation of soliciting sexual favours as a bribe).[158] Around 1580 a group of "poor men" complained to the Earl of Lincoln about the behaviour of Edmund Slyfield (c.1520–1591), a Surrey JP who had been appointed to the bench in

---

155. McSheffrey, "Sanctuary Seekers in England, 1380–1557" (Online companion to *Seeking Sanctuary*, 2017).

156. Rosemary Horrox (ed.), *Fifteenth century Attitudes: Perceptions of Society in Late Medieval England* (Cambridge: Cambridge University Press, 2008), p. 38.

157. Lander, *English Justices of the Peace*, pp. 94–95.

158. SHC LM/COR/3/652.

about 1552. He was accused of, inter alia, abusing his position to further his own private business, assaulting people, ordering that his daughter's maid be put in the stocks in Leatherhead for speaking out against her, and blocking a highway in Shere.[159]

Richard Bostock (c.1530–1606), of Tandridge and Crowhurst, in Surrey, a member of the Inner Temple, was a JP for Surrey from 1579, and sheriff of the county in 1585. Despite this, at the end of the 1580s he became involved in a lengthy dispute with a gentleman named Foster, possibly following his part in the trial and hanging of two of the latter's servants for highway robbery. This culminated in a lethal affray between Foster and Bostock and their respective servants as the latter was on his way to church. Bostock subsequently rejected Foster's allegation that the death of one of his retainers, a man named Holloway, had been caused by the disturbance; he counterclaimed that one of his own men and his nephew (and future JP) Bostock Fuller had been seriously hurt.[160]

In 1601 Edward Glascock made an allegation of widespread corruption on the part of the "inferior sort of Justices".[161] Several JPs were prosecuted in the Star Chamber for such behaviour.[162] More insidiously, as the Bishop of Exeter observed, JPs might be exposed to the "winks of a great neighbour". Ideally, these would be ignored; in practice, this was often much easier said than done, in a society in which contacts and influence were of vast importance, and the seeking and granting of favours was the common currency of everyday life. In 1587 Lord Burghley received a letter from Edwin Sandys, the Archbishop of York, complaining about local JPs whose failings meant that they deserved to be removed from the commission. In Yorkshire, at least, it was apparently "very hard to choose fit men" to be JPs. One magistrate was a "great fornicator" of "small wisdom, and less skill".[163]

Despite such incidents, the sixteenth century saw an improvement in the average quality of JPs, although this was, perhaps, not difficult,

---

159. SHC LM/1043/2.
160. SHC LM/COR/3/441.
161. J. R. Kent, "Attitudes of Members of the House of Commons to the Regulation of 'Personal Conduct' in Late Elizabethan and Early Stuart England", *Bulletin of the Institute of Historical Research*, Vol. 46 (1973), pp. 52–53.
162. Heal and Holmes, *The Gentry in England and Wales*, p. 175.
163. T. A. Morris, *Tudor Government* (London: Routledge, 1999), p. 69.

given the poor state of the late medieval magistracy.[164] Active steps were taken to encourage this after the early 1500s. Thomas More noted that, when he was Lord Chancellor, and acting on secret information about personal unsuitability, he had put some men out of their commissions of the peace. In these situations he would "never tell them who told me the tales that made me [act] so".[165] Nevertheless, one of the most problematic issues was magisterial laziness, rather than active wrongdoing.

Indolence

Many Tudor JPs, once appointed, were reluctant to conduct legal work, whether in or out of sessions. Of course, some had been appointed with no expectation that active service would ensue, such as the prominent aristocrats and national statesmen who were traditionally included in "most of the commissions of all the shires of England" (see above).[166] Unfortunately, many non-noble, county-resident JPs, appointed in the hope that they would serve actively, were also fairly modest in their contributions, both out of court and at sessions.

As a result, in each county a small coterie of fairly industrious men carried out a disproportionate amount of legal business, while a significant number did very little.[167] This was not a new state of affairs: it had been the case in the early fifteenth century.[168] For example, between 1422 and 1442 just 42 magistrates conducted judicial work in Norfolk and Suffolk, although far more men were appointed to the counties' commissions of the peace during this period.[169] In the 1460s the Kentish JP John Alfey sat at quarter sessions for 55 out of a possible 56 days for which records have been preserved. (These figures are based on the four shillings daily payment for "commoner" magistrates below the rank of knight banneret.) He headed a small group of committed men who were at the core of the

---

164. Lander, *English Justices of the Peace*, p. 157.
165. Elizabeth M. Nugent (ed.), *The Thought & Culture of the English Renaissance: An Anthology of Tudor Prose*, Vol. 1 (The Hague: Martinus Nijhoff, 1969), p. 243.
166. Smith, *De Republica Anglorum*, p. 103.
167. Joseph Hall, *Characters of Virtues and Vices* (London: Melch. Bradwood, 1608), Book 1, p. 58.
168. Lander, *English Justices of the Peace*, p. 64.
169. Philippa C. Maddern, *Violence and Social Order: East Anglia 1422–1442* (New York: Clarendon Press, 1992), p. 62.

Kent Commission. By contrast, others in the county at this time were almost totally inactive.[170] Similarly, small groups of lawyers and officials, often drawn from the middling ranks of the gentry, had conducted a disproportionately large amount of work on the West Riding bench in Yorkshire in the late fifteenth century.[171]

This pattern of (in)activism continued throughout the Tudor era. As Lord Keeper Bacon noted in 1565, some magistrates were "drones" who sought the office merely "for reputation's sake".[172] Such men were often reluctant to attend quarter sessions and assizes. By the 1580s, Edwin Sandys could note that absentees who lived "much in London" were affecting attendance in Yorkshire (a problem that would become much more significant over a century later).[173] Thus, in most years during the 1530s and 1540s, only half of the then Kent Commission of around 40 resident justices attended at least one sitting of quarter sessions annually.[174] Similarly, of the local men named as JPs on the various commissions of the peace for Devonshire issued around the middle of the sixteenth century, only an average of about 30 per cent appeared at quarter sessions; half of these men did not attend more than three times during their entire time in office, leaving a small group to do the lion's share of the work.[175] More than half a century later, little had changed. In the years between 1603 and 1625, only between ten and 18 magistrates in the North Riding of Yorkshire normally attended quarter sessions with any frequency, out of an average total of 59 JPs on the commission.[176]

Even these modest attendance figures might be slightly exaggerated; that a JP was recorded as attending a particular quarter sessions did not necessarily mean that he was present at all of it. Just after the Tudor period, King James' orders of 23 June, 1605 required that JPs should attend for the whole of quarter sessions, from beginning to end, unless

---

170. Lander, *English Justices of the Peace,* p. 64.
171. C. Arnold, "The Commission of the Peace for the West Riding of Yorkshire, 1437–1509", in *Property and Politics: Essays in Later Medieval English History,* Tony Pollard (ed.) (Gloucester: A. Sutton, 1984), pp. 116–138.
172. Heal and Holmes, *The Gentry in England and Wales,* p. 168.
173. Morris, *Tudor Government,* p. 69.
174. Zell, "Early Tudor JPs at Work", p. 138.
175. Zmarzly, *Justices Of The Peace,* p. 97.
176. Lander, *English Justices of the Peace,* p. 157.

they had good cause to leave early.[177] This was a response to the fairly common practice of justices' attending at the start of sessions and then slipping away.

However, there was considerable variation from county to county. At the assizes held at Chelmsford in July 1566 it was noted that there were then 30 county magistrates and 15 honorary JPs for Essex. Of the former, 19 were present. (Interestingly, five of the latter also attended, showing that there was not a hermetic divide between the two).[178] More generally, at the end of the period, approximately one-quarter to one-third of the county magistracy would be present at any given quarter session in Hertfordshire and Essex; however, when the honorary appointments are removed, attendance increases to almost half the resident JPs. Thus, in Hertfordshire, to take random quarter sessions, it was 14 out of 28 men in 1592, exactly 50 per cent, while 75 per cent attended in 1598 (an unusually high figure) and 47 per cent in 1602. In Essex it was 35 per cent in 1591, 55 per cent in 1598, and 36 per cent in 1602.[179]

It was not just court attendance that was affected by a reluctance to serve actively. Some JPs were also inactive when it came to out-of-sessions work, such as issuing warrants, taking depositions, examining and committing suspects for trial, or binding witnesses over to give evidence.[180] In July 1604, just before Parliament was prorogued, the Lord Keeper addressed the MPs, many of whom were also JPs in their counties and about to return home. He deprecated magistrates who, on their return to the country "fall to hawking, and yf any man comme about Justice, they send him to their next neybur Justice".[181] To deal with the problems that this occasioned, it seems that JPs who were active "out of sessions" often apportioned de facto areas of responsibility. For example, many

---

177. Hamilton, *Quarter Sessions*, p. 68.

178. Cockburn, *Calendar of Assize Records: Essex Indictments, Elizabeth I*, p. 44.

179. Jefffery R. Hankins, *Local Government and Society in Early Modern England: Hertfordshire and Essex, c.1590–1630*, Louisiana State University, PhD thesis, 2003, p. 336.

180. Malcolm Gaskill, *Crime and Mentalities in Modern England* (Cambridge: Cambridge University Press, 2000), p. 243.

181. Isaac Herbert Jeayes (ed.), *Letters of Philip Gawdy of West Harling, Norfolk, and of London to Various Members of His Family, 1579–1616* (London: J. B. Nichols and Sons, 1906), pp. 147–148.

recognisances taken by JPs in Elizabethan Essex related to individuals located within a five-mile radius of where they resided.[182]

Patterns of Activism

There was often some variation as to where even active JPs concentrated their legal efforts. Some appear to have focussed on attending court hearings, while others concentrated on out-of-court matters. Some were all-rounders, making a major contribution to out-of-sessions work and also attending court on a regular basis, though generally the lowest-performing magistrates in both categories were the same. Even among those who went to court there might be differences in attendance patterns; some focussed on the quarter sessions, some on the assizes, while others divided their attendance proportionately between the two forums.

For example, at the end of the Tudor period, Thomas Wilford attended only ten per cent of the Kent assizes hearings but got to 75 per cent of the county's quarter sessions. By contrast, Edward Filmer managed to get to 70 per cent of the former, but none of the latter. However, Thomas Fludd was remarkably diligent, attending all the sessions of both courts. Furthermore, Fludd also processed 29 cases out of sessions. In the east of the county, between 1598 and 1602, Stephen Thornhurst attended almost half of all assizes but no quarter sessions. However, he was also reasonably active out of court, processing (or helping to process) some 17 cases for assizes and six for quarter sessions during the same period. In the same area, Peter Manwood made a balanced and active contribution, attending about two-thirds of both assizes and quarter sessions hearings and processing 41 cases out-of-sessions. In West Kent, Thomas Potter attended no quarter sessions and only ten per cent of the assizes, but processed some 26 cases out-of-court. By contrast, Martin Barnham of Hollingbourne attended nearly all assizes but almost no quarter sessions, and only processed 13 cases.[183]

Of course, poor attendance at sessions was not solely down to indolence or the pressures of other business. Bouts of sickness, like long-term

---

182. Hankins, *Local Government and Society*, p. 147.
183. Knafla, *Kent at Law 1602*, pp. 21–22 and p. xxiv.

bad health (see above), could also produce such an outcome. In a letter sent to Lords Riche and Darcy, Henry Medeley, and James Morice, a pair of Essex JPs during the Elizabethan era, apologised for their recent absence from quarter sessions "syns at this tyme neyther of us is well able to travayle".[184] In June 1559 Sir Thomas Cawarden wrote to William More, the High Sheriff for Surrey, to inform him that he had broken his legs, making it doubtful that he could attend the following assizes. (He died later that year.)[185] Mental illness could also prevent a justice from attending. In September 1575, Thomas Stoughton (1521–1576), a Surrey JP wrote to William More noting that his colleague John Agmondesham had gone mad.[186]

However, physical incapacity did not necessarily preclude JPs from doing out-of-sessions work from their homes. In 1574, in a letter to the Clerk of the Peace for Essex, Edward Bury of Rayley noted that he was sending him various recognisances that he had taken, set down on paper "for lacke of parchementt", and explaining his own inability to appear at the forthcoming quarter sessions: "as for my comyng to do my dewtye I desyre you to consyder that I am olde and lame, assuryng you that yyt is great trouble and payne to me ether to ryde or go".[187]

Even so, laziness or distaste for the work involved appears to have been a far more important explanation for inaction than physical incapacity. Some men were quite open about their reluctance to serve. The first Baron (John) Lumley (1533–1609), a well-known Surrey aristocrat and art collector, was effectively an honorary appointment to the county bench; typically, he was listed but absent from the assizes held at Croydon in July 1563 and Southwark in March 1565.[188] In February 1564, Lumley wrote to Sir Henry Weston and William More, apparently returning a commission and an accompanying letter from the Privy Council, explaining that he was extremely busy elsewhere in the country, in the absence of which he claimed he would willingly have helped in the execution of

---

184. ERO Q/SR 68/59.
185. SHC LM/COR/3/21.
186. SHC LM/COR/3/185.
187. ERO Q/SR 48/26.
188. Cockburn, *Calendar of Assize Records: Surrey Indictments, Elizabeth I*, p. 35 and p. 41.

justice.[189] Much more commonly, many JPs simply shirked such service after appointment.

Official Concern

Magisterial inactivity was a matter of permanent concern to the authorities. Even so, dealing with the problem was not easy. In theory, indolent JPs could have been excluded from their commissions (see below). It appears that justices who were low down the order of precedence on the Lancashire commission often fulfilled their duties very conscientiously.[190] Presumably they realised that poor performance might lead to their being left off their county commission when it was reissued, and it is likely that this situation was replicated elsewhere. However, in practice, dismissal was sometimes not a realistic option, especially when more powerful men were involved.

Instead, less drastic methods might be employed. For example, at the Croydon Assizes in February 1572, JPs from the county working commission who were absent were each fined £5.[191] In January 1593 the Privy Council wrote to the Surrey justices ordering that the names of JPs attending and, more pertinently, those who failed to attend, assizes, be returned to them, suggesting that similar punishment might be forthcoming.[192] Magistrates were certainly concerned about criticism and possible sanctions for non-attendance, especially in the latter stages of the Tudor era. In July 1604, John Hammond, who was resident at Nonsuch, wrote to Sir George More apologising for not having been at the Summer Assizes for Surrey.[193]

Indicative of the problem, King James I's orders of the 23 June, 1605, made at the Court in Greenwich, and aimed at the better preservation of "peace, order and obedience", required, that all JPs attend all quarter sessions, and that the clerk of the peace report those not attending to the assize judges. These men were then to report those without a reasonable

---

189. SHC LM/COR/3/43.
190. Wilkinson, "The Commission of the Peace in Lancashire", p. 43.
191. Cockburn, *Calendar of Assize Records: Surrey Indictments, Elizabeth I*, p. 99.
192. SHC 643/1/8.
193. SHC 6729/12/34.

excuse for non-attendance (which was to be properly investigated) to the Lord Chancellor, who would pass on the information to the King and Privy Council. Judges were also required to enquire into, and report on, JPs who were inactive or negligent out-of-sessions.[194] These orders were widely distributed by the Privy Council. For example, in July 1605 the Surrey JPs, like those of other commissions, were sent a copy.[195] They even filtered down to lower-ranking officials. In October 1605 Richard Fleming sent a copy to the constables, churchwardens, and officers of the poor in Broughton-in-Furness, Hawkshead, Colton, and Cartmell in North Lancashire.[196] However, they were always a statement of good intentions, rather than rules that were ever likely to be followed to the letter.

Dismissal

The commissions of the peace for each county were frequently revised, sometimes more than once a year, especially where there had been major changes in composition in the meantime. For example, in Devon, the February 1540 commission listed Thomas Cromwell as an ex officio member, but that for July 1540 omitted him. By then Cromwell was imprisoned in the Tower of London and heading for execution.[197] More commonly, commissions were issued yearly, but occasionally this occurred after a lapse of several years.

New JPs would be added to the list, and those who had died or were deemed surplus to requirements, for whatever reasons, whether indolence or political unpopularity, would be left off. Typically, in June 1559, just a few weeks before his death, Sir Thomas Cawarden wrote to William More, the High Sheriff of Surrey, sending him copies of the latest commission of the peace for the county to distribute to gentlemen in his part of the shire. He noted that he had arranged for More's name, and that

---

194. Hamilton, *Quarter Sessions from Queen Elizabeth to Queen Anne*, pp. 67–68.
195. SHC 663/1/15.
196. J. A. Bennett and Richard Ward (eds.), *The Manuscripts of S. H. Le Fleming, Esq., of Rydal Hall* (London: HMSO, 1890), p. 12.
197. Zmarzly, *Justices Of The Peace In Mid-Tudor Devon*, p. 25.

of a gentleman named Birch, to be inserted in the commission, and that of a magistrate named Baker, who had died, to be erased.[198]

Many Tudor JPs suffered the humiliation of premature dismissal from their county commissions during these revisions. For example, in early 1583 Sir Arthur Heveningham turned up at the Epiphany Quarter Sessions for Norfolk to take his place on the bench, only to discover, when the commission was publicly read, that he was no longer a JP. Most men had a little more notice. In August 1575, John Skinner, a JP from Reigate, in Surrey, wrote to William More, complaining that he had been turned out of the prestigious quorum (a special group of senior and experienced JPs), and his cousins John Agmondesham and Edmund Saunders had been dismissed from the commission altogether. He suggested that More had been responsible for bringing about these changes "through some misliking you have of the parties".[199] As this comment suggests, rivalry, personal animosity, and political influence sometimes played a part in such disposals.

As a result, much of the gossip between prominent late medieval and Tudor gentlemen — and some gentlewomen — concerned who was likely to be excluded, and who added, to their county commissions. In May 1465 Margaret Paston urged John Paston to replace a Norfolk JP with her brother purely for personal advantage: "I wold ryght fayn that John Jenney werre putte oute of the Comyssyon of the Peas, and that my brother Wyll. Lumner wer set yn hys stede, for me thynkyth it wer ryght necessere that ther were such a man in that county that oght you gode wyll".[200] Almost a century later, in March 1564, Lawrence Ashburnham wrote to William More, noting Lord Lincoln's agreement to their seeking the removal from the Surrey commission of men to whom they both objected, and Ashburnham's rebuttal of a rumour that he and More had plotted to remove John Amersham from the same commission.[201] In September 1575 Thomas Stoughton, a Surrey JP and MP for Guildford, wrote to William More with the draft of a letter that he

---

198. SHC LM/COR/3/21.
199. SHC LM/COR/3/185.
200. James Gairdner (ed.), *The Paston Letters, A.D. 1422–1509*, Vol. 4 (London: Chatto & Windus, 1904), p. 141.
201. SHC 6729/1/5.

proposed to send to Edmund Saunders about Saunders' dismissal from the commission of the peace, with a view to getting More's opinion on such a delicate matter.[202]

However, it was not merely personal machinations that brought about dismissal from the commission but also factional pressures or the search for better, more hardworking, and politically or religiously "reliable" magistrates. Even so, the process was not always very well organized or scientific. Occasionally a simple administrative error was the cause. For example, during their year in office sheriffs were usually left off the commissions for their county. In July 1581 John Southcote, a judge of the Court of Queen's Bench, wrote to Sir William More, observing with surprise and regret that, since serving as Surrey sheriff for the year to 1580, More had been left out of the county commission. (He had been reappointed shortly before Southcote wrote.)[203] In 1593 Sir John Wolley, the Latin Secretary to the queen, wrote to Sir William More claiming that some men were on the Surrey Commission "that were not here at the Court named to be commissioners at all. I know not, I assure you, how they came in".[204]

During the religious strife of the mid-sixteenth century, groups of JPs were sometimes excluded because they were not deemed sufficiently Catholic (under Mary) or Protestant (under Elizabeth). For example, the total number of JPs commissioned for Devon during Henry VIII's rule peaked at 54 men in 1544. However, this number dropped by more than a third at the start of Mary's reign, a trend that has been discerned in many other counties, such as Hertfordshire and Kent. One possible explanation is that there was a purge of overtly Protestant JPs (another is that many of those who died between the end of Henry VIII's reign and the beginning of Mary's were not replaced).[205] Similarly, some Marian-appointed MPs were excluded from their commissions at the start of the Elizabethan period. For example, the first commission issued in Kent, after the new queen's accession in 1558, left out John Tooke and three other men who had served on the 1556 heresy commission for the

---

202. SHC LM/COR/3/185.
203. SHC 6729/7/67.
204. SHC LM/COR/3/524.
205. Zmarzly, *Justices Of The Peace In Mid-Tudor Devon*, p. 26.

Canterbury diocese.[206] Similarly, Sir Edward Gage (1521–1568), a Surrey JP, was removed from the commission after the queen's accession. According to John Trewe, Gage had been behind the burning of several Protestants in Lewes in 1556, and had placed him (Trewe) in the pillory, as well as cutting off his ears, without due cause.[207]

However, groups of magistrates were purged for many reasons, not just religious ones. In Elizabeth's reign alone there were widespread sackings of JPs in 1559, 1564, 1572, 1580, 1582, 1587, 1593, 1595, 1596, 1601, and 1603. Lord Burghley's papers list 330 men put out of the commissions of the peace in 1587. Amongst them were 13 JPs who were dismissed in Devon, a similar number in Somerset, 14 in Suffolk, and nine who went from Norfolk, including prominent men like Sir Thomas Knevett. Some sacked JPs eventually managed to secure reappointment.[208]

Even so, most JPs served for a significant period of time (at least five years), and often until death or ill health ended their careers. There were some local exceptions. If the 51 JPs in Devonshire who received per diem payments (i.e. non-noble members of the commission) between 1538 and 1570 are considered, it appears likely that eleven served for little more than a single year (or less) and just under half for three years or less. However, even there, five men served for more than a decade, while two men served for 19 years.[209] Nationally, a few individuals served for several decades. For example, in Kent, Sir Thomas Cheyney was a JP from 1524 (if not before) until his death in 1558. More generally, of the 42 men on the first Edwardian commission of the peace in that county (i.e. after January 1547), 30 per cent had been JPs since at least 1532.[210] Sir Thomas Denys, the longest-serving justice in sixteenth century Devon, was first appointed in 1504 and active until he died in 1561.[211]

206. Zell, "Kent's Elizabethan JPs at Work", pp. 4–5, and p. 10.
207. ERO Z/407/MSLb.508.
208. Wall, "'The Greatest Disgrace,'" p. 313 and p. 318.
209. Zmarzly, *Justices of the Peace in Mid-Tudor Devon*, p. 41.
210. Zell, "Early Tudor JPs at Work", p. 128.
211. Zmarzly, *Justices Of The Peace in Mid-Tudor Devon*, p. 26. and p. 40.

Number of JPs

The number of JPs appointed in each county during the Tudor era varied considerably, depending on its size, population, judicial needs, the amount of important local gentlemen who were keen (or at least willing and able) to discharge the office, and the local culture with regard to such matters. It also changed greatly over time. Throughout the period, the quantity of JPs was on a generally upward trend, although there were periodic reductions, for a variety of reasons, in which a significant number were "culled", temporarily reversing the situation. For example, in 1521 the Kent commission's strength was greatly reduced, for unknown reasons, but it had recovered by 1524.[212]

During the medieval period, the number of JPs had been quite limited. The commission for East Yorkshire comprised just seven men between 1361 and 1364.[213] Indeed, there had been a major reduction in the size of many commissions in 1389, when statute confined each county to no more than eight JPs. A legal writer expressly reiterated this requirement as late as 1506.[214] However, by the early sixteenth century this was slightly unusual in practice, although the Buckinghamshire Commission of February 1514 still contained just eight local men.[215] Nevertheless, by then, the majority of counties had far more, as the restrictions on manning levels had been tacitly ignored for years. For example, in Norfolk, between 1436 and 1504, the number of resident knights and gentlemen on the county commission had increased from seven to 25 men.[216]

Even so, there was little pattern to the number of JPs found in the various late fifteenth century commissions of the peace; some were large and others comparatively small, their sizes not always being contingent on that of the relevant county, although the general trend was upwards. For example, in Cumberland, during the 1460s, there was an average of 12.6 magistrates on the commission, with an average of 4.3 men being members of the quorum. Between 1497 and 1509 the comparable figures

---

212. Zell, "Early Tudor JPs at Work", p. 126.
213. Forster, *East Riding Justices,* p. 12.
214. Anon, *The Boke of Justices of Peas,* p. 1.
215. Cornwall, "The Early Tudor Gentry", p. 469.
216. Lander, *English Justices of the Peace,* p. 160.

were 14.5 and five men, respectively. In Cornwall, between 1461 and 1470, there was an average of 13.6 men, of whom 5.4 were in the quorum. Between 1497 and 1509, the numbers had increased to 24 and nine men, respectively. In Gloucestershire, in the 1460s, the figures were 21.4 men, 5.4 of them on the quorum. Between 1497 and 1509 these numbers had risen to 39.5 and 9.8, respectively.[217]

The number of JPs continued to increase during the course of the sixteenth century, especially after about 1530, due to a growth in legal work and the enhanced prestige of the office, even if significant population increase meant that the per capita expansion in the number of JPs was less striking.[218] For example, in the decade prior to 1525, the Buckinghamshire commission grew from eight to 15 local men.[219] In Wiltshire the resident commission of the peace had been made up of 25 local men in 1562 but reached 46 in 1600.[220] Some commissions were even larger. Kent had grown from about 40 in 1550 to approximately 90 men by the end of the century.[221]

Although Middlesex was close to the capital, its number of JPs grew relatively slowly at first. In 1558 there were 34 names on its commission, including six who were government officials, peers, and senior lawyers (the Attorney General among them), the rest being members of the local gentry (or at least "genteel" individuals). There were still only 42 JPs in 1584, despite the burgeoning size of the metropolis. Thereafter, numbers on the Middlesex bench increased significantly. As a result, in 1596 there were 68 names on the county commission, and in 1610 there were 87. Of course, as elsewhere in the country, some local appointees were attracted by the status of the office, and rarely attended sessions.[222]

At the close of the Tudor era, an average of more than 40 JPs per county was common in most parts of England.[223] By 1621 there were some 2,000 non-clerical and non-noble justices in the various commissions of

217. *Ibid*, p. 39.
218. Lambarde, *Eirenarcha*, p. 32; Zell, "Early Tudor JPs at Work", p. 125.
219. Cornwall, "The Early Tudor Gentry", p. 469.
220. Hurstfield, *Freedom, Corruption and Government*, p. 253.
221. Zell, "Early Tudor JPs at Work", p. 126; Zell, "Kent's Elizabethan JPs at Work", p. 4.
222. King, *The Middlesex Justices*, p. 40.
223. Cynthia B. Herrup, *The Common Peace* (Cambridge: Cambridge University Press, 1987), p. 44.

England and Wales.[224] Nevertheless, even with this major expansion, the number of active JPs often appeared relatively limited for the growing judicial and administrative duties entrusted to them.

Rewards

Although Parliament stipulated that the men chosen to be JPs should not need to be rewarded for their work, by an act of 1389, non-noble magistrates received a fairly generous subsistence allowance of four shillings a day for sitting at quarter sessions. This was still frequently claimed during the late fifteenth and sixteenth centuries (unlike later years), and provides important information as to attendance at such hearings. JPs also received a small amount of direct remuneration from their office from modest fees granted for specific legal services. It appears that a few magistrates were at least partly motivated by financial considerations, especially those recruited where there was a dearth of suitable gentlemen ready to actively take on the office, and the minimum property requirement for service was accepted.

Criticism

Although many contemporary observers claimed to admire the office of JP and the men who held it, the magistracy also faced a constant groundswell of informed criticism during the Tudor period. Towards the end of the sixteenth century, this became increasingly widespread and severe. One of Queen Elizabeth I's Lord Keepers even warned that their failings meant that professional judges might have to be appointed in their place, a theme that would be periodically revisited for the next two centuries until being realised (to a modest extent) in 1792: "Her Majesty may be driven, clean contrary to her most gracious nature and inclination, to appoint and assign private men for profit and gain sake to see her penal laws to be executed".

---

224. Landau, "The Justices and their Quarter Sessions", p. 242.

Queen Elizabeth herself complained that there were "more justices than justice"; many of them were "unlearned, negligent, and indiscreet" men.[225] The queen's flirtation with provost martials, at the end of 1589 may have been, in part, a public rebuff to the JPs, who were, according to the preamble to her proclamation of that time, not executing the vagrancy statutes properly. Where established, the provost marshals would, inevitably, provide competition to the magistracy.

Professional Knowledge

Inevitably, like all amateur judges, JPs suffered from a lack of legal expertise, a problem that became more serious as their duties and responsibilities increased during the sixteenth century. This was not an entirely satisfactory situation; although a JP might "be not fully wel versed in the lawes, yet it behoveth him to have some knowledge therin, and chiefly in thinges belonging to his office".[226] The explorer Sir Humphrey Gilbert (1539–1583), arguing for the establishment of a London Academy, thought that even aristocrats who sat as JPs should have some "judgement in the office of a justice of the peace". In its absence, they were often so ignorant of the law that they were subject to the views of their social inferiors on the bench.[227]

In theory the widespread Tudor practice of gentlemen joining and spending time at the Inns of Court when young ought to have ameliorated this situation, as they provided a legal education of sorts. As early as 1475, William Worcester was lamenting that many gentlemen had chosen to "lerne the practique of law" rather than skill at arms.[228] Their numbers increased greatly during the sixteenth century. On some estimates, a third of the resident and active magistrates in Kent in 1562 fell into this category; the proportion had increased to almost 40 per cent by 1584, and about half in 1608.[229] According to another estimate, 47 per cent of

225. Cockburn, *A History of English Assizes 1558–1714*, p. 58.
226. Humfrey Braham, *The institucion of a gentleman* (London: 1568, second ed.), p. 40.
227. Wilfrid R. Prest, *The Inns of Court under Elizabeth I and the Early Stuarts, 1590–1640* (Lanham, Maryland: Rowman and Littlefield,1972), p. 221.
228. Deborah Youngs, *Humphrey Newton (1466–1536): An Early Tudor Gentleman* (Martlesham, Suffolk: The Boydell Press, 2008), p. 41.
229. Zell, "Kent's Elizabethan JPs at Work", p. 10.

new JPs in Essex in the years from 1562 to 1571 were members of an Inn of Court, although the proportion gradually declined thereafter, falling to 27 per cent in the years between 1592 and 1601. Perhaps unsurprisingly, such men tended to be more active magistrates than those without a legal background. At least 10 of the 24 JPs (i.e. more than 40 per cent) whose attendance can be traced at Elizabethan quarter sessions in Essex, and who appeared at 15 or more sessions, were members of an inn.[230]

Nevertheless, the significance of this phenomenon can easily be exaggerated. Even in the 1460s, Sir John Fortescue had observed that, as well as providing legal education, the inns were a kind of academy, teaching the manners and skills needed by high status men. Dancing and singing classes were particularly popular. This aspect of student life became even more important over the ensuing century, and was often conducted to the neglect of legal studies. In the 1590s Paul Hentzner thought that many of those who frequented the inns and did not intend to practise law as a career failed to take their studies seriously.[231] At about the same time, Robert Parsons was scathing about the way in which it had become a custom "much increased these later years, that either all, or the most part of Noblemen's Children do repair to the Inns of Court, and Chancery, under pretence of studying the Common Laws of England".[232] Shakespeare's fictional Gloucestershire magistrate (and member of the quorum for that county), Justice Shallow, remembering his time at the Inns of Court and Chancery, primarily recalled that on one occasion he had had a fight with a fruiterer behind Gray's Inn.[233] Those who did take their legal studies seriously often concentrated on land law, which was invaluable to gentlemen who would inherit estates.

In practice, most early Tudor JPs acquired their knowledge of criminal law from their colleagues, in private discussions, on the quarter-sessions bench, or at assizes, when they sat with the judiciary. This gave them a valuable opportunity to learn the criminal law from both the presiding

---

230. F. G. Emmison, *Elizabethan Life: Disorder* (Chelmsford: Essex Record Office Publications, 1970), pp. 322–324.
231. Paul Hentzner, *Travels in England During the Reign of Queen Elizabeth* (London: Cassell, 1889), p. 43.
232. Parsons, *The Jesuit's Memorial*, p. 249.
233. *Henry IV, Part 2*, Act III, Scene 2.

judge and the assize clerk.[234] After the early decades of the sixteenth century, JPs also made increasing use of the specialist manuals that were starting to become available.[235] These eventually included Lambarde's *Eirenarcha*, the publication of which was partly motivated by the author's own service as a JP in Kent.[236] It first appeared in 1581 and went through numerous subsequent editions until being (largely) replaced by Michael Dalton's handbook after 1619. It was considered so authoritative that, in 1603, two JPs examining potential prosecution witnesses in a murder case in Devon, finding that they did not have a bible to hand, used a copy of Lambarde's work to swear them in.[237]

A variety of expedients were employed to remedy the lack of legal knowledge found amongst many JPs and the concern that this engendered in central government.

The Quorum and Lawyer JPs

One late medieval response to a lack of ability on the bench was to bifurcate the commission into ordinary magistrates and a special group, the quorum, who were supposed to be men of experience and proven competence or those possessed of legal qualifications, and who were entrusted with special powers and responsibilities. Sometimes, they had to be present before jurisdiction could be exercised, something that was often expressly specified in Tudor enabling legislation. Their presence was also required at all quarter sessions.[238]

Originally, membership of the quorum had extended to only a small proportion of a county's justices in the fifteenth and early sixteenth centuries. For example, in the three ridings of Yorkshire, in the early 1400s, many of the resident gentry who were members of the quorum were also

---

234. Braddick, *State Formation in Early Modern England,* p. 37.
235. Wilfrid Prest, "Legal Education of the Gentry at the Inns of Court, 1560–1640", *Past and Present,* Vol. 38, No. 1, pp. 20–39.
236. Terill, "William Lambarde", pp. 157–176.
237. Heal and Holmes, *The Gentry in England and Wales,* p. 178.
238. Raphael Holinshed, *The First Volume of the Chronicles of England, Scotland and Ireland* (London: George Bishop, 1577), p. 75.

qualified lawyers, whether practising locally or at Westminster.[239] Similarly, in Hampshire — admittedly one of the most professionally run counties in this respect — during the early years of the reign of Henry VIII, the quorum was largely made up of lawyers (often chosen with the support of the diocesan bishop); as a result, its members dominated proceedings at quarter sessions.[240] An acute local shortage of willing and able candidates, combined with a reluctance to extend the status gratuitously, meant that in March 1526 Geoffrey Lancaster was, for a time, the only member of the quorum for Cumberland.[241]

However, the standard required for membership of the quorum was greatly watered down during the course of the Tudor era, and far more men appointed, especially after the middle of the sixteenth century. For example, by 1544, 44 per cent of the Kent Commission held this status. Even so, they were still more likely to have had some form of legal experience, if only attendance as a student at the Inns of Court, and were of slightly higher than average social status than the commission as a whole. They were also more likely to be veteran and experienced magistrates. Nevertheless, by the end of Elizabeth's reign, the Kent quorum had expanded even further, so that some 80 to 90 locally resident JPs — the great majority of its commission — enjoyed this status, even though most were not specially qualified for such a position.[242]

The same pattern can be detected elsewhere in the country. In 1547, 17 of the 36 JPs in Somerset were members of the quorum, while the figures were exactly the same in Northamptonshire, and proportionately slightly higher in Worcestershire (25 of 49). By 1584 these numbers had increased to 33 of 49 in Somerset, 34 of 43, in Northamptonshire, and 45 of 55 in Worcestershire.[243]

It has been suggested that the significant expansion in the quorum after the 1550s, albeit the continuation of an already established trend, may have been linked to the advent of the Marian statutes in that decade. As

239. Simon Walker, "Yorkshire Justices of the Peace, 1389–1413", *The English Historical Review*, vol. CVIII, Issue 427, p. 292.
240. Lander, *English Justices of the Peace*, pp. 158–159.
241. Etty, *Tudor Revolution?*, p. 120.
242. Zell, "Early Tudor JPs at Work", p. 140.
243. Langbein, *Prosecuting Crime in the Renaissance: England, Germany, France* (Cambridge: Harvard University Press, 1974), pp. 113–115.

JPs became less likely to try serious felonies (which increasingly went to the assizes), it became less important to identify magistrates of proven ability to preside over such hearings and the status became largely honorific.[244] It may also reflect a modest general improvement in magisterial quality; there was less need to protect quarter sessions from "rogue" members of the bench.

The establishment of the quorum was not the only expedient employed to ensure competence on the bench. From the late fourteenth century, statute required that all commissions of the peace include at least two "men of the law" in their quorums — that is, qualified apprentices/barristers or serjeants-at-law, not simply former students at the Inns of Court. Furthermore, the physical presence of these men (lawyers) was necessary if gaol delivery was held at quarter sessions. As a result, and for example, John Boteler, a serjeant-at-law from West Malling, in Kent, who eventually became a judge of the Common Pleas in 1508, was a regular attender at quarter sessions during his 16 years of service as a JP in the reign of Henry VII.[245] Successful lawyers could expect to be appointed to the commissions of their counties once they were well-recognised within their profession, even if their social position in the shire would not otherwise justify it, and were exempt from the £20 property requirement. Thomas Kebell, a serjeant-at-law, was made a Leicestershire JP in 1474, eight years before his older brother.[246] Similarly, Robert Townshend, the lawyer second son of a leading Norfolk gentry family, was most active on his county bench after being appointed to its commission in 1526. He had entered Lincoln's Inn in 1515, was made serjeant-at-law in 1540, and Recorder of Lynn (a part-time judge) shortly thereafter (before being knighted and appointed a justice of the Chester, Denbigh and Montgomery Circuit in 1545). Townshend helped to enforce the Reformation in Norfolk, as well as putting down low-level disorder and gaining high-level approval in the process. At one point, the Duke of Norfolk even wrote to Thomas Cromwell expressing a wish to see three or four men "such as Master Townshend in every shire". (This officiousness also made him somewhat

244. *Ibid.*
245. Lander, *English Justices of the Peace*, p. 66.
246. E. W. Ives, *The Common Lawyers of Pre-Reformation England: Thomas Kebell: A Case Study* (Cambridge: Cambridge University Press, 1983), p. 227.

132

unpopular locally, and there was trouble in three of his manors during Kett's Rebellion in 1549).[247] Of course, assizes judges were often made JPs in one or more of the counties situated on the circuits they served and could also sit at quarter sessions, satisfying the legal requirement when they were present.

Far more than two qualified lawyers could be appointed to the bench, if they could be found. According to one Elizabethan observer, the Crown made a "special choice of lawyers to be justices of the peace". In this respect, much would depend on the county involved, especially on how remote and prosperous it was. In some, particularly those far from London without many resident apprentices (later barristers) or serjeants, the minimum possible (two men) might be found, while in others qualified lawyers made up more than a fifth of the commission. An examination of six English counties suggests that the proportion of qualified barrister JPs stood at an average of 14 per cent during the mid-sixteenth century and subsequently increased further.[248] (There is a slight tendency to underestimate the number of lawyers appointed during the 1500s because of the frequent difficulty in identifying their affiliation, unless they were prominent members of their profession.)

Liaison Across County Lines

In an unprecedentedly mobile society, Tudor JPs would often have to liaise with their counterparts in other shires to ensure that a felon who crossed county lines did not escape. So important were these relationships that, in April 1579, Sir Richard Norton, a Hampshire JP, felt obliged to write to his Surrey counterpart Sir William More to deny saying to one Henry Knight that a man could not live near More "quietly, but that he must grease your hand" (an allegation of corruption). According to Norton, Knight was a "Jack" (knave) whom he had earlier expelled from Hampshire for lewd behaviour. He urged More to punish him, feeling that allowing such stories to go unchallenged was a certain way to

---

247. C. E. Moreton, "Mid-Tudor Trespass: A Break-in at Norwich, 1549", *The English Historical Review*, Vol. 108, No. 427 (1993), pp. 389–390.

248. Wilfrid R. Prest, *The Rise of the Barristers: A Social History of the English Bar 1590–1640* (Oxford: Clarendon Press, 1986), p. 8 and p. 237.

"hinder her Majesty's service to take away good opinion of such as hath the administration of justice that thereby we should not deal together hereafter as hitherto we have done for matters of each shire".[249]

A selection of cases is indicative of this inter-county action. In August 1571, for example, Henry Cheyne, a Bedfordshire magistrate, responded to a letter from John Agmondesham, a Surrey counterpart, about one Anthony Parvise, who was suspected of horse theft in the latter's county. He had examined Parvise and sent Agmodesham a record of what he had established. He offered to send the suspect to Surrey, if Agmondesham wished, for further examination.[250] In September 1574, Sir Henry Wallop, a Hampshire JP, wrote to Sir William More, a Surrey magistrate, asking that Thomas Hampton, a shoemaker in Farnham, in Surrey, be arrested to answer a charge of burglary perpetrated against a farmer in Coldwaltham, in Hampshire, some seven years earlier.[251] In June 1580 John Apsley of Thakeham, a Sussex JP, wrote to Sir William More, who had asked him to search for a group of men accused of robbery. He suggested that other Sussex JPs, in the jurisdictions of Chichester, Arundel, and Lewes, were better placed for this purpose.[252] In January 1596 Thomas Ive, a Norfolk JP, wrote to John Sammes, in Essex, noting that a man named Pudney whom Sammes had committed to gaol for a robbery in Essex, was wanted for a similar crime in his own county, for which he had been outlawed. Ive asked that, if Pudney was acquitted of the Essex robbery, he not be released but sent by *habeas corpus* to King's Bench.[253]

Bald Patches

Although appointment as a justice of the peace became increasingly sought after during the Tudor era, and the number of magistrates increased steadily, some parts of the country still lacked adequate coverage by active JPs. For example, during the early Tudor era, quarter sessions could sometimes not be held in the Border areas of Northumberland and

249. SHC 6729/1/74.
250. SHC LM/COR/3/119.
251. SHC LM/COR/3/168.
252. SHC 6729/1/3.
253. ERO Q/SR 132/51.

Cumberland because of a lack of substantial gentry willing to undertake what, in that region, was often a hazardous task.[254] In August 1526 Thomas Magnus, a clergyman, administrator, and diplomat, wrote to Cardinal Wolsey, advising him that there were so few JPs in Northumberland, especially experienced men of the quorum, that quarter sessions had not been held for a long time. To remedy this situation, he enclosed a list of new men from the area whom he and Sir William Evers (an experienced Border soldier) thought suitable for appointment.[255] In Cumberland that same year, Sir Christopher Dacre complained that he and Geoffrey Lancaster were the only active JPs within the county, and that no sessions of the peace could be held until this was remedied. (By 1528 their numbers had increased to four.)[256]

At the start of the Elizabethan era there was often a problem finding resident JPs in or near the sparsely populated villages in the forested Kentish Weald and the damp and unhealthy parishes found in the same county near the Thames Estuary and on Romney Marsh. In 1564 Archbishop Parker complained that in these areas "we have too few justices; betwixt Canterbury and Dover none". Again, steps were taken to remedy the situation, largely by appointing more men in the east of the county, so that by the end of the Tudor era the dearth of resident justices was largely confined to marsh parishes, where very few gentlemen lived.[257] In 1587 a report to the Privy Council concluded that it was necessary that more JPs be permitted in Sussex than in some other parts of the country, because of the presence of coast and forest "in which two places commonly the people be given much to rudeness and willfulness".[258]

In such locations, "inferior" men were sometimes appointed to the commission to ensure satisfactory coverage. However, in a few parts of the country, this was not possible or was unsuccessful, so that "bald" patches, where active magistrates were few and far between, remained to the end of the period. In a not entirely successful attempt to remedy

254. Steven Ellis, "Frontiers and Power in the Early Tudor State", *History Today*, Vol. 45, Issue 4, pp. 35–42.
255. J. S. Brewer (ed.), *Letters and Papers, Foreign and Domestic, Henry VIII, Vol. 4, 1524–1530* (London: HMSO, 1875), pp. 1081–1093.
256. Etty, *Tudor Revolution?*, p. 119.
257. Zell, "Kent's Elizabethan JPs at Work", pp. 1–44, p. 7.
258. Herrup, *The Common Peace*, p. 11.

this, King James I's orders of 23 June, 1605, required that all counties be divided into divisions of suitable size and JPs assigned to each one, so that no-one had to travel more than eight miles to see a magistrate.[259]

Urban Magistrates

Tudor England had more than 100 incorporated boroughs. For example, there were two in Hertfordshire (St Albans and Hertford) and three in Essex (Colchester, Harwich, and Maldon). Colchester was the largest of the latter, with a thriving cloth trade and a population of nearly 5,000 people, but many other corporate boroughs around the country were very much smaller, and a few, such as Dunwich, in Suffolk, were tiny.[260] Such boroughs had successfully excluded the surrounding county JPs' jurisdiction during the medieval period, under the terms of their newly issued charters. Instead, municipal politicians, normally the mayor and senior aldermen or their locally named equivalents, would provide the town's magistrates.

For example, by the terms of a charter issued in 1467, the Mayor of Doncaster was the only magistrate of the town. However, under a fresh charter, issued in 1505, his responsibilities were shared with three aldermen. Similarly, in Winchester, the mayor, senior aldermen, and the city's recorder all acted as magistrates. In like manner, after the Colchester governing council expanded during the sixteenth century, the two "bailiffs", two of the eight aldermen, and the recorder served as justices for the borough. In Maidstone, under a charter of 1549, there were 13 jurats (the local term for aldermen) at any one time, chosen from (and by) the Common Council, and elected for life. Some of them, usually the mayor, former mayors, and senior jurats, were also sworn in as municipal magistrates and able to sit in the borough's courts.[261]

Borough magistrates, like those in urban counties such as Norwich, were not subject to the county JPs' £20 property requirement, which did not extend to "suche Cytyes and borowes, that be cou~tes encorporate

---

259. SHC 663/1/15.
260. Hankins, *Local Government and Society,* p. 250.
261. Judy Buckley, *For the Good of This Town: The Jurats of Maidstone, 1549–1660* (Maidstone: Miscellany Books, 2009), p. 2.

of them selfe, nor to cyties, townes, and borowes, that haue Iustyce of peace of the inhabytantes by commyssyon or graunt of the kynge or his progenytours".[262] However, this did not necessarily mean that they were poor or uneducated men. For example, the individuals chosen to be jurats in Maidstone were usually drawn from the most prosperous elements in what was a relatively wealthy town. John Beale and his son Robert, who died in 1461 and 1490, respectively, both of whom served in this capacity, were wine merchants. Between 1549 and 1590, at least nine other jurats were in the cloth trade (mercers, drapers, a fuller, and a weaver); another was a mason, one a glazier, one a pewterer, and at least one was a yeoman farmer. John Eppes, an Elizabethan jurat for the town, was a lawyer. It appears that the average total value of movable goods or bequests left by 14 of the 16 jurats who died between 1580 and 1600 was just under £340, a very significant sum.[263]

In Essex, Tudor Colchester had a total of 98 aldermen. Tax assessments show that in 1524 and 1525 all of them had at least £40 in movable goods, and everyone in the town with £100 or more in such goods was made an alderman.[264] A little more modestly, William Shakespeare's father, John, was bailiff, and so a magistrate, in Stratford-upon-Avon. He was a skilled and prosperous glover and leatherworker.

Nevertheless, smaller and poorer incorporated towns were sometimes forced to have recourse to very much less wealthy (and educated) men as their officials and magistrates. Like the county magistracy, the municipal bench was subject to pressure on appointment and retention to be of the same religion as the Crown. For example, four Edwardian jurats in Maidstone who had later been removed from the bench for Protestant sympathies were reinstated after the death of Queen Mary.[265]

Some incorporated boroughs with their own sessions, especially the larger towns, had a recorder. This official was its chief legal officer, provided relevant expertise to the town, and was also usually made one of its magistrates by dint of his position, being appointed automatically under its charter. Such men were normally professional lawyers with local roots

---

262. Anon, *The Boke for a Justyce of Peace*, pp. 8–9.
263. Buckley, *For the Good of This Town*, p. 9.
264. Higgs, *Godliness and Governance*, p. 24.
265. Buckley, *For the Good of This Town*, p. 3.

or connections. However, many recorders did not reside permanently in their towns (even if this was a theoretical requirement of the position), especially as the Tudor era advanced, and were not expected to attend all meetings of its council. Instead, they spent much of their time exercising their profession in Westminster or representing the town's interests in the capital.[266] For example, in Colchester the recorder was not normally resident after 1532, although London was not very far away. Such absence could also make it difficult to attend borough sessions, although some recorders would make an effort to be present at such hearings, especially when power of gaol delivery was being exercised. Even so, some such appointments became near sinecures. Despite being a barrister by training, Sir Francis Walsingham, principal secretary to Queen Elizabeth, had little time to be actively involved in Colchester's affairs during the last 12 years of his life, when he was also the town's recorder.[267]

Although usually independent of the magistracy for the surrounding county, borough justices might liaise with its senior JPs, especially if these men had contacts with central government. For example, in February 1552 William Parr, the Marquess of Northampton, wrote to the Surrey JP William More. He had been informed that people in Guildford were keeping greyhounds, ferrets, and nets for hunting hares, deer, and rabbits in Guildford Park and other private grounds near their town. He asked More to require the mayor and his fellow officials to search the houses of "idle persons" who may have committed such offences, and restrain them from roaming around the countryside. Presumably, Parr wrote to More because he did not know the mayor, while the latter officer would know that More was forwarding a message from a prominent courtier.

266. Robert Tittler and Norman Jones (eds.), *A Companion to Tudor Britain* (Hoboken: Wiley-Blackwell, 2009), p. 121.
267. Higgs, *Godliness and Governance*, p. 247.

CHAPTER 6

The Coroner and his Inquest

Introduction

In 1194, King Richard I formally established the office of county coroner as a general-purpose royal functionary, entrusted with protecting the Crown's interests, something that also explains the title. The first borough coroners followed in 1200. Among their duties were investigating sudden, unexpected, suspicious, or violent deaths.[268] By the start of the Tudor era this was the royal official's most important function. As a result, in 1487 statute reiterated his vital role in prosecuting homicides and complained that, because such officials had been neglecting their duties, "great boldness is given to slayers and murderers".[269]

However, coroners still had several other responsibilities within the wider criminal justice system (and one or two outside it), these related to the outlawry, sanctuary, abjuration, appeal, and approvement procedures, for as long as they lasted, as well as with preventing felony suspects from alienating their property prior to trial, and helping to secure their possessions afterwards if they were convicted.[270] These aspects of their work are dealt with in other chapters of this book.

Coroners also investigated all deaths that occurred in custody, even if they were not obviously suspicious or unexpected. The risk of mistreatment by jailers was probably the original reason for requiring such hearings, but the vast majority of such deaths were due to disease. For

---

268. R. F. Hunnisett, *The Medieval Coroner* (Cambridge: Cambridge University Press, 1961), p. 1.
269. Daniel R. Ernst, "The Moribund Appeal of Death: Compensating Survivors and Controlling Jurors in Early Modern England", *The American Journal of Legal History*, Vol. 28, No. 2, p. 166 and p. 174.
270. R. A. Houston, *The Coroners of Northern Britain c.1300–1700* (London: Palgrave Pivot, 2014), pp. 9–10; R.F. Hunnisett, *Sussex Coroners' Inquests 1485–1558* (Lewes: Sussex Record Society, 1985), p. xiv.

example, the coroner for the City of London, Thomas Wilbraham, conducted a total of 35 inquests during the summer and autumn of 1590. Of these, ten concerned prisoners in Newgate Gaol. All had succumbed to a "pyninge sickness" and were held to have died "by the visitation of God" (*ex visitatione divina*), having been ill for between one day and six weeks.[271] Similarly, six inquests were carried out at Horsham Gaol in Sussex in 1578, and an equal number in 1587 and 1598 (a small number of years saw no inquests being held in the same prison).[272]

Types of Coroner

There were three main types of coroner. By far the most important (by number of inquests held) were those appointed for the counties, some of which had four designated officers, as the original 1194 legislation had stipulated that three knights and a cleric be elected to this role in every shire. The clergyman was probably added because he would be able to write. Within a few years, another knight frequently replaced the cleric, albeit that the number of men of this status serving as coroners also waned swiftly after about 1300. However, many counties had just two coroners, and some had more than four. Thus, in Hertfordshire, in 1581, there were two men, George Drywood and Henry Mayne.[273] Sussex was the same, despite its substantial size. By contrast, Kent had four men in February 1559, and five in July of the same year.[274] (This was also the normal complement in Kent during the late medieval period.)[275] A few counties had six coroners.

Although county coroners were empowered to act in any place within their shire that did not have its own franchise or borough coroner (see below), they would normally have a de facto area of responsibility. For example, in Sussex one man covered the three western rapes (county

---

271. Thomas R. Forbes, "London Coroner's Inquests for 1590", *Journal of the History of Medicine and Allied Sciences,* vol. xxviii, No. 4, p. 378.
272. R. F. Hunnisett, *Sussex Coroners' Inquests, 1558–1603* (London: PRO Publications, 1996), p. xxxi.
273. Cockburn, *Calendar of Assize Records: Hertfordshire Indictments, Elizabeth I,* p. 35.
274. J. S. Cockburn, *Calendar of Assize Records: Kent Indictments, Elizabeth I* (London: Public Record Office, 1979), p. 1 and p. 4.
275. Musson and Powell, *Crime, Law and Society,* p. 139.

subdivisions) and the other the east of the county; they were usually expected to reside and own land in their respective parts.[276] Similarly, in Wiltshire one officer covered the north of the county, another the south. Indicative of the typical "spacing" of such men in medium-size shires, Thomas Moore, a resident of Dagenham, and Thomas Drywoode, who lived in Danbury, were both coroners for Essex in 1592; their homes were about 25 miles apart, as the crow flies.[277]

The county system did not prevail everywhere. Franchise jurisdictions and a tiny number of individual manors had their own coroners, independent of those for the surrounding county. For example, John Wylegose and Robert Chalcrofte were coroners for the abbot of the liberty (a form of hundred) of Battle, in Sussex, and investigated deaths that occurred there during the 1520s. The Hastings rape in the same county also had its own coroner, so that its officer, Sir Nicholas Tufton (1479–1538), examined several corpses that were found within his territory at about the same time. There were even special coroners for the lands within Sussex that were under the control of the Archbishop of Canterbury and of the Duchy of Lancaster. The duchy (the personal estate of the Monarch as Duke of Lancaster since 1399) had numerous coroners nationally, as it held substantial amounts of land in many counties. For example, in 1592 Charles Chute, the duchy coroner in Essex, was frequently mentioned in official records for the shire.[278]

Much more significantly, on a statistical basis, individual incorporated boroughs often had their own officers (usually one or two men), having successfully excluded the coroner for the surrounding county during the medieval period. Typically, when Much Wenlock acquired its borough charter in 1468, it allowed the Shropshire town to appoint its own coroner and prevent recourse to the county officers.[279] In Sussex, borough coroners could be found at, inter alia, Rye, Chichester, Battle, Arundel, Bosham, and East Grinstead.

---

276. Hunnisett, *Sussex Coroners' Inquests, 1485–1558*, p. xxiii.
277. ERO Q/SR 120/2.
278. *Ibid.*
279. A. P. Baggs et al., "The Liberty and Borough of Wenlock", in C. R. J. Currie (ed.), *A History of the County of Shropshire: Vol. 10, Munslow Hundred (Part), the Liberty and Borough of Wenlock* (London: Victoria County History, 1998), pp. 187–212.

Taken together, the existence of three types of coroner meant that numerous officers might operate within a county. Thus for most of the sixteenth century there were 18 coroners in Sussex at any one time, a level that was not unusual on a national basis.[280] Even so, despite the large number of jurisdictions in a relatively confined area, coroners normally appear to have worked out their individual responsibilities in a fairly amicable manner. Sometimes there was even a degree of fluidity between officials investigating deaths when it came to jurisdictions; the coroner's office was not always guarded with quite the same zeal as other territorial legal rights, perhaps because it attracted fewer perquisites.

For example, the county coroner carried out almost half the inquests conducted in Sussex's Bramber Rape during the Elizabethan period, although the rape had its own officer.[281] Similarly, although Chichester had its own coroners, those for the surrounding county sometimes held inquests within the city, as occurred in June 1512, when John Royce, a Sussex coroner, conducted a hearing there, even if the circumstances were slightly unusual: the death had occurred in Chichester, but the injuries were inflicted some distance away.[282] Occasionally such coroners even worked together. For example, an inquest held in the Liberty of the Manor of Writtle, in Essex, into the death of one Henry Collyn, was conducted before both Thomas Knott, a county coroner, and Edward Bell, the coroner for the liberty (a verdict of manslaughter was returned).[283]

Even so, although serious conflict between coroners was rare, it was not unheard of. There were periodic disputes, and in 1553 there was a violent confrontation between a county coroner for Oxfordshire and one of his counterparts for the city of Oxford, as to which should investigate the death of a woman found hanged in a house in Walton. Both men claimed jurisdiction, and there was an armed standoff between large numbers of their supporters. The matter ultimately resulted in a Star Chamber suit.[284]

---

280. Matthew Lockwood, *The Conquest of Death: Violence and the Birth of the Modern English State* (New Haven: Yale University Press, 2017), p. 59.
281. *Ibid*, p. 61.
282. Hunnisett, *Sussex Coroners' Inquests, 1485–1558*, p. xxxv.
283. ERO T/A 418/13/29.
284. Lockwood, *The Conquest of Death*, p. 63.

Social Background and Appointment

Tudor county coroners were nearly always identified as "gent", even if most were drawn from what Sir Thomas Smith termed the "meaner sort" of gentlemen. They were usually recruited from men who were just below the social rank that provided sheriffs and JPs. A few more socially prominent individuals and some who might more properly be described as well-to-do yeomen supplemented their ranks, in a pattern that had been established by the 1400s. For example, Thomas Denys has been described as a textbook example of an upwardly mobile fifteenth century man, one who was on the margins of gentility. He received some legal training at Lincoln's Inn in the years after 1421, and held office as a coroner in Norfolk later in the century, as well as providing legal services to gentlemen in the county.[285] Although all county coroners in Elizabethan Sussex were described as gentlemen, few were titled "esquire", and none was a knight, although men of this status were occasionally found in the position elsewhere in the country. (They had been far more common in the medieval period.) One Sussex coroner, Magnus Fowle, was described in correspondence from 1560 as a prosperous yeoman but as "esquire" elsewhere.[286]

Almost no Tudor county or borough coroners had a medical background, and, although it was very much more common, only a minority, like Denys, had any form of legal training; when they did, it was often as an attorney, although a few were more prominent members of the legal profession. For example, at the end of the Tudor era, the East Riding of Yorkshire had two coroners who usually seem to have been local attorneys.[287]

Those appointed for a county were normally elected, when a position came vacant, by county freeholders voting at quarter sessions (if there was more than one nomination). In 1593 the Privy Council was forced to intervene after there were reports that JPs at Brecon, in Wales, had

285. Hannes Kleineke and James Ross, "Just Another Day in Chancery Lane: Disorder and the Law in London's Legal Quarter in the Fifteenth Century", *Law and History Review*, Vol. 35, No. 4, pp. 1017–1047.
286. Hunnisett, *Sussex Coroners' Inquests, 1558–1603*, p. xxxi.
287. G. C. F. Forster, *East Riding Justices*, p. 7.

assembled an armed crowd to make sure that their preferred candidate was chosen.[288] County coroners held their post for life unless removed for misconduct (very rare) or deciding to retire (much more common); ill health was often the reason for the latter, perhaps unsurprisingly, given the considerable travelling attendant on the position.

Even so, some men served for very long periods. In sixteenth century Sussex, William Playfere was a county coroner for more than 25 years and presided over at least 125 inquests that survive in the National Archives and, presumably, some others that do not. In the same county and century, Magnus Fowle served for 22 years and presided over at least 100 inquests.[289] In Elizabethan Essex, Thomas Knott served for 19 years and sat on at least 118 inquests, while his colleague William Vernon served for 14 years and presided over a minimum of 46 inquests.[290] Thomas Wilbraham became Coroner of the City of London in 1590 and served for a decade, dealing with hundreds of inquests in his crowded jurisdiction.[291] At the other extreme, a few men lasted just a year or two.

Where a liberty had its own coroner, its lord or his steward normally made the appointment.[292] Similarly, borough coroners were often appointed to their positions, or held them ex officio along with another local political office. For example, in the early 1500s, Peter Moreff (or Moryff) was a merchant, burgess, and coroner for tiny Dunwich, in Suffolk.[293] At about the same time, John Fletcher was both coroner and mayor for Rye, and examined deaths that occurred in the Cinque Port.[294] Inevitably, such men rarely acquired the experience of their county counterparts.

288. Kesselring, *Making Murder Public: Homicide in Early Modern England, 1480–1680* (Oxford: Oxford University Press, 2019), p. 44.
289. Carol Loar, "Medical Knowledge and the Early Modern English Coroner's Inquest", *Social History of Medicine*, Vol. 23, No. 3, pp. 475–491.
290. Samaha, *Law and Order*, p. 167.
291. Forbes, "London Coroner's Inquests", p. 386.
292. Lockwood, *The Conquest of Death*, p. 68.
293. J. S. Brewer (ed.), *Letters and Papers, Foreign and Domestic, Henry VIII, Vol. 1, 1509–1514* (London: HMSO, 1920), pp. 203–216.
294. Hunnisett, R. F., *Sussex Coroners' Inquests, 1485–1558*, pp. 20–30.

Pay

Tudor coroners were unsalaried, and not even paid for most of the inquests that they conducted (a situation that would survive until 1752).[295] This did not encourage diligence, and there were periodic, but very long-standing, claims that some officers would hold inquests only if bribed to do so; it was also claimed that others embezzled money. Furthermore, it seems that, although it was not mandatory, some towns voluntarily paid coroners a fee for conducting inquests, if only to ensure that the process ran smoothly.[296]

Nevertheless, from 1487 onwards, statute allowed coroners 13s 4d (one mark) for an inquest that led to a homicide (murder or manslaughter) verdict that was subsequently brought to trial. This was supposed to be recovered from the felon's goods and property.[297] In practice, it seems that the town where (or near which) a death had occurred sometimes paid the fee, even if a suspect lacked assets or had fled so that no trial took place, provided the coroner brought the resulting documents to the next gaol delivery in the county.[298] This may have been because it was responsible for the killer's escape, and the fee could be taken from its fine. As Sir Anthony Fitzherbert noted, the "coroner shal haue for his fee .xiii. s~. iiij. d. of the gooddes of the Murderer. And yf he haue no goodes, then to haue his fee of such amerciament as shalbe set vpon the towneshyppe for the scape".[299]

This payment encouraged a modicum of official diligence when it came to investigating potential murders and manslaughters, so much so that in 1510 another statute reminded coroners to hold inquests into deaths occasioned by simple misadventure (accident) or unexpected

---

295. John Weaver and David Wright (eds.), *Histories of Suicide: International Perspectives on Self-Destruction in the Modern World* (Toronto: University of Toronto Press, 2009), p. 101.

296. Hunnissett, *The Medieval Coroner*, p. vii and p. 118.

297. Sara M. Butler, *Forensic Medicine and Death Investigation in Medieval England* (New York: Routledge, 2015), p. 53.

298. Katherine D. Watson, *Poisoned Lives: English Poisoners and their Victims* (London: Hambledon and London, 2006), p. 155.

299. Anthony Fitzherbert, *In this booke is contayned the offices of shyriffes, bailliffes of liberties, escheatours co[n]stables and coroners [and] sheweth what euery one of the[m] maye do by vertue of theyr offices, drawen out of bokes of the comon lawe [and] of the statutes*, 1538, p. 66 (present author's pagination, original is unnumbered).

medical causes (visitation of God), which they had, apparently, often neglected since the advent of payment for homicide inquests. Assizes judges and JPs were given authority to punish them for failures in this regard.[300] Nevertheless, most Tudor coroners did not make enormous sums from investigating homicides. Although he served for more than 25 years, William Playfere was eligible to receive payment in only 14 cases, or just eleven per cent of his (preserved) caseload. The total of just over £9 was less than a single £10 fine he received from assizes for defective performance while in office in 1577.[301]

Coming to the Coroner's Attention

A hundred or liberty bailiff, constable, high constable, sheriff, JP, or other reputable individual, such as a village squire, confronted by an unexpected or suspicious death reported to him by a local "first finder" (the person who discovered the body) or parish "searcher" (a woman who laid out corpses), was required to summon a coroner to investigate the matter. Inevitably, this could be a weakness in the system, especially in cases that were only marginally suspicious and might not be reported at all. In 1551 William Nott and his brother obtained a Wiltshire JP's permission not to report a death that looked suspiciously like murder; this was partly on the basis that the noxious odours that the decayed body emitted posed a danger that required swift interment.[302]

Usually local notables would choose the nearest coroner with jurisdictional responsibility for the place where the death occurred, whether it was one of the county coroners or the man who served for a specific borough or liberty that was outside the county system. In 1589 Richard Bostock, fearing that he would be accused of the death of an elderly man named Holloway after an affray, urged Surrey JPs to ignore the suggestion that the inquest take place in Crowhurst, where Holloway's wounds

---

300. S. J. Stevenson, "The Rise of Suicide Verdicts in South-East England, 1530–1590: The Legal Process", *Continuity and Change*, Vol. 2, No. 1, p. 39.
301. Lockwood, *The Conquest of Death*, p. 85.
302. Kesselring, *Making Murder Public*, p. 53.

had allegedly been inflicted; he submitted that it should be held in Kent, where Holloway eventually died (which was what the law required).[303]

That coroners came expeditiously when summoned was important, as bodies were not supposed to be moved from the place where they were found before their arrival. Thus, one April evening in 1579, a passer-by discovered the murdered body of a London hosier named Abel Bourn lying in a deep gutter next to a road in the city. He told a local constable, who then informed a coroner and, with other local men, guarded the body in situ for the remainder of the night.[304] Corpses were also not supposed to be interred before the coroner arrived; on the rare occasions that they were, he would order that they be exhumed. However, very occasionally, if there was going to be a significant delay, and there was a fear of disease, a body might be temporarily buried in a shallow grave. Once under the supervision of a coroner, the corpse could not be legally buried without a warrant being issued permitting it.

In theory, without a body (however decayed) there could be no inquest, which was a potential weakness in the investigative system. "The Coroner hathe no power to enquyre of mannes deathe, but onely vppon viewe of the bodye, and if he do, it is frustrate and voyde".[305] However, and unusually, it was noted that inquests conducted after the demise of two prisoners in Nottingham Gaol in January 1538 (one had died a week earlier, the other nearly five weeks earlier) were "held upon the deaths and not on view of the bodies". The same situation applied to another two deaths that occurred in the prison the following February.[306] This procedure does not seem to have been unique to this prison and time, suggesting that the requirement may occasionally have been relaxed in gaol inquests, at least where death by sickness was suspected.

Most coroners arrived reasonably swiftly when summoned. Unsurprisingly, those for boroughs and small liberties usually held their inquests very rapidly; often on the same day a death was reported. However, this

---

303. SHC LM/COR/3/440.
304. Anthony Munday, *A view of sundry examples Reporting many straunge murthers, sundry persons perjured, signes and tokens of Gods anger towards us* (London: William Wright, 1580), p. D.111.
305. Fitzherbert, *In this booke is contayned*, 1538, unnumbered page.
306. R. F. Hunnisett (ed.), "Calendar of Nottinghamshire Coroners' Inquests, 1485–1558", *Thoroton Society Record Series*, vol. xxv, pp. 84–85.

was not invariably the case; although Christopher Marlowe was killed in a brawl in Deptford on the evening of 28 May 1593, the inquest was not conducted until 1 June (immediately following which his body was buried in the local churchyard).[307]

The county coroners, who normally had much further to travel, sometimes as much as 30 miles or more, might take longer to arrive. Even so, the majority of county inquests in Elizabethan Sussex were held within 10 days of a body's discovery, and most were conducted much more quickly.[308] Fairly typically, in the early sixteenth century, after Thomas Mitchell, of Cannington in Somerset, murdered his wife, Joan, and her sister Eleanor, and then committed suicide, it took the county coroner three days to get to the scene of a death.[309] Perhaps surprisingly, given that it was such a heinous crime, the Kentish coroner who investigated the deaths of three children who were murdered by their father and an accomplice near Ashford in 1590, took five days to get there.[310] Against this, on 27 October, Nicholas Lewkenor, a Sussex coroner held an inquest in West Grinstead into the killing that same morning of a local woman named Alice Ford.[311]

Even in more remote parts of the country, the process was usually fairly swift. In late medieval (and early Tudor) County Durham, coroners seldom let more than five or six days go by before examining a corpse.[312] Similarly, after Roger Crockett was murdered in Nantwich in 1572, it took just three days for one of Cheshire's two county coroners to hold an inquest. In the meantime, his body was put on display near the tavern he owned, presumably to attract witnesses, although few men could approach it "for the horribleness of the smell".[313]

---

307. J. Leslie Hotson and G.L. Kittredge, The Death of Christopher Marlowe (London: The Nonesuch Press, 1925), p. 38.
308. Hunnisett, *Sussex Coroners' Inquests, 1558–1603*, p. xxxvii.
309. Gladys Bradford (ed.), *Proceedings in the Court of the Star Chamber in the Reigns of Henry VII and Henry VIII* (London: Harrison, 1911), p. 32.
310. James Moore, *The Tudor Murder Files* (Barnsley: Pen and Sword, 2016), p. 150.
311. Hunnisett, *Sussex Coroners' Inquests, 1485–1558*, p. 43.
312. Cynthia J. Neville, "'The Bishop's Ministers': The Office of Coroner in Late Medieval Durham", *Florilegium*, Vol. 18, No. 2, p. 48.
313. Steve Hindle, "'Bleedinge Afreshe'? The Affray and Murder at Nantwich, 19 December 1572", in Angela McShane and Garthine Walker (eds.), *The Extraordinary and the Everyday in Early Modern England* (Basingstoke: Palgrave Macmillan, 2010), p. 232.

The enthusiasm with which Tudor coroners carried out their duties was influenced by such diverse factors as personal inclination, local pressure and expectations, the state of the roads, the clemency of the weather, the demands placed on their time by other official duties such as attending assizes (a requirement of the position), personal business interests, the needs of their estates (even if very modest), and social lives.[314] Sometimes coroners might have to visit London on official business, such as to give evidence at the Court of King's Bench. In these situations, they would not be able to investigate suspicious deaths until they returned, although another county coroner might make a longer than normal journey to cover for them. The possibility of remuneration (see above) might also be an important factor in their degree of activism.

Raising a Jury

On arrival at the scene of a suspicious death, the coroner would issue warrants to the parish constable or a local hundred bailiff, and those of the (up to) four immediately adjacent parishes or townships, ordering them to summon a jury from their householders. In practice, by the Tudor era, the focus was often on recruiting men from the immediate neighbourhood or parish in which the body had been found. Unlike trial jurors (by the middle of the sixteenth century), this proximity meant that it was still very common for inquest jurors to have a detailed knowledge of the people involved in a case, and the background to a killing or accident. Indeed, in 1522, three men who found the body of a 12-year-old girl named Lucy in a pit of water at Battle, in Sussex, served as jurors at her inquest.[315] Similarly, in 1589, at an inquest held at Little Bardfield, in Essex, into the body of a female baby, one of the jurors was the "first finder" of the diminutive corpse (it was discovered in his haymow). As with many other first finders, it was carefully noted at the inquest that he was a man of good reputation (and so unlikely to have been involved in what had occurred).[316]

---

314. Stevenson, "The Rise of Suicide Verdicts", p. 41.
315. Lockwood, *The Conquest of Death*, p. 156.
316. ERO Q/SR 110/68.

Interestingly, when inquests were held in gaols, on deaths in custody, it appears to have been common practice for some of the jurors to be drawn from other inmates, as was the case with six of the 13 men who sat on the deaths of two prisoners in Nottingham Gaol in January 1538.[317] This was not just a provincial phenomenon. In the period from December 1530 to February 1531, John Torre, an inmate in the King's Bench Prison who was being held in connection with a London burglary, served as a juror on two coroner's inquest juries for fellow prisoners who had died of sickness or other natural causes.[318]

The Jurors

Coroners' juries were not confined to a dozen men; they could have up to 24 members, although this was unusual. More typically, when, in April 1532, the coroner for the Abbot of Westminster's liberty convened an inquest into the death of Sir William Pennington, 16 jurors were present.[319] In 1572 the jury at the inquest into the death of Roger Crockett in Cheshire also had 16 men.[320] In a more routine case, the jury that looked into the death of Joan Broker's newborn baby in Surrey in December 1580 was made up of 15 men, two of them being a father and son.[321] The same number sat on the inquest into the killing of John Morris, held at Westfield in Sussex in May 1594. Indeed, during the Elizabethan period West Sussex inquests averaged 15 jurors, while those for East Sussex were slightly smaller, with an average of 14 men.[322] However, not a few coroners' juries had the bare minimum of 12 jurors.

The modest property requirement for inquest jurors meant that they came from a very wide range of backgrounds, more so than most other jurymen of the era. It seems that less than one per cent of those who sat on Sussex inquest juries between 1560 and 1660 would qualify as

317. Hunnisett, "Calendar of Nottinghamshire Coroners' Inquests, 1485–1558", pp. 84–85.
318. *McSheffrey*, "Sanctuary Seekers in England, 1380–1557" (Online companion to *Seeking Sanctuary*, 2017).
319. Shannon McSheffrey, "The Slaying of Sir William Pennington: Legal Narrative and the Late Medieval English Archive", *Florilegium*, Vol. 28 (2011), p. 172.
320. Hindle, "'Bleedinge Afreshe'?", p. 233.
321. Cockburn, *Calendar of Assize Records: Surrey Indictments, Elizabeth I*, p. 216.
322. Lockwood, *The Conquest of Death*, p. 151.

gentlemen. However, at least one or two men from the "upper orders" (broadly construed) might be present if the investigation involved someone of the same class. For example, the coroner's inquest that considered the death of Gaynesford's maid at his wife's hands (see above) included two men described as "gentlemen" and another as an "esquire".[323]

If an inquest was politically sensitive, special efforts might be made to assemble an enhanced body of men, as was the case with the jury selected to sit on the inquest into the notorious death of Richard Hunne, found dead in his cell in 1514 while awaiting trial for heresy. In 1560 Lord Robert Dudley, Queen Elizabeth's favourite, demanded that the coroner presiding over the inquest into his wife's death from a fall "make no choice of light or slight persons, but the discreetest and [most] substantial men, for their juries".[324] Similarly, after Henry Percy, Earl of Northumberland, was found dead in the Tower of London in 1585, an apparent suicide, his extremely high social status meant that there was a "very substantiall [coroner's] jurie, chosen among the best commoners of the Citie".[325]

Despite such cases, the great majority of Tudor inquest jurors were yeomen, husbandmen, and craftsmen, such as saddlers and shoemakers. Many, especially in rural areas, had to mark, rather than sign, the official document produced at the end of the process. However, they could not have been convicted of a felony and were supposed to be drawn from the "wiser" men of their parishes. A few may even have been local medical practitioners of some description, appointed to bring some specialist expertise to the hearing.[326] Sixteenth century coroners' jurors often had previous experience of sitting on an inquest; in some areas up to half of them had served on at least one earlier occasion, and a few had participated in as many as five over a ten-year period.[327]

---

323. Cockburn, *Calendar of Assize Records: Surrey Indictments, Elizabeth I*, p. 96.

324. G. W. Bernard, *Power and Politics in Tudor England* (Abingdon: Routledge, 2016), pp. 161–166.

325. Anon, *A true and summarie reporte of the declaration of some part of the Earle of Northumberlands treasons deliuered publiquelie in the Court at the Starrechamber by the Lord Chauncellour and others of her Maiesties most Honourable priuie Counsell* (London, C. Barker, 1585), pp. 1–22.

326. Butler, *Forensic Medicine*, pp. 99–101.

327. Loar, "Medical Knowledge", p. 475.

Juror Bias

A coroner had the power to exclude potentially biased men from his jury, although suspects (if present) could not challenge them in possible homicide cases. After Roger Crockett was murdered in Nantwich in 1572, Richard Crewe was summoned to sit on the inquest, but "set asyde" due to his name. He was, it seems, related to the chief suspect, one Edmund Crewe.[328] However, this was not always done, even if the coroner was aware of the potential conflict of interest. In 1571 an inquest that sat on the body of a maid who had allegedly been killed by physical chastisement inflicted by the wife of the prominent Surrey gentleman, John Gaynesford, included a man, Erasmus Gaynesford, who appears to have been related by marriage to the suspect. (The jury produced a verdict of felonious killing—i.e. manslaughter).[329] Much more significantly, as outsiders, county coroners were often unaware of likely juror bias one way or the other, and so unable to do much about it unless told (see below).

Conduct of the Inquest

Once assembled, the coroner and his jury would formally view the body, even if it were in an advanced state of decomposition. An example of this occurred in 1547. In June of that year, Thomas Edwards was suffering from "French pokkes" or syphilis (which had arrived in Europe from the New World in the late fifteenth century). He went for a cure to a surgeon who lodged him in the house of Ursula Wicombe, a widow who lived in Hardham, in Sussex. The surgeon's cure appears to have been based on administering special baths to the sick man (referred to by Shakespeare in *Timon of Athens*), but was unsuccessful, and Edwards died while actually in such a bath. To avoid funeral expenses or bad publicity, it appears that Wicombe and the surgeon then threw Edwards' corpse across a horse and carried it to an outhouse, where a hole was dug and he was buried. Some six months later this was discovered, the

---

328. Hindle, "'Bleedinge Afreshe'?", p. 233.
329. Cockburn, *Calendar of Assize Records: Surrey indictments, Elizabeth I*, p. 96.

coroner called, and the body dug up, although there cannot have been much left of it beyond the skeleton. It was examined and an inquest duly held, which eventually concluded that this was a case of natural death followed by irregular burial rather than murder.[330]

Most coroners and their juries appear to have been reasonably conscientious when conducting the examination of a dead person's body, looking for damage that would suggest the physical cause of death, and expressly noting if there were no external injuries. Bruising, fractures, and lacerations were carefully described, and the depth of wounds accurately measured and recorded.[331] For example, it was noted that the stab wound to the right shoulder that killed Thomas Butcher in Lewes (Sussex) in 1585 was seven inches deep and one-and-a-half inches wide. Similarly, it was recorded that the three knife wounds that killed an unknown man in Northchapel in the same county and year were from half an inch wide and one inch deep to one inch wide and four inches deep.[332] In 1589, at the inquest into the death of Mary Bundocke of Black Notely, in Essex, the coroner's jury specifically noted that she had died instantly from four mortal axe wounds, two on the top of her head, both an inch long and half-an-inch deep, another on the back of her head that was an inch-and-a-half long and an inch deep, which had penetrated into her brain, and another on the right side of her head, of similar dimensions, which had also gone through her skull.[333]

The ensuing hearing might be held in a local tavern, the dead man's own house (if large enough), a church, church porch, barn, some other substantial building, or even, weather permitting, outside. Thus, after Roger Crockett was murdered in Nantwich in 1572, his inquest was held in the local church.[334] According to Sir Thomas Smith, writing in the 1560s, even if held indoors, it was common for certain stages of proceedings to be conducted outside: "The empanelling of this enquest, and the viewe of the bodie, and the giving of the verdict, is commonly in the streete in an open place".

---

330. Hunnisett, *Sussex Coroners' Inquests, 1485–1558*, pp. 41–42.
331. Loar, "Medical Knowledge", p. 475.
332. Hunnisett, *Sussex Coroners' Inquests, 1558–1603*, pp. 72–73.
333. ERO T/A 418/51/48.
334. Hindle, "'Bleedinge Afreshe'?", p. 233.

Witnesses would then be called and questioned, as would any suspects. Unlike criminal trials, coroners' inquests could be adjourned after they had started, to allow further enquiries to be made before a verdict was returned. As Sir Thomas Smith noted, their jurors were allowed to "goe at large, and take a day, sometime of xx or xxx daies, more or lesse, as the fact is more evident, or more kept close, to give their evidence". They would then return their verdict to the coroner in person. For example, the inquest into Thomas Edwards' death (see above) saw several adjournments for a month at a time, at the request of the jurors, while they made enquiries (itself indicative of their activism).[335]

Nevertheless, such delay was very unusual. It occurred in only eight cases (of all types) out of more than 240 inquests preserved from Sussex between 1485 and 1558. All but one adjournment was for a matter of weeks or, at the most, months. However, in a particularly extreme case, the inquest into the murder of Marion Wyatt in Sussex in December 1528 was adjourned several times over a period of years because the jurors felt that they were not sufficiently well-informed to return a verdict. Thus they met again almost a month after they first assembled, when they were still not satisfied, and it was not until 1536 that they decided that a Felpham clergyman and his female servant had stabbed her to death with a "prag" (stiletto dagger) while she slept. By then several members of the original inquest jury had been replaced, and only eight of the men who had viewed the body back in 1528 were still present. The accused cleric successfully argued at King's Bench that he should not have to answer such a defective inquest at trial.[336]

Even so, the relatively leisured environment found at a coroner's inquest often allowed more evidence to be called about a homicide than would be the case at the corresponding trial at assizes. At Rowlande Cramphorne's hearing for petty treason (killing his master) in 1608, it was noted that a dozen witnesses were produced who had previously given

---

335. Hunnisett, *Sussex Coroners' Inquests, 1485–1558*, pp. 41–42.
336. *Ibid*, p. xxxix and p. 19.

evidence to the coroner's inquest, but pressure of time meant that only those with the most germane evidence could be called.[337]

Furthermore, inquests were often fairly active, indeed enterprising, when investigating the deaths that came before them. Coroners' juries regularly conducted "views" of the immediate environs to the death and other places that were relevant to the investigation. Typically, in 1617 the jurors in a drowning case, who were personally aware (being local) that the dead man regularly fished in the nearby River Thames, examined his favourite angling spot. They found that part of the bank which the water had undermined, had "newly fallen into the said River". The jurors then threw a stick into the water to see where the current would take it. It washed up close to where the man's body had been found, leading them to conclude that the cause of death had been an accident (few people could swim at this time) rather than foul play.[338] Jurors could suggest their own lines of inquiry to the coroner as well as personally asking questions of testifying witnesses when trying to establish how a death occurred.

This jury activism has led some observers to suggest that early modern inquests were held "before" rather than "by" coroners, although this is an exaggeration. The coroner did the majority of the questioning and made most decisions on investigations, and his power to direct the inquest jury meant that he wielded considerable influence over their verdicts. This was widely recognised by contemporary observers. Indicative of this, in 1572 the widow of Roger Crockett thought that a Cheshire county coroner who was presiding over the inquest into her husband's murder was corruptly trying to shield a group of local men who she believed were behind the killing. She thought that he had packed the 16-man jury, and given the jurors a heavy-handed and misleading summary of the evidence before they made their decision blaming the murder on just one man. Subsequently, she went further, and claimed that the same coroner had a well-established reputation for corruption, having "cloaked" at least

---

337. Anon, *A bloudy new-yeares gift, or A true declaration of the most cruell and bloudy murther, of maister Robert Heath, in his owne house at high Holbourne, being the signe of the fire-brand which murther was committed by Rowland Cramphorne, seruant and tapster to the said Heath: on new-yeares day last past in the morning, 1609* (London, 1609), pp. 1–3.
338. Loar, "Medical Knowledge", p. 475.

two-dozen murders in the county.[339] She was not alone in having a negative view of her local coroner. In 1589 Richard Bostock urged that an inquest not be held in front of a Surrey coroner, in part because he was concerned that the latter was in league with the dead man's master.[340]

Furthermore, coroners could refuse to accept an inquest verdict and ask jurors to reconsider their initial decision. This was often successful. At an inquest held in York during the sixteenth century, evidence was given that a man named Robinson had been responsible for a homicide. However, the inquest jurors initially declined to return a murder verdict. As a result, the coroner, John Dixon, "refused to accept the same verdicte and caused them to make an other verdicte". Robinson was then tried on this at the following assizes.[341] If jurors were not amenable to a coroner's directions, and refused to change their decision, all they could do was to refuse to return any verdict at all, although this was unusual and risked punishment at assizes, Star Chamber, or King's Bench.

Inquest Verdict

Once the inquest jury had heard and considered all the available evidence, and been directed by the coroner, it returned its verdict. Its members would usually give a brief narrative account of the victim's death and either classify it as a murder/manslaughter, suicide, accident, or visitation of God (essentially sickness) or return what would today be termed an open verdict, stating that they did not know how (or why) the dead man met his death. Although the reports vary in length and the amount of detail provided, they were usually fairly brief, perhaps 300 words in total. They were normally written in Latin, on rectangular strips of parchment or paper. The coroner and jurors all signed or marked the document.

The decision of the coroner's jury had to be unanimous. In a letter to his (knighted) namesake and relative in June 1470, John Paston noted that, along with two others, the four of them had been indicted at the Norwich Sessions for firing a gun at Caister that had killed two men.

---

339. Hindle, "'Bleedinge Afreshe'?", p. 244.
340. SHC LM/COR/3/440.
341. Lockwood, *The Conquest of Death*, p. 165.

This prosecution was apparently being conducted on the basis of the coroner's inquest into the double killing. However, having received advice from others, the author (very tentatively) held hopes that the inquest had been flawed because two jurors had not concurred on all aspects of the decision, without being excluded, so that its "verdytt is voyd, for ther wer ij. of th'enqwest that wold not agre to th'endyttment. And in as myche as they ij. wer agreyd in othyr maters, and not in that, and that they two wer not dyschargyd fro the remnant at syche tym as that verdyth of yowyr endytment was govyn".[342]

From 1487 (and until 1752) statute (3 Henry VII, c 2) required coroners to hand over all the inquest records to the visiting assize judges twice a year, although this did not always happen. The judges then returned those that did not result in criminal trials to the King's Bench. Inquests delivered in Lent were normally forwarded in the Easter term, while those delivered to the summer assizes appear in the Michaelmas term files for the Westminster court. However, inquests which produced homicide verdicts, whether murder or manslaughter, and led to criminal hearings, were usually left with the indictments for the relevant circuit. (Because London and Middlesex were anomalous jurisdictions, without assize courts, their inquisitions were treated somewhat differently).[343]

As the Paston example suggests, in cases of homicide the inquest verdict could serve as the equivalent of an indictment: a suspect — often questioned at the coroner's hearing and committed to custody by that officer — could be brought to trial under it, without a murder or manslaughter bill needing to be "found" by an assize or quarter sessions grand jury. As Sir Thomas Smith noted of an inquest, "For whosoever they doe finde as guiltie of the murder, he is streight committed to prison, and this is against him in the nature of an inditement". For example, at the Hertfordshire Assizes in July 1596, Catherine Trott was indicted on a coroner's inquisition for feloniously killing another woman by knocking her to the ground and inflicting injuries from which she subsequently died. "Felonious killing" seems to have been used as a synonym for less

---

342. James Gairdner (ed.), *The Paston Letters, AD 1422–1509*, Vol. 5 (London: Chatto & Windus, 1904), p. 746.
343. Stevenson, "The Rise of Suicide Verdicts", p. 41.

culpable forms of killing, i.e. manslaughter, and in later centuries was often used when a defendant stood trial purely on an inquisition, rather than on a grand jury indictment. In this case, the trial jury acquitted Trott outright, having decided that the victim "died by divine visitation".[344]

This power to bring a matter to trial was particularly important if the victim was a stranger who could not be recognised, as there would be no relatives to take an interest in any prosecution. For example, in September 1560 an inquest was held at Leytonstone on the body of an unknown woman before Thomas Knott, an Essex county coroner. The 13 jurors concluded that, a month earlier, between 8 am and 9 am, in a local wood next to the highway, George Hunt had struck the woman a mortal blow on the head with a "bearinge bill" (a hooked blade mounted on a staff), from which wound she died instantly. He then cut off her arms and legs. Unsurprisingly, the jurors concluded that he had murdered her. The woman was never identified, but Hunt was convicted of her murder at the Essex Assizes and hanged.[345]

An inquest could also find that a suspect who was still at large (and so not produced before them) had committed a killing, and send the relevant papers on to the next sitting of the assizes in their county, so that the person could stand trial if captured in the meantime. For example, in November 1599 Richard Ap Bevan, a Lewes peddler, raped a girl who was just under seven years-of-age; as a result of her injuries, she "lingered" until the following March (well within the year-and-a-day limitation for homicide that then appertained) and then died. An inquest was held some 13 days later, in Bevan's absence, and the matter referred to the assizes, although when they were held Bevan was still at liberty.[346]

Because the coroner often fulfilled many of the same functions in homicide cases as an examining JP, the Marian statute of 1556 extended to him (see *Chapter 7*), so that, under section 3 of the act, they were required to "put in writing the effect of the evidence given to the jury before him, beeing material". They were also required to commit suspects to gaol, and to bind-over by recognisance to attend and give evidence at

344. Cockburn, *Calendar of Assize Records: Hertfordshire Indictments, Elizabeth I*, p. 122.
345. Cockburn, *Calendar of Assize Records: Essex Indictments, Elizabeth I*, p. 23; ERO T/A 418/5/33.
346. Hunnisett, *Sussex Coroners' Inquests, 1558–1603*, p. 133.

a subsequent gaol delivery, anyone who could "declare any thing materiall to proue the said murther, or manslaughter".

It should be noted that even if a coroner's jury returned a "benign" verdict, such as accident, it did not preclude a death being investigated further as a potential homicide, or even from coming to trial on a grand-jury indictment (rather than an inquest) if suspicions developed after the hearing. People were sometimes held in gaol or bailed pending further investigation for deaths that had initially been found by an inquest jury to have been caused by misfortune or natural causes.[347] The experiences of Brian Gunter, the rector of North Moreton, in Berkshire, during the 1590s, are indicative.

During a football match in May 1598, Gunter fatally injured two local yeomen, John and Richard Gregory. It appears that, in the course of the game, a general melee developed, in which his relative William Gunter became involved. Brian then joined in, or attempted to break up, the disturbance (opinions differed), by striking the two young men on the head with the pommel of his dagger. Despite his claim to have only inflicted a "little harm", both were dead within two weeks. The verdict of the subsequent coroner's inquest into Richard Gregory's death has survived. Perhaps rather surprisingly, it concluded that he had died from divine visitation (*ex visitatione divina*), and not as a result of his head injuries, a point that was expressly set out in the document. Doubtless there was a considerable reluctance to implicate a prominent local man like Gunter. Even so, three men from the village, a relative of the dead men and two players from the football match, attended the ensuing assizes at Abingdon with a view to bringing a homicide prosecution against him. However, their tendered bills of indictment were thrown out by the grand jury there, which appears to have reached, or accepted, the same conclusion as the inquest jury.[348]

Suspects might also be prosecuted for murder following a grand-jury indictment, even if the inquest verdict had merely been for manslaughter, although this was not nearly as common in the Tudor era as it would

---

347. Sharpe and Dickinson, "Revisiting the 'Violence We Have Lost,'" p. 297.
348. James Sharpe, *The Bewitching of Anne Gunter: A Horrible and True Story of Deception, Witchcraft, Murder and the King of England* (London: Profile Books, 1999), pp. 17–18.

be in the early eighteenth century. However, in April 1584 Nicholas St John wrote to the Surrey JP Sir William More about his bad-tempered son Oliver, who had killed the explorer George Best in a violent quarrel (it may have been a duel). At the inquest the coroner's jury returned a verdict of manslaughter against St John. Although this was normal for deaths arising in such situations, Nicholas feared that his son's enemies intended to go to the sessions to "exhibit new bills whereby to find the fact to be murder". He asked More's attendance there to oppose this. (Oliver was eventually pardoned and pursued a military career in the Low Countries.)[349] Similarly, in November 1595, George Carey wrote to Sir Robert Cecil, discussing the killing in Devon of one John Harris by John Neale. The two men had quarrelled, and Neale, apparently acting in self-defence, had mortally wounded Harris. Before his death a week later, Harris confessed that he had actively sought out the quarrel and honourably absolved Neale from any blame. A coroner's inquest was held, and a verdict of manslaughter was duly returned. This decision was apparently displeasing to a local JP (since put out of the commission), who ensured that Neale was indicted for murder at trial.[350]

If the inquest did commit a suspect for trial, or identify a suspect who had fled, it was supposed to secure his assets, to accommodate forfeiture for felony should he be convicted (see *Chapter 12*). According to one sixteenth century legal manual, in cases of homicide and suicide the coroner and jury should immediately identify all of the killer's goods and chattels "as if they should straightway be sold".[351] In practice, coroners' juries often returned a formal verdict to the effect that the suspect lacked such goods, especially if he was poor. However, in 1537, after Thomas Barr killed Thomas Hopper at Eastwood, in Nottinghamshire, and fled, the inquest held on Hopper's body concluded not only that Barr was a murderer, but also that he had goods and chattels worth £4 4s 4d, including several cows, sheep, and mares, as well as domestic utensils. They were

---

349. SHC 6729/7/77.

350. Mary Anne Everett Green (ed.), *Calendar of State Papers Domestic: Elizabeth, 1595–97* (London: HMSO, 1869), pp. 121–138.

351. Carol Loar, "'Under Felt Hats and Worsted Stockings': The Uses of Conscience in Early Modern English Coroners' Inquests", *The Sixteenth Century Journal*, Vol. 41, No. 2, pp. 393–414.

put into the keeping of Richard Bradshaw, the parish constable.[352] Similarly, after an inquest held in the Liberty of Writtle, in Essex, concluded that Edward Harrys had attacked and mortally wounded Henry Collyn with a "hedgeying byll", it was noted that Harrys' goods were worth £6 13s 4d, and were being held by Edward Bell, the coroner for the liberty.[353] The Kent coroner's jury that considered the death of Agnes Smith at the hands of her husband in October 1563 was particularly thorough, producing a detailed inventory of William Smith's goods, listing dozens of items, down to a small cushion and an "old iron pot".[354]

Inquest Juries and Corruption

Although the very localised nature of the inquest process was one of its strengths, it also had some disadvantages. It could lead to local pressure to return "acceptable" verdicts, something that might be enhanced by the careful selection of jurors, of which the coroner could be unaware. This phenomenon has been well-marked in cases of suicide (a felony), which might lead to the dead person's possessions' being forfeited to the Crown rather than being inherited by their family. For example, after William Ponder killed himself in Dodford, in Worcestershire, one of his neighbours, Thomas Baylie, went to the local bailiff's home to help him select suitably sympathetic men from the village and adjoining parishes to serve as inquest jurors. He then reassured the dead man's widow that her husband's goods would not be confiscated. The jury returned a verdict of accidental death, the coroner accepted this, and the widow kept her property.[355]

However, by the 1580s the King's Almoner or one of his deputies, who had the right to receive, on behalf of the Crown, most of the goods and chattels forfeited in cases of suicide, as well as deodands (animals or objects that had caused accidental deaths, which were also forfeit), was becoming stricter about monitoring inquests. As a result, many instances

---

352. Hunnisett, "Calendar of Nottinghamshire Coroners' Inquests, 1485–1558", p. 80.
353. ERO T/A 418/13/29.
354. Cockburn, *Calendar of Assize Records: Kent Indictments: Elizabeth I*, p. 45.
355. Kesselring, "Felony Forfeiture And The Profits Of Crime In Early Modern England", *The Historical Journal*, Vol. 53, No. 2, p. 281.

of such local corruption were identified. For example, after Thomas Chennell was found drowned in a Surrey pond in 1591, the almoner pursued three of the inquest jurors for bribing a local pauper to flee the area, so as to give the impression that he had murdered the dead man, with a view to saving the latter's family from the loss of property that would be consequent on a suicide verdict.[356]

Similarly, in 1619 a King's Almoner accused a group of jurors with acting contrary to their consciences after Francis Marshall drowned in a pond. The coroner's jury ruled that he had been murdered, but the almoner believed that Marshall had killed himself. The almoner also alleged that the jurors concerned had illegally removed Marshall's body from the pond before the coroner arrived and then inflicted numerous wounds on his head to create the impression that he had been attacked. Once at Marshall's house, where the body was placed for examination, they reportedly added yet more injuries to heighten the effect. Not content with this, after the coroner arrived, they managed to insinuate some of their number onto the inquest jury and to persuade others to conceal evidence. It was claimed that the jury then ignored evidence suggesting that Marshall had drowned himself as well as the coroner's directions to return a verdict of suicide. According to the almoner, they were determined to "give no other verdict although in their consciences they knew that [Marshall] had killed himself".[357]

It is almost certain that the same thing happened in possible but not blatant cases of homicide that involved a popular, unpopular, or influential victim or suspect. For example, in 1560 Amy Dudley, the first wife of Lord Robert Dudley, was killed when she broke her neck after falling down a short flight of stairs. As with most such cases, a coroner's inquest was held. The death raised the possibility of accident, suicide, or murder. That Dudley may have played a nefarious role in what had occurred was raised fairly early on, although it appears unlikely. Nevertheless, one reason that he was suspected (even if unfairly) was that he seems to have had some contact with the jury foreman prior to the

---

356. Lockwood, *The Conquest of Death*, p. 2.
357. Loar, "'Under Felt Hats and Worsted Stockings,'" pp. 393–414.

inquest, if only indirectly. The jurors swiftly concluded that it was an accidental death and returned a finding of "mischance".[358]

Less notorious cases of potential homicide could also manifest a local bias. For example, in June 1596 Thomas Griffin, a labourer from Orsett, in Essex, noisily heckled and interrupted the Reverend John Adams while he was conducting evening prayer. In response, the local constable, one William Garreth, and the churchwarden, William Bright, assisted by several other villagers, tried to put Griffin in the parish stocks. They secured his right leg but he resisted vigorously, being injured in the process. The inquest jurors subsequently concluded that he had managed to "bruse and surfet" his internal organs, which were already weak from a recent fall, during the struggle so that he died the following afternoon. Precise responsibility for his injuries must have been hard to apportion, but it seems likely that the jurors gave the benefit of the doubt to their respectable if rather "rough" neighbours, rather than to an obstreperous heckler.[359]

Medical Knowledge and Assistance

For much of the twentieth century, Tudor England was thought to have lagged behind most continental countries in the use of forensic medicine, rarely having recourse to the evidence of physicians and surgeons at inquests, let alone using formal post mortems on corpses to assist the coroner's jury to reach its verdict. By contrast, in 1514 the Pope ordered that the body of the English Cardinal Christopher Bainbridge, who had been murdered in Italy, be "opened" when it was reported that he had been poisoned.

Coroners were not required to have any medical experience, and there was no legal necessity for medical testimony to be presented at inquests. England did not come close to matching the provision for such things set out in the Carolina Code (*Constitutio Criminalis Carolina*) that was declared Imperial law in 1532 and probably constitutes European best practice at this time. This would become an important influence on the

---

358. Bernard, *Power and Politics*, pp. 161–166.
359. TNA KB 9/693c/306, cited in http://tudoraccidents.history.ox.ac.uk

development of legal medicine in Germany, as, under Article 147 of the code, the courts were often required to hear evidence from physicians, barber surgeons, or midwives in cases of abortion, infanticide, and other forms of homicide. Court records from the sixteenth century municipal archives of Frankfurt am Main suggest that the medico-legal investigation of killings was normally conducted by committees made up, at the very least, of several surgeons, while in difficult cases they would be joined by a physician with an academic education in medicine. At trial physicians and barber surgeons were questioned as expert witnesses and based their evidence on the victim's manner of living as well as on autopsies and partial autopsies.[360]

Of course, such thoroughness was not typical of the whole of continental Europe. More pertinently, an absence of medical evidence was not necessarily as significant as might at first be thought. Most English homicide inquests had direct evidence of a killing in the form of eyewitness testimony, while the medical techniques of the period, often fairly primitive, were of limited value. However, English backwardness can also be exaggerated: historians have sometimes assumed that an absence of evidence of medical assistance is evidence of its absence. The typical inquest report of the time, however, was brief and fairly formulaic, providing little more than the names of the coroner, jurors, the subject, any suspects, and the verdict. That it did not refer to medical evidence does not mean that medical practitioners never became involved.

Sara Butler's work suggests that both physicians and surgeons did sometimes participate in medieval inquests, acting as expert witnesses and occasionally even becoming coroners themselves. Similarly, during the Tudor era there was a willingness to use medical men at inquests, if they were available and willing to assist voluntarily, or could be cajoled or paid to do so (and the necessary money was forthcoming). Obviously this favoured inquests conducted in towns rather than remote rural areas.

For example, in 1504 a maid named Christian died in Sandwich, in Kent. It was widely reported that this was the result of a beating administered by her master's wife. However, a local surgeon (as well as a chaplain)

---

360. H. F. Brettel and D. Emrich, "Criminal Law and Forensic Medicine in the 16th Century", *Beiträge zur gerichtlichen Medizin*, Vol. 49, February 1991, pp. 171–174.

examined her body, and the former deposed that the girl had "ii or iii sorys off pestilence and therof died, and not upon no manner beating of her mistress as the clamor renyth".[361] Towards the end of the century, in 1589 Richard Bostock of Crowhurst, in Surrey, wrote to the JPs Sir William More and William Howard about an affray between himself and a man named Foster. He denied that the later death of one of Foster's retainers, an (allegedly) old and sickly man named Holloway, was caused by the disturbance. He asked More and Howard to write to a clergyman who was apparently skilled in physic and surgery, to discover the truth.[362] Presumably he was asking that the cleric examine the body and testify at the inquest.

A case involving one Henry Robson's wife, who died a lingering death in Rye, in Sussex, during the 1590s, is also worthy of consideration. Her husband, who desired to be rid of her so that he could sell up and start a new life, had inserted a mixture of ratsbane (arsenic trioxide) and powdered glass into her "privy parts" while they were in bed together, although it is not clear if this was done during sexual intercourse or while she was asleep. The physicians who attended her prior to what was a very painful death were convinced that she had been poisoned. As a result, they prevented her burial and "having obtained license of the officers, they caused her to bee ripped [dissected], where they found in euerie vaine both glasse and Ratsbane".[363] At about the same time, in another part of Sussex, Edward Skinner hit Robert Mullenex over the head with an iron pot, apparently occasioning injuries from which Mullenex died. Three surgeons were present when a fourth, Thomas Gunter of London, opened Mullenex's skull. Gunter testified that the "skull was cracked and broken and that the contused or bruised blood did lay in great abundance upon the brain, which was the cause of death".[364]

In a particularly notorious case of 1597, Richard Anger, an elderly barrister and former reader at Gray's Inn, disappeared and was found

---

361. Karen Jones, *Gender and Petty Crime in Late Medieval England: The Local Courts in Kent, 1460–1560* (Woodbridge, Suffolk: Boydell Press, 2006), p. 35.

362. SHC LM/COR/3/440.

363. Anon, *The examination, confession, and condemnation of Henry Robson: fisherman of Rye, who poysoned his wife in the strangest maner that euer hitherto hath bin heard of* (London: R. Walker, 1598), pp. 1–10.

364. Loar, "Medical Knowledge", p. 480.

several weeks later in the River Thames. A letter sent to the Recorder of London by the Privy Council noted that several "skilfull surgeons" had examined his corpse and concluded that Anger had been murdered and his body placed in the river to suggest an accidental drowning.[365] The following year, when Avery Blasse died after "lingering" for almost a month, having been stabbed during a fight with one Thomas Oliver in Newhaven, in Sussex, the inquest jurors asked a local surgeon to help them determine whether the wounds had caused his death.[366] In most of these inquests the formal inquest report did not mention an autopsy being held. Doubtless the details of many cases involving medical assistance have been entirely lost.

Furthermore, inquest verdicts often reveal a significant level of medical understanding on the part of coroners, and sometimes jurors, even if they had no formal training in this area. Reports describing fatal head injuries often stress that the skull was penetrated through to the brain.[367] An early sixteenth century oath book from Doncaster expressly advised local coroners, in cases where the cause of death appeared to be drowning, to check carefully that it was not in fact murder. It advised them to examine bodies thoroughly to exclude the possibility of "throttling".[368]

How the Coroner's Jury Worked

In a *cause célèbre* from 1514, Richard Hunne, a suspected Lollard who had been involved in a bitter dispute with the London diocese, was found dead, an apparent suicide by hanging, while in custody in the Bishop of London's prison (the so-called Lollard's Tower in Lambeth Palace). The Lord Mayor, George Monoux, instructed the Coroner of London, William Barnwell, to empanel a jury to investigate the death, as it was sudden and violent, and had occurred in jail. As a result, 24 citizens (the maximum allowed) from neighbouring wards were sworn in. Their work was fairly thorough. They carefully examined the body in situ and

---

365. *Ibid*, p. 475.
366. Kesselring, "Detecting 'Death Disguised,'" *History Today*, Vol. 56, Issue 4, pp. 20–26.
367. Gunn and Gromelski, "For Whom the Bell Tolls", pp. 1222–1223.
368. Butler, *Forensic Medicine*, p. 47.

received evidence from all available witnesses, which was (unusually) also recorded.

It quickly became obvious to the jurors that Hunne could not have killed himself: the noose was too small to accommodate his head; marks on his wrists suggested that his hands had been tied beforehand; the serrations round his neck had been caused by a metal object rather than a belt; the corpse was devoid of any "drivelling or splurging", an absence inconsistent with death by hanging, and the chair from which Hunne would have had to jump was too precariously situated for anyone to have perched on it. There was also a lot of blood in a corner of the cell, away from the body, and on Hunne's discarded jacket. Furthermore, the dead man had clearly been tidied up post mortem. As a result, the jurors concluded that "it appeareth plainly to us all that the neck of Hunne was broken, and the great plenty of blood was shed before he was hanged. Wherefore all we find, by God and all our consciences, that Richard Hunne was murdered".

However, the jury was able to go even further, because Charles Joseph had confessed to the killing while being held in the Tower of London. Relying on Joseph's testimony, the jury concluded that Joseph and two other named men had broken Hunne's neck and then strung him up. Indictments were issued against the three men, who included the prison gaoler, John Spalding. The unspoken implication was that the bishop had been the prime mover in the murder.[369]

A far less famous (and so more typical) case of 1554, in which a bailiff named Roger Barnes died shortly after a beating by three men, is also indicative of jury thoroughness and activism in such forums. The inquest faced competing narratives as to the cause of Barnes' death: was it the result of the assault (i.e. a case of homicide), or of a pre-existing medical condition (natural causes)? After hearing a female witness claim that the dead man's right leg was so badly broken by the beating that his foot could be placed on his thigh, two of the inquest jurors tried this experiment for themselves, manipulating the relevant limb on the corpse. One later reported that he "took the thigh in his hand and Walter Donne

---

369. Richard Dale, "Death at St Paul's", *History Today*, Vol. 64, Issue 12, pp. 10–16.

took the foot and they could not make it bend". The wounds appeared clean and had not festered, so that the jurors had to consider other evidence, suggesting that Barnes may have died of colic and stone: they observed that the "privy members of the lower part of his body was black and swollen". A surgeon sent them a letter stating that he had treated Barnes for both his beating-induced injuries and his existing illness, and attributing his death to the latter. Another physician, whom the dead man had consulted on an earlier occasion, also sent a letter and was then visited by the entire inquest jury; he told them that he had seen blood in Barnes' urine prior to the beating and concluded that he was already terminally ill. Several of the dead man's friends and family gave evidence that Barnes had had difficulty urinating and had declared before he was attacked that he was a "gone man". Perhaps unsurprisingly, the jury concluded that he died of natural causes and not because of the beating.[370]

In another case, from early 1566, John Plankney, a New College student, was found drowned in Oxford. The death might have been occasioned by murder, accident or, most likely, suicide. The coroner took considerable care to establish its true cause. Depositions were taken from 28 people at the ensuing inquest: five Oxford jurymen; four of the townsmen who retrieved Plankney's body from the water; the two women who prepared the corpse for burial (and gave evidence about its condition); three people who had found the student's cloak and boots (weeks before the body itself was located); five passers-by; and nine fellow students who had known Plankney at the college. Some of the students discussed his emotional state. Another testified that Plankney had suffered from severe headaches shortly before Christmas. Numerous questions were asked about the precise state of the corpse and the garments that clothed it.[371]

In a case from 1591, which was not entirely dissimilar to the Hunne affair, inquest jurors who examined the corpse of Peter Courtopp claimed that, although he was found hanging, an examination of his body revealed the presence of wounds that, they argued, could not have been self-inflicted. Instead, they ruled that Courtopp had been murdered and

---

370. Kesselring, "Detecting 'Death Disguised,'" pp. 20–26.
371. Jennifer Thorp, "An Inquest of 1566", *New College Notes* 5 (2014).

then hung up by somebody attempting to conceal the killing. The jurors emphasised the evidence of numerous heavy blows to his corpse and the presence of: "many dangerous bruises as were upon his head and breast and other parts of this body".[372]

---

372. Loar, "Medical Knowledge", p. 475.

CHAPTER 7

Entering the Criminal justice System

Introduction

At the start of the Tudor era, some people accused of felony still entered the criminal justice system as a result of complainants and victims reporting their crimes directly to JPs assembled at quarter sessions. These justices might then order that a bill of indictment be prepared to go before the grand jury, after which (if found to be "true"), efforts would be made to secure the suspect.[373] This had been common practice for much of the medieval period, and may explain why, as late as January 1464, 90 per cent of people indicted at the Cheshire County Court Sessions (the palatinate's equivalent of assizes and quarter sessions) were still at large.

However, by then, and as a 1467 parliamentary petition on bail suggests (see below), most suspects were being physically detained and then brought before a JP who would either commit them to prison pending trial at quarter sessions/assizes or discharge them. Illustrative of this, in October 1465 Margaret Paston wrote to John Paston indignantly complaining that the latter's cook and two other men had been arrested at "Heylesdon be the balyf of Ey[e] callid Bottisforth, and led for to Cossey, and ther thei kepe hem yet with ought any warant or autoryte of Justice of Peas".[374] By the start of the Tudor era this was by far the most common way in which a felon entered the criminal justice system, making the JP fundamental to the entire process.

Because of this, even the threat to involve a magistrate could sometimes settle a heated dispute. For example, in 1601 three local men forced their way into the home of Tabatha Adams' mother in Westwell, in Kent.

---

373. Baker, *Oxford History*, pp. 270–271.
374. Gairdner, *The Paston Letters, AD 1422–1509*, Vol. 4, p. 616.

They threw Tabatha's spindle to the ground, consumed ale they found on the premises, and flung bread around the cottage. The men refused all entreaties to leave, until one of Tabatha's sisters "threatned to complayne to the nexte justice if they did not departe and then they departed all from thence to an alehowse in Westwell Strete".[375] However, JPs did not (normally) personally arrest suspects.

Arrest

Felony suspects could be arrested in a variety of ways, by a range of people. They might be detained by warrant or simply seized and frog-marched to a JP. As Sir John Smith noted, it might be by "hue or crie, [or] by the Constable or anie other who doth pursue the malefactor". In this situation "anie other" often referred to the victim and likely prosecutor, but could, in theory, be anyone. Frequently, a combination of victim, parish constable, and various members of the public would become involved.

Caught Red-handed

Victims or passersby caught many felony defendants red-handed or in the immediate aftermath of their crimes. For example, during the Eliza-bethan period, the ten-year-old Robert Paine from Minster, on the Isle of Sheppey (Kent) cut a woman's purse in a small crowd at Eastchurch hoping to secure enough money to buy cakes. His victim quickly realised that it was missing and looked around her. She noticed that the tassels of her purse were hanging out of Robert's pocket. She retrieved the purse, "which he confessed he did cutt". Perhaps surprisingly, given the boy's age, she also involved the authorities, so that a local JP examined Rob-ert. He immediately made further admissions.[376]

The experiences of Thomas Dreywood, from Warley, in Essex, were also fairly typical. One Sunday evening in June 1576, he was coming from

---

375. Elizabeth Melling, *Kentish Sources VI: Crime and Punishment* (Maidstone: Kent County Council, 1969), pp. 41–42.
376. *Ibid*, p. 35.

church when he came across an outsider, John Arget, who was loitering suspiciously in one of his fields with a woman, while also carrying a reinforced wooden staff. Dreywood challenged him and received a torrent of abuse in reply. The sturdy Dreywood then disarmed and arrested Arget in the name of the queen, ordering the intruder to accompany him to the nearest constable. A group of local people came to assist, and together they forcibly took the two suspects into Warley. The pair were duly delivered to a parish constable, as rogues and vagabonds, then marched before a JP.[377]

At a much more serious level can be considered the arrest of John Rowse. Although this occurred in 1621, it was indicative of practice for much of the sixteenth century. The severely depressed Rowse drowned his two small daughters rather than see them begging for sustenance in Ewell. When his wife returned home and discovered their bodies, a fairly standard sequence of events ensued: "Presently the constable was sent for, who took him into his custody". Rowse was then taken before a magistrate, where his "examination was very brief, for he confessed all the whole circumstances of the matter freely". He was then sent to the White Lion, a former inn that was the common prison for Surrey, where he remained for almost 15 weeks before being indicted at the Surrey Assizes in June. At trial he made a "free confession at the bar". As a result, he was condemned to death for murder, and executed shortly afterwards at the county gallows in Croydon.[378]

Taken After Personal Pursuit

In other cases, a felon, although not taken red-handed, would be captured by an immediate pursuit that was personally conducted or arranged by the victim, self-help being of the essence in the justice system of the time. For example, in February 1518 the Marquess of Dorset wrote to Cardinal Wolsey, noting that James Higgenson, a tailor, had stolen two horses

---

377. ERO Q/SR 58/5aaz5.
378. John Taylor, *The Unnaturall Father: or, the cruell Murther, Committed by one John Rowse, of the Towne of Ewell* (London, 1621), pp. 1–9.

from the stable of one of his employees. In response, the marquess sent 12 of his servants to search for the thief, and captured him at Doncaster.[379]

At a more quotidian level, in 1572, John Hammond was taken on for a trial period as an apprentice "sewmaker" at Billericay, in Essex. One night he took the opportunity to steal £3 from his master and fled to South Benfleet and then over the Thames to Rochester, in Kent, where he spent some of the money. However, he was tracked down by his employer and returned to Essex.[380] In 1598 Sir Stephen Thornhurst and Matthew Hodde, two Kentish JPs, wrote to their counterparts in Essex, noting that they had been reliably informed that a man named William Clibury, who said he was from Halstead, in Essex, had tricked numerous people in Kent out of "divers sums of money" before disappearing. They asked that the Essex magistracy assist the bearers of their letter — four men who appear to have gone across the Thames to track him down — if they managed to locate Clibury in his claimed county of origin. If he was found, they were to bind him over to appear at the Kent Quarter Sessions.[381]

In like manner, in 1600 Margery Corker, a London widow, went into a mercer's shop at Gravesend, in Kent, where she purchased a small amount of cloth. After she had left, the shopkeeper noticed that a large piece of cambric, worth 39 shillings, was missing. He immediately suspected Corker and followed her to Rochester, where he tracked her down. When Corker denied involvement in the theft and failed to return the cambric, the mercer summoned a local constable and charged the officer with her. The constable took her into a private yard and asked her to produce the cloth, which she did (presumably fearing a personal search if she held back). When subsequently examined by a JP, she merely said that she had found the fabric on the ground in the mercer's shop and taken it. (Perhaps surprisingly, she appears to have been acquitted at trial).[382]

Of course, such personal initiatives had potential dangers. In the summer of 1578 a journeyman tailor was walking with his master when

---

379. J. S. Brewer (ed.), *Letters and Papers, Foreign and Domestic, Henry VIII, Vol. 2, 1515–1518* (London: HMSO, 1864), pp. 1220–1236.

380. ERO Q/SR 41/4.

381. ERO Q/SR 142/25.

382. Melling, *Kentish Sources VI: Crime And Punishment*, pp. 40–41.

another (presumably rival) tailor attacked the older man. He suddenly stepped out of a hedgerow and beat him with a "crabbe tree kydgell", knocking him down, and breaking his leg. Fortunately, another man rode by at the same time, and the assailant fled. The journeyman pursued him, until threatened with violence by the fugitive, "and so he escaped".[383]

The more organized and official pursuit of the "hue and cry" could reduce some of these risks, as well as reaching much greater distances.

The Hue and Cry

The 1285 Statute of Winchester introduced the "hue and cry", by which a felon who was not arrested in the immediate aftermath of his crime might be pursued over a wider area. This was especially common in cases of highway robbery and murder, but could be employed for much more mundane offences. In a letter sent to Lord Riche, two Elizabethan JPs from Essex, Henry Medeley and James Morris, noted that one John Founten had recently been apprehended upon hue and cry at Chipping Ongar and brought before them. His crime involved obtaining money by deception, so that it may, technically, have been a misdemeanour. He had gone to various clergymen, claiming kindred to senior local clerics, and demanding their contribution to the queen's subsidy. Some of his marks had been successfully "cozened" into paying him money.[384] At the start of 1619 Joane Friend, who seems to have run an alehouse in Brixham, in Devonshire, found that a poor man who had spent the day drinking in her establishment had slipped away with her husband's shirt, which she subsequently "found about him in the afternoon of the same day upon hue and cry". (When examined by a JP, he claimed to have paid her 18 pence for it.)[385]

In serious cases, a victim of, or witness to, a felony whose perpetrator had escaped was supposed to alert a constable or JP in the first village that he reached, describing the suspect and the direction in which he

---

383. ERO Q/SR 68/58.
384. ERO Q/SR 68/59.
385. Charmian Mansell and Mark Hailwood (eds.), *Court Depositions of South West England, 1500–1700*, University of Exeter http://humanities-research.exeter.ac.uk/womenswork/court-depositions; accessed 26/9/19.

had taken. The constable would then "raise the parish to aide him" in a search for the offender. In theory, all able-bodied men between the ages of 15 and 60 were obliged to participate in the pursuit on receipt of such a request. (Given the time involved and the potential for a violent confrontation, the practice could be quite different.) Traditionally, it was a fairly noisy business, with much sounding of horns and shouting of "Out! Out!" Local people would then turn out with whatever weapons they could find to hand.[386]

If the felon was not found quickly, the constable would send notice, personally or by a messenger, to his counterparts in adjacent parishes, especially those in the direction in which the criminal had fled. These officers would then raise a search in their own parishes, while transmitting the notice on to their neighbouring villages, so that "this hue and crie from parish to parish is caried, till the theefe or robber be founde". Typically, in 1557, after Francis Draycotte fled following a fatal stabbing in Nottingham, John Strilley, a local gentleman, raised the hue and cry and unsuccessfully pursued him through four neighbouring townships.[387]

Inevitably, the system sometimes failed to operate properly, let alone to capture fugitives. Constables were periodically presented at quarter sessions for not raising the hue and cry after learning of a serious crime, or breaking the "chain" when they received notice from elsewhere. This occurred in 1574, after a mare belonging to the constable of White Notley, in Essex, was stolen. Unsurprisingly, given his personal loss, he made hue and cry to his counterpart in neighbouring Black Notley, three miles to the Northwest, who neglected to take it up. In 1584, following a robbery in Goldhanger in the same county, the constable in Layer de la Haye expressly refused to join a hue and cry, because a JP had not initiated it, although a magistrate's authorisation was not normally required. Interestingly, and perhaps revealingly, the Goldhanger constable had already crossed six other parishes to get to Layer de la Haye, presumably passing on the message as he went, rather than leaving it to the chain of constables, until he was far from home.[388] In October 1578 a leet court

---

386. Butler, *Forensic Medicine*, p. 43.
387. Hunnisett, "Calendar of Nottinghamshire Coroners' Inquests, 1485–1558", p. 155.
388. Emmison, *Elizabethan Life*, p. 306; ERO Q/SR 89/11.

fined two constables from Cannock in Staffordshire a shilling each for failing to raise the hue and cry after a felony was committed locally and reported to them.[389]

The need to react speedily to a request for hue and cry meant that the legal or factual basis for calling it out was not always properly examined before it was initiated. In the summer of 1566 Nicholas Kidwelly raised the hue and cry against two of his servants, apparently suspecting them of stealing from him and fleeing. Although they were eventually detained, the Surrey JPs had to send a man to ascertain the precise charges levied against the pair.[390] The system could also be abused, although maliciously raising the hue and cry was an offence. In the late 1570s, William Courtney wrote to Sir William More, complaining that one of his servants, a man named Bryant, had been mistreated by a Bagshot innkeeper named Baker, who had raised the hue and cry against him on very thin grounds. He asked More to find out if Baker was genuinely able to bring any charge of felony against Bryant.[391]

The hue and cry could work very well over short and even medium distances. For example, one afternoon in 1595, at Sutton-at-Hone, in Kent, a labourer's wife returned from harvest work to find that someone had broken into her house and stolen clothes and other household items. She immediately made an outcry and shortly afterwards "Hue and Cry was made and theruppon 2 men were fownd at Crayford passing towards London, who had about them the goods of this examinant [the husband]". These items were then held as exhibits by the local borsholder (constable) pending trial.[392] The distance between Sutton-at-Hone and Crayford is just under five miles. In the same county, in December 1602, James Romney encountered Clement Nuce while riding on the highway near Strood. Nuce's horse accidentally bumped into Romney's and an altercation arose, which ended in a sword fight (both individuals were described as gentlemen). Romney stabbed Nuce with his rapier, mortally wounding him, and then fled to Maidstone, a distance of some 12

389. Andrew Barrett and Christopher Harrison (eds.), *Crime and Punishment in England: A Sourcebook* (Abingdon: Routledge, 1999), pp. 72–74.
390. SHC LM/COR/3/60.
391. SHC LM/COR/3/698.
392. Melling, *Kentish Sources VI: Crime And Punishment*, p. 35.

miles, where the hue and cry caught up with him and he was arrested. (He was subsequently convicted of manslaughter but successfully pleaded benefit of clergy.)[393]

Some felons pursued in this manner were forced to take drastic steps to escape. After the notorious Gamaliel Ratsey and two companions robbed a wealthy man on the highway in Essex it was noted that they only narrowly got away "for hue & crie went foorth in everie place, but they spared no Horse-flesh till they Coasted the Countrie and came to Saffron-walden".[394]

Occasionally the hue and cry seems to have operated effectively over very much longer distances, and lengthy periods of time. In one remarkable case from the 1590s, two men murdered a Welsh drover on his way home from London. When the hue and cry was raised with the assistance of a suspicious fellow traveller's description, it went "to London, toward Wales, & euery way". One of the suspects was subsequently captured in Wales, the other at his home in London.[395]

A surviving aspect of communal responsibility for local crime, one set out in the Statute of Winchester of 1285 (13 Edw. I, St. 2), was that if the hue and cry failed to catch a robber who had operated in daylight, having been properly summoned by one of his victims, the hundred in which the offence occurred would be answerable for his loss, and have to make financial reparation. It could also be fined, although this did not always happen.

The system was slightly modified by statute in 1585. The preamble to this Act noted that the hue and cry was being raised increasingly frequently, and had often proved burdensome to hundreds where a crime had been committed, as the neighbouring hundreds were reluctant to join in a pursuit, knowing that they would not be forced to pay for any failure to capture a fleeing criminal. It was also feared that the existing system encouraged victims to be negligent about pursuing felons. The

---

393. Knafla, *Kent at Law 1602*, p. 22.
394. Anon, *The life and death of Gamaliell Ratsey a famous theefe of England, executed at Bedford the 26. of March last past* (London, 1605), pp. 1–10.
395. Anon, *Two notorious murders one committed by a tanner on his wiues sonne nere Horne-church in Essex, the other on a grasier nere Ailsburie in Buckinghamshire: with these is intermixt another murdrous intending fellonie at Rislip in Middlesex, all done this last month* (London, 1595), pp. 8–9.

statute transferred half the potential cost of damages to adjacent hundreds that failed to raise their own hue and cry in these circumstances.[396] With this in mind, in July 1598 the Bishop of Winchester wrote to a Surrey JP, Sir William More, asking his support for a man who had been robbed in the latter county and considered some of its hundreds chargeable for his loss because of the inadequacy of the hue and cry that had been raised.[397]

The 1585 statute also established a procedure for distributing the burden of paying damages to all the inhabitants of a hundred by means of the imposition of a special rate. Victims were required, inter alia, to give notice of the commission of a felony with as much "convenient speede as may be", and to be examined before a JP about its circumstances within 20 days if they were to have a valid claim.[398]

In practice, payments for failing to raise a proper hue and cry were not made lightly. One reason was suspicion of fraudulent claims. In August 1569, John Wyatt and Richard Sturmye attempted to defraud the inhabitants of the Kingston and Elmbridge hundreds in Surrey. Wyatt tied up Sturmye and left him lying by the highway near Walton-on-Thames. Sturmye subsequently claimed that he had been robbed of almost £12 and demanded that the hundred reimburse him, as required by the 1285 Act. Wyatt was convicted at the Surrey Assizes in March 1571, after the fraud was exposed. (Sturmye was then still at large.)[399] This form of crime would continue to crop up periodically over the next two centuries.

Perhaps more commonly, genuine victims might exaggerate their losses. In the late 1580s officials in the Surrey hundreds of Brixton and Wallington wrote to Sir William More seeking recompense for excessive compensation paid to three people who had been robbed in separate incidents within their bounds, where a hue and cry had not initially caught the perpetrators. In one case a man named Shelly claimed to have been robbed of £60 in Coulsdon Lane in August 1585, but one of the robbers involved subsequently declared at the gallows that only £20 had been taken. In another, Thomas Fenner, a butterman who had been robbed

---

396. David Dean, *Law-Making and Society in Late Elizabethan England: The Parliament of England, 1584–1601* (Cambridge: Cambridge University Press, 2002), p. 192.
397. SHC 6729/9/27.
398. Dean, *Law-Making and Society*, p. 192.
399. Cockburn, *Calendar of Assize Records: Surrey Indictments, Elizabeth I*, p. 93.

at Smithden Bottom in July 1587, claimed £100 had been taken, but the robber, who was apprehended almost immediately, had only 5s 7d on him.[400] A quarter of a century after the Tudor era, John Clavell claimed that such exaggeration was a fairly common occurrence.[401]

Identifying Suspects

Of course, hot pursuit required a suspect. In some cases, a suspect and his or her place of residence could readily be identified, even if he or she was not taken at, or pursued from, the crime scene. These facts might then be reported to a local magistrate, who could issue an arrest warrant. As Sir Thomas Smith noted, as soon as a JP received such a complaint, he would write to the constable of the relevant parish ordering him to bring the man before him for examination. For example, in 1597 one of Robert Gibson's maids stole some goods from her master at North Deighton, in Yorkshire, and ran away. A man named Ramsden then harboured her in the nearby village of Spofforth. Learning of this, Gibson secured a warrant from a local JP, Sir Richard Mawliverer, addressed to the constable of Spofforth, requiring him to arrest her.[402]

A slightly more complicated case occurred in Kent in 1601. About 10 pm one summer evening, Richard Read, a butcher from the small North Downs village of Stalisfield, stole a wether (castrated male) sheep in the nearby village of Charing from a Kentish gentleman named Christopher Dering. It would have been dark by then, providing him with cover. Unfortunately, Henry Perrin, a Charing labourer, woke at about the same time and remembered that he had left his scythe outside. He went out to retrieve it and saw Read running alongside the sheep. His curiosity aroused, he followed him, while Read unsuccessfully tried to hide the animal's mark (used by Dering on all his sheep) from Perrin's sight, and behaved in a generally suspicious manner. The next morning, when Perrin learned that Dering had lost a sheep overnight, he reported what he had seen, and went with a constable to search Read's premises;

---

400. SHC 6729/11/70.
401. J. Clavell, *A Recantation of an ill led Life,* London, 1628, pp. 33–39.
402. Lister, *West Riding Sessions Rolls,* p. 87.

the animal was found, and the thief arrested and taken before JP Nicholas Gilbourne for questioning.[403]

Nevertheless, in many cases, an obvious suspect could not be immediately identified, let alone pursued. Some form of detection would be required for anyone to be prosecuted. The absence of a professional police force imposed major limitations on the ease with which this could be done, as it was often left to the victim of the crime. It was, in part, for this reason that faith was sometimes placed in supernatural means of detection. However, as will be seen, a variety of more practical stratagems were also employed to identify suspects.

Supernatural Detection

One of the centuries-old skills of a cunning man or wise woman (essentially forms of "white" witch) was the ability to find stolen property and identify thieves and arsonists (as well as malefic witches). Of course, in many cases the victim had conveniently supplied them with the names of potential suspects, and often intimated those against whom suspicion was strongest, the cunning person merely confirming this suspicion using various magical techniques, such as looking into crystal balls or cutting cards.

There was also a strong faith in the capacity of divine intervention to directly expose particularly heinous crimes. Many thought it the "grosest part of folly" to imagine that the Almighty would allow such offences to go unmarked by earthly ministers of justice.[404] In particular, it was thought that God would ensure that "murder cannot be hidde".[405]

In one such case in Lincolnshire during the 1590s, a tavern keeper's wife stabbed a sleeping traveller in the throat to secure his money, and then successfully made the death appear to be suicide. A few months later, she took his severely blood-stained smock to a poor woman and asked her to clean it. The wife claimed that the large amount of blood

---

403. Knafla, *Kent at Law 1602*, p. 171.
404. Anon, *The araignement & burning of Margaret Ferne-seede for the murther of her late husband Anthony Ferne-seede* (London, 1608), pp. 1–16.
405. Anon, *A World of Wonders. A Masse of Murthers. A Covie of Cosonages* (London: William Barley, 1595), p. 9.

on the garment was the result of slaughtering a pig. However, the more the woman washed it, the fresher the blood appeared, which so troubled her that she could not rest until she had told the local constable "who immagining what after prooved trueth, tooke other of his neighbours and went to the Inkeepers wife who after some examinations confessed the matter".[406] She was convicted at the Lincoln Assizes and executed. Of course, it may be that rumours had been circulating in the area, and simply producing the stained garment for cleaning was enough to prompt action, the story then being embellished.

Cruentation, one of the most dramatic examples of supernatural detection, was occasionally used to identify murderers. Although it tapped into a tradition of tests that sought the judgment of God, there is only limited evidence for its use in medieval England.[407] However, it experienced a minor flourishing during the Tudor period.[408] In theory, as James VI of Scotland (and future King of England) noted in his treatise *Daemonologie* in 1597, in cases involving a secret murder, "if the deade carcase be at any time thereafter handled by the murtherer, it wil gush out of bloud".[409] In 1572, in Cheshire, another proponent of the technique thought that the corpse would also "expel excrements" in such circumstances.[410]

The test was considered a form of divine judgment manifested by the "indignation" of the victim's corpse when in the presence of its killer. It had some official (i.e. forensic) respect in both England and Scotland until at least the early seventeenth century, and continued in popular use until well into the 1700s. The practice was referred to by William Shakespeare in *Richard III,* when Lady Anne, standing before the body of Henry VI, says to Richard, "Dead Henry's wounds/Open their congeal'd mouths and bleed afresh./Blush, blush, thou lump of foul deformity,/ For 'tis thy presence that exhales this blood/From cold and empty veins where no blood dwells".[411]

---

406. *Ibid,* p. 9.
407. Butler, *Forensic Medicine,* p. 122.
408. Robert P. Brittain, "Cruentation: In Legal Medicine and in Literature", *Medical History*, Vol. 9, Issue 1, pp. 82–88.
409. James VI of Scotland, *Daemonologie* (Edinburgh, 1597), pp. 80–81.
410. Hindle, "'Bleedinge Afreshe'?", p. 233.
411. Act I, Scene 2.

Under the fullest procedure (it was often attenuated), the corpse was laid naked on its back and the suspect walked around it several times, calling on it by name, before lightly touching the wounds. Occasionally, numerous people might be walked past a corpse. In some cases, guilty people do appear to have been moved to confess their crimes, but this usually resulted from applying psychological pressure.[412]

The use of cruentation was reported in chapbooks detailing several instances of murder, such as that carried out by William Sherwood in 1581, in which it was claimed that after he was "brought to the slaine bodie, the blood which was settled, issued out a freshe".[413] Similarly, after Thomas Hill killed his mother in Faversham, in Kent, he had her buried very speedily, before his brother could attend her funeral, claiming that she had died of plague. His sibling became suspicious, and insisted on the corpse being exhumed. After noting that there were no signs of disease, Thomas was brought before it, whereupon the corpse allegedly "bled both at the nose and at the mouth; whereupon hee confessed".[414] (He subsequently hanged himself in prison.) In 1591, after Arnold Cosby, who had murdered Lord Burke, approached the dead man's body, it was claimed "his wounds bled more freshlie then when they were first given".[415]

However, in 1572 the Cheshire coroner presiding over the inquest into the death of Roger Crockett refused to allow such a test to be conducted on a group of men suspected of involvement by the dead man's widow. Although this might suggest that he was sceptical about its value, the test was used periodically (albeit very rarely) at inquests over the following century, and the widow thought that the coroner was corruptly trying to shield the guilty men.[416] Perhaps more pertinently, although the Lord Chamberlain announced the positive result of the test in the

---

412. Brittain, "Cruentation", pp. 82–88.
413. Anon, *A true report of the late horrible murther committed by William Sherwood prisoner in the Queenes Bench, for the profession of Popery, the 18 of June. 1581* (London: Charlewood and White, 1581), pp. 1–8.
414. Moore, *Tudor Murder Files*, p. 11.
415. W. R. (a servant of Lord Bourgh), *The most horrible and tragicall murther of the right honorable, the vertuous and valerous gentleman, John Lord Bourgh, Baron of Castell Connell Committed by Arnold Cosby*, (London: R. Robinson, 1591), pp. 1–16.
416. Hindle, "'Bleedinge Afreshe'?", p. 233.

Cosby case to the Surrey Assizes, he did so only after the jury had retired to consider its verdict, suggesting doubts about its forensic value.[417] In practice, conventional detective methods were much more important than supernatural ones.

Conventional Investigative Techniques

Private individuals carried out much detection on their own initiative. At a very basic level, in a case from 1602, two men in Kent suspected that a local married woman, Alice Bett, had stolen beans from one of their grandfather's fields under cover of darkness. Eventually, they staked out the bean patch overnight and, in the small hours of the morning, caught the suspect and her daughter loading a sack with vegetables.[418] On other occasions, marked coins or goods would be used to trap suspected thieves, especially if they were servants, colleagues, or employees.

Many people instinctively grasped basic detective reasoning. For example, in February 1551, when Thomas Ardern's corpse was found in a muddy field near his Faversham home, with reeds (the floor covering of the room where he had been killed) sticking to his shoes, it did not take a huge leap of imagination to infer that he had been murdered indoors and then dumped outside.[419]

As the Tudor era advanced, the more energetic type of JP became increasingly involved in the active investigation of very serious crimes.

JPs as Detectives

It has been suggested that, even in the early seventeenth century, most JPs were still essentially stay-at-home interrogators, dealing with cases, and reacting to pieces of evidence that were brought to them.[420] This is certainly true of many Tudor magistrates, especially when it came to dealing with less serious crimes. However, throughout the era, even at its start, some JPs went very much further and actively investigated grave

---

417. G.B. Harrison, *An Elizabethan Journal* (New York: Doubleday, 1965), p. 6.
418. Knafla, *Kent at Law 1602*, p. 195.
419. Bellamy, *Strange Inhuman Deaths*, p. 121.
420. Herrup, *The Common Peace*, p. 86.

felonies, playing a significant role in building a case against those who perpetrated them. Magistrates had been urged to actively pursue murderers from at least the late fifteenth century, and this became steadily more widespread as the era advanced.[421] In these situations, JPs might seek out and question suspects and witnesses, test various hypotheses, and prepare cases for trial.

For example, in 1532 Sir John Gaynesford, a veteran JP and sometime Sheriff of Surrey actively sought out and examined witnesses and potential suspects in a local robbery and murder case.[422] (The latter were eventually indicted at the Surrey Assizes, but no convictions seem to have resulted).[423] This magisterial function entered popular consciousness. In what appears to have been the early Elizabethan period, the inhabitants of Ashtead, in Surrey, wrote to the Lord Chief Justice asking that Thomas Browne, William More, and other local JPs be instructed to investigate the disappearance of one Joan Ingate, who, they suspected, had been murdered and secretly buried by her master and his wife.[424]

It was not just homicide that warranted such treatment.[425] For example, in May 1546 Mighell Mallett, a Somerset JP, personally investigated a fairly modest burglary at Spaxton. More speculatively, in 1574 John Skinner, a magistrate from Reigate, in Surrey, received a letter from More enclosing the examination of a man named Watford from the Reigate area. Skinner replied, observing that he had been watching Watford for a long time, because of his generally suspicious behaviour. He had also learned that Watford had been prosecuted at the previous assizes in neighbouring Sussex for stealing a poor woman's horse (presumably he was acquitted). He suggested that More should not bail Watford.[426] Clearly, Skinner had been seeking Watford's indictment for a considerable period of time.

Once a suspect was detained for a crime, JPs might attempt to obtain a confession to other offences of a similar type that had been committed in

421. Gaskill, *Crime and Mentalities*, p. 243.
422. Robison, "Murder at Crowhurst", pp. 32–36 and pp. 44–45.
423. James Gairdner (ed.), *Letters and Papers, Foreign and Domestic, Henry VIII, Vol. 7, 1534*, (London: HMSO, 1883), pp. 61–68.
424. SHC LM/371.
425. Zell, "Early Tudor JPs at Work", p. 126.
426. SHC LM/COR/3/149.

the same area. For example, at some point prior to 1576 Thomas Cooper of Thorpe, in Surrey, wrote to William More and Richard Polsted (JPs for the same county). One John Tanner, from Chertsey, had apparently, and possibly informally, confessed to the theft of one of Cooper's calves, and been temporarily placed in the stocks; however, he refused to implicate others involved in the crime, declaring that he would say nothing "although he be pulled and racked to pieces" (more than a little unlikely in the circumstances). Cooper was convinced that Tanner and his associates had been involved in the theft of a dozen sheep the previous Christmas, and possibly several sheep and lambs at Easter. He sent Tanner to the two JPs in the custody of the Chertsey constables (who also carried his letter), asking that they pursue the matter further.[427]

Securing Suspects

Finding a magistrate to examine a suspect and commit him to prison (if appropriate) might require a journey that could be anything from a few hundred yards to more than ten miles, depending on how far away the nearest "active" JP lived. If arrested at night, on the Sabbath (when JPs would not normally sit), or in remote areas, a suspect would have to be detained. In substantial villages, towns, and cities he might be held in a local gaol or purpose-built lock-up. In other places, he might have to be secured in a more improvised manner, by placing him in the public stocks or a confined place, such as the cellar of a private house. These were not always secure, especially if the detained man was resourceful or had assistance from friends. In 1585 John Gouldesburye of Colchester was arrested by the constable of Abridge, in Essex, who then "set him in the stockes and hanged a locke upon ye stockes, and this examynate [Gouldesburye] picked the locke and ranne his wayes".[428] Similarly, in November 1616, when a man named Toller was brought before Bostock Fuller in Surrey, accused of stealing a goose, the JP charged the constable to "laye him by the heeles all night" and bring him back the following

---

427. SHR LM/COR/3/681.
428. ERO Q/SR 95/67.

morning. Unfortunately, during the night, Toller "brake the stocks and ran away".[429]

November was quite late in the year to put a man out overnight, which was not possible when it was very cold. An alternative solution was used in a case from October 1608. Early one Sunday morning, Simon and Alice Cripple from Egerton, in Kent, found two geese in their shop. They immediately suspected that their temporary lodger, Isaac Loveless, who had come in late the previous night, had stolen them. Local men, including the parish constable, were summoned, and Loveless was questioned. He quickly admitted to stealing the birds. This meant that he had to be secured until the following morning, when he could be produced for examination before a JP. The constable asked two men to guard him in the Cripples' house overnight "or else he should be dryven to sett him all nighte in the stockes". The pair agreed and remained "sittynge up all the night with him". Unfortunately, the following morning Loveless bribed his way to freedom.[430]

The Early Tudor Examination

In 1500 a visiting Venetian noted (with some exaggeration) that once a JP received notice of an identifiable malefactor from a complainant, he "causes him immediately to be thrown into prison".[431] Unsurprisingly, in these circumstances, it seems that a practice also developed by which the JP would examine those detained for serious offences, especially murder, about their involvement in the alleged crime, along with the most germane prosecution witnesses.[432] To some extent, such questioning was necessary, if only to decide whether a case warranted committal, and to avoid the consequences of purely malicious allegations. It also allowed an informed decision to be made on the issue of bail in the years after 1484.

For example, in a case from 1481, mentioned in the *Year Books*, it was noted that JPs might question robbery victims on oath about the

---

429. Granville Leveson-Gower, "Notebook of a Surrey Justice", *Surrey Archaeological Collections*, Vol. 9, 1888, p. 215.
430. Melling, *Kentish Sources VI: Crime And Punishment*, p. 46.
431. Anon, *A Relation, or Rather A True Account*, pp. 33–34.
432. Powell, *Kingship, Law, and Society*, p. 81.

circumstances of the crime. It seems that a written record was also sometimes made of what suspects and important witnesses said, which might then be referred to quarter sessions or assizes.[433] In December 1488, Thomas Andrew wrote to William Paston, a Norfolk JP, asking for what appears to have been the outcome of Paston's examination of a suspected coiner: "Sir, now I beseche you to send me a copy of thes mony makers confeschon, and ther namys, for I ame bothe sworne on the quest of the *oyer determiner*, and also on the quest at large, and of that we most make our verdyte at the sessyons after Crystmes for the quest at large".[434]

In part, this development was probably encouraged by a modest (and far from universal) improvement in magisterial quality. It required a significant number of JPs who were willing to give up time for the common good and who were also literate, as was normally the case with prominent gentlemen by the late fifteenth century. It is also explained by the imperatives created by the decline of the self-informing jury during the fifteenth century. In the high medieval period, there was no need for the state to marshal evidence against suspected criminals because the jury knew or had collected that information on its own. As late medieval jurors became increasingly ignorant of the facts of an alleged crime before they came to court, the state actively encouraged JPs to help assemble the prosecution case against a suspect.[435]

The JP's changing role in this regard appears to have slowly evolved over as much as a century.[436] However, various early Tudor statutes gave an impetus to such developments. For example, one of the first Acts (1 H. VII c. 7) passed during Henry VII's reign, a rather arcane measure intended to combat hunting under the cover of darkness or in disguise, provided that, after receiving information that someone was suspected of such activity, a JP was to issue an arrest warrant and then examine him when produced. If the suspect immediately made admissions, the case could be dealt with as a misdemeanour at ensuing quarter sessions.

---

433. Bellamy, *Criminal Trial in Later Medieval England,* p. 106.
434. Gairdner, *The Paston Letters, AD 1422–1509,* p. 1028.
435. Daniel M. Klerman, "Was the Jury Ever Self-Informing?", *Southern California Law Review,* Vol. 77, No. 1, 2003, pp. 123–150.
436. Green, *Verdict According to Conscience,* p. 111.

If he denied it, the matter would go for trial as a felony.[437] A number of similar specific statutes followed (albeit that some new offences could be determined summarily after examination).

By the start of the sixteenth century it seems to have been fairly common practice amongst conscientious JPs to conduct examinations when confronted by serious crimes in their localities, even when statute did not require it. In 1503 Sir John Paston (1444–1504), a former sheriff of Norfolk and Suffolk (in 1486) and, it seems, a Norfolk JP, sent his cousin Richard Lightfoot and his brother William, then in service with the Earl of Oxford, what appears to have been a volume of criminal depositions made against a group of suspects; he called it a "booke of the seying of dyvers folkis, whiche testyfiee ayenst Thomas Rutty and others. I prey yow shewe it to my lordys good lordshepe, and that I may know hys plesur ferther in as hasty wyse as may be, that I may ordre me ther aftyr". Sir John went on to note that a crucial witness in the case was a woman who had previously been in service with Rutty and overheard all of his conversations. She had also impeached several other men, including one Thomas Bange, supposedly a notorious thief, who was then in prison at Norwich. Bange had been questioned by Sir John, who stressed that he had not done so brutally; the interview had been unproductive, as "he wyll nowghte confesse, nor I handelyd hym not sore to cause hym to confesse". Rutty and others were apparently due to be indicted at the Norwich Sessions.[438] In February 1518 the Marquess of Dorset sent Cardinal Wolsey a copy of the examination of one James Higgenson, who had been questioned over the theft of two horses from a stable and duly confessed.[439]

A case from the following decade is more revealing. In 1521 Thomas Bennett, an inmate of the sanctuary at Beaulieu, and the former keeper of Weeley Park, in Essex, made a lengthy confession to his involvement in a murder committed some four years earlier. Its circumstances were indicative of the growing role of JPs in the processing of suspected felons in very serious cases, especially homicides, but also of a degree of

---

437. Pickthorn, *Early Tudor Government*, pp. 63–64.
438. Gairdner, *The Paston Letters, AD 1422–1509*, p. 1071.
439. Brewer, *Letters and Papers, Foreign and Domestic, Henry VIII, Vol. 2, 1515–1518*, pp. 1220–1236.

amateurism in the procedure, something that would linger until the Marian statute of 1556. In 1516, Bennett had started an affair with the wife of Alan Osborn, from nearby Thorpe. In 1517 Bennett met Osborn in Weeley Park and picked a quarrel with him. He eventually hit Osborn with an ash staff that he had ready to hand, so that his victim "fell to the ground struck dead". The lovers subsequently agreed to say that Osborn had gone to Baddow wearing certain distinctive clothes, taken from his wardrobe, which they then hid. That night they buried Osborn in a sawpit a few hundred yards from where he had been killed.

However, the affair had become common knowledge, so that Bennett was forced to promise his master, Sir John Raynsford (1482–1559), a county JP and future high sheriff, that, henceforth he would not "keep company" with Elizabeth. When he failed to keep this promise, Sir John warned her to leave Thorpe, on pain of being set in the pillory. In the meantime, rumours had started to circulate that Bennett had murdered Osborn, becoming stronger when servants discovered the hidden clothes that he was supposed to have been wearing. These rumours could not be tested in a coroner's inquest, as there was no body. However, they appear to have entered official channels, and prompted a formal investigation, as soon afterwards Sir John sent for Bennett, asking the latter to meet him, along with another county JP, William Pirton (1469–1551), and several other prominent men.[440]

It appears that this meeting was intended as a formal examination, one that might have led to charges, and Bennett being committed to Colchester Gaol (the prison for the county) pending trial at the Essex Assizes, if evidence of the killing had emerged. However, and slightly strangely, Pirton seems to have warned Bennett in advance that it was widely rumoured that he had murdered Osborn, and that, if he had done it, he could not expect favours because of his position: "Thou must not trust to thy master for he will not help thee". Subsequently, Sir John also warned Bennett that if he had slain Osborn "the devil is on thee that thou are here now". Was this a kindly warning to a popular employee that he should vacate the area (as eventually occurred)?

---

440. J. S. Brewer (ed.), *Letters and Papers, Foreign and Domestic, Henry VIII*, Vol. 3, 1519–1523 (London: HMSO, 1867), p. 395.

Nevertheless, Bennett continued to deny the crime, even though Sir John reminded him that there was "never murder done but it will come out". Sir John also intimated that he would send for Elizabeth so that she, too, could be questioned. She was duly examined at Cranfield Hall. Bennett secretly waited nearby, so that he could see her arrive and depart, being concerned that she might blurt out the truth. When he saw Elizabeth leave, he stopped her and asked how the examination had gone. To his relief, she replied that she had been very afraid but had confessed nothing. Even so, by late 1518 Bennett appears to have appreciated that the net was closing in. An old man named Thomas Christmas even warned him to sell his possessions and flee if he was guilty, pinning his hopes on paying a gentleman to secure a royal pardon once he had done this. (The suspiciously modest sum of 20 marks or £13 8s was mentioned for this service.)

Having sold his property, Bennett came across Sir John Raynsford, who intimated that he knew that Bennett was "about to go thy way". This seems to have prompted Bennett to contemplate making a clean breast of matters, but Sir John quickly warned him against this, not wishing to be compromised in his magisterial capacity: "Nay, tell me nothing. God be with thee". Just before Easter, Sir John, William Pirton, and several other gentlemen questioned Bennett once more, when Sir John observed that it was being rumoured that it was only his influence and the fear he engendered that prevented Bennett's arrest for murder. However, he warned Bennett that, in reality, if he had the evidence, he would personally arrest him. He then addressed the other JPs and gentlemen present, inviting them to arrest Bennett if they felt they had sufficient evidence, but "there was no man that answered anything". Clearly, the lack of hard proof was still problematic. John Sinclair, one of those present, freely accepted that there was not enough evidence even to satisfy a grand jury: "Where shall we find 12 men that will indict him?" Even so, Sir John fired Bennett from his employment, until such time as he could clear himself. A week or so later, Bennett fled to the prominent (and permanent) sanctuary of Beaulieu Abbey in Hampshire.[441]

---

441. Euan Roger, *Tudor Trials: Confessions from the Star Chamber*, The National Archives Podcast Series, 2017.

Privy Council Involvement

Sometimes the questioning of suspects was done with the express encouragement of the Privy Council, at others it was carried out by the council itself, which in the Tudor period took on some of the aspects of a prosecuting authority, a development that was strongly supported by Thomas Cromwell. A case from 1532 is indicative of the (then newly established) Privy Council's interest in local law enforcement. After Sir John Gaynesford, a Surrey JP, failed to obtain a confession from the principal suspect in a routine case of murder for gain (i.e. not a political crime), during his own examination of the man the JP took him before the Privy Council, which then questioned him directly.[442] (This power was only formally abandoned in the early nineteenth century.)

In the same decade, the Privy Council asked groups of Kentish JPs to inquire into various murders in their county. For example, in 1533 they asked Edward Thwaites and two other JPs to look into the killing of one William Gerrard. Sometimes magistrates in Kent also sought guidance from the council about other types of crime. In 1537 John Fogge, a prominent gentleman and JP in the Ashford area, was approached by several local people who complained about William Marshall, the vicar of Mersham, alleging extortion and disloyalty to the Crown. Fogge wrote to Thomas Cromwell, asking the Lord Privy Seal to issue a letter authorising him to investigate the allegations with two other JPs. Cromwell did this very quickly, and the magistrates interviewed dozens of the cleric's parishioners. They quickly concluded that there was little more to the accusations than a property dispute over a church living, reporting back to Cromwell that they had supervised a settlement of the matter between the vicar and his opponents.[443]

It was not just the Home Counties that saw Privy Council involvement. In 1540 three Devon JPs — the Bishop of Exeter, Sir Hugh Pollard, and Lewis Fortescue — were the principal investigators in a murder that had occurred in the county, after Thomas Cromwell personally called

442. Robison, "Murder at Crowhurst", p. 46.
443. Zell, "Early Tudor JPs at Work", pp. 133–135.

the cleric into the investigation.[444] This involvement in local, non-political investigations and prosecutions was to continue to the end of the Tudor era. In September 1599 the Privy Council sent a commission to Sir George More, Richard Drake, and Lawrence Stoughton, to enquire into the alleged murder of a child of Lady Jane Browne (1575–1629) at Stoke D'Abernon in Surrey.[445]

However, as the Bennett case suggests, local JPs often conducted such examinations on their own personal initiative, without waiting for orders from higher-up. For example, the mayor and other ex-officio magistrates in Norwich took extensive pre-trial depositions from witnesses in 1519, after John Ganton was fatally stabbed in a violent argument over dice in a city tavern. At least five men (including potential suspects) gave detailed accounts of the entire incident, all of which were carefully written down.[446]

Similarly, in the spring of 1530, the burglary of a wealthy widow's home in London, and the attendant murder of her maid—a "conventional" albeit heinous crime with a fairly well-connected victim—led to the careful pre-trial examination of two of its suspected perpetrators, John Laurence and Robert Turner. Sir John Dunham and a pair of Thomas Wolsey's officials, William Disney and Hugh Fuller, conducted the questioning in the (now out-of-favour) Cardinal Archbishop's home in Nottinghamshire. (The two felons, who appear to have headed north after committing the crime, were arrested there, and then produced at the cleric's home.) Wolsey had held high administrative and legal positions from the early 1510s until November 1529. However, in June 1530, after his fall from grace, he was merely the Archbishop of York, living at his manor in Southwell. Even so, and as with other prominent statesmen, he had been named to the local commission of the peace in 1528, and may have still been part of it two years later. More pertinently, it is likely that Dunham, who had been born about 1498 in Scrooby, in Nottinghamshire (the seat of this prominent family), and would have been 32 at the relevant time, was on the local commission. The questioning

---

444. Zmarzly, *Justices of the Peace*, p. 55.
445. SHC LM/1077.
446. Langbein, *Prosecuting Crime in the Renaissance*, pp. 98–103.

of the two men was neatly recorded on several sheets of paper, with a heading setting out the place of examination, the names of those examined and their examiners, and the former's responses and confessions, as well as an inventory of the goods they had stolen.[447]

By the early 1530s, almost a quarter of a century before the Marian statute requiring examination of suspected felons (see below), Thomas More could note that statements were regularly being taken from witnesses by justices of the peace in their counties and then adduced at trial, "afterward those depositions with such contrary oaths and all the circumstances therewith given in evidence to the jury at the bar, in the face of the King's ordinary court, sitting upon the deliverance of the prisoner".[448] At about the same time, Christopher St Germain also suggested that such examinations were widespread when stressing that, even where a defendant had confessed his guilt when questioned by a magistrate, he must be subject to full legal proprieties at trial.[449]

Of course, such examination could bring its own dangers when conducted by a JP without a judicial temperament. When Philip Witherick's wife was coerced into falsely supporting her son's malicious accusation of murder against her husband (his father), at the St Edmundsbury Assizes, in Suffolk, in 1538, the pressure placed on her by examining magistrates was acute. Most important, it seems that a local JP threatened that she would be treated as an accessory to the alleged (but non-existent) murder, and tried herself, if she did not agree with what her son (the principal prosecution witness) had said. Although initially resolute, she eventually weakened.[450] (It is not clear if she simply made a statement implicating her spouse or actively testified against him at trial.)

In May 1546, the examination Mighell Mallett, a Somerset justice of the peace, conducted into a burglary, was more professional. He appears to have summoned the local constable and the victim of the alleged crime,

447. Shannon McSheffrey, "The Murder of Mistress Lacey's Maid: Ad Hockery and the Law in England circa 1530", in John Witte et al. (eds.), *Texts and Contexts in Legal History: Essays in Honor of Charles Donahue* (Berkeley: Robbins Collection, 2016) pp. 331–347.
448. John Guy, Clarence H. Miller, and Ralph Keen (eds.), *The Complete Works of St. Thomas More, Vol. 10: The Debellation of Salem and Bizance* (New Haven: Yale University Press, 1988), p. 151.
449. T. F. T. Plucknett and J. L. Barton (eds.), *St. Germain's Doctor and Student, Second Dialogue, 1530* (London: Selden Society, 1974), p. 285.
450. Bellamy, *Strange, Inhuman Deaths*, pp. 94–95.

along with the chief suspect in the burglary, a man named Credelond, for questioning. The first two confirmed the case against Credelond, who remained obdurate when examined, and the JP, obtaining no confession, took a recognisance with sureties for his appearance before the next Somerset Assizes. At the hearing Mallett repeated to the jury all that had been told him. The detail with which he did so suggests that he must have kept a written record of what he had heard. He was one of only four prosecution witnesses called, along with the victim and two neighbours.[451]

Although these developments should not be exaggerated—the *Year Book*s run to 1536 but rarely mention the JPs' examination—it is apparent that, to a considerable extent, the Marian statute of 1556 formalised and made compulsory for all felonies what was already fairly longstanding and relatively widespread (but not universal) good practice for serious crimes, especially murder. It seems that Michael Dalton was badly mistaken in believing (almost a century later) that 1556 marked a new beginning in this respect. To some extent, the development of the JPs' examination was a slightly belated recognition that, if a jury was not to be self-informing but, instead, dependent on court-adduced evidence, steps would have to be taken to enhance the quality of that evidence. Even so, the Marian statute was a significant development.

The 1556 Act

The statute of 1556 (2 & 3. P. & M. c. 10) required justices of the peace to examine detained suspects and potential prosecution witnesses in felony cases at special committal hearings, and then to reduce the results of such questioning to writing for production at trial. (The statute placed very similar requirements on coroners presiding over inquests in homicide cases.) It closely followed an earlier Act of 1555 (1 & 2 Philip & Mary c. 13), that was primarily concerned with bail, but which had also required a certified examination of those to whom liberty was granted pending trial (see below).

---

451. Ezra Ripley Thayer, "A Sixteenth Century Jury", *The Green Bag*, Vol. 25 (1913), p. 297; Bradford, *Proceedings in the Court of the Star Chamber*, p. 256.

Perhaps because, in many ways, the 1556 statute merely made universal what was already common practice amongst JPs, it entered popular consciousness very swiftly, and quickly became almost universal. For example, in 1557, just a year after the statute came into force, Lord Stourton initially appears to have considered invoking the criminal law against a father and son named Hartgill after he forcibly seized them for a supposed felony. He called two local JPs to examine them, although for what crime is not clear. The magistrates asked that the men be committed to prison but made no effort to ensure that this was done before they left; doubtless such a powerful aristocrat intimidated them.[452] In June 1584, almost 30 years after the Act came into force, William Lambarde could note as a routine matter that he and another JP "took at Cobham Hall the examination of John Poulterer and the information against him for a cow and a calf stolen from John Miller of Friendsbury".[453]

So fundamental was this process that, in 1598, when Earth Bickley of Crediton went with her father to make a rape complaint directly to the Devonshire Assizes at Exeter, they appear to have been sent away because there had not been a magistrate's examination. They arrived with the "intent and purpose to proffer a bill of indictment against him [the alleged rapist], but stayed their purpose therein, in so much as the matter was not examined before any Justice of the Peace".[454] (Even so, grand juries normally appear to have been willing to receive complaints of felony directly.)

In urban areas, borough magistrates undertook the same task. Thus, and typically, in the autumn of 1578 a tailor named Robert Ellis was taken before John Hunwicke, one of the bailiffs for Colchester, and Robert Mydleton and Robert Mott, two aldermen for the town (all of them being borough magistrates) for questioning in connection with a suspected felony.[455] It was not merely suspects and victims who were examined. Other potential prosecution witnesses might be questioned, and statements taken from them. For example, in June 1599 Robert

---

452. Moore, *The Tudor Murder Files*, p. 87.
453. Conyers Read (ed.), *William Lambarde and Local Government* (Ithaca: Cornell University Press, 1962), p. 146.
454. Mansell and Hailwood, *Court Depositions of South West England, 1500–1700*, accessed 26/9/19.
455. ERO Q/SR 68/58.

Smith, a goldsmith, was examined in connection with a theft from Shotwick Church, in Cheshire. He had unknowingly spoken to one of the thieves, who tried to sell him a bible for an angel (a gold coin introduced in 1465 and worth ten shillings after 1550).[456]

The justice (or, more commonly, his clerk) would record the statements made by suspects and potential witnesses, which might then be read back to them and which they would usually be invited to sign (or, if illiterate, mark). This was not normally a verbatim record but a summary of the magistrate's questions and answers, though there might be direct quotation of key phrases, especially incriminating ones. In theory, the JP had two days to write this down, making it clear that the parliamentary draftsmen had not envisaged a word-for-word transcription. Even so, the best JPs would ensure that the statement was prepared very swiftly, and organize the depositions into a coherent narrative, at least for serious cases.[457]

The suspect was not usually sworn prior to being questioned. However, potential prosecution witnesses would often be examined on oath during the sixteenth century, and this became normal practice thereafter. The written results of these examinations were then certified to the trial court, as required by the 1556 statute. For example, in the summer of 1585 William Lambarde noted, "At the gaol delivery holden at Maidstone, 5 July, 1585, I certified the examinations etc. concerning Atkinson and Prebble".[458] This was one reason that suspects would often be examined by two justices, even though there was no legal requirement that this be done. If one JP was unable to attend the sessions to certify their examinations, the other would. (Pairing-up also allowed the justices to pool investigative experience and gave them the power to grant bail if appropriate.)

This system had some disadvantages. It imparted a fairly strong prosecution bias to English pre-trial procedure, with the JP often helping the complainant to assemble evidence rather than serving as a neutral

---

456. Cheshire RO ZQSE/5/129.
457. Holger Schott Syme, *Theatre and Testimony in Shakespeare's England: A Culture of Mediation* (Cambridge: Cambridge University Press, 2011), p. 37.
458. Read, *William Lambarde*, p. 150.

investigator, seeking all relevant material.[459] By the second half of the Tudor era, an increasing number of diligent magistrates viewed themselves almost as public prosecutors when it came to serious felonies, actively pursuing local miscreants and building cases against them that would stand up in court. For example, in January 1582, Richard Lewknor, a Surrey JP, wrote to his more senior and experienced colleague, Sir William More, about a case of illegal hunting in East Dean Park. He noted that, although he was personally satisfied from his questioning of a young witness that John Standen and Parson Brett had hunted there, he feared that the jury would not be convinced by the boy's evidence on its own. As a result, he would not proceed against them until he had examined another female witness, who, it was thought, might be able to give relevant supporting evidence.[460]

Sometimes examinations were conducted on fairly thin grounds, primarily to harass suspected miscreants. For example, a request to a Surrey JP from the mid-to-late-sixteenth century from an unknown author in London, asked that a man named Gendy be brought in for questioning should he appear again in Shere, where he had "lingered" for three months without apparent cause. He was suspected of breaking into barns and stealing corn there, not least because he had earlier been imprisoned in London for stealing goblets. His brother apparently had a reputation for stealing fish. The writer hoped that questioning Gendy would discourage him from spending time in Shere.[461]

The Role of Reputation

Reputation could be a vital commodity when examining JPs were making a decision on whether to prosecute, especially where the evidence was not clear-cut and particularly if "respectable" people were willing to vouch for suspects. In October 1581 Walter Covert of Slaugham, in Surrey, dispatched a letter to Sir William More, to accompany one of his servants who was suspected of a felony and was being sent to the

---

459. Langbein, *History of the Common Law*, p. 586.
460. SHC LM/COR/3/324.
461. SHC LM/1329/176.

busy JP for examination. Covert did not claim to know that the man was innocent, but noted that he had served him well for six years, and had been safely entrusted with more than 1,000 marks in that time, suggesting that he was not inherently dishonest.

Similarly, in January 1596 Sir Thomas Lucas, an Essex JP, wrote to his fellow magistrate John Sammes about a man that the latter had asked him to question. George Rawlyn had been committed to the county gaol in Colchester after confessing, when examined by Sammes, that he had stolen a horse. In the process, Rawlyn also appears to have (loosely) implicated an Aldham alehouse keeper named Borrowdale as a possible accessory to the crime. Lucas told Sammes that he did not feel there was any basis for action against Borrowdale, with whom he was familiar. He had never previously heard him to be suspected of a crime, or to be a friend to thieves; instead, he was a well-thought-of man whose victualling house was kept in a generally orderly manner. By contrast, Rawlyn was a "most badd fellowe" whose insinuations should not be enough to prompt action against a respectable man, something that would occasion Borrowdale great trouble and expense.[462]

In cases that were both very serious and factually or legally difficult, several examinations of the same suspect might be held, over a period of time, sometimes by different magistrates, with the outcomes being discussed and further evidence sought before a decision whether to prosecute was taken and the appropriate crime identified, as some JPs adopted a prosecutorial approach to "building" cases against some suspects. In a few cases further questioning might even occur after the decision to indict had been made, with a view to securing more evidence or admissions. Whether this was authorised by the 1556 statute, and so entirely legal, would be debated over ensuing centuries.

For example, and fairly mundanely, in April 1598 an Essex mercer's apprentice was examined twice concerning theft of cash from his master and the alleged burning of his apprenticeship indenture.[463] A suspected murder case from Shere, in Surrey, in late 1592 was much more complicated, and led to several examinations as further investigations were

---

462. ERO Q/SR 132/47, 47a.
463. ERO ZQSE/5/116.

conducted. Edmund Tilney (1536–1610), the local JP who carried out the initial questioning, wrote to Sir William More, sending him the details he had taken of the matter.[464] However, in early 1593 Tilney wrote to More again, asking that if he (More) and other county JPs re-examined the witnesses, they should first be asked to affirm the earlier statements the suspects had made to him (Tilney).[465] In 1608 it was noted that Margaret Ferneseede, accused of the murder of her husband, Anthony, maintained her innocence when first questioned and throughout "all her examinations taken before severall Justices".[466]

Having examined a suspect, a JP would decide whether to commit them for trial and, if so, for what offence, and to what forum. If magistrates did decide that a matter should be tried they would also bind-over the prosecutor and (sometimes) important prosecution witnesses to attend the hearing. As Sir Thomas Smith noted in the 1560s, this might be for as little as £10 or as much as £100 or more, with £20, £30, and £40 being fairly common sums, depending on the gravity of the crime and the magistrate's discretion. These sums would be forfeit if those bound over failed to go through with the matter. As Sir Thomas Smith summarised the procedure, as soon as a suspect was brought before a JP he would "examine the malefactor, and writeth the examination and his confession: then he doth binde the partie that is robbed or him that sueth, and the Constable, and so manie as can give evidence against the malefactor to be at the next sessions of gaole deliverie to give their evidence for the Queene".

Status of Examinations

The Marian statutes said nothing about whether the written statements were meant to take the place of testimony at trial, i.e. to constitute evidence. In the judicially supervised pre-trial examinations of suspects and witnesses in much of continental Europe by this time, the investigating magistrate usually compiled an authoritative written dossier on which,

---

464. SHC LM/COR/3/699.
465. SHC LM/COR/3/700.
466. Anon, *The araignement & burning of Margaret Ferne-seede*, pp. 1–16.

to a significant extent, the final judgment was based; such statements were indeed evidence.[467] Traditionally, this was not the case in England. As the Venetian envoy observed in 1500: "Nor are proceedings carried on in this country by the deposition of any one, or by writing".[468]

At first sight this situation might seem to have changed in England after 1556. According to Sir Thomas Smith, the written examinations and statements JPs produced were being formally read out to the court at the start of a trial in the early 1560s. Thus, when three alleged witches were tried at Chelmsford in July 1589, it was noted that "their inditements were read, and their examinations also".[469] In the 1590s the Somerset JP Edmund Hext thought that the personal attendance of an examining magistrate at trial was very important for this reason, as well as for case management; he could: "inform both judge and jury what he found by examination; and likewise see that the party robbed give true evidence to the petty jury that he can".[470]

However, the practice of reading out depositions does not seem to have persisted much beyond the end of the sixteenth century. More pertinently, it is apparent that, even in the late 1500s, the examinations did not displace the then still relatively new (i.e. post-self-informing jury) dominance of oral testimony given in court that had developed towards the end of the medieval period. For example, in the 1560s Sir Thomas Smith suggested that, in the absence of witnesses to testify for the prosecution after arraignment, the accused was normally "without difficultie acquitted". Thus, in a witchcraft case from Elizabethan Colchester, it was noted that a witness who had made an allegation in a magistrate's examination prior to trial at borough sessions had failed to repeat the charge at gaol delivery, and so the case had to be dropped, despite its having been indicted by the town's grand jury.[471] Evidently, reading out pre-trial statements would not usually be enough to secure a conviction.

---

467. Langbein, *Prosecuting Crime in the Renaissance*, p. 33.
468. Anon, *A Relation or rather a true account of the Island of England*, p. 32.
469. Anon, *The Apprehension and confession of three notorious Witches. Arreigned and by Justice condemned and executed at Chelmes-forde, in the Countye of Essex, the 5. day of Julye, last past.* (London,1589), p. 5.
470. John Strype, *Annals of the Reformation ... in the Church of England* (Oxford: Clarendon Press, 1824), p. 406.
471. Samaha, *Law and Order*, p. 69.

It seems that the draftsmen of the Acts never intended to establish a system of written evidence, and this did not occur in practice.[472]

Even so, there was not a rigidly binding rule excluding pre-trial statements from being read out, perhaps unsurprisingly, given the very rudimentary nature of the hearsay rule at this time. At the Surrey Assizes held at Southwark in 1590, the (legally advised) Puritan cleric John Udall, accused of having published a "wicked, scandalous, and seditious libel" contrary to statute (23 Eliz. cap. 3), argued that most of the evidence against him, being in the form of written depositions made by witnesses in an earlier action in the Court of High Commission, would not be permitted in many civil actions, let alone at a trial for capital crimes. His reaction clearly indicates that it was normal in criminal matters for witnesses to testify "live". Even so, Serjeant John Puckering (presiding over the hearing) firmly rejected Udall's considering the "witnesses against you the less lawful, because the parties were not present". (Udall was convicted but ultimately pardoned.)[473]

Rather belatedly, when Lord Morley was tried for murder before the House of Lords in 1666, after killing his opponent in a duel, the Westminster judges resolved, prior to his hearing, that a deposition made by a witness other than the accused before a coroner or JP was admissible only if its maker was dead, too sick to travel, or kept away from court by or at the behest of the accused himself.[474]

Nevertheless, whatever their precise status, Tudor jurors would often be exposed to such pre-trial statements, and influenced by them, at least to some extent. They could also be used for other forensic purposes. For example, it seems that assize judges sometimes had sight of them in advance of trial, to help them arrange the presentation of a case. More important, they could be employed to refresh a witness' memory and as a basis for cross-examination where the makers of such statements departed from them when testifying in court.

---

472. Langbein, *Prosecuting Crime in the Renaissance*, p. 15.
473. William Cobbett, *A Complete Collection of State Trials and Proceedings for High Treason and Other Crimes and Misdemeanours, Vol. 1* (London: R Bagshaw, 1809), pp. 1278–1302.
474. Robert K. Kry, "Confrontation under the Marian Statutes", *Brooklyn Law Review*, Vol. 72, No. 2, p. 498.

Even more significantly, confessions contained within the statements could be admitted against their maker if the magistrate to whom they were made (or his clerk) was in court to adduce them, as was usually the case; eventually this would become an acknowledged exception to the emerging hearsay rule. This could be vital, but according to Sir Thomas Smith was not enough, on its own, to secure a conviction in the absence of other prosecution evidence. For example, in Elizabethan Colchester Robert Man confessed to stealing a "mortar brazier" from Thomas Gladwyn of Lexden. But when Gladwyn did not come to court to prosecute him, the bailiffs were unprepared to rely on Man to repeat the same story in court when his life was at stake, and nervous about relying purely on his out-of-court admissions.[475]

Because the justices' pre-trial examinations were written down, unlike most in-court testimony, they were often important if a jury was brought before the Star Chamber, as occurred after Roger Life, who had been tried at assizes in Hereford for the manslaughter of Richard Rowe, was acquitted. The Star Chamber considered the depositions taken before an examining JP as well as the testimony of other witnesses given at the original trial (presumably reported by the presiding judge with the aid of the court clerk), something that led the court to conclude that the jury "ought to have found the same Life guilty of the manslaughter".[476]

More generally, the Marian examination enhanced the traditional English system of de facto private prosecution. It made it difficult and costly for those who had approached a magistrate to withdraw their allegations when their blood had cooled, and the expense and trouble of indicting a matter or testifying at trial became apparent. It also deterred people from making frivolous allegations that would not be pressed (a common problem).

For example, in September 1595 two men had a heated argument in an Essex tavern, at the end of which one accused the other of uttering seditious words. He then reported the matter to a local JP who suspected that the allegation was partly influenced by personal hostility. Noticing

---

475. Samaha, "Hanging for Felony", p. 770.
476. Charles Hamilton, "Star Chamber and Juries: Some Observations", *Albion: A Quarterly Journal Concerned with British Studies*, Vol. 5, No. 3, p. 239.

that the complainant seemed to change his story when required to repeat it, the magistrate insisted that he set down in writing the precise words used, which he did with evident reluctance. The justice then examined other men who had been present in the tavern. In light of these investigations, he noted that the complainant "beyng oppressed with anger had added somwhat to ye speaches to make them ye more heynouse and wolde ye next day have retracted ye wrytynge". The magistrate refused to allow this. The parties and independent witnesses were bound over to the following quarter sessions.[477]

The procedure also helped to ensure that avoidable evidential gaps in prospective cases were filled prior to trial, increasing the likelihood of conviction. For example, in a Surrey homicide case of 1593, the JP Edmund Tilney requested that his colleagues take the sworn evidence of the main suspect's young servant as to whether the victim had turned when stones were thrown at him. He appeared to have been killed by a blow from a pitchfork to the back of the head, but Tilney allowed for the possibility that it was given in self-defence, despite believing that this was a deliberate murder stemming from long-held "malice".[478]

The Marian statutes only required that justices conduct examinations in cases of suspected felony. However, well before the end of the era, they were often holding them for serious misdemeanours, something that would become even more common in the seventeenth century.[479] Robert Greene alluded to this in his celebrated defence of con men of 1592. The narrator of this fictional work says that an Exeter tanner he tricked out of two shillings (a misdemeanour) had him arrested by a constable, and the next day he was carried before a JP, "whereupon after strict examination I was sent to the jail".[480] In November 1583 the Surrey JP William More formally examined John May about his fishing at Frensham Ponds.[481]

---

477. ERO Q/SR 131/34.
478. SHC LM/COR/3/700.
479. T. G. Barnes, "Examination Before a Justice in the Seventeenth Century", *Somerset and Dorset Notes and Queries,* Vol. 27, 1955, pp. 39–42.
480. Anon, *The Defence of Cony-Catching or The confutation of those two injurious pamphlets published by R. G. against the practitioners of many nimble-witted and mystical sciences* (London: Thomas Gubbins, 1592), p. 2.
481. SHC LM/558/6.

At its best, the system worked well, especially after 1555. For example, following a fatal sword fight in New Romney, in Kent, in 1587, magistrates from the small town prepared extremely thorough interrogatories to determine where the fight occurred, the nature of the wound, how the victim died, the location of the body, who was suspected of committing the crime, whether it was a case of murder or manslaughter, etc.[482] In the early seventeenth century, in June 1618, Bostock Fuller, a Surrey JP, noted that he had sent out warrants for a variety of witnesses, so that they could be "examined concerning the murther of William Darye of Reygate [alleged] against Robert Cotes, & the 27th I examined 7 persons & the said Cotes, & sent him to the White Lyon [prison]".[483]

Successful prosecutions were often founded on such examinations. However, not all JPs had the time, ability, or inclination for them. In 1596 Edward Hext complained about the lack of interrogative experience and energy amongst many English magistrates, fearing that criminals were often brought before a JP who either lacked the experience to examine a cunning thief or would not "take the pains that ought to be taken in sifting him upon every circumstance and presumption". In part to counter this, William Lambarde, in the 1588 edition of his *Eirenarcha*, expressly identified matters that examining JPs should view as engendering suspicion. Many were fairly obvious examples of circumstantial evidence. For example, if a crime required physical strength, was the suspect sturdy or weak and sickly? These factors were similar to many expressly identified in the German Carolina Code of 1532.[484]

Magistrates treated some suspects unfairly. The late seventeenth and eighteenth centuries were to see increasing concern about the manner in which examining JPs obtained confessions from those accused of capital felonies. However, there was less anxiety about such niceties in the Tudor era. In 1598 George Harvey, an Essex JP from Tolleshunt D'Arcy, examined a long-suspected local thief named Edward Tunbridge about numerous crimes, many of them perpetrated against the magistrate himself (something that was not then considered improper). Although

---

482. Gaskill, *Crime and Mentalities*, p. 243.
483. Leveson-Gower, "Notebook of a Surrey Justice", pp. 175–178 and pp. 206–207.
484. Langbein, *Prosecuting Crime in the Renaissance*, pp. 42–43.

Tunbridge initially denied everything, Harvey appears to have broken him in just 15 minutes of questioning, as he subsequently boasted in a letter to his fellow JPs: "I Charged him with causes wch he most vehemently denied … and I doe assure you I made [him] wthin lesse them a quarter of an hower after confesse all to be trewe".[485] Similarly, in 1595, a young man's stepfather and brother-in-law decided to murder him so as to inherit his property. They ambushed and killed him near Hornchurch. Suspicion quickly fell on one of the men, and although "at the first he sought to face it out, yet before a Justice he confessed it presently".[486]

Sometimes blatant trickery was employed. In about 1590 John Parker and Anne Brewen were questioned in London about the murder of Anne's husband two years earlier, after neighbours overheard them arguing about the killing. Anne was carried before Alderman Haward (an ex-officio magistrate for the City of London) to be examined, while Parker was taken to one Justice Younge. Initially both of the suspects firmly denied everything, but "in the ende shee [Anne] was made to beleeve that Parker had betrayed the matter, whereupon she confessed the fact".[487] Similarly, in 1598, after Henry Robson was suspected of poisoning his wife in Rye, the mayor, jurats, and recorder (all of them ex-officio magistrates for the town) questioned him. The recorder, a lawyer named Boulton, went first and resorted to deception to get Robson to confess, telling him that his accomplice had been arrested and had implicated him.[488] Adopting a different tack, the Essex JP Brian Darcy, investigating the St Osyth witches in 1582, offered Ursula Kemp an inducement to make a confession, even though it would not be honoured and ultimately helped lead to her conviction and execution.[489]

At other times, a rather "robust" or even aggressive form of questioning is hinted at. One night in January 1577 Alice Neate slit her sister-in-law's throat in Colchester. The testimony of Alice's daughter, Abigail,

---

485. ERO Q/SR 143/23.
486. Anon, *Two Notorious Murders*, pp. 1–10.
487. Thomas Kyd, *The Truth of the Most Wicked and Secret Murdering of John Brewen, Goldsmith of London, Committed by His Own Wife, Through the Provocation of One John Parker Whom She Loved* (London, 1592), p. 6.
488. Anon, *The Examination, Confession, and Condemnation of Henry Robson*, pp. 1–10.
489. W. W., *A true and just Recorde, of the Information, Examination and Confession of all the Witches, taken at S. Oses in the countie of Essex* (London, 1582), pp. 1–20.

was devastating to her case at trial. However, initially Abigail had firmly maintained her mother's innocence when questioned. It was only under the pressure of what was coyly termed "straight examination" that she finally admitted that her mother had persuaded her to conceal the homicide, and that she had been an eyewitness to the killing.[490]

In about 1590 Sir John Norris (1547–1597) wrote from Portsmouth to Sir William More. A man had been charged with robbing one of the queen's servants. Norris was convinced of his guilt, but the absence of those who could give evidence against him was delaying matters. Norris had threatened the man with service in Brittany and asked More to interrogate him again, and, if he would still not confess, to "impress him as a soldier" and send him to Norris, a senior officer in Portsmouth, who would extract the truth in a military environment and send him back at his own expense.[491]

Even so, some suspects still refused to cooperate. After Elizabeth Caldwell made a full confession when questioned about the murder of her husband, her two accomplices, who had been arrested on the strength of her statement, "very stoutly denied all, afferming that they were not guiltie to any such action, although her confession in her Examination did manifest against them, beeing layd to their charge".[492] Similarly, in 1576 a sophisticated confidence trickster remained silent when questioned by two Essex JPs: "We would have examyned the partie of this his lewde dealinge but he would answeare nothinge directly".[493]

However, even if some examining JPs showed excessive zeal, others were aware of its dangers. In the early 1600s, Sir Richard Grosvenor (1585–1645), a Cheshire JP and sometime high sheriff for the county, knew the dangers of excessively pressuring those brought in for questioning, and urged that magistrates "labour to discover the truth, but entrap not poor simple men in their own words. Let them thoroughly understand

---

490. Samaha, "Hanging for Felony", p. 763.
491. SHC 6729/1/73.
492. Gilbert Dugdale, *A true discourse of the practises of Elizabeth Caldwell, Ma: Ieffrey Bownd, Isabell Hall widdow, and George Fernely, on the parson of Ma: Thomas Caldwell, in the county of Chester, to haue murdered and poysoned him* (London, 1604), pp. 1–10.
493. ERO Q/SR 68/59.

themselves before you record their examinations".[494] Doubtless he had many Tudor predecessors of equal probity.

Nevertheless, it seems that many suspects (who were legally unrepresented) made admissions when questioned where they would have been better advised to remain silent, as there was only limited evidence against them. For example, in about 1590, when Alice Shepherd, her mother, grandmother, and a midwife broke the neck of Alice's newborn boy and buried his body in a Salisbury churchyard, a JP examined all four women. They swore (although it was unusual for suspects to be questioned on oath) that the baby had been stillborn, and, despite the brutal nature of the killing, they were discharged. As they left, the midwife was overheard to reproach herself for her false oath, and the group were re-examined. On this occasion "after a faint denial they generally confessed". They were convicted and sentenced to death at the following assizes.[495]

In exceptional cases, especially but not solely in or near the capital, a senior judge who was also a local JP, whether because he had a territorial connection with the county or covered its assizes, might be asked to conduct the examination, so as to employ his investigative and interrogative expertise. For example, in 1595 a Middlesex man burgled his neighbours' house at Ruislip in full view of their ten-year-old son. He then viciously and repeatedly stabbed the boy, before leaving him for dead. Amazingly, the child survived and identified his assailant. Even so, this was not initially taken as conclusive, as the suspect denied the deed "with many bitter curses". He was released on bail. However, pressure from the child's parents made the authorities bring him before Lord Anderson, "who so sifted him that he confessed the fact". The irascible Edmund Anderson was Chief Justice of the Court of Common Pleas, but had also had been born in Holborn and was a member of the Middlesex Commission of the Peace. (At trial, the child gave evidence against the burglar, who was duly convicted and executed.)[496] Similarly, in 1591, William Fleetwood, the Recorder of London and a Surrey JP of some 20 years' standing,

---

494. Richard Cust and Peter G. Lake, "Sir Richard Grosvenor and the Rhetoric of Magistracy", *Historical Research*, Vol. 54, Issue 129, pp. 40–53; Herrup, *The Common Peace*, p. 88.
495. Anon, *Sundrye strange and inhumaine murthers lately committed* (London, 1591), pp. 1–16; Bellamy, *Strange, Inhuman Deaths*, p. 214.
496. Anon, *Two Notorious Murders*, p. 7.

examined a servant to Sir Owen Hopton at another magistrate's request, about a robbery in Surrey. The servant was eventually discharged in light of his good character and after producing a sound alibi.[497]

In the close-knit society of rural England, finding a JP who was entirely independent of an investigation could pose problems, so this did not occasion undue concern in the sixteenth century (as it would by the late 1700s). Nevertheless, in 1595 the Essex magistrate Arthur Herry wrote to Sir Thomas Mildmay and the rest of the county's JPs. He noted that William Thrustell and Thomas Byndar of Danbury had had an argument in an alehouse, during which Byndar was alleged to have uttered seditious words, which were duly reported to him by Thrustell. Herry unavailingly urged Thrustell to prefer them to another magistrate, apparently because he had earlier employed Byndar as a farrier, and so might be thought to favour him in any ensuing examination.[498]

The Test for Committal

Foreigners were often struck by the relative ease and indiscriminate manner with which private individuals could activate the criminal process by making accusations to a JP, even though it would often entail a suspect being committed to custody until his or her trial. In 1500 a visiting Venetian thought that it was the "easiest thing in the world" to get someone sent for trial in England, a situation that was made worse by the country's lack of effective punishment for slanderous and malicious allegations.[499] In theory it seems that if a complainant was prepared to swear to a suspect's having committed an indictable offence, and the JP was satisfied that such a crime had been committed, even if he had serious reservations about the identity of its perpetrator, he was required to commit the matter for a hearing. This lack of "quality control" in assessing criminal accusations was to be a permanent issue until well into the eighteenth century.

---

497. SHC LM/COR/3/503.
498. ERO Q/SR 131/34.
499. Anon, *A Relation, or Rather A True Account*, pp. 33–34.

However, in practice, it seems that even Tudor JPs were slightly more willing to make an assessment of the strength of the prosecution case than the theory might allow. Of course, the frequency with which allegations of felony made to a JP were dismissed out of hand because of a lack of evidence is almost impossible to assess. Such cases produced few, if any, records. Nevertheless, it appears that, like granting bail (see below), it was slightly more common than is sometimes suggested. For example, on one occasion John Cooper, a young servant in Elizabethan Dedham in Essex, was accused of stealing wool from his master. William Cardinal, a distinguished local JP and a barrister of some standing, examined the boy extremely thoroughly but "fyndinge nothinge againste him, let him goe".[500]

Interlocutory Matters

If an examining magistrate decided to commit a matter for trial, he would have to make several ancillary decisions with respect to the case. For example, the JP would have to decide whether to send the matter to quarter sessions or assizes, whether to bail the suspect in the meantime, and whether to bind-over the prosecutor and other key prosecution witnesses to attend court to pursue the matter or give evidence, and, if so, in what sums. As with so many areas of the justice system, the recognisance played a vital role in this regard.

The Recognisance

A recognisance consisted of two sections. The first was a bond acknowledging a specified debt to the Crown, which could be anything from five to many hundreds of pounds; this would have to be paid if the condition(s) set out in the second section were not fulfilled, but would be voided if they were. The condition(s) ranged from attending court to stand trial (if bail was granted to a defendant) to indicting/giving evidence

---

500. Samaha, "Hanging for Felony", p. 769.

for the prosecution.[501] (A comparable power to bind-over individuals to keep the peace was also used to deal with conflict between individuals.)

For example, in February 1590 it was noted that a man named Chandler who had conspired to murder his lover's husband (the plot did not come to fruition) had been bailed prior to a hearing at the Essex Quarter Sessions, failed to attend, and then disappeared. As a result, a justice noted, his "recognysaunce [was] forfyted by Chanundeler who I dought wyll no more be founde".[502] However, if there were special mitigating reasons for failing to perform the specified act, the person bound over might be excused by the justices from forfeiting some, or all, of the relevant sum. In September 1574 Robert Dudley, the Earl of Leicester, wrote to the Surrey justices asking for indulgence to be shown towards John Milton, a servant to the master of the queen's buckhounds. Milton had accompanied his employer to Warwickshire in July, after Leicester asked the latter to travel there. As a result, Milton had failed to attend the quarter sessions held at Guildford at this time, and was now at risk of forfeiting the recognisance he had entered into to do so.[503]

Both the person who was the subject of the recognisance—a suspect seeking bail, someone being bound over to prosecute, etc.—and third parties (usually friends, relations, and neighbours) acting on his behalf, or a combination of the two, could provide such sureties. For those being bailed, it was fairly common for these sureties to be provided by the defendant and two others, if they were deemed to be satisfactory. However, tendered sureties were not always accepted. In 1585 Thomas Gent, an Essex JP, noted that one Charles Hopkyn had been summoned before him to be bound over to keep the peace against two men whom he had earlier abused. When Hopkyn appeared before the magistrate, he urged Gent to take two "very mean sureties" for his future good behaviour. Both were poor or landless men. Aware that Hopkyn had a reputation for being quarrelsome, Gent decided that these were inadequate, and asked him to find better-quality individuals. When Hopkyn responded angrily, Gent committed him to the custody of a Steeple Bumpstead constable

---

501. Joel B. Samaha, "The Recognizance in Elizabethan Law Enforcement", *The American Journal of Legal History*, Vol. 25, No. 3, p. 189.
502. ERO Q/SR 112/8.
503. SHC 6729/13/21.

for production at the imminent quarter sessions, where the assembled JPs could give the matter more detailed consideration.[504]

Those who stood surety did not always entirely trust the suspects whose appearance they guaranteed. A few subsequently asked to be released from their obligations. In a convoluted transaction in 1524, Arnold Chandler of Godalming, in Surrey mortgaged land to John Glover as security for a pledge (recognisance) that Glover had provided for Chandler on a charge of felony.[505]

A selection of cases is indicative of the operation of recognisances in securing prosecution and prosecution evidence. For example, after a robbery in the autumn of 1556, Henry Peter and John Green, two labourers from Takeley in Essex, entered into recognisances to prosecute the suspects, while Thomas Horensbye, a butcher from Elsenam, entered into a recognisance to ensure that his identically named ten-year-old son appear to give evidence at the same trial.[506] In October 1581, the Kentish JP William Lambarde and another magistrate examined one William Greves from Gravesend who had been arrested on suspicion of stealing 30 sheep. He also took the "informations" of three witnesses on the same matter and bound over two of them in the sum of £20 each to give evidence against Greves at trial. (Presumably one of them was also the prosecutor.) In January the following year Lambarde committed Richard Hanwood, an assistant butcher, to stand trial for stealing £24 from his master, William Latham. Latham was bound over "to sue etc." (i.e. to prosecute the matter). Lambarde also advised Latham on preparing for the hearing. He warned him to bring to the trial at least one of two men who were with him when Hanwood was apprehended, presumably as corroboration, although they were not formally bound over to testify. Lambarde also reminded him to send for the borsholder (constable) of Milton, who had arrested Hanwood and counted the recovered money.[507] In April 1594, Thomas Gladwin, a servant to Lord Henry Cock, was personally bound over in the sum of £10 to appear at the next Middlesex

---

504. ERO Q/SR 94/26, 27 and ERO Q/SR 94/29.
505. SHC 5410/2/3/23.
506. ERO Q/SR 173/110.
507. Conyers Read, "William Lambarde's 'Ephemeris,' 1580–1588", *Huntington Library Quarterly*, Vol. 12, No. 2, pp. 137–138.

Sessions to give evidence against John Tucker for highway robbery.[508] In 1596, John Sorrell of Essex entered into a recognisance in front of the JP Edward Grimeston to appear at the next assizes or quarter sessions with gaol delivery (wherever the case was brought) to give evidence against John Sparling of St Osyth for stealing four milk cows.[509]

Bail

Most suspected felons, if committed for trial, would be remanded in custody to await their hearings. As Sir Thomas Smith observed, frequently the same constable who had brought them in for questioning would then be asked by the examining JP to take them to gaol to await their hearing. However, this was not invariably the case. In 1361 JPs had been empowered by statute to grant bail, under prescribed conditions, for certain offences. However, the system occasioned problems, especially as the nature of the country's legal system evolved. Indicative of the changing nature of prosecutions, in 1467 the House of Commons requested that the king take note that innocent men throughout the realm were being "arrested daily on suspicion of felony, of which they are not guilty, and thereupon have been taken to various of your gaols, where by law they must remain in prison until the coming of your commissioners for gaol delivery". They asked that Edward IV decree that JPs have authority to bail suspected felons "out of sessions". The King promised to consider the matter, but no action was taken until 1484, when Richard III's only Parliament, lasting 27 days between late January and late February 1484, passed a statute that was similar to the proposals made some 17 years earlier. It extended the law governing bail to those who had not yet been indicted because, according to the parliamentary rolls, people were regularly being arrested and imprisoned as suspected felons, "sometimes out of malice and sometimes on vague suspicion, and thus kept in prison without bail or mainprise [a closely linked doctrine] to their great vexation and trouble". It was also ordered that every county JP or borough magistrate should have the power to grant bail or mainprise at

---

508. Jeaffreson, *Middlesex County Records: Vol. 1, 1550–1603*, pp. 219–225.
509. ERO Q/SR 135/76.

his discretion to such prisoners, just as they could for prisoners indicted for the same crimes at quarter sessions.[510]

Nevertheless, even this system did not prove satisfactory. In 1485 the newly crowned Henry VII demanded that JPs refuse bail to any man "knowing and deeming him to be felon".[511] Parliament complained that the 1484 statute, which allowed every JP and borough magistrate to grant bail or mainprise at his discretion, had produced a situation in which many people who should not have been released from custody were being bailed: "against the proper form of the law, whereby many murderers and felons escaped".

In response the 1487 Parliament ordered that one or more justices of the peace involved in granting bail should "certify it at the next general sessions of the peace, or at the next general gaol delivery of any such gaol in every such county, city or town, following the taking of any such bail or mainprise; upon pain of forfeiting £10 to the king for every recorded failure". This statute also required that a minimum of two JPs, acting together, authorise bail. The 1487 Act allowed the assize judges to fine magistrates who did so improperly. It was probably for this reason, and in the hope of some formal action being taken, that the Cambridgeshire JP Sir John Huddelston wrote to Thomas Cromwell in October 1539, complaining about the conduct of his colleagues in a homicide case: "Roland Morton and Ric. Rede, justices, who let the said murderers to bail contrary to law".[512]

Nevertheless, like its predecessor, the 1487 Act occasioned problems. In March 1540 Thomas Amys of Brewham, in Somerset, complained about John Webb, a servant to William Hargyll of Kylmynton, in the same county. Some nine years earlier Webb had stolen a mare and colt belonging to Amys and fled, although one of his accomplices had been executed for the felony and another forced to seek sanctuary at the charterhouse in Witham. However, Webb had apparently returned to Hargyll. Amys

---

510. William F. Duker, "The Right to Bail: A Historical Inquiry", *Albany Law Review*, Vol. 42, pp. 50–56.

511. C. H. Williams (ed.), *English Historical Documents, 1485–1558*, Vol. 5 (London: Eyre & Spottiswoode, 1967), pp. 532–534.

512. James Gairdner and R. H. Brodie (eds.), *Letters and Papers, Foreign and Domestic, Henry VIII, Vol. 14, Part 2, August–December 1539* (London: HMSO, 1895), pp. 137–160.

had Webb arrested and prosecuted for the horse theft, but Hargyll and his sons apparently "rescued" him, and the next morning secretly sent him to another JP, who bailed him until the following assizes.[513]

As a result, there was a further statutory reform of bail under Queen Mary. The preamble to this Act complained that some JPs had been abusing their powers in "sinister" fashion to bail the worst felons. A lone JP, perhaps conniving with a suspect, could easily procure the required second signature from one of his fellow justices without the latter being "party nor privy unto the case". Only one man, therefore, made the decision. The felon who was released on bail might then abscond. The judges at assizes had no way of knowing whether the original decision to grant bail was reasonable, and so were unable to punish abuse of the procedure.

Under the Marian bail statute of 1555, a minimum of two JPs was required to grant bail "out of sessions", at least one of whom was of the quorum, and both had to be physically present when granting a suspect his freedom. Furthermore, the assize court was given a proper basis for reviewing the propriety of bail decisions by the Act's requirement that depositions be taken from those who received the privilege. Even so, the problems attendant on bail were not entirely resolved. In April 1578 the Privy Council wrote to Francis Gawdy and John Southcote, judges on the Home Circuit, ordering that they require JPs in Hertfordshire, Essex, Surrey, and Sussex to take better sureties from bailed felons than had become the practice.[514]

Bail in Practice

Throughout the Tudor era, there was a strong presumption against bail in felony cases. However, in the right circumstances bail could be granted for the most serious crimes, especially if the evidence seemed weak, the suspect could provide substantial recognisances (that would be forfeit for non-appearance), and was a man with strong local ties or of superior social status. For example, in May 1507, at the Winchester Borough Sessions, four men from Hampshire stood bail for Thomas Godby of Basingstoke,

---

513. *Ibid, Vol. 15, 1540* (London: HMSO, 1896), pp. 150–181.
514. SHC Z/407/MSLb.221.

who had been arrested in the city on suspicion of felony, guaranteeing his appearance at the next general session of the peace. The four men were each bound in the sum of £10, while the suspect himself was placed "under a penalty of £20" for his non-appearance, so that £60 would be forfeit if he absconded. Inflation may have encouraged an increase in the sums pledged as the century advanced. In December 1581, William Lambarde and his JP father-in-law bailed Andrew Brewer to appear at his trial for burgling a widow's house. Brewer himself entered into a recognisance of £40, while two other men entered into recognisances in the sum of £20 each (a total of £80) to secure his attendance.[515] This seems to have been a common arrangement in this county at the time. In October the following year Lambarde and another JP examined George Pelsot about the theft of a sheep. Once again bail was allowed on the basis that Pelsot be personally bound over in the sum of £40, and his father and another man for £20 each.[516] However, in January 1594 John Haynes, a Middlesex JP, took recognisances of just £40 for each of three gentlemen (two of them local), "to answer to fellony layde againste them by one Story".[517]

Where suspects were wealthy and the allegations extremely grave, the sums specified for recognisances could be very much greater. In December 1575, William Lusher wrote to his fellow Surrey JP William More, describing the examination of several men with regard to the theft of a bag and apparel from a chest. He noted that he had taken surety of £500 from one of the suspects for his appearance at trial, but that the others were poor men.

Inevitably, mistakes were sometimes made. In 1602, after the very genteel Francis Cartwright had attacked and mortally wounded the Minister of Market Rasen, he fled to his father's house, where a crowd of people came to arrest him. Cartwright senior pacified them until the constables arrived and carried him before a justice of the peace. Despite his crime, "either for lacke of their due information of the truth, or by the corrupt, and favourable affection of the magistrate, or both, there was a very slender baile taken, and the malefactor by this sleight sent

---

515. Read, "William Lambarde's 'Ephemeris,'" p. 138.
516. *Ibid*, p. 140.
517. Jeaffreson, *Middlesex County Records: Vol. 1, 1550–1603*, pp. 219–225.

away". He promptly absconded. In fairness to the JP, it should be noted that the minister took eight days to die, so that (technically) he may not have been dealing with a felony at the time he granted bail.[518]

Bail could be revoked. In 1574 the Surrey JP Thomas Browne wrote to his fellow magistrate William More noting that he (Browne) and a colleague had recently examined Stephen Smith on suspicion of committing a robbery but had allowed him bail. However, in light of what they had since heard about Smith, and what More had written about him in a letter sent to them, the two JPs wanted to withdraw bail and send him to gaol, if they could apprehend him again. Brown warned More that Smith was thought to be in his local area and asked that he be detained.[519]

Bail for Misdemeanours

Misdemeanours and cases of petty theft were bailed very much more readily than felonies; provided that relatively modest recognisances were available, suspects would be allowed to make their own way to court. For example, in 1602 Phillip Lacon stood surety for his cross-dressing wife Anne's appearance at the Middlesex Sessions in the sum of £20. Two other men stood surety for £10 each. Anne had been "taken at Hamersmith wearing of man's apparel and for the same committed to the Gaole of Newgate".[520] Frequently the recognisances required were much smaller, sometimes as little as £5.

However, transients might have difficulties meeting even the smallest demands, if only because of their lack of local connections. In early 1590 Edward Hubbard, an Essex JP, was faced by a difficult decision in this regard. Elizabeth Clifford and her husband, John, had been staying at an alehouse in Dunmow for a week. John, a former soldier, who was originally from York and probably a total stranger in the county, had been having surgery on his leg, which had been "hurt with a shott". Money was undoubtedly tight. However, while at Dunmow, Elizabeth was accused of petty theft (described as a "misdemeanour") by a blacksmith named

---

518. Anon, *The manner of the cruell outragious murther of William Storre*, p. 4.
519. SHR LM/COR/3/148.
520. Jeaffreson, *Middlesex County Records: Vol. 1, 1550–1603*, pp. 276–282.

Browning. The evidence was not strong, and Elizabeth claimed that she had obtained the minor sum involved from the complainant in exchange "for the use of her body which he denyeth and sayth she tooke his purse from him and toke out the money". This was the sort of case where a suspect would normally have been bailed on a small recognisance to appear at the following quarter sessions. Unfortunately, it was noted that Elizabeth's impoverished husband "cannot put in any surety for her forthcoming at the next Sessions". As a result, and with the husband's consent, Hubbard sent Elizabeth to the local house of correction pending her appearance at trial. Apparently aware that this was a rather draconian solution to the problem, he urged the constables to take "specyall care of the safetye of the bodye of this woman so that she be safe delivered at the howse of correccon and safelye brought to the Quarter Sessyons".[521]

The Journey to Prison

Having decided that there was a case to answer, and assuming that bail was not granted, the examining JP would commit the suspected felon to the county gaol or borough prison. Usually a constable or two would escort them there; frequently, as Sir Thomas Smith noted, this might be the same officer who had brought in the suspect for questioning. Such officers would be given a *mittimus*, the formal document committing a suspect to prison, which would be handed to the gaoler on arrival. Depending on the security risk, other sturdy men might be encouraged, paid, or ordered to help take the prisoner to the gaol. In 1556 Edward Hart and Thomas Johnson of Orsett were indicted at the Essex Quarter Sessions for refusing a JP's order that they aid the local constables in carrying a prisoner to Colchester.[522]

If questioned by a JP late in the day, suspects who had been committed to prison might have to be held overnight before being taken on to the gaol. In 1615 Margaret Vincent murdered her two young children in Acton, then a village five miles west of London. She was taken before a Middlesex JP in Willesden, where she confessed to the crime. The

---

521. ERO Q/SR 112/44.
522. ERO Q/SR 3/45.

magistrate duly filled in a *mittimus* committing her to Newgate. However, by then the evening was quite advanced, so the constable had to lodge her in his own house, having arranged to have her guarded throughout the night, before making the journey the following morning.[523]

Perhaps unsurprisingly, some suspects escaped between examination and arrival at prison. For example, in the summer of 1596 Edward Haddesley of Takeley, in Essex, was arrested on suspicion of horse theft. He was examined by Edward Hubbard and then committed to the custody of John Meadow, a local constable, who was required to escort him to the county gaol at Colchester. Unfortunately, as they passed through Coggeshall, Haddesley assaulted the officer and fled.[524] Similarly, in November 1603, Thomas Turner was caught in the Essex village of Marks Tey while trying to steal a canvas shirt that had been left drying on a hedge. Parish officers took him before Thomas Waldegrave, a JP in Bures, who examined him and decided to commit him to the county gaol. However, as Robert Tibbold, a constable, and two local men, were taking him there, the "felone runn into the ryver by Northe bridge nere Colchester, beinge verye deepe of water that wee were not able to followe him". Turner escaped, and, despite all their efforts to find him, was still at liberty a month later and, they thought, probably gone for good. The constable and one of his assistants were indicted for negligently allowing the escape.[525]

The Absence of Torture

By the end of the thirteenth century, judicial torture was well-established in France, Italy, Germany, and most other continental countries. There were a few peripheral exceptions, such as Sweden (Stockholm apart), but these were unusual. In the 1460s Sir John Fortescue, then in exile in France, and a former Chief Justice of the King's Bench under Henry VI, touched on some of the tortures found in his country of exile, while noting that most Roman and civil-law countries used the same techniques.

---

523. Anon, *A pittilesse mother. That most unnaturally at one time, murthered two of her owne Children at Acton within sixe miles from London uppon holy thursday last 1616* (London, 1616), pp. 1–30.
524. ERO T/A 418/63/74.
525. ERO Q/SR 182/18.

Some suspects were stretched on the rack: "... till their very sinews crack, and the veins gush out in streams of blood: others have weights hung to their feet, till their limbs are almost torn asunder, and the whole body dislocated: some have their mouths gagged to such a wideness, for a long time, whereat such quantities of water are poured in, that their bellies swell to a prodigious degree".[526] Torture was used on a regular basis on the Continent until the late 1600s, when it started a slow but terminal decline, though it was not formally abolished in most European countries for another 100 years.

The use of torture was often necessary in these countries to obtain the level of forensic proof required under the Roman or civil law canon of evidence, with its precisely articulated standards of persuasion, in which "full proof" in the form of a confession or the testimony of two independent eyewitnesses was usually needed to convict in cases of serious crime.[527] A confession produced by torture was acceptable. It might also be used in cases of "half proof", where there was a single witness or weighty circumstantial evidence (neither being enough on their own for a conviction). As a result, confessions became the "queen of proofs" on the Continent.[528]

For example, in 1514, after Cardinal Christopher Bainbridge, the Archbishop of York, was poisoned while in Italy, the chief suspect, his steward Rinaldo de Modena, initially refused to say anything, although subjected to a thorough examination. He was then tortured and swiftly confessed to putting poison into the cardinal's potage, at the desire of Silvestro de' Gigli, the Italian Bishop of Worcester. (The latter cleric denied any involvement.)[529]

Like many late medieval Englishmen, Fortescue thought that torture was both barbaric and a source of totally unreliable confessions.[530] His countrymen still held such views a century later. In 1551 Daniele Barbero,

---

526. Francis Grigor (ed.), *Sir John Fortescue's Commendation of the Laws of England* (London: Sweet & Maxwell, 1917), p. 33.
527. Heikki Pihlajamäki, "The Painful Question: The Fate of Judicial Torture in Early Modern Sweden"', *Law and History Review*, Vol. 25, Issue 3, p. 557.
528. Jonathan L. Pearl, *The Crime of Crimes: Demonology and Politics in France, 1560–1620* (Waterloo, Canada: Wilfrid Laurier University Press, 1999), p. 33.
529. Brewer, *Letters and Papers, Foreign and Domestic, Henry VIII, Vol. 1, 1509–1514*, pp. 1347–1367.
530. Grigor, *Sir John Fortescue's Commendation*, p. 33.

the Venetian diplomatic agent in London, noted that they thought torture made men confess to crimes they had not committed, so that it could injure both the body and life (through execution) of an innocent person.[531] It was also widely recognised that appropriate compensation could not be made to an innocent man who had been tortured.

Many English observers did not, however, appreciate that, at least in theory, there had to be a clear prima facie case against the suspect or, as the Carolina Code of 1532 put it, a "sufficient indication of the crime", before torture could be administered in most continental countries. Furthermore, the interrogators who used torture were advised to seek verifiable corroborating details, rather than simple admissions, to enhance its reliability.[532]

English exceptionalism in this regard was not purely a matter of national temperament; the survival of the *peine forte et dure* would suggest that deliberately inflicting pain was not inimical to the populace. More substantive reasons were the country's relative lack of career bureaucrats and its reliance on highly localised amateurs to administer justice; this would have made the use of judicial torture, which normally required professional control, supervision, and application, problematic. Most important, under its unusual (in European terms) system of trial adjudication, jurors could, in theory convict on less evidence than was needed to justify torture in many continental countries. (In practice this does not appear to have occurred).

It is also a mistake to say that England never used torture. It was employed occasionally during the century after 1540 and may have been used before then (although infrequently), possibly as early as the mid-fifteenth century. It was last employed in 1640, but by then its use had declined greatly since the early seventeenth century. During the previous 100 years it had been administered on at least 81, probably 101, and possibly even more occasions, its use reaching a peak during the Elizabethan period. Torture was normally conducted in London. Initially, this was at the Tower of London, but between 1589 and 1603 it was carried out

---

531. Rawdon Brown (ed.), *Calendar of State Papers Relating To English Affairs in the Archives of Venice, Vol. 5, 1534–1554* (London: HMSO, 1873), p. 340.
532. Langbein, *Prosecuting Crime in the Renaissance: England, Germany, France* (Cambridge, Mass: Harvard University Press, 1974), pp. 179–183.

in the Bridewell Prison. Occasionally, it took place at other venues near the capital. A handful of cases of torture were carried out in provincial cities, such as Bristol.

Most of those tortured were questioned for political or religious (and so political) offences, such as treason and sedition. However, from the 1550s to the 1590s, torture was also employed in at least 20 "ordinary" cases of serious felony, including murder, robbery, and burglary. The last such case to be investigated in this manner occurred in 1597, when Richard Anger, an elderly barrister, was found dead several weeks after disappearing from his chambers. His son and a Gray's Inn porter were suspected of the crime. The Privy Council ordered that either or both of them be put "to the manacles in Bridewell". In this case, the council felt that there were great "presumptions" against the two men.[533]

The use of torture may also, very occasionally, have been threatened, if only to make suspects more cooperative, even if it was not ultimately carried out. In December 1574, Robert Dudley, the Earl of Leicester, wrote from the Court to the Surrey magistrate William More, directing him to examine the bearer of the letter, a man named Rumsey, who, under threat of being sent to the Tower, had promised to reveal the names of his companions.

English torture was often (though not quite invariably) aimed at securing information rather than judicial proof; in Francis Bacon's words, it was employed "for discovery, and not for evidence". However it came about, and for whatever reason, it was a grim experience. The Jesuit priest John Gerard (1564–1637) wrote a book describing his experiences in England shortly after his escape to the Continent. Among them was his torture in the Tower in 1594, which included being suspended from chains on the dungeon wall. Gerard was invited to confess but refused to do so. A variety of other tortures were then applied to him until he fainted. (The primary aim of the torturers in this case was to identify the London lodgings of Henry Garnet.)[534] Despite his comments, a more modest range of tortures was employed in England than on the

---

533. John H. Langbein, *Torture and the Law of Proof: Europe and England in the Ancien Régime* (Chicago: University of Chicago Press, 2006), p. 136; John Gerard, *The Autobiography of a Hunted Priest* (San Franciso: Ignatius Press, 2012), p. 133.
534. Gerard, *Autobiography*, p. 133.

Continent, usually just the manacles or the rack. Both involved stretching, the former by the force of gravity and the latter by a pulley system.

Even so, torture was never institutionalised as part of English criminal procedure in the way that it was in Europe. Instead the Privy Council ordered it on an occasional, ad hoc, extra-legal basis, whether as a manifestation of the royal prerogative or of sovereign immunity (and that of the sovereign's agents). The council had to issue a special warrant, specifically naming investigators, when doing so. It normally included one or two government legal officers, such as the Attorney General, or common law judges, and even specified the method of torture to be used. (Gerard was tortured in the presence of the Attorney General, who had a warrant authorising such treatment). Such warrants effectively constituted a legal derogation from the established common law position that torture was unlawful, granting the process the stamp of legality.[535] Ironically, some of the men identified in these warrants, such as Robert Beale, Clerk to the Privy Council and one of those directly involved in the torture of Edmund Campion, observed on other occasions that their fellow countrymen condemned the "racking of grievous offenders as being cruel, barbarous, and contrary to law and the liberty of English subjects". Most common lawyers viewed the existence of torture as something of an embarrassment.[536]

It should also be noted that, at least at the end of the medieval era and start of the Tudor age, those held in connection with serious crimes were sometimes subject to extra-legal mistreatment by gaolers, with the aim of obtaining a confession, even if recourse was not made to formal torture. Thus in 1456 it was noted that several men who had been falsely accused by a supposed accomplice were imprisoned and "suffered many great pains, and that was so they should confess and accord unto his false appealing".[537] Such brutality was eventually made a felony.

---

535. Langbein, *Torture and the Law of Proof,* p. 207.
536. Danny Friedman, "Torture and the Common Law", *European Human Rights Law Review,* 2006, Issue 2, pp. 180–182, and p. 188.
537. Musson and Powell, *Crime, Law and Society in the later Middle Ages,* p. 176.

PART III

PROSECUTION, THE COURTS, TRIAL, AND PUNISHMENT

CHAPTER 8

Methods of Prosecution for Felony

Introduction

When Henry VII came to the throne there were three methods for bringing suspected felons before the courts. One of them was clearly dominant, another was still moderately significant but just a few years away from rapid and almost terminal decline, and the third was already moribund. They are considered in ascending order of importance.

Approvement

From the twelfth century onwards a man who was accused of a felony could confess his guilt and ask to turn "approver". Permitting this was a Crown privilege, so that, if the royal judges (who made the decision) allowed such a course of action, he was called the King's Approver or *probator regis*. The approver would then be assigned a coroner who would record his admissions to crimes that he had personally committed and the accusations he made against his former accomplices; he would also provide details of the latters' whereabouts. Those implicated had to be men who had actively participated in the same crimes as the approver, or at least acted as the receiver for goods stolen during them, not merely those who had committed offences of which the approver was personally aware.[1] One medieval illustration is a case from 1383, in which Richard II wrote to the sheriffs of London ordering them to arrest John Colbrond and Alice Longe (the former's "concubine"), and three other people, all of whom were resident in the City, if they could be found (a variety of

---

1. Frederick C. Hamil, "The King's Approvers: A Chapter in the History of English Criminal Law", *Speculum*, Vol. 11, No. 2, p. 238.

general addresses were provided). They were then to be kept in prison until produced for trial to "make answer unto us as to certain felonies, of which, by an approver, now in the prison of our Marshalsey, they have been accused".[2] Given the frequent absence of willing private prosecutors, the procedure allowed the Crown to turn a felon into an officer of justice. Although the process by which the approver's alleged accomplices were prosecuted was termed an appeal, it should be distinguished from the (related) private appeal of felony (discussed below).

In theory, if not quite always in practice, women, children, and men who had been maimed or who were over the age of 70 years, were excluded from turning approver, not least because, and as with the appeal of felony, those implicated might opt for trial by battle — a judicially supervised duel — rather than by jury. Where this occurred, the parties would be bare-headed, bare-legged from the knees downward, sleeveless from the elbows, armed with long batons with "crooks" made of horn or iron, and protected by four-cornered leather shields. They fought until one of them died, yielded by crying "craven", or the evening stars appeared.[3]

During the thirteenth century, such combat occurred quite regularly. It appears that in 1274 a single approver convicted 13 of his erstwhile accomplices through trial by battle, whilst in 1249 another defeated and convicted ten appellees in the same manner.[4] However, by the early fourteenth century, this method of adjudication was no longer a regular feature of approver cases (or, as will be seen, appeals), and it declined further thereafter. Only two cases of approvers' battles have been positively identified in England for the fifteenth century, while a thorough scrutiny of East Anglia during the same period has found none at all in what was then an important region.[5] Nevertheless, such a combat appears

---

2. H.T. Riley (ed.), *Memorials of London and London Life in the 13th, 14th and 15th Centuries* (London: Longmans Green, 1868), pp. 476–482.
3. Sanjeev Anand, "The Origins, Early History and Evolution of the English Criminal Trial Jury", *Alberta Law Review*, Vol. 43, No. 2, p. 413.
4. James Corbyn, *KB27/648: An Unsuccessful Case of Approver's Appeal*, Royal Holloway, University of London, MA thesis, 2015, p. 8.
5. A.J. Musson, "Turning King's Evidence: The Prosecution of Crime in Late Medieval England", *Oxford Journal of Legal Studies*, Vol. 19, No. 3, 1999, p. 473; Philippa C. Maddern, *Violence and Social Order: East Anglia 1422–1442* (Oxford: Clarendon Press, 1992), p. 71.

to have taken place as late as 1456, being conducted in the traditionally stipulated fashion. In this case, Thomas Whitehorn, a notorious false approver, fought one of the innocent men he had implicated, at the latter's request, near Winchester. The bout included extensive recourse to grappling and biting. Whitehorn eventually yielded, and admitted that his allegations were false. He was executed shortly afterwards.[6]

Some observers have suggested that it is very unlikely that there were any instances at all of trial by battle in Tudor times (whether on an approver's or a private appeal). William Stanford, a sixteenth century judge and legal writer, even thought it probable that it could only be claimed if there was a "bare accusation" against the accused, unsupported by other evidence.[7] Nevertheless, in a case from 1556, it seems that one Richard Reade appealed several men for his brother's murder. When one of them offered him trial by battle he demurred and abandoned the action, and was even ordered to pay damages to the suspects.[8] Formal abolition of trial by battle was considered in the early seventeenth century but ultimately waited until 1819.

Some approvers appealed only a handful of accomplices, others as many as 40 of them. In an extreme case, William Rose named 54 men in 1389. The system was particularly effective in breaking up bands of robbers and thieves, something that explains why it survived the institution of the presentment jury in the years after 1166.[9] In exchange for such services, the approver enjoyed a significant delay (months or even years) to his own trial. This also allowed him the possibility of making an escape in the meantime. For example, one John Tyler, who turned approver early in 1393, escaped while the ensuing process was still incomplete, some three years later. The need to occasion such delay may explain why some approvers' appeals involved legal process in widely distant counties; for example, one man cited felonies in both Devon and Suffolk.

Alternatively, if the approver secured the arrest and conviction of a sufficient number of his erstwhile accomplices he might be allowed to

---

6.   Anthony Musson, *Medieval Law in Context: The Growth of Legal Consciousness from Magna Carta to the Peasants' Revolt* (Manchester: Manchester University Press, 2001), p. 176.
7.   Ernst, "The Moribund Appeal of Death", pp. 164–188.
8.   Kesselring, *Making Murder Public*, p. 83.
9.   Hamil, "The King's Approvers", pp. 239–240.

abjure the realm, or even secure a full pardon and release. However, as the judges of the courts of both Common Pleas and King's Bench noted in 1442, the commonwealth had to gain a benefit from the approver if the latter was to be considered. In its absence, for example, if those implicated were abroad and so not prosecuted, or if they were acquitted after being brought to trial, the approver would be hanged.[10] There was no set figure for the number of successful appeals required to secure a pardon, although some commentators spoke of at least five being necessary. In practice, few approvers received such mercy.[11] The penalty for failure to secure sufficient convictions was death, the approver's conviction based on his initial confession to the coroner.[12]

Of course, there was always a danger that desperate men might invent accomplices to delay matters or, even worse, make up allegations against innocent people to whet the authorities' interest and buy time, just as they would when turning "Crown evidence" in later centuries. For example, in the 1450s, the thief Thomas Whitehorn (see above) was sent to the prison at Winchester after being captured in the New Forest. Once there, he "appealed many true men, and by this means he kept his life albeit living it in prison". Some of these innocent men were, apparently, subsequently convicted and executed.[13] Less disastrously, in a King's Bench case of 1454, a Southwark yeoman named John Owden, sentenced to death for felony, attempted to save his own life by turning approver and accusing eleven Bristol burgesses of various capital offences, including plotting treason with the French. Investigations into Owden's story quickly revealed it to be a total fabrication, and he was duly executed.[14]

Furthermore, improper pressure may have been placed on some potential approvers to implicate others. William Nethercote, who eventually claimed benefit of clergy in 1394 (and whose ability to read meant that he was never in fear for his life), ultimately withdrew his appeals, claimed that they were formulated for him, and revealed that his original consent

10. *Anon.* (1442) Jenkins 84, 145 E.R. 59.
11. Musson and Powell, *Crime, Law and Society*, p. 103.
12. Hamil, "The King's Approvers", p. 238.
13. Musson, *Medieval Law in Context*, p. 176.
14. Peter Fleming, "Time, Space and Power in Later Medieval Bristol", Working Paper, University of the West of England, Bristol, 2013, p. 201.

to this course of action had been obtained by the use of thumbscrews.[15] On another occasion, four men claimed that they were forced to turn approvers after being hung up by their hands and feet by the constable of Worcester Castle, while a Norwich approver testified that he had been kept naked while in gaol, and without food or drink, for three nights, during which he was tortured by the sheriff and constables.[16] Unsurprisingly, in these circumstances, there was often considerable distrust of approvers' appeals, and the great majority that went to trial ended in an acquittal.[17]

Even so, the use of approvers continued on a fairly regular basis throughout the early 1400s, albeit founding only a small minority of total prosecutions. They were employed extensively during the reign of Henry V, particularly to deal with professional counterfeiters in the Midlands, and secured a significant number of convictions in the Court of King's Bench.[18] However, their use seems to have petered out rapidly during the second half of the fifteenth century, perhaps because, by then, they were no longer producing many guilty verdicts.

Nevertheless, in 1468 a petition from the House of Commons requested that justices of the peace (rather than just royal judges or officials) be permitted to authorise approvements, so as to prevent lengthy delays during which potential approvers might escape or seek ordinary pardons. This suggests that the method was still in use at the time, and still valued. In 1470 a Surrey labourer named Richard Wilkinson confessed before a coroner in the Marshalsea Prison to the theft of several oxen, and appealed four men of aiding him in the crime, and a butcher of abetting it. King's Bench decided that the appeal against the butcher was not good, because it was not for the same crime as that committed by Wilkinson. Just one of the other appellees was arrested, tried, and acquitted, after which the unsuccessful approver was duly hanged. Two years later, a *Year Book* mentions a pair of further cases, while the King's Bench records for Michaelmas 1487 suggest that one John Terry had appeared before the court and admitted a murder at Westminster the previous year, but

15.   Bellamy, *The Criminal Trial*, pp. 39–42.
16.   Musson, "Turning King's Evidence", p. 470.
17.   Bellamy, *The Criminal Trial*, pp. 39–42.
18.   Musson, "Turning King's Evidence", p. 476.

called for a coroner with a view to turning approver and giving evidence about his co-accused. Unfortunately, the king's attorney told him that the monarch had already ordered him to refuse any offer by Terry to become an approver, so that he was sentenced to death.[19]

Legal writers were still discussing approvement in the sixteenth century, suggesting that it may have been used on a handful of occasions in the early 1500s, although almost no formal records have been found of this.[20] Even so, in April 1515, when David Jones fled to the parish church at Croughton, in Northamptonshire, and confessed to a county coroner that he had stolen clothing and other items from a local cleric, he attempted to appeal two men. He claimed that the previous month they had joined him in assaulting an unknown man in Lancashire and robbing him of 20 marks. Jones eventually abjured, perhaps because it was clear that his attempt to appeal the others would not be successful. More pertinently, in December 1532 a coroner's memorandum records that a man named Glasewright took sanctuary in the parish church of Heybridge, in Essex, and confessed that the previous August he and two named men had fatally assaulted and robbed an unknown man on the highway near Newmarket. The King's Bench record suggests that Glasewright *may* (it is by no means certain) have subsequently turned approver with regard to these men, who were duly outlawed in Trinity 1534.[21] At about the same time, in *The Debellation of Salem and Bizance* of 1533, Thomas More noted that, even then, some convicted felons unavailingly sought to become "approvers when they were cast, and called for a coroner".[22]

Approvement was never formally abolished. As late as 1775 Lord Mansfield claimed that it remained part of the common law, although long abandoned and, in practice, replaced by the informal arrangements under which accomplices turned king's evidence. The latter may have been operative by the second half of the Tudor era. In December 1556

---

19.   McSheffrey, "Sanctuary Seekers".
20.   Bellamy, *The Criminal Trial*, pp. 41–42.
21.   McSheffrey, "Sanctuary Seekers".
22.   Guy et al., *The Complete Works of St Thomas More, Vol. 10*, p. 107.

Gregorie Carpenter tried to stab a co-defendant who, it appears, had "given witnesse against him" in the Old Bailey.[23]

Perhaps more pertinently, the highwayman Gamaliel Ratsey's notorious and lengthy criminal career came to an end at the Bedford Assizes in 1605, after a former member of his gang, a man named Snell, was arrested for (unclergyable) horse theft in London. When examined before a justice about this crime, and about to be committed to prison, Snell "appealed to ye justice for fauour, tolde him hee would helpe him to one *Ratsey* of whome such fame went for many robberies, if he weld be good unto him for his life". The justice promised to do so, Snell gave him the information, and Ratsey was arrested and committed to Newgate, along with Snell and other gang members. As was to become common in such cases, Snell eventually asked the justice to move him to the King's Bench prison "for feare least one of ye other shold doe him some suddaine mischiefe for revealing of *Ratsey*".[24]

The Appeal of Felony

The criminal appeal—the appeal of felony or murder—was a medieval form of private prosecution for felony. It did not normally extend to prosecuting misdemeanours and had nothing to do with challenging the safety of a conviction. Very crudely, it was a combination of criminal and civil action, one that had originally been introduced to England by the Normans and initially required that the prosecuting party (the "appellor") make an oral accusation at a series of meetings of the county court, duly witnessed by a coroner, and for the defending party (the appellee) to deny the accusations or to object to them on technical grounds.[25] (After the fifteenth century the appellor could initiate such an action by issuing a writ in the king's courts in Westminster). When the court decided that the accusation had been properly made and answered, the appeal was ready to be tried. In theory, this could be by battle, if the appellor was healthy, male, and not elderly, and by ordeal if the appellor was a

---

23. John Stow, *The Annales, or General Chronicle of England* (London, 1615), p. 1066.
24. Anon, *The Life and Death of Gamaliell Ratsey*, pp. 1–46.
25. Musson, *Medieval Law in Context*, p. 154.

woman, or a man who was exempt from battle due to age or health. After the Fourth Lateran Council in 1215, the opinion of neighbours, gathered together in a jury, was used instead of ordeal, and, in practice, this method of determination also swiftly extended to cases where the parties were healthy men who might otherwise have been tried by battle. Although, in theory, the last process remained available for appeals until 1819, when the whole action was abolished (after an appellee unexpectedly asked for trial by battle), and as with approvers' appeals, it had largely fallen into disuse, in favour of a jury hearing, well before the Tudor period (see above).[26]

Appeals differed from prosecutions on indictment conducted in the name of the Crown in several important respects. Proceedings were entered on the plea side of the King's Bench, and trial at assizes was, in theory, at *nisi prius*, although there was very little overt difference from criminal trials on indictment.[27] In cases such as false imprisonment, theft, robbery, and arson, an appeal was normally brought by the victim, as the appellor had to have a personal interest in the matter.[28] For example, in 1406 William Hegge was arrested in London while in possession of more than £40 of stolen goods taken from the shop of Margaret Normantone, a prosperous widow. It was alleged that Hegge had broken into the premises at night. She duly appealed him for the crime.[29]

In the case of murder, where victim suit was, of course, impossible, an appeal had to be brought by the slain person's nearest relative, being commenced by a writ or bill issued by their (un-remarried) widow, heir, or closest male kin (in that order) within a year-and-a-day of the victim's death.[30] For example, in 1573 Henry Lobery, the brother and heir of John Lobery, appealed Hugh Yenans, a London shoemaker, for murdering his sibling.[31]

26. Margaret H. Kerr, "Angevin Reform of the Appeal of Felony", *Law and History Review*, Vol. 13, No. 2 (1995), p. 351.

27. John Baker, *The Oxford History of the Laws of England: 1483–1558, Vol. VI*, p. 513.

28. M. J. Russell, "II Trial by Battle and the Appeals of Felony", *Journal of Legal History*, Vol. 1, Issue 2, p. 135.

29. H. T. Riley (ed.), *Memorials of London*, pp. 561–566.

30. G. Jacob, *Laws of Appeals and Murder* (London, 1709), pp. 3–6.

31. Jeaffreson, *Middlesex County Records: Vol. 1, 1550–1603*, pp. 78–85.

Magna Carta itself had stipulated, "No one shall be arrested or imprisoned upon appeal of a woman for the death of anyone except her husband". If it transpired that the marriage of a homicide victim to his (supposed) wife was invalid or that his widow had remarried, she lost her right to bring such an action. (As would a son if it transpired that he was illegitimate). It was for this reason that Sir John Paston intimated, in a letter written in December 1469, that two widows who had appealed his brother for the murder of their husbands had married again and that as a result their appeals might be "abated". His brother supported this analysis, although he had been informed that the two women had already been "bowndyn in a gret some that they shall sue a peel ayenst me".[32] Unsurprisingly, in these circumstances, a prosecution by appeal was brought in the complainant's name, as with a civil action, not that of the Crown (as with prosecution on indictment).[33]

The use of appeals peaked in the late twelfth century, declining sharply thereafter. By the end of the thirteenth century, only a relatively small number of criminals were being prosecuted in this way, compared to those being tried on indictment. This was probably due to increasing judicial hostility to the process and because out-of-court settlements between felons and appellors ceased to preclude the former from being sent for trial on indictment.[34]

Additionally, appeal was an expensive and potentially hazardous way of bringing someone suspected of a serious crime to justice—if only due to the possibility of healthy men opting for trial by battle—compared to prosecution on indictment, encouraging use of the latter mechanism. This was exacerbated because, unlike defendants in trials on indictment, appellees were permitted counsel at their hearings, allowing them to take advantage of legal flaws in the notoriously complicated procedure. Typically, Margery Webb noted in a bill of supplication to one of Henry VIII's Lord Chancellors that she had sought justice for her husband's death by an appeal, but had then seen the action quashed for a simple

32. Gairdner, *The Paston Letters, AD 1422–1509, Vol. VI*, p. 740.
33. Thomas Smith, *De Republica Anglorum* (London, 1583), p. 123.
34. Daniel Klerman, "Settlement and the Decline of Private Prosecution in Thirteenth century England", *Law and History Review*, Vol. 19, Issue 1, p. 3.

naming error.[35] In the medieval period it was sometimes claimed that representation was forbidden in trial on indictment (unlike appeal) because the king was a party to proceedings. Even so, in the sixteenth century Christopher St Germain struggled to justify the difference. He suggested, slightly implausibly, that representation was allowed because whenever an appeal was brought there was a general assumption that the appellant harboured personal malice against the appellee, as might be expected, for example, with a widow whose husband had been murdered. As a result, if the judges presiding over appeals attempted to instruct the appellees/defendants on the law, as they were supposed to do in a trial on indictment, the appellants would complain and think them biased.[36]

Nevertheless, the appeal had some advantages. It obviated the need for a grand jury to approve an indictment, and so was not as susceptible to outside pressure as trial on indictment. If the victim of a crime was known to be the enemy of a local magnate or (more commonly) someone who owed such a powerful man allegiance, the chances of a bill of indictment's being found "true" by a grand jury were greatly reduced. This was a particularly serious problem during the Wars of the Roses, but could not happen with an appeal. It has been suggested that this made it particularly popular with "outsiders" or those victims who were, for whatever reason, unpopular in their localities. Appeals also seem to have produced a higher conviction rate than trial on indictment during the fifteenth century. One important advantage they had was that, after securing a conviction, the appellor could recover any stolen property that was still in the convict's hands rather than seeing it forfeit to the Crown, something that would not be possible in a trial on indictment until 1529. Finally, unlike those found guilty on indictment, the Crown could not pardon people convicted on appeal, any more than it could remit the damages awarded in a civil action for battery, as Francis Cartwright discovered shortly after the death of Queen Elizabeth (see below).

As a result, appeals were not uncommon during the 1400s, and in a few places they were even quite a regular occurrence. For example,

---

35. Kesselring, *Making Murder Public,* p. 85.
36. Christoper St Germain, William Muchall (ed.), *The Doctor and Student. or Dialogues Between a Doctor of Divinity and a Student in the Laws of England* (Cincinnati: Robert Clarke, 1886), p. 258.

in Yorkshire (on the Northern Circuit) appellees made up 23 per cent of those prosecuted between 1439 and 1460. Nevertheless, most other counties produced much smaller totals; appeals made up only 12 per cent of criminal cases tried on what was then termed the Eastern Circuit between 1437 and 1441. Furthermore, the number of appeals heard fell significantly in the late 1400s, although they remained a (declining) feature of the criminal justice system during the first three decades of the sixteenth century. There were 28 cases pending in King's Bench alone in 1500. Most were for murder or (less commonly) robbery, although a few were for rape or mayhem (essentially a grave form of wounding).

Appeals became much less popular in the years after 1529, when restitution of stolen goods was extended by statute to convictions secured on indictment (21 Hen. VIII c. 11). This was vitally important; even at the end of the Tudor period, justices were reluctant to release apparently stolen goods back to their original owners without a court decision. In December 1593, Sir George Paulet, a Surrey JP, expressed doubts about handing over items that had been recovered without the suspected thief first being convicted, although eventually agreeing to do so on a guarantee that the man would be prosecuted when arrested.[37] Prior to 1529 this would not have been legally possible.

This provision helps to explain some early-sixteenth century appeals. For example, at a trial held at Oxford Castle in July 1512, William Brounyng appealed a man named Davy for the theft of his horse. In a more serious case from February 1518, Gerard Hughes appealed William Burbage for stealing a gold cross worth £5, a diamond ring and loose precious stones valued at £15, and various gold rings and ornaments.[38] If the authorities had recovered the horse or jewellery, their owners would have wanted to get them back.

After 1529 the use of appeals declined very rapidly, and for most crimes the action was moribund by the middle of the sixteenth century. There are only five preserved cases (all of them for murder or robbery) from the entire Home Circuit during the reign of Elizabeth I.[39] Most of these were

---

37. SHC LM/COR/3/525.
38. McSheffrey, "Sanctuary Seekers".
39. Bellamy, *The Criminal Trial*, pp. 35–38.

from Surrey. The extensive surviving assize records for Elizabethan Essex do not reveal a single instance in that important county. Of course, they were probably slightly more common at the Old Bailey, and certainly much more common at Queen's Bench, to which many such actions were brought or removed.

By way of illustration, in July 1563, after William Newnam was indicted at the Croydon Assizes for grand larceny, accused of stealing a horse and saddle from Thomas Barnard, his victim appears to have been unhappy, feeling that this did not properly reflect what had occurred. He successfully appealed Newnam for robbery the following year. (Strangely, although Newnam was found guilty, he seems to have been pardoned; perhaps this was with the agreement of Barnard.) At the same forum, in March 1578, a "gentleman" named Jasper Swift appealed Richard Frayne for robbery, although he had been indicted, in his absence, for the same crime in July the previous year. There is no more information as to what occurred on this occasion, or why.[40]

Appeals in cases of murder provided a limited exception to the general pattern of decline, continuing a modest existence until 1819. In the late medieval period it was still common for an appeal to be accompanied by a parallel prosecution on indictment. For example, in February 1435 several powerful men were indicted, at the Suffolk Quarter Sessions in Bury St Edmunds, for the ambush and murder of James Andrew. However, although the court's JPs included the two assize judges for the county, the accused were too well connected to be dealt with locally, so that in April 1435 a *certiorari* was issued to send all the indictments (and their attendant documents) for trial at King's Bench in London. Even so, during the Easter and Trinity terms of 1435, Margery, the dead man's widow, also brought appeals in the King's Bench for the murder of her husband (several of those so appealed were acquitted by a Suffolk jury in 1438). During the five years after 1435, the Crown's indictments and Margery's appeal proceeded simultaneously. The case eventually appears

---

40.   Cockburn, *Calendar of Assize Records. Surrey Indictments: Elizabeth I,* pp. 33–34, p. 158, and p. 166.

to have petered out.[41] After 1485 indictments in these types of case were usually tried before any appeals were heard.

However, a homicide defendant could still be subject to an appeal, even though he had been acquitted by the petty jury in a trial on indictment. This remained the case after 1487, when statute made an acquittal on indictment a bar to a subsequent appeal for other types of felony.[42] This exemption could mean that "si le murderer soit acquyte deins lan all sute le roy, il sera autre foitz en appele arrayn deis mesme lan al sute de party".[43] For example, in October 1553, William Smith punched his wife in the neck while in a "rage". She started bleeding from the nose, "lingered" for ten days, and then died. Although indicted for feloniously killing her (manslaughter) at the Kent Assizes, he was acquitted. Even so, William Bishop, her son by an earlier marriage, appealed Smith for murder.[44] In a few cases, capital convictions were obtained by such appeals, and executions resulted.

An appeal could also provide an opportunity for the next of kin of a slain man to get a case to trial where a coroner's inquest and/or a grand jury had declined to indict the matter. For example, in 1572 a Nantwich coroner's inquest refused to find that all members of a large group of men had murdered Roger Crockett, confining itself to the most obvious suspect. Eighteen months after his death, the widow sought to appeal the rest. Some 21 men were initially accused and came before the Chief Justice of Cheshire; six were bailed and bound-over to the Michaelmas Sessions, where they were all discharged by proclamation, the appeal apparently not having got very far.[45]

The viability of an appeal when the defendant had been convicted of manslaughter, rather than murder, following trial on indictment, was less certain. In 1571 Anne Gaynesford, a gentleman's wife, thrashed one of her maids, Agnes Rayner, with a "wand", beating her about the head and body. (Disciplining female domestics was usually left to women.)

---

41. Roger Virgoe, "The Murder of James Andrew: Suffolk Faction in the 1430s", *Proceedings of the Suffolk Institute of Archaeology and History*, Vol. 34, pp. 264–265.
42. J. H. Baker, "Criminal Courts and Procedure at Common Law 1550–1800", in J. S. Cockburn (ed.), *Crime in England 1550–1800* (London: Methuen, 1977), pp. 17–18.
43. Richard Pyson, *Diversite de Courts et lour Jurisdictions* (London, 1526), f. Bv.
44. Cockburn, *Calendar of Assize Records. Kent Indictments: Elizabeth I*, p. 45.
45. Hindle, "'Bleedinge Afreshe'?", p. 224.

Unfortunately, Rayner died of her injuries. Gaynesford was indicted for, and convicted of, manslaughter at the Surrey Assizes. Although this was a clergyable offence, Anne could not claim the privilege because she was a woman. Perhaps unsurprisingly, she successfully pleaded her belly. In these circumstances, it was always likely that she would, eventually, have been quietly released or pardoned, as happened the following year, rather than being hanged after giving birth or proving not to be pregnant (see *Chapter 15*).[46]

However, Rayner's brother Peter, a London ironmonger, her next of kin and heir, was unhappy about the result, and appealed the matter, which was removed into King's Bench in Easter 1572.[47] It does not appear to have produced a conviction. This is unsurprising. In many situations the next of kin of the dead person used an appeal to force the suspect into making financial compensation in exchange for withdrawing the action. Gaynesford was from a wealthy family, and this may well have occurred in her case.

An appeal could still be brought even if the Crown had pardoned a homicide, because, unlike trial on indictment, the action was not brought in the name of the monarch. For this reason, it was only after John Pauncefote's widow, Bridget, had abandoned her appeal against his killer, Sir John Savage, in King's Bench, early in 1520, that the latter dropped his claim that he had been unlawfully removed from sanctuary and presented a royal pardon for the relevant homicide.[48] Similarly, six months before the death of Elizabeth I, a notorious killing took place in Lincolnshire, when the minister of Market Rasen, the Reverend William Storre, was murdered by one of his parishioners, a young, bad-tempered, and very well-to-do man named Francis Cartwright. Cartwright was intensely annoyed with Storre because of the position the clergyman had taken on a local dispute over land enclosure. Eventually, he ambushed and stabbed Storre with a specially sharpened sword before leaving him in the road to die. Despite being terribly wounded, the minister survived

---

46. Kesselring, *To Pardon and to Punish: Mercy and Authority in Tudor England*, Queen's University, Ontario, PhD thesis, 2000, p. 48.

47. Cockburn, *Calendar of Assize Records. Surrey Indictments: Elizabeth I*, p. 96 and p. 103.

48. Peter Gwyn, *The King's Cardinal: The Rise and Fall of Thomas Wolsey* (London: Barrie & Jenkins, 1990), p. 133.

for several days and identified his attacker. In the meantime, Cartwright escaped via a circuitous route to London and then on to the Continent.

Being well-connected and wealthy, Cartwright eventually secured a pardon from the Crown. This spared him trial on indictment and allowed him to return to the capital. Even so, Storre's widow decided to bring an appeal against him, and travelled to London to do so. In Cartwright's own words, many years later: "The wife of the slaine sueth an Appeale against me, notwithstanding my Pardon".[49] This threat, and a further question about the validity of the Crown's pardon, initially forced Cartwright to go into hiding again in the capital, where he "lurked in secret amongst his friends". He then had recourse to the two traditional methods of dealing with an appeal before it went to trial: finding a legal flaw in the notoriously complicated proceedings or paying off the complainant. Unfortunately, Cartwright's counsel could not find an error that "might hold plea in law to stop her suit". Furthermore, despite having five children to support, the minister's widow refused to compound the matter (still legal in appeals) and to "accept the large offers made daily to her". As a result, Cartwright was forced to flee abroad again.[50] However, he later returned, "the Appeale beeing crossed, and finding my Pardon firme".[51]

Of course, ignoring a royal pardon by appealing a murderer who had received such clemency was not done lightly, as it thwarted the monarch's decision, adding to the difficulties of pursuing such an action and risking his displeasure. In 1533 Sir William Pennington's widow, Frances, appears not to have pursued an appeal against Richard Southwell, who had killed her husband, after he was pardoned, even though that option was open to her. She had become the Duke of Suffolk's dependent following her husband's death, living in his household, and may have been deferring to Suffolk's wishes in not pursuing the matter.[52] Similarly, Bridget Pauncefote's decision to abandon her case against the

---

49. Francis Cartwright, *The life, confession, and heartie repentance of Francis Cartwright, Gentleman for his bloudie sinne in killing of one Master Storr, Master of Arts, and minister of Market Rason in Lincolnshire* (London, 1621), pp. 1–36.

50. Anon, *The manner of the cruell outragious murther of William Storre*, pp. 1–12.

51. Cartwright, *The life, confession, and heartie repentance*, pp. 1–36.

52. McSheffrey, "The Slaying of Sir William Pennington", p. 178.

man who killed her husband, after securing 1,000 marks from him, may have been influenced by the fact that he had also received a pardon on the indictment from the Crown (on payment of an even greater sum of money).[53] Essentially, he had bought off both parties.

If the defendant was found guilty in an appeal of murder, he was attainted and executed, just as he would be if convicted on indictment. If he was found guilty of manslaughter, the killer could plead benefit of clergy and escape hanging, but would still suffer the consequences of attainder (forfeiture of chattels and any title, and the inability to pass the latter on), as would those who had been convicted on indictment.[54]

Trial on Indictment

Trial on indictment was by far the most common procedure by which serious crimes were determined during the Tudor era; it could be used for all felonies and the vast majority of misdemeanours. By the fourteenth century "indictment" was the technical word used for a written accusation that was not an appeal by an individual (see above), but the outcome of an enquiry into the commission of offences. As this suggests, originally, such cases were supposed to have come to a court's attention by dint of a presenting jury's own observation. Presentment juries were assembled from communities of different sizes, whether a hundred, borough, liberty, or the whole county (the last being the so-called grand jury), to report collectively on anyone from their area suspected of committing a crime.

The grand jury traced its origins to Henry II's Assize of Clarendon of 1166, which called for inquiry to be made by the oath of 12 "good and lawful men" drawn from every hundred in a county, and another four from each township within it, of those who were suspected of robbery, murder, or theft. The list of offences to be inquired into was gradually expanded over ensuing years to include almost all serious crimes. To some extent, this instituted a form of public prosecution. The grand jurors presented suspected criminals before royal justices, and their guilt

---

53. Peter Gwyn, *The King's Cardinal: The Rise and Fall of Thomas Wolsey* (London: Barrie & Jenkins, 1990), p. 133.
54. Ernst, "The Moribund Appeal of Death", p. 170.

or innocence was then determined by trial. Up to 1215 this was often by ordeal. Thereafter it was by decision of a petty jury, producing the double jury hearing that lasted in England, to a modest extent, until the twentieth century.[55]

The system was premised on a belief that in the close-knit, mainly rural, relatively static society of most of the medieval period, with its communitarian open fields, such jurors would readily be able to discover who had committed crimes in their area, and be equipped to make a decision on who should properly be charged with an offence. When they "presented" such an offender, he would have to stand trial before a petty jury on the accusation.[56]

However, during the late medieval period the social basis of the system started to fail. New modes of agriculture, increasing population mobility, and greater urbanisation all undermined it. When it came to the grand jury, and the prosecution of felonies, this process was largely complete before 1485, especially at assizes. Even so, lower-level presentment juries continued to operate throughout the Tudor era. Thus, in Hertfordshire, hundred juries averaged six or seven presentments per quarter session, even at the close of the sixteenth century.[57] However, such juries tended to present low level misdemeanours and regulatory offences rather than serious crimes, especially at quarter sessions.

For example, in 1571, the presentment jury for the Hundred of Ongar and Harlow in Essex noted, "The Jury do present one bredg lying in the paresh of Witham called Machyns mell bredge that is in rewin". It was claimed that the local gentleman (and JP) Bryan Darcy had the responsibility for repairing that bridge. Furthermore, they noted that a portion of the highway in the parish of Shelley was in a poor state and ought to be repaired by local people.[58] A majority of parishes did not produce presentments of any sort. Thus at Easter 1566, most of the villages of Barstable Hundred in Essex simply declared that they had

55. Bellamy, *The Criminal Trial*, p. 20; Richard H. Helmholz, "The Early History of the Grand Jury and the Canon Law", *University of Chicago Law Review*, Vol. 50, p. 613.
56. Edward Powell, *Kingship, Law, and Society: Criminal Justice in the Reign of Henry V* (Oxford: Oxford University Press, 1989), p. 67.
57. Hankins, *Local Government and Society*, p. 336.
58. ERO Q/SR 38/5.

nothing to present and that "all thinges is well in that parishe". Exceptions included several parishes whose archery butts were "owte of reparacion". However, in Mucking and Stanford-le-Hope, named individuals were presented for buying foodstuffs such as chickens, butter, and eggs and selling them on without the appropriate licence. Other parishes presented illicit alehouses.[59]

Even in the early fourteenth century, the assizes grand jury was presenting far more cases for trial that had been put before it by private citizens bringing bills of indictment than those based on its collective awareness of local crimes. By 1485 this was also clearly the grand jury's main function at quarter/borough sessions, although presenting crimes on its own initiative remained slightly more important at these forums than with their senior counterpart. Even so (and like the hundred jury), these presentments were often for regulatory offences rather than felonies. For example, at the Michaelmas Quarter Sessions for Essex held at Chelmsford in 1573, the county grand jury presented two bridges on the road from Chelmsford to Roxwell as being decayed, and required Lady Anne Peter, lady of the manor in which they were situated, to repair them. They also presented Richard Swayne, an innkeeper of Little Waltham, for allowing servants to play "att unlawfull games that ys to saye att cards dyce and tables in ye nightes and other unlawfull tymes".[60] Similarly, in 1576, at the Epiphany Quarter Sessions for Essex, the "body of the county" (i.e. the county grand jury) presented John Sterling of Thaxted for having kept a common alehouse without a license.[61] Even so, during the Elizabethan period, William Lambarde urged quarter sessions grand juries to be more active in presenting offences, reminding them that their "duty is not only to hear and receive what others shall bring but also to inquire and present what yourselves do know".[62]

Although prosecution on indictment became the usual way of beginning criminal proceedings during the late medieval period, the legal consequences of its origins lingered well into the Tudor period, even at assizes. For example, until 1529, when a defendant was convicted on

---

59. ERO Q/SR 18/46.
60. ERO Q/SR 46/58.
61. ERO Q/SR 56/51.
62. Read, *William Lambarde and Local Government*, p. 88.

indictment of theft (for example), any stolen property still in his possession could not be returned to its original owners, even if they had been the effective prosecutor and main prosecution witness in his trial. Instead, they reverted to the Crown, or a Crown nominee. One example can be seen in a case of 1473 in which Thomas Calowe, a labourer from Bridgnorth, stole a foal from John Markes in the Manor of Worfield, in Shropshire; this became forfeit to the lord of the manor (who had this right as a grant from the Crown) on his conviction, instead of being returned to the victim. There were several other similar cases in the manor at about the same time.[63] The rationale behind this was that the victim could have brought an appeal of felony (see above) whose success would have allowed him to recover stolen items. If he could not be bothered to do this, and relied instead on a grand jury to take notice of a crime (even though this was no longer the reality), he could not complain.

Reality of Private Prosecution

Although prosecution on indictment was brought in the name of the Crown, until the end of the Tudor period (and well beyond), an ordinary individual, usually but not invariably the victim (homicide cases apart), rather than a public prosecutor, normally initiated the process; he would find potential witnesses, arrange for them to be examined by a JP, and then ensure that they appeared at trial to give evidence, often covering any out-of-pocket costs they might incur. Furthermore, complainants were not usually forced to initiate a prosecution, even if it had come to the attention of a JP, although pressure might be brought on them to do so, if a magistrate was so inclined. Occasionally, this was done by threatening them with the rather vague doctrine of misprision of felony. Thus, in Canterbury, in the early years of the sixteenth century, several men were prosecuted before the city's borough sessions for failing to indict thieves (often their employees). For example, in 1506 Thomas Berry's servant stole clothing allegedly worth £2, but after he recovered his possessions he "lett her escape unponysshed" and refused

---

63. Spike Gibbs, "Felony Forfeiture at the Manor of Worfield, c.1370-c.1600", *The Journal of Legal History*, Vol. 39, Issue 3, pp. 253–255.

to indict the maid. He was subsequently fined five shillings.[64] In 1594 Arthur Pryce (aka Paul Davy), a butcher from Stanway, in Essex, was committed to gaol for a fortnight, and then required to enter sureties for his good behaviour and appearance at the next quarter sessions, because he resolutely resisted pressure from the court to indict such matters as (the court thought) he could against one Peter Tuke (possibly a local JP) and others.[65] However, such actions were not common.

More typically, in November 1613, Bostock Fuller, a Surrey JP, issued an arrest warrant against Robert Allingham after receiving a complaint that he had stolen a "swine and akernes [acorns] in a bag" from a local widow. However, the "woman would not pursue it as felonye". Fuller had the thief brought before several JPs at Godstone the following month, where "after muche reasoning they lett him goe".[66] In June of the same year, Amias Gullock, another transient (he was originally from the West Country), was brought before Fuller by parish officers from Gatton, in Surrey, accused of stealing a petticoat that had been found in his possession: "But the partie [the owner] would not accuse him of ffelonye, & he [Gullock] said he boughte it". Without a complainant willing to pursue the matter, there was no prospect of a formal prosecution. Instead, Fuller dealt with Gullock as a low-level vagrant: "I caused him to be whipte & sent to the place of his byrthe at Combe by Charde in Somersetshire". Given that, if the matter had gone for trial, it would probably have ended in a conviction for petty theft (at the most), for which Gullock would have been whipped and discharged, this course of action had many attractions.[67]

Problems Attendant on Private Prosecution

Any system premised on gratuitous private prosecution occasions numerous problems. The usual dependence of JPs on victim initiation inevitably meant that they were often faced by allegation and counter-allegation. For example, in 1569 Robert Cockerell, of Much Maplestead,

---

64. Jones, *Gender and Petty Crime*, p. 41.
65. ERO Q/SR 128/70 and Q/SR 128/61.
66. Leveson-Gower, "Notebook of a Surrey Justice", pp. 198–199.
67. *Ibid.*

in Essex, claimed that he had been attacked and threatened by a gentleman named Edward Glascock. He had subsequently failed to settle the matter informally, and make Glascock "come to some reasonable talke and order with hym". Eventually he went to Robert Kempe, a local JP, who granted him a warrant for Glascock's arrest. However, on learning this, Glascock went to Sir Thomas Golding, another, more prominent, justice, denied the allegations, and took out a *supersedeas*, which was a writ commanding a stay of proceedings under another writ (in this case, the original warrant). As a result, Cockerell claimed that he was still in fear of Glascock.[68]

More generally, there could be serious disadvantages to indicting a crime, discouraging victims from doing so. The prosecutor was not financially reimbursed for the significant costs involved, such as court fees and witness expenses, let alone for the large amount of time necessarily expended in travelling to find a JP, going to court for the hearing, and then waiting there for a case to be called. In addition, Sir Thomas Elyot was certainly not alone in the 1530s when he suggested that a reluctance to indict a felony was often motivated by pity for the offender and potential prosecutors' fears of burdening their consciences with a man's death, especially for non-violent property offences. Furthermore, anyone who sought to enforce the letter of the law in less serious cases might be the subject of popular opprobrium.[69] Little had changed 50 years later. According to Edward Hext, many simple countrymen were loath to procure a man's death for theft, especially if they had recovered their stolen property.[70] Additionally, prosecution might make dangerous enemies (the defendant himself if he was acquitted, or his kith and kin if executed), particularly if plaintiff and suspect were neighbours.

As a result, those who were prosecuted for a middle-ranking felony, such as grand larceny or housebreaking (rather than murder, rape, or robbery), tended to fall into certain categories. They were often outsiders, strangers to the communities where they had offended and been caught, without local people who would speak on their behalf or harbour grudges

---

68. ERO Q/SR 30/1.
69. Thomas Elyot, *The Boke Named The Governour* (London: J.M. Dent, 1962), p. 120.
70. R. H. Tawney and Eileen Power (eds.), *Tudor Economic Documents, Vol. 2* (London: Longmans, Green, 1951), p. 341.

against their accusers. If local, they were often recidivists who had been caught, and informally dealt with, on several earlier occasions, but had not reformed and had finally exhausted the patience of other villagers. Frequently they were poor and drawn from the margins of society.

Of course, there were exceptions. A few defendants were unfortunate or unwise enough to have targeted thick-skinned or vindictive people who were impervious to local pressure and keen to have their day in court. During the reign of Henry VIII, it was even suggested that many of the criminal laws were not being enforced "unless it be by malice, rancour and evil will".[71] However, this was a slight simplification of prosecutors' motives. There were practical benefits to indicting some cases. A wish not to be seen as weak by local offenders (which might encourage repeat victimisation); the chance, after 1529, of recovering stolen goods; and the possibility of compounding a crime for financial advantage (see below), whether or not this was legal, all played a role.

Even so, for many victims none of these factors was enough. By their very nature it is impossible to establish the proportion of such cases, although Edward Hext suggested that it might be more than 80 per cent. If they *were* forced to attend trial, having been bound to do so by recognisance, some prosecutors and their witnesses would give "feynt evidence" so that the defendant was acquitted, but their recognisance was not estreated.[72]

Even at the time, many observers thought this situation unsatisfactory. In the first year of Henry VII's reign, Lord Chief Justice Hussey, addressing the Westminster judges, noted that while there were plenty of good laws on the statute book, their lack of enforcement was a national problem.[73] This would become a regularly reiterated theme over ensuing decades and centuries, enunciated by men such as Sir Thomas Elyot, and particularly popular amongst Puritans in the Elizabethan period. Thus

---

71. Gary Slapper, *How the Law Works* (London: HarperCollins, 2007), p. 176; T.F.T. Plucknett, "Some Proposed Legislation of Henry VIII", *Transactions of the Royal Historical Society*, Vol. 19, pp. 125–133; Yue Ma, "Exploring the Origins of Public Prosecution", *International Criminal Justice Review*, Vol. 18, Issue 2, p. 195; Gairdner, *Letters and Papers, Foreign and Domestic, Henry VIII, Vol. 7*, pp. 599–627.

72. Tawney and Power, *Tudor Economic Documents, Vol. 2*, pp. 340–341.

73. S. B. Chrimes et al. (eds.), *Fifteenth Century England 1399–1509* (Stroud: Sutton Publishing, 1995), p. 77.

Phillip Stubbes would urge people to enforce the country's many laws and godly statutes: "The want of the due execution wherof, is ye cause of all these mischiefs, which both rage and raigne amongst us".[74] However, it should be noted that this tradition, which was based on what has been termed an "authoritarian, patriarchal ideology", never gained general acceptance, amongst either governors or governed.[75]

Even so, in 1534 Henry VIII proposed the creation of a very limited system of official public prosecution, wondering why so many penal laws had been passed if they were not to be "put in due and perfect legislation". Under this scheme, six "Justices or Conservators of the Common Weal", three of them qualified barristers, would sit in a special court based in Whitehall or elsewhere, and take over responsibility for dealing with penal statutes passed since 1485. Their court would have its own seal, with a plough and spade on it, signifying where the strength of the country came from. However, it would employ common law procedure when trying cases, including use of a jury, and, under section 10 of the proposed statute, could also refer a matter for trial before the Westminster judges at assizes if they felt it desirable (as was done at quarter sessions).[76]

Vitally, further officials, based in every county, termed "sergeants or servants of the common weal", would be appointed under sections 3 and 4 of the proposed legislation. These men would finance their operations out of forfeited property when they secured convictions; they were empowered to search out local offenders (a little like the French *procureur du roi*) and prosecute before the conservators anyone detected and accused of a crime. However, as a safeguard against abuse, acquitted defendants would be able to recover generous costs and damages against the searjeants. Conversely, under section 8 of the proposed act, guilty pleas would secure a considerable mitigation in punishment. It was also hoped that this system would help replace the use of common informers.

---

74. Phillip Stubbes, *The Anatomie of Abuses contayning a discouerie, or briefe Summarie of such Notable Vices and Imperfections, as now raigne in many Christian Countreyes of the World,* (London, 1583), p. 254.

75. Andy Wood, "The Deep Roots of Albion's Fatal Tree: The Tudor State and the Monopoly of Violence", *History,* Vol. 99, Issue 336, p. 405.

76. Slapper, *How the Law Works,* p. 176; Plucknett, "Some Proposed Legislation", pp. 125–133. Yue Ma, "Exploring the Origins", p. 195; Gairdner, *Letters and Papers, Foreign and Domestic, Henry VIII, Vol. 7, 1534,* pp. 599–627.

The proposal was defeated in Parliament, to become an intriguing "road not travelled" in English criminal justice history.[77]

However, the problems occasioned by a lack of public prosecution should not be exaggerated. Many felons who did not come to trial were still punished financially, often heavily, by compounding (see below). Furthermore, the death-for-felony rule would necessarily have to have been reformed if any more felons were convicted (which, of course, might have been a good thing).

Compounding

Throughout the Tudor period (and well beyond), compounding a crime—accepting payment for not prosecuting it—was widespread. In 1605 Sir William Selby, discussing a generally improving situation in law and order in the northern counties and the cities of Durham, Newcastle, and Carlisle, identified the composition of felonies as a continuing impediment to progress in the region. It was so endemic that, although many serious crimes were committed, very few came before the courts.[78]

At the start of the Tudor era, compounding was entirely legal, even for felonies, albeit frowned upon and not binding in preventing a subsequent indictment, if means other than the original complainant's evidence could be used to prove the matter in court. Compounding misdemeanours, such as assault and some forms of wood theft, remained both legal and commonplace to the end of the period (and well beyond). Thus in 1586 Thomas Pettes and William Rivett of St Osyth, in Essex, apparently broke into the close of Henry Coleman at Weeley (in the same county), cutting down wood and brush to the value of 30 shillings. Although the matter entered the criminal justice system, a composition was made and the prosecution abandoned.[79]

---

77. Slapper, *How the Law Works*, p. 176; Plucknett, "Some Proposed Legislation", pp. 125–133; Gary Slapper, "History on Trial", *The Journal of Criminal Law*, Vol. 79, Issue 6, pp. 357–377; Yue Ma, "Exploring the Origins", p. 195; Gairdner, *Letters and Papers, Foreign and Domestic, Henry VIII, Vol. 7, 1534*, pp. 599–627.
78. M.S. Giuseppi (ed.), *Calendar of the Cecil Papers in Hatfield House: Vol. 17, 1605* (London: HMSO, 1938), pp. 374–409.
79. ERO Q/SR 96/48.

However, in 1576 (18 Eliz. c. 5) it was (temporarily) made illegal to compound felonies without permission, something that became permanent nine years later (27 Eliz. c. 10), after which it seems that permission was very rarely granted. When in 1598 a work associate of Richard Thrasher raped the latter's wife in Devonshire, there appear to have been attempts to negotiate a financial settlement, the accused man telling him that he "might do it very well without offence in law, saying that it was no matter for the Queen.[However, subsequently] he was enformed by diverse that the foresaid matters did concern the Queen's Majesty and in that respect he could not end the same".[80]

The two statutes made compounding such crimes an indictable misdemeanour. As a result, at the Essex Quarter Sessions held at Easter 1590, Thomas Shovelard, a High Ongar tailor, was accused of receiving money from various people in Great Dunmow and High Roding under pretext of making compositions for offences that they had (allegedly) committed against various penal statutes. He had obtained five shillings from John Moyne, ten shillings from John Bridge, ten shillings from the Reverend Richard Vaugham, and 2s 6d from John Choppyn, contrary to the 1576 act. He was convicted and sentenced to stand in the pillory at Dunmow Market.[81]

Even so, this relatively minor offence was very rarely prosecuted, and, as Shovelard's case suggests, punished fairly leniently on the few occasions when it was, and convictions were secured, even when committed maliciously; many other cases merely produced fines. As a result, the practice continued on a large scale.

Of course, paying compensation for stolen items, especially those of modest value, could easily merge into compounding, even if it involved a felony. In 1590 a Yorkshire shoemaker who was examined by the Surrey JP Anthony Maxey noted that one allegation made against him, for taking three hens unlawfully, had been dealt with privately; after a complaint was made to a constable, he had paid 18 pence for them in "recompence".[82]

80. Mansell and Hailwood, *Court Depositions of South West England, 1500–1700*, accessed 26/9/19.
81. ERO Q/SR 112/68.
82. ERO Q/SR 113/40.

The notion of compounding with court permission appears strange to modern observers, and was, apparently, a rare occurrence even in the years immediately after 1576. However, according to William Lambarde, in September 1585, Edward Mylett, a tailor from Strood, in Kent, informed him of a composition he had made along with his accomplice, one Thomas Harrys, and their victim, Johr. Champe, "for iiii li. To be paid concerning certain cloth stolen out of the shop of the said Harrys at Cobham, of the privity thereof the said Champe and Myllet were accused by one that was executed".[83] Similarly, in April 1607, at the Newcastle Assizes, Robert Hall was capitally convicted of a burglary that had been committed almost 12 years earlier and compounded at the time, apparently with the permission of the then Lord Warden, something that was freely admitted at trial by the prosecutor. (The injustice occasioned by bringing such a matter before the courts meant that Hall was reprieved for 40 days to allow time for a royal pardon to be considered).[84]

Indeed, it seems that some agreements to compound minor offences, such as assault and petty larceny, were arranged by JPs themselves, while supervising mutually acceptable settlements between complainants and suspects. Although this appears to have been much more common in the early 1700s than it was in the sixteenth century, the roots of such mediation can be traced back to the Tudor era. An anonymous pamphlet of 1555, *The Institution of a Gentleman*, saw this function as fundamental to the office: "To bee a justice in the cuntrye, [meant acting] as a stay for symple men & helper of theyr causes by way of arbitrement, or otherwise to end their contentions, and stynt thwyr strives".[85] In 1594 even the prosecution-minded William Lambarde thought that a JP should be as much a "Compounder as a Commissioner of the Peace".[86] In the same decade, Robert Parsons appreciated that to avoid vexing lawsuits it was necessary that justices of the peace "may hear matters first, and compose

---

83. Read, *William Lambarde and Local Government*, p. 151.
84. M. S. Giuseppi and D. McN. Lockie (eds.), *Calendar of the Cecil Papers in Hatfield House: Vol. 19, 1607* (London: HMSO, 1965), pp. 84–96.
85. Lander, *English Justices of the Peace*, p. 84.
86. Lambarde, *Eirenarcha*, p. 10.

and take them up, with the consent of both parties, or otherwise favour him that hath the most right".[87]

Indicative of this function, in January 1589 Matthew Parker, the Archbishop of Canterbury, wrote to three Surrey JPs, asking that they attempt to resolve a dispute between two of their neighbours, John Grove and Thomas Purdam and, with regard to another matter, to "compound the matter betwixt the mother and son concerning his demands of costs, as also for her imprisonment".[88] In April 1608 Bostock Fuller informally dealt with a case of wood theft: "I ended the matter between Pycknett and Jo: Knolden for which I had sent my warrant: viz. Knolden was to doe twoo dayes worke for Pycknett & never he himselfe nor his wife or servants to poll his hedges &c".[89]

Rewards

The employment of informers who were motivated by rewards to initiate cases stretched far back into the medieval period, and their use was fairly widespread during the Tudor era. Statute sometimes gave informers a share of the fines imposed on those whose convictions they had secured, or of their goods, if seized. This was especially common with regard to regulatory matters and lesser "economic" offences. For example, in the summer of 1593 Rowland Buckley went before the Essex JPs and gave information that Thomas Wood, had shot at a buck at Messing with a "fowling peace", despite not having lands, fees, annuities, or an office to the annual value of £100. This was against the statutory provision aimed at discouraging all but the rich from possessing firearms. He was fined £10, of which Buckley claimed half.[90]

However, the granting of such rewards was inevitably fraught with danger, encouraging malicious accusations and blackmail, something that occasioned concern, even at the time. At some point in the mid-Elizabethan period, Sir Walter Mildmay was one of the commissioners

---

87. Parsons, *The Jesuit's Memorial*, p. 257.
88. SHC 6729/6/4.
89. Leveson-Gower, "Notebook of a Surrey Justice", p. 174.
90. ERO T/A 418/58/52.

who inquired into the "abuses and extortions of informers".[91] Perhaps because of these dangers, rewards were often relatively modest, and not normally available in felony cases, unlike the statutory regime that would develop after 1692, with its very substantial payments, something that would occasion numerous problems and miscarriages of justice during the early eighteenth century.

Malicious Prosecution

In any system premised on personal prosecution there is always a risk that people will indict non-existent crimes out of vengeance or spite or as part of a blackmail attempt. In Tudor England this was a regular allegation in both misdemeanour and felony cases. Of course, some of these claims were themselves unfounded, whether knowingly or because one man's legitimate indictment could easily be construed as another man's malicious prosecution. Nevertheless, a selection of cases is indicative of the potential for abuse.

For example, at a gaol delivery (the trying of felons held in the local gaol) at Gloucester in early November 1536, Lady Anne Berkeley (Lord Thomas' widow) caused John Barlo, the Dean of Westbury, and several of the cleric's friends, to be indicted by her servants for various misdemeanours, one of which was more than a year old.[92] Lady Berkeley was, apparently, not sympathetic to the religious reforms sweeping through the country, and had been accused of shielding William Norton, a priest who was hostile to the breach with Rome, when Barlo and Sir Nicholas Poyntz tried to seize him the previous year. This explained her desire for revenge.[93]

In March 1579, William Aubrey wrote from London to the Surrey JP William More, asking the latter to show favour towards Aubrey's neighbour and former servant (also the bearer of the letter), who claimed he was being threatened by two brothers, John and Edward Hind, who had

91. SHC 6729/11/34.
92. James Gairdner (ed.), *Letters and Papers, Foreign and Domestic, Henry VIII, Vol. 11, July–December 1536* (London: HMSO, 1888), pp. 418–435.
93. Caroline Litzenberger, *The English Reformation and the Laity: Gloucestershire, 1540–1580* (Cambridge: Cambridge University Press, 2009), pp. 37–38.

bound him over to appear at the quarter sessions. Aubrey suggested that this was because the man had testified in King's Bench against one of the brothers when he was accused of usury.[94]

In October 1591 Sir Owen Hopton, a recent lieutenant of the Tower of London, wrote to Sir William More; he informed him that his (Hopton's) servant Edward Brice had been examined by the Recorder of London, as requested by More, in connection with a robbery in Surrey, but discharged as innocent. Brice had a good alibi and was of known good character; Hopton thought that the original allegation made against Brice "was done upon malice".[95]

In a slightly bizarre case at the start of 1596, the Bishop of London wrote to Sir Thomas Mildmay, Sir John Petre, and other Essex JPs, noting that two men in Elmstead had preferred indictments against the local vicar, the Reverend Reginald Medcalfe, for stealing cheeses. This was an allegation that the bishop felt was inherently unlikely, probably being made maliciously, and smacking strongly of "practice against the poor minister and conspiracy". He urged the JPs to prevent the matter going further, and asked that if Medcalfe was required to go to trial, it should be at assizes, not at the county quarter sessions.[96] Even so, at the end of 1596 Medcalfe was indicted at the latter forum for stealing 12 cheeses worth 10 shillings in total, belonging to one Henry Wayte, and another worth 2s. 4d, belonging to John Kempe.[97] Wayte and Kempe had been bound over to prosecute the cleric, who was bailed pending his hearing after the Reverend Lionel Foster from Little Tey provided a surety for the cleric's appearance at trial.

Perhaps indicative of the confessional tensions of the era, in August 1601, Thomas Sackville, Lord Buckhurst, wrote to the Surrey JP Sir George More, who had been appointed to investigate a "foul offence" that Sir Matthew Browne (a Surrey MP) alleged had been committed by Buckhurst's kinsman Maurice Sackville, then the rector or vicar of Ockley. Sackville claimed that Browne was pursuing the case with a "very hard mind" for personal reasons. He also suspected some kind of

---

94. SHC 6729/1/7.
95. SHC LM/COR/3/503.
96. ERO Q/SR 132/53.
97. ERO Q/SR 131/31, 32.

conspiracy had been fomented by several "lewd persons" to deprive Sackville of his living. It was claimed that Browne had already attempted to prosecute Sackville at the assizes on the evidence of two "rogues" who lived in earth-covered cabins on a local common and obtained their living by begging.[98] Sackville survived and continued as rector of Ockley until his death in 1615.

Although absolutely fundamental to the system, the role of the unrewarded private individual in prosecution on indictment can also be exaggerated. There were numerous cases in Tudor England in which nobody was willing or able to pursue a matter but the public interest required such action. As a result, a number of exceptions to the general rule of victim prosecution developed. Homicide is an obvious example. Coroners would ensure, where possible, that murderers were identified, indicted by inquest, and committed to prison pending their hearings, and that relevant prosecution witnesses were found and bound-over to appear at trial to give evidence. At times a local constable might also be bound-over to indict such matters as part of his duties, whether by a coroner or JP. For example, in early 1602 Sir Edward Denny, an Essex magistrate, felt obliged to write to his colleagues at quarter sessions about an alleged infanticide committed by William Bright "because the constable is since deed who should have informed againste him".[99] The role of coroners in homicide cases is considered in *Chapter 6*. However, such non-victim prosecutions were not unique.

Non-Victim Prosecution

Parish officers might prosecute minor offences in their own capacity, sometimes at the behest of local magistrates. For example, in 1572, JPs for the Hundred of Ossulton, in Middlesex, appointed "searchers" to detect and prosecute those eating or dressing flesh on fast days.[100] In April 1589 Simon Askewe was bailed by John Mauchell, a Middlesex JP, to appear

98.   SHC 6729/2/19.
99.   ERO Q/SR 156/30.
100. Robert Lemon (ed.), *Calendar of State Papers Domestic: Edward VI, Mary and Elizabeth, 1547–80* (London: HMSO, 1856), pp. 439–442.

at the next county quarter sessions "upon the complaint of the Constable of Norton Folgate for frequenting suspected houses in that liberty".[101]

Furthermore, although victims were often prosecutors in ordinary felony cases, there was no requirement that this be so. In theory, anyone could prosecute a felony provided that they could assemble sufficient evidence to satisfy an examining JP. As a result, throughout the Tudor period some cases were tried on indictment, even though the victims refused to become involved. Occasionally, this might be for a misdemeanour or petty theft. For example, in 1484, Thomas Kelly stole two barrels of beer from Thomas Biggs' house in Sandwich, in Kent. Although Biggs was not willing to pursue the matter, Kelly was paraded around the town; his ear was nailed to a cartwheel in the market, and he was banished. Similarly, in 1556, although the "certen person" who had been the victim of a petty theft would not pursue the matter, John May, the perpetrator, was whipped at the cart's tail and expelled from the same town.[102]

More significantly, a scrutiny of the assize sessions held on the Home Circuit during the Elizabethan period reveals a surprising number of prosecutions for both forms of larceny (grand and petty) and a few for more serious felonies, such as rape and robbery, where the victim was not identified, being simply described as an "unknown" man or woman. As a result, it is clear that they could not have been pursuing the matter personally, or even have been called to testify at trial, so that these cases must indicate an ability to prosecute such felonies in the absence of a victim complainant. Although this remained possible in ensuing centuries, it was very rare by 1700, as legal concern about firmly establishing the *corpus delicti* of an offence increased and (perhaps) the hearsay rule strengthened.

By contrast, some of these Tudor prosecutions were successful, even if the conviction rate was below the average for the same offence when actively pursued by a victim. These cases may suggest that the notion of a "system" of private prosecution has been slightly overstated for the sixteenth century. Although victim prosecution was the prevalent and

---

101. Jeaffreson, *Middlesex County Records: Vol. 1, 1550–1603*, pp. 182–189.
102. Jones, *Gender and Petty Crime*, p. 41.

dominant mode of bringing non-homicide proceedings for felony, it was neither requisite nor universal. A selection of cases is indicative.

For example, at a Newgate gaol delivery held in October 1507, a man named Rowland was accused of stealing 20 shillings from an unknown victim at Acton, in Middlesex.[103] In July 1562 Isabel Wilson was convicted of grand larceny at the Surrey Assizes after stealing 10s 8d from an "unknown" person in Croydon. At the same forum, in February 1591, John Marten pleaded guilty to petty theft after stealing 12 hens from another unknown person (the birds had clearly been artificially down-valued to eleven pence, but by whom is unclear).[104] In July of the same year, and again at the Surrey Assizes, John Vaughan, a labourer from Newington, was convicted of grand larceny after stealing six sheep from an "unknown" man. (He was clergied). In another case from the same sessions, Thomas Vele was indicted for petty larceny, accused of stealing a lamb from another unknown person that was (down) valued at ten pence, but in this case he was acquitted.[105]

Moving county, in 1591 Percival Wattes and George Watters, a tailor and blacksmith respectively, from Dartford, in Kent, were indicted for stealing five quarters of wheat worth £5, ten shillings' worth of peas, and two shillings of oats from an unknown man. In like manner, at the Essex Assizes in March 1571, Henry Thorne, from Foulness, was convicted of grand larceny having been accused of stealing a purse containing just two shillings from an unknown man in his home town. Such a figure might (and often would) have been down-valued by the jury to petty theft; clearly, whoever brought the prosecution viewed the crime as unusually reprehensible. Although found guilty, Thorne was remanded, suggesting that the trial judge, at least, had concerns about the defendant's being executed in these circumstances (presumably he could not read and so claim clergy).[106]

More seriously, in 1561 four men pleaded guilty at the Old Bailey to beating and robbing an unknown man on the highway at Marylebone, in Middlesex, taking just 20 pence from him. Two (perhaps three) of

---

103. McSheffrey, "The Slaying of Sir William Pennington", p. 178.
104. Cockburn, *Calendar of Assize Records. Surrey Indictments: Elizabeth I*, p. 362 and p. 367.
105. *Ibid*, p. 26.
106. *Ibid*, p. 85.

them were sentenced to death, while one was reprieved.[107] Similarly, at the Essex Assizes held in March 1593, George Hocker was tried for highway robbery; it was claimed that he stole (with an accomplice) cattle from two named men, but also 22 heifers from another "unknown man" at Boxted. Somewhat strangely, he was acquitted of the first two counts and convicted of the last, despite the apparent lack of a victim-prosecutor.[108] Even more notably, in February 1568 two men were convicted before the Surrey Assizes of raping an "unknown woman" in Newington.[109]

These prosecutions, especially the successful ones that were contested, have to be reconciled with Sir Thomas Smith's view, expressed in the early 1560s, that an out-of-court confession, even to a magistrate, that was unsupported by prosecution witnesses, would not normally found a conviction in felony cases: "If none come in to give evidence although the malefactor hath confessed the crime to the Justice of the peace, and that appear by his hande and confirmation, the xii. men will acquite the prisoner".[110] Exactly how such prosecutions occurred must involve a measure of speculation. However, Smith did not say that the victim had to be the witness who testified at trial. It was common practice to arrest those (especially strangers) who were in possession of goods or cash that appeared incompatible with their social status if they could not explain their ownership in a satisfactory manner. It is possible that, in these situations, a confession by the suspect to a JP accompanied by circumstantial evidence and, perhaps, hearsay testimony provided by bystanders or parish officers (or, even better, a non-victim eyewitness to events) would be enough.

In these situations, an examining magistrate may have bound over an arresting constable or other local official to pursue the matter to trial. That English courts did not like deposition evidence does not mean that live witnesses called to give evidence were forbidden from repeating orally what another person had told them. The rules governing hearsay began to form properly only in the latter decades of the seventeenth century. It appears that such evidence was rarely excluded during the 1500s, even

107. Jeaffreson, *Middlesex County Records: Volume 1, 1550–1603*, pp. 37–44.
108. Cockburn, *Calendar of Assize Records. Essex Indictments: Elizabeth I*, p. 395.
109. Cockburn, *Calendar of Assize Records. Surrey Indictments: Elizabeth I*, p. 67.
110. Smith, *De Republica Anglorum*, p. 113.

if it sometimes occasioned mild concern. For example, there was nothing to prevent a constable from repeating what a victim or bystander had said to him, even if that victim or witness subsequently vanished.

Nevertheless, it remains the case that these were exceptions to the general situation in which victims (homicide cases apart) normally initiated prosecutions.

CHAPTER 9

The Criminal Courts

Introduction

This chapter considers the main jury courts found in Tudor England that were charged with trying felonies and serious misdemeanours. For most of the country this meant the assizes and quarter or borough sessions. The Star Chamber was not a jury court, and manorial leet courts, although employing juries, rarely heard serious felonies, though they did deal with many misdemeanours. (They are considered in the next chapter). However, the lack of "system" at this time meant that there were a number of important but localised variations to the general pattern, some of which will also be considered.

In the early thirteenth century felons were as likely to be prosecuted before local jurisdictions as in the king's courts. The power to try felonies was then gradually centralised in the Crown, which sought sole jurisdiction over serious offences. By the middle of the fifteenth century, trial by royal courts was the usual method by which felony was prosecuted, and these forums also determined most serious misdemeanours.

The first major effort at imposing royal justice in the provinces, the General Eyre, a system of itinerant courts established in the twelfth and early thirteenth centuries, proved too slow and cumbersome. Two options were open to the Crown for replacing it and with more effective criminal tribunals. One was to improve on the Eyre but still employ royal justices sent from London to preside over hearings. The other was to rely on prominent men in the localities to try serious offences. For several centuries, recourse was made to both, and the two co-existed.[111]

---

111. James Masschaele, *Jury, State, and Society in Medieval England* (New York: Palgrave Macmillan, 2008), p. 71.

During the reign of Henry III (1216–1272) it was accepted that judges assigned to deal with the possessory assizes might also cover gaol delivery; this eventually gave rise to the assizes system.[112] In 1340 a statute restricted those appointed to preside over these forums to judges and senior serjeants-at-law drawn from the Westminster courts. This promoted centralised royal control (and a degree of uniformity) over the trial of serious crimes outside London and ensured a degree of legal competence in those who conducted such hearings.

However, the county gentry, who provided the great majority of justices of the peace, resisted this process. They were keen to secure greater power in their own localities, even if it was at the expense of central government and its judiciary, something that encouraged them to press for JPs to be granted the power to try felons. They found a ready forum for their demands in the House of Commons, which they dominated.[113] (A considerable majority of MPs were, or had served as, JPs). As a result, they gained and lost the power to determine felonies at quarter sessions several times in the first half of the fourteenth century before acquiring it on a permanent basis, with an Act of 1394 even encouraging them to exercise gaol delivery at this forum.[114]

Although in theory gaol delivery could be exercised under the JPs' general commissions of the peace without further authorisation, after the early decades of the Tudor era this was not always seen as sufficient, and it was often carried out as a result of special ad hoc commissions. For example, in April 1531, prompted by prison overcrowding, the Corporation of Salisbury wrote to Thomas Cromwell: "As we have had no sessions for gaol delivery a long time, considering the number of the prisoners, their great hunger and misery, we beg commissions may be sent for this purpose".[115]

Even so, there were additional safeguards in place when quarter sessions' JPs exercised the power of gaol delivery. A statute from the reign

---

112. J. B. Post, "Local Jurisdictions and Judgement of Death in Later Medieval England", *Criminal Justice History*, Vol. 4, p. 1 and pp. 10–14.

113. Powell, *Kingship, Law, and Society*, p. 16.

114. Post, "Local Jurisdictions and Judgement of Death", p. 1 and pp. 10–14; R.H. Helmholz, "Crime, Compurgation and the Courts of the Medieval Church", *Law and History Review*, Vol. 1, No. 1, pp. 1–26.

115. Gairdner, *Letters and Papers, Foreign and Domestic, Henry VIII, Vol. 5*, pp. 82–94.

of Richard II required that "two men of lawe shoulde be in any comyssion of peas to procede to delyverence of felons".[116] This requirement, which did not extend to the trial of misdemeanours, remained in force throughout the Tudor period.[117] The "men of lawe" had to be qualified apprentices/barristers and serjeants-at-law.

A number of county resident JPs were usually able to satisfy the requirement, even if they had not always enjoyed the most distinguished legal careers. For example, in 1590 there were several "professional" common lawyers who were not then assize judges in the Surrey Commission. Amongst them was Serjeant William Fleetwood, the Recorder of London (who only narrowly missed advancement to the Exchequer bench); Serjeant John Cooper was another.[118] A number of local career lawyers were also present on the Essex bench, and regularly attended quarter sessions. They included Serjeant William Bendlowes (1516–1584), who eventually served as a justice of assizes on the Midland Circuit and was also Recorder of Thaxted in his native county.[119] (His overt support of the Marian regime may have cost him preferment under Elizabeth.)

Of course, Essex, like Surrey, was close to London and so favoured in this regard; a legal career in the capital and its courts was easier to combine with local residence and service as a county JP. Nevertheless, resident JPs who were legally qualified were found in much more remote locations. In 1592 the Devonshire bench included several local lawyers, although they were sometimes absent because of engagements in the capital. Among them were: Edward Drewe, a serjeant and Recorder of both Exeter and (eventually) London, who became an assize judge on the Home Circuit in 1594; Thomas Harris, another serjeant; and John Hele, who was made Recorder of Exeter in 1593 and serjeant the following year.[120]

Most important of all, the assizes and quarter sessions were not rigidly separated. After 1344 it became normal practice to include judges

116. Glazebrook, *The Boke of Justices of Peas*, f.Aii.
117. William Fleetwood, *The Office of a Justice of Peace* (London: W. Lee, 1657), p. 96.
118. Cockburn, *Calendar of Assize Records. Surrey indictments: Elizabeth I*, p. 340.
119. Samaha, *Law and Order*, p. 75.
120. Alexander Henry Abercromby Hamilton, *Quarter Sessions from Queen Elizabeth to Queen Anne; Illustrations of Local Government and History Drawn from Original Records (Chiefly of the County of Devon)*, (London: Sampson Low, 1878), p. 343.

for the former in the commissions of the peace for the counties they covered while on circuit. When so appointed, they were, unsurprisingly, also included in the quorums of those commissions.[121] For example, the general issue of county commissions in July and November 1389 added a pair of judges to each of the counties on their circuits; John Cassy and William Gascoigne were added to those in the East Anglian (later the Norfolk) Circuit and John Wadham and William Hankford those on the Home Circuit.[122] On a broader scale, nine of the 94 JPs appointed to the commissions (and quorums) of the three Ridings of Yorkshire during the adult rule of Richard II and the reign of Henry IV were judges of the Westminster Courts or senior serjeants-at-law who had served as assize judges.[123]

During the late medieval period a practice also developed of holding some quarter sessions with power of gaol delivery at approximately the same time as the assizes; judges on circuit could therefore sit at the former in their capacity as legally qualified JPs, satisfying the prerequisites for those sessions to exercise gaol delivery, even if no other professional lawyers were present.[124] Thus in fifteenth century Yorkshire, when the Westminster judges' visits for the assizes coincided with quarter sessions, they held what were, effectively, joint sessions.[125] Typically, in a letter written to Henry V in 1420, Robert Waterton (a trusted Crown servant in the North) noted: "And opun Wednesday next shall your justices sit at York upon the deliverance of the gaol there and a session of the peace also".[126]

The holding of such simultaneous sessions gradually waned during the sixteenth century. For example, although, in the late medieval and early Tudor period, the Durham Midsummer Quarter Sessions were sometimes timed to coincide with the August Assizes, so as to allow the Westminster judges to attend them, this practice ceased some time after 1557.[127]

---

121. Powell, *Kingship, Law, and Society*, p. 17.
122. Edward Powell, "The Administration of Criminal Justice in Late-Medieval England: Peace Sessions and Assizes", in Eales and Sullivan, *The Political Context of Law*, p. 59.
123. Walker, "Yorkshire Justices of the Peace", p. 283 and pp. 289–290.
124. Glazebrook, *The Boke of Justices of Peas*, p. Aii.
125. Walker, "Yorkshire Justices of the Peace", p. 283 and pp. 289–290.
126. Musson and Powell, *Crime, Law and Society*, pp. 128–129.
127. C. M. Fraser (ed.), *Durham Quarter Sessions Rolls, 1471–1625* (Woodbridge: Boydell & Brewer, 1988), p. 9 and p. 23.

Nevertheless, some "judicial" JPs continued to sit at quarter sessions, even if they did not do so while on circuit.[128] This was especially likely for quarter sessions that were held close to London. Thus two assize judges who were also county JPs were always in attendance at the minority of Essex Quarter Sessions that determined serious felonies in the years immediately after 1584. These were "special" gaol deliveries, often (but not solely) held immediately after the routine misdemeanours at the Epiphany Quarter Sessions had been heard, though on different days. They lasted until the end of the reign of Queen Elizabeth. Their records were filed with those for the quarter sessions to which they were appended, albeit wrapped and bound by themselves.[129]

For example, at the start of 1591 one Geoffrey Nightingale wrote to Sir Robert Clarke, a judge of the Exchequer Court, who frequently presided over the Essex Assizes and was also an active member of the county commission of the peace. He noted that he had recently been robbed of three bullocks at his home in Newport, and, after much "sending about", the thief, a man called Andrew Howe, had been captured and committed to prison. Nightingale and one of his farmhands had been bound-over before Sir Thomas Lucas, a county JP, to prosecute the matter at the next (Lent) assizes for Essex.

However, Nightingale had since learnt that Clarke intended to deliver the county gaol at the forthcoming Epiphany Quarter Sessions, some weeks earlier than the assizes, which would include presiding over Howe's trial; unfortunately, he would not be able to attend because of his involvement in some important legal business elsewhere. Nightingale noted that his farmhand was able to attend the quarter sessions, and could give just as full evidence as he could. Howe had apparently also confessed to stealing the bullocks when questioned by Sir Thomas Lucas, "as shall appear by the examination taken by him". As was normal practice in felony trials, Sir Thomas had promised to personally bring or send (probably by his clerk) the written examination to the quarter sessions.[130]

---

128.   Glazebrook, *The Boke of Justices of Peas*, f.Aii.
129.   Samaha, *Law and Order*, p. 97.
130.   ERO Q/SR 115/28; Samaha, *Law and Order*, p. 97.

Sir Robert Clarke attended 20 quarter sessions, the great majority in the 1580s, but he was by no means the only Westminster judge to do so, even in Essex. William Ayloff, a judge of the Court of Queen's Bench, was present at five that were held in the county between 1562 and 1571. Anthony Brown, from the same forum, attended two quarter sessions in the same decade, while Thomas Meade, also from Queen's Bench, was present at 14 of them during a career that covered much of the Elizabethan era. Even more impressively, Thomas Gente, another Baron of the Exchequer, attended 28 Essex quarter sessions in the 1570s and 1580s alone.[131]

The Assizes System

By the start of the Tudor period, the assizes system was already long established. However, the general absence of surviving records for the century after about 1460 has led to their late medieval and early Tudor history being neglected, with many studies focussing on the better-documented period after 1558. Even so, there is enough evidence to indicate that the assizes functioned fully throughout the reign of Henry VIII and, it seems, that of his father.[132] Indeed, it appears that they continued to function at the height of the Wars of the Roses, prior to the advent of Henry VII. For example, records show that the Summer Assizes on the South-western Circuit were conducted despite the uncertainty created by the Battle of Northampton in 1460, albeit that there were many fines for non-attendance.[133]

The assizes were usually held twice a year in the Tudor era (they had been held three times annually in earlier centuries), during the Lent and long vacations (the latter normally in July and August) in the Westminster courts. Timings might be varied in emergencies, but this was quite unusual. Arranging the assizes to coincide with the lengthy periods outside

---

131. *Ibid*, p. 75.
132. Amanda Bevan, "The Henrician Assizes and the Enforcement of the Reformation", in Richard Eales and David Sullivan (eds.), *The Political Context of Law* (London: Hambledon, 1987), pp. 61–62.
133. Rosemary Horrox (ed.), *Fifteenth century Attitudes: Perceptions of Society in Late Medieval England* (Cambridge: Cambridge University Press, 1994), p. 33.

term time in the central courts allowed judges and senior serjeants-at-law to preside over them without disturbing their primary work in London.

Occasionally, additional special assizes might be held to deal with sudden specific problems in a particular county, especially if it was not too far from London. For example, in December 1564 special assizes were held in Southwark to clear the county gaol for Surrey. These were conducted between the normal Summer Assizes, held the previous July, and the forthcoming Lent Assizes, to be held in March 1565. On this occasion, the relevant gaol delivery commission was issued in late November to Judge John Southcote and Attorney General Gilbert Gerard, the normal assizes judges for the county. They dealt with a fairly full list, with cases of highway robbery, grand larceny, and the county's first murder by witchcraft (under the then recent 1563 statute) being tried.[134] Additional sessions were not, it seems, held at this time for the other counties on the Home Circuit.

Similarly, in September 1571 the Surrey JPs wrote to Lord Howard, the Lord Chamberlain, asking for a special commission to try seven felons, most of them "notable thieves", who would otherwise be held in gaol until the following Lent Assizes, with the "leisure not only to increase in evil themselves, but also to instruct others in the like". They thought that quick trials would act as a public deterrent to other criminals. Surrey was, of course, very close to Westminster, reducing the inconvenience that this would occasion.[135] However, in April 1607 the Bishop of Carlisle and Sir Wilfred Lawson noted that what appears to have been an additional assizes held at Newcastle was so confused and disorganized that, although it did not transact a huge amount of work, it began on Thursday and sat on Friday and Saturday until 10 pm, not finishing until Monday, at 3 pm.[136]

Along with their Crown side work, the assizes also had a civil jurisdiction dating back to the Statute of Westminster in 1285 — that of *nisi prius* — which allowed a matter entered in one of the three major common law courts in the capital, especially King's Bench and Common

---

134. Cockburn, *Calendar of Assize Records. Surrey indictments: Elizabeth I*, pp. 38–40.
135. SHC 6729/11/57/2.
136. Giuseppi and Lockie, *Calendar of the Cecil Papers in Hatfield House: Vol. 19, 1607*, pp. 84–96.

Pleas, to be tried in the claimant's county. One of the two judges assigned to each circuit would preside over such hearings at sessions, at least some of the time. Nevertheless, most of the court's work was criminal, and unlike civil matters, criminal cases were initiated and dealt with locally rather than by Westminster.[137]

Even early in the Tudor era, some observers, both foreign and domestic, felt that the delay attendant on using occasional, and centrally administered, courts for very serious provincial crimes was not conducive to efficient crime control.[138] Such views were reiterated during what was seen as a crisis engendered by a combination of high levels of vagrancy, the presence of numerous recently discharged soldiers and sailors, and the straitened economic conditions in the winter of 1589–1590. George More, briefly the Provost Marshal as well as being a Surrey JP and MP for Guildford, suggested that a standing commission of oyer and terminer should be established to deal with murders, highway robbery, and burglaries in the counties adjoining London.[139] Even more significant, London and, by the fifteenth century, Middlesex (which had been on what became the Home Circuit as late as the 1330s) were excluded from the national system and serviced by the Old Bailey, which held many sessions (see below).

The Circuits

England had been divided into six circuits in 1328, these replacing the four circuits established (from yet older roots) by statute in 1292. Each of them was made up of groups of adjoining counties.[140] A few shires moved between circuits during the first two centuries of their existence. By 1500 the Western Circuit covered the counties of Devon, Berkshire (which later moved to the Oxford Circuit), Cornwall, Dorset, Somerset, Hampshire, and Wiltshire. The Home Circuit encompassed the counties around London: Hertfordshire, Essex, Kent, Surrey, and Sussex (the last was the only one not adjacent to the capital or Middlesex). The misleadingly named

---

137. Hentzner, *Travels in England*, p. 80.
138. Anon, *A Relation, or Rather A True Account*, p. 33.
139. SHC 6729/3/29.
140. Cockburn, *A History of English Assizes 1558–1714*, p. 17.

Norfolk Circuit included Bedfordshire and Buckinghamshire as well the East Anglian counties. The equally misnamed, and very large, Oxford Circuit covered eight counties, including Gloucestershire, Staffordshire, Herefordshire, and Shropshire; it acquired Monmouthshire in 1541. The Midland Circuit held the central counties—Rutland, Lincolnshire, Warwickshire, and Leicestershire. The Northern Circuit comprised Durham, Westmorland, Cumberland, Northumberland, Yorkshire, and Lancashire.

A few major provincial cities had become urban counties during the medieval period, and were placed on the same circuit as the wider county in which they were situated. Bristol achieved this status in 1373, partly as a result of its lavish support for Edward III's war efforts, and partly in response to a petition by the townsmen pointing out that their city straddled two counties, and it was enormously inconvenient to make journeys of 30 miles on heavily rutted roads to assizes at Gloucester and Ilchester.[141] Norwich followed in the early fifteenth century. During the 1530s Henry VIII further added to their number when he made Exeter "a county of it self", independent of surrounding Devonshire. This meant that the city (like Norwich and Bristol) was host to two assizes, the county assizes that were held in its castle and the city assizes that were, very occasionally, convened in its Guildhall. (The latter were rare because the king also granted the mayor and aldermen the right to sit as justices of the peace with full power of gaol delivery, reducing the need for assizes.)[142]

Wales was sui generis, although subject to the same common law and procedure as England. After 1542 the principality had four circuits, together known as the Great Sessions. Each circuit comprised three or four contiguous Welsh counties. The Brecon Circuit was made up of Breconshire, Glamorganshire, and Radnorshire; the Carmarthen Circuit encompassed Cardiganshire, Carmarthenshire, and Pembrokeshire; and the North Wales Circuit covered Anglesey, Caernarvonshire, and Merionethshire. The Great Sessions also included the Chester Circuit,

---

141. Fleming, *Time, Space and Power*, p. 7; Francis B. Bickley (ed.), *The Little Red Book of Bristol*, *Vol. 1* (Bristol: W. Crofton Hemons, 1900), pp. 115–26.
142. Mark Stoyle, "'It Is But an Olde Wytche Gonne': Prosecution and Execution for Witchcraft in Exeter, 1558–1610", *History*, Vol. 96, Issue 322, pp. 129–135.

which comprised Cheshire in England as well as Denbigh, Flintshire, and Montgomeryshire in Wales.

In each English county there would be at least one and sometimes two or more towns where the judges might sit for their assizes, although only one would be used on any single circuit. As a result, up to 50 towns and cities were visited nationally each year. A few counties had a policy of sharing their assizes among their major towns, not least because they were good for local trade. In many others, certain towns and cities, such as Ipswich in Suffolk, Exeter in Devonshire, Oakham in Rutland, and Chelmsford in Essex, were regularly employed as assizes towns where the vast majority of the shire's sessions were held.

These venues were usually "le principal et chiefe villes de les counties".[143] However, occasionally, a smaller town might become a regular place for assizes because it was convenient for transportation and the movements of the circulating judges. Thus East Grinstead, the normal location for the Sussex Assizes, was only just inside the county, facilitating easy access for the judiciary when they were proceeding around the Home Circuit.

Nevertheless, even counties with regular assize venues occasionally varied locations. For example, Lewes and Horsham were sometimes pressed into service in Sussex, while, in Essex, Brentwood, Colchester, and Witham sometimes stood in for Chelmsford.[144] In Elizabethan Hertfordshire, assizes were sometimes held at Bishop's Stortford, St Albans, and Hitchin, as well as in Hertford (the usual choice).[145] Occasionally such variation might take place for special reasons, such as the presence of plague in the customary venue. In exceptional situations, disease could also lead to the circuits' being curtailed, as occurred with the "sweating sickness" in 1527.[146]

Judges would usually visit the counties and their assizes towns in the same sequence on each circuit. Thus the summer assizes for the Western Circuit were often held at Winchester (Hampshire), Salisbury (Wiltshire),

143. Richard Crompton, *L'Authoritie et Jurisdiction Des Courts de la Maiestie de la Roygne* (London, 1594), p. 226.
144. Cockburn, *Calendar of Assize Records. Sussex Indictments: Elizabeth I*, p. 152 and p. 108; Samaha, *Law and Order*, pp. 158–159.
145. Cockburn, *A History of English Assizes*, p. 27.
146. Elyot, *The Boke Named The Governour, Vol. 1* (London: Kegan Paul, Trench, 1883), p. 53.

Dorchester (Dorset), Exeter (Devon), Bodmin or Truro (Cornwall), and either Wells or Bridgwater (Somerset), and attended in that order. The Home Circuit normally began with Maidstone or Canterbury (Kent); this was followed by East Grinstead (Sussex); Croydon, Kingston, or Guildford (Surrey); and Hertford (Hertfordshire). The circuit finished at Chelmsford (Essex). Even so, there was no requirement that this occur, and temporary variation sometimes took place, while more permanent change in the order of towns or counties visited also occurred from time-to-time.

By dint of a statute from 1340 the assize judges were primarily drawn from the two Lord Chief Justices and (eventually) the Lord Chief Baron of the Courts of Common Pleas, King's Bench, and Exchequer in Westminster, supplemented (by the Tudor era) by the nine or so puisne judges from these courts. In their absence, whether due to illness, infirmity, or the need to discharge other legal duties, assizes judges might be drawn from experienced serjeants-at-law who were members of the country's tiny but senior legal profession, a majority of whom would themselves ultimately go on to be full-time members of the judiciary.

Nearly all serjeants eventually went on circuit in a judicial capacity. For example, of the 30 men in service during the reign of Henry VII, 22 acted as judges of assizes. Seven of the remaining eight either died or got appointed to the full-time bench before they could be called upon in this capacity. Only Serjeant John Yaxley seems to have been deliberately ignored. Quite frequently, during the early Tudor period, a third of assizes commissions were made up of serjeants, and in the spring of 1507 and 1508 they constituted half the judges on circuit.[147] They continued to serve in this capacity to the end of the period (and beyond). For example, both Francis Gawdy and Thomas Owen had been serjeants when first sitting as judges on the Elizabethan Home Circuit before being appointed as puisne judges (to King's Bench and Common Pleas, respectively), after which they continued to cover the same circuit. The Crown's most senior law officers also sometimes served as assizes judges during the sixteenth century. Thus in February 1540 William Whorwood,

147. Ives, *Common Lawyers*, p. 74.

the newly appointed Attorney General, covered the Midland Circuit, along with Sir Walter Luke from King's Bench.[148] In the summer of 1562 Gilbert Gerard, the Attorney General from 1559 to 1581, sat with a serjeant on the Home Circuit.[149]

Although the men chosen necessarily included the most eminent lawyers in the nation, not all of them proved adept at circuit work, especially when first appointed.[150] Serjeant John Hele was made Queen's Serjeant (a legal adviser to the monarch) in the summer of 1602, and shortly afterwards rode the Home Circuit with Sir Francis Gawdy, a judge of the Queen's Bench. Unfortunately, it was claimed that he swiftly made himself both "odious and ridiculous" while doing so. By then he was a relatively old and unpopular man, something that may have influenced the assessment of his abilities; the last years of his career were to be mired in scandal.[151]

The two judges would usually travel together around the circuit, moving from one assizes town to another, dispensing justice as they went. When, as was normally the case, both judges were present, one man might preside over the criminal or Crown side (accompanied by local JPs), the other over the civil or *nisi prius* trials, at least until the latter were complete, after which he might assist his colleague with criminal matters. If loads were light, the judges might sit together for both types of work.

In an emergency—if, for instance, one judge was taken ill—a single judge might have to travel alone and do his best to cover the most urgent cases, while adjourning less pressing matters to the following assizes or referring them down to quarter sessions. It also seems that, very occasionally, the clerk of assizes (always a qualified barrister) stood in for the missing man in such situations, at least during the sixteenth century. For example, in the preamble to the gaol calendars returned from the Western Circuit in the winter of 1560, Thomas Andrews, its clerk, was described as one of the two judges of gaol delivery for most

---

148. James Gairdner and R. H. Brodie (eds.), *Letters and Papers, Foreign and Domestic, Henry VIII, Vol. 16, 1540–1541* (London: HMSO, 1898), pp. 267–281.

149. Cockburn, *Calendar of Assizes Records. Essex Indictments: Elizabeth I*, p. 531.

150. Cockburn, *A History of English Assizes*, pp. 120–127.

151. Mary Anne Everett Green (ed.), *Calendar of State Papers Domestic: Elizabeth, 1601–3, With Addenda 1547–65* (London: HMSO, 1870), pp. 246–253.

of the counties. Similarly, the long-serving John Glascock, an alumnus of Eton College, Oxford, and the Inner Temple (of which he eventually became a bencher), was so described for all the counties on the Home Circuit in the summer of 1570. A year later, the calendar for the Oxford Circuit suggests that the assizes clerk there, William Fowler, deputised in Berkshire and Oxfordshire until Serjeant William Lovelace could, belatedly, join the circuit and bring its complement of two Westminster judges up to strength.[152]

During the sixteenth century, the time it took to complete an assizes circuit varied with location and caseload. It had increased substantially since the first half of the fifteenth century. For example, during the 1420s and 1430s the assizes rarely sat for more than a day in each location on the Norfolk Circuit, so that the six-county tour took about 12 hectic days.[153] During the Tudor era two to three days in each location became normal. By the 1580s the Oxford Circuit, which covered eight counties, and was the longest in the country, lasted 28 days. The shortest, the Northern, lasted 16 days in the summer and just a week during the winter, when, because of road conditions and security considerations, it was confined to York and Lancaster. This meant that Cumberland, Westmorland, Northumberland, and Durham had to make do with one assizes a year.[154] They were not unique in this. It seems that Sussex often saw just one sessions (in the summer) each year until 1568, and the City and County of Norwich, which had become a separate assizes jurisdiction (with a hinterland covering a few square miles) in 1404, also normally saw only one sessions annually, as did some other cities that had achieved assizes status.

Apart from the journey to and from London, judges could cover over 200 miles on circuit, although travelling almost anywhere in Tudor England could be arduous, and was always fairly slow, especially in winter. Those going to and from the north of England during the Elizabethan period would have to allow up to six days each way (particularly in the

---

152. Cockburn, *A History of English Assizes*, pp. 77–78.
153. Maddern, *Violence and Social Order: East Anglia 1422–1442*, pp. 58–59.
154. Cockburn, *A History of English Assizes*, p. 25; D. R. Bentley (ed.), *Select Cases from the Twelve Judges' Notebooks* (London: John Rees, 1997), p. 2; J. S. Cockburn, "The Northern Assize Circuit", *Northern History*, Vol. 3, Issue 1, p. 122.

winter) for the journey from the capital, on top of the time taken for the actual circuit; those going to the Midland and Western Circuits also had to allow for a significant, if more modest, amount of travelling time to and from their starting and finishing points.[155] The two judges would normally share a coach, ideally pulled by six horses, especially during the Lent Sessions, when the roads were particularly poor. Sometimes, especially in parts of the Northern Circuit, they might have (or prefer) to ride on horseback.

The Crown empowered assizes judges with five temporary commissions, those of general gaol delivery; assize; the peace; oyer and terminer (after 1537); and *nisi prius*. The most important for criminal matters (*nisi prius* was purely for civil actions) were those of gaol delivery and oyer and terminer.[156] The commission of gaol delivery allowed the judges involved to deal with every prisoner in the county jail "for what offence soever he be ther". Ideally, by the end of each assizes, the local prison should have been completely cleared, although this only rarely happened in practice.[157]

A circuit was usually initiated by a commission of gaol delivery being issued to a group of judges, senior serjeants, and law officers, authorising any two of them to hold the assizes in a specified county at a set time. In the early sixteenth century this group normally consisted of three or (less commonly) four men. Thus the commission of gaol delivery for the Midland Circuit in February 1522 was issued to Sir Humphrey Coningsby (a justice of the King's Bench), John Carell, and John Jenour (second prothonotary, or clerk).[158] By the end of the century, it seems that the commission was usually issued to five judges or serjeants, as occurred on 25 January, 1597, with regard to the Hertford Assizes that were to be held the following March.[159]

In the 1560s the selected judges would gather in Serjeants' Inn towards the end of the Hilary and Trinity terms, where they would choose their forthcoming circuits on the basis of personal preference, granted

---

155. Prest, *The Rise of the Barristers,* 1986, p. 46.

156. Baker, *Oxford History,* p. 256.

157. Francis Bacon, "The Use of the Law", in *The Works of Francis Bacon, Lord Chancellor of England, Vol. 3* (Philadelphia: Carey and Hart, 1841), pp. 247–253.

158. Brewer, *Letters and Papers, Foreign and Domestic, Henry VIII, Vol. 2, 1515–1518,* pp. 392–409; *Ibid, Vol. 3, 1519–1523,* pp. 883–892.

159. Cockburn, *Calendar of Assize Records. Hertfordshire Indictments: Elizabeth I,* p. 125.

according to seniority. The two Lord Chief Justices and the Lord Chief Baron would have first pick, the puisne judges following in order of appointment to the bench, with any remaining vacancies being filled by serjeants-at-law. Occasionally, political factors influenced allocation. The very reliable Edmund Anderson was given the Norfolk Circuit in the 1580s, although still only a serjeant, specifically to suppress Brownists (early dissenters), even though it ranked with the Midland Circuit as one of the most attractive choices, frequently being chosen by the chief justices. (After about 1586, the Western seems to have replaced the Midland by preference). The Northern was distant from London, requiring a long journey to and from the circuit, and could also be physically arduous and insecure; the judges would often carry weapons and normally be escorted by a significant number of well-armed local men. It also carried only modest judicial allowances.[160] These factors could make it unattractive.

Perhaps surprisingly, the Home Circuit was also unpopular amongst judges during the latter part of the Tudor era, even though it required the least amount of travelling to and from London. This had not always been the case. In the 1490s it was seen as clearly preferable to the hazardous Northern Circuit, whose judges moved to the Home Circuit when they could, and appears to have been ranked in the top three circuits by judicial preference, along with the Norfolk and Oxford Circuits, only occasionally being covered by serjeants.[161]

The Home Circuit might, in part, have been unpopular during the latter decades of the sixteenth century because, by then, the South-eastern counties (along with those on the Northern Circuit) had the smallest per diem financial allowances for the judiciary. It was these, rather than the fee for serving, which was usually under £20 per circuit even at the end of the Tudor era, that made such work remunerative. Furthermore, Home Circuit caseloads were often heavy during the final decades of the century, while the terrain was generally poor for hunting, for those judges who had the inclination and (much less commonly) the time for

160. Cockburn, *A History of English Assizes 1558–1714*, pp. 49–50.
161. Ives, *Common Lawyers*, pp. 75–76, and p. 67.

such sport. It also seems that proximity to London did not guarantee cleaner, more comfortable, quarters, or even safer surroundings.[162]

As a result, at least one of the judges covering the Elizabethan Home Circuit would normally be a serjeant, and his partner was usually a relatively junior puisne judge. Sometimes, and unusually in a national context after the mid-century, both would be serjeants, as occurred at the Brentwood Assizes of February 1559, when Ralph Cholmley and Thomas Carus presided over the hearings.[163] This had also been the case on the then unpopular Western Circuit at the start of the Tudor era, when 30 of 47 assizes circuits during the reign of Henry VII were covered by two serjeants, and only a tiny number had a pair of Westminster judges present.[164] This changed as the Western Circuit became more attractive to the London judiciary.

When they acquired sufficient seniority, some judges would opt for more favoured circuits. For example, Sir Robert Clarke, a Baron of the Exchequer, was made an assizes judge on the Home Circuit in 1587, but changed to the Norfolk Circuit in 1593. Nevertheless, judges might continue choosing the apparently less desirable circuits even after they had alternatives because they were familiar with the counties involved, valued continuity, had been appointed to their commissions of the peace, or had become friendly with local dignitaries. For example, almost immediately after the confirmation of his patent as serjeant-at-law by Henry VII in 1503, Richard Elyot (father of Thomas) received a commission to act as justice of assize on the Western Circuit, and from that time until his death in 1522 he always rode the same circuit, even after becoming a judge of the Common Pleas in 1513.[165] Similarly, from July 1596 to March 1601, Thomas Walmsley, another judge of the Court of Common Pleas, and Edward Fenner, from the Queen's Bench, took all the assizes on the Western Circuit.[166] Even the Home Circuit saw a quota of senior judicial figures, albeit many were in the first half of the Tudor

---

162. Herrup, *The Common Peace*, p. 57.
163. Cockburn, *Calendar of Assize Records. Essex Indictments, Elizabeth I*, p. 1.
164. Ives, *Common Lawyers*, pp. 75–76 and p. 67.
165. Elyot, *The Boke Named The Governour*, p. 44.
166. William Durrant Cooper (ed.), *The Expenses of the Judges of Assize Riding the Western and Oxford Circuits, Temp. Elizabeth, 1596–1601* (Sydney: Wentworth Press, 2016), p. 3.

era. Sir John More (c.1451–1530), father of the more famous Thomas, was appointed a serjeant-at-law in 1503, an assizes judge in 1513, to the bench of Common Pleas in 1518, and to King's Bench in 1520. He died at the end of 1530, having ridden the Home Circuit with Sir Thomas Inglefield (1488–1537), a judge of the Common Pleas, during the Lent Assizes in the same year.[167] Judges had to get express permission to sit on circuits in which they had their own residences, to reduce the risk of bias, although such authorisation was usually forthcoming if requested, and not uncommon.

According to Sir Thomas Smith, during the 1560s at least, details of the judges' assizes itinerary were written-up and displayed in the Exchequer at the end of the law term immediately prior to the judges' going on circuit. Those selected for the duty would write to the sheriff of each county, sending a precept (writ or warrant) informing them of the forthcoming assizes and its dates, and requesting them to make the necessary logistical arrangements (accommodation, etc.), as occurred in January 1567 when Serjeant John Southcote wrote to the Sheriff of Surrey and Sussex (it was a combined position) asking for assizes to be held at Kingston-on-Thames for the former county.[168] The sheriff would then reply, confirming that he had made suitable arrangements and providing the judge with details of any complicated cases he would be asked to preside over. (The opportunity for legal research on circuit was often limited). For much of the era, the sheriff would bear many of the judges' substantial charges personally, subsequently seeking reimbursement from the Exchequer. Thus, in 1564 the Sheriff of Suffolk claimed £93 for lodging and entertaining the judges at Bury St Edmunds during the Lent Assizes. On one occasion the Sheriff of Westmorland was even advised by central government to reduce expenditure on circuit dinners.

This financial obligation helped to make the shrievalty increasingly unpopular. In February 1574, the Privy Council wrote to the Sheriff of Surrey (and others holding the same position), noting that many gentlemen who were eligible for the position had complained in Parliament about how onerous it was, while others had refused to take up the office

167. SHC LM/961/1–16.
168. SHC LM/970.

when it was offered to them, because of the great expense of the "large diets and other charges of the Justices of Assize and Gaol Delivery". However, the council also noted that, as a result, the Queen had decided to pay for much of this out of her own coffers, across the nation. (Sheriffs were still asked to assist the judges' servants in finding appropriate lodgings.)[169] More generally, in about 1575 the council wrote to the justices of assize, urging them to discourage sheriffs from giving expensive entertainments while they were on circuit.[170]

Judicial accommodation during assizes might be provided in rented houses, in the homes of local county dignitaries, such as the high sheriff or the lord lieutenant (after the 1540s) and other prominent gentlemen, or in the better inns. Wealthy men might donate beer, wine, and meat for consumption at the attendant social events. For example, in July 1570 Viscount Montague wrote to William More, offering him a buck for his guests during the forthcoming Guildford Assizes.[171] At one assizes held on the Western Circuit in the late 1590s, 89 gallons of beer were donated and consumed in three days at Winchester, 90 gallons over two days at Salisbury, and a further butt of beer in five days at Chard and Exeter.[172] Such gifts meant that much of the judges' per diem allowances could be retained as pure profit. Towards the end of the Elizabethan period they could amount to more than £100 a year for those on the Western Circuit, and £70 on the Oxford Circuit.[173]

The assizes were conducted with considerable ceremony, something that reinforced the authority of central government. The sheriff's deputy would escort the judges from the boundary of each county to a point near the relevant assizes town, where the sheriff would greet them and lead them to their lodgings. Wearing scarlet and ermine robes, they would meet other local dignitaries before attending a special service at a major parish church or cathedral, along with trumpeters, javelin men, court officers, lawyers, and the sheriff and under-sheriff of the county.

---

169. SHC 6729/11/60.
170. Lemon, *Calendar of State Papers Domestic: Edward VI, Mary and Elizabeth, 1547–80*, pp. 508–513.
171. SHC 6729/8/32.
172. Cooper, *Expenses of the Judges*, p. 11.
173. Cockburn, *A History of English Assizes 1558–1714*, p. 56.

After the Reformation took hold, they would often listen to a special assizes sermon delivered by a prominent local clergyman. Such sermons normally stressed a legal and religious theme. For example, towards the end of the Tudor era, the Reverend William Westerman, a minister from Sandridge in Hertfordshire, warned the congregation at Hertford about the perils of taking private revenge rather than seeking public redress through due process of the law.[174] Although Justice Gawdy, sitting at the Lent Assizes for Sussex in 1579, claimed that he and his brother judge had gained "great fruite and comforte" from hearing such a sermon, just before they started their lists, some lawyers found them tedious.[175] In September 1596 the irascible Lord Chief Justice Anderson was apparently greatly aggrieved by the preachers at both the Northampton and Leicester Assizes.[176]

Very few English courts were purpose-built for criminal hearings during the Tudor era, especially in its early decades. Instead, the county shire hall (often found in or near a castle) was frequently used as an ad hoc venue. Thus, John Leland, who produced a valuable account of Tudor England during his travels around the country in the 1530s and early 1540s, noted that Launceston, in Cornwall (the county town), had a castle within which there was a "hawle for syses and sessions, for a commune gayle for al Cornwayle is yn this castel".[177] This proximity of gaol and sessions venue, while very common, was not universal. Although the assizes in Sussex were normally held at East Grinstead, the county gaol was a highly inconvenient 18 miles away.[178]

In most cases the court furnishings were portable, and stored when not in use. The presiding judge would usually sit on a raised platform, flanked by senior JPs, with less prominent magistrates sitting on a bench below them, along with other minor dignitaries. Beneath these was often

---

174. William Westerman, *Two Sermons of Assise: The one Intituled A prohibition of Revenge, the other A Sword of Maintenance* (London, 1600).
175. William Overton, *A Godly, and Pithie Exhortation made to the Judges and Justices of Sussex, and the whole Countie, assembled together, at the general Assizes* (London, 1579), p. Aiii.
176. Harrison, *Second Elizabethan Journal*, p. 135.
177. Lucy Toulmin Smith (ed.), *The Itinerary of John Leland in or about the Years, 1535–1543*, Parts I to III (London: George Bell and Sons, 1907), p. 325.
178. Herrup, *The Common Peace*, p. 58.

a table where the under-sheriff and clerks sat and worked.[179] There would be a jury box or benches (frequently divided in two, sitting six apiece) and an improvised dock for the defendant.

JPs were supposed to attend their county assizes, and central government tried to encourage this, although their presence was slightly less important (as they were not presiding over the hearing) than it was at quarter sessions. On average, a little over half of all non-honorary JPs in Surrey attended assizes at some point in the year during the late sixteenth century (a better attendance rate than many counties), although numbers varied. For example, there were about 35 JPs on the Surrey Commission in 1590, apart from eleven men who might (more or less) be defined as honorary appointments plus the county's two assizes judges. Of these, just 15 attended the assizes held at Southwark in March 1590. However, at other assizes sessions, 20 or so magistrates might be present.[180]

The assizes were major social and commercial events for the county gentry. As a result, many men made an effort to attend, even if they were not JPs. The judges would often entertain local notables to dinner in the evening, passing on central government concerns while themselves acquiring information, scouting potential JPs, and learning about local concerns that might be transmitted back to government when they made their formal post-circuit report.

Black Assizes

Dozens of witnesses, judges, JPs, jurors, and members of the public were crammed into a relatively confined space at the hearing. A general lack of hygiene, and the press of people, meant that, throughout the sixteenth century (and well beyond), there were periodic "Black Assizes" in which disease, usually typhus or "gaol fever", as it was called at the time, was spread by lice from prisoners to court personnel and even, through them, to residents of the town. For example, many lawyers and other people, Sir John Cut and Sir Giles Alington among them, died during a major case at the Lent Assizes held at Cambridge Castle in 1522. The prisoners themselves appear to have been immune on this occasion. One of

---

179. Smith, *De Republica Anglorum*, p. 111.
180. Cockburn, *Calendar of Assize Records. Surrey Indictments: Elizabeth I*, p. 340.

the most famous of these epidemics occurred at Oxford, in the summer of 1577. Among the many dead were the Lord Chief Baron, Sir Robert Bell; the High Sheriff of the county, Sir Robert D'Oyly; many of the jurors; and up to 300 people in the city and some 200 in the surrounding countryside.

In March 1586, the Devonshire Assizes, held at Exeter Castle and presided over by Sir Edmund Anderson, also resulted in many deaths. Anderson's coadjutor, Edward Flowerdew, died, as well as eleven members of the petty jury, up to eight attendant JPs, and numerous constables and townsmen. This is, perhaps, not entirely unsurprising. A large number of the prisoners had been so ill when produced from the local gaol that they had to be brought to court in wheelbarrows. Another Black Assizes occurred on the Northern Circuit in 1598. Among the dead on this occasion were Judge Francis Beaumont of the Court of Common Pleas and Serjeant Edward Drewe.[181] This threat explains why the new, post-1539, Old Bailey building had one side open to the elements. However, it was not just gaol fever that posed a danger to sessions. In 1593 it appears that the Summer Assizes for Surrey were held in a large barn at St George's Fields, in Southwark, specifically to reduce the risk of plague (an even more virulent disease), which had broken out in the vicinity.[182]

Circuit Administration

A clerk of assizes was responsible for most of the administration on each circuit, so that there were normally at least six at any one time in the country. They had originated as private clerks to the judiciary, the position becoming a barristers' monopoly in the late fourteenth century, although a statute of 1541 (33 Hen. VIII, c. 24) forbade those appointed from practising law on the circuit they served.[183] Although clerks were not usually drawn from the elite of the legal profession, several were highly successful and noteworthy men during the sixteenth century, as the salary and fees available for both criminal and civil matters made the position attractive. For example, Sir Thomas Elyot (1490–1546), a

---

181. Green, *Calendar of State Papers Domestic: Elizabeth, 1598–1601*, pp. 45–59.
182. Cockburn, *A History of English Assizes 1558–1714*, p. 29.
183. J. S. Cockburn, "Seventeenth century Clerks of Assize — Some Anonymous Members of the Legal Profession", *The American Journal of Legal History*, Vol. 13, No. 4, p. 317.

diplomat and scholar, was clerk to the Western Circuit between 1511 and 1526, initially accompanying his father, who was a judge on the same circuit. He received a salary of 800 marks a year. On his resignation, the office was bestowed on Robert Dacres, the nephew of the Master of the Rolls.[184] For most of the reign of Queen Elizabeth, John Glascock, who had attended Eton and Oxford, was made an Inner Temple bencher in 1568, and was evidently highly regarded, was clerk on the Home Circuit.[185]

Several assizes clerks held positions in the central common law courts at the same time, serving as, *inter alia,* prothonotaries (the chief clerks to the Courts of King's Bench and Common Pleas). In the years from 1498 to 1510, all three prothonotaries were clerks of assizes, on the Norfolk, Home, and Western Circuits, although none of them combined the two roles in the 1520s.[186] Clerks would frequently be based in an assizes town on their circuit, although many spent a considerable amount of time in the capital. It seems that they often kept the circuit records in their own residences, explaining why so many have been lost.

Even when they did not serve as emergency judges (see above) the role of clerks was often significant, especially on the Crown side. Judges, particularly those not drawn from the Court of King's Bench, spent most of their professional lives engaged in civil, not criminal, matters. As a result, they were often heavily dependent on the clerk's expertise in criminal law and procedure, especially when first appointed.

The clerks' pre-trial role was primarily to supervise and coordinate, as two or three associates usually supported them. The latter were also legally qualified, whether as barristers or attorneys; they would draw up many of the formal documents (such as indictments) employed by the court, under the clerk's direction, and kept some of the court's files. They often combined this work with a clerkship or deputy clerkship of the peace or service as a borough coroner. Unlike the clerks of assizes, they were not forbidden to conduct private legal work on their circuits, something that could be professionally unhealthy, given their positions.[187]

184. Elyot, *The Boke Named The Governour,* p. 40 and p. 56.
185. Cockburn, *A History of English Assizes,* p. 75.
186. Baker, *Oxford History,* p. 262.
187. Thomas G. Barnes (ed.), *Somerset Assize Orders 1629–1640, Vol. 65* (Frome: Somerset Record Society, 1959), p. 34.

A few of these men eventually became clerks to the assizes themselves, when a vacancy presented itself, as was the case with Thomas Warren on the Midland Circuit in 1604.

Below the associates were several general or assistant clerks, legally less or unqualified, who were available to assist with routine administration. The assizes courts would also usually have a couple of unsalaried marshals and a cryer who were paid fees as and when they performed their duties. The former were responsible for courtroom order and swearing-in of witnesses and the latter for proclamations and some clerical and courier work.[188] The precise complement for each circuit differed and varied over time. On the pressured Home Circuit in 1602, it consisted of the clerk, three associates, and up to eight assistant clerks.[189]

Quarter Sessions

The quarter sessions in each county, along with their equivalent forums in chartered boroughs (see below), were the lowest criminal courts that could try serious crimes on indictment before a jury, a power that they had held since at least 1368. (Following an act of 1462, they also acquired some of the legal work previously carried out by high sheriffs.) They were found in most parts of England, although the palatinate counties of Cheshire (see below) and Durham acquired them only after reform in 1536. There were also a few special sub-county peculiars, such as the Royal Liberty of Havering-atte-Bower, in Essex, which was created in 1465 by royal charter, and comprised the very large parish of Hornchurch, including Havering and Romford. It had its own court of quarter sessions, which survived until 1892.[190]

Justices of the peace, rather than professional Westminster judges, presided over these hearings, albeit that the latter were often appointed as JPs and so might be found on the bench (see above). One of those present, usually a senior and experienced magistrate, would normally preside over the hearing by, for example, addressing the jury and controlling other aspects of proceedings. (Some boroughs would appoint

---

188. Cockburn, *A History of English Assizes*, p. 84.
189. Knafla, *Kent at Law 1602*, p. xviii.
190. F. G. Emmison (ed.), *Guide to the Essex Quarter Sessions and Other Official Records* (Colchester: Essex Archaeological Society, 1946), p. 81.

a professional lawyer as their recorder to do this). For example, at the Essex Quarter Sessions at Chelmsford in 1595, Sir Thomas Mildmay, who had been a magistrate for the county since 1571 and was a major local gentleman, performed this important function.[191]

Even so, there was always a degree of collegiality in the decisions of a quarter sessions bench. This sometimes became fractured, occasioning problems in a forensic environment. In September 1574, William More noted that John Agmondesham had been awkward at the recent Surrey Quarter Sessions held in Kingston (the two magistrates had a difficult relationship), taking the side of two men accused of various offences, including stealing rabbits from a park, against the views of the rest of the justices on the bench.[192] Such disagreements might influence the manner in which the trial jury would be directed on a case.

At quarter sessions, the JPs would receive professional assistance and legal advice from the clerk of the peace for the county, who was usually a man of reasonable social standing, with some education and legal experience, albeit normally inferior in this regard to the clerk of assizes. For example, in Elizabethan Essex, all the clerks of the peace had attended an Inn of Court, but none had been called to the Bar, and only one had obtained a university degree.[193] Clerks of the peace normally served for a period of years, sometimes decades, acquiring considerable experience. For example, in Wiltshire, Christopher Dysmers was clerk between 1537 and 1567; his successor, Walter Berington, served for 13 years.[194] This position had been salaried from its inception in the late 1300s.[195] As the JPs acquired extensive administrative functions, the holder of this post became one of the county's main professional administrators.[196]

At quarter sessions, the clerk of the peace would enroll proceedings, read out indictments, commissions, and writs, become involved in the preparation of bills of indictment and other documents, arraign prisoners,

---

191. ERO Q/SR 131/2–5.

192. SHC LM/COR/3/647.

193. Samaha, *Law and Order*, p. 90.

194. R. B. Pugh and Elizabeth Crittall (eds.), *A History of the County of Wiltshire: Vol. 5* (London: Victoria County History, 1957), pp. 80–110.

195. Forster, *The East Riding Justices*, p. 13.

196. Ben Howell, *Law and Disorder in Tudor Monmouthshire* (Chesterfield: Merton Priory Press, 1995), p. lxxiv.

and (sometimes) advise the JPs, as well as conducting various administrative functions. Several inferior clerks and scribes supported them.

Until 1545 the position of the clerk of the peace was in the gift of the Crown; this seems to have risked unqualified men being appointed as an exercise in local patronage, and after that time the *Custos Rotulorum* — the most senior of the JPs and often, after the 1540s, the lord lieutenant of the county — usually acquired this responsibility, and the clerk held his position on the former's sufferance.[197] Nevertheless, legal offices in the palatinate of Lancaster continued to be granted by the Crown, and these included the clerk of the peace, who was appointed, usually for life, by letters patent issued under palatinate seals. These were normally given in exchange for a substantial payment to the Crown (seen as an investment on future returns). Non-legally qualified office-holders continued to be appointed in Lancashire, employing a lawyer deputy to do the work on their behalf. (It was not a sinecure, and any failure to carry out the duties properly could lead to a cancellation of the letters patent.) Thus, in May 1589 Roger Rigby purchased the clerkship of the peace in the county. He was not a lawyer, and so chose his cousin, Alexander Rigby, as his deputy. Alexander was an attorney, and had (in part) been educated at Gray's Inn. He received half the annual fees and profits after the first £20 had been paid to Roger.[198]

An Act of 1388 provided that quarter sessions were to be held, as their name suggests, every three months, and it remained the rule that: "Justyces of Peas shall holde theyr Cessyons iiii tymes of the yere". In 1414 statute regulated the times when they would be conducted. They were usually held at Epiphany, Easter, the Feast of St Thomas, and Michaelmas. At the appropriate time, the clerk of the peace would draw up a precept (writ or warrant) for holding the sessions; this was then signed by the county JPs, and directed the sheriff to return panels of grand and petty jurors.[199]

It seems that, very occasionally, a few counties failed to meet the quarterly requirement. Thus, in Essex, during the early Elizabethan era,

---

197. Baker, *Oxford History*, p. 268.
198. Bagley, "Kenyon V. Rigby", pp. 34–37.
199. DRO DQS p. 8 and p. 17.

they were sometimes held only three times a year, although later in that period the requisite four sessions were being conducted. It may, occasionally, have happened in Devonshire. According to John Hooker, the gaol fever at the Black Assizes at Exeter in 1586 prompted Lord Chief Justice Anderson to try to reduce the prison population by insisting that quarter sessions were "not to be passed anie more over, as in times past until the assises". By contrast, if pressure of business made it convenient, counties could hold "more [Quarter] cessyons if nede be after theyr dyscrecyon".[200] These were often termed "special" or "statute" sessions, frequently limited to a specific hundred, and presided over by a minimum of two magistrates, at least one of whom was of the quorum. For example, in December 1603 special sessions were held at Stanway for the hundred of Lexden and half-hundred of Winstree before two Essex JPs, Charles Chilborne and John Darcey.[201]

Such sessions were a fairly regular phenomenon. In the early years the reign of Henry VIII, Kentish JPs held extra quarter sessions at Canterbury in December 1522, 1524, 1530, and 1533, and at Maidstone in December 1528.[202] In the same county, in June 1582, William Lambarde noted: "I and others held a special gaol delivery at Maidstone, for the rogues, at which we adjudged 17 and punished them".[203] Similarly, special sessions of the peace were held on at least three occasions in Wiltshire during the years from 1574 to 1592, these being at Salisbury in August 1584 (before just two JPs); Hyndon in October 1586; and Salisbury in December 1592 (before at least six JPs). However, in this last county they were primarily held to deal with administrative matters rather than to conduct criminal trials.

There was a huge variety in the arrangements produced by differing shires for holding their quarter sessions.[204] The four regular dates did not necessarily mean that each part of a county would be covered by four sessions. Large shires were often subdivided for this purpose. Thus, in Kent, although there was only one commission of the peace from the

---

200. Glazebrook, *The Boke of Justices of Peas*, f. Aiii.
201. ERO Q/SR 182/18.
202. Zell, "Early Tudor JPs at Work", p. 137.
203. Read, "William Lambarde's 'Ephemeris,'" p. 139.
204. B. W. Quintrell (ed.), *Proceedings of the Lancashire Justices of the Peace at the Sheriff's Table During Assizes Week, 1578–1694* (Liverpool: Record Society of Lancashire and Cheshire, 1981), p. 4.

mid-fifteenth century onwards, the justices acted in two divisions. The eastern division would normally hold their quarter sessions at Canterbury, the western at Maidstone. Justices mainly acted in the division in which they resided, although a small coterie of assiduous men from the mid-Kent area covered both locations and helped preserve consistency of approach between benches in the West and East. Many lower-ranking officials attended only one division.

During the sixteenth century, quarter sessions were held only twice in each part of Kent: at Epiphany and Midsummer in the East, and at Easter and Michaelmas in the West. William Lambarde thought this deplorable, as it meant that each division (effectively) had only a biannual court.[205] It should also be noted that, at various times, several other Kentish towns (to Maidstone and Canterbury) were pressed into service to host quarter sessions for their halves of the county. For example, Dartford was used in August 1515, Goudhurst in June 1520, Sittingbourne in July 1519, Sevenoaks in February 1520 and August 1542, Gravesend in January 1522, and Wingham in May 1545.[206]

The venues for the Wiltshire Quarter Sessions were not rigidly fixed during the Tudor era, but from the final decades of the sixteenth century they tended to follow a fairly consistent pattern: Salisbury for the Hilary Quarter Sessions; Warminster for those held at Easter; Devizes at Midsummer; and Marlborough at Michaelmas. This was not a binding arrangement, and there was considerable variation, especially between 1575 and 1587. (At various times, Calne, Chippenham, Hindon, and Trowbridge all hosted quarter sessions). Unlike Kent, each location would serve for the entire county.[207]

In sixteenth century Norfolk, quarter sessions were often held four times a year at each of four venues, Norwich, Bishop's (the future King's) Lynn, Little Walsingham, and Swaffham, so producing sixteen 'sittings.'[208] In Cheshire there were four locations for the post-1536 county quarter sessions, but unlike Norfolk (and like Wiltshire) normally only one sitting per quarter. These were held at Chester at Epiphany, Knutsford

---

205. Melling, *Crime and Punishment*, p. 9 and p. 44.
206. Zell, "Early Tudor JPs at Work", p. 137.
207. Pugh and Crittall, *A History of the County of Wiltshire: Vol. 5*, pp. 80–110.
208. NRO C/S 3/roll 1.

at Easter, Nantwich at Midsummer, and Northwich or Middlewich at Michaelmas.[209] In County Durham, quarter sessions were first held in 1312, and were usually conducted in Durham Castle, but were also sometimes held in Bishop Auckland, Stanhope, and other locations.[210] In Lancashire the quarter sessions met four times a year in each of four locations (as in Norfolk), although JPs usually attended only their local court. By the late sixteenth century, only the *Custos Rotulorum*, the clerk of the peace, and his staff would normally make the journey through the whole of Lancashire, attending each sitting in turn.[211]

Yorkshire, the largest county in England, was divided into three ridings, each of which had much of the administrative status of a county, although they shared a high sheriff. Each riding had its own court of quarter sessions, sitting four times a year. In the West Riding the location and number of sittings for quarter sessions varied greatly, according to the season. In 1598 its Epiphany Sessions were held at Doncaster, Leeds, and Wetherby over one January week. There was just one sitting at Easter, held at Pontefract and four sittings, spread out over several weeks, at midsummer, at Knaresborough, Skipton, Barnsley, and Wakefield. At Michaelmas there were three sittings over a week in early October, these being held at Rotherham, Wakefield, and Knaresborough.[212] Lincolnshire, the second-largest county, was also subdivided, in this case into three "parts" (Lindsey, Kesteven, and Holland), each of which had their own system of quarter sessions.

Of course, in most counties, and as with the assizes, JPs from peripheral areas would not be able to commute to quarter sessions daily from their homes, and would have to stay at inns or with local gentlemen. Thus, in about 1552, William Fitzwilliam asked the Surrey JPs what day they had appointed for their next quarter sessions, noting that "if you will sit on your commission in these parts I pray you with the rest of the gents to take a bed with me".[213]

---

209. J. S. Morrill, *The Cheshire Grand Jury 1625–1659, A Social and Administrative Study* (Leicester: Leicester University Press, 1976), p. 9.

210. Durham Record Office DQS 9.

211. Quintrell, *Proceedings*, p. 7.

212. Lister, *West Riding Sessions Rolls*, p. xl.

213. SHC LM/COR/3/235.

Urban counties, such as Norwich, had their own quarter sessions. For example, when, in 1537, Henry VIII gave the city of Exeter this status, he also granted its mayor and aldermen the right to sit as justices of the peace with the power of gaol delivery. As a result, there were two courts of quarter sessions based in Exeter, one for Devonshire and one for the urban county itself. The latter's JPs presided over the Exeter Quarter Sessions with the assistance of a recorder.[214]

Court Buildings

Quarter sessions were often held in the same buildings used for assizes. For example, those conducted for Essex in March 1594 were heard at the Sessions House in Chelmsford, just two weeks after the Lent Assizes had been held in the same place.[215] This meant that, as with the assizes (and unlike Elizabethan Chelmsford), most quarter sessions were not conducted in purpose-built buildings. Typically, the Rutland Quarter Sessions were held in the same great hall in Oakham Castle used by the higher jury court.[216]

Duration

Sittings at Tudor Quarter Sessions could last from a day to three days (the normal maximum). Typically, each quarter sessions in Kent during the 1540s lasted between one and two days, as they had done since late medieval times. There appears to have been a slight increase in average length during the late sixteenth century, as workloads grew, so that a minimum of two days became standard in this South-eastern county. Thus a total of seven days were spent sitting in 1520, and again in 1527, 1536 and 1537. Sittings took four days (a day per sessions) in 1540 and 1545, but eight days (two days per sessions) in 1542 and 1552.[217] Under the early Stuarts, the Wiltshire Quarter Sessions usually lasted one or

---

214. Stoyle, "'It Is But an Olde Wytche Gonne,'" 2011, pp. 129–135.
215. Samaha, *Law and Order*, p. 96.
216. T. H. McK. Clough, *Oakham Castle: A Guide and History* (Oakham: Rutland County Council, 1999), pp. 14–17.
217. Zell, "Early Tudor JPs at Work", p. 139.

two days, and only occasionally extended to three days.[218] In the East Riding of Yorkshire, entries in the Treasury records for wages paid to the clerk of the peace suggest that one or two days was usually sufficient.[219]

JPs' Attendance

Magistrates' attendance at quarter sessions varied greatly. Many county JPs went to only one a year, some to two, a few to three, and only a handful of diligent men attended all four. In a few years and counties, half the members of the commission did not appear at all.[220] Attendance at individual quarter sessions within a county also fluctuated greatly, depending on locality, season, decade (numbers increased as commissions expanded), and the administrative arrangement employed by the county. Winter was unpopular in some counties, although in Essex, in the late Elizabethan period, the frequent addition of a gaol delivery to the Epiphany Sessions seems to have encouraged more JPs to be present, despite the weather.

For example, on one occasion in 1526 the Essex Quarter Sessions were held at Chelmsford before just four JPs, albeit all men of rank: Sir Thomas Nicolls, Sir Thomas Franke, Sir Mathias Bradbury, and Sir Edward Riche.[221] By contrast, towards the end of the century, a dozen JPs were in attendance at the Michaelmas Quarter Sessions held at Chelmsford in 1595, even though they were general sessions, with no gaol delivery, and dealt only with minor matters.[222] (Elizabethan Essex generally saw good levels of attendance). In Kent the Midsummer Sessions held at Maidstone in 1539 had six JPs present, but those at Canterbury the following Michaelmas were attended by 15 men.[223] In Wiltshire, during the late sixteenth century, quarter sessions would normally attract between eight and eleven JPs, but sometimes there were far fewer. At those held at Devizes in July 1576, only three justices were present, and at the

---

218. Pugh and Crittall, *A History of the County of Wiltshire: Vol. 5*, pp. 80–110.
219. Forster, *The East Riding Justices of the Peace*, p. 30.
220. Hurstfield, *Freedom, Corruption and Government*, p. 259.
221. ERO Q/SR 17/52.
222. ERO Q/SR 131/2–5.
223. Zell, "Early Tudor JPs at Work", p. 138.

Michaelmas Sessions in the same town some 15 months later it seems that the (legal) minimum of two men were in attendance. Similarly, at the Michaelmas Sessions held two years further on again at Chippenham, just two justices appeared. However, the Easter Sessions at Warminster in 1586 saw the presence of 16 magistrates.[224] In Lancashire, even in the late sixteenth century, the sessions benches rarely mustered more than a dozen magistrates and sometimes as few as three or four.[225]

Borough Sessions

By the start of the Tudor era, many incorporated towns had long excluded county JPs from their affairs and conducted their own quarter sessions, which were often termed borough sessions, pursuant to royally granted charters. For example, in 1468, and largely at the behest of Lord Wen-lock, the Chief Butler of England, Edward IV granted a charter giving Much Wenlock in Shropshire the status of a "free borough incorporate". Among the many privileges conferred was the right to hold its own sessions.[226] It was not the only borough in Shropshire to acquire this status, which was also granted, at various times, to Bridgnorth, Lud-low, Oswestry, and Bishop's Castle. Similarly, in Essex the boroughs of Colchester, Maldon, Harwich, Saffron Walden, and Thaxted also held borough sessions. Although Brightlingsea did not have such status, it was exempt from county quarter sessions as a limb of the Cinque Port of Sandwich (the only one north of the River Thames).[227]

In some chartered towns, borough sessions were not necessarily held four times a year (whatever the theory). For example, under Colchester's charter of 1447, sessions were normally called just three times annually, with extra sessions being scheduled on an ad hoc basis to deal with special situations. Thus additional borough sessions appear to have been held in the town before the bailiffs and four other justices in December 1516,

---

224. Pugh and Crittall, *A History of the County of Wiltshire: Vol. 5*, pp. 80–110.
225. Quintrell, *Proceedings of the Lancashire Justices of the Peace*, p. 7.
226. A. P. Baggs, G. C. Baugh, D. C. Cox, Jessie McFall, and P A Stamper, "The Liberty and Borough of Wenlock", in G. C. Baugh (ed.), *A History of the County of Shropshire: Vol. 10, Munslow Hundred (Part), the Liberty and Borough of Wenlock* (London: Victoria County History, 1998), pp. 187–212.
227. Emmison, *Guide to the Essex Quarter Sessions*, p. 30.

to deal with the consequences of a local riot.[228] Another ad hoc sessions was held there in 1538 to deal with the aftermath of an enclosure disturbance. By contrast, Winchester, which had first been granted the right to hold its own court of quarter sessions by Henry VI in 1442, always held the full four sessions a year.

In these boroughs, the magistrates who heard interlocutory criminal matters (the examination of suspects etc.) and presided over borough sessions were normally drawn from senior officeholders. Typically, in Winchester, the mayor, recorder, and aldermen acted as JPs. In Colchester hearings were normally presided over by the mayor, its two bailiffs, and four senior members of its complement of aldermen. In Much Wenlock the recorder and bailiff (the latter elected by its burgesses) provided its justices of gaol delivery and of the peace.[229]

Judicial personnel aside, borough sessions were very similar to the quarter sessions held for the surrounding county. In 1514 a newly appointed town clerk in Colchester noted that they functioned by "hearing and determining divers felonies and other misdeeds".[230] These included capital cases. Much Wenlock periodically convicted and executed felons when exercising its power of gaol delivery from the end of the 1460s. Despite the small size of the town, three convicts were hanged there on a single occasion in February 1541.[231]

After the first half of the sixteenth century, and like county quarter sessions, some chartered towns began to remit their very serious cases, such as local murders, to the county assizes for determination. For example, in April 1596 the Mayor and Recorder of Oxford initially proposed to try a townsman named Winckle, who was accused of murdering the Warden of New College's servant, by virtue of their Commission of Oyer and Terminer. The Privy Council, aware that a locally-recruited jury might be partial towards a townsman, advised that Winckle be tried at the county assizes to prevent such suspicion arising.[232] However, a handful of

228. ERO D/B 5 Sr1.
229. Baugh, *A History of the County of Shropshire: Vol. 10*, pp. 187–212.
230. Higgs, *Godliness and Governance*, p. 17.
231. Charles Henry Hartshorne (ed.), *Extracts from the Register of Sir Thomas Butler, Vicar of Much Wenlock, in Shropshire* (Tenby: R. Mason, 1861), p. 11.
232. Harrison, *A Second Elizabethan Journal*, p. 90.

boroughs, such as King's Lynn and Great Yarmouth, in Norfolk, jealously guarded their charter rights, successfully resisted the centralising forces coming from London, and preserved their right to determine the most serious crimes in their own forums, and to execute those found guilty in their towns, even during the seventeenth and eighteenth centuries.

Most boroughs used their civic buildings as a forum for such hearings. However, Much Wenlock acquired a fine courtroom for borough sessions in 1540, after the dissolution of the local priory. (It was also the forum for local petty sessions, the bailiff's court, and a manorial leet court).[233]

Distribution of Work in Assizes and Quarter Sessions

Throughout the Tudor era there was an almost total overlap between the criminal cases that could, in theory, be tried on indictment before JPs and a jury sitting at quarter, special, or borough sessions and those that could be heard by a judge and jury at assizes or the Old Bailey. Treason was the only significant exception; it could not be heard in the lower jury court because JPs did not have authority to determine such matters; as a result, several coining offences were also excluded from their purview.

More significantly, during the late medieval and early Tudor period, there was also a significant overlap in practice in trial jurisdiction. Unsurprisingly, the quarter sessions spent a great deal of time dealing with misdemeanours, such as assault, lesser forms of poaching, playing unlawful games, practising surgery without a licence, and harbouring idle persons.[234] Nevertheless, they also dealt with many serious felonies. For much of the fifteenth century, homicide cases were regularly heard before quarter sessions, if not as frequently as they were at assizes. For example, in January 1472 the Durham Quarter Sessions conducted the trial emanating from a murder that had occurred in Weardale, in which eight labourers armed with axes and clubs had attacked and killed one Richard Warde.[235] In September 1506 Richard Pulham was indicted and convicted at the Canterbury Quarter Sessions for killing John a Wode

233. Hartshorne, *Extracts from the Register of Sir Thomas Butler*, p. 11.
234. Baker, *Oxford History*, pp. 272–273.
235. Durham Record Office DQS p. 21.

with a pikestaff the previous month.[236] A scrutiny of just under two-thirds of the records for the Norfolk Quarter Sessions, held in Norwich, Walsingham, and Lynn from 1532 to 1533 (about 330 parchment slips in total), probably the oldest that have been preserved for a shire county in England, reveal at least two murders, one of the victims being a woman.[237]

The Norfolk papers also include at least three rapes, as well as numerous cases of burglary and theft, along with the usual litany of assaults, instances of hunting with dogs without the necessary qualifying wealth, pulling down houses, etc.[238] Closer to London, in 1536, Thomas Stidolph, a Surrey JP, suggested to the Privy Council that the trial of a heinous case involving rape, robbery, and what appears to have been attempted murder, would set a good and timely example to local troublemakers if held at Surrey Quarter Sessions.[239]

Conversely, it was always accepted that the assizes might determine misdemeanours and petty thefts if they had the time and inclination to do so (as was often the case). The experience of John Barlo, the Dean of Westbury, in Wiltshire, in 1536, is indicative of this overlap between forums for minor offences. In November that year, he wrote to Thomas Cromwell, complaining that the previous Michaelmas Day, as he was riding to the quarter sessions at Gloucester, he came across 14 "evil-disposed" people playing the unlawful game of "tennis" during morning service at Yate, in Gloucestershire. They fled when they saw him, but he obtained some of their names, with a view to prosecuting them at the very quarter sessions to which he was travelling. (Given its timing, the matter might also have been referred to an ecclesiastical court). Unfortunately, Yate was where the powerful dowager Lady Anne Berkeley (the widow of Thomas, Lord Berkeley) dwelled, and some of the tennis players were her retainers. When he reached Gloucester, Barlo found that another group of Berkeley's servants was to serve as petty jurors at the sessions. Convinced that this would preclude any possibility of a conviction, he

---

236. McSheffrey, "Sanctuary Seekers".
237. NRO C/S 3/1; I am grateful to Tom Townshend at the Norfolk Record Office for this information.
238. *Ibid.*
239. Robison, "Murder at Crowhurst", p. 60; NA SP III 03/220.

deferred prosecuting the players to the next assizes.[240] Similarly, numerous cases that were indicted as petty theft were still being heard at the Surrey Assizes in the early 1600s.

This situation began to change during the mid to late Tudor period, at least with regard to the lower jury forum's willingness to try grave felonies. Even as sixteenth century JPs acquired dominance over the trial of minor criminal matters at the expense of leet courts and other low-level forums, they gradually lost responsibility for trying serious crimes, ceding it to the justices of assizes. Several factors contributed to the JPs' withdrawal from such work.

As the sixteenth century advanced, there was increasing concern at the legal competence of many magistrates presiding over quarter sessions. As early as 1489, they had been required to read out a proclamation at the start of the sessions, clearly defining their powers and noting that grievances against a JP or his decisions could be referred to an assize court or direct to the king. (The evidence suggests that this rarely happened.)[241] Nevertheless, there were regular complaints about their performance. In 1539 the Bishop of Llandaff wrote to Thomas Cromwell, claiming that John Horsley, before giving up the shrievalty of Northumberland, had arranged what he called a privy sessions and gaol delivery, which had been poorly conducted by local JPs. The bishop complained that an impoverished "pykar" (pilferer) had been executed for grand larceny after stealing out of need, while a wilful murderer and two other felons had been acquitted.[242]

This slowly developing reluctance to send the most serious crimes to the lower jury forum appears to have accelerated swiftly after the advent of the Marian statutes in the mid-1550s. According to William Lambarde, writing in 1581, the provision in these acts by which JPs were directed to certify their examinations to the "next general Gaol Delivery" was often interpreted as meaning to the following assizes, rather than their own quarter sessions. Although this did not reduce the JPs' theoretical powers

240. Gairdner, *Letters and Papers, Foreign and Domestic. Henry VIII: Vol. 11*, pp. 418–435.
241. Roger Lockyer and Andrew Thrush, *Henry VII* (Abingdon: Routledge, 2014), p. 47.
242. James Gairdner and R. H. Brodie, *Letters and Papers, Foreign and Domestic, Henry VIII, Vol. 14, Part 1, January-July 1539* (London: HMSO, 1894), pp. 22–29.

(which continued unabated), it made it less likely that they would actually exercise them.[243]

Furthermore, by the Elizabethan period, the Privy Council was regularly reiterating the importance of reserving serious matters to the assizes. This was also stressed by the reformed commission of the peace of 1590, which, although still permitting quarter sessions to determine felonies, qualified this with a *casus difficultatis* clause, inserted at the instigation of Lord Chief Justice Wray, insisting that difficult cases be sent to the higher jury forum. This was sometimes interpreted to mean that felonies likely to result in actual, not commuted, death sentences if proved, as well as cases that were legally complicated (the proper interpretation of the clause), should be left for the superior court.

As a result, clerks of the peace at quarter sessions might pass on indictments that had been entered in their own forums to the assizes for trial, where JPs felt this appropriate in light of their gravity or complexity. (Local convenience also played a role, and clerks of assizes sometimes sent lesser matters to the lower jury court if they were under pressure of time). For example, the Essex Assizes held at Brentwood in February 1559 heard as many cases (and more defendants) that had been returned *billa verra* (granting an indictment) several months earlier by a quarter sessions grand jury, and then committed to the higher court, as it did offences that had been processed by its own grand jury. Most of the former had been considered by a 15-man grand jury at the Michaelmas Quarter Sessions held at Chelmsford in early October 1558, although the Epiphany Quarter Sessions conducted at the same town at the beginning of January 1559 sent up one man for trial. Such individuals were committed to the higher forum for burglary, horse theft, cattle theft, and serious cases of grand larceny.

Interestingly, the four-man bench at the county's October Quarter Sessions in 1558 included Richard Weston (1527–1572), the Solicitor General, who had been an Essex JP since 1554, and who would go on to be a serjeant-at-law and judge of the Common Pleas. Also present was Sir Humphrey Brown (1522–1558), already a judge of that court, who owned

---

243. Langbein, *Prosecuting Crime*, p. 106.

a manor in the same county. Ostensibly, it would seem that the requirement that two men who were learned in the law should be present to exercise gaol delivery at the lower jury court had been met. The decision to send a case up from the hearing at Epiphany is less surprising. The sessions had, apparently, been presided over by just two men. One of them, William Bendlowes, was an active professional lawyer (and noted legal author) having been a serjeant-at-law since 1555. However, the other JP, William Strangman, may not have been legally qualified.[244] Similarly, two years later, indictments for burglary and grand larceny approved by the county quarter sessions at Chelmsford in January 1561 were referred to the assizes that were held in the same town the following March, although Richard Weston (who was a judge by then) and William Bendlowes were present on the bench.[245]

As a result of these developments, from the 1550s onwards many quarter sessions began to focus the bulk of their attention on petty theft; misdemeanours, such as assault, poaching, and trespass; regulatory prosecutions, such as drunkenness, selling ale without a licence, lesser forms of vagrancy, swearing, gaming, Sabbath-breaking, and harbouring rogues; and prosecutions of those who had abused or neglected an appointed office, such as lazy or incompetent parish constables. Essentially, the courts would "inquyre of the common annoyances of the king's leege people".[246]

Nevertheless, lesser felonies (in addition to petty theft) were still heard at most of the country's lower jury courts. Thus in 1595 the judge Sir Robert Clarke, who regularly presided over the assizes for Essex and was also on its commission of the peace, urged its sheriff to hold a gaol delivery at the following quarter sessions, at the "request of the Keeper of the Gaol of Colchester because he is charged with many more prisoners than he is able to maintain and the offences are of no great moment". As it transpired, Clarke himself sat on the bench at this quarter sessions, by dint of his position as a JP.[247]

---

244. Cockburn, *Calendar of Assize Records. Essex Indictments: Elizabeth I*, pp. 3–4.
245. *Ibid*, pp. 18–19.
246. Holinshed, *The First Volume of the Chronicles*, p. 75.
247. Langbein, *Prosecuting Crime*, p. 108.

By then, grand larceny was by far the most common felony prosecuted at quarter sessions. In some counties, such as Worcestershire, it was almost the only such crime that was still tried at this forum (ignoring petty theft). There were good reasons for this. It did not occasion the popular alarm that some other felonies did. There were also numerous opportunities to make it a non-capital offence in all but the most undeserving cases. Frequently only the gravest examples of the crime, established on the most unequivocal evidence, produced a conviction for the full offence rather than one for petty larceny (see *Chapter 14*). For example, at the Michaelmas Quarter Sessions for Essex in 1591, Matthew Crabb was indicted for stealing a scythe worth two shillings, a kettle worth four shillings, and 30 pounds of feathers worth ten shillings. He was found guilty of petty larceny to the value of ten pence for the scythe, and acquitted of the remaining offences.[248] Even when a conviction for the full offence was returned, magistrates could, in suitable cases, encourage the granting of clergy or a finding of pregnancy.

By the final years of Queen Elizabeth's reign, a few county quarter sessions were even becoming slightly reluctant to hear cases of clergyable grand larceny. For example, only three instances came before those in Worcestershire in 1600 and 1601. Thus, in 1600 Roger Phillips of Bredon was accused of stealing a cartload of wheat. At the same sessions George Saunders was indicted for stealing a cartload of hay (worth 20s). More seriously, the following year, William Graynger was prosecuted for entering a dwelling house and stealing £6 8s.[249] By then, the Wiltshire quarter sessions were equally cautious about hearing such cases. This helps to explain the view of the magistrate and legal author William Lambarde, expressed as early as 1581, that JPs were no longer heavily involved with the trial of felonies, and would normally defer a serious felony "til the coming of the Justices of asizes".[250]

Nevertheless, a few counties apart, this was an exaggeration. Large numbers of often quite serious cases of theft would be heard at such

---

248. ERO Q/SR 118/104.
249. J. W. Willis Bund (ed.), *Worcestershire County Records: The Quarter Sessions Rolls, Vol. I: 1591–1643* (Worcester: Worcestershire County Council, 1900), pp. 28–39.
250. Peter Lawson, "Property Crime and Hard Times in England, 1559–1624", *Law and History Review*, Vol. 4, Issue 1, p. 101.

courts until well into the eighteenth century. More pertinently, felonies that had been put beyond the remit of clergy, such as horse theft, pick-pocketing, and burglary, were still being heard at quarter sessions in at least some parts of the country long after 1581, while occasional rapes, robberies, manslaughters, and even murders were also sometimes found at these forums.

For example, at the Shropshire Quarter Sessions held at Shrewsbury in November 1580, 25 people were convicted of capital felonies, with four being executed.[251] Similarly, in the year from 1576 to 1577, at quarter sessions for the Anglo-Welsh county of Monmouthshire, four death penalties were passed after conviction for unclergyable felonies. Thus, at those held in Newport in January 1577, John Lewis and George Baker were sentenced to death for stealing a purse containing £3. (Interestingly, this disposal may have been reviewed at the county assizes.) At the same sessions, John Jevan was convicted and sentenced to death for horse theft. Most seriously, at the Usk Quarter Sessions in June 1577, John Williams Sr. was convicted of murdering John Williams Jr. (his son?) with a dagger and sentenced to death. By contrast the two county assizes sessions passed just five death sentences in the same year (at least four for animal theft).[252]

One reason for the continuing involvement of at least some quarter sessions in trying serious felonies was the sheer amount of criminal work found in parts of the country. As a result, county magistrates in these areas still committed many felony cases to such forums *ab initio*, while the local assizes often remitted felonies that they did not have time to try back to the lower court. Indicative of this overlap, in 1585 Henry Gray wrote to Sir Thomas Mildmay and the other JPs attending the forthcoming Essex Quarter Sessions, noting that one Edward Bell had stolen his sparrowhawks and been bound over to appear before them for trial. Unfortunately, Gray's business commitments meant that he could not attend the hearing himself. Even so, he asked that Bell might have the same judgment that others had had when tried at the assizes for similar

---

251. Barrett and Harrison, *Crime and Punishment,* p. 65.
252. Howell, *Law and Disorder,* p. 30 and p. 69.

offences.[253] Similarly, in September the following year, William Cecil, Lord Burghley and Thomas Bromley, the Lord Chancellor, wrote to the Surrey JPs asking that Reynold Underwood, who was in the White Lion Prison in Southwark accused of stealing geldings and mares from three men, be tried at the next quarter sessions in Kingston.[254] That these counties were both on the Home Circuit may not have been a coincidence.

The situation in Kent is indicative of the impact on court allocation of the generally high caseloads found in some parts of the South East, even at the very end of the period. In 1596 concern about the "great number" of inmates being held in the county and their attendant expense prompted the authorities to urge all JPs in the lathes (administrative divisions) of Aylesford and Sutton-at-Hone to send the recognisances and examinations that they had taken for burglaries and "small felonyes" to the following quarter sessions, as a matter of urgency.[255] In the following two years, Kent JPs sitting at quarter sessions were commissioned to hold nine gaol deliveries, above and beyond those being heard by the assizes, although only about 60 cases were tried, and 25 men, mainly (unclergyable) horse thieves and burglars, were convicted and condemned to death. A few years further on again, in 1602, the Kent Quarter Sessions tried 51 cases of grand larceny, nine more than the county assizes, including a higher number that were valued at over £5. In the same year, they determined five cases of horse theft, eight of burglary, and even one case of (clergyable) manslaughter.[256]

There were some logistical advantages in using quarter sessions to deal with felonies. If a crime were processed just after the assizes, the suspects would have to remain in prison for about six months before coming for trial, rather than a maximum of three if it could be heard at the following quarter sessions. Furthermore, a delay of even a few months might not assuage public concern about heinous offences, such as cold-blooded murder, and would undermine the deterrent effect of the law, particularly in the counties around London. This had been stressed in 1557, during the reign of Queen Mary, when the Surrey magistrates had been

---

253. ERO Q/SR 94/28.35.
254. SHC 6729/11/31.
255. Melling, *Crime and Punishment*, p. 212.
256. Knafla, *Kent at Law 1602*, p. xxi.

urged by the Crown to deal swiftly with murders according to a special commission of oyer and terminer. More specifically, in February 1564 the Privy Council, then at Windsor Castle, wrote to the Surrey JPs Sir Henry Weston, William More, and Richard Bydon noting that it had procured a special commission of oyer and terminer under which the three magistrates were to arraign three people named in earlier letters as having robbed and murdered a man from Walton-on-Thames. However, the council stressed that they should not go further, and "deliver" the whole county gaol. All other prisoners in custody were to be tried at the following assizes in July or August.[257]

In early November 1593, the Surrey JPs reported to the court on the arrest of seven men suspected of burglary from a barn at Ewhurst. Their alleged ringleader, a man named Edmund Strudwick, was being held in Guildford Prison. The magistrates asked that a commission of oyer and terminer be issued to deal with them, as the gang had placed people in fear not only of being robbed but also of being physically harmed, as some of their victims had been tortured with firebrands and lit candles to make them reveal where their cash was hidden.[258] Two weeks later, Sir John Wolley (a member of the Privy Council) sent a message to William More with a commission of oyer and terminer for proceeding against the men. He thought that executing the chief offenders would be a terror to the rest.[259]

Even so, the South East was certainly not unique in having its quarter sessions determining unclergyable felonies in the final decades of the Tudor period. In September 1596, the Somerset JP Edmund Hext noted that it was vital that the lower jury forum of the county deliver its gaol, as the numbers incarcerated would not otherwise be manageable.[260] Devonshire, on the same Western Circuit, was something of an extreme case in this regard, even at the close of the era. For example, in 1598, at Epiphany Quarter Sessions, 18 felons out of 65 who had been tried were convicted and hanged. At the Easter Sessions that year, 12 out of 41 prisoners were convicted and executed. At the Midsummer

---

257. SHC 6729/10/24.
258. LM/COR/3/523.
259. LM/COR/3/524.
260. Key and Bucholz, *Sources and Debates*, pp. 128–129.

Sessions, eight out of 35 prisoners came into this category. The Michaelmas Sessions for 1598 produced a much more modest death toll. Just one felon out of 25 who were tried was hanged. This produces a total of 39 executions for the year. By contrast, at the Lent Assizes for Devon in the same year, only 17 convicts were sentenced to death. At the next (and slightly belated) assizes, held in the autumn of 1598, 18 prisoners out of 87 were hanged, producing a total of 35 for the year. Thus over half of the annual total of 74 convicts that were sentenced to death came from the county's quarter sessions rather than its assizes.[261]

The defendants tried at the Devonshire Quarter Sessions in July 1598 can be considered in more detail. They included, among others, one horse thief, three pickpockets, a housebreaker, a sheep thief, and a woman who received stolen goods. In one case the crime is unknown, as the document has become corrupted. The first four were accused of unclergyable offences. The housebreaker's crime may have fallen into the same category, depending on circumstances. However, seven people were convicted of grand larceny and clergied, and another seven were acquitted of theft and receiving stolen goods. Thirteen people were flogged, which is indicative of convictions for petty theft. Some of these were most likely indicted for petty larceny *ab initio*; for example, William Ackland was accused of stealing some cheese. However, others, such as Phineas Horsham and Gregory Talman, separately accused of sheep stealing, must have been the beneficiaries of complainant or (more likely) jury down-valuing in what (legally) should have been grand-larceny indictments.[262]

Thereafter, the number of hangings originating in this forum fell quickly. No-one was executed in Devon after conviction at quarter sessions in 1601, and the annual total never again exceeded seven people during the ensuing 30 years.[263] Nevertheless, such cases continued to occur, on a modest scale, for many years after the turn of the century.

For a detailed and specific example from the West Country, can be considered the case of Thomasine Short, who was tried for capital witchcraft (under the 1563 act) at the (county of) Exeter Quarter Sessions in

---

261. Hamilton, *Quarter Sessions*, p. 30.
262. *Ibid*, pp. 33–34.
263. Cockburn, *A History of English Assizes*, pp. 94–95.

1581. During the 1530s Henry VIII had granted its mayor and aldermen the right to sit as justices of the peace with the power of gaol delivery. Short was probably already known to the city magistrates, which cannot have helped her case. Less than 20 years earlier she appears to have been ducked in the city's river for "scolding", and some years after that she may have been bailed for an unspecified felony. On this occasion it was alleged that in September 1580 she had threatened the family members of a local weaver, several of whom had subsequently died. Short was accused of murdering them by witchcraft, and committed to prison by the mayor in his capacity as an *ex officio* justice for the city. The sessions' grand jury returned all three allegations against her as "true bills". Twelve witnesses were called to testify for the prosecution at trial, and the petty jury convicted. Short was sentenced to hang. However, perhaps nervous of passing a death sentence at such a forum, the bills were also marked *reprehensa sine judicio* (re-imprisoned without judgment). Even so, no reprieve was ultimately granted, as Short was subsequently executed and buried in the churchyard of St Sidwell's church in the city.[264]

In the North, the records for quarter sessions held in the West Riding of Yorkshire (almost a county on its own) can also be considered. Although these begin only in 1597, most records have survived for the five years after this date. They show that this forum was still hearing a significant number of cases of clergyable grand larceny, while several unclergyable offences, including five cases of horse theft and one involving the rape of Jenettam Scolefield also came before it.[265] Similarly, in January 1598 a grave case of burglary was tried at the Epiphany Quarter Sessions for Durham. A widow's house had been targeted, just before midnight the previous August; she was assaulted during the crime, and 20s in cash, five gold pieces, and a silver heart were stolen.[266] Even more significantly, two murders were tried at the same sessions. In both cases the victims were women. One, in August 1597, was exceptionally heinous. Four men staged a home invasion in Shincliffe, terrifying an entire family and killing Matthew Noble's wife, Margaret, with a blow from an

---

264. Stoyle, "'It Is But an Olde Wytche Gonne,'" pp. 129–135.
265. Lister, *West Riding Sessions Rolls*, p. xi and p. 156.
266. DRO DQS p. 8 and p. 10.

iron bar ("solidus"). In the other crime, which occurred just a few days before the sessions began, John Garner from Southfields assaulted Katherine Brughe, a local spinster, threw her to ground, and kicked her in the belly and chest. She "lingered" for three days, then died.[267] Durham, being one of the most northern counties of the Northern circuit, had only one assizes a year (in the summer); the suspects in the Noble case would have had to be incarcerated for almost an entire year before they could be tried in that forum, encouraging recourse to the lower court.[268]

Even so, by the latter decades of the sixteenth century the assizes, even in the South-east, were dealing with the great majority crimes that were deemed to threaten the security or fabric of society. Thus most cases of murder, infanticide, manslaughter, witchcraft (especially those producing a death), robbery, and rape were heard before the Westminster judges on circuit. Such cases were thought to be deserving of the majesty and solemnity of the higher court. This reasoning was alluded to in January 1601, when Sir Francis Gawdy wrote to Sir Thomas Mildmay and other Essex JPs, noting that he had been informed by George Longworth and Christopher Bell that they had been violently attacked and robbed of several pounds on a highway in the county by William Elkyn and three other named men who had been bound-over to appear at the next quarter sessions. Gawdy thought that this was clearly inappropriate for a "very foul" crime that ought to be thoroughly investigated and punished accordingly: "I do therefore require and pray you that you would forbear to proceed against those offenders at the said Sessions, and to bind all the four offenders over with good and sufficient sureties to appear at the next assizes and general Gaol Delivery". He also asked them to bind-over the two victims to appear at the same assizes to give evidence against the four men, and personally undertook to have the matter thoroughly examined in the meantime.[269]

As a result of such attitudes, in 1602, for example, eight of nine indicted robberies in Kent, all seven of its murders, and 14 of its 15 manslaughters were tried at the county assizes. Unsurprisingly, in these circumstances,

---

267. DRO DQS pp. 102–103.
268. DRO DQS p. 8 and p. 102.
269. ERO Q/SR 152/30.

the proportion of convicted defendants from this forum (of all types) who were hanged in the early 1600s, some 36 per cent, was enormously higher than the one per cent of convicts from the county quarter sessions who met the same fate.[270]

Furthermore, by the early years of the seventeenth century, change was in the air. In 1611, Judge David Williams (of the King's Bench), while riding the Norfolk Circuit, attempted to distinguish between the type of work that should go to assizes and that which could be dealt with at quarter sessions. He felt that the latter should deal only with petty larceny and "small" felonies, such as simple (clergyable) grand larceny, along with their normal diet of misdemeanours. This distinction was picked-up and popularised by Michael Dalton in his justices' *vade mecum* of 1618 and slowly became accepted practice throughout the country.[271] As a result, during the seventeenth century the trial of potentially capital felonies largely disappeared from county quarter sessions and most (but not all) borough sessions. One of the last death sentences that was imposed and carried out by the former forum appears to have taken place in Norfolk in 1665.[272] Even so, a handful of powerful borough sessions, such as King's Lynn and Great Yarmouth, would continue to pass sentence of death until the late eighteenth and early nineteenth centuries.

However, although very serious crimes were increasingly being monopolised by the assizes by the end of the Tudor era, the converse did not occur. Large numbers of minor cases continued to be determined at the higher jury forum, throughout the period (and beyond), rather than being reserved for quarter sessions, even on the pressured Home Circuit. For example, at the Hertford Assizes held in July 1593, Helen Hogg was acquitted of petty larceny after being accused of stealing two "kerchiefs" valued at just two pence from a widow in Ware.[273] At times the Kent Assizes determined more cases of petty larceny during the Elizabethan period than did the county quarter sessions. Numerous misdemeanours also continued to go to the higher forum. In March 1598, in what was otherwise a very full calendar for the Hertford Assizes, four alehouse

270. Knafla, *Kent at Law 1602*, p. xxi, pp. 21–22 and p. 29.
271. Cockburn, *A History of English Assizes*, p. 92.
272. Norma Landau, "The Justices and their Quarter Sessions", p. 248.
273. Cockburn, *Calendar of Assize Records. Hertfordshire Indictments: Elizabeth 1*, p. 103.

keepers from Royston were tried for exercising the trade of baker without serving the statutory seven years' apprenticeship.[274]

At some times such cases were listed at the higher jury forum for administrative convenience, as might be the case when petty crimes were committed just before the assizes were held. At others this might be done to flesh out an otherwise thin judges' list or because the case raised legal complications or was thought to require special publicity. However, although widespread, this practice was not always welcome by the higher court. On one occasion, John Glascocke, the clerk of the assizes on the Home Circuit for much of the Elizabethan period, complained to the Essex clerk of the peace that his (higher) court was being bothered with too many trivial crimes which should more properly have gone to quarter sessions. This led to a diminution in the number of misdemeanours appearing at the Essex Assizes in subsequent months.[275]

Special Jurisdictions

Tudor England was notably lacking in uniformity in its criminal justice system, so that every generalisation must necessarily be qualified by numerous exceptions. This was especially the case in 1485, but still fairly marked in 1603, although even contemporary observers sometimes appear to have ignored the level of variation. It has been suggested that only a "slender majority" of counties corresponded to the neatly ordered administrative structure, with its quarter sessions and assizes, that early modern legislation and conciliar directives often appear to have assumed was the "standard" pattern.[276] This section will briefly consider some (not all) of the forums where felonies could be tried that were outside this model.

The Palatine Counties

The three counties palatine (literally "from the palace") constituted one of the largest variations to the "national" system. Technically, the Isle of Ely (see below) was a royal franchise, not a county palatine, for most

---

274. *Ibid*, pp. 138–139.
275. Samaha, *Law and Order*, p. 89.
276. Quintrell, *Proceedings of the Lancashire Justices*, p. 3.

of the period, although very similar to, and sometimes confused with, the former trio. Two of these palatinates, Chester and Durham, had enjoyed their special status from time immemorial, while Edward III had expressly granted Lancaster's privilege to Henry Plantagenet. As a result, at one time the Earl of Chester, the Bishop of Durham, and the Duke of Lancaster held the same legal powers as the Crown over justice in their dominions. However, only Durham had survived in the hands of a subject (the bishop), the earldom of Chester being united to the Crown by Henry III and the Duchy of Lancaster being forfeited to the Crown during the reign of Edward IV. Nevertheless, to an extent, they continued an independent legal existence during the Tudor period, albeit brought more firmly within royal control.[277]

For example, from the late fifteenth century the Durham gaol delivery commissions normally included one or more of the king's judges, whether they were on circuit or (less commonly) sent specially from Westminster. It should be stressed that these counties and their forums were subject to exactly the same common law and trial procedure as the rest of the country. For reasons of space, only Cheshire, which was in many respects the most singular of these jurisdictions, will be considered in further detail.

Cheshire

During the fifteenth and early sixteenth centuries, Cheshire was not part of the assizes system and did not have quarter sessions (or even JPs). Instead, the Cheshire County Court usually sat nine times a year, for about two days at a time, always commencing its sessions on a Tuesday. It sat in various locations, in addition to Chester, and had jurisdiction over all civil and criminal cases from the county. The Justice of Chester or his deputy presided over the court. Because the former was often a figure of national importance (in 1464 it was Lord Stanley, the future Earl of Derby) it is probable that the deputy heard most trials. Even so, in most respects the procedure for trial on indictment was identical to that found at assizes and quarter sessions. Cases went before a grand jury

---

277. Cockburn, *A History of English Assizes*, p. 43.

of 17 or so local gentlemen, most of whom had considerable experience in this role. If they produced a finding of "*verum est*" on a bill (literally, "it is true", the local equivalent of "*billa verra*"), it would go for trial by a petty jury. If rejected, the bill would be torn up (common practice in other places with unsuccessful bills of indictment). The petty jury of 12 men was drawn from a panel of about 20 or 21 summoned individuals.[278]

Under a Henrician statute of 1536, and further Acts from the early 1540s, the powers of the counties palatine were considerably reduced, and they were more fully integrated into the Tudor state.[279] Even so, their special character survived, to some extent. In Cheshire this continuing independence from the centre was reinforced as a byproduct of the incorporation of Wales into the English polity. Under statutes of 1541 and 1543 (34 and 35 Henry VIII c. 26), courts of great sessions were set up for all the newly-established Welsh counties. The same Acts ordered that the Justices of Chester, who were officers of the palatinate, also hold the sessions for Denbighshire, Flintshire, and Montgomeryshire. As a consequence, Cheshire became associated with the Welsh courts of session rather than the assizes that exercised criminal jurisdiction elsewhere in England. It lost its old County Court and acquired its Court of Great Sessions, remaining outside direct Westminster control.

This new forum had cognisance of all Crown pleas with regard to crime. Twice a year it sat as a court of assize to determine felonies. It also had its own Chief Justice of Chester and an assistant puisne judge, normally recruited from outside the judicial personnel of the Westminster courts, together with a permanent administrative staff. The chief justiceship was desirable both on its own merits and as a rung on the ladder of judicial promotion in the national scheme.[280] The court procedures were almost identical to those of the assizes courts elsewhere, and in contemporary documentation for the county it was often even referred to as the assizes.[281] The 1536 Act also provided that justices of

---

278. B. E. Harris and Dorothy J. Clayton, "Criminal Procedure in Cheshire in the Mid-Fifteenth Century", *Transactions of The Historic Society of Lancashire and Cheshire*, Vol. 128, pp. 161–162.
279. William Blackstone, *Commentaries on the Laws of England, Vol. 1* (Oxford: Clarendon, 1765), p. 113.
280. Morrill, *The Cheshire Grand Jury*, p. 6.
281. Sharpe and Dickinson, "Revisiting the 'Violence We Have Lost'", p. 295.

the peace should be appointed in Cheshire for the first time and sit at newly created quarter sessions for the county.

The Isle of Ely

Until drainage works in the 1620s, the cathedral city of Ely was surrounded by fenland, making it an island. From 1109 until 1836 it was under the jurisdiction of its bishop, who exercised temporal as well as ecclesiastical powers within its bounds. For example, the bishop appointed a chief bailiff, who held the position for life, and acted as its high sheriff. It also had its own assizes, held at Ely (Lent) and Wisbech (Summer); its own quarter sessions, held twice every year at each of these two locations (Easter and Michaelmas being at Ely); and its own jails and houses of correction. As a result, although part of Cambridgeshire, it was almost a separate county.

For much of this time, the bishop also appointed a Chief Justice of Ely, who usually presided over its assizes, to the exclusion of the Westminster judges who covered the Norfolk Circuit, including those held for the rest of Cambridgeshire. For example, in 1575, the Wisbech Assizes were held before John Goldewelle, Chief Justice of the Isle. It also had its own commission of the peace. This was quite modest, reflecting its small size. In 1487 and 1489 there were a dozen names in the commission, in 1490 only eight. However, as elsewhere, some of these were honorary appointments, men such as the Archbishop of Canterbury and the Attorney General. In the late sixteenth and early seventeenth centuries, Privy Council letters were addressed to groups of from three to seven JPs, which probably reflects the working commission at the time (it expanded thereafter).

Although the Isle of Ely may, originally, have been almost a (sub) county palatine, an Act of 1535 ended this status, so that its JPs were appointed by letters patent issued under the great seal, like those found elsewhere in England, albeit remaining separate from those for the rest of Cambridgeshire. Similarly, warrants were issued in the king's name. Both Henry VII and Henry VIII attempted to assert closer royal control over the isle, often by means of the Privy Council. As a result, during the Tudor era the bishop sometimes merely endorsed the royal recommendation as to the Chief Justice. On other occasions, it seems that a Westminster judge presided over its assizes. This may explain why, during the reign of Queen Mary, Sir Clement Heigham (1495–1571), Lord Chief Baron of the Exchequer Court and one of her privy councillors, sat as the "king's and queen's justice" at Wisbech when the local Protestant house painter Robert Pigot was presented for heresy. This was also encouraged by a vacancy in the see from 1581 to 1600, helping to explain why several prominent royal judges, such as Edward Flowerdew and Sir John Popham, presided over assizes in the isle during this period.

Nevertheless, Ely emerged from the Tudor period with less abatement than most medieval franchises and, in theory, the bishop retained exclusive jurisdiction in civil and criminal matters. Indicative of this, in 1565 it was even issued with its own commission for repressing pirates. From 1600 onwards, the usual president at assizes in the isle was the Chief Justice of the Liberty rather than a Westminster judge. Some of them were men of distinction in the wider legal world. For example, Sir Robert Hitcham, Chief Justice in 1610, was the Attorney General. Ely remained a separate royal liberty or franchise until 1836.[282]

London and Middlesex

By the start of the Tudor era the county of Middlesex, which bordered those parts of the City of London that were not delineated by the River Thames, had long been outside the assizes system. Instead, it shared a court of equivalent rank with the City, which was effectively a powerful urban county. Prior to the fifteenth century, gaol delivery sessions at this forum were usually held twice a year, in the Great Hall of Newgate Prison (which held inmates from both Middlesex and the Square Mile), one being the sheriff's responsibility and the other the Lord Mayor's. However, by 1475 up to six sessions were being held annually at this location.[283] During the Tudor era their number often increased further, so that they were conducted between five and eleven times a year. Between 1537 and 1539, these sessions were moved from the Great Hall to the new,

---

282. R. B. Pugh (ed.), *A History of the County of Cambridge and the Isle of Ely: Vol. 4, City of Ely; Ely, N. and S. Witchford and Wisbech Hundreds* (London: Victoria County History, 2002), p. 15.

283. Christine Winter, *Prisons and Punishments in Late Medieval London*, Royal Holloway, University of London, PhD thesis, 2013, p. 122.

purpose-built Old Bailey court, adjacent to the prison and open to the elements on one side. There they were heard before collegiate benches containing various combinations of the Recorder of London, the Lord Mayor, Aldermen from the City, a small number of Westminster judges on temporary assignment, and several JPs from Middlesex (the last group being at the bottom of the hierarchy of prestige). Otherwise, trial procedure was exactly the same as at assizes, and one of the bench would sit in a presiding capacity, like an assizes judge.

The special provision made for the area was necessary, as its growing population, and increasing number of poor people, often living close to conspicuous wealth, contributed to a significant level of crime, a problem made politically sensitive by its proximity to the centre of government. For example, Queen Elizabeth's palaces were burgled on numerous occasions, and her personal silver saltcellars were stolen from the Bishop of London's palace at Fulham during a royal visit. Burglars also targeted Sir Walter Raleigh's house in Westminster and removed silk-embroidered and gold-embroidered pillowcases. In 1592 three men even broke into the Tower of London and stole several barrels of gunpowder.[284]

By an Act of 1456 Middlesex was allowed to hold two (rather than four) general "quarter" sessions because it had to bear the cost of numerous other legal forums. Ironically, however, by the Tudor era, the high level of crime in the county and the fact that its grand juries normally decided whether there was a case to answer for matters that would be heard at the Old Bailey meant that it sat in adjourned sessions almost as frequently as the Bailey, and more often than its equivalent forum in most other counties. Although, like other quarter sessions, those for Middlesex could try both misdemeanours and felonies under its commissions of the peace and oyer and terminer, most of the latter, even if quite modest, were tried at the Old Bailey.

Neither the Middlesex nor the City of London Quarter Sessions was held at the Old Bailey, even after a purpose-built court became available. During the late Tudor period, the Middlesex justices held their sessions in whatever halls or large public houses they could find near the

---

284. King, *The Middlesex Justices*, p. 25.

City, such as the Castle and Windmill taverns just north of Smithfield. However, in 1601 Sir Baptist Hicks funded a new purpose-built court building for the Middlesex Sessions (the first in the county), which eventually opened in 1612. After 1411 the sessions of the peace for London were usually held in the City's imposing Guildhall (also sometimes the setting for important state trials).

The Northern Border and March Law

The Scottish Border counties were notorious for the poverty of royal justice that they received, something that did not change after the accession of Henry VII. The area was highly singular. No Anglo-Scottish peace was signed between 1333 and 1502, although there were periodic truces. This meant that defence of the Border often took priority over what might be deemed "good governance", forcing the Crown to rely on powerful local magnates with extended ties of kinship to protect the frontier. It also encouraged the development of a militarised society.[285] For example, although Lord Dacre periodically executed a few thieves during the early sixteenth century, often when under acute pressure from London, vigorous action would have destroyed his following on the Border. As a result, there were numerous complaints from the gentry of Northumberland and Durham that he failed to keep order there. In 1518 many of these were addressed to the justices of assize.[286]

At the same time, the terrain was wild and its inhabitants were often quite poor. Many supplemented their living by raiding, not just across the border but also in their own lowlands. In June 1522 the Bishop of Carlisle reported that more theft and extortion was being committed by English reivers than by Scottish marauders. If their victims resisted or reported them to the authorities, the criminal justice system could not prevent reprisals. The cleric feared that Cumberland and Northumberland were going "to waste". Bands of several dozen men were normal, though they could be far larger. In April 1525 a group of 400 "riotous" thieves and reivers from Tynedale, Bewcastledale, and Gilsland, accompanied

---

285. Etty, *Tudor Revolution?*, p. 254.
286. Steven G. Ellis, "A Border Baron and the Tudor State: The Rise and Fall of Lord Dacre of the North", *The Historical Journal*, Vol. 35, No. 2, p. 266.

by a large group of Scotsmen, raided Ingoe and Kirkheaton, in Northumberland, and came within eight miles of Newcastle.[287]

Of course, Scotsmen also played a major role in such depredations, on their own initiative. As late as 1596, Walter Scott (1550–1629) of Harden led a group of 400 men into England, taking 300 cattle, burning 20 houses, and stealing £400 in gold. In 1603, when Elizabeth I died, Hutcheon Graham and his wider family and retainers decided that, at least until James VI of Scotland reached London, to be crowned as James I of England, there was an opportunity. In what was later termed "ill week" they raided the English West March as far south as Penrith, capturing 5,000 cattle, doing almost £7,000 worth of damage to property, taking over a dozen men for ransom, and killing another six.[288]

As a result, many of the Tudor indictments for those parts of Northumberland between Berwick-on-Tweed, on the Scottish border, and Newcastle, had a slightly distinctive character. It is easy to identify instances of largescale cattle rustling, arson, kidnapping for ransom, extortion, and attacks on the area's bastle (fortified) houses among numerous more quotidian offences.[289]

All parts of England adjoining the Scottish Border were within the Northern Circuit, and so the assizes system. However, throughout the era the northern assizes visited Northumberland, Westmorland, and Cumberland, just once each year (see above), and, when they did, the assizes judges spent no more than a week covering Newcastle, Carlisle, and Appleby; even these visits were often curtailed because of war. In 1524 Wolsey tacitly acknowledged the inadequacy of the system, commanding Thomas, Lord Dacre, to impose summary justice (presumably march law) on felons whose trial would usually have been reserved for the justices of gaol delivery, because waiting for the sessions might encourage other potential offenders.[290]

Furthermore, the power of gaol delivery was not exercised frequently in the region's quarter sessions, if only because of their comparative

287. Etty, *Tudor Revolution?*, pp. 129–133.
288. George MacDonald Fraser, *The Steel Bonnets* (London: Barrie & Jenkins, 1971), p. 361 and p. 367.
289. *Ibid*, pp. 90–96.
290. Etty, *Tudor Revolution?*, p. 105.

rarity. In August 1526 Thomas Magnus, a cleric and administrator, wrote to Cardinal Wolsey, informing him that there were so few working justices in Northumberland that quarter sessions had not been kept there for a long time. In April 1528 William, Lord Dacre (Thomas' successor), wrote to Wolsey, begging him to add more local inhabitants to the quorum of the Cumberland commission of the peace. Sessions could not go ahead, because non-resident members of the quorum (presumably these included the Westminster judges) "never come in these parts but once in the year, at the general assize".[291]

To address some of these problems, an alternative system of criminal justice developed in the Border counties during the medieval period, operating alongside (and supplemental to) that exercised by the quarter sessions and the Northern Circuit Assizes. This was the special regime of march law (from the Old French for "boundary"), under which local forums in Northumberland, Cumberland, and Westmorland were empowered to hear very serious cases that had a cross-border element, such as those involving Scottish felons or mixed bands of Scottish and English criminals. It incorporated, inter alia, elements of both common law and military law, and was thought better suited to the problems attendant on an artificial (to Border families) boundary, where the threat posed by bandits meant that justices and constables were sometimes absent or unwilling to carry out their duties.

Border law survived for centuries, despite opposition from several English monarchs, including Edward I, who attempted to abolish it in favour of relying solely on the standard system of common law. However, the significance of this system should not be exaggerated. It never replaced the assizes, which kept going even in periods of acute cross-border strife. Indeed, during the sixteenth century, it was of far less significance than the common law courts, which determined most criminal cases in the normal manner, even where they might, theoretically, have been dealt with by march law. For example, and fairly typically, at the sessions of gaol delivery held at Appleby Castle, Westmorland, in September 1454, a Scottish labourer named John Short was tried and convicted by a jury

---

291. Etty, *Ibid*, p. 105 and p. 118.

in the normal manner for stealing a horse and saddle worth 20 shillings, despite his nationality. He was sentenced to death like any other felon found guilty at assizes. The system of Border law came to a formal end with the Union of the Crowns in 1603.[292]

The Court of King's Bench

The King's Bench was the highest court of common law in England and Wales, and the only Westminster court with jurisdiction over both civil and criminal actions. The latter were dealt with on the court's Crown Side, which had three separate jurisdictions. These were: original jurisdiction over all matters of a criminal nature as the *Custos Morum* or "keeper of morals" of all subjects within the realm; supervisory powers over inferior courts; and a local first-instance jurisdiction over Middlesex and its subordinate jurisdictions, such as Westminster and the Tower Hamlets, after the court became permanently situated there in the fifteenth century. By the start of the Tudor period this last jurisdiction was largely discharged by periodically delivering its own gaol (the Marshalsea). Even so, the Old Bailey remained the normal forum for criminal cases from these areas.[293]

Because of this multiplicity of jurisdictions, the criminal cases determined by the court could range from the gravest cases of high treason to relatively petty matters. Nevertheless, as has been seen elsewhere, a significant number of prominent Tudor men were prosecuted for felonies in this forum *ab initio* or, most commonly, had their cases transferred to its jurisdiction from an inferior court. Thus, in Michaelmas 1488, 50 cases that were before the court had originated in another forum, including 32 from commissions of oyer and terminer and nine from sessions of the peace (others came from leets, sheriffs' tourns, and coroners' inquests). Few poor defendants reached the court, other than the thieves produced from the Marshalsea.[294]

---

292. Cynthia J. Neville, "Keeping the Peace on the Northern Marches in the Later Middle Ages", *The English Historical Review*, Vol. 109, pp. 1–25; Etty, *Tudor Revolution?*, p. 254; Cockburn, "The Northern Assize Circuit", p. 122; Cynthia J. Neville, "Border Law in Late Medieval England", *The Journal of Legal History*, Vol. 9, p. 335.
293. Marjorie Blatcher, *The Court of King's Bench, 1450–1550: A Study in Self-Help* (London: Athlone Press, 1978), p. 47.
294. *Ibid*, p. 51.

CHAPTER 10

Lesser Courts

Introduction

Unsurprisingly, lesser courts normally determined lesser crimes, whether they were regulatory offences or breaches of by-laws being heard at manorial leets, or spiritual lapses being determined by the Archdeacon's Court (part of the country's ecclesiastical court structure). These are largely outside the remit of this book. However, during the Tudor era, these forums also dealt with many mainstream offences that might otherwise have been indicted as serious misdemeanours or even felonies at quarter/borough sessions or assizes. One extreme (and very unusual) example was a case from 1537 in which a man was convicted of rape and successfully claimed clergy in a local court in Kent.[295] As a result, they merit brief consideration.

Leet Courts

The manorial system covered much (but not all) of late medieval England. Manors were substantial estates administered as single units. They were easily the most important subdivision for local administration until the end of the fourteenth century, when the parish very slowly started to displace them. Manors varied greatly in size: they might be situated within a parish, be the same size as a parish, or (in a small number of cases) cover several parishes. For example, the substantial manor of Kirtlington, in North-east Oxfordshire, had an area of 3,582 acres and was the largest of two manors in a parish of the same name, the other being the

---

295. Jones, *Gender and Petty Crime*, p. 35.

much smaller manor of Northbrook.[296] Close to London, Hackney, in Middlesex, contained three manors: Lordshold, which was held by the Bishop of London until 1550; Kingshold, held by the Priory of St John of Jerusalem before the Reformation and which reverted to the Crown in 1537 (it was subsequently granted to the Earl of Pembroke); and the much smaller Grumbolds, which had also been held by the Bishop of London before 1550.[297]

Manorial courts flourished during the late medieval period, developing both presentment and trial by jury, their procedures increasingly following those of the higher royal courts, with their records being written in a compressed form of Latin.[298] Most contemporary observers divided them into two types, distinguishing the leet court, which was viewed as a petty criminal court, from the court baron, which was essentially a civil forum, although there was often a significant overlap in jurisdiction.[299]

Virtually all manors had a court baron. This forum handled its administration, including the enforcement of manorial customs (such as the use of common land for pasture), settled disputes between tenants, protected the rights and interests of the lord, and helped regulate land holding. However, it also imposed fines on tenants for breaking the rules and by-laws of the manor. For example, in 1452, a court baron in the manor of Writtle, in Essex, fined John Croucheman after seven of his animals strayed onto the land of another tenant and ate some drying hay.[300]

By contrast, leet courts were by no means universal. This was for historic reasons. Almost every English county was subdivided into hundreds, each of which had a court with a criminal jurisdiction dating back to Saxon times, known as the sheriff's tourn; traditionally, these were held twice a year.[301] In the centuries after the Norman Conquest, royal courts slowly assumed responsibility for serious crimes, so that the jurisdiction

---

296. Griffiths, "Kirtlington Manor Court", p. 261.
297. LMA M/79/G (Grumbolds); M/79/KH (Kingshold); M/79/LH (Lordshold).
298. John S. Beckerman, "Procedural Innovation and Institutional Change in Medieval English Manorial Courts", *Law and History Review*, Vol. 10, No. 2, pp. 197–198.
299. Griffiths, "Kirtlington Manor Court", p. 265.
300. ERO D/DU 886/3.
301. John Selden, *A Briefe Discourse Concerning the Powers of the Peeres and Comons of Parliament* (London, 1640), p. 2; George J. Edwards, *The Grand Jury* (Philadelphia: G. T. Bisel, 1906), pp. 4–7.

of the hundred courts gradually became confined to lesser offences and anti-social conduct.[302] The significance of the tourn waned rapidly after 1461, when, following much criticism of the court, the sheriff was obliged by statute to send all indictments and presentments to quarter sessions and the JPs.[303]

Nevertheless, individual manorial lords had been able to apply to the Crown to have the jurisdiction of the hundred courts transferred to their own manors (within their bounds). This "contracting-out" process allowed them to exercise the criminal jurisdiction of the sheriff's twice-yearly tourn in a smaller, more local forum known as the leet or the "view of frankpledge". As a result, the leet can be described as a royal court that was in private hands, which adjudicated offences against the public. Nevertheless, by no means all manorial lords applied for, or were granted, such a privilege.[304] Manors that possessed only courts baron left minor criminal jurisdiction to the hundred courts for as long as they operated, and to the rapidly expanding jurisdiction of the JPs thereafter.

However, leets continued to determine criminal matters long after the hundred courts had ceased to do so, effectively (though not juris-dictionally) restricting the role of quarter sessions in their areas. Leet courts were cheap to run, and convenient to attend, because they sat near those who used them. This was important, as all males other than small children, whether freeholders or cottagers, living within a manor, were supposed to attend their sessions. On average, more than 40 people attended each of the five "views of frankpledge" that met at Kirklington between Michaelmas 1520 and Michaelmas 1524, a figure that was still being matched between 1585 and 1589.[305]

During the sixteenth century, many leets still met twice each year under the presidency of the court steward, as they had often done in the medieval period.[306] Thus in Burgh by Sands, in Cumberland, the

---

302. Griffiths, "Kirtlington Manor Court", p. 265.
303. Musson and Powell, *Crime, Law and Society*, p. 136.
304. Smith, *De Republica Anglorum*, p. 103.
305. Griffiths, "Kirtlington Manor Court", p. 263.
306. Maureen Mulholland, "Trials in Manorial Courts in Late Medieval England", in Mulholland and Brian Pullan (eds.), *Judicial Tribunals in England and Europe 1200–1700*, Vol. 1 (Manchester: Manchester University Press, 2003), p. 84.

leet met during the months immediately after Michaelmas and Easter.[307] Occasionally such forums met three or more times a year, and some met just once. Nevertheless, in other places, the administrative distinction between baron and leet courts had become eroded. At Kirklington there was often a unitary manorial court exercising both jurisdictions (leet and baron) at the same meeting.[308] Similarly, during the Elizabethan period, no clear distinction was made between the leet and the court baron in the Manor of Headley, in Surrey, and the proceedings of the latter were formally recorded in continuation of those for the leet. That both forums could deal with some types of regulatory matter facilitated this process.

Composition

Leets were jury courts presided over by a steward. The latter were often minor gentlemen, as the position required some education. Frequently, but not invariably, they were lawyers of some description, usually attorneys, more rarely barristers. Humphrey Newton (1466–1536) was typical example of such men. Newton had inherited a small estate in the north of Cheshire in 1497, and supplemented his income by being employed as a steward on several large estates in the same county and in neighbouring Staffordshire during the early sixteenth century. He presided over various manorial tribunals, including several leets, had a good working knowledge of the law, and was not merely literate but also knew the legal languages of Latin and Law French.[309]

The constitution of the leet's jury varied from manor to manor. In some, tenants were chosen in rotation, in others by the stewards. In some rural areas it may have been left to the bailiff to decide. At Coventry, the mayor and his council chose the jury. At least a dozen men would eventually be sworn in as jurors; if the jury were larger, at least 12 of them had to agree to return a verdict.[310] Defendants could challenge them for partiality, just as they could jurors at assizes and quarter

---

307. Cumbria Record Office: D/Lons/L5/2/41/49.
308. Griffiths, "Kirtlington Manor Court", p. 266.
309. See generally, Youngs, *Humphrey Newton*.
310. Walter J. King, "Leet Jurors and the Search for Law and Order in Seventeenth century England: 'Galling Persecution' or Reasonable Justice?", *Social History*, Vol. 13, p. 309.

sessions.[311] Perhaps surprisingly, even Star Chamber occasionally took notice of jury misbehaviour in leet courts. In 1562 the court punished a man who gave the steward of the Earl of Arundel's leet court a blank sheet of paper and told him that it was his verdict, and should stand for the next seven years. He was ordered to stand with a paper on his head confessing his "contemptuous behavior and putting in a blank paper into this leet being sworn one of the jury".[312]

The degree to which leet juries were primarily involved in presentment, rather than the determination in court of an allegation, has been a matter of considerable debate. Some observers have suggested that surviving leet rolls give a misleading impression, so that modern investigators conclude, erroneously, that leets equated presentment with guilt. Instead, it is argued, jurors were not committed to a certain verdict before trial, and often changed their minds during the course of the hearing.

Criminal Jurisdiction

Tudor leets had two main responsibilities when dealing with crime. They could prepare and present indictments for serious felonies and treason to the higher jury courts, whether assizes or quarter sessions. Thus, in 1507 the manor court of the Liberty of Havering, in Essex, presented a female servant for feloniously stealing wool, yarn, and money from her master's house for trial at the county assizes.[313] In the early sixteenth century, Humphrey Newton even processed a murder case on its way to the higher jury forum. (After 1534 the Court of King's Bench expressly discouraged this in homicide cases).[314] The leets' willingness to investigate and present felonies to the royal courts declined during the sixteenth century, and they increasingly returned a formal answer that denied any cognisance of such crimes. Typically, in 1611 the Southampton Leet merely

---

311. John S. Beckerman, "Toward a Theory of Medieval Manorial Adjudication: The Nature of Communal Judgments in a System of Customary Law", *Law and History Review*, Vol. 13, No. 1, pp. 1–23.

312. Hamilton, "Star Chamber and Juries", pp. 239–240.

313. McIntosh, *A Community Transformed*, p. 310.

314. Christopher W. Brooks, *Law, Politics and Society in Early Modern England* (Cambridge: Cambridge University Press, 2008), p. 256.

noted: "Itm we present the like concerninge Treasons, peteet Treasons and felonies we have heere of non neither of there accessories".[315]

However, leets could also deal with minor criminal matters, and handed down punishment in several types of case. Obviously there were a large number of regulatory offences pertaining to the manor, such as breaking hedges, cutting down trees, and cleaning hemp in ponds and rivers that were also used to water cattle. Where necessary, societal norms could be legally accommodated by the use of locally created by-laws. A fine and an award of compensation might be imposed. Thus, in the years between 1497 and 1508 presentments at the view of frankpledge for the manor of Albury, in Surrey, included those for failing to repair a footbridge, overstocking a common with sheep, providing inadequate fences between closes, failing to repair gates, and failing to scour local ditches.[316]

Additionally, leets punished the sellers of "corrupt victuals" and took steps to enforce the Assize of Bread and Ale. This law regulated the price and quality of these necessities and the measures they were sold by. For example, in 1474, at a view of frankpledge at a leet court in Writtle, Thomas Elkyn, a baker, was amerced eight pence for selling bread that was short in weight to one of his customers. In 1483, in the same manor, seven women were each fined a penny as regrators of ale, after selling the beverage by the cup.[317] Similarly, in 1542, at the view of frankpledge of the manor of Limpsfield, in Surrey, Peter Harman was presented for breaking the king's assize of ale.[318]

Many other leet prosecutions were designed to preserve village harmony, so that "scoulders", "common barratours", and "evesdroppers" were presented. Others were intended to promote morality, so that "keepers of bawdry" might also be prosecuted.[319] Thus, during the early 1540s, the Coventry leet court administered small fines for disobeying the constable

---

315. F. J. C. Hearnshaw and D. M. Hearnshaw (eds.), *Court Leet Records, Vol. 1, A.D. 1550–1624* (Southampton: H. M. Gilbert and Son, 1905), p. 436.

316. SHC 1322/1/2.

317. ERO D/DP M278 and D/DP M287.

318. SHC 2186/1/14.

319. Anon, *The Order of Keeping a Court Leet and Court Baron* (London, 1650), p. 10.

while he was in the execution of his duty, being a "very scold", and running an alehouse while maintaining "bawdery and evyll".[320]

However, and more significantly for the purposes of this study, leets also had a general jurisdiction to determine criminal offences of a more mainstream and conventional type that might otherwise have been prosecuted at quarter sessions or even assizes. In theory, they could deal with every common law offence that had not been expressly removed from their purview by statute. They had dealt with quite serious property crimes during the early medieval period. At the leet held for Conesford, in Norfolk, in February 1288, Beatrice la Qwyte and her associate, Acilia, were presented for stealing sheep fleeces and a surcoat valued at 40 pence from a house, while Richard Cokard was presented for habitually stealing geese and hens over the previous seven years.[321]

However, by the fourteenth century the jurisdiction of the leet had been heavily limited by legislation, which removed to the royal justices cases of arson, burglary, robbery, counterfeiting, and homicide.[322] Nevertheless, this left misdemeanours involving non-lethal violence as well as cases of petty theft. In practice, albeit only occasionally, some leets still dealt with more serious common law property crimes, such as grand larcenies, even if their legal basis for doing so was sometimes uncertain (see below).

No newly created statutory offences came within the leet's purview unless this was expressly stated in the enabling act. Even so, during the Tudor era a number of new minor crimes did contain such a provision, as was the case with the law of 1541 (33 Hen VIII cap. 6) prohibiting popular possession of handguns. Similarly, the law for preserving pheasants and partridges of 1580 (23 Eliz., cap. 10), which placed a fine of 20 shillings on those poaching the former bird, and ten shillings for the latter, provided that, as well as being dealt with at assizes and quarter sessions, the provision could be punished by "stewards of leets".[323] Even

320. Levi Fox, "Some New Evidence of Leet Activity in Coventry, 1540–1541", *The English Historical Review*, Vol. 61, pp. 235–243.

321. William Hudson (ed.), *Leet Jurisdiction in the City of Norwich, Vol. 5* (London: Selden Society, 1892), pp. 4–6.

322. Mulholland, "Trials in Manorial Courts", p. 92.

323. F. J. C. Hearnshaw, *Leet Jurisdiction in England, Especially as Illustrated by the Records of the Court Leet of Southampton* (Southampton: Cox & Sharland, 1908), pp. 128–129.

more important, the late Tudor statutory laws dealing with wood-stealing and hedge-breaking expressly authorised leets to determine such cases. (It has been argued that this legislation acted as something of a rejuvenating agent for leet courts in some areas.)[324] For example, early Stuart leet records mention 27 accusations made against individuals for taking underwood from Prescot Wood in Lancashire and a further 98 for unlawfully taking wood that had been obtained for other purposes.[325]

Violence

Tudor leets dealt with many cases of assault and affray, most of which were legally defined as misdemeanours. For example, at the view of frankpledge held in the manor of Shalford, in Surrey, in August 1503, John Materus was presented for assaulting William Preston and drawing blood.[326] In 1548 William Persons was fined the small, but frequently used, sum of four pence at the Kirtlington leet in Oxfordshire, after he beat Henry Hogekyns so badly with a cudgel that he was unable to work for a week. Even more seriously, William Arundel and Richard Turner were fined a similar amount after they attacked another man, threw him from his horse, dislocated his shoulder, and wounded him in the head.[327] In April 1560, at a leet court held at Limpsfield, in Surrey, Thomas Blackman was presented for assaulting a stranger with a fork handle and, again, drawing blood.[328] In April 1574, at the Cannock and Rugeley Leet Court in Staffordshire, William Harryman was fined four pence for an affray committed against Richard Attye. In October the same year, John Wolsley, described as a "gentleman", and so presumably better off, was fined 1s 8d for a similar offence in which blood had been drawn. The leet even fined the local vicar for using his fists.[329]

This aspect of Tudor leet court work should not be exaggerated. Punishing violence did not make up a substantial proportion of its business. A

324. Newton and McIntosh, "Leet Jurisdiction in Essex Manor Courts", p. 3.
325. Walter J. King, *Social History*, "Early Stuart Courts Leet Still Needful and Useful", *Social History*, Vol. 23, No. 46, p. 279.
326. SHC 1322/1/2.
327. Griffiths, "Kirtlington Manor Court", p. 279.
328. SHC 2186/1/15.
329. Barrett and Harrison, *Crime and Punishment*, pp. 72–74.

sample of leets in 113 parishes with a Yorkshire bias suggests that, during the second half of the 1500s, such cases made up just 7.5 per cent of their total caseload. Normally, only one or two people were presented at each leet for assaults and affrays. Only in very large and active manors were nine or ten violent offenders punished in a single year.[330] Nevertheless, during the Tudor (and Jacobean) era, people in the (declining) number of parishes that still had an active leet were very much more likely to prosecute "offences against the person" before such forums than they were to take them to quarter sessions. Frequently, offenders would be put before a local JP and sent to quarter sessions or assizes only if they had committed extremely serious crimes of violence that went beyond the limits of local toleration and resolution or the community had run out of patience with the accused person.

For example, between 1603 and 1623 Ralph Whalley was charged at the leet court at Upholland, in Lancashire (which preserved active leets for much longer than many other counties), 25 times for assault and four times for being drunk and disorderly. At the same forum, Nicholas Taylor was accused of 23 assaults and eleven cases of gambling. Taylor was only once brought before a JP during this period, for fighting with a constable, which may have been viewed as a more serious form of the crime.[331] Similarly, on one assessment, as late as the years between 1615 and 1660, only two per cent of those who perpetrated assaults in Prescot, in Lancashire (that is, some 27 of 1,280 cases), were presented at quarter sessions rather than the local leet. However, and as elsewhere in the country, as a general rule, the graver the assault, the more likely it was to be sent to the higher forum. Seventy per cent of the 27 people indicted at quarter sessions with assault had drawn blood, but only 22 per cent of those charged with the same crime at Prescot's leet had done so.[332]

---

330. Brodie Waddell, "Governing England through the Manor Courts, 1550–1850", *The Historical Journal*, Vol. 55, Issue 2, pp. 279–315.

331. King, "Leet Jurors and the Search for Law and Order", p. 312.

332. King, "Early Stuart Courts Leet", p. 277.

Property Crimes

Tudor leets continued to try some common law felonies involving the theft of property. For example, at the Ingatestone Leet in 1530, a man was fined for having broken into a house and stolen a cup worth 12 pence.[333] Presumably this was simply prosecuted as a petty larceny, the crime occurring during the day. In early sixteenth century Cheshire, the leet court steward Humphrey Newton presided over several trials for petty theft.[334]

As these cases suggest, most such crimes were minor ones; this became more marked after the middle of the sixteenth century. A legal guide of 1556 even suggested that leet courts deal with "any small theves amonge you that steal geese, capons, hennes, chickens, sheeves of corne in harvest, or ani other geare in menes windows pryvely that passeth not the value of 3d".[335] However, that figure was frequently exceeded in practice, with thefts of up a shilling routinely going to the forum.

For example, virtually all petty larcenies committed in Stock (Essex) during the second half of the Tudor era (and presumably before) were dealt with at its leet. Normally, only grand larcenies (thefts involving a shilling or more in value) committed in the village went to quarter sessions, and only half a dozen of these were sent there during this period. By contrast, the only petty theft sent to the higher forum involved a clear case of down-valuing by the prosecutor, helping to explain the decision. In 1602 Dorothy Norrington was found guilty of stealing a smock and a sheep from another Stock resident, albeit that the crime had merely been indicted as petty larceny (she pleaded guilty).[336]

As elsewhere in the country, prosecution in the leet usually benefitted those found guilty, as its punishments were normally milder than the customary whipping imposed on those convicted of petty theft at quarter sessions and assizes, let alone the death sentence given to those who stole goods worth one shilling or more but were not literate (and so could not plead benefit of clergy). In Stock a majority of those convicted

---

333. Newton and McIntosh, "Leet Jurisdiction in Essex Manor Courts", p. 12.
334. Youngs, *Humphrey Newton*.
335. Anthony Fitzherbert, *The Contentes of this Booke. Fyrst the booke for a Justice of Peace. The Boke that teacheth to kepe a courte baron, or a lete* (London, 1556), p. 85.
336. Robey, *The Village of Stock*, pp. 202–206.

were merely fined between four and 12 pence.[337] As late as 1614, the leet at Upholland in southwest Lancashire merely ordered Roger Gaiskell, who had stolen a chicken, to sit in the stocks on a Sabbath for six hours "with a hen tied unto his foot".[338]

Very occasionally, a much more serious crime that was clearly outside its theoretical jurisdiction would be dealt with by a leet court, perhaps to limit the legal consequences for the accused. Sometimes this might be done in a subtle manner. At the Cannock and Rugeley Leet Court, in Staffordshire, in October 1579, John Fisher was fined 6s 8d for putting his own sign on a stray sheep. This was a veiled way of accusing him of theft. However, much more blatant examples occurred at the same forum. In 1551 a case involving the theft of four horses (an unclergyable felony) was heard.[339] Had it gone before the royal courts, it would have been capital if proved.

Decline

The number of leets that were willing and able to hear mainstream crimes started to decline after about 1530. The speed with which this occurred varied greatly, from region-to-region, and even on a local basis. A majority, but by no means all, of the leets in the southern half of England had either disappeared or abandoned much of their criminal jurisdiction by 1600, a process that continued during the early decades of the seventeenth century.[340] Where leets did survive in the south, they increasingly confined themselves to offences dealing with roads, drainage, and fences, the management of common lands and local immigration.[341] Those in parts of the North, such as Lancashire, and in some areas in the West, tended to last, and be willing to hear minor felonies, for longer.[342]

However, leet survival also varied greatly on a local, infra-county basis. For example, by the Elizabethan period, many Essex villages, unlike

---

337. *Ibid.*
338. King, "Early Stuart Courts Leet", p. 271.
339. Barrett and Harrison, *Crime and Punishment*, p. 40 and pp. 72–74.
340. Marjorie Keniston McIntosh, *Controlling Misbehaviour in England, 1370–1600* (Cambridge: Cambridge University Press, 1998), pp. 43–45.
341. Waddell, "Governing England", p. 275.
342. McIntosh, *Controlling Misbehaviour*, pp. 43–45.

Stock, were sending criminal cases, especially those involving dishonesty, to quarter sessions as a matter of course.[343] Thus, the leet for Weathersfield tried no felonies between 1558 and 1603. However, Stock was not unique. Two property felonies were tried at the leet for Ingatestone between 1558 and 1579.[344] Similarly, even in Surrey, as late as April 1592, the Manor of Headley's "view of frankpledge and court baron" included the presentment of Thomas Kempsall for theft.

The decline in the criminal jurisdiction of leets was partly encouraged by their gradual loss of powers of non-financial punishment. At the start of the Tudor era, they had used the stocks, the tumbrel or cucking stool (aka ducking stool), eviction from the community, and the threat of whipping.[345] Banishment was a particularly effective weapon in their penal armoury, although it was much more likely to be used against recent arrivals than longstanding residents. For example, early in the reign of Henry VIII, a leet for the Manor of High Roding, in Essex, ordered that a woman leave the village by Michaelmas for being a common scold, upon pain of a fine of five shillings.[346] In the same county, a "pety bryber" was ordered to quit Ingatestone in 1533.[347]

In a few places, such punishments lingered late into the sixteenth century. At the Manor of Headley in April 1592, Margaret Weller was presented as a common scold, and punished "cum supplicio de le Tumbrell".[348] Similarly, in Elizabethan Ingatestone, those who abused their neighbours or sowed discord (usually women) were put on "le kuckyng stole".[349] Nevertheless, by the end of the Tudor period, many forums would only impose fiscal penalties, which were of limited value when those sentenced were impoverished.[350]

Many leets also failed in the latter decades of the 1500s because of the lord of the manor's neglect, so that their criminal duties were necessarily

343. Robey, *The Village of Stock*, pp. 202–206.
344. Samaha, *Law and Order*, pp. 165–166.
345. McIntosh, *A Community Transformed*, pp. 63–65.
346. ERO D/DU 886/3.
347. Newton and McIntosh "Leet Jurisdiction in Essex Manor Courts", p. 12.
348. SHC 439/1.
349. *Ibid*, p. 8.
350. King, "Leet Jurors and the Search for Law and Order", p. 322.

taken over by local JPs.[351] Sometimes, as in Havering, in Essex, this was a drawn-out and gradual process.[352] Similarly, the manorial court at Ingatestone manifested a gradual reluctance to hear all but administrative crimes between the 1570s and the end of the Tudor era.[353] At other times, the end of the leet's criminal jurisdiction occurred more abruptly, as happened after the manor at Earls Colne, in Essex, was sold to Roger Harlakenden (a county JP) in 1592.[354]

JPs and Summary Justice

During the late medieval and Tudor period JPs acquired several judicial powers that could be exercised summarily, without a jury. Some gave them summary jurisdiction over specific, usually fairly minor, offences that had been, or still were, dealt with by manorial courts, so that it was a matter of moving between low-level forums. Among them was the theft of timber from woods (see above). As a result, in March 1614, Bostock Fuller dealt summarily with several men and a woman at the behest of Richard Killicke of Oxted, in Surrey, who complained that they had been "pulling his hedges and stealing his woode". William Browne confessed to the offence, and, this being the "first tyme of his conviction", was merely ordered to make satisfaction to Killicke in the sum of two shillings. The others were also fined 1s 6d each.[355] At the very end of the Tudor period, some cases of cutting grain growing in fields, and vegetable and fruit theft from orchards and gardens, were dealt with summarily under an Elizabethan statute from 1601 (43 Eliz. I, c. 7). Under this provision, if the thief was unable or unwilling to pay a fine or damages to their victim, he or she could be whipped.[356]

351. Steve Hindle, "Hierarchy and Community in the Elizabethan Parish: The Swallowfield Articles of 1596", *The Historical Journal*, Vol. 42, Issue 3, pp. 835–851.
352. McIntosh, *A Community Transformed*, p. 310.
353. Samaha, *Law and Order*, p. 166.
354. Robert von Friedeburg, "Reformation of Manners and the Social Composition of Offenders in an East Anglian Cloth Village: Earls Colne, Essex, 1531–1642", *Journal of British Studies*, 1990, Vol. 29, No. 4, pp. 358–9.
355. Leveson-Gower, "Notebook of a Surrey Justice", pp. 206–207.
356. Robert Shoemaker, *Prosecution and Punishment: Petty Crime and the Law in London and Rural Middlesex, 1660–1725* (New York: Cambridge University Press, 1991), p. 36.

"Petty" Sessions

In the early Tudor period, the requirement that two JPs be present to exercise some legal powers, and the growing responsibilities placed on magistrates, encouraged the modest, and often very ad hoc, emergence of what, in later centuries, would be termed "petty sessions" — that is, meetings of local groups of magistrates outside quarter sessions. (In the Tudor era the phrase "petty sessions" was often used to refer to meetings of high constables to consider cases suitable for presentment). In 1495, Parliament even empowered JPs to hear and determine all statutory (not common law) offences short of felony by information, without indictment or a jury hearing, in appropriate circumstances. Under this provision, two or more magistrates (one of them of the quorum) could punish misdemeanours such as using false weights and measures. This potentially important power did not last long. Henry VIII's first Parliament removed it.[357] Allegedly this was because it was being abused by means of "sinister and crafty feigned and forged information".[358]

However, the increasing burden of administrative and criminal justice matters being placed on JPs meant that de facto non-jury sessions, often based on local hundreds, were sometimes used to supplement quarter sessions, especially after the 1520s.[359] It also led to an attempt in 1542 to create formal sessions that would be held by two magistrates, sitting without a jury, in every hundred in a county, six weeks before the shire's quarter sessions, at which statutes regulating vagabonds, laws enforcing compulsory archery practice, and similar minor matters would be enforced. This was abandoned after three years as it was felt to be inconvenient and too rigid. Even so, the informal, local, organization of sessions of two or more justices continued.[360] In 1557, during the reign of Queen Mary, JPs were expressly encouraged to associate in subdivisions

---

357. Pickthorn, *Early Tudor Government*, p. 65.
358. Baker, *Oxford History*, p. 522.
359. DeLloyd J. Guth and John W. McKenna (eds.), *Tudor Rule and Revolution: Essays for G. R. Elton from His American Friends* (New York: Cambridge University Press, 1982), pp. 202–203.
360. Geoffrey Elton, *The Tudor Constitution: Documents and Commentary* (Cambridge: Cambridge University Press, 1960), p. 466.

to promote order in their areas. This was to be reiterated shortly after the Tudor era, in 1605.

Vagabond Powers

By the final decades of the era (and probably well before) JPs were using their extensive powers against vagabonds to deal summarily with various forms of petty crime, something that would become much more marked in ensuing centuries. It was also occasionally done with more serious offences, in the absence of a willing prosecutor or where a case appeared evidentially weak. For example, just after the Tudor era, in April 1608, Bostock Fuller and several other Surrey JPs rounded-up a group of four vagrants, two of them female, on Blindley Heath. They took them to Godstone for examination. The four were suspected of stealing two ducks, and when questioned each blamed the others for the crime. Rather than go to the considerable trouble of what might be an inconclusive prosecution for theft, they were dealt with as vagrants, Fuller noting: "I went to Mr. Evelyns & there we saw them whipped & made them passports to Devonshire and Somersetshire".[361]

Nevertheless, to the end of the sixteenth century, JPs sitting without a jury normally determined only the most limited forms and amount of conventional crime.

Church Courts

Both before and after the Reformation, the Church had its own system of courts in which various types of offender could be tried and punished. Most were dealt with for spiritual or moral failings, such as non-attendance at divine service, Sabbath violation, non-payment of tithes, fornication, adultery, and clandestine marriages. For example, in the early sixteenth century, the Cistercian abbey of Whalley, in Lancashire, possessed an ecclesiastical jurisdiction embracing the royal forests of Pendle, Blackburnshire, Trawden, Bowland, and Rossendale. A surviving

---

361. Leveson-Gower, "Notebook of a Surrey Justice", p. 198–199.

Act Book covering the years from 1510 to 1537 records proceedings before the commissaries who exercised this jurisdiction on behalf of the abbey and, after its dissolution, by royal authority. Fornication and (to a lesser extent) adultery made up a high proportion of the offences that came before the court.[362] Indeed, it was the high level of cases of sexual immorality that led to the Archdeacon's Court, normally the lowest forum in the ecclesiastical hierarchy, being called the "bawdy court".

Such prosecutions continued after the Reformation. Thus in June 1566 Gavin Lemyng, a prosperous farmer from Balderton in Nottinghamshire, was brought before an ecclesiastical court for requiring his workers to mow at least 15 acres of barley on the Sabbath the previous summer. He admitted the allegation and was required to undergo penance in church, it being ordered that the following Sunday, during divine service, he would "declare unto the people that he is sorie for that he so abused the sabothe daie in causing mowers to fell his corne upon the same contrarie to the lawes of God and the quenes majesties injunctions". Had he failed to do so, he might have been excommunicated. The following month, Thomas Wilkinson, from the parish of Barnby, was cited before the same forum for "absentinge himself from his parishe churche".[363] This sort of offence is outside the remit of this book.

However, sometimes defendants before the church courts were charged with what might be considered "conventional" crimes, even if they sometimes had an ecclesiastical connection. Infanticide, by far the most serious of these, which was largely dealt with by church courts during the first 75 years of the Tudor era, is considered in *Chapter 17*. Nevertheless, there were others.

In the late medieval period, and at the very start of the Tudor era, thefts were occasionally dealt with by ecclesiastical forums, although it appears that these actions were sometimes brought with a view to securing a formal declaration of innocence by someone who had been publicly accused of such a crime; they might also have been brought to

---

362. Margaret Lynch, Nigel Tringham, and John Swain (eds.), *Life, Love and Death in North-East Lancashire, 1510 to 1537: A Translation of the Act Book of the Ecclesiastical Court of Whalley* (Manchester: Chetham Society, 2006), p. 29.
363. R. F. B. Hodgkinson (ed.), "Extracts from the Act Books of the Archdeacons of Nottingham", *Transactions of the Thoroton Society*, Vol. 29, pp. 19–67.

pre-empt a prosecution in a royal court (the suspect having his compurgators ready), or to settle what was essentially a personal dispute through the mediation of a church court. One example of the last scenario was a case in which a priest accused his chaplain of breaking into his rectory and stealing various items; the archdeacon's official duly arbitrated.[364]

Nevertheless, in 1457 John Steven from Faversham, in Kent, was accused of having entered a common privy, where he accosted "lame Wilbur" and forcibly took a sum of money from him, in what appears to have been a purely secular robbery. No cleric had been involved, and the incident did not occur on consecrated ground, or involve the theft of ecclesiastical goods, but even so the case went to a church forum. (The result is unknown.) However, the number of such cases was always small. The diocesan court at Canterbury dealt with an average of about three a year between 1455 and 1457, the Commissary Court of the diocese of Hereford heard roughly one case of secular crime a year in the 1440s, and in 1470 the London Commissary Court dealt with only four such cases. Furthermore, their incidence waned quickly after 1485.[365]

Domestic violence also featured in the work of the ecclesiastical courts, particularly that of the archdeacon. For example, they might deal with spousal abuse and children who threatened or used physical violence towards their parents. (Significantly, almost no cases involving the physical abuse of children by parents, other than infanticide prior to 1563, were heard by these forums.) Thus, in the consistory court of Rochester in 1458, John Hanschawe was prosecuted for having "laid violent hands upon his mother". At the commissary court at Hereford in 1495, Thomas Cock was prosecuted for committing the same offence against his father. In 1503, before the Archdeacon of Canterbury's court, John Goldache, from Chilham, was cited for having on several occasions thrown beer and milk into the face of his father "against the natural disposition of a son and contra bonos mores". Three years earlier, Alice Kemp from

---

364. David J. Harvey, *The Law Emprynted and Englysshed* (Oxford: Hart, 2015), pp. 54–55.
365. Helmholz, "Crime, Compurgation and the Courts", pp. 1–26.

Shoreham had been summoned by the same court for having "laid violent hands upon her mother".[366]

Such prosecutions were never particularly frequent, and the punishments allotted were extremely mild. Sometimes penance was imposed, which might require standing in penitential (white) garb before the assembled parish on Sunday. In most cases, the court simply ordered that a child publicly seek the forgiveness of his or her parent. For instance, the prosecution of Elizabeth Gyles at Oxford in 1598 ended with a simple requirement that she "ask her father's forgiveness" before parishioners drawn from her neighbourhood. (As this late Tudor case suggests, no significant change in the substance of spiritual court practice seems to have occurred in this regard after the Reformation.)[367]

The ecclesiastical courts also dealt with some assaults on clerics by both fellow clergy and laymen, and with a few cases involving only laymen, that took place in church, churchyards, or on ecclesiastical premises. For example, in 1595 Elizabeth Wheeler (alias Rundles) was brought before Stratford-upon-Avon's bawdy court, held at Holy Trinity Church, for brawling on sacred ground. She was defiant, declaring: "A plague of God on you all, a fart of one's arse for you". Wheeler was duly excommunicated.[368]

---

366. R. H. Helmholz, "And were there children's rights in early modern England? The Canon Law and 'intra-family violence' in England, 1400–1640", *The International Journal of Children's Rights*, Vol. 1, Issue 1, pp. 27–28.

367. *Ibid*, pp. 27–28.

368. E.R.C. Brinkworth, *Shakespeare and the Bawdy Court of Stratford* (Chichester: Phillimore, 1972), p. 122 and p. 128.

CHAPTER 11

Trial on Indictment

Introduction

Procedure at trial on indictment was the same for all Englishmen, apart from the country's nobles. Those of the status of duke, marquess, earl, viscount, and baron were very few in number, because their ranks were restricted by primogeniture, although supplemented by the bishops (the Lords Spiritual). Nevertheless, such men enjoyed a range of legal privileges, including, inter alia, being excused from serving on "normal" juries or needing to read when they claimed benefit of clergy.[369] Most important, they were entitled to trial by their peers if accused of a felony or treason, whether they were prosecuted on indictment or appeal, something that many new statutes of the time, such as the Witchcraft Acts of 1563 and 1604, expressly reiterated.

By contrast, foreign nobles who committed crimes in England were treated as, and so were tried by, commoners, as occurred in 1610 after the Scottish Baron Lord Sanchar was accused of murder.[370] John Fisher, the former Bishop of Rochester, who was accused of treason in 1535, was also tried by an ordinary jury (albeit one specially made up of knights and esquires) rather than by peers, because an Act of Attainder deprived him of his ecclesiastical position, so that he reverted to being a commoner.[371]

English noblemen would be tried before the full House of Lords when Parliament was sitting (rarely more than a couple of months a year), while the Court of the Lord High Steward of England, a prerogative creation of Henry VII, would hear cases involving peers of the realm when it was

---

369. *Anonymous* (1456) Jenkins 107, 145 E.R. 902.
370. *Lord Sanchar's Case* (1612) 9 Coke Reports 117, 77 E.R. 902.
371. John Hostettler, *The Criminal Jury Old and New: Jury Power from Early Times to the Present Day* (Winchester: Waterside Press, 2004), p. 45.

in recess. In practice, almost all peers tried during the Tudor era came before the latter forum.[372] In this situation, the monarch would have the Lord High Steward summon a small number of lords to serve as jurors, although, unlike ordinary trial juries, they usually exceeded a dozen men, could convict by majority verdict, and could not be challenged, whether peremptorily or for cause.

For example, 20 peers were summoned from a national total of about 50 to try the Duke of Buckingham for treason in 1521.[373] Similarly, in 1536 the Duke of Norfolk, as Lord High Steward of England, issued a precept to 26 peers living in or relatively close to London (they were given just two days' notice) to form a jury for the trial of the queen, Anne Boleyn, and her brother, Lord Rochford, that was conducted at the Tower of London.[374] More prosaically, in 1503, Edward Sutton, Lord Dudley, was either acquitted or pardoned after trial for a conventional felony before this forum.[375] Similarly, and very unwisely as it transpired, Thomas Fiennes, Baron Dacre, pleaded guilty to a (non-political) murder, committed while out poaching deer, before this forum in 1541.

For everyone else — knights, esquires, gentlemen, yeomen, husbandmen, or even vagabonds — the criminal trial was the same, at least in theory.[376] In practice, as the trial of Bishop John Fisher at King's Bench suggests, informal steps were often taken to accommodate high-status but non-noble defendants. When a gentleman was accused of a crime there might be some effort to ensure that more "substantial" men than normal were on the petty (trial) jury, as had been noted by Sir John Fortescue in the fifteenth century, and which was acknowledged by the elderly Fernando Pulton just after the close of the Tudor period. Even so, ostensibly there were no formal differences in procedure.

---

372. Colin Rhys Lovell, "The Trial of Peers in Great Britain", *The American Historical Review*, Vol. 55, No. 1, p. 70.
373. Peter Gwyn, *The King's Cardinal: The Rise and Fall of Thomas Wolsey* (London: Barrie & Jenkins, 1990), p. 162.
374. Margery S. Schauer and Frederick Schauer, "Law as the Engine of State: The Trial of Anne Boleyn", *William & Mary Law Review*, Vol. 22, Issue 1, p. 60.
375. Barbara Harris, "The Trial of the Third Duke of Buckingham — A Revisionist View", *The American Journal of Legal History*, Vol. 20, Issue 1, p. 16.
376. Smith, *De Republica Anglorum*, p. 119.

Trial on indictment was also broadly the same whether it was held at the JP-dominated quarter sessions or at the (usually) better-documented, and Westminster-judge-dominated, assizes, Old Bailey, or Crown Side of the Court of King's Bench. For example, hearings at the Exeter Quarter Sessions followed much the same procedure as those of the Devonshire Assizes, held in the same city, although the opening formalities differed slightly. (At their start a JP, often the magistrate who would sit in a presiding role, rather than a judge, would read out a "charge" to the jurors, describing their role in the process and some of the crimes that they were likely to deal with.) Thus a group of men were sworn in to serve on the grand jury (see below) or "grand inquest", as it was usually termed at the lower forum, and privately determined which of the bills of indictment drawn up against those accused of crimes were "true". A trial jury was then sworn in to consider the evidence adduced in court. Finally, all of those who had been convicted were brought before the justices (rather than the judges found at assizes) to be sentenced.[377]

Popular Esteem

Many late medieval and Tudor Englishmen professed to admire their national system of criminal trial: the noted Victorian legal historian James Fitzjames Stephen later referred to those writing in this tradition as "panegyrists". Such men were impressed by its public nature (unlike the hearings found in many continental jurisdictions), its reliance on lay factfinders (jurors), and its apparent lack of "artifice". It was widely felt that this was encouraged by the general absence of lawyers from the hearing. As the use of in-court testimony increased, and the self-informing jury waned, they also admired its reliance on openly presented oral evidence.

However, such praise was certainly not universal. Towards the end of the Tudor era, the (admittedly biased) Jesuit Robert Parsons was just one of a number of observers who thought the common law criminal trial inherently unfair. He compared it unfavourably with those conducted under the civil law systems of most other European countries, basing

---

377. Mark Stoyle, "'It Is But an Olde Wytche Gonne': Prosecution and Execution for Witchcraft in Exeter, 1558–1610", *History*, Vol. 96, Issue 322, pp. 129–135.

his criticism on the brevity of the hearing, the disorientating nature of the experience to uneducated men suddenly produced from harsh custodial conditions, the poor quality of the petty jurors who determined their guilt, and the lack of legal representation afforded to the accused. Parsons, who proposed that free lawyers be provided for defendants, thought it almost impossible to identify flaws in the Crown's case, and potential defences, in such an environment.[378] Interestingly, at his treason trial in 1535, even an eminent lawyer like Thomas More (previously held in the Tower) was moved to warn that his ability to defend himself was compromised by his "long detention in prison and the illness and bodily weakness that now afflict me".[379]

Of course, a few defendants still rose to the occasion. Although Nicholas Throckmorton publicly lamented that he had never previously studied law, he proved adept at challenging the evidence at his treason trial in 1554. One of his prosecuting counsel, serjeant-at-law William Stanford (1509–1558), admitted that, if he had appreciated this in advance of the hearing, "I would have been better provided for you".[380] However, Throckmorton was by no means typical.

Not a few late Tudor observers shared Parsons' particular reservations about trial by jury, despite fairly regular encomiums to that institution. In 1591 the innately pessimistic William Lambarde feared for its very future, gloomily noting that juries were already being dispensed with in certain situations, and very slowly "shred off and diminished, very like also in short time to be utterly lost and taken from us if you lay not better hands and hold upon it". Lambarde cited the Star Chamber as an example of an effective court that did not use a jury, as well as the then recent introduction of a provost marshal with some summary powers.[381]

---

378. Parsons, *The Jesuit's Memorial,* p. 249.
379. Henry Ansgar Kelly, Louis W. Karlin, and Gerard B. Wegemer (eds.), *Thomas More's Trial by Jury: A Procedural and Legal Review with a Collection of Documents* (Woodbridge: The Boydell Press, 2011), p. 187.
380. Sil, "'My Bitter Comedie,'" p. 390.
381. Derek Dunne, "Re-assessing Trial by Jury in Early Modern Law and Literature", *Literature Compass*, Vol. 12, Issue 10, p. 519.

Arrival at Court

Early in the morning on the first day of sessions, shackled prisoners from the local gaol would be brought to court, while those on bail would arrive there independently, as would their prosecutors. The latter would normally produce appropriate bills of indictment, written on slips of parchment, or preparatory drafts in paper. These might have been prepared with the help of examining (or other) JPs. For example, in July 1574 Thomas Lyfield, a Surrey JP, wrote to his more experienced colleague William More, noting that he had sent him Robert Wyse's confession to stealing a horse and asking More to draw-up an appropriate indictment.[382] If these documents did not arrive ready prepared with prosecutors, they could be drawn-up with the assistance of the court clerk.

The Grand Jury

At all trials on indictment (but not on appeal), whether at quarter sessions, borough sessions, or assizes, a grand jury would first have to scrutinise and approve the tendered bills of indictment before they could go for a hearing in front of a petty (trial) jury; this had been expressly required by medieval legislation and was done to ensure that accusations were not being made maliciously.[383]

By the Tudor era, grand juries did not normally present significant criminal offences from their own knowledge, as had occurred in the high medieval period, although they might occasionally initiate prosecutions for regulatory matters, such as the repair of roads and bridges, especially (but not solely) at quarter sessions (see *Chapter 1*).[384] However, at the lower forum, hundred juries would still present a significant number of bills for consideration by the quarter sessions grand jury, albeit that most would (again) be of a regulatory nature.

---

382. SHC LM/COR/3/153.
383. Langbein, *History of the Common Law*, p. 218.
384. *Ibid*, p. 216.

Grand Jury Scrutiny

Grand juries would consider the tendered bills of indictment in private. Ostensibly, this was done to prevent external influence being brought to bear, alerting offenders still at liberty that they were being sought, and garnering adverse publicity for those whose bills were thrown out. Grand jurors usually sat in a room, house, or inn that was close to the main court. However, by 1500 the London area may have been an exception in this regard, with bills of indictment for the Newgate or Old Bailey Sessions normally being considered at (almost) simultaneously held City and Middlesex Quarter Sessions, rather than the forum itself, a situation that would continue in ensuing centuries.

"True bills" found by quarter sessions grand juries could also be referred to the assizes for trial, if the lower court thought fit, without the need for further scrutiny by the higher forum's own grand jury. A significant number of trials at assizes during the Tudor period (especially in its latter years) were held on indictments that had been approved earlier by quarter sessions grand juries, where the JPs had then declined jurisdiction. For example, the Surrey Assizes held at Guildford in the summer of 1530 to try prisoners being held in gaol at Southwark, determined several indictments approved at the county quarter sessions at Kingston the previous Michaelmas.[385] Nevertheless, the lower jury forum's increasing reluctance to hear serious felonies made it much more common towards the close of the Tudor era.

Grand jurors were merely required to hear enough evidence from the prosecutor and his witnesses to establish a prima facie case against the accused. They did not normally listen to defence evidence, however relevant it might appear. This also meant that the defendant did not have to be in custody, or even in court, to be indicted. As a result, Sir Thomas Smith thought that "commonly men be indicted absent, not called to it, nor knowing of it". For example, John She was indicted in his absence for stealing a gelding at the Surrey Assizes in February 1559.[386]

---

385. SHC LM/961/1.
386. Cockburn, *Calendar of Assize Records. Surrey Indictments: Elizabeth I*, p. 2.

This may have been a fairly frequent occurrence during the late medieval period, when criminal complaints were still sometimes first raised at sessions. In an extreme example, of the ten men indicted at the Cheshire County Court Sessions (the palatinate's then equivalent of both assizes and quarter sessions) held on 10 January 1464, only one, Lawrence Priestwood, was in custody or on bail. The other nine were still at large.[387] However, despite Sir Thomas' belief, it was not very common by the sixteenth century, when suspects were being committed to prison by JPs prior to their appearance at court, and very few people were indicted while totally unaware of the proceedings against them, especially at assizes.

When this did happen, it was most likely to occur when a group of men had committed a crime but only one (or some) of them had been captured; the grand jury would consider bills against absentee suspects at the same time as they did that of the detained man or men. Typically, in 1586, when Christopher Phillips, a professional horse thief, was capitally convicted at the Hertford Assizes the grand jury also indicted Thomas Hayward as an accessory, even though he was still at large. Presumably the indictment was left on the file in the hope that he would eventually be arrested and produced for trial.[388] Such a situation might also occur when a suspected felon was on bail, and then failed to appear at court for his hearing.

There is little firm evidence as to how the Tudor grand jury was informed when making its decisions. To some extent, this may have varied with time, circuit, and forum. Nevertheless, it is apparent that evidence would usually be given by oral testimony. For example, when the Warboys witches came for trial at the Huntingdon Assizes in 1593, it was noted that, after their indictments were delivered to the grand jury, an extensive list of witnesses, including the victim's father and various clerics, gave evidence, albeit testifying very speedily, even by the standards of the main trial, and this was probably typical of such hearings. After hearing them, "The graund Jury made no great delay, but found

---

387. Quintrell, *Proceedings of the Lancashire Justices*, p. 3; Blackstone, *Commentaries, Vol. 1*, p. 115; Harris and Clayton, "Criminal Procedure in Cheshire", pp. 161–162.

388. J. S. Cockburn, *Calendar of Assize Records. Hertfordshire Indictments: James I* (London: HMSO, 1975), p. 62.

them all guiltie [i.e. *billa verra* in this context]".[389] Similarly, just after the Tudor era, it was noted that the two main prosecution witnesses against the notorious pickpocket John Selman — his final victim and his captor respectively — gave extensive verbal testimony to the 18 man "grand inquest" at King's Bench.[390]

Even so, Sir Thomas Smith, writing about 1565, spoke of indicted defendants at assizes being acquitted without difficulty if no-one attended trial to testify against them. By definition, this presupposes that their case had got through the grand-jury hearing; if the prosecution witnesses were not in court, it could be argued that the grand jurors must have had other material to base their decisions on. Certainly, the Marian committal statute of 1555 required examining JPs to submit the depositions they had taken in advance of the assize sitting and then (normally) to attend in person. It is possible that, at the assizes, magistrates or the clerk of assize took these depositions to the grand jury, perhaps with the aid of an arresting constable, and that the grand jurors sometimes made their decision on the basis of these documents, at least in part, if only to expedite the process. Against this, the matter might simply have been approved by a quarter sessions grand jury and referred to the higher court for trial.

If the grand jury found a bill to be "true", they normally wrote *billa verra* or a regional variation on it and then sent it to the courtroom so that the matter could be tried. If they did not find a case to answer they would usually write *ignoramus* on it, and the defendant would be released by proclamation, although this did not constitute an acquittal that would preclude a better-evidenced case being brought in future. This was rare, but did sometimes occur. For example, in July 1615 the Reverend John Lowes faced four counts of witchcraft at the Suffolk Assizes, but the grand jury threw out all of them. Even so, one of the counts was later renewed and, on this occasion, successfully reached a jury trial, though

---

389. Anon, *The Most Strange and Admirable Discoverie of the Three Witches of Warboys* (London, 1593), p. 108.

390. Anon, *The araignment of John Selman, who was executed neere Charing-Crosse the 7. of January, 1611. for a felony by him committed in the Kings Chappell at White-Hall upon Christmas day last, in presence of the King and divers of the Nobility* (London, 1612), p. 12 and p. 13.

a not guilty verdict was then returned.[391] Very unusually, in a notorious murder case of 1624, a man named Smethwick, the only one of a group of people who avoided committal for trial at the Somerset Assizes after receiving a finding of *ignoramus* from the grand jury, was not released. Instead he was "recommitted unto the Gayle of *Ilchester,* to the intent that time might produce stronger proofes against him".[392]

The grand jury process was exactly the same at the lower jury court, if a little less formal and, it seems, with little or no use of deposition evidence, even in the latter decades of the sixteenth century (whatever may have been the situation at the higher forum). As the jurist Sir Francis Bacon observed, at the start of quarter sessions an accuser was usually called into court and asked to prepare a bill of indictment against the prisoner, and then to go with it to the grand jury, where he would "give evidence upon their oaths, he and the [prosecution] witnesses".[393] Nevertheless, in a witchcraft trial in Elizabethan Colchester, a witness who had made an allegation in a magistrate's examination prior to trial at the borough sessions failed to repeat the charge at the gaol delivery. The case was dropped, despite having been indicted by the grand jury, suggesting that that body may have used his written examination to reach their decision.[394]

Unlike the trial jury, the number on a grand jury was not limited to a dozen men, and, as the Venetian envoy's comment suggests, decisions were reached by simple majority rather than unanimously, although at least 12 jurors had to agree that there was a case to answer before they could indict a matter. Occasionally, grand juries of up to 27 men might be found at the assizes. However, 24 jurors was the normal maximum, and much smaller numbers were far more common. Grand jurors were, effectively, selected from a small panel, as it was not uncommon for one or two of the summoned men to be rejected or excused at court, for whatever reason, so that not all of those called served.

---

391. Malcolm Gaskill, *Witchfinders: A Seventeenth century English Tragedy* (London: John Murray, 2005), p. 140.
392. C. W., *The crying murther Contayning the cruell and most horrible bu[tchery] of Mr. Trat, curate of old Cleave* (London, 1624), p. 10.
393. Bacon, "The Use of The Law", p. 250.
394. Samaha, *Law and Order,* p. 69.

The (very) late medieval and Tudor assizes grand jury did not have the exalted social status it was to acquire in the late seventeenth century. For example, none of the 19 men on the grand jury panel for the Cheshire County Court Sessions in January 1464 was given the title of knight or esquire.[395] Some men served on both types of jury, grand and petty. Nevertheless, its members were usually, on average, of a higher rank than those found on the trial jury, and often included several men drawn from what might very loosely be termed the upper social orders.

Thus, and for example, at the Surrey Assizes in the mid-1580s, the grand jury normally numbered at least 17 men, with 19 jurors being the most common figure, and the odd jury being up to 21 men in strength. Most juries included three or four individuals (loosely) described as "gents", although the total in this category varied between none and seven. Typically, at the assizes held at Croydon in July 1586, 19 men served, of whom four were described as gentlemen. This profile was precisely matched at the Southwark Assizes in February 1587 and at those held at the same forum a year later.[396] The situation in Essex was similar, with between 17 and 21 men normally found on assizes grand juries, with two or three usually being accorded the status of "gent". However, of the 18 men on the grand jury at the Chelmsford Assizes in February 1598, a remarkable 12 were accorded this title.[397]

A much higher proportion of grand jurors had previous experience of service than did their counterparts on the petty (trial) jury. Two examples from fifteenth century Cheshire are illustrative. Peter Minshull served on 41 grand-jury panels between 1450 and 1477, while John Bunbury sat on 28 between 1460 and 1481. These are extreme cases, but neophyte grand jurors were in a small minority in Cheshire at the start of the Tudor era. This general pattern can still be identified in the same county in the mid-seventeenth century.[398] It was matched in Essex and appears to have been the situation nationwide.

---

395. Harris and Clayton, "Criminal Procedure In Cheshire", p. 162.
396. Cockburn, *Calendar of Assize Records. Surrey Indictments: Elizabeth I*, p. 285, p. 295, and pp. 311–312.
397. Cockburn, *Calendar of Assize Records. Essex Indictments: Elizabeth I*, p. 479.
398. Harris and Clayton, "Criminal Procedure In Cheshire", p. 162.

At quarter sessions, the grand jury was typically made up of about 16 or so "discreet" freeholders chosen from a panel of 24 individuals summoned by the sheriff, although figures varied from as few as 13 to well over 20 men.[399] A handwritten guide to running quarter sessions of 1590 suggested one or (unusually) even two grand juries of "14 or 15 substantial freeholders".[400] For example, at the Durham Quarter Sessions held in March 1511, there were 26 grand jurors present, albeit that, for most of the sixteenth century, a jury of 13 to 15 men was more normal at this forum.[401] The social complexion of grand jurors at the lower jury tribunal was more modest than at assizes, but still, on average, higher than that for the trial jury sworn in at the same forum. At the Monmouthshire Quarter Sessions held at Usk in June 1572, three of the 15 grand jurors were even described as gentlemen while at the same forum held at Monmouth in July 1577, almost half (seven of 15 men) were accorded this status.[402]

The considerable pressure placed on grand juries to reach decisions expeditiously, so that trials could proceed, meant that although there was nothing to stop them returning one true bill at a time to the court, they often did so in batches. At the start of the Hilary Assizes held in Essex in 1594, groups of six or seven indictments were being returned. However, towards its end, the grand jury sent back one batch of 25 decisions.[403] Once a man had been formally indicted by a grand jury, he would be treated more strictly, perhaps even losing his liberty pending the outcome of the trial if he had been on bail.[404]

Grand jurors (like trial jurors) could be referred to the Star Chamber or council if a presiding judge or other royal official thought that they had improperly refused to indict a matter, although this happened very seldom. However, in February 1528 those who returned a bill of indictment in a murder case as *ignoramus*, in a matter the Crown considered to be clearly suitable for trial, after allegedly ignoring the prosecution's

399. Bacon, 'The Use of The Law", p. 250.
400. HRO KAcc148/5/G/310.
401. DRO Durham Quarter Sessions DQS 15.
402. Howell, *Law and Disorder*, p. 69 and p. 81.
403. Samaha, *Law and Order*, p. 100.
404. Smith, *De Republica Anglorum*, p. 105.

"pregnant and manifest" evidence, were presented by the king's solicitor and committed to the Fleet Prison on the orders of the Council. New bills were ordered, and a fresh jury empanelled to reconsider the matter (the finding of *ignoramus* not constituting an acquittal).[405] Similarly, in 1561 a grand jury in Derby was imprisoned, fined, and forced to wear papers confessing its guilt by the same forum for returning a bill *ignoramus* when, it was claimed, the evidence warranted a murder indictment.[406]

It is apparent that the Tudor grand jury process was not a formality. A significant number of allegations were thrown out, as can be seen from the number of cases in which co-defendants came before grand juries, where some bills were found *billa verra* and others *ignoramus*. (In these situations a reference to the latter is much more likely to have survived than in situations where no-one was indicted.) For example, at the Chelmsford Assizes in March 1595, Richard Loveday and Thomas Wendell were accused of stealing a pig. A true bill was found against Loveday (albeit that he was acquitted at trial), but not his alleged accomplice.[407]

However, it is difficult to establish the precise proportion of cases dismissed by grand juries after assessing their merits, as most bills of indictment that were endorsed *ignoramus* were eventually (and unfortunately for historians) destroyed. Although such men and women were formally delivered by proclamation, this was also done when no one appeared to prosecute an accused person. Nevertheless, at the Hertford Assizes in March 1597, it seems that about a quarter of all suspects were eventually released for these two reasons.[408] In Somerset the year before, the JP Edmund Hext, writing to the Lord Treasurer, noted that at the Lent Assizes some 134 prisoners had gone before the grand jury; at the end of the sessions nine of these were executed and 14 clergied after conviction for felony, and 15 were whipped after being found guilty of petty larceny (the majority probably as a result of down-valuing by the jury).[409] This produces 38 convictions out of 134 bills of indictment (about 30 per cent). Again, it is not clear how many of the latter were thrown out by

405. Bellamy, *The Criminal Trial*, p. 33.
406. Hamilton, "Star Chamber and Juries", pp. 239–240.
407. Cockburn, *Calendar of Assize Records. Essex indictments: Elizabeth I*, p. 433.
408. Cockburn, *Calendar of Assize Records. Hertfordshire Indictments: Elizabeth I*, p. 131.
409. Strype, *Annals of the Reformation*, p. 404.

the grand jury as *ignoramus*, or because they produced not guilty verdicts at trial, but, given late Tudor conviction rates (often about two-thirds) it must have been significant, and possibly higher than the 12 per cent of cases that one scrutiny of gaol calendars suggests was thrown out at assizes in the seventeenth century.[410]

This double jury hearing (grand and petty) was confusing to foreign observers. In 1500 a Venetian envoy inaccurately observed that in a grand jury "if the greater number vote that he has [committed the crime], he is considered to be guilty. He is not, however, punished at that time; but it is necessary that twelve other men should be chosen, who must hear the cause over again: and if their verdict should agree with the former one, the days of the delinquent are brought to a close".[411]

The Indictment

Tudor indictments, like most other legal documents of the time, were written in Latin (as they would be until 1733), although translated verbally into the vernacular by the court clerk for both defendants and jurors. They tended to be lengthy and prolix. In part, this was because, in theory, they had to be extremely precise, especially as courts were reluctant to allow them to be amended once a trial was under way.

The Statute of Additions (or Additional Information) of 1413 (1 Henry V c. 5) required that an indictment provide, inter alia, not just the defendant's name but also his place and county of residence as well as his "estate". In 1503 Sir Thomas Marowe could suggest that indictments had five essential components: the name and "addition" (occupation and residence) of the defendant; the date and place of the offence; the name of the victim (if known); and details of any goods stolen in a theft, or weapons used in a crime of violence. These were viewed very seriously, and a failure to provide such information could lead to a legal challenge.[412]

This was not a new phenomenon in 1485. For example, during the mid-fifteenth century, a significant number of those tried at gaol delivery

---

410. Cockburn, *A History of English Assizes*, p. 127.
411. Anon, *A Relation, or Rather A True Account*, p. 33.
412. Powell, *Kingship, Law, and Society*, p. 67.

in the Border counties, such as Northumberland, were released *sine die* (without an appointed date for resumption and effectively a dismissal) after their indictments were examined and dismissed by the judges for being "insufficient in law" or *minus sufficiens in lege*. Frequently this was on highly technical grounds (often based on the 1413 Act), such as a failure to note the name of the county in which the suspect's home village was located. More often it was because indictments failed to note details such as the defendant's occupation, the name of a murder victim, the value of the goods stolen, or the place and date of the alleged felony.[413]

This need for accuracy and completeness continued in the Tudor era. Thus, during the reign of Henry VII, an indictment alleged that a man had killed another on the Feast of St Peter. However, this was held to be bad because there was more than one feast day for the very important saint each year, and the precise one had not been specified. During his son's reign, in *R v Hardwyk*, heard at the Court of King's Bench in 1532, a man was indicted for stealing ten wether sheep. No value for the animals was set out in the indictment, and it was held that this rendered it "void", as they could, in theory (although not in reality), have been worth less than a shilling, making the case one of non-capital petty theft.[414] Furthermore, many specific offences had to incorporate particular words if they were not to fail. Thus an indictment for rape that did not use the word "rapuit" was bad, as was one for murder in which "murdravit" was misspelled "murderavit".[415]

This precision did not just apply to indictments relating to felonies. In 1591 John Perry was prosecuted at the Essex Quarter Sessions for what appears to have been a misdemeanour (possibly keeping an unlicensed "tippling house"), and challenged his indictment. Henry Longe, his attorney — active legal representation in court was allowed for the lesser category of crime — claimed that it was insufficient in law. One reason given was that it did not give Perry's trade or occupation, contrary to the ostensible requirements of the 1413 Act and common law. It

---

413. C. J. Neville, "Gaol Delivery in the Border Counties, 1439–1459: Some Preliminary Observations", *Northern History*, Vol. 19, Issue 1, pp. 54–55.
414. John Spelman, *The Reports of Sir John Spelman* (London: Selden Society, 1977), p. 98.
415. Geoffrey de C. Parmiter, "Tudor Indictments, Illustrated by the Indictment of St. Thomas More", *Recusant History*, Vol. 6, Issue 3, pp. 145–147.

was also challenged as to the dates at which it was alleged that Perry had kept the tippling house, as well as "divers other causes".[416] Similarly, at the Kent Quarter Sessions held at Canterbury in January 1602, Thomas Crayford was accused of shooting duck with a gun loaded with shot, contrary to several statutes, including one from 1548 (2 & 3 Edward VI c. 14). However, the indictment was deemed to be insufficient, and so void, because it lacked the words "a handgun".[417]

As some of the above cases suggest, a common way for defendants to challenge felony indictments during the Tudor era was to have them removed by a writ of *certiorari* into the Court of King's Bench for further consideration. King's Bench, the highest court of common law, enjoyed supervisory powers over inferior courts. As was noted (in Law French) in 1526, its judges had: *"poier de proceder et termyner inditements presentementes prises en alcun counte deins le royalme"*.[418] Recourse to this procedure was often effective, especially in the early decades of the era. This was widely known. When Sir John Huddleston wrote to Thomas Cromwell in 1539 about the murder of William Jackson (one of his servants) some two years earlier, he noted that one of the men indicted for the crime had had his case "removyd up un to the kyngis bench by the kyngis wrytt to the intent that he schall be savyd, the wyche where grett pettye".[419]

For example, in July 1503 a coroner's inquest in Kent concluded that Agnes Berry had fatally poisoned her husband, Richard, the previous March. She initially fled to sanctuary, but later surrendered for trial. However, Berry appeared before King's Bench in 1507 and pleaded that her indictment was insufficient, because it did not identify in what place or county she lived, as required by the 1413 act. The court agreed, and she was released; the matter eventually went *sine die*.[420]

Similarly, in 1539 William Gawger, a yeoman and bailiff to the Earl of Essex, was accused of murdering a miller at Chelsworth, in Suffolk. It was alleged that he had stabbed him in the side of the head with a dagger.

416. ERO Q/SR 115/53.
417. Knafla, *Kent at Law, 1602*, p. 39.
418. Richard Pynson, *Diversite de Courtz et lour Jurisdictions* (London, 1526), f. Aiii.
419. McSheffrey, "Sanctuary Seekers".
420. *Ibid.*

A coroner's inquest was held, and the jury held Gawger responsible for murder. It is likely that he was sent for trial at the Bury Assizes on their presentment. However, he was not arraigned there. A writ of *certiorari* removed the case to King's Bench. When Gawger came for trial there, and despite being prosecuted by the Attorney General, he challenged the indictment on the basis that it stated that he came from Dunmow, in Essex, although there was no village of this precise name (in fact, there was Great Dunmow and Little Dunmow). He called witnesses to establish this point, and was discharged on the technicality, after spending two years in prison.[421]

Many Tudor indictments contained inaccuracies; discrepancies with other documents, such as pre-trial examinations; and flaws that, it might be thought, should have provided fertile grounds for legal challenge.[422] Nevertheless, these were, apparently, usually ignored by clerks of assizes, judges and grand juries, and only a very small proportion of all indictments were referred to King's/Queen's Bench for review.

In part this was for practical reasons; such actions were extremely expensive. That John Perry had a lawyer is significant. Most defendants did not have access to legal advice, even outside the courtroom, and did not appreciate that they could challenge indictments on these grounds (competent lawyers might have made short work of at least some of them). Furthermore, a copy of the indictment, vital for identifying such flaws, was not given to the accused person as of right. Even Anne Boleyn did not see her indictment prior to trial in 1536.[423] In practice, it seems that the legal niceties that sometimes afforded the rich, educated, and well-connected loopholes to avoid the reach of the criminal law, were often ignored in routine trials of ordinary people.

Nevertheless, by the Tudor era at least, whether all of the details required in an indictment had to be accurate, rather than precisely set out, is also questionable. Some were quite obviously mistaken without

---

421. Bellamy, *Strange, Inhuman Deaths*, p. 108.

422. J. S. Cockburn, "Trial by the Book? Fact and Theory in the Criminal Process 1558–1625", in J. H. Baker (ed.), *Legal Records and the Historian* (London: Royal Historical Society, 1978), pp. 62–64.

423. Margery S. Schauer and Frederick Schauer, "Law as the Engine of State: The Trial of Anne Boleyn", *William & Mary Law Review*, Vol. 22, Issue 1, p. 60.

occasioning undue concern, and it may be that this was not solely due to a blind-eye being cast over them, but because the defects were not thought to have major legal implications. For example, provided that a valuation was given to stolen goods that clearly identified whether the case was one of petty or grand larceny, its precise accuracy may not have been important. Similarly, the exact date of an offence was not necessarily vital. Furthermore, some documentary discrepancies in the occupation and status of the accused may have been more apparent than real, being due to defendants' holding more than one occupation; for example, bakers often doubled up as brewers, while a clergyman might also be a farmer.

Other differences may have been matters of terminology. The 1413 statute (1 Henry V c. 5) required that an accused's "estate or degree or mystery" be given in the indictment; clearly, just one of these was sufficient. Quite often, an apparent discrepancy between a document and an indictment in this regard can be explained by one having given a precise occupation, for example "bargeman", and the other a broad status, such as "labourer". It may be that only gross discrepancies, such as that found in a case in which an attorney of the Court of Common Pleas was discharged when he proved that he was not a "husbandman", would be deemed significant. It should also be noted that people changed occupations, status, and residence at a faster pace during the Tudor era than is sometimes appreciated. Apparent inaccuracies in identifying the place from which the accused came can often be explained by geographical mobility. A defendant may have been born in one place, had legal settlement in a second, worked or owned property in a third, and temporarily resided in yet another, making them all "valid".[424]

Arraignment

Once the grand jury had approved a bill of indictment the prisoner would have to plead to it. As Sir Thomas Smith observed: "No man that is once indicted can be delivered without arainement. For as xij have given a prejudice against him, so xij againe must acquite or condemne him".

---

424. Alan Macfarlane, "Review of 'Calendar of Assize Records. Essex Indictments: Elizabeth I'", *American Journal of Legal History*, Vol. 24, pp. 171–177.

The plea had to be unequivocal. When, at the Newgate gaol delivery in January 1512, Robert Williamson, a London tailor, was arraigned for grand larceny and pleaded not guilty but, at the same time, asked that he be acquitted on the ground that he had been forcibly removed from sanctuary, his plea was held (slightly unusually) to be insufficiently clear. He was ordered to undergo *peine forte et dure* (see below), although it does not seem to have been imposed (he remained in prison until 1523, when he presented a pardon at King's Bench).[425]

If defendants could not respond to the arraignment because they were "mute by the visitation of God", that is physically unable to speak, a not guilty plea would be entered on their behalf. Early in the reign of Henry VIII, a deaf mute was indicted for homicide, raising questions as to what to do with him, as he could not follow evidence, and his reasons for standing mute could not be investigated properly; some legal observers thought he should be "perpetually" detained in prison without trial as a result.[426]

However, standing "mute of malice", i.e. refusing to enter a plea (even if the defendant explained his reasons for such a refusal) was extremely unusual, as it had fearful consequences. As Christopher St Germain noted in the 1530s, in the context of a homicide allegation, if a man was arraigned "at the king's suit [i.e. on indictment], and thereupon standeth dumb, and will not answer; there he shall not be attainted of the murther, but he shall have Paine fort and dure, that is to say, he shall be pressed to death".[427] As a result, when, in December 1550, William Hill, a Sussex glover living in Whitechapel, broke into a house and stole 60lb of wool, and refused to plead guilty or not guilty when indicted at the Old Bailey the following month, he was committed to the *peine*, his bill of indictment being marked: *"Pd. Will's noluit ponere se ipsum in jur' illam sed recusavit resp' sc'd'm legem. Ideo judicium dat' est p' Cur' scz, fort et dure"*.[428]

---

425. McSheffrey, "Sanctuary Seekers".
426. Spelman, *Reports of Sir John Spelman*, p. 67.
427. St. Germain, *The Doctor and Student*, p. 227.
428. Jeaffreson, *Middlesex County Records: Vol. 1, 1550–1603*, pp. 7–8.

Peine Forte et Dure

In theory, the *peine forte et dure* involved being pressed to death by huge weights being placed on a board over the breast and a sharp stone under the back.[429] Although in 1586 Margaret Clitherow had a fist-size rock placed underneath her, Sir Thomas Smith thought that this feature (intended to break the suspect's spine) was often left out of the process, the accused man or woman merely being "layd upon a table, and an other uppon him, and so much weight of stones or lead laide uppon that table, while as his bodie be crushed". Doors were sometimes used instead of tables.

Pressing, and the hard dietary regime that traditionally preceded or accompanied it, was a relic of the situation prior to 1215 in which an accused person had to choose trial on indictment rather than trial by ordeal. If he was reluctant to choose, he had to be "encouraged" to do so. Originally, under the Statute of Westminster of 1275, it seems that those receiving the *peine* were merely imprisoned and starved into submission, with a tiny amount of unsalted barley bread daily alternating with a small quantity of dirty water.[430] However, in 1406, at the very latest (and probably earlier), pressing to death was added to the regime, perhaps as a result of a growing need for expeditiousness in the trial process. In theory, the combination produced a hybrid means of persuasion, though by the Tudor era the weights killed the defendant long before he could find the diet more than an irritant.

When sentence was passed on Margaret Clitherow in March 1586, her assizes judge ordered that she be "stripped naked, laid down, your back upon the ground, and as much weight laid upon you as you are able to bear, and so to continue three days without meat or drink, except a little barley bread and puddle water, and the third day to be pressed to death, your hands and feet tied to posts, and a sharp stone under your back". However, in Clitherow's case (and most others), it seems that weights were not applied until their final, fatal, imposition. The process

---

429. William Harrison, *Elizabethan England* (London: W. Scott, 1889), p. 244.
430. Musson and Powell, *Crime, Law and Society*, p. 168.

would normally be carried out in (or close to) a gaol that was local to the trial court.

Noblemen, like females, were subject to the *peine* in the same way as male commoners.[431] When Lord Stourton, tried by his peers for murder in 1557, hesitated to enter a plea to his indictment, he was warned of the dire consequences if he persisted in his recalcitrance. Margaret Clitherow was made of sterner stuff; she was pressed to death in the tollbooth on Ousebridge (next to the prison where she was incarcerated) for repeatedly refusing to enter a plea at the York Assizes to the new statutory felony of harbouring Catholic priests (27 Eliz I c. 2).

According to Father John Mush, Margaret Clitherow's confessor, local beggars were drafted in to carry out the gruesome procedure, although the two York sheriffs, other peace officers, and several women were also present. Clitherow died after just 15 minutes: "Upon her was laid to the quantity of seven or eight hundred-weight at the least, which, breaking her ribs, caused them to burst forth of the skin". (Others in this situation lasted much longer.) It seems that Margaret's own house door was employed in the process. Her dead (and near naked) body remained under the weights for six hours, and then the serjeants present were ordered to bury her in an obscure part of the city; allegedly, they chose a spot "beside a dunghill" when interring her in the middle of the night.[432]

However, pressing was not necessary in cases of high treason (as opposed to felony and petty treason) because in these situations the defendant's silence was treated as tantamount to a guilty plea. For this reason, the religious fanatic William Hacket's refusal to give a clear, unequivocal plea to the second count on the indictment at his treason trial at the Old Bailey in 1591 automatically produced a conviction.[433] Similarly, silence in the face of misdemeanour indictments was also treated as a guilty plea, precluding its use in minor cases. Furthermore, the *peine* applied only to trial on indictment, not to a felony prosecuted by appeal, where silence also constituted a formal admission.[434]

---

431. J. H. Baker, "Criminal Justice at Newgate 1616–1627", *The Irish Jurist*, Vol. 8, No. 2, p. 316.
432. Katharine M. Longley, "The 'Trial' Of Margaret Clitherow", *Ampleforth Journal*, Vol. 75, No. 3, p. 340.
433. Richard Cosin, *Conspiracie, for pretended Reformation* (London, 1591), pp. 72–80.
434. St. Germain, *The Doctor and Student*, p. 227.

Suffering the *peine* was a horrific way to die, and, unsurprisingly, Lord Stourton was not the only man to waver when threatened with it. Such individuals normally appear to have been allowed to change their minds, even after the procedure had been ordered. Margaret Clitherow was repeatedly urged to enter a plea after the *peine* was passed on her, even being visited in prison to this end, the presiding judge telling her that the court would be indulgent if she changed her mind.[435] At the Essex Assizes in July 1607, David Barton, accused of grand larceny, was recorded as standing "mute". However, he was sentenced at the following assizes, so he must have been allowed to enter a plea.[436]

Nevertheless, there could be significant benefits to enduring such torment for those with the requisite fortitude, especially if facing an unanswerable prosecution case, explaining why some people had recourse to it. Most important, the "death of the party before conviction dischargeth all proceedings and forfeitures".[437] By contrast, in theory, a convicted felon would forfeit all his goods and chattels to the Crown, and all lands to the lord of the fee, after the king had taken the profit of those lands for a year-and-a-day. As a result, they were permanently lost to his family, although there was some legal confusion, and considerable local variation, as to precisely what would be forfeit, particularly in Kent (where land was never given up), Gloucester, and the Redesdale Valley of Northumberland. Furthermore, after 1547 statute allowed the widows of felons to retain their dower in an executed husband's freehold land, and in ensuing years there were further changes with regard to heirs' rights to felons' estates under specific statutory crimes.[438]

Those who died before conviction avoided subjecting their families to such losses. Nevertheless, suicide was shameful, a grave sin, and a special felony resulting in forfeiture, despite the absence of a conviction. In late 1554, after the mentally-disturbed and severely depressed judge Sir James Hales deliberately drowned himself in a Kentish stream (as was found by a coroner's inquest), Sir James Dyer, the Lord Chief Justice, declared

---

435. John Morris, *The Troubles of our Catholic Forefathers Related by Themselves* (London: Burns and Oates, 1872, p. 417.
436. Cockburn, *Calendar of Assize Records. Essex Indictments: James I*, p. 29.
437. Francis Bacon, *Cases of Treason* (London, 1641), pp. 12–13.
438. Kesselring, "Felony Forfeiture", pp. 272–273.

that the "forfeiture of the goods and chattels, real and personal, of Sir James shall have relation to the act done in his lifetime". The Crown then seized his property.

However, if the state killed a defendant before he was convicted, by application of the *peine*, this did not occur. John Gerard, a celebrated Catholic priest in Elizabethan England, was convinced that this was one of the reasons the authorities were reluctant to put the *peine* into effect after it was ordered for the prosperous Catholic widow Jane Wiseman, accused of harbouring priests in 1598: "What they were after was her property for the Queen. And had she been executed [pressed in this context], this would have gone, not to the Queen, but her son, my host".[439] (It was Queen Elizabeth who ultimately ensured that the *peine* was never carried out, and Wiseman was pardoned and released a few years later).

Unsurprisingly, few extremely poor men refused to enter a plea, having little to save that was of interest to the Crown, or reason for preserving it. Nevertheless, for the few defendants with substantial assets, such as the major Warwickshire landowner Lodowick Greville, who was pressed to death in the King's Bench Prison in Southwark after standing mute to a murder indictment at King's Bench in November 1589, confiscation remained a serious concern (his fortitude allowed his son Edward to inherit his estate), while for those with a modest amount of possessions this danger could not be disregarded.[440]

Furthermore, those who refused to enter a plea escaped being publicly humiliated at trial. This may have been a factor in 1595, when Richard Weekes, one of a pair of highway robbers who had attacked a man in Southall and stolen more than £46 from him, refused to enter a plea, although his co-accused pleaded guilty. He was committed to the *peine*. Weekes was described (perhaps a little optimistically) as a gentleman, while his colleague was merely termed a yeoman, and it is possible that he sought to preserve his honour as well as his estate.[441] By contrast, it

439. Gerard, *Autobiography of a Hunted Priest*, p. 65.
440. Jan Broadway, "Aberrant Accounts: William Dugdale's Handling of Two Tudor Murders in '*The Antiquities of Warwickshire*,'" *Midland History*, Vol. 33, No. 1, p. 14; Moore, *The Tudor Murder Files*, pp. 140–141; Smith, *De Republica Anglorum*, p. 112.
441. Jeaffreson, *Middlesex County Records: Vol. 1, 1550–1603*, pp. 225–230.

seems that Margaret Clitherow refused to plead to prevent her children and servants being called and pressured to testify against her.

The *peine* appears to have been administered slightly more frequently in the metropolitan area than in the provinces, if only because of its large population. Typically, in December 1551 a grand jury at the Old Bailey found a true bill against William Hill, a glover from Robertsbridge, in Sussex, who was accused of breaking into a house at Whitechapel, in Middlesex, and stealing a large quantity of wool. Refusing to plead guilty or not guilty, Hill was subjected to the *peine*.[442] In 1595, at least two men were ordered for pressing at the Old Bailey, in separate cases; this was probably about the annual average for the decade.

Outside London use of the *peine* was relatively rare. No cases are recorded for the Elizabethan assizes in Hertfordshire, albeit that no records are preserved from before 1573. At the Essex Assizes, during the 43-year period after 1560, only two men are recorded as having stood mute of malice, on separate occasions, so that the court ordered that they be pressed (some records are missing). Michael Lyster, a butcher from Theydon Garnon, had been accused of grand larceny after stealing a black ox and a similarly coloured "runt". Lyster may have been a moderately prosperous man, perhaps explaining his decision. The other individual, Francis Morris, was, it appears, a habitual burglar. His two colleagues pleaded not guilty and were convicted. It is possible that Morris had accrued enough wealth from his criminal career to make it worth the torment.[443] Similarly, only two such cases are preserved for Essex during the entire Jacobean period.

However, rare though it was, Clitherow was not alone in the North in standing mute. For example, in Chester, at the start of the seventeenth century, the poisoner Elizabeth Caldwell's lover, Geoffrey Bownd, refused to plead, whether due to "evill counsell giuen him, or for his owne obstinacie". He was sentenced to the *peine* on a Saturday, so that he was pressed at nine o'clock on Monday morning, "where to every mans judgement there present, hee made a very penitent end".[444]

---

442. *Ibid*, pp. 7–8.
443. Cockburn, *Calendar of Assize Records. Essex Indictments{ Elizabeth I*, p. 67.
444. Dugdale, Gilbert, *A true discourse of the practises of Elizabeth Caldwell* (London,1604), pp. 1–10.

The Plea

According to the elderly Ferdinando Pulton, writing in 1609, not guilty was the "most common and usual plea" in a felony case.[445] In the 1560s Sir Thomas Smith claimed that felons normally entered such a plea even if they had been caught red-handed or confessed to their crime when examined by a JP. Even earlier, in the 1530s, pleading not guilty was viewed as positively desirable by Christopher St Germain's "Student", even in apparently well-evidenced cases, not least because innocent men could sometimes appear guilty at first sight.[446]

A guilty plea would also deny the trial jury any chance to down-value the subject matter of the indictment in a theft case, or of exercising some other form of jury equity. For example, at the Epiphany Quarter Sessions for Essex held in 1591, Jerome Heckford appears to have pleaded guilty ("acknowledges") to a very minor case of grand larceny, after being accused of stealing socks and a petticoat worth a total of two shillings from another villager in Marks Tey. He could not read (and so claim clergy), and was duly sentenced to death. This was exactly the sort of case that a trial jury at this time, given the opportunity, would have been likely to down-value below a shilling to non-capital petty theft.[447]

Even so, guilty pleas for capital felonies appear to have been much more common during the second half of the Tudor era (if not earlier), particularly at some venues, than in the seventeenth century, let alone the 1700s, when whole assizes regularly passed without a single accused felon formally admitting his guilt. By contrast, at the Old Bailey during the 1550s, and for reasons that have yet to be fully explained, guilty pleas can almost be described as the norm. They remained fairly common at this forum until the end of the reign of Queen Elizabeth. For example, in Hackney in 1571, a London shoemaker named John Sheppard stabbed a butcher to death with a meat knife. After pleading guilty to the crime, Sheppard was sentenced to death.[448] Similarly, in June 1601

---

445. Ferdinando Pulton, *De Pace Regis et Regni; Viz. A Treatise Declaring Which Be the Great and Generall Offences of the Realme* (London, 1609), p. 196.
446. St. Germain, *The Doctor and Student*, p. 258.
447. ERO Q/SR 115/108.
448. Jeaffreson, *Middlesex County Records: Vol. 1, 1550–1603*, pp. 68–73.

Henry Bowyer was indicted at the Old Bailey for the unclergyable crime of stealing ten horses in and about London and Middlesex the previous year. At the head of each bill was noted the abbreviation "Cogn' Indictamentu' Sus'" — i.e. he confessed the indictment (pleaded guilty), and was sentenced to be hanged.[449] After the early 1600s, it seems that "Not guilty" became an increasingly standard response to arraignment in the metropolitan area. On the Elizabethan Home Circuit, guilty pleas were less common than in the capital, even in the early 1560s, perhaps helping to explain Sir Thomas Smith's views. Nevertheless, they were still far more common than they would be 200 years later.

As a result, it appears that formal admissions of guilt were not nearly so strongly opposed by the judiciary at the late Tudor Old Bailey, and less vigorously opposed by assizes judges in the provinces than was to be the case in later years. They might sometimes even have been tacitly encouraged. This may have been done, at least in part, to address the increasingly heavy caseloads seen from the 1560s onwards; in some forums, work nearly doubled during the 30 years to 1590, placing the justice system under acute stress.[450] For example, Essex produced about eight indictments per 10,000 people in the 1560s but 20 by 1600.[451] Exceptional population growth in the London area during the sixteenth century also created considerable pressure of work at the Old Bailey, perhaps helping to explain the situation there.

Of course, sometimes, those who admitted their crimes in court were confident that they could claim clergy (men) or pregnancy (women). For example, in December 1563 John Crofton pleaded guilty at the Old Bailey to stealing three linen shirts in Highgate, and immediately and successfully asked for his "book". However, as Bowyer's case suggests (see above), this was by no means always the situation. A significant number of guilty pleas were made by the obviously illiterate, who had no such hope, or were made to crimes that had been withdrawn from clergy. Thus in September 1562 two men pleaded guilty to robbing a London

---

449. *Ibid*, pp. 257–266.
450. Dunne, "Re-assessing Trial by Jury", p. 521.
451. J. S. Cockburn, "The Nature and Incidences of Crime in England 1559–1625: A Preliminary Survey", in J. S. Cockburn (ed.), *Crime in England 1550–1800* (London: Methuen, 1977), pp. 53–54 and p. 70.

poulterer named Thomas Wilkinson on the highway at Edgware in Middlesex, and taking his horse, saddle, boots, clothes, sword, and cash. By then, neither highway robbery nor horse theft was clergyable, and the pair were sentenced to death.[452]

Throughout the Tudor era, pleas of guilty to misdemeanours and petty theft, which were always non-capital offences, were very much more common than for felonies, even at assizes, just as they would be for the ensuing two centuries. For example, at the Hertford Assizes in July 1591, all three (separate) cases indicted as petty larceny produced guilty pleas. At the same forum in March 1601, only one defendant out of eight accused of petty theft in five different cases pleaded not guilty.[453]

A guilty plea brought proceedings to a close, apart from the passing of sentence, which was often done communally at the end of sessions (subject to pleas of clergy and pregnancy). By contrast, after a defendant had entered a not guilty plea he would be asked how he wished to be tried, to which the prisoner had to reply, "By God and my country".[454] A jury would be sworn in or assembled, the defendant identified (by raising an arm), and the indictment explained to them by the clerk. A trial would then ensue.

The Trial Jury

In England, the trial or petty jury (rather than the older grand jury) had emerged as a result of the exclusion of priests from involvement in trial by ordeal after the Fourth Lateran Council in 1215. This forced the development of an alternative method of adjudication. Continental Europe was (eventually) to follow a different path in this regard, so that the English bifurcation of its tribunal between that of law (the judge) and fact (the petty jury) was always noteworthy for visitors from Roman law countries, where the two functions were normally combined in the judiciary. As a German traveller observed in the 1590s, the trial jury "sit

---

452. Jeaffreson, *Middlesex County Records: Volume 1, 1550–1603*, pp. 44–50.
453. Cockburn, *Calendar of Assize Records. Hertfordshire Indictments: Elizabeth I*, p. 86 and pp. 160–162.
454. James Fitzjames Stephen, *A History of the Criminal Law of England, Vol. I* (London: Macmillan, 1883), pp. 298–299.

upon facts, and return their verdict to the judges (who in England are only such of the law, and not of the fact)".[455]

The high sheriff was responsible for summoning county juries as part of his duties. Thus, and typically, in October 1540 a writ was issued to John Sackville, the Sheriff of Surrey from 1540 to 1541, requiring jurymen from Croydon to appear at the next assizes to be held in the town.[456] In practice, his assistants did much of this work. Jury service was confined to males between 21 and 70, although many men in their twenties were unable to satisfy the property qualification required to serve, while those in their sixties who were frail might not be called; most jurors were in their thirties, forties, and fifties. It seems that, although clergymen were technically qualified to serve, it was not customary to call them, and they may even have been entitled to be excused if summoned. In *Beecher's Case*, in 1577, a gentleman of the Middle Temple was ordained the day before being summoned. He objected to doing jury service "according to the privilege of those of the ministry". However, the Court of Common Pleas insisted that he be sworn because at the time of his selection he was a layman.[457]

More generally, the sheriff was warned against accepting "notorious" characters for service. Given the difficulties involved in finding appropriate numbers of suitable men (see below), and the poor quality of contemporary record-keeping, it is likely that previous convictions were overlooked or ignored unless they were for grave matters. None of the jurors in Hertfordshire during the late sixteenth century appears to have been convicted of a felony, but several had been indicted for assault.[458]

Trial jurors were normally drawn from what might very loosely be termed the "middling" social orders.[459] Theoretically, more than three-quarters of adult males were not qualified to sit on even a quarter sessions petty jury, because a 40 shillings requirement (lands or revenues to at

---

455. Hentzner, *Travels in England*, p. 80.
456. SHC 5410/6/5.
457. Rosemary Pattenden, "The Exclusion of the Clergy from Criminal Trial Juries: An Historical Perspective", *Ecclesiastical Law Journal*, Vol. 5, Issue 24, p. 155.
458. P. C. Lawson, "Lawless Juries? The Composition and Behavior of Hertfordshire Juries, 1573–1624", in J. S. Cockburn and Thomas A. Green (eds.), *Twelve Good Men and True: The Criminal Trial Jury in England 1200–1800* (Princeton: Princeton University Press, 1988), p. 121.
459. Grigor, *Sir John Fortescue*, p. 48.

least that value a year) was the general rule in royal courts for the late medieval period and much of the sixteenth century, as a result of a statute from 1414. (It had been 20 shillings prior to that date.) It was feared that, in the absence of such a qualification, jurors would be susceptible to bribery.[460] As a result, and as Sir Thomas Smith observed, they came from a very different social milieu from most of those whose fates they determined, although this may have been more marked at the Old Bailey in London than at assizes and (even more so) quarter sessions in the counties.[461]

Even so, by the start of the Tudor era, there were longstanding claims that the 40 shilling qualification was inadequate. In the fifteenth century Sir John Fortescue had suggested that, for serious felonies at least, it was desirable to have men with annual lands and revenues "to the value of a hundred shillings". As a result, and following earlier failed attempts at enhancing it, an Elizabethan statute of 1585 (27 Eliz. c. 6) raised the requirement to £4 (80 shillings) a year of lands, rent, or tenements and (in theory) imposed a fine of 20 shillings on sheriffs for each person wrongfully empanelled.[462] (Initially, the parliamentary bill had also provided that the new qualification should be confined to real estate, but this requirement was dropped in its passage through the House of Commons).[463] The sum selected seems to have been viewed as the starting point for what most observers deemed to be substantial yeoman status.[464]

Although, in many counties, there was a modest social difference between those who sat as trial jurors at quarter sessions and those summoned for the same duty at the more exalted assizes, this was not invariably the case, and some sat at both. Typically, rural petty jurors would include a large admixture of yeomen or tenant farmers and the more skilled type of village craftsman, such as blacksmiths. Urban trial jurors were often lesser tradesmen, merchants, and, again, well-to-do craftsmen, including those found only in towns, such as silversmiths.

---

460. *Ibid*, p. 40.
461. Green, *Verdict According to Conscience*, p. 133.
462. Grigor, *Sir John Fortescue*, p. 24 and p. 48.
463. David Dean, *Law-Making and Society in Late Elizabethan England: The Parliament of England, 1584–1601* (Cambridge: Cambridge University Press, 1996), p. 207.
464. Alexandra Shepard, *Accounting for Oneself: Worth, Status, and the Social Order in Early Modern England* (Oxford: Oxford University Press, 2015), p. 109.

The difficulties involved in assembling a suitably qualified petty jury were aggravated because such service was time consuming, inconvenient, and sometimes even dangerous, as prisoners could carry disease. As a result, it was often unpopular, especially among well-to-do people. Illustrative of this, in September 1580 Nicholas Saunders wrote an angry letter to Sir William More, Sheriff of Surrey and Sussex, claiming that he had been unjustly called as a trial juror at the Surrey Assizes after being placed on a panel on which "there was no other gentleman".[465]

In these circumstances, incompetent or corrupt sheriffs or, very much more commonly, under-sheriffs and bailiffs, might overlook suitable men as favours or accept bribes to excuse them from service. On at least one occasion, the Court of Star Chamber punished an under-sheriff for extorting money in exchange for excusing people from jury duty. More typically, James Chapman, a Chelmsford bailiff, was prosecuted at the Essex Quarter Sessions in 1578 for taking bribes of between two and four shillings from six people, "under colour of his office", to excuse them serving as jurors at quarter sessions or gaol delivery.[466]

As a result, sheriffs were sometimes forced to fill out jury panels (and so juries) with men who did not quite meet the relevant qualification, and parties withheld their challenges because they were unaware of this, in order to avoid delay, or because they did not envisage being prejudiced by it.[467] Many contemporary observers thought that the presence of unqualified men made the trial jury one of the weak links in the system.[468] Robert Parsons believed that juries were largely made up of "silly men". William Lambarde complained about their frequent "slothfulness", and a few years later even James I acknowledged that jury service was often left to the "simple and ignorant".[469] The King's Proclamation of 1607

---

465. SHC 6729/1/87.
466. ERO Q/SR 68/28.
467. David J Seipp, "Jurors, Evidences and the Tempest of 1499", in John W. Cairns and Grant McLeod (eds.), *"The Dearest Birthright of the People of England": The Jury in the History of the Common Law* (Oxford: Hart, 2002), p. 75.
468. Cockburn and Green, *Twelve Good Men and True*, p. 160.
469. James C. Oldham, "The Origins of the Special Jury", *University of Chicago Law Review*, Vol. 50, Issue 1, pp. 142–144.

was aimed at restoring the ancient credit and integrity of an institution that, he freely accepted, had fallen into some disrepute.[470]

As with so many aspects of the criminal justice system of the period, the validity of such criticism depends on time, place (counties varied greatly in this regard), and forum — assizes, quarter sessions, or borough sessions. The last of these often faced the greatest problems in assembling suitable jurors. In some urban areas it could be difficult even to find enough members of the "middling orders", even with that definition generously construed, to serve on borough sessions. In the 1560s Sir Thomas Smith claimed that, in many, the lack of available yeomen allowed the poor, who normally had no voice or authority in society, to sit on inferior juries.[471] Trial juries for the borough sessions of Elizabethan Colchester sometimes included alehouse keepers and, occasionally, even day labourers.[472]

When there were not enough jurors available at court, as sometimes happened, particularly if there had been numerous challenges (albeit that this was unusual), the justices might have recourse to those on the *nisi prius* panel (called to hear civil matters); they could also issue a writ of *tales de circunstantibus* to the sheriff and bailiff, allowing them to haul in bystanders from inside or near the courtroom — the so-called talesmen — to join a trial jury.[473] Talesmen were not required to have the property qualifications of jurors summoned in the normal manner, so that they were "men of all sorts", although many had, at least, the leisure to be at court, and occasionally their number included comparatively well-to-do men drawn from the grand jury. (After 1532 grand jurors could be challenged as of right if they sat on the petty jury that tried the bill that they had found to be true, although it seems that occasional instances continued to occur).[474]

The Elizabethan tightening-up of jury qualifications, which significantly reduced the pool of eligible men and (in theory) helped concentrate

---

470. Derek Dunne, *Shakespeare, Revenge Tragedy and Early Modern Law: Vindictive Justice* (Basingstoke: Palgrave Macmillan, 2016), p. 54.
471. Smith, *De Republica Anglorum*, pp. 76–77.
472. Samaha, "Hanging for Felony", p. 769.
473. Seipp, "Jurors, Evidences and the Tempest of 1499", p. 75.
474. Oldham, "The Origins of the Special Jury", pp. 142–144; Cockburn and Green, *Twelve Good Men and True*, p. 161.

it within a class that was often reluctant to serve, may have contributed to the growing use of talesmen towards the end of the Tudor era, making the change counter-productive.[475] Their employment would increase further during the early Jacobean period.

Unlike many grand jurors, most trial jurors sat just once or twice during their lives. Of the 6,408 men sworn to assizes jury service on the Home Circuit between 1559 and 1603 (some records are missing), only 22 per cent were called three or more times. However, a handful sat extremely frequently, appearing up to 40 times.[476] In his 1607 Proclamation for Jurors, James I complained that such men often became case hardened.[477] Nevertheless, there was a rationale behind their appointment. They could help instruct neophyte and less experienced fellow jurors, and were better equipped to pick up hints on appropriate verdicts from the bench, so greatly expediting the pressured trial process and helping to produce what would be deemed "correct" decisions. They were much more likely to be made jury foremen than were neophytes.

There were 35 peremptory challenges available to each defendant in the early sixteenth century, a figure that was reduced to 20 in 1530, but returned to the original 35 for cases of treason a few years later. These allowed defendants to reject potential jurors without any need to show cause.[478] Fernando Pulton thought that such challenges were usually based on "opinion or phantasie". The original limit prevented a defendant rejecting three entire trial juries (36 men) without providing valid reasons for doing so. If this was not sufficient, he could challenge "as many as he hath cause of challenge to if he can prove it".[479] The accused, therefore, could request the removal of any number of jurors who, for example, had a known personal animosity towards him. As today, any challenges had to be made before the jurors were sworn. In theory, co-defendants could pool their challenges, every prisoner peremptorily challenging his full number of potential jurors: *R.* v *Salisbury* (1553) 1 Plowd 100. In

475. Green, *Verdict According to Conscience,* p. 114.
476. J. S. Cockburn, "Twelve Silly Men? The Trial Jury at Assizes, 1560–1670", in Cockburn and Green, *Twelve Good Men and True,* p. 161 and p. 165.
477. Oldham, "The Origins of the Special Jury", pp. 142–144.
478. Grigor, *Sir John Fortescue,* p. 44.
479. St. Germain, *Doctor and Student,* p. 63.

this case chaos had ensued when five murder defendants challenged an entire panel at the Shropshire Assizes, and then the talesmen called in to replace them. Ultimately the trials went ahead after a threat to sever the indictment and proceed to separate hearings.

Salisbury's case was exceptional, challenges of both types being uncommon, even at assizes, if only because of the defendant's ignorance — most did not know much about their jurors (they did not have sight of the names on the jury panel prior to trial) or their rights to reject them. The lack of legal representation, the speed of the trial process, and a reluctance to annoy the substitute jurors who would then be called also played a part. Nicholas Throckmorton's challenge to as many as ten jurors in 1554 was considered unusual. This was fortunate, as Tudor jury panels were often only 24 men strong, and sometimes even less; by exercising their full rights, defendants might have brought some assizes to a halt. Either they did not appreciate this, or they were actively "discouraged" from doing so.[480]

Juries per medietatem linguae

A foreign defendant could be tried *per medietatem linguae* ("by half tongue"); that is, if he could find six of his fellow countrymen or, at the very least, foreign nationals who were sympathetic towards his country, on the petty jury. This procedure had originated in Norman times and was only ended in 1870, although withdrawn from treason cases in 1554.[481] In theory, it helped prevent foreign defendants from prejudice.[482] However, it could be inconvenient, especially outside London and other major ports where aliens were not easily found.

For example, in March 1571 two men — John Androwes, a sailor, and Henry Davy, a labourer — were accused of murder at the Surrey Assizes after attacking another man with a dagger and a pikestaff. Androwes

---

480. Green, *Verdict According to Conscience,* p. 132.
481. Deborah Ramirez, "The Mixed Jury and the Ancient Custom of Trial by Jury de Medietate Linguae", *Boston University Law Review*, Vol. 74, pp. 784–786.
482. Judy M. Cornett, "'Hoodwink'd by Custom': The Exclusion of Women from Juries in Eighteenth century English Law and Literature", *William & Mary Journal of Women and the Law*, Vol. 4, Issue 1, pp. 16–17.

claimed to be a Spaniard (he may have been from the Spanish Nether-lands), and asked to be tried by a jury that was *de medietate linguae*. This required separate trials and juries for the two men. Androwes' jury did not have a large number of individuals with obviously Spanish names, but some might have come from Spanish possessions in Europe. Amongst them were Remerus Clerck, Martin Deleue, and Simon Byllere. Both defendants were convicted.[483]

Claud Purnell was more fortunate when he appeared at the Sussex Assizes in July 1585. Accused of murdering an unknown man in North-chapel (where he resided), he asked to be tried by a jury half of whose members spoke his language (probably French), and his trial was post-poned to the next assizes the following February to facilitate this. At these sessions, he was merely convicted of manslaughter, and successfully pleaded benefit of clergy. Assuming that he was given a normal Bible or Psalter for the literacy test, his command of written English, at least, must have been fairly good, or the court very indulgent.[484]

Scotsmen were not deemed to be aliens (any more than Welshmen and Irishmen), even though they came from a separate legal jurisdiction, as lowlanders spoke what was considered to be a dialect of English.[485] Furthermore, because the procedure had been ordained for the benefit of aliens, and it was claimed that English rogues were often associating with gypsies, and even counterfeiting their speech and apparel so that the two could not be readily distinguished, all "Egyptians" were withdrawn from the privilege in 1531 (22. H. 8. 10). As a result, gypsies accused of a felony, even if they were recent arrivals from abroad, would be tried by a jury that was "altogether Englishmen".

The Move from a Self-Informing Jury

During the late thirteenth and early fourteenth century, the criminal trial jury was largely (but not entirely) self-informing, its members serving as a species of witness as well as the tribunal of fact. At least some, if not

---

483. Cockburn, *Calendar of Assize Records. Surrey Indictments: Elizabeth I*, p. 90.

484. Hunnisett, *Sussex Coroners' Inquests, 1558–1603*, p. 72.

485. Mortimer Levine, "A More than Ordinary Case of 'Rape,' 13 and 14 Elizabeth 1", *The American Journal of Legal History*, Vol. 7, Issue 2, p. 159.

most, trial jurors came to court with extensive personal knowledge of the facts of a case, acquired by living near to where the alleged crime had occurred, a principle reflected in the requirements of vicinage.[486] (They were not supposed to be close friends of the defendant.)[487] Jurors largely based their verdicts on information they had witnessed, gathered in anticipation of trial, or had heard as a result of living in small, tight-knit communities, where gossip kept most people apprised of neighbourhood affairs.[488] This made most trials exceptionally brief, perhaps just 20 minutes or less, as jurors would not receive significant amounts of evidence in public before making their decisions.[489] It also allowed popular mores and communal beliefs to influence verdicts, as jurors manipulated the facts before them to do equity in particular cases, despite an ostensibly harsh and inflexible legal system.[490]

Nevertheless, even in the fourteenth century, criminal jurors probably learned a modest amount from in-court testimony rather than their own knowledge.[491] This may have been provided by the defendant speaking during his hearing; the prosecutor (in appeals) speaking in court; local officials, such as the coroner or sheriff, testifying; or (less frequently) others with relevant information speaking-up at trial. These may well have made a modest contribution to the jurors' opinions, as did the judge's questioning of the accused. Although the jury was self-informing, this did not necessarily mean that its verdict was irreversibly settled before its members were sworn in to consider a case.

However, by the early to middle decades of the fifteenth century, it seems that jurors were becoming increasingly dependent on in-court testimony to reach their decisions, despite Fortescue's idealised (and slightly anachronistic) belief that the English jury of the 1460s still merged

---

486. Mike Macnair, "Vicinage and the Antecedents of the Jury", *Law and History Review*, Vol. 17, No. 3, pp. 537–590, p. 546.
487. Musson, "Twelve Good Men and True?", p. 132.
488. Daniel M. Klerman, "Was the Jury Ever Self-Informing?", *Southern California Law Review*, Vol. 77, pp. 123–127 and p. 149.
489. Powell, *Kingship, Law, and Society*, p. 78.
490. Sara M. Butler, "Local Concerns: Suicide and Jury Behavior in Medieval England", *History Compass*, Vol. 4, Issue 5, pp. 820–821.
491. Niamh Howlin, "Irish Jurors: Passive Observers or Active Participants?", *Journal of Legal History*, Vol. 35, Issue 2, p. 144.

witnesses and triers of fact drawn from the neighbourhood of the crime.[492] The "active" medieval assizes and quarter sessions jury had started to give way to the passive triers of fact found in the modern courtroom.

This development was probably due to greatly increased population mobility after the Black Death of 1348, a linked decline in communal open-field agriculture, and other social and administrative changes in the wider society.[493] As relatively static and interdependent agrarian communities were replaced by more mobile societies, with larger numbers of wage earners, fewer people had a deep personal knowledge of their neighbours' lives.[494] For example, the provenance of jurors on the Midland Circuit by the early 1400s suggests that many of them could not have been personally familiar with the facts of the crimes they heard, not least because they were drawn from different (and even distant) parts of the county from those where the offences had been committed.[495]

Several contemporary observers spoke of evidence being delivered in "open court" during the fifteenth century, and by the early decades of the sixteenth century both Thomas More and Christopher St Germain treated the proposition that jurors were primarily judges of forensic fact, not witnesses, as common knowledge.[496] By then most jurors required testimony at the bar to inform them of a case and learned the majority of the information they needed to reach their verdicts in court.[497] Indeed, in 1537 the King's Council examined the foreman of a petty jury specifically because he and his fellow jurors had convicted purely on the "noise of the country", without considering forensic evidence.[498]

This development was, indirectly and rather belatedly, acknowledged in 1563 by an Act punishing those "as shall procure or commit any willful Perjury". Such a power had not been necessary when jurors supplied their own information, although there may have been a vague common law power to punish such behaviour, and the Star Chamber had dealt

492. John Fortescue, *The Governance of England* (Westport, Conn: Hyperion Press, 1979), p. 65.
493. Klerman, "Was the Jury Ever Self-Informing?", pp. 125–127 and p. 149.
494. Langbein, *History of the Common Law*, p. 227.
495. Powell, "Jury Trial at Gaol Delivery", p. 111 and pp. 115–116.
496. Barbara J. Shapiro, *A Culture of Fact: England 1550–1720* (Ithaca, New York: Cornell University Press, 2000), p. 12.
497. Baker, *Oxford History*, p. 361; Guy et al., *The Complete Works of St. Thomas More, Vol. 10*, p. 149.
498. Bellamy, *The Criminal Trial*, p. 127.

with some cases of this type. The 1563 Act claimed that its introduction was necessary as the "sinister Procurement of false Witnesses, hath nevertheless greatly increased". Anyone who committed perjury was to be fined £20 or pilloried, and imprisoned for six months.[499]

Continuing Jury Familiarity

Even so, during the Tudor period, especially its first half, at least some assizes and quarter sessions jurors might still be familiar with the facts of a case and the reputations of the people involved before it came to trial, particularly in more "stable" parts of the country. (London may have been different in this regard.) Such knowledge certainly did not disqualify them from service, as it would today.[500] As late as 1499 it was noted that, in theory, there was no need for a jury to receive any evidence in court before returning a verdict, as jurors might use personal knowledge that they had acquired prior to trial.[501] Around 1530 Christopher St Germain (1460–1540) considered a hypothetical situation in which one of the 12 jurors was aware of the "very truth of his own knowledge, and instructs his fellows thereof, and they will in no wise give credence to him".[502]

Occasionally a significant number of petty jurors knew a great deal about a matter before a hearing, and this cannot have been purely a coincidence. For an example, can be considered a bizarre case involving a jury that acquitted an alleged burglar at the Somerset Assizes in 1546. The presiding judge subsequently reported them to the Court of Star Chamber for returning false verdicts.[503] The defendant, John Wynscott, had entered the house of the alleged victim, John Boldy, in Spaxton during the small hours and then got into bed with him. The occupant summoned neighbours and a constable after he woke-up and noticed his new sleeping companion. Subsequently a bag of money was found to be missing and the suspect was carried before a JP for examination.

---

499. Richard H. Underwood, "False Witness: A Lawyer's History of the Law of Perjury", *Arizona Journal of International and Comparative Law*, Vol. 10, No. 2, pp. 243–245.
500. Klerman, "Was the Jury Ever Self-Informing?", pp. 125–127 and p. 149.
501. *Lucas v. Cesse* (1499) Trin. 14 Hen. VII.
502. William Forsyth, *History of Trial by Jury* (Clark, New Jersey: The Lawbook Exchange, 1994), p. 206.
503. Hamilton, "Star Chamber and Juries", p. 237.

At trial, despite there being some evidence of admissions by this man, and to the astonishment of the assizes' judge, the jury acquitted. In their defence to the Star Chamber, the jurors explained why they had found the prosecution evidence unconvincing. In part this was because they personally knew about the characters of the defendant and prosecutor and also some of the background to the case. This knowledge was not surprising, given that two of them had been among the neighbours called to the scene by the alleged victim. They also knew that, although Wynscott was "accustome[d] to be drunk", he was still considered a "true man". Furthermore, he had once lived in the house in question, possibly making his actions an error due to intoxication. They also suspected that Boldy's account was a "feyned tale" made maliciously to vex Wynscott. (There is no evidence as to how the case was eventually dealt with by the prerogative court.)[504]

Occasionally the same level of personal knowledge could be found among jurors at the lower forum. Interestingly, as late as 1596 Sir Thomas Mildmay issued a writ to summon a jury from the neighbourhood of Bulphan, in Essex, for the following Easter Quarter Sessions to determine whether one John Hurt, from the same village, was guilty of assaulting a man named Robert Cock and committing other misdemeanours. Edward Sulyard, the county sheriff, who would be responsible for summoning the jurors, specifically endorsed the writ to this effect.[505] Clearly such jurors would have had a great deal of private knowledge about the matter and Hurt's character, which was, presumably, why Mildmay wanted them.

However, by the early 1600s, this may have been changing. In a particularly gruesome West Country murder case from 1624, Lord Chief Baron Tanfield was careful that the assizes grand jury, at least, should "avoyd all partiallity which consanguinity or acquaintance might impose". He directed that it be composed of men who did not live in the part of Somerset where one of the defendants, himself a former grand juryman for the county, resided.[506]

---

504. Thayer, "A Sixteenth century Jury", pp. 298–300.
505. ERO Q/SR 133/16.
506. C.W., *The crying murther,* p. 10.

The Hearing

In the 1560s Sir Thomas Smith noted that, at the start of the trial, the court crier or clerk would publicly announce that the prisoner was standing at the bar, and ask that "if any man can say any thing against him, let him now speake". If no-one appeared to prosecute or testify, he would be discharged by proclamation. However, if a good reason, such as illness, had been advanced at or before the hearing for a prosecutor or witness not attending, the case might be remitted to a later date (with the suspect usually remaining in gaol in the meantime).

For example, at the start of 1591 Israel Amyce, an Essex JP, wrote to Baron Clarke of the Court of Exchequer and a fellow magistrate in the same county, noting that one John Browne was due to be tried at a gaol delivery at the forthcoming Epiphany Quarter Sessions. However, it would be impossible to hear the case as the prosecutor, who had been bound-over to attend the next (Lent) Assizes, where it had originally been intended that the matter would be heard, was then in Wales and would not return until Candlemas (February 2). As a result, Amyce asked that the matter be adjourned back to the assizes rather than dismissed for non-prosecution, if only because Browne was "supposyd to be as strong a thefe as ever apperyd before you".[507]

More commonly, witnesses would come forward to testify against the defendant, if only to avoid losing their recognisances, and a trial would ensue. Sir Thomas Smith described a criminal hearing that was quite informal, in which the unrepresented accused engaged in a heated give-and-take with the prosecution witnesses, who normally included the alleged victim. Defendants would respond to each prosecution allegation as it came up, so that the witness and accused would "stand a while in altercation" while exchanging their stories. In the absence of lawyers—not allowed to defendants in felony cases and, though not legally forbidden, not normally employed by prosecutors—judges had to prevent proceedings from getting bogged down in irrelevancies. It is likely that the judiciary prompted the complainant/prosecutor as he

---

507. ERO Q/SR 115/27.

testified, with the aid of pre-trial depositions if available, to ensure that the evidence remained focussed.[508]

Trials were not only informal but also extremely brief, so that the defendant would normally stand (unshackled) throughout. (Thomas More successfully asked for a chair, but his trial was much longer than that seen in a typical criminal matter). Even allowing for the long working days found at assizes which, depending on caseloads and the number of guilty pleas, might sit from eight am to midnight (if necessary), it seems that many contested hearings lasted significantly less than 30 minutes, and not a few under ten. Even so, there were periodic exceptions, involving grave and complicated matters, which stretched to several hours and heard more than a dozen prosecution witnesses. In an extreme case in 1605, the trial of two witches at the Lent Assizes for Oxfordshire lasted at least eight hours, with the jury not retiring to consider its verdict until 10 pm.[509] Trials could not be adjourned once started.

Of course, the lack of "technicality" in the criminal trial of the period meant that hearings were much faster at adducing evidence than their modern counterparts. Even so, when there was a lot of potential prosecution evidence, less significant witnesses might not be called, even if available. In 1593, at the trial of the Warboys witches, the prosecution evidence had eventually been closed because of indications from the tribunal that it was sufficient, and due to limitations of time "which was five houres, with out intermission or interruption".[510] Similarly, at the murder trial of Rowland Cramphorne in 1608, the prosecution called only the "proofes that were most pregnant".[511]

Many defendants did not call witnesses to support their own cases, and at times there even appears to have been a strong judicial reluctance to allow this, especially in state trials. However, this was not a rule of law, as the Crown periodically made clear, and such witnesses did sometimes testify for the accused. Nevertheless, by the middle decades of the Tudor era, defence witnesses, like the defendant (but unlike the prosecutor and

---

508. Green, *Verdict According To Conscience*, p. 133.
509. Brian P. Levack, "Possession, Witchcraft, and the Law in Jacobean England", *Washington and Lee Law Review*, Vol. 52, Issue 5, p. 1623.
510. Anon, *The Most Strange and Admirable Discoverie*, p. 108.
511. Anon, *A bloudy new-yeares gift*, pp. 1–3.

his witnesses), could not give evidence on oath, a situation that would persist until the early eighteenth century; the accused himself would wait until 1898 to give sworn testimony, despite a parliamentary suggestion for reform in 1610. (In the early Tudor period, there is very occasional, if passing, reference to defence witnesses other than the accused being sworn). Where the rule came from, and its justification, is not obvious. Sir Edward Coke thought that it could be traced to no statute or case, although a few observers thought that, like the ban on defendants testifying on oath, it helped prevent perjury.[512] It was also the subject of parliamentary criticism in the early seventeenth century.[513]

By modern standards the atmosphere at Tudor trials could be decidedly noisy and irreverent. At Margaret Clitherow's hearing in 1586, a Puritan preacher named Giles Wiggington stood up in open court to address the judge, but the "murmuring and noise in the Hall would not suffer him to be heard". Members of the judiciary were also robust in running their courts. In September 1596 it was noted that, during his then recent circuit, Lord Chief Justice Anderson (a notoriously hot-tempered judge) had been so irritable, angry, and abusive that prominent local people had taken considerable offence.[514] However, the judiciary did not always overawe other court users. In 1547 a jury was committed to the Fleet Prison by the court of Star Chamber, in part for returning a verdict against the evidence, but also "for lewd words by them spoken at the above, saying the said [assize] Justices were very shifty with them".[515] In 1554 Nicholas Throckmorton even interrupted his trial judge's summing-up.

In-Court Evidence

The existence of a primarily self-informing jury until late in the medieval period may help to explain why firm rules regulating oral evidence, delivered in open court, arrived so late in the English criminal trial.

---

512. Barbara Shapiro, "Law and the Evidentiary Environment", in Hutson, *The Oxford Handbook of Law and Literature, 1500–1700*, pp. 260–261.
513. Lorna Hutson, *The Invention of Suspicion: Law and Mimesis in Shakespeare and Renaissance Drama* (Oxford: Oxford University Press, 2011), p. 89.
514. Harrison, *A Second Elizabethan Journal*, p. 134.
515. Charles Hamilton, "Star Chamber and Juries: Some Observations", *Albion: A Quarterly Journal Concerned with British Studies*, Vol. 5, No. 3, p. 241.

They were not necessary when in-court witness testimony was of minor importance, and many jurors were personally well-informed about a matter before the trial.[516] Such rules would slowly emerge after jurors came to court to "hear" rather than "speak", but only fully flourish after the arrival of defence counsel in felony cases during the 1700s, long after the end of the Tudor era.

This lack of regulation could have some strange results. In October 1594, Ralph Mepham killed his wife by cutting her throat with a knife, in the presence of his five-year-old son. He then set their house on fire. The woman's body was recovered before being consumed by the flames, and the boy was rescued from the blaze. The child implicated his father in the killing at an inquest presided over by Magnus Fowle, an experienced Sussex coroner. Even more remarkably, despite his youth, he appears to have been the chief prosecution witness at the ensuing assizes, where his father was convicted of murder and then executed on his evidence. The boy was, apparently, mature for his years, and spoke in a "voice laudable" without any "blushing fear", unlike most other infants of that age.[517]

Although rare, such cases were thought to be legally quite proper, albeit sometimes occasioning concern even then. At Margaret Clitherow's trial in 1586, a cleric warned the presiding judge that, because her case involved life and death, he ought not "either by God's laws or man's, to judge her to die upon the slender witness of a boy; nor unless you have two or three sufficient men of very good credit to give evidence against her". The judge, ignoring any spiritual considerations, simply replied, quite accurately, "I may do it by law". As this also suggests, outside treason and perjury cases, a single witness could suffice, and there was then no rule preventing a five-year-old testifying.[518]

Ensuing years would see more focus on witness competence, and greater care to exclude the evidence of convicted felons and perjurers, small children, and lunatics.[519] By the eighteenth century, a child of five, however mature, would not have given sworn evidence, and would not

---

516. Klerman, "Was the Jury Ever Self-Informing?", pp. 123–50.
517. Ken MacMillan, *Stories of True Crime in Tudor and Stuart England* (Abingdon: Routledge, 2015), p. 50.
518. Morris, *Troubles of our Catholic Forefathers*, p. 416.
519. Shapiro, *A Culture of Fact*, p. 13.

normally have been allowed to testify without being on oath. Of course, there were dangers in such latitude; as Margaret Clitherow told the York Assizes: "With an apple and a rod you may make [child witnesses] to say what you will".[520] Even so, certain general evidential trends can be tentatively identified during the 1500s.

Hearsay

The formal hearsay rule of exclusion still lay far in the future during the sixteenth century. As late as 1647, a case at King's Bench suggested that the provenance of such evidence went to weight, and so was to be "left to the jury" rather than going to admissibility, even if its original maker may not have been competent to testify. It became a rigid rule only in the latter decades of the eighteenth century.[521]

Typically, during the trial of the Warboys' witches at the Huntingdon Assizes in 1593, unexpected witnesses came forward during the hearing to testify for the prosecution "who spake som things of their owne knowledge, and some of the reporte". Among them was the Reverend Robert Poulter, vicar of Brampton, who repeated in court what one of his parishioners, then confined to bed by sickness, had told him.[522] The witch trial pamphlets of the era recount many such examples, but there is no suggestion that such testimony was special to this type of case, even if encountered more commonly with regard to such allegations.[523]

However, some of the hearsay rule's most distant roots were already faintly present, and accorded some respect. Most important, there was a marked preference for first-hand oral testimony where it was both available and vital to a case. For example, at his trial for treason before the Lord High Steward of England in 1521, the Duke of Buckingham requested that the prosecution "witnesses", whose depositions had been read out during the hearing, be brought into court. The Duke of Norfolk (presiding as Lord High Steward) agreed. A serjeant then led in three

---

520. Morris, *Troubles of our Catholic Forefathers*, p. 415.
521. Langbein, *History of Common Law*, p. 456.
522. Anon, *The Most Strange and Admirable Discoverie*, p. 110.
523. Orna Alyagon Darr, *Marks of an Absolute Witch: Evidentiary Dilemmas in Early Modern England* (Farnham: Ashgate, 2011), p. 237.

of Buckingham's servants and Nicholas Hopkins, a Carthusian monk who had predicted that Buckingham would succeed Henry VIII. One of the servants apparently testified orally, and the duke tried to answer the allegations that he made as they were advanced (the forensic "altercation" discussed above).[524] Interestingly, the use of read-out depositions to bolster important live witnesses seems to have occurred almost 70 years later, in July 1579, when three witches were tried at Chelmsford; the author of an account of the trial noted that several witnesses were called whose oral evidence secured convictions when taken "together with the depositions of sundrye other witnesses".[525]

Nicholas Throckmorton's treason trial at the Guildhall in 1554 was unusual because the Crown case against him consisted largely of hearsay evidence, particularly read-out depositions of potentially available witnesses who did not themselves testify at trial. These included the deposition of the Duke of Suffolk, which contained several statements that the duke supposedly heard from his brother (i.e. of multiple hearsay). Several of the makers of these read-out depositions were even present in court, something that the defendant made an issue of: "Master Crofts is yet living and is here this day: How happeneth it he is not brought face to face to justify this matter".[526] The trial was also notable because, almost uniquely in this type of case, the jury acquitted. It seems that, at least in part, they refused to convict because of the Crown's reliance on hearsay, even if they would not have recognised the term.[527]

Similarly, when, in November 1603, Sir Walter Raleigh was convicted of treason at Winchester, largely on what appears to have been hearsay evidence, the verdict appears to have occasioned considerable concern. Some observers were particularly troubled by the sworn confession of Raleigh's friend Henry Brook, Baron Cobham, which implicated him, and which was produced in Cobham's absence, despite Raleigh's repeatedly requests

524. Barbara Harris, "The Trial of the Third Duke of Buckingham — A Revisionist View", *The American Journal of Legal History*, Vol. 20, Issue 1, p. 20.
525. Anon, *The Apprehension and confession of three notorious Witches*, p. 5.
526. Sil, "'My Bitter Comedie,'" pp. 381–405.
527. Justin Sevier, "Popularizing Hearsay", *Georgetown Law Journal*, Vol. 104, p. 645.

that he and his "accuser come face to face", and Cobham being in custody and so readily available to the Crown.[528]

It was not only "political" cases that produced concern about hearsay from available witnesses. In the Star Chamber case *Brown and Hales* v *Richeman* of 1546, a jury, accused of perversely failing to convict a burglar on apparently very strong evidence, was forced to explain the basis for its acquittal. One of the grounds was that an examining JP named Michael Mallett had testified at the assizes as to what he had learnt from various observers, some of whom, such as the local constable, were (again) present at court, but who did not themselves give evidence. It was hearsay, even if the word was not used: "The seyd evidence of the seyd Mallett was but by report of the seyd constable and others as is aforeseyd, not sworne, and some of them were present at the assyz and give not the seyd evidence themselves". (It was also suggested that some of these "witnesses" had contradicted their testimony to the examining JP with other out-of-court tales.)[529]

Even then, certain types of out-of-court statement were being given significance above other forms of hearsay. Confession evidence was one of them (as it still is today), especially after the Marian examination produced increased numbers of written and signed or marked records of suspects' admissions to JPs. Indicative of this, in September 1579 the courtier Sir Edward Horsey, who had been made a JP for Hampshire and the Isle of Wight ten years earlier, wrote to Sir William More, his Surrey counterpart, noting that he had arrested and examined two men named Syggins and Christopher. He also sent More their confessions so that they could be charged at the next gaol delivery for Surrey.[530]

An account of the major witch trial held at the Huntingdon Assizes in 1593 noted that the confession elicited during Alice Samuel's pre-trial examination was presented to the jury as evidence of her guilt: "So also was read the confession of the saide mother Samuell made at Burkden afore saide the 29 day of December 1592 before ... Justices of her Maiesties

---

528. *Ibid*, p. 655.
529. Bradford, *Proceedings in the Court of the Star Chamber*, p. 259.
530. SHC 6729/1/54.

peace within the countie of Huntington, which also is before specified. After these confessions redd, and deliuered to the Jury".[531]

Nevertheless, in the 1560s, Sir Thomas Smith still thought that such a confession on its own, even if signed or marked, was unlikely to be sufficient to found a conviction. For example, when the three witches were tried at Chelmsford in 1570 (see above), it was noted that, despite making full, detailed, and carefully recorded confessions, which were sufficient to prove the indictment, and that were read out in court, "yet to make the matters more apparent, sundry witnesses were produced to give evidence against them".[532]

In the seventeenth century, the dying declaration was to become a common law exception to the then slowly emerging hearsay rule. However, its roots were considerably older, originating during the medieval period and being based on the principle *Nemo moriturus praesumitur mentiri*, i.e. that no-one on the point of death should be presumed to be lying. At the Surrey Assizes in July 1559, Henry Colson appears to have reported to the court what his dying brother Richard had said about the origins of his injuries and, more particularly, that if he died it was because of a blow inflicted by one Richard Harrison and another man; even so, and perhaps significantly, both defendants were acquitted.[533] However, at the same forum in 1591, the mortally wounded Lord Burke's account as to how Arnold Cosby had tricked and murdered him were vital evidence at the latter's trial, which did produce a murder conviction and execution.[534]

Circumstantial Evidence

In theory, purely circumstantial evidence could found a conviction in England, which, unlike most Roman law countries, did not normally have rigid rules about the level and quality of evidence required to prove a criminal case. In practice, Tudor juries were often reluctant to convict purely on "circumstances" and "presumptions", as such evidence was sometimes termed, unsupported by either direct testimony or confessions,

---

531. Anon, *The Most Strange And Admirable Discoverie*, p. 110.
532. Anon, *The Apprehension and confession*, p. 5.
533. Cockburn, *Calendar of Assize Records. Surrey Indictments. Elizabeth I*, p. 6.
534. Harrison, *An Elizabethan Journal, Vol. 1*, p. 6.

unless it was exceptionally strong. Judges shared this nervousness. Their concern is partly explained by the speed of criminal trials, which did not allow proper consideration of alternative explanations for such evidence (always a possibility). The frequent (and necessary) dependence of witchcraft cases on circumstantial material made them slightly unusual in this regard. Alluding to this, Sir Edmund Anderson, Chief Justice of the Court of Common Pleas, warned an Old Bailey trial jury in 1602 that the number of witches would soar if juries were unwilling to "convict them without their own confession or direct proofs, where the presumptions are so great and the circumstances so apparent".[535]

Nevertheless, witchcraft cases were not quite unique in this, as such evidence was often vitally important in poisoning and fraud cases as well.[536] Very strong circumstantial evidence could be enough in other cases. Sir Walter Raleigh was reminded of this at his treason trial in 1603, when he complained that the case against him was not founded on "direct proofs, but all by circumstances". Mr Justice Warburton, the presiding judge, firmly rejected this as a ground of complaint and pointed out that it was decisive in some conventional felony trials, so that "many horse-stealers may escape, if they may not be condemned without [eye] witnesses".[537]

More generally, circumstantial evidence might bolster direct testimony. For example, in the trial of a long-past robbery and murder case, that the alleged perpetrators had renovated their property at the time of the alleged killing, although neighbours "knew not from whence" the money to do this had come, might be relevant in supporting direct evidence of the crime.[538]

---

535. P. G. Maxwell-Stuart, "The New King and the Crucible of the Act: King James' Experience of Witches, and the 1604 English Witchcraft Act", in John Newton and Jo Bath (eds.), *Witchcraft and the Act of 1604* (Leiden: Brill, 2008), p. 43.
536. Shapiro, "Law and the Evidential Environment", p. 270.
537. Katharine Eisaman Maus, "Proof and Consequences: Inwardness and its Exposure in the English Renaissance", *Representations*, No. 34, pp. 31–32.
538. Ken MacMillan and Melissa Glass, "Murder and Mutilation in Early-Stuart England: A Case Study in Crime Reporting", *Journal of the Canadian Historical Association*, vol. 27, Issue 2, p. 69.

Identification

Identification was often an issue at trial where a suspect had not been taken red-handed. It could lead to dramatic courtroom confrontations.[539] Where it was questioned, alibi evidence could be crucial, and was often advanced at trial. Sometimes it might be investigated prior to the hearing, presumably having been raised during the JPs' examination, and, if well founded, prosecutions could be abandoned. For example, in March 1597 Lord Howard wrote to Sir William More in Surrey asking that a charge of robbery against three men be dropped, as there was evidence that they were elsewhere at the relevant time.[540]

Nevertheless, those who were not caught *in flagrante* could secure fabricated alibis fairly easily, and this seems to have been a common occurrence.[541] For example, in January 1535, Matthew Bourne claimed that a thief named John-a-Baron had stolen two horses in Dorking, in Surrey. The man and his wife kept a tavern in Lambeth, and his spouse apparently gave him a false alibi, saying that he was at home on the night the animals went missing.[542]

Judicial Summing-up

During the Tudor era, judicial charges to juries were usually extremely brief, and there was little meaningful separation between the judge's comments on the evidence as it was adduced during the trial and his directions to the jury before they retired. For example, according to Reginald Pole, the judges at Thomas More's treason trial in 1535 shouted out "Malice! Malice!", even though the evidence for this appeared weak, which was something that "fixed in [the] ears and minds" of the jury before they returned their verdict.[543] Similarly, in 1602 Lord Chief Justice Anderson was open about rebutting the expert evidence of Edward

---

539. Smith, *De Republica Anglorum*, p. 114.
540. SHC LM/COR/3/565.
541. Thomas More, "The Debellacyon of Salem and Bizance 1533", in *Works of Sir Thomas More* (London, 1577), pp. 996–998.
542. Gairdner, *Letters and Papers, Foreign and Domestic, Henry VIII, Vol. 8, January-July 1535*, pp. 24–32.
543. Kelly, *Thomas More's Trial by Jury*, pp. 200–201.

Jorden, a physician, who had argued that Mary Glover was not the victim of bewitchment but was suffering from a kind of hysteria, "I care not for your judgement".[544] However, the summing-up might contain the most direct statement of the judge's personal opinion on the merits of a case (if he had one), even if he did not discuss the individual pieces of evidence on which it had been based. The judge's charge also normally invoked the jurors' duty to God and their own consciences. Its conclusion brought the hearing to an end, after which the jury's decision process began.[545]

Reaching a Verdict

Tudor jurors would normally (though not invariably) retire to deliberate on a batch of trials rather than considering their verdict on each case as it finished; the latter did not become widespread practice until the early eighteenth century. It was not a new system even in the 1500s, having been present in the 1420s and 1430s, and something that probably reduced the impact of the trial judge's charge in individual cases.[546]

On one assessment, late medieval juries tried an average of three to five defendants before retiring, although in Derby it has been noted that, at times, as many as eight or nine cases may have been determined together.[547] The Tudor era was broadly the same, albeit that, in the 1560s, Sir Thomas Smith thought that trial jurors would frequently complain if asked to consider more than three cases at once, and were often charged with just one or two.[548] However, on the Home Circuit, between 1559 and 1625, it seems that each assize jury was charged with an average of almost seven defendants.[549] Quarter sessions would sometimes produce a similar profile, but, indicative of the diversity and variation of practice, at one sitting of the Monmouthshire Quarter Sessions in Abergavenny, in 1577, each of three consecutive contested trials was heard by a fresh jury.[550]

---

544. Maxwell-Stuart, "The New King and the Crucible of the Act", p. 43.
545. Green, *Verdict According to Conscience*, p. 144.
546. Maddern, *Violence and Social Order*, p. 59.
547. Powell, *Kingship, Law, and Society*, p. 79.
548. Smith, *De Republica Anglorum*, p. 114.
549. Cockburn, "Twelve Silly Men?", p. 178.
550. Howell, *Law and Disorder*, at p. xcix.

It appears that, while the initial jury considered its verdicts, another jury was sometimes sworn in, so that further matters could be tried, and precious and pressured court time was not wasted, especially at the higher forum. For example, at the Hertfordshire Assizes held between 1573 and 1624, an average of 2.5 juries sat at each sessions. Only rarely did a juror sit on more than one jury, and only once did a jury have to sit on a second "group" of cases.[551] At the busy assizes held at Hertford in March 1597, four juries were empanelled. There is an interesting variation between their workloads. Two of them determined an extensive list of cases, one 15 and the other 17. The other two juries tried just four and two cases, none of them of any apparent complexity. It is possible that these juries were sworn in to hear cases while the two "main" juries considered their verdicts; alternatively, they may have been empanelled when the judge determining *nisi prius* cases had finished his civil list and was able to assist his colleague on the Crown side.[552]

Once they retired to deliberate — they may simply have huddled together on their benches to discuss verdicts if all their cases were straightforward — jurors were isolated in a special room or a nearby house under the supervision of a bailiff appointed to keep them together and ensure that no-one spoke to them until they had reached their verdicts. The effectiveness of jury sequestration was important, as it provided a degree of protection from external, including judicial, pressure while they were making their decisions.[553] Interestingly, there were almost no contemporary literary or theatrical portrayals of juries or their deliberations during the Tudor era. It appears that the dramatic potential of jury debate, such as disagreements and prejudices, was culturally "off limits", even though it must have been present in many cases. Portraying this would undermine the unanimity and certainty of a verdict delivered by "the country". Juries spoke with a united voice, whatever had gone on in private.[554]

---

551. Cockburn and Green, *Twelve Good Men and True*, p. 127.
552. Cockburn, *Calendar of Assize Records. Hertfordshire Indictments: Elizabeth I*, pp. 125–131.
553. Robert Tittler, "The Sequestration of Juries in Early Modern England", *Historical Research*, Vol. 61, Issue 146, p. 301.
554. Holger Schott Syme, "(Mis)representing Justice on the Early Modern Stage", *Studies in Philology*, Vol. 109, No. 1, p. 84.

Sir Thomas Smith thought that juries would often be sent out to consider their decisions while the judges and justices went to dinner, after which they would return to court to receive criminal verdicts; if these were not ready, they might deal with some civil matters "to drive out the time". Unlike jurors in *nisi prius* cases, those from the Crown side at assizes could not return a "privy verdict" that was delivered privately to the judge in his lodgings after the court had risen. This encouraged speedy decision-making, if only to avoid spending a night in the jury room.[555] This would have been very uncomfortable.

In a legal discussion held by the Westminster judges in the Exchequer Chamber in 1499, Sir John Vavasour (1440–1506), a puisne judge of the Court of Common Pleas, opined that jurors were treated almost like prisoners after they were charged with cases. They were required to agree on their verdicts before they had access to any form of refreshment or sustenance. In theory, heating, lighting, and even seating would also be withheld from them. In 1500 a Venetian envoy observed that they were shut up in a room without "fire, or means of sitting down". Some 65 years later this was reiterated by Sir Thomas Smith, who thought that the bailiff would make sure that "they have neither bread, drinke, meate, ne fire brought to them".[556]

How strictly these provisions were enforced is debatable. In winter, it seems that some form of warmth was occasionally provided. In 1530 Christopher St Germain suggested that the rigidity of the rules on food was also slightly exaggerated; for example, at the court's discretion, sick jurors might be allowed sustenance, as might those who were deadlocked over reaching agreement and needed more time.[557] In a criminal trial of 1533, it was noted that one man's wife had given divers members of the jury meat in sight of others. The jurors were, apparently, quite famished at the time.[558] However, it is clear that refreshment was not normally permitted, even if chairs and a stove might sometimes have crept in. Between 1500 and 1588 numerous jurors were fined up to £5 after being

555. Baker, *Oxford History*, p. 261.
556. Smith, *De Republica Anglorum*, p. 114.
557. St. Germain, *Doctor and Student*, p. 293.
558. Gairdner, *Letters and Papers, Foreign and Domestic, Henry VIII, Vol. 6*, pp. 386–404.

caught with Tudor "snack foods", such as raisins, plum jam, dates, figs, pippins, preserved barberries, and liquorice.[559]

The reasoning behind such denial was freely acknowledged. As Serjeant Kebell warned early in the Tudor period, if jurors were allowed to eat and drink they would be much less likely to reach a speedy decision. In these circumstances, as the Venetian envoy also noted (in about 1500), verdicts could sometimes be decided by a process of attrition, as "those who cannot bear the discomfort, yield to the more determined, for the sake of getting out sooner". This may have occurred when William Levenyng was tried at York in March 1537 for complicity in Bigod's Rebellion two months earlier (admittedly, an untypical offence). Apparently five of his trial jurors were ready to convict him, but the other seven, who knew him as a neighbour in Acklam (further evidence that the self-informing jury was not entirely dead), believed that the main prosecution witness had given evidence against him out of malice. The "hung" jury was locked in the jury room at nine o'clock on a Friday morning. On the afternoon of the following day, the Duke of Norfolk sent an usher to find out if they were agreed on a verdict, but a minority still held out, one juror strongly urging a conviction. As a more effectual way of promoting unanimity, they were then deprived of all means of warmth, suggesting that the theoretical embargo on fires had not initially been applied in what was still late winter. At night the duke sent to them again, and the 12 men prayed for guidance, after which they returned their verdict of not guilty.[560]

Contemporary observers were convinced that a small group of men dominated jury deliberations because of their social status, forceful personalities, or previous experience as jurors. It does seem that jurors who were in a small minority often deferred to the majority to achieve unanimity. In *Watts* v *Brains* (1599) Cro Eliz 778, jurors were fined for giving a collusive verdict in a homicide case. Essentially, they returned an acquittal against the directions of the trial judge, who then questioned each man on his decision. Two jurors admitted they had been in favour of a conviction but had gone with the majority.

---

559. Seipp, "Jurors, Evidences", p. 61.
560. Gairdner, *Letters and Papers, Foreign and Domestic, Henry VIII, Vol. 12, Part 1*, pp. i-xl.

Jurors were largely dependent on their memory (another reason not to overburden them); they had nothing in writing given to them, apart from the indictment, which was in Latin, although the court clerk would reiterate "the effect of it" in English before they retired. However, after they were sequestered, jurors could still seek advice from the presiding judge and even rehear and question evidence that had been adduced at trial and, exceptionally, hear entirely fresh material that, for some reason, had not been called, such as the testimony of witnesses who had "come late" to court. Although this violates modern notions of "closing the case", it did at least make some allowance for the era's problems with listing and communication.[561] For example, in 1616, a jury at the Old Bailey retired from court to consider its verdict on a case in which a servant was accused of taking goods from his employer and putting them in a metal trunk; they subsequently asked if there was evidence that the trunk had ever been removed from the house.[562]

It has been noted that the maxim "innocent until proven guilty" cannot readily be found in English court cases or jurisprudential treatises before about 1800.[563] However, this absence is slightly misleading. Although the precise standard of proof in criminal matters was still rather vague, it was generally accepted by the late medieval period that, for serious felonies at least, the benefit of any significant doubt should normally be found in the defendant's favour, and that it was better that "twenty guilty persons should escape the punishment of death than that one innocent person should be condemned and suffer capitally".[564] Interestingly, given its draconian reputation, the Star Chamber reiterated this principle in almost identical terms in 1607; it was also reflected in the high late medieval acquittal rate and the smaller, but still substantial, level of not guilty verdicts in the Tudor period. In part this may have been rooted in the anxiety that medieval and early modern Christians experienced when contemplating the dangers of mistaken acts of judgment,

561. Smith, *De Republica Anglorum*, p. 114.
562. Hutson, *Invention of Suspicion*, p. 85.
563. Kenneth Pennington, "Innocent Until Proven Guilty: The Origins of a Legal Maxim", *The Jurist*, Vol. 63, pp. 106–7.
564. Grigor, *Sir John Fortescue*, p. 45.

resulting in blood punishments, to their souls.[565] In 1612 Thomas Potts, an associate clerk of assizes observed to a jury: "I would alwaies intreat you to remember, that it is as great a crime (as *Salomon* sayth, *Prov.* 17) to condemne the innocent, as to let the guiltie escape free".

The national feeling on such matters was also noteworthy to several foreign observers, even though they often came from Roman law systems with strict formal rules on evidential sufficiency, suggesting that such requirements did not necessarily enhance the reliability of a conviction. Typically, in 1551 the Venetian diplomat Daniele Barbaro observed that Englishmen thought that it was much fairer to release a guilty person than to condemn someone who was blameless.[566] Nevertheless, the burden and standard of proof were much less clearly enunciated than in the modern era.

Jury Discretion

From their inception in the early 1200s, trial juries had been able to exercise a considerable degree of discretion when assessing evidence and reaching their verdicts, something that often allowed them to nullify the substantive criminal law. Their members might have a number of reasons, both laudable and malign, for believing that a guilty defendant did not deserve death: they might have thought that there were mitigating circumstances or that execution under the death-for-felony rule was too grave a punishment for what had occurred. Bribery, personal bias, and favouritism might also have played a part.[567]

During the medieval period, and despite a low conviction rate, judges do not normally appear to have pressured juries to return guilty verdicts in ordinary criminal (rather than treason) cases, although there were a few notable exceptions and records are limited. The Crown seems to have been reluctant to punish them when they failed to convict.[568] One

---

565. James Q. Whitman, "The Origins of "Reasonable Doubt", Yale Law School Legal Scholarship Repository, March 2005.

566. Brown, *Calendar of State Papers*, p. 340.

567. T. A. Green, "The Jury and Criminal Responsibility in Anglo-American History", *Criminal Law and Philosophy*, Vol. 9, Issue 3, p. 427.

568. Bellamy, *The Criminal Trial*, p. 14.

explanation for this reticence can probably be found in the high medieval trial jury's largely self-informing character. This gave its members a considerable ability to ignore black-letter law. Because little evidence was presented in court, judges could not identify verdicts as perverse, or prevent jurors from deciding cases according to their own notions of culpability.[569]

However, the situation (like the nature of the jury) changed during the early Tudor era, when judicial pressure on ordinary felony juries to return certain verdicts could sometimes be extremely robust, and recalcitrant jurors might be punished. This development should not be exaggerated. Jurors still retained an extensive degree of discretion, although precisely how far this extended was an issue that would exercise lawyers over the course of the sixteenth century.[570] It is apparent that the Tudor judiciary did not intervene in jury decision-making lightly. Many cases boiled down to assessments of witness credibility, which the bench was usually happy to leave to juries, the judge merely providing an indication of the range of potentially appropriate verdicts.[571] In 1607 James I's Proclamation for Jurors freely observed that English law did not rigidly tie jurors to the evidence produced in court, but left the "discerning and credit of testimony to the juries' consciences and understanding". This had always been the case with regard to in-court evidence. In a felony trial from 1533 a correspondent noted that divers men from Montacute and Northover, in Somerset, were sworn and gave evidence in court, but were given little credit by the jury.[572] More dramatically, juries artificially down-valued cases of grand larceny on numerous occasions, sometimes in extreme circumstances, without demur from trial judges, and even attributed homicides to fictitious characters such as "John at Death" without judicial criticism or challenge.

Illustrative of this official acceptance of a broad realm of jury discretion is a letter written by the Duke of Norfolk in March 1537 to Thomas Cromwell. The duke promised to obtain the names of jurors who had acquitted defendants in several recent *causes célèbres*. However, he also

569. Klerman, "Was the Jury Ever Self-Informing?", pp. 123–50.
570. Loar, "'Under Felt Hats and Worsted Stockings,'" pp. 393–395.
571. Green, *Verdict According to Conscience*, p. 144.
572. Gairdner, *Letters and Papers, Foreign and Domestic, Henry VIII, Vol. 6, 1533*, pp. 386–404.

expressed concern that if action were taken against them it would lead to rumours that "men should be compelled to pass otherwise than [where] their conscience should lead them". (He also noted that, in his opinion, several of the acquittals were justified on the evidence).[573] Interestingly, if William Rastell is to be believed, just two years earlier Cromwell had threatened and intimidated an initially reluctant petty jury, presiding over the treason trials of four Carthusian monks, to convict the accused. This was something that subsequently made the jurors "ashamed to show their faces".[574]

Of course, if a jury convicted, when a judge had encouraged an acquittal, the latter could ensure that a reprieve was issued. If a jury returned a not guilty verdict where the judge had urged a conviction, he (perhaps advised by attending JPs) was not always entirely devoid of measures that could be taken against the acquitted defendant, if he felt it appropriate (usually not the case). For example, in three trials held at the Hertford Assizes in March 1587 not guilty verdicts were not quite the end of the matter for the accused.

William Conway (one of the three defendants), a London silk weaver, was acquitted outright of stealing two cheeses in Hemel Hempstead, worth just three shillings, but indicted as grand larceny (perhaps because he was a stranger). Even so, he was remanded to the house of correction (presumably as a vagabond) rather than being released. Another man, John Freed, allegedly stole four steers worth £13 in his own village of Furneux Pelham. Although acquitted, he was bound-over to be of good behaviour as a man of ill repute: i.e. he would forfeit a set sum of money if he misbehaved in future. The third individual, Randolph Haunce, who had been acquitted of burglary in his home village of Stanstead Abbots, received the same disposal.[575] Furthermore, in homicide cases, where the evidence appeared very strong, judges could encourage the next of kin of the victim to appeal prisoners who had been found not guilty, as occurred at the Hertford Assizes as late as 1629.[576]

---

573. *Ibid, Vol. 12, Part 1*, January-May 1537, pp. 323–354.
574. Kelly, *Thomas More's Trial by Jury*, p. 113.
575. Cockburn, *Calendar of Assize Records. Hertfordshire Indictments: Elizabeth I*, pp. 66–68.
576. Ernst, "The Moribund Appeal of Death", p. 166 and p. 177.

Nevertheless, Tudor jurors in ordinary felony cases were sometimes rebuked, lectured, and sent out to reconsider a verdict with which the trial judge did not agree, in the often justified hope that they would change their minds. In these situations, they might be threatened with punishment, if they continued to "pronounce not guiltie the prisoner against whome manifest witnesse is brought in". In practice, juries who failed to succumb to such pressure were not necessarily penalised, as this was felt to be contrary to the liberty and customs of England.[577] Even so, some trial juries in routine felony cases *were* actively punished for returning not guilty verdicts after resisting judicial encouragement to convict or where the trial judge thought the evidence very strong.

Jury Punishment

Petty juries could be disciplined in a variety of ways. At the start of the period, the grand jury, which had reviewed the evidence before trial, often had a role in this process, and might act "yf it apere unto the graund jurye in theyr conscience, that the petty jury wylfully of som corrupt mynde regarded not the wytnesses". At the Essex Assizes held in July 1560, jurors were bound-over in the sum of £10 to appear at the following sessions for acquitting Robert Mylborne of a high-value grand larceny, supposedly against the evidence. (The outcome is not known.)[578] Alternatively, and more commonly as the sixteenth century advanced, the judge could ensure that they appeared before the royal council or (its effective successor) the Privy Council: "If the Jury likewise regard ye witnesses so sleightly, that the Judges think they quyt the felon against their owne conscience they bind them sometime to apere before ye King's Counsel".[579]

However, from the late fifteenth century this was often done indirectly, by their being required to appear before the Star Chamber. By then this forum actively punished jury misconduct, in both civil and criminal cases, including situations in which jurors were deemed to have

---

577. Smith, *De Republica Anglorum*, p. 120; Cockburn, 'Twelve Silly Men?', p. 158.
578. Cockburn, *Calendar of Assize Records: Essex indictments, Elizabeth I*, p. 23.
579. More, "The Deballacyon of Salem and Bizance", p. 998.

perversely and unreasonably returned a not guilty verdict against what the trial judge perceived to be the evidence, whether through affection for one of the parties or as a result of personal corruption.[580]

The importance of the Star Chamber in this regard seems to have increased after the early sixteenth century, something that may reflect both Thomas Wolsey's legal activism (he made the court a much more efficient forum) and the fact that, after 1540, Henry VIII did not have judges (and so judicial expertise) in his comparatively new Privy Council, which was much smaller (only about 20 men) than the traditional Royal Council. Queen Elizabeth also excluded the judiciary from her Privy Council. For example, allegedly corrupt juries went before Star Chamber in 1516, 1517, 1520, 1523, 1527, and 1529.[581] Others have suggested that most terms saw early Tudor jurors, whether grand or petty, fined by the Star Chamber for returning perverse verdicts.[582]

However, punishment of a jury does not appear to have had any affect on the validity of the verdict (usually an acquittal) that its members had returned.[583] In 1554 Nicholas Throckmorton's jury may have been heavily fined and imprisoned (up to £220 and six months each) after Queen Mary was made sick for three days by their verdict (if a Burgundian diplomat is to believed), but the monarch accepted their decision, even if Throckmorton was sent back to the Tower for another year while other charges were considered. He was then released on a £2,000 bond, and subsequently regained some favour with the Queen.[584]

A few of these cases, like that involving Throckmorton, had political overtones. Nevertheless, this was unusual, as juries in political trials nearly always convicted, even if they later admitted that it had offended their consciences to do so, as was the case with those who found John Fisher, the former Bishop of Rochester, guilty of treason in 1535.[585] Most juries presented before the Star Chamber had heard routine, conventional,

---

580. Whitman, "Reasonable Doubt", p. 258.
581. J. A. Guy, *The Court of Star Chamber and its records to the reign of Elizabeth I* (London: HMSO, 1985), p. 53.
582. Bellamy, *The Criminal Trial*, p. 122.
583. Baker, *Oxford History*, p. 373.
584. Sil, "'My Bitter Comedie,'" pp. 381–405.
585. Hostettler, *The Criminal Jury Old and New: Jury Power from Early Times to the Present Day* (Winchester: Waterside Press, 2004), p. 45.

felonies and even the occasional misdemeanour. Most had sat at assizes, but a few were sent there from the lower jury forum, and one or two even came from leet courts. For example, in July 1556 the jurors at the Essex Quarter Sessions held at Rochford were each bound-over in the sum of £5 to appear before the Star Chamber on a set Wednesday after the following Michaelmas.[586] A selection of cases is indicative of the forum's work in this regard.

The Somerset Assizes jury that was reported to Star Chamber by an astonished trial judge after it acquitted in a burglary trial in 1546, setting what he felt was an "evyll example" to others, has already been considered, although the outcome is unknown.[587] This is not the situation with a case from the Oxford Assizes in 1554, where it was claimed that a jury had acquitted four thieves against the evidence. The Attorney General brought the case before the Star Chamber, which convicted the jurors of willful perjury and committed them to the Fleet Prison. In another case about the same time, the "principal offender" in a jury that "failed to do its duty" when trying two felonies was bound by recognisances of £200 to appear before the court. (How this man was identified is not clear.) When he failed to attend, the sum was forfeited. In 1580 the Star Chamber tried a jury that failed to convict two murder defendants at the Gloucestershire Assizes. It decided that this was contrary to the evidence presented at trial, and, as a result, sentenced the jurors to wear papers on their heads at Westminster Hall setting out their offence. They were also to stand with the same papers on their heads at the "next assizes in Gloucester and in the Cathedral Church whilst a sermon is made for that purpose, and to pay £40 a piece for a fine". (Star Chamber fines were sometimes commuted.)[588]

A document in the Ellesmere collection gives a particularly full account of a "perjured jury" case heard by the Star Chamber in 1581. Agnes Hobbes and John Paynter were accused of murdering Agnes' husband. According to the report made to the forum, the trial court was confronted with three problems. Had the husband been murdered and,

---

if so, by whom? Did the jury verdict reflect the evidence at trial? The court had no difficulty proving that Hobbes was murdered. The notion (presumably offered by the defendants) that he died by falling from his bed, which was only a short height from the floor, did not seem plausible. There were other telling indications of foul play, such as broken bed staves and blood on his pillow and sheets. The evidence also suggested that Agnes and Paynter murdered Hobbes. Agnes had publicly stated that she "loved Paynter better in the sole of the foot, than she did him [her husband] in his whole body". Furthermore, her behaviour on the night of the murder was suspicious, as was her marriage to Paynter immediately after their acquittal at assizes. Equally damning evidence was presented against Paynter. This led to the conclusion that he was the "principal actor with the woman in this unnatural and horrible murder". It was also clear to the Star Chamber that the jury had perjured itself in acquitting them, having been misled by its affection for the defendants and their friends. Before sentencing its members, the court noted that a case from the same county had come before it the previous year (see above), perhaps encouraging exemplary action. As punishment, the jurors were imprisoned in the Fleet, fined 100 marks (about £66), and forced to wear papers acknowledging their guilt both at Westminster and at the next Gloucestershire Assizes.[589]

Considerable detail is also available about a case from late 1586, in which a jury on the Northern Circuit returned a lesser verdict of guilty to clergyable manslaughter on three men who had been indicted for murdering one William Clavering, and acquitted another defendant outright, which the trial judge thought was manifestly unreasonable. The matter was referred to the Star Chamber, along with the names of six witnesses for the prosecution and an abstract of their depositions (possibly made in court, but much more likely their pre-trial examinations). It was claimed that the jury were biased towards the accused, that their verdicts were against the law and evidence adduced at trial, and that all four defendants should have been convicted of murder. It appears that a member of the jury had subsequently said that they made their decision

---

589. *Ibid*, p. 240.

because the men were soldiers, apparently acting under the orders of an absent superior, although the Attorney General was adamant that this defence applied only to legitimate military operations, not manifestly unlawful acts.[590]

Although jury referrals to the Star Chamber were comparatively rare, very strangely, at the Lent Assizes for Sussex in 1568 two juries were remanded to the following assizes or Star Chamber (whichever was more convenient) for returning verdicts "against the evidence" in three very ordinary cases, only one of which was even particularly serious. Perhaps Serjeant Christopher Wray, one of the two judges covering the circuit, was presiding, and his inexperience was reflected in this unusual level of judicial activism.

Such matters still had to be proved to the Court of Star Chamber's satisfaction, even though there was no jury in this forum; this was not a formality. In most cases of this type, the jurors involved defended themselves by claiming that they had evidence of their own justifying their verdicts (still often the case) or that the evidence presented in court seemed inconclusive. Occasionally, some individuals claimed that their co-jurors had persuaded them to decide as they did, against their initial inclinations. More generally, they asserted their right to assess the evidence as they saw it and denied having acted out of corrupt motives.[591] Nevertheless, an increased willingness to punish jurors for returning the "wrong" verdict may have made a contribution to the Tudor increase in conviction rates.

Conviction Rates on Indictment

The late medieval conviction rate for trial on indictment (as opposed to appeal) fluctuated greatly with time and place, but was always extremely low. Such evidence as is available suggests that, during the thirteenth and fourteenth centuries, approximately 70 per cent of indicted felons were acquitted.[592] Even during the great famine of 1315–1317, when the

---

590. Green, *Calendar of State Papers Domestic: Elizabeth, Addenda 1580–1625*, pp. 196–199.
591. Green, *Verdict According to Conscience*, p. 142.
592. Powell, *Kingship, Law, and Society*, p. 82.

number of felony indictments in Norfolk, Yorkshire, Essex, Somerset, and Herefordshire doubled, the conviction rate remained the same in these counties, at 23 per cent.[593] For more than 100 years afterward it did not increase. Indeed, it does not appear to have exceeded 25 per cent at any point between the arrival of the Black Death in 1348 and the reign of Edward IV (1461–1483). Sometimes it was much lower. For example, in the counties of what would eventually become the Western Circuit, it stood at only ten per cent between 1415 and 1430.[594] In the highly unusual environment of the far North of England, with its Scottish border, the figures were even lower. Between 1335 and 1457 only 36 of 522 suspects tried at 19 gaol deliveries in Cumberland (just under seven per cent of the total) were convicted.[595] Very similarly, of 618 (preserved) cases tried at gaol delivery in Northumberland, Cumberland, and Westmorland during the 1440s and 1450s, only 33 produced verdicts of guilty (less than six per cent).[596]

In part the lack of guilty verdicts was explained by the frequent failure of the accuser even to appear at trial. However, it also reflects the effect of (still largely self-informing) jury notions of "equity" and reluctance to convict in cases that jurors felt did not warrant the death penalty. There were probably many other, as yet only partially understood, factors involved.[597] Nevertheless, at some point after the middle of the fifteenth century the situation started to change. Exactly when this occurred is unclear, as there is a dearth of assizes and quarter sessions gaol delivery evidence between about 1460 and 1559. It is likely that it differed with geographic location.

For example, 43 cases can be identified from six Bristol gaol delivery rolls (the equivalent of three years' worth of trials) that were held in the city's guildhall during the years just after the middle of the fifteenth century. They covered a range of crimes, from murder to theft. In seven the verdict is illegible. However, in 21 of the remaining 36 cases, the

---

593. Hanawalt, "'Good Governance' in the Medieval and Early Modern Context", *Journal of British Studies*, Vol. 37, Issue 3, p. 252.

594. Bellamy, *The Criminal Trial*, pp. 94–97.

595. Henry Summerson, "Crime and Society in Medieval Cumberland", *Transactions of the Cumberland and Westmorland Antiquarian and Archaeological Society*, series 2, Vol. 82, p. 112.

596. Neville, "Gaol Delivery in the Border Counties", p. 59.

597. Powell, *Kingship, Law, and Society*, p. 82.

jury convicted, and the convicts were, it seems, executed. The other 15 defendants were acquitted. This produces a felony conviction rate of just over 58 per cent.[598] It would be dangerous to extrapolate too many conclusions from such a tiny and localised sample, but it does suggest that change may have been in the air in this regard before the end of the medieval era, at least in a few places. It probably occurred very much later in most others.

Whenever the change took place, by the Elizabethan era there had been a sea change from the situation that prevailed in the early 1400s. During the years between 1559 and 1572, the majority of those tried on the Home Circuit assizes were convicted, the figure for Kent being 56.5 per cent and that for Essex (easily the highest) 63.6 per cent. This was an increase of between 50 per cent and 80 per cent in Kent and fully a doubling in Essex on the conviction levels apparently pertaining around the middle years of the fifteenth century. More specifically, but fairly typically, at the Hertford Assizes held in February 1584, eleven people were indicted in ten trials. Five (about 45 per cent) were acquitted outright. Six (about 55 per cent) were found guilty, albeit that two other defendants who had been indicted for grand larceny were merely convicted of petty theft, the trial jury down-valuing the stolen items (including a sheep that was initially valued at five shillings).[599] The situation was broadly the same when it came to felony trials at the lower jury forum. For example, at the Easter Quarter Sessions for Essex in 1566, 22 people were indicted for felony. Of these, eight were acquitted after trial, so that some two-thirds were convicted.[600]

Moving north, and just after the Tudor era, in April 1607 the Bishop of Carlisle and Sir Wilfrid Lawson noted the results of what appears to have been an additional assizes held at Newcastle to deliver the local gaol, which was groaning under the pressure of dozens of prisoners. Thirty people (some of them on bail) were ultimately indicted, a majority for comparatively minor felonies. Of these, 17 (over half) were convicted. Three of these were for non-capital petty theft, while another

---

598. Fleming, *Time, Space and Power*, p. 243.
599. Cockburn, *Calendar of Assize Records. Hertfordshire Indictments: Elizabeth I*, pp. 30–33 and pp. 51–52.
600. ERO Q/SR 18/41.

three received benefit of clergy, so that eleven people were sentenced to death (one of these was temporarily reprieved so that a pardon could be considered).[601]

Of course there was considerable variation in conviction rates for different offences. For example, of the 258 people indicted at assizes on the Home Circuit under the new Elizabethan Witchcraft Act, between 1563 and 1600, just 59 (23 per cent) were found guilty (making the average even higher for "conventional" offences).[602] Furthermore, compared to Victorian conviction rates, those in Tudor England were still relatively modest. Even so, the increase from those found in the medieval period has been termed a "virtual revolution" in the criminal justice system.[603]

Appeals Against Conviction

It was very difficult to challenge a jury verdict. As Sir Thomas Smith observed, once the foreman had pronounced a defendant guilty or not guilty neither judges (at assizes) or JPs (at quarter sessions) could "reverse, alter or chaunge that matter". Common law did not normally allow an appeal against conviction. The writ of error could only be used to challenge technical defects in the trial that were apparent on the record, and the general absence of defence counsel and the normal practice of withholding a copy of the indictment from the accused, made identifying even these fairly difficult.[604]

In its lack of a proper appeal process, English law differed from many of the hierarchical civil law systems in continental Europe. For example, the complicated judicial structure of sixteenth century France had up to four tiers of potential appeal. At its summit were the king and his personal judicial court, the *Grand Conseil*. Below them were the *parlements* and *cour des aides*, followed by the *bailliages* and *sénéchaussées*. The lowest courts were the *prévôtés*, which conducted local trials. A commoner in a

601. Giuseppi and Lockie, *Calendar of the Cecil Papers in Hatfield House: Vol. 19, 1607*, pp. 84–96.
602. Malcolm Gaskill, "Witchcraft and Evidence in Early Modern England", *Past & Present*, Vol. 198, Issue 1, p. 40.
603. Bellamy, *The Criminal Trial*, pp. 94–97.
604. Langbein, "The Origins of Public Prosecution at Common Law", *American Journal of Legal History*, Vol. 17, p. 317.

small town could, in theory (whatever the reality), appeal a verdict from a *prévôté* to a royal court, such as a *bailliage*, then to a local *parlement,* and even, if the king was interested, to the monarch himself through the *Grand Conseil.*[605]

There had been less need to introduce such a procedure in medieval England, as the assize judges who presided over the majority of serious trials already came from, and spent most of their professional lives at, the central courts in Westminster, giving the Crown effective legal control in the localities.[606] As a result, as Sir Thomas Smith observed in the 1560s, "appeale which is used so much in other countries, it hath no place in England". This situation had some negative consequences. It was, of course, unfortunate for those who were convicted on dubious or inadequate evidence. More generally, the lack of a proper review procedure meant that criminal law was sometimes unclear or underdeveloped.

However, by the 1500s the judge in a criminal trial that produced a conviction at assizes or the Old Bailey could reserve a point of law from the case about which he was personally uncertain for further consideration. The issue would then be examined by as many of the 12 (or more) judges who manned the three Westminster Courts as were available, and who met for this purpose, two or three times a year, usually at Serjeants Inn or the Exchequer Chamber. (The procedure did not apply to cases from quarter sessions.) If they decided that a conviction was wrong as a matter of law, they could recommend a pardon.[607] Similarly, a jury could give a "special" verdict, which established specific facts as proven but asked for senior judicial consideration as to the correct verdict that should be returned on them. This was usually done with the active encouragement of the presiding judge.

For example, at the Essex Assizes in August 1594 four men were indicted for highway robbery after assaulting Thomas King in Purfleet and stealing a sporting gun and 24 shillings from his person. However, the alleged "highway" in this case was actually the River Thames, not a

---

605. Lauren Kim, "The Judicial Court Structure of Sixteenth century France", *Torch Trinity Journal*, Vol. 16, No. 1, p. 37.
606. R. C. Van Caenegam, *Judges, Legislators & Professors: Chapters in European Legal History* (Cambridge: Cambridge University Press, 1987), p. 2.
607. Bentley, *Select Cases*, p. 9.

road, and King had been in a boat when the crime occurred. The petty jury returned a special verdict, formally setting out the facts that they had found to be established. They then noted that "if this be fellonye and roberye accordinge to the Indytement, then we finde them giltie … and if yt be not fellonye and roberye accordinge to the Indytement, then we finde them not guiltea".[608]

---

608. Cockburn, *Calendar of Assize Records. Essex Indictments: Elizabeth I*, p. 425.

CHAPTER 12

Punishment

Introduction

The English penal regime revolved around the death penalty, the ostensible punishment for all felonies, apart from petty theft (discussed in *Chapter 1*), even if ultimately avoided via clergy, pardon, or pregnancy (discussed in *Chapter 15*). The heavy use of capital punishment in England marked it out from many continental jurisdictions and often struck European visitors, such as the Venetian chaplain Horatio Busino, who expressed surprise (slightly inaccurately in that he ignored petty larceny) that in England "the slightest theft is punished with death".[609]

By contrast, a survey of thefts and robberies tried at Peronne, in France, between 1510 and 1520 shows a range of punishments being imposed on those convicted, from banishment for a cutpurse *brasseur* caught at a fair, to the hanging of a vagabond caught breaking into a building.[610] The Great Assizes of Poitou (a large province in West-central France), held in 1531, issued just 13 death sentences to men of all social backgrounds, and carried out only seven of them, the remainder being commuted.[611]

Of course, France was not Europe. England was not unique. Some smaller jurisdictions on the Continent also administered the death penalty fairly freely. In Lucerne, in the Swiss Confederation, the use of death for theft increased dramatically at the start of the sixteenth century, so that execution was the outcome in 68 per cent of cases during the first

---

609. Thomas Platter and Horatio Busino, Peter Razzell (ed.), *Journals of Two Travellers in Elizabethan and Early Stuart England*, (London: Caliban, 1995), p. 148.
610. David Potter, "'Rigueur de Justice': Crime, Murder and the Law in Picardy, Fifteenth to Sixteenth Centuries", *French History*, Vol. 11, Issue 3, p. 272.
611. Stuart Carroll, *Blood and Violence in Early Modern France* (Oxford: Oxford University Press, 2006), p. 262.

decade, and 77 per cent in the second, before falling again.[612] Between 1573 and 1615, the Free Imperial City of Nuremberg, with just 40,000 inhabitants, executed 361 criminals. Between 1575 and 1603, in the principality of Ansbach, with about 100,00 subjects, 474 people went to the gallows. They were executed — in a variety of ways, depending on their crime — not just for murder and rape but also for theft, forgery, and bigamy.[613] Nevertheless, throughout the sixteenth century, England differed from most major European countries in its ready recourse to execution.

Lack of Secondary Punishments

The death-for-felony rule was partly premised on a belief that as only a few cases would come for trial and result in conviction, it was necessary to make examples of those that did. However, this was not the only explanation for such draconian disposals. Even in the 1590s, Robert Parsons appreciated that an important reason for the sanguinary nature of the English penal system was its lack of secondary punishments, especially for property crimes. In its turn, this can, at least in part, be explained by a lack of professional bureaucrats and administrators, who would have been required to administer such punishments, unlike the situation in many continental countries. In part it probably also reflects cultural differences towards constraining physical liberty and concern about cost.

For example, Venice, Spain, France, Naples, and several other European countries, all regularly used penal service in galleys as a punishment during the sixteenth century. In the Neapolitan galleys, convicts seem to have made up between half and three-fifths of the state oarsmen (slaves and volunteers constituted the balance) during the 1500s. Service was normally for between one and seven years, although for a few men it was much longer. It was backbreaking work, with harsh overseers and a significant mortality rate due to the rigors of life on the rowing bench, poor diet, and frequent outbreaks of disease below decks. Perhaps because of this, even the most serious offences might receive such a disposal.

---

612. Laura Stokes, *Demons of Urban Reform: Early European Witch Trials and Criminal Justice, 1430–1530* (New York: Palgrave, 2011), p. 111.
613. Robert A. Selig, "Eye for an Eye? Crime and Punishment in Early Modern Germany", *German Life: Culture, History, Travel*, December 1998, p. 23.

In 1562, about 26 per cent of men sentenced in Naples to the galleys had been convicted of murder, 21 per cent found guilty of other acts of violence, 37 per cent of theft, and three per cent of sexual offences. The availability of such a disposal greatly limited the need for and use of death sentences, so that, in practice, some serious offences in Venice almost never resulted in executions. As with any time-limited punishment, compulsory galley service could also be variegated quite easily to reflect the gravity of a particular offence.[614]

In England there were periodic suggestions as to possible substitutes for the death sentence for minor felonies other than petty theft. In 1621 Parliament briefly considered a proposal (it did not come to fruition) whereby those "being adjudged to die for small faults they may be saved and condemned as slaves during life and be used as in other countries unto any public works in the kingdom". Those who performed well might be released after eight years, and reacquire their good characters "never after to be taxed or twitted in the teeth either with their bondage or with their crimes for which they were so punished".[615]

The Incidence of Execution

Despite the presence of the death-for-felony rule in the late medieval period, levels of capital punishment appear to have been relatively modest, if only because of the general inefficiency of the criminal justice system, marked as it was by extremely low rates of both prosecution and conviction for capital offences (see *Chapter 1*). For example, just 13 people were hanged for felony in Warwickshire between 1377 and 1397; this execution rate seems to be indicative of wider patterns in England.[616] Some evidence suggests that the number of death sentences passed for less serious crimes was even declining in the early fifteenth century, something that may have been explained by a reluctance to assist what

---

614. Antonio Calabria, "The Cost of a Man's Life in Sixteenth century Naples: Galley Rowers On The Early Modern Mediterranean", *Essays in Economic & Business History*, Vol. 22, Issue 1, pp. 1–8.
615. TNA SP. 14/119, fols. 132, 131, identified by Krista Kesselring.
616. Richard Ward (ed.), *A Global History of Execution and the Criminal Corpse* (Basingstoke: Palgrave Macmillan, 2015), p. 3.

nature and war had done to population levels through plague, famine, and military conflict.[617]

By contrast, the Tudor execution rate quickly became very much higher than that found in the early 1400s.[618] There appears to have been a particularly sharp increase in its levels during the early sixteenth century, especially after Henry VIII came to the throne in 1509, as the criminal justice system became much more efficient at processing felons. In 1529, one official correspondent could complain that, since the by then out-of-favour Thomas Wolsey had become the king's main counsellor and strong promoter of an efficient justice system, "We have hanged, pressed, and banished more men ... than have suffered death by way of justice in all Christendom beside".[619] Such a change was hinted at in July 1513, when the Italian Peter Martyr d'Anghiera noted that Sir John Style, the English ambassador to Spain, had said that wagons bringing the king money for his French war had been attacked by robbers, but that the king had caught and hanged 80 of them.[620] By 1516, when Thomas More's fictional English lawyer in *Utopia* praised the severe punishment meted out to thieves in England, he noted that there were sometimes 20 felons being hanged at the same time on a single gallows.

Although attributing the high incidence of execution to Henry VIII or Wolsey would be unfair, there is some truth to Sir Walter Raleigh's retrospective observation that the former was a "merciless prince". It has been estimated that, during his 38-year-reign (1509–1547), between 57,000 and 72,000 people suffered judicial execution. The latter figure was suggested by Raphael Holinshed, some 35 years after the king's death, and may have been a slight exaggeration. Nevertheless, surviving letters from judges and government officials indicate that between six and 14 people were normally executed after each assizes or quarter sessions. This might suggest that at least 40 people a year would be hanged in each county, or about 1,600 annually in England. This would amount to about 60,000 during Henry's 38-year reign, or more than two per cent of

---

617. McGlynn, "Violence and the Law", pp. 53–59.
618. Bellamy, *The Criminal Trial*, pp. 155–156.
619. Brewer, *Letters and Papers, Foreign and Domestic, Henry VIII, Vol. 4, 1524–1530*, pp. 2548–2564.
620. *Ibid, Vol. 1, 1509–1514*, pp. 952–967.

the then 2,800,000 inhabitants.[621] Others have proposed a slightly lower total. Much also depends on whether mass executions for treason after rebellions such as the Pilgrimage of Grace (political crimes) are included in the total. Whatever the precise figure, it was clearly substantial. For example, in June 1541, when Sir John Neville was executed for treason (failing to report a conspiracy) in York, it was noted that 30 ordinary prisoners were hanged with him for various conventional felonies.[622]

The reigns of the later Tudors were only slightly less sanguinary in this regard. As a result, it is apparent that the Tudor state was far more willing to have recourse to judicial violence than its late medieval predecessor and its seventeenth century and eighteenth century successors. It is likely that more English people were hanged between 1580 and 1630 than were executed between 1630 and the abolition of capital punishment in 1965.[623] Many observers suggest that even in the latter decades of Elizabethan England between 600 and more than 1,000 people were being put to death every year.[624] On one modern assessment, of the 75,000 people executed during the century before 1630, between 18,000 and 20,000 were hanged in the years from 1580 to 1610. However, the execution rate had started to fall significantly by the 1620s.[625]

Even so, the incidence of capital punishment also varied considerably around the country during the Tudor era (making estimates difficult). In Chester about nine offenders were being put to death each year in the 1580s, a fairly modest total.[626] Similarly, the Sussex port of Rye, a town of about 4,000 people in the mid-sixteenth century that had power of gaol delivery (like all its fellow Cinque Ports), produced just nine executions in the 45 years between 1558 and 1603.[627] By contrast, according to the diarist Henry Machyn, writing in October 1556, 40 people were

621. Jasper Ridley, *Henry VIII* (London: Penguin, 2002), p. 281.
622. Gairdner and Brodie, *Letters and Papers, Foreign and Domestic, Henry VIII, Vol. 16, 1540–1541*, pp. 444–465.
623. Wood, "Deep Roots", p. 406.
624. Kesselring, *Mercy and Authority in the Tudor State* (Cambridge: Cambridge University Press, 2009), p. 200.
625. Wood, "Deep Roots", pp. 406–408.
626. Ward, *Global History*, p. 3.
627. J. S. Cockburn, "Punishment and Brutalization in the English Enlightenment", *Law and History Review*, Vol. 12, No. 1, 1994, p. 159.

condemned to death on just one occasion at a then recent Oxford Assizes (although this figure appears to have been based on hearsay).[628]

Unsurprisingly, given its size and crime problems, the metropolitan area witnessed a particularly high level of executions. In the late 1590s the German lawyer Paul Hentzner reported that more than 300 people were being hanged there annually. Most executions took place at Tyburn (near present-day Marble Arch), an hour's journey from Newgate. However, there were several other venues in the capital and its environs that were used for occasional or specialist executions, such as Smithfield, Lincoln's Inn Fields, and Execution Dock in Wapping (the last being employed for those convicted at Admiralty Sessions).

After every Old Bailey sessions (held between five and eleven times a year for most of the Tudor era), those to be hanged would be carried west in a procession from Newgate. In 1557 Henry Machyn noted that, on one day alone, 17 people were hanged at Tyburn, including a 90-year-old woman. In February 1562, Machyn saw five cartloads of felons, including four women, heading for Tyburn.[629] Given the numbers involved, it is, perhaps, not surprising that the Tyburn "Triple Tree", a permanent rather than temporary gallows, was erected in 1571. A horizontal wooden triangle, raised high off the ground, and supported by three legs, it allowed up to 24 felons to be hanged at the same time. In the 1590s the Swiss traveller Thomas Platter observed, "Rarely does a law day in London in all the four seasons pass without some twenty to thirty persons — both men and women — being gibbeted".

Other convicts were executed near the site of a particularly grave crime, on temporary ad hoc gallows, to set a public example. For example, in 1583 it was noted that a Worcestershire servant convicted of petty treason had received such a disposal, it being ordered that he "bée carried to the place where he did ye déed: there to be first hanged dead".[630]

628. J. G. Nichols (ed.), *The Diary of Henry Machyn, Citizen and Merchant-Taylor of London, 1550–1563* (London: Camden Society, 1848), pp. 109–123.

629. Nichols, *The Diary of Henry Machyn*, pp. 123–141 and pp. 274–286.

630. Anon, *A briefe discourse of two most cruell and bloudie murthers, committed bothe in Worcestershire, and bothe happening unhappily in the yeare 1583* (London, 1583), pp. 22–24.

Age and Gender Profile

When the visiting German Lupold von Wedel described a mass Tyburn execution in the 1580s, he noted that, among the 18 people hanged together, were "two women and two boys".[631] As this suggests, throughout the country most of those executed were adult males, but both females and children were represented. Women constituted about a tenth of those hanged. This is unsurprising; they made up a fairly small minority of convicted felons, but could not claim benefit of clergy during the Tudor era, although they were more likely to be reprieved than men. The presence of children was more disturbing to foreign observers.

By the seventeenth century, a lower age limit of seven years for criminal responsibility had been accepted at common law; this was extrapolated from older cases and principles, and seems to have been present in Tudor England. However, for defendants between seven and 12-years-of-age (by the 1600s, between seven and 14) the prosecution also had to establish that the child knew right from wrong, which eventually became the (so-called) presumption of *doli incapax*. As a result, below seven years-of-age Tudor children were presumed incapable of guilt, and above that age but below 12 or 14 years (depending on decade), the possession of a criminal discretion had to be proved to secure a conviction. This was a lower age of responsibility than that found in many Roman law countries.[632]

As von Wedel's account suggests, some of those hanged at Tyburn and elsewhere *were* very young. In April 1562 Henry Machyn noted that a "boy" was among a group of nine people carried to execution there, while at the start of the seventeenth century the Spanish Catholic missionary Luisa Carvajal y Mendoza was still shocked to find that amongst the 25 or more people executed every month or two, some were allegedly "children of ten or eleven years old".[633] Such juvenile executions were not confined to the capital. In April 1546 Alice Glaston, an eleven-year-old

---

631. Gottfried von Bülow, "Journey through England and Scotland Made by Lupold von Wedel in the Years 1584 and 1585", *Transactions of the Royal Historical Society, New Series*, Vol. 9, p. 267.
632. Thomas Crofts, "The Common Law Influence over the Age of Criminal Responsibility in Australia", *Northern Ireland Legal Quarterly*, Vol. 67, No. 3, pp. 284–287.
633. Nichols, *The Diary of Henry Machyn*, pp. 274–286; Glyn Redworth, *The She-Apostle: The Extraordinary Life and Death of Luisa de Carvajal* (Oxford: Oxford University Press, 2011), p. 131.

girl, was convicted and executed in Much Wenlock, in Shropshire, for an unknown felony, making her the youngest female known to have been hanged during the Tudor era (or subsequently). She was buried with two other felons in front of the door to the Lady Chapel of the local church.[634] It was claimed that John Dean, convicted of arson (a very dangerous crime) at the Berkshire Assizes at Abingdon in February 1629, after burning two buildings in Windsor, was between eight and nine years-of-age when hanged, becoming the youngest person known to have been executed in early modern England. His trial judge, Mr. Justice Whitelock (1570–1632) of King's Bench, apparently found signs of malice and cunning in the crime, and so did not recommend a reprieve.

However, such cases were very unusual. Many youthful suspects were not even prosecuted, while only a tiny minority of felony convicts were 10 to 12-years-of-age, let alone younger, and most were boys rather than girls. Even if found guilty, sentence of death was not normally imposed on defendants of this age. Thus, and fairly typically, at the Essex Assizes held at Chelmsford in July 1592, Richard Goodwyn was convicted as a cutpurse (an unclergyable crime), but remanded without judgment because he was aged just ten-years-old.[635] At the same forum, in July 1602, Rachel Brackley was convicted of two counts of grand larceny, in which goods and cash worth almost £2 had been taken. As a female she could not have pleaded clergy. Even so, she was remanded without sentence, specifically because she was less than eleven-years-old.[636]

Lack of Variegation

Execution was the standard punishment for felony in England (petty theft apart), and hanging the standard means of inflicting it. As Sir Thomas Smith noted, for those sentenced to death, whether for murder or unclergied grand larceny, there was usually "no other punishment, but to hang till they be dead".[637] Despite the high incidence of capital punishment, its imposition was not normally variegated.

---

634. Hartshorne, *Extracts from the Register of Sir Thomas Butler*, p. 11.
635. ERO: T/A 418/56/4.
636. Cockburn, *Calendar of Assizes Records. Essex Indictments: Elizabeth I*, p. 540.
637. Smith, *De Republica Anglorum*, p. 117.

In this, England was unlike many continental countries, which employed aggravated forms of death for particularly heinous offences, such as drowning, burying alive, tearing with pincers, dismembering while still living, or being "broken on the wheel". The last of these entailed the criminal's being tied to a large wheel, spread-eagled, and then being beaten with a blunt object so that his limbs and other bones were broken, producing a slow and agonising death. Although used rarely, it was sometimes seen in Scotland. In 1603 Robert Weir, a servant, was broken on a cartwheel in Edinburgh for murdering the Lord of Warriston at the behest of the latter's wife (who was beheaded). After being secured to a wheel, Weir was repeatedly struck with the coulter of a plough, wielded by the local hangman, until he was dead. His corpse was then publicly displayed, still lashed to the wheel.[638]

However, in England, noblemen condemned to death for felony might be granted (by the monarch) the privilege of being beheaded, although, as the cases of Lord Dacre in 1541 and Lord Stourton in 1557 show, there was no guarantee that this would occur. Heretics, including almost 300 Protestants during the reign of Queen Mary and two Anabaptists during that of her sister, were burned at the stake. Nevertheless, there were a limited number of other variations to the general rule, of which by far the most important was treason.

Treason

Treason (a different criminal classification from felony) was *sui generis* in the method of execution. As John Florio (c.1553–1625), the English-born son of an Italian Protestant refugee, and a resident of Elizabethan London, noted, special punishment applied "onely [to] the traytours, the which are quartered".[639] Typically, when Anthony Babington was executed in 1586 for plotting the murder of Queen Elizabeth, he was told that he would be drawn on a hurdle to the gallows, where he would be hanged and then cut down while still alive, after which his body would

---

638. Robert Pitcairn, *Criminal Trials and Other Proceedings Before the High Court of Judiciary* (Glasgow: Maitland Club, 1831), p. 450.

639. John Florio, *First Fruits, which yield Familiar Speech, Merry Proverbs, Witty Sentences, and Golden Sayings* (London, 1578), p. 16.

be opened, his heart and bowels plucked out, and "…your privy members cut off and thrown into the fire before your eyes. Then your head to be stricken off from your body, and your body shall be divided into 4 quarters". These would be disposed of at the Queen's pleasure. However, the full punishment was sometimes mitigated if the convict's crime was not deemed to have been particularly heinous. In February 1595, Robert Southwell, a Catholic priest who had prayed for the Queen before being "turned off", attracted so much sympathy from the crowd at Tyburn that he was granted the indulgence of not being cut down for quartering until he appeared to be completely unconscious.[640] Nevertheless, aristocrats, like high born felons, might be granted the indulgence of beheading, while, if only for reasons of public decency, women convicted of high treason (a rare occurrence) were not hanged, drawn, and quartered, but drawn on a hurdle to the place of execution, and there "burned to death".

Although some forms of coining were legally defined as treason, only the initial part of the execution ritual was normally applied to men convicted of the crime. As a result, in 1577, when Michael Cox was found guilty at the Essex Assizes of counterfeiting shillings and sixpences, he was sentenced to be drawn to the place of execution on a hurdle, but then to be hanged in the normal manner.[641] Unfortunately, it seems that women capitally convicted of coining were not only drawn to the place of execution on a hurdle but also burned, receiving no mitigation to their gender's normal disposal for treason.

Petty Treason

Those convicted of petty treason — the killing of a husband or master/clerical superior — would suffer a special type of execution. According to Sir Thomas Smith, "If the wife kill her husbande, shee shall bee burned alive. If the servaunt kill his master, hee shal bee drawen on a hurdle to the place of execution". Essentially, a woman who was convicted of the crime received the standard female punishment for high treason, being drawn on a hurdle to the place of execution and burned. However, and

---

640. Harrison, *A Second Elizabethan Journal*, p. 15.
641. Cockburn, *Calendar of Assize Records. Essex Indictments: Elizabeth I*, p. 158.

as with coining, the male punishment was attenuated to the purely symbolic first part of the punishment (being drawn to the gallows on a hurdle), after which a normal hanging would ensue. As a result, when, in the 1580s, a woman and a servant in Worcestershire, who had had an adulterous affair and then killed the man who was their husband/master, were executed for petty treason, the judge ordered that the wife should be burned and the servant merely drawn on a sledge and hanged. On the appointed day she was "laide upon an hurdle, & so drawne to the place of Execution, which was without the town: & there béeing bound to ye stake, & the fire made to burne about her, her wretched carkas was soone dissolved into ashes".[642]

In the latter decades of the seventeenth century a merciful practice developed whereby women who were to be burnt for petty treason were first usually strangled with a rope-and-pulley system shortly before the fire was lit. However, during the Tudor and early Jacobean period this was not normally done. As a result, in 1609 Margery Wilkes, who had poisoned her husband in Nantwich, was burned while still alive, and reduced to ashes at the stake.[643] The same year, when Mary Perkins was convicted of poisoning her husband in Worcester, she was even ordered to pay for the kindling required to make the fire, the iron links used to secure her to a stake, and the wages of the six men tending to the conflagration (necessary to prevent it spreading to domestic premises). This was not necessarily a trivial sum. When Alice Ardern was burned for killing her husband, the cost of her execution, combined with the hanging of a co-defendant, came to 43 shillings.[644]

Poisoners

The worst form of aggravated death in Tudor England was that imposed on poisoners for a 15-year period during the reign of Henry VIII. Under a statute from 1531 it was ordered that they be "boyled to death".[645]

---

642. Anon, *A briefe discourse of two most cruell and bloudie murthers*, pp. 22–24.
643. Sharpe and Dickinson; "Revisiting the 'Violence We Have Lost'", p. 304.
644. John Bellamy, *Strange, Inhuman Deaths*, p. 224; Kathy Lynn Emerson, *A Who's Who of Tudor Women*, tudorwomen.com
645. Smith, *De Republica Anglorum*, p. 117.

According to William Harrison, the Act extended to the inchoate offence as well, although this had not been contemplated in the original draft, so that a poisoner was to be: "boiled to death in water or lead, although the [poisoned] partie die not of the practise".[646] The passing of the Act was prompted by the case of Richard Roose, a cook who had attempted to poison John Fisher, the then Bishop of Rochester. Several other people (but not the cleric) died after ingesting the tainted food. It was feared that such an insidious form of crime might spread if there was not condign punishment.[647] As a result, and with the personal support of the king, under a retrospectively operative statute, Roose was repeatedly dunked in boiling water in a cauldron in Smithfield, being secured in a chain and "pullyd up and downe with a gybbyt at dyvers tymes tyll he was ded".[648] While being executed, "He roared mighty loud, and divers women who were big with child did feel sick at the sight of what they saw, and were carried away half dead".[649] This disposal greatly increased his suffering, but also had a symbolic function. Roose had mixed the poison in porridge or gruel, so that boiling him to death in a cooking pot re-enacted the crime and dramatised its relationship with his punishment.[650]

The 1531 statute was not invoked frequently. It seems that only two other people, both women, definitely met their deaths in this way, one (like Roose) in 1531 and another, Margaret Davey, in 1542. Davey was executed for poisoning the family for whom she worked in London: "*Margaret Dauie* a mayde seruant [was] boyled in *Smithfeeld* for poysoning of thrée seuerall houshoulders with whome she had dwelled".[651] There may have been a fourth case of boiling, but details are sparse.

Sir Thomas Smith argued that this special punishment was inflicted so infrequently because poisoning was almost unknown in England, despite considerable evidence to the contrary.[652] More likely, it was often difficult

646. Harrison, *A Description of England*, p. 225.
647. Kesselring, "'A Draft for the 1531 'Acte for Poysoning'", *English Historical Review*, Vol. 116, Issue 468, pp. 894–899.
648. J. G. Nichols (ed.), *Chronicle of the Grey Friars of London* (London: Camden Society, 1852), p. 35.
649. Moore, *The Tudor Murder Files*, pp. 51–54.
650. William R. Stacey, "Richard Roose and the Use of Parliamentary Attainder in the Reign of Henry VIII", *The Historical Journal*, Vol. 29, Issue 1, p. 5.
651. Anon, *A World of Wonders*, unpaginated.
652. Smith, *De Republica Anglorum*, p. 117.

to find a suitably large cauldron, especially outside the capital. The Act appears to have been repealed, along with several other late Henrician statutes, in 1547, during the brief reign of Edward VI, although several legal observers seem to have been unaware of this for some years afterwards. There was an unavailing attempt to restore it in 1563.

Amputation of Hands

In cases of murder, Harrison claimed that there was still occasionally some aggravation in the manner of execution, with the convict's hand being struck off near the site of the crime before he was hanged.[653] Even so, this does not appear to have been a common occurrence. Nevertheless, in April 1555, in a non-homicide case, a former monk from Ely who had married and was, it seems, unhappy with the return of Catholicism under Queen Mary, attacked a priest during mass at St Margaret's Church in Westminster. He struck the cleric on the arm with a wood knife, occasioning a severe injury. After the perpetrator was sentenced to death, it was ordered that prior to execution he should have the "hand that hurt the prest cut off".[654]

More significantly, it was normal during the Tudor era to cut-off the offending hand of a convicted felon prior to execution if he had assaulted a witness, judge, juror, or law officer in open court. This practice seems to have reached back to at least the fourteenth century.[655] Thus, in December 1556 Gregorie Carpenter tried to stab his co-accused, who had testified against him at the Old Bailey; his hand was cut off before he was hanged from an ad hoc gallows erected next to the Justice Hall (for exemplary purposes).[656]

The Scaffold Ceremony

In late medieval England it does not appear to have been customary for an executed convict to make a speech at the scaffold and, if they did,

---

653. Harrison, *Elizabethan England*, p. 242.
654. Nichols, *The Diary of Henry Machyn*, pp. 79–90.
655. Bellamy, *The Criminal Trial*, p. 154.
656. Stow, *The Annales*, p. 1066.

it was often done to proclaim their innocence. However, during the sixteenth century this changed, and a carefully scripted speech became increasingly commonplace, and was actively encouraged by attending officials and clergymen.[657] Thus, in 1572, when John Kynnestar went to the gallows in Bristol for murdering his wife, "The preacher went hym by, Exhortyng hym, saiyng repent, Prepare thy self to dye".[658] The condemned convict would often cooperate in what became a theatre of social obedience, praising the justness of the state's actions, accepting both his guilt and the religious ministrations offered at the scaffold, and setting a public example of repentance in what was an act of social reconciliation.[659] This was important, as significant crowds might be attracted to watch an execution, especially in an urban environment, and particularly in London. Of course, not all those who were condemned complied. William Sherwood (see below) was certainly not alone in refusing to confess, and others were openly defiant.

Conduct of a Hanging

Where there were only one or two people to be hanged, as was sometimes the case, especially in the provinces, they might ascend a ladder set against the scaffold, having first been attached by a noose to the crossbeam. The ladder was then suddenly twisted away, so that they fell off and were suspended by their necks, beginning the process of strangulation. The recusant and prison murderer William Sherwood's nerve broke at the gallows erected on the Old Kent road in 1581, after he climbed up such a ladder. When he concluded that there was no prospect of a public confession from the condemned man, the sheriff in charge (as part of his office) ordered that the execution proceed. Sherwood, perceiving that his death was at hand, fled down the ladder to escape, so that the hangman was forced to "undo the Halter which he had fastened to the

657. Katherine Royer, *The English Execution Narrative, 1200–1700* (Abingdon: Routledge, 2016), pp. 53–58.
658. Anon, *A true reporte or description of an horrible, wofull, and moste lamentable murther doen in the citie of Bristowe by one Ihon Kynnestar* (London, 1573), p. 11.
659. Gerald Broce and Richard Wunderli, "The Final Moment before Death in Early Modern England", *The Sixteenth Century Journal*, Vol. 20, No. 2, p. 274.

gibbet, and to put it about his neck below, and so by little and little to draw him up". Sherwood was then successfully "turned off".[660]

Alternatively, and especially where there were several felons to be executed (almost always the situation at Tyburn), convicts might remain in the carts that had drawn them to the place of execution with a rope already tied about their necks. The hangman would then fasten each rope to the crossbeam, and, when prayers had finished, drive the cart from under the gallows, so that the convicts were left suspended in the air.

Early modern gallows, lacking a "long drop", normally brought about death by strangulation rather than via the broken neck of late Victorian times. The thick hemp ropes of the era meant that this could be quite a slow process, taking several minutes or even longer, with much depending on luck, the physical qualities and weight of the felon, and the skill of the executioner.

Several convicts sought to expedite their deaths, as they would for centuries to come, by leaping from the gallows, hoping to break their necks or at least tighten their ligatures. After being convicted of sodomy at the Court of King's Bench in 1607, Humfrey Stafford considered this option when executed at St Thomas-a-Watering on the Old Kent Road. Shortly before being "turned off" a ladder, he admitted that he had initially planned to accelerate the process: "I had thought (saide he) to have leaped off, which yet I will not doe, least I should bee thought to dye desperately".[661]

Some observers sought to speed up the deaths of friends and loved ones who were being executed, and this seems to have been tolerated by the authorities. As the visiting German Lupold von Wedel noted in the 1580s, when the cart in which certain prisoners had been carried to Tyburn was driven away: "Their friends came, pulled them by the legs, and struck them on the chest, to end their lives the sooner".[662] Clearly this made an impression on foreign visitors. In the following decade,

660. Anon, *A true report of the late horrible murther committed by William Sherwood prisoner in the Queenes Benche, for the profession of Popery, the 18. of June. 1581* (London, 1581).
661. Anon, *The arraignement, iudgement, confession, and execution of Humfrey Stafford gentleman Who on the tenth of this present month of June, 1607. suffered, at Saint Thomas of Waterings* (London, 1607), pp. 1–22.
662. von Bülow, "Journey through England and Scotland, p. 267.

Thomas Platter the Younger also noted that criminals' friends would attempt to speed up the process of strangulation by pulling on their feet. Almost two decades further on again, Horatio Busino, the chaplain to the Venetian Ambassador in London, observed relatives of those executed at Tyburn not just pulling on their legs but also throwing brickbats at their chests to hasten their deaths.[663]

Post-Mortem Disposal

Having died, and then hung for (usually) an hour or more, executed convicts were taken down from the gallows and normally buried in a nearby cemetery. As Lupold von Wedel noted, "When life was gone, they [friends of executed felons] cut them off and buried them".[664] Henry Machyn more specifically recorded the hanging of the murderer William North and his accomplice on improvised gallows near St Paul's Cathedral on the morning of 10 January 1560 (the location was used for just a handful of executions). The corpses of the two men were left suspended for up to six hours before being cut down and summarily buried, in a rather degrading manner, but still within consecrated ground: the hangman "cared [them] in-to sant Gregore chyrche-yerd, and ther was a grayff mad, and so they wher strypyd of all, and tumbelyd nakyd in-to the grayff".[665]

Not everyone who was executed had friends willing or able to arrange such a disposal. However, prior to the Reformation the Hospitallers sometimes allowed parts of their graveyards to be used for executed felons and suicides, and occasionally even arranged such burials for unclaimed convicts, their black-draped carts being seen waiting beneath gallows.[666]

Even so, a few of the most heinous offenders, especially those executed for murder or highway robbery, might be publicly displayed or "gibbeted" after death. Although this only became a formal part of the punishment for grave crimes in the eighteenth century, offenders had occasionally been hung in chains after execution, on an ad hoc basis, from at least the

663. Platter and Busino, *Journals of Two Travellers*, p. 148.
664. von Bülow, "Journey through England and Scotland", p. 267.
665. Nichols, *The Diary of Henry Machyn*, pp. 221–239.
666. Gregory O'Malley, *The Knights Hospitaller of the English Langue, 1460–1565* (Oxford: Oxford University Press, 2005), p. 16 and p. 19.

late fourteenth century. As Sir Thomas Smith observed, notable murderers would, by royal decree, "bee hanged with chaines while they rotte in the ayre". As this suggests, normally the king or his council ordered such a disposal, as it was an extra-judicial punishment.

For example, in 1530 a London chronicle noted that three of the perpetrators of a particularly brutal murder had been hung in chains after they were separately convicted and executed over a period of two years. The first occurred in July that year, when a man was "hangyd in chayns in Fynsbery fyld for kyllynge mastres knevytt's mayd in sente Auntolyns paryshe".[667] Similarly, in the aftermath of the notorious murder of Thomas Ardern in Faversham, the Privy Council ordered that several of the perpetrators who had been hanged should be publicly displayed. Thus, George Bradshaw was hung on a gibbet in Canterbury. In like manner, in 1583, after being convicted of the killing of his master (petty treason), Christopher Tomson was returned to Worcester for execution, where, to set an example, "according to his judgment he hangeth in chaynes".[668] Once displayed, a felon's corpse would normally remain on view "till his bones consume to nothing".[669] This was a fairly regular phenomenon in and about London, but less common elsewhere.

In 1540, following the amalgamation of the barbers and surgeons into one body, Henry VIII granted the new Barber Surgeons Company the statutory (32 Hen. VIII, c. 42) right to use the corpses of four executed felons a year for anatomical study. (Again, this disposal would become much more common in the eighteenth century). Most would necessarily come from the London area. Thus, after the burglar Charles Courtney was executed at Tyburn his body was "begd by thee Barbar surgeons for an anatomie".[670] In 1587 the chronicler John Stow claimed that an "executed" felon had even revived while being prepared for dissection, something that would occur periodically over ensuing centuries.

---

667. McSheffrey, "Sanctuary Seekers".
668. Anon, *A briefe discourse of two most cruell and bloudie murthers*, pp. 22–24.
669. Harrison, *Elizabethan England*, p. 242.
670. Pamphlet 1612, p. 16.

Felony Forfeiture

As mentioned in *Chapter 11*, with regard to the *peine forte et dure*, conviction for felony, whether on indictment or appeal, led to attainder or "corruption of blood", even if the crime was pardoned or the subject of a successful plea of benefit of clergy. This resulted in forfeiture of property to the monarch, unless the Crown expressly remitted it (as sometimes occurred when a pardon was granted).[671] Forfeiture was one of the defining characteristics of felony and treason and a cardinal legal distinction between these crimes and those classified as misdemeanours.

There had to be a finding of guilt before such forfeiture could occur. The Ricardian Parliament of early 1484 had addressed a situation in which felony suspects were sometimes being deprived of their property after they had been taken into custody but before conviction. A statute that year provided that "no sheriff or escheator, bailiff of a franchise or any other person shall take or seize the goods of any person arrested on suspicion of felony before the person thus arrested and imprisoned has been convicted or attainted of the felony according to the law". Those deprived of their property in these circumstances could sue for double their value in damages.

Nevertheless, steps could be taken prior to trial and conviction to prevent assets being squandered or alienated and to ensure that sheriffs were well placed to seize property if a guilty verdict was returned. For example, in August 1533 John Bedell of Godstone, in Surrey, entered into a recognisance to hand over to the sheriff the goods and chattels of a murder suspect that he was holding if the man was convicted at trial.[672]

Of course, forfeiture was not usually a concern for the truly destitute, as they had little to leave to their families. It was once thought that this situation gradually extended up the social scale, as Tudor juries increasingly returned a formalised answer, irrespective of the truth, when asked what property a convict possessed after convicting them: "Their common answer is, none to our knowledge".[673] This response was customary

---

671. Ernst, "The Moribund Appeal of Death", p. 166 and p. 174.
672. SHC LM/963/2.
673. T. W., *The Clerk of Assize* (London: Timothy Twyford, 1660), p. 16.

by at least the middle of the sixteenth century, if not earlier. However, as Sir Thomas Smith noted at the time, this was not conclusive of the issue. Recent research suggests that, despite such a jury finding, sheriffs could and did make active enquiries about a convict's property and take action to seize it for the Crown. Furthermore, they did not confine their attention solely to the wealthy.

For example, the petty jurors that convicted Henry Mellershe of murder at the Surrey Assizes in 1579 produced the traditional formulaic answer as to his property. Even so, the local sheriff seized a horse and cash from his family. The same thing happened when William Payne, an Essex labourer, was convicted of manslaughter in 1594; the county sheriff seized goods from him valued at £5.[674]

As a result, it seems that forfeiture for felony (and treason) remained a real and tangible fear for many offenders throughout the Tudor era and beyond, as can be seen by a selection of contemporary cases. At the end of 1511, Charles Joseph was alarmed at the possible consequences of his involvement in the murder of Richard Hunne. Late one evening, shortly before fleeing to sanctuary, he came home with three bakers and a blacksmith from Stratford (an Essex village east of London) to pre-empt such a seizure, should he be convicted: "And the same night they carried out of Charles' house all his goods by the field side to the Bell at Shoreditch. And early on the morrow conveyed it with carts to Stratford".[675]

Similarly, in the 1530s a village bailiff in Suffolk, attempting to persuade a woman to implicate her husband in a murder, offered to ensure that if he were convicted she would not be left destitute by forfeiture. In particular, he declared that she would at least keep her "raiment" and a third of her husband's goods. Subsequently, the bailiff suggested that he might be able to arrange for all her husband's property to be returned to her if he were found guilty.[676] After Anne Myle's spouse committed a murder in 1601, she swiftly began distributing various household items to her friends and acquaintances, so that the under-sheriff would not note them prior to her husband's conviction and execution. A local

---

674. Kesselring, "Felony Forfeiture", p. 274.
675. Anon, *The enquirie and verdite of the quest paneld of the death of Richard Hune which was founde hanged in the Lolars tower* (Antwerp, 1537), pp. 8–10.
676. Bellamy, *Strange, Inhuman Deaths*, pp. 94–95.

widow named Malbye hid a brass pot for her, and even the vicar became involved, storing corn malt and other items.[677]

Some years after the Tudor era, in 1621, when the mentally troubled John Rowse murdered his daughters, he tried to pre-empt the financial consequences of the crime for his wife by asking a local woman, who was unaware of what had happened to the girls, to help carry his goods from the family home; he told her: "... that he feared that the sheriff of Surrey would come and seize upon all. But the woman not thinking of any of the harm that was done, imagined that he had meant that his goods would be seized for debt and not for murder".[678]

Not everyone approved of felony forfeiture. In the 1530s and 1540s, several writers criticised it for unfairly punishing the innocent, as wives, heirs, and even creditors were made to pay for a criminal's sins. In the early 1540s, the London evangelical Protestant and former Franciscan Friar Roderick Mors produced a treatise or "complaynt" in which he alleged that felony forfeiture was a cruel law and doubted its additional deterrent value to potential offenders. He also thought that it was dangerous, as its presence led to false allegations of felony by those who hoped to secure the rights to an executed man's property and "helped many an honest man to his death, by the covetousness of the officers that farm such things of the King".[679] Certainly, there were documented cases of this occurring. In 1524 Joan Burleton was pardoned following conviction for murdering her husband (petty treason) after it was appreciated that the prosecution had been brought at the behest of several malicious gentlemen "desiring her goods and tenements".[680]

In response, others defended forfeiture as a valuable deterrent for this very reason, arguing that a potential offender might not commit a crime out of concern for the wellbeing of his kin or (perhaps less plausibly) his creditors. It was necessary that the punishment create real hardship for

---

677. Kesselring, "Coverture and Criminal Forfeiture in English Law", in Richard Hillman and Pauline Ruberry-Blanc (eds.), *Female Transgression in Early Modern Britain* (Burlington, Vt.: Ashgate, 2014), p. 199.
678. Taylor, *The Unnaturall Father*, p. B3.
679. Gairdner and Brodie, *Letters and Papers, Foreign and Domestic, Henry VIII, Vol. 20, Part 2, August-December 1545*, pp. 330–349.
680. Kesselring, *Mercy and Authority*, p. 131.

intimates if it was to have any influence on their actions.[681] Interestingly, the 1621 Parliament discussed making the estates of convicted felons liable for their debts before forfeiture, though nothing came of this.

However, where forfeiture would occasion acute and entirely undeserved hardship, in circumstances where the threat of confiscation could not possibly have influenced the felon's conduct, especially if those prejudiced were "genteel", it might be remitted, in whole or in part, by an exercise of royal discretion. When Agnes Hungerford was convicted of murdering her first husband in 1522, all that she had inherited on the (natural) death of her second spouse, Sir Edward Hungerford, was forfeited to the Crown. Even so, it was eventually returned to her innocent stepson.[682] In about 1599 Fulke Underhill poisoned his father, William, in Warwickshire. (William Shakespeare had earlier bought a house in Stratford-upon-Avon from the latter). On one account (it has been questioned), the murder was discovered, so that Fulke was prosecuted, convicted, and executed at the Warwick Assizes, and so attainted as a felon. As a result, his estates were escheated to the Crown; even so, they were returned to his younger brother, Hercules, when he came of age in 1602.[683]

In some respects, the history of felony forfeiture in late medieval and Tudor England is unusual. Even as most criminal justice powers, such as the right to pardon convicts, were being centralised in the Crown, the monarch's right to a convict's property was often being farmed out. Sometimes this was on a permanent basis, the entitlement being given to manors, boroughs, and other corporate bodies whose felons were found guilty. For example, in 1446 the Manor of Prescot in Lancashire, owned by King's College, Cambridge, was given the right to take the chattels of all convicted felons who were tenants or inhabitants of college property.[684] Similarly, by the late medieval era the Lord of the Manor of Worfield, in Shropshire, had long held the right to the chattels and, it

---

681. Kesselring, "Felony Forfeiture", pp. 274–275.
682. Carole Levin, Anna Riehl Bertolet, and Jo Eldridge Carney (eds.), *A Biographical Encyclopedia of Early Modern Englishwomen* (Abingdon: Routledge, 2017), s. 2.2.
683. Ronald L. Dotterer (ed.), *Shakespeare: Text, Subtext, and Context*, (Cranbury, N.J.: Associated University Presses, 1989), p. 17.
684. F.A. Bailey, "The Court Leet of Prescot", *Historic Society of Lancashire and Cheshire*, Vol. 84, p. 65.

seems, some of the lands forfeited by felons resident within its bounds. As an account of the manor for 1602 reiterated: "If any copieholder committ treason or felionie his copiehold lands ought to escheat to ye lord". (Although it was normal for a felon's lands to return to the lord of a fee after the king had taken their profits for a year-and-a-day that of traitors usually went to the king in perpetuity). Instances of forfeiture in the manor declined during the early Tudor period before increasing again in its final two decades. Although some of the felonies that led to forfeiture are not identified, suicides accounted for at least four of them between 1493 and 1596, with thieves also being well-represented.[685] In like manner, under the Elizabethan iteration of its charter, the mayor and burgesses of Newcastle-upon-Tyne were granted all fines and felons' goods recovered in the city and its liberties.[686]

At other times, the right to a specific felon's possessions was awarded to private individuals, whether for a fee or as a favour. For example, in April 1533 Thomas Hall wrote to Thomas Cromwell, noting that Henry Lorde, a prosperous man from Leighton in Huntingdonshire, had recently died without direct heirs, so that his land had descended to his brother, Thomas Lorde, who was then one of three prisoners being held in Lincoln Castle for a robbery committed the previous summer. Hall thought (correctly) that he was likely to be convicted and attainted for this crime. Assuming this occurred, he urged Cromwell not to allow the property to be alienated to anyone else, as it "would be much to my comfort if I had them by the King's gift". In October 1533 Hall wrote a reminder to Cromwell, noting that he (Cromwell) had taken the office of receiver and "begging you to remember what I said to you of the lands at Leighton, which have descended to Thos. Lorde, attainted of felony at the last gaol delivery, wherein I desire your favour".[687] Similarly, in 1556, after the execution of Alice Ardern for the notorious murder of her husband, Thomas, in Faversham, a local family acquired his property. The Arderns' daughter and heiress subsequently petitioned for its return

---

685. Gibbs, "Felony Forfeiture", pp. 253–255.
686. Ralph Gardiner, *England's Grievance Discovered, in Relation to the Coal Trade* (North Shields: Philipson and Hare, 1849), pp. 169–171.
687. Gairdner, *Letters and Papers, Foreign and Domestic, Henry VIII, Vol. 6, 1533*, pp. 497–514.

(or the equivalent in money), and itemised the goods taken. The chattels alone came to over £45 in value.[688]

Occasionally the individual grant of a felon's property was given as a mark of royal favour. Bizarrely, an early sign that Catherine Howard had won the approval of Henry VIII was that she was given the rights to the possessions of two convicted murderers. In June 1540 John Berde sent a receipt to Christopher More, the Sheriff for Surrey, for £15 worth of cattle and sheep that had previously belonged to the murderer William Ledbetter, which Berde was to deliver to "Mistress Katherine Howard".[689] Almost three decades later, in November 1568, William Cecil wrote from Hampton Court to William More, a Surrey JP, asking him to make an urgent survey of the lands held in Godalming by a gentleman named John Scarlett who had, apparently, committed a murder. These particular lands, which included a moiety of the manor of Westbrooke, would be escheated to the Crown on conviction, and, should this happen, the Queen wished to grant them (or their value) to one of her privy chamber.[690] Courtiers and other influential people, who kept an eye on assizes dockets and petitioned for particular grants, probably acquired the rights to property in many of the most lucrative cases of felony forfeiture.[691]

On a more commercial basis, Queen Elizabeth sometimes granted forfeitures to individuals in exchange for a fixed share of the proceeds.[692] This saved the Crown the trouble of seeking recovery, which was not always a legally straightforward issue. For example, in September 1570 William Pelham wrote from London to William More, asking for the latter's help in recovering a horse and equipment that were being held in Godalming as a suspected felon's goods. The felon, a Southwark grocer, was in prison awaiting trial. It was claimed that a poor man named Thomas Browne (the bearer of the letter) had lent (not given) the animal and its harness to him. As the grocer did not own them, he could not forfeit them, even if convicted.[693]

---

688. Patricia Hyde, *Thomas Ardern in Faversham: The Man Behind the Myth* (Faversham: Faversham Society, 1996), p. 106.
689. SHC 6729/13/2 and SHC LM/965/1.
690. SHC LM/COR/3/90 and LM/572.
691. Kesselring, "Felony Forfeiture", pp. 278–280.
692. *Ibid*, pp. 276–277.
693. SHC 6729/1/82.

Nevertheless, felony forfeiture was not usually a source of great wealth. Nationally, even the Crown made only relatively small sums from the procedure. It obtained just £41 6s from felons' goods in 1551, although such a small amount was unusual, and it made at least £605 in 1589. Those corporate bodies that had acquired local rights to such assets also normally secured only modest sums. For example, Great Yarmouth, which had the right to its felons' possessions, recovered a total of £73 between 1581 and 1612, and some £24 of this came from just one case in 1599. Even so, and as this last instance suggests, there could be occasional windfalls in which major sums from particularly rich convicts became available. In 1597 Edmund Dockett paid Plymouth £132 to redeem the goods he had forfeited to the town after being found guilty of manslaughter.[694]

Various explanations have been advanced for the small amount of money secured from the country's felons. Obviously, many convicts came from poor backgrounds. However, it seems that others proved fairly adept at illicitly hiding or alienating their wealth prior to conviction. Sometimes this was even done with legal advice or assistance. In *Serjeant Brown's Case*, heard in the Star Chamber in 1540, the king committed serjeant-at-law Humphrey Brown to the Fleet Prison. In part this was for hunting in Waltham Forest, but it was also because he had "given counsel to felons or prisoners in the tower to sell their goods to avoid forfeiting them".[695] In 1601 it was claimed, perhaps with a little exaggeration, that the goods of felons and traitors were "now so concealed that hardly the twentieth part is paid".[696]

Corruption may also have played a role. In 1552 it was suggested that, nationally, sheriffs and their inferior officers were under-declaring what they had secured and then pocketing some of the proceeds of confiscations. In Somerset, after a murder-suicide involving a man named Thomas Mitchell, it was alleged that the under-sheriff had personally driven off some of the dead man's cattle to Bridgwater. Perhaps significantly, in August 1593, when Sir John Wolley wrote from the Court to Sir William More, he asked the latter to use his influence with the sheriff to

---

694. Kesselring, "Felony Forfeiture", pp. 278–280.
695. Spelman, *The Reports of Sir John Spelman*, p. 183.
696. Green, *Calendar of State Papers Domestic: Elizabeth, 1601–3, with Addenda 1547–65*, pp. 137–140.

ensure that the goods of a man named Chapman, which had been confiscated for a murder, pass to the Crown "and not be embezzled". (The Queen had, apparently, promised them to one of Wolley's friends.)[697]

There were even occasional allegations that JPs became involved in such nefarious activity. In about 1566, Sir William More wrote to his fellow Surrey magistrate Richard Bydon, informing him that the wife of an executed felon named Maybank, who came from Chiddingfold, had alleged that, after her husband's death, Bydon had taken deeds relating to land her spouse had purchased locally.[698] Bydon denied knowing anything of the case, but recalled a man named Hamond who was executed for sheep stealing and who had bought a house and mill in the area, which his heirs had inherited, while "for his goods, I think the Queen's Majesty is answered of them". (More remained doubtful about Bydon's claims.)[699]

Lesser Punishments

Flogging

Public flogging was to become a major punishment during the sixteenth century, combining pain and shame. It was used to deal with various forms of immorality, such as bastard-bearing and prostitution. Thus, at the Devonshire Quarter Sessions held at Easter 1598, it was ordered that the mothers and putative fathers of several illegitimate children be whipped. Perhaps more important, whipping was also employed for some forms of vagrancy. Under the Vagabonds Act of 1530 (22 Henry VIII c. 12), sometimes colloquially referred to as the Whipping Act, rogues and vagabonds were to be "tied to the end of a cart naked and beaten with whips throughout such market town till the body shall be bloody". Most important of all, especially for the purposes of this book, it was the standard punishment for petty theft, meaning that it was imposed on a regular basis after both quarter sessions and assizes.

The whipping might be inflicted with birch rods or knotted leather cords, with the recipient stripped to the waist (even if female), tied to

---

697. SHC 6729/3/168.
698. SHC LM/COR/3/652.
699. SHC 6729/8/14; SHC LM/COR/3/651.

the tail of a cart, and beaten while being paraded through a populous area near where the crime had been committed. However, after legislation in 1597, the use of a stationary whipping post for such punishment became more common. The number of such posts proliferated rapidly; frequently they would be set up next to a town pillory and stocks.[700] Typically, the Waltham Abbey whipping post of 1598 was made of oak, with iron clasps for the hands. (The use of clasps for the feet allowed it to double as stocks.)[701] Occasionally the number of strokes to be imposed was stipulated by the sentencing court, which might order that a "dossyn good lashes" or "xii strypes at the least" be inflicted, but this was rare. More commonly, it would be stipulated that a convict's back be bloodied.[702] In Ferdinando Pulton's words, after sentencing most offenders would be returned to the gaol or stocks, and after a week or two the suspect was taken to the town or village where he had offended, or some other stipulated place to be "tied to a carte, stripped from the girdle upward, and whipped untill his bodie doe bléede, once, twice, or thrice, &c. according to the justices discretion". In practice, a single flogging was fairly usual for petty theft, and it was frequently carried out almost immediately after conviction, or within a few days, the recipient then being released without more ado. For example, at the West Riding Quarter Sessions in 1598, William Prate was convicted of stealing two sheep, severely undervalued at ten pence, for which he was sentenced to be whipped the following Monday in Leeds marketplace, the "constable of Wortley safelie to keepe hym in the meane tyme".[703]

The punishment could be attenuated to some degree to allow for the age, health, and gender of the recipient. Nevertheless, there would come a point at which people were too frail to be dealt with in this manner. This may explain why, in 1598, when Edmund Harrison admitted stealing six chickens, down-valued to below a shilling in total worth, it was ordered that he be "sett in the Stocke att Tonge with ffeathers picked

---

700. Graeme R. Newman, *The Punishment Response* (Abingdon: Routledge, 2017), pp. 120–121.
701. William Andrews, *Bygone Punishments* (London: William Andrews, 1899), p. 211.
702. Martin Ingram, "Shame and Pain: Themes and Variations in Tudor Punishments", in Simon Devereaux and Paul Griffiths (eds.), *Penal Practice and Culture, 1500–1900* (Basingstoke: Palgrave Macmillan, 2004), p. 57.
703. Lister, *West Riding Sessions Rolls*, p. 79.

in his apparaile".[704] It is possible that he was too fragile to be whipped, too poor to be fined, and being humiliated in such a public manner, in the place where he had committed the crime, was felt to be sufficient.

Stocks and Pillory

The main purpose of both the stocks and the pillory was to humiliate offenders, identify miscreants to their neighbours, and serve as a deterrent example so that others would not offend. The stocks, which confined convicts by their ankles, were used to punish very minor crimes such as drunkenness, swearing, and dishonest trading (selling underweight goods, etc.). Manorial leet courts often imposed such punishments. The pillory, which confined by neck and wrists, was a more draconian punishment, being employed for misdemeanours such as perjury and, after 1563, minor forms of witchcraft. Those in the stocks or (even more so) pillory could be pelted with rotten food, eggs, and dirt. The latter punishment was not fully abolished until 1837, and the former continued in use until 1872.

Fiscal Penalties

Fines were used to punish many misdemeanours, especially assaults. They were also sometimes used for those who were considered too genteel to be placed in the pillory. The sums imposed would reflect both the gravity of the offence and (to some extent) the means of the recipient.

Imprisonment

England had a plethora of prisons. All counties had their own gaols, as did most chartered boroughs. For example, there was already one major prison in Exeter in 1537, the "high gaol" for Devon, which stood within the precincts of Exeter Castle, and came under the jurisdiction of the Crown (rather than the city authorities). However, when Exeter became an urban county that year, Henry VIII gave the citizens the right to set up a gaol of their own, and by 1556 this had become established in the

---

704. Lister, *West Riding Sessions Rolls*, p. 119.

South Gate, in the suburban parish of St Sidwells. Similarly, amongst the rights acquired by Much Wenlock when it received its borough charter in 1468 was the privilege of having its own prison.[705]

The mid-Tudor metropolis, including its environs and extensions South of the Thames, was particularly well-served for custodial institutions, having 14 major prisons, although some were primarily for holding debtors or petty offenders. They included the Tower of London (usually reserved for state prisoners and felons of particular note); the Gatehouse; the Fleet (for debtors); Newgate (for both criminals and debtors); Ludgate, Poultry Counter, Wood Street Counter, Bridewell (largely vice-related crimes), White Lion (for the county of Surrey), the King's Bench, Marshalsea (debtors and Admiralty offenders), Southwark Counter, the Clink, and the Liberty of St Katherine's prison.[706]

Nevertheless, in England imprisonment was primarily used as a means to secure suspected felons before trial, or convicts prior to execution (or the award of a reprieve), rather than as a punishment. Imprisonment could not normally be imposed as a sentence for felony. However, this principle was qualified in a number of ways. In theory, if a convict was clergied after 1576, he could be sentenced to a year in custody, at the discretion of the court. In practice this rarely occurred, if only because of a lack of space in the country's gaols. There were also a number of moderately serious statutory crimes for which custody was or could be the designated punishment, albeit that some were fairly arcane. For example, under the 1563 Witchcraft Act, lesser forms of malefic witchcraft, such as injuring but not killing another person, could result in a year's imprisonment (and four sessions in the pillory).

Furthermore, short-term imprisonment in one of the post-1553 bridewells or "houses of correction" (as they also became known), frequently combined with hard labour and regular whippings, was used as a punishment for many minor offences after the mid-Tudor period, especially those involving vice, pilfering, and lesser forms of vagabondage. The Bridewell Palace had originally been built for Henry VIII in the years after 1515, and was named after the nearby holy well of St Bride. It served as

---

705. Baugh, *A History of the County of Shropshire: Vol. 10*, pp. 187–212.
706. Peter Ackroyd, *London* (London: Vintage, 2001), pp. 260–261.

a royal palace for only a short period. By 1531 it was leased to the French Ambassador. In 1553 Edward VI gave it to the City of London as a home for orphans and a prison for punishing petty offenders. Queen Mary confirmed Edward's gift the same year, after his death.

When Lupold von Wedel visited the London Bridewell in 1584, he noted that the prison was centred on two large courtyards. Male inmates were forced to tread a mill which ground flour at the same time, while female prisoners were required to work at other menial tasks, unlike the situation in normal prisons, where formal work was not usually provided. Both men and women were normally whipped twice a week. Most of the female inmates were prostitutes.[707] As a result, in 1599, another foreigner, Thomas Platter observed that a whore would be "taken to Bridewell, the king's palace, situated near the river, where the executioner scourges her naked before the populace".[708]

The London Bridewell served as a model for many other, similar prisons for petty offenders in urban centres, which opened across much of the country and often took the same name as well as being known as houses of correction. (Their introduction can be seen as part of the era's general search for order.) Thus Oxford followed suit in 1562, Salisbury in 1564, Norwich in 1565, and Ipswich in 1569. In 1571 the Lord Treasurer observed that he desired a "Bridewell in every Town". With this encouragement, further institutions were established. For example, Acle, in Norfolk, opened in 1574 and Chester in 1575. A permissive act of 1576 encouraged the voluntary establishment of houses of correction, prompting further expansion. A house of correction was established at Bodmin that same year, at Bristol in 1577, and others, including those at Worcester, Exeter, Winchester, Devizes, and Plymouth followed shortly afterwards.[709] At the Winchester house, established at a cost of £1,000 in 1578, the 80 inmates would spool yarn, grind wheat, comb wool, make nails, and draw water if male, while women would spin, card wool, and

---

707. von Bülow, "Journey through England and Scotland", p. 233.
708. Andrew Gurr, *Playgoing in Shakespeare's London* (Cambridge: Cambridge University Press, 2004), p. 257.
709. Austin Van der Slice, "Elizabethan Houses of Correction", *The Journal of Criminal Law & Criminology*, Vol. 27, Issue 1, p. 53.

knit hose, among other tasks. All those committed to the establishment would be flogged on arrival and for any failings in their work.[710]

However, ensuring that a suitably strict regime of work and whippings was kept up in such institutions, so that they did not regress to being simple prisons, proved difficult. As early as 1589 Sir Edmund Huddleston and Anthony Maxey wrote to Sir Henry Gray and the rest of the Surrey Commission about the results of their investigation into an acrimonious dispute between the two governors of the county house of correction, amid allegations of laxness. They concluded that neither man was blameless when it came to the performance of their duty "partlie by slackness in lookeinge unto there chardge, and partlie by overmuche lenytie showed towardes some bad persons committed to theire custodie".[711] Nevertheless, during the sixteenth century such institutions were not normally used to deal with conventional felonies.

Prison Conditions and Security

Tudor prisons were usually squalid and insecure institutions, with high inmate mortality rates and regular escapes. Occasional efforts were made to improve this situation. In 1532 a statute (23 Henry VIII, c. 2) required that gaols in England be edified and made more secure, so that fewer inmates would break out, while more provision was to be made to ensure that the "relyeff & charyte of the people shall be to the prisoners mynystred". The JPs of 22 counties were ordered to build new prisons, although this provision, like several others in the statute, often appears to have been ignored or carried out in a half-hearted manner.[712]

Sixteenth century prisons were often overrun with rats and mice, inmate nutrition was usually poor, the provision of bedding bad or nonexistent, and artificial warmth a luxury, even in winter. As a result, disease was an ever-present threat. The surviving assize court records (some have been lost) for the Home Circuit between 1559 and 1625 produce coroners' inquests into some 1,291 deaths that occurred in custody, the vast

710. *Ibid*, p. 63.
711. SHC Q/SR 109/16.
712. John Charles Cox, *Three Centuries of Derbyshire Annals* (London: Bemrose, 1890), p. 3.

majority due to sickness.[713] Frequently, this was typhus (although there were many others), often known as the "pryson syknesse", which was given as the cause of the suspected felon Henry Warren's death in September 1566 as he was being held in the dungeon of Nottingham Gaol.[714]

Andrew Boorde had a shrewd idea about the sort of conditions that encouraged such disease, even if he was unaware of the pathogen. He attributed gaol sickness to the: "corruption of the ayer, and the breth and fylth the which doth come from men, as many men to be together in a lytle rome, having but lytle open air". Boorde suggested purchasing some perfumes to hide the smell and, more usefully, keeping the prison clean. He also thought that friends on the outside could provide inmates with practical assistance.[715]

Perhaps due to their proximity to the capital, Surrey prisons were particularly prone to epidemics, and it seems that between 1558 and 1625 more than 500 prisoners died in them.[716] More specifically, in about 1560 William More received a petition from a group of prisoners (described by the magistrate as "Egyptians", or gypsies) who were confined in the White Lion Prison in Southwark, in Surrey. They begged to be released from the jail, warning that they would lose the use of their limbs if they continued to be held there.[717] At the Summer Assizes for the county in 1587, three defendants could not be produced for trial because they had died in the meantime.[718]

Conditions in the houses of correction were just as bad. Shortly after the London Bridewell opened in the mid-1550s, stories of ferocious thrashings, inadequate and maggot-laced food, and appalling accommodation started to circulate in the streets outside.[719] When John Gerard, a Catholic priest, visited a recusant in the Bridewell during the Elizabethan period, he noted that one man had recently died there of starvation

---

713. J.S. Cockburn (ed.), *Calendar of Assize Records. Home Circuit Indictments: Elizabeth I and James I: Introduction* (London: HSMO, 1985), p. 36, p. 39, p. 125, pp. 145–171.
714. Hunnisett, "Calendar of Nottinghamshire Coroners' Inquests", p. 153.
715. Boorde, *The fyrst boke of the introduction of knowledge*, p. 72.
716. Cockburn, *Calendar of Assize Records, Elizabeth I and James I, Introduction*, p. 35.
717. SHC Z/407/MSLb.210.
718. Cockburn, *Calendar of Assize Records. Surrey indictments: Elizabeth I*, p. 309.
719. Paul Griffiths, "Contesting London Bridewell, 1576–1580", *Journal of British Studies*, Vol. 42, Issue 3, p. 283.

while the subject of his visit was covered in lice and "wasted to a skeleton and in a state of exhaustion from grinding at the treadmill".[720]

However, in most gaols, better-off inmates could avoid some of the privations of prison life, although no-one could entirely escape the risk of sickness. The entrepreneurial character of English prisons was already well-established by Tudor times, and would endure for centuries to come. Keepers made much of their income from selling superior accommodation, bedding, food, alcohol, and freedom from irons and shackles to inmates. As a result, in 1491, the inmates of the King's Bench Prison in Southwark complained that they were only able to purchase ale at the steep prison rate of half-a-penny a pint.[721] For this reason, the position of keeper was often sought after; in July 1580 Lord Buckhurst wrote to Sir William More, requesting that one of his servants be given the place of the recently deceased gaoler of Lewes as a favour: "I pray you good cousin most heartily, to grant it to him".[722]

Nevertheless, even the small minority of suspects who could initially afford the greatly inflated prices involved in ameliorating prison life would often see their money run out after a few weeks in custody, and be forced to endure the basic conditions and strict security of the ordinary prisoners in the common wards, unless they could find someone else to fund them. For example, in the early stages of his incarceration, William Sherwood was able to afford good treatment in the Queen's Bench Prison. Unfortunately, it happened after "about six weekes, that *Sherwood* for want of paiment was removed from his lodging, well shakeled, to the common Gaile, whose misery being pitied by this young man [his eventual victim], was also reléeued by his meanes". (A fatal quarrel was to develop between the two men over this money.)[723]

Detained felons (whether suspected or convicted) were entitled to only a modest bread allowance, usually not more than a penny's worth a day. In September 1596 the Somerset JP Edmund Hext noted that criminals in the county prisons were allowed six pence a week in loaves; even so,

---

720. Gerard, *Hunted Priest*, p. 5.
721. Steven Gunn, *Henry VII's New Men and the Making of Tudor England* (Oxford: Oxford University Press, 2016), p. 59.
722. SHC 6729/9/32.
723. Anon, *A true report of the late horrible murther*, pp. 1–16.

there were so many people in custody that Somerset had paid out about £73 (2,920 man-weeks, or the equivalent of a permanent prison population of almost 60 people) over the previous year.[724]

Not all counties were so generous. At the Epiphany Quarter Sessions held at Chelmsford in 1578, the keeper of the common gaol at Colchester informed the court that so many vagabonds had been put into his charge that the annual allowance of 20 marks (about £14) granted for their relief was woefully inadequate. The resulting lack of food meant that "of late moste of the roges ther have ben by famyn in grete perill of deathe". It was even claimed that some had died from malnutrition, despite the gaoler using his own resources to help them. In response, the JPs ordered that the yearly allowance paid by the county be doubled, the extra money to be raised by high constables within their hundreds as a matter of urgency. They also agreed to monitor whether the new figure of 40 marks a year was adequate.[725]

Fortunately, the basic bread allowance was often supplemented by gifts brought into prison by the relatives of those detained and by charitable donations. A common bequest for wealthy people of the time, one that stretched back into the medieval period, was to leave money to those held in the country's gaols.[726] Inevitably, testators usually had a local focus, leaving money to inmates in their native counties or towns. However, this was not invariably the case. For example, a serjeant-at-law whose will was proved in 1502 left money to four London prisons but also provided legacies for gaols in York and Hull. A knight from Kent whose will was proved in 1525 left money to prisons in Nottingham and Lincoln.[727]

Some bequests were substantial, occasionally running to hundreds of pounds. Much more typically, on his death in 1597, and among many other charitable gifts set out in his will, Charles Hoskins of Oxted, in Surrey, left £14 to the poor prisoners in the two Counters and Newgate and Ludgate prisons in London, and £2 each to those in the King's Bench,

724. Key and Bucholz, *Sources and Debates*, pp. 128–129.
725. ERO Q/SR 65/70.
726. Shannon McSheffrey, "Sanctuary and the Legal Topography of Pre-Reformation London", *Law and History Review*, Vol. 27, No. 3, pp. 483–514.
727. Ralph B. Pugh, *Imprisonment in Medieval England* (Cambridge: Cambridge University Press, 1968), p. 324.

the Marshalsea, and the White Lion prisons in Southwark.[728] Other poor inmates were either able to beg through the bars of their gaols or were even released into the community for short periods to do so; some provided services for wealthier fellow prisoners for cash.

Despite the privations, a few inmates did survive for long periods in Tudor gaols. Simon Godfrey lasted eleven years in Horsham Gaol after being charged with recusancy in 1588 and then being repeatedly remanded in custody for failing to meet the terms needed for release. He eventually died from "natural causes" in 1599.[729] Doubtless, possession of a strong natural immune system and robust constitution, along with outside assistance, was a great help in such cases.

There was no expectation that prison would improve inmates. In 1621 an anonymous parliamentary proposal for penal reform noted that long imprisonment in common prisons made those incarcerated "more obdurate and desperate when they are delivered out of the gaols, they being then poor, miserable, and friendless, [and] are in a manner exposed to the like mischiefs, they not having means of their own, nor place of habitation".[730] Even so, the poor conditions and prospects faced by prison inmates generated limited concern amongst contemporary observers. The physician Andrew Boorde (1490–1549), like many contemporary observers, and despite having spent time in the Fleet Prison himself, was robust about the best cure for harsh prison conditions; it was to live in such a righteous manner as not to end up being incarcerated.[731]

Security

Security in Tudor gaols was often extremely basic, not least because many had not been built as carceral institutions. For example, the Common Gaol for the City of Norwich (separate from that for Norfolk) was

---

728. SHC 212/81/1.

729. Hunnisett, *Sussex Coroners' Inquests*, 1558–1603, p. 131.

730. *An Act for keeping in servile works such persons as shall be convicted of petit larceny and felony capable of the benefit of clergy, and such as shall be convicted for cheaters or incorrigible rogues*, held at NA SP. 14/119 fols. 131 and 132.

731. Andrew Boorde, *The fyrst boke of the introduction of knowledge made by Andrew Borde, of physycke doctor. A compendyous regyment; or, A dyetary of helth made in Mountpyllier* (London: Early English Text Society, 1870), p. 72.

situated in the cellars of the Guildhall from 1412 until 1597, when it was moved to a building that had formerly been the Lamb Inn. This encouraged the use of dungeons, shackles, and leg-irons to prevent escapes. Even so, breakouts were a regular occurrence, sometimes on a large scale. However, not all were successful. An attempt at a mass escape from the Essex county gaol in Colchester Castle, on Christmas Day 1502, led to the deaths of 28 prisoners, including Agnes Scalys, the only woman in the group. The inmates were being held in the dungeon of the castle, a space some 30 feet long, 14 feet wide, and 12 feet high, with thick stone walls. Nineteen of them were chained to a wooden beam. They smuggled in some firewood and sulphur, and the means to ignite them, then broke the bolt on the chain so they could get loose before setting fire to the door. Unfortunately, instead of providing a way out, the burning door filled the dungeon with smoke and flames, and all the inmates were overcome. They must have hoped that the distraction of Christmas celebrations would make for an easy getaway.[732]

Prison keepers were personally liable for inmates who escaped or were rescued from their custody, especially if they had been negligent. For example, in 1602, Francis Clayse, the keeper of the county gaol in Colchester, was indicted (albeit acquitted) at the Michaelmas Quarter Sessions for allowing one Robert Warner to escape from custody. The Statute of Escapes (1504) even laid down a tariff of fines for the loss of an inmate. These ranged from about £5 if the escapee was suspected of felony, to more than 100 marks if they had been indicted for high treason.[733] In extreme cases, keepers may also have lost their positions, or even been imprisoned themselves. At the start of the Tudor era at least, liability may, sometimes, have extended to high sheriffs, who were, ostensibly, responsible for county gaols.

732. Steven Gunn and Tomasz Gromelski, *Everyday Life and Fatal Hazard in Sixteenth century England*, https://tudoraccidents.history.ox.ac.uk
733. Winter, *Prisons and Punishments*, p. 118.

PART IV
AVOIDING THE DEATH-FOR-FELONY RULE

CHAPTER 13

Sanctuary and Abjuration

Introduction

Two historic privileges allowed felons to evade prosecution, rather than merely avoid execution after conviction, as was the case with benefit of clergy and pleas of pregnancy. These were sanctuary in a church and abjuration of the realm. In many respects, the two privileges were closely intertwined, the latter normally following the former when it was invoked. They were still significant in the first 50 years of the Tudor era, and even grew in importance during the final decades of this half century. In part this reflected the increasing effectiveness of England's criminal justice system, which meant that more people were encouraged to find ways to escape its expanding net, at a time when the mid-Tudor "softening" in the strictness with which benefit of clergy was awarded, and claims of pregnancy entertained, had yet to get fully under way (See *Chapter 15*). Both privileges disappeared fairly swiftly after the mid-1530s, although James I formally abolished the last remnants of criminal sanctuary only in the early seventeenth century.

Sanctuary

Sanctuary was found in much of early modern Europe prior to the Reformation, and in a small number of (mainly Catholic) states for a few years afterwards, although its terms and scope varied significantly in each country. This ubiquity is unsurprising. Christian teachings about clemency emphasised the need to pardon repentant sinners and influenced its early development. It also had an ancient scriptural basis in the six cities of refuge for unpremeditated homicides, such as Golan, in Bashan, discussed in *Numbers* and *Exodus* in the Old Testament.[1] These roots, together with classical traditions of intercession, combined to create the formal right of sanctuary during the late fourth and early fifth centuries.[2]

For more than a thousand years afterwards, the right of a criminal to some protection within a consecrated building or land was widely accepted in Latin Europe, albeit that the privilege was subject to a variety of restrictions and intrusions.[3] By the thirteenth century, it had become central to the canon law of the Church, being addressed in the Decretals of Pope Innocent III in the *Compilatio Quarta* of 1216.[4] In England the privilege was older than (and so always part of) the common law, probably going back to the advent of Christianity in the late sixth century, and being expressly recognised by Anglo-Saxon kings such as Aethelberht of Wessex (reigned AD 860–865), who had particularly strong views on its inviolacy.[5]

Common Sanctuary

Under the right to "common" or general sanctuary, a suspected felon could take refuge for up to 40 days (a peculiarly English time limit) in any church by placing himself physically within its bounds. (Some observers argued that the designated time began only after a coroner had attended on the sanctuary seeker.) English lawyers often abbreviated this process to "fled to Church". Thus, and typically, when John Lukas, a Newark gentleman, stabbed Henry Kyrkehouse in the heart with his sword one December afternoon in 1526, he fled to the Church of the Observant Friars in the same town and claimed 40-day sanctuary.[6]

---

1.   Teresa Field, "Biblical Influences on the Medieval and Early Modern English Law of Sanctuary", *Ecclesiastical Law Journal*, Vol. 2, p. 223.
2.   Karl Shoemaker, *Sanctuary and Crime in the Middle Ages, 400–1500* (New York: Fordham University Press, 2010), p. 30.
3.   R. H. Helmholz, *The* ius commune *in England: Four Studies* (Oxford: Oxford University Press, 2001), pp. 16–18.
4.   Victor M. Uribe-Uran, "'Iglesia me Llamo': Church Asylum and the Law in Spain and Colonial Spanish America", *Comparative Studies in Society and History*, Vol. 49, No. 2, pp. 446–472.
5.   J. H. Baker, "The English law of Sanctuary", *Ecclesiastical Law Journal*, Vol. 2. No. 6, p. 8.
6.   R. F. Hunnisett (ed.), *Thoroton Society Record Series, Vol. XXV: Calendar of Nottinghamshire Coroners' Inquests, 1485–1558* (Nottingham: Derry and Sons, 1969), p. 47.

The privilege extended to sanctified grounds as well as the ecclesiastical building itself. As a result, when John Makyn stabbed Thomas York to death with a dagger on the highway near Dunham, in Nottinghamshire, he immediately "leapt into Darlton churchyard in order to save his life". (He was still there two days later when the inquest into York's death was held nearby.)[7] If there was no consecrated ground outside a religious building, and it was locked, sanctuary could (in theory) be claimed by grasping its door handle or knocker. Durham became noted for the latter, but no cases of its knocker being used for this purpose are recorded for the medieval period, while its sanctuary register records that Thomas Wadeson rang the cathedral bell to seek the privilege in 1479, some two years after beating a man to death with a club in Sedbergh.[8]

Not all church owned ground was consecrated, and so able to offer protection. In 1534 a group of men killed one Amos Burdett in York. Six of them sought sanctuary with the nearby Whitefriars. They were allowed to frequent gardens and other grounds nearby which, though legally belonging to the friars, were unconsecrated, something that led to the men being arrested while out walking.[9] In a similar case, heard at the Lent Assizes at Coventry in 1520, a man named Spencer claimed that he had been removed from sanctuary in the Greyfriars' garden in the city. However, it was ruled that the garden was a profane place, not within the ambit of the religious house, and so did not afford protection. He was convicted and hanged.[10]

Sanctuary was open only to felons, not those accused of misdemeanours or petty theft. After 1486 care was taken to restrict the number of sanctuaries that could shelter those accused of high treason (see below), although this aspect of the privilege was only totally abolished in 1534. In its final years, sanctuary was sometimes not allowed to convicted criminals who had subsequently escaped punishment. In 1518 a man accused of heresy was denied sanctuary on the basis that he could not benefit from an ecclesiastical privilege, as he had rejected the tenets of the church.[11] For

7.   *Ibid*, p. 42.
8.   McSheffrey, "Sanctuary Seekers".
9.   Brooks, *Yorkshire and the Star Chamber*, p. 8.
10. McSheffrey, "Sanctuary Seekers".
11. McSheffrey, *Seeking Sanctuary*, p. 50.

obvious reasons, one of the bars to seeking the privilege was committing a felony inside the sanctuary itself, although its perpetrator could then flee to another church to make a claim. However, even this limitation appears to have been quietly ignored in 1532, when Richard Southwell unlawfully killed Sir William Pennington within the Westminster sanctuary, but then sought the privilege in the same place.[12]

Violation of Sanctuary

Whatever the theory as to its inviolability, during the fourteenth, fifteenth, and early sixteenth centuries breaches of sanctuary occurred on a fairly regular, albeit not frequent, basis. Some Lollards and traitors were forced from churches, and the same thing sometimes happened to those accused of "conventional" crimes. For example, in 1378 a major breach of sanctuary occurred at Westminster Abbey when Sir Alan de Buxhall and 50 soldiers broke into the church; a squire named John Shakel was seized, and another, Robert Hauley, chased round the chancel before being beaten to death. This precipitated a major debate about Westminster's privileges when Parliament met at Gloucester in 1378; John Wyclif spoke on the issue.[13] Even so, the law emerged unchanged.[14]

On a much larger scale, in a Chancery suit brought in 1466, the master of the Dominican order in Bristol alleged that a number of prisoners had escaped from the city prison and taken sanctuary in his friary. However, the Bristol gaoler was determined to recapture them (if only to avoid a heavy fine for allowing their escape) and laid siege to the house with 60 well-armed men. Eventually, they scaled the walls with ladders, broke through the inner gates, and then threatened the terrified friars into giving-up the prisoners.[15]

In the early years of the Tudor era, when the government was preoccupied with putting down sedition, the granting of sanctuary for high treason was scrutinised more closely and limited to specific establishments.

---

12. McSheffrey, "The Slaying of Sir William Pennington", p. 178.
13. Field, "Biblical Influences", p. 224.
14. Karl Shoemaker, *Sanctuary and Crime in the Middle Ages, 400–1500* (New York: Fordham University Press, 2011), p. 163.
15. Fleming, *Time, space and power,* p. 243.

This followed a case in 1486, when, after an abortive attempt at rebellion, the brothers Thomas and Humphrey Stafford sought chartered protection (see below) in the church at Culham, in Oxfordshire. The Manor of Culham belonged to the abbey of Abingdon, which had hitherto served as a sanctuary for debtors and may also have claimed to shelter others. Even so, Henry VII had the brothers forcibly removed by John Savage and a band of men. Humphrey was brought before King's Bench, where he based his defence on this violation of privilege, and demanded to be returned to Culham. The judges, who were under considerable pressure from the Crown, listened carefully to legal arguments, including those of the abbot, but eventually acquiesced in the King's view that sanctuary could not be pleaded in cases of high treason at this particular establishment (although it may well have had other sanctuary privileges). This decision may have signalled a more restrictive approach to treason cases than the situation that had prevailed during the Wars of the Roses; Humphrey was duly sentenced to a traitor's death and executed.[16] The King apparently pardoned the younger Thomas.

The breaking of sanctuary in this case prompted protests to the Pope. However, in August 1486, Innocent VIII accepted a slightly more circumscribed view of the general privilege. A papal bull was issued the following year. It provided that the King might appoint keepers to supervise anyone who took sanctuary for treason and prevent their escape. Furthermore, it provided that, where a man left sanctuary and committed fresh crimes, as was often alleged against those in places such as Westminster, he lost the privilege if he returned to the religious house. (Articles against recidivism had been passed earlier in the century but applied only to Saint Martin's Le Grand in the City of London.) Furthermore, the goods of men claiming sanctuary were not to be protected from their creditors.[17]

In 1487 two more alleged traitors, Thomas and Herbert Redshawe, were dragged from sanctuary in Hexham and executed.[18] Four other

---

16. C. H. Williams, "The Rebellion of Humphrey Stafford in 1486", *The English Historical Review*, Vol. 43, No. 170, pp. 186–188.

17. Thomas John de' Mazzinghi, *Sanctuaries* (Stafford: Halden & Son, 1887), p. 17; Peter Iver Kaufman, "Henry VII and Sanctuary", *Church History*, Vol. 53, Issue 4, p. 473.

18. John A. F. Thomson, *The Early Tudor Church and Society, 1485–1529* (Abingdon: Routledge, 2014), p. 101.

sanctuary seekers were forced from St Martin-Le-Grand in 1493. It seems that they had displayed treasonous placards attacking the government and supporting the pretender Perkin Warbeck.[19] However, only one of them, Thomas Bagnall, relied on violation of the privilege at trial rather than defending the merits of the allegation against him. The other three were convicted and executed, but Bagnall's claim may have succeeded; he appears to have been reprieved, although committed to the Tower.[20]

A significant number of less celebrated cases of sanctuary being violated, in which the defendants were accused of conventional felonies, occurred during the late 1400s and early 1500s. The men involved sometimes refused to enter a plea when arraigned, having carefully explained the basis for their actions to the court, if only to avoid the *peine forte et dure*. Judges usually took such allegations seriously, and would often put the matter back for further investigation; the defendant would be kept in prison in the meantime. If a violation was established, he might be restored to sanctuary, as occurred with the burglar and robber George Sawyer in 1500, after his plea of sanctuary at the Court of King's Bench was successful in the Easter term of 1500.[21]

Sometimes alleged violations of sanctuary were specifically referred to King's Bench by other courts for further consideration. For example, at a Newgate gaol delivery held in October 1507, a man named Rowland claimed that shortly after stealing some money he had fled to sanctuary in the parish church at Bray, in Berkshire, but had been forcibly dragged-out of the building. He asked to be returned to the church, and was sent back to prison while the legal position was considered. The matter was then sent up to King's Bench in November 1507. (The outcome is unknown.) In a similar case from 1521, judges at King's Bench ruled that one Thomas Wrexham be restored to the church from whence he had been removed.[22] Even if they were not returned to their sanctuaries, successful claimants were sometimes pardoned.

---

19. McSheffrey, *Seeking Sanctuary*, p. 49.
20. Kaufman, "Henry VII and Sanctuary", pp. 469–470; Thomson, *The Early Tudor Church*, p. 101.
21. Peter Iver Kaufman, *The "Polytyque Churche": Religion and Early Tudor Political Culture, 1485–1516* (Macon, Ga.: Mercer University Press, 1986), p. 146 and pp. 469–470.
22. McSheffrey, "The Slaying of Sir William Pennington", p. 178.

As with a previous claim of benefit of clergy, it appears that whether someone had been wrongly taken from sanctuary was usually left to a jury to decide. For example, in an appeal of felony heard at King's Bench during Trinity Term 1507, Roger Thornedon accused Peter Beauregard of burgling his house in London and stealing cloth worth more than £6. Beauregard claimed that he had taken sanctuary at the church of St Mary Magdalen, in Southwark, on the same December day as the crime, but was forcibly removed from the building, to which he asked to be restored. The plea was put to a jury, and a legal issue arose as to whether its members had to have the same 40 shillings property qualification as those used to try a felony (answered affirmatively). There is no record of their verdict.[23]

In other cases, jurors were asked to determine whether a seized felon was physically in or out of the bounds of a sanctuary when taken. The King's Bench roll records that in early November 1501 a man named Henley pleaded sanctuary in response to an indictment for a theft committed the previous month, in which cloth valued at £30 had been taken from one Peter Hall in Middlesex. Henley claimed that a few weeks after the crime he had taken sanctuary in the cemetery of the parish church of St Mary Magdalen in Southwark, but that on the same day he was violently removed from there. The King's attorney replied that he had in fact been taken outside the churchyard. A jury decided that he had not been within sanctuary when detained. Henley then pleaded not guilty to the indictment, but was convicted and hanged in 1504.[24]

Despite such decisions, the general right to sanctuary for felony was normally respected, and violating it could lead to punishment, both ecclesiastical and (occasionally) secular. Sir Alan de Buxhall suffered excommunication in 1378, and this was lifted only on payment of a substantial fine. In 1487, Archbishop Rotherham of York threatened the city sheriffs and their servants with excommunication after they took two men from the sanctuary of a local church, unless the men were returned within 15 days.[25] It seems that at no time during his reign did Henry VII

23. McSheffrey, "Sanctuary Seekers".
24. *Ibid.*
25. Thomson, *The Early Tudor Church*, p. 98.

contemplate root-and-branch reform, let alone abolition, of sanctuary for ordinary cases of felony. Indeed, he was actively conciliatory towards the ecclesiastical authorities on this issue. In a letter he admitted that the Redshawes (see above) had been forcibly removed from Hexham, but stressed that they had been accused of high treason and not merely felony. He promised to do nothing against Hexham's historic "privileges and franchises" with regard to the latter form of crime.[26]

Perhaps indicative of this general respect can be considered a case from 1491 in which Margery Ludlow, the widow of Thomas Ludlow, an Oxford serjeant (a municipal law enforcement officer in this context), felt it necessary to petition the Crown against giving in to what appears to have been mounting pressure to return his killer, John Wells, to sanctuary after a possible violation of the privilege. Wells was a very violent man. The previous December he had killed one Robert Phylipson and immediately fled to a church to claim sanctuary. He subsequently obtained mainprise, the release of a prisoner from custody on providing sureties (analogous to bail), perhaps because the death occurred during an altercation. He was allowed his liberty and returned home before the felony was reported to a local coroner and properly investigated. However, this being done, bailiffs and serjeants, including Thomas Ludlow, entered Wells' house with an arrest warrant in early January (some ten days after the initial incident). Wells responded to this intrusion by killing Ludlow, seriously wounding a bailiff, and injuring several other men. He then fled to the same church he had used previously.

However, once in sanctuary Wells refused to confess his crime to the city coroners so as to start the abjuration process (see below). When this was reported to local constables, the enraged officers violated sanctuary and seized him, before committing him to the Bocardo Prison. Margery subsequently became aware that several people were making strenuous efforts to have Wells returned to the church, so remedying the violation, despite the two homicides. She urged that royal letters rejecting such pressure be sent to both the ecclesiastical and secular authorities in Oxford.[27]

26. Kaufman, *The "Polytyque Churche"*, p. 146 and pp. 469–70.

27. Anon, "Petition to the king against sanctuary rights of a homicide: Archives of the borough of Bridgwater", in H. E. Salter (ed.), *Snappe's Formulary and Other Records* (Oxford: Oxford Historical Society, 1923), pp. 252–253.

Escape from Common Sanctuary

During a felon's first 40 days in common sanctuary, he could be fed by local people or visitors. After this period had elapsed, a sanctuary seeker who refused to abjure the realm (see below) or submit to royal officials (as some did) could be starved out. It was forbidden to give over-stayers sustenance. In the early 1520s an assembly of Westminster judges reaffirmed that "after the forty days no-one can give him food or drink".[28] Anyone who did so could be charged as an accessory to the man's crimes. In theory, even speaking to over-stayers was forbidden. However, the secular authorities were usually reluctant to secure such men by force, as shedding blood would mean violating holy ground.

As a result, escape was normally the only option for those in common sanctuary who had not abjured and who were unwilling to surrender to trial. Those resident near the relevant church were supposed to prevent this happening. Local constables might set up a nocturnal guard; they could be indicted, and the wider community fined, for allowing an escape. However, keeping watch was an onerous and time-consuming function, and was frequently neglected.[29] As a result, escapes were often attempted, especially at night, and not a few succeeded.

Illustrative of such cases, in 1504 two constables in the City of London's jurisdiction in Southwark were indicted for permitting the escape of John Sampyre and Richard Cooper, who had fled to sanctuary in a local church. A coroner had quickly attended them, but they had indicated that, although they sought sanctuary, they would not abjure immediately, waiting instead for their 40 days to expire before doing so. In reality, they were "scheming to escape", which they did a few days later.[30] Of course, outside assistance made this much easier. In 1516 a man named Bewesbury mortally wounded one John Hudson with a knife, then fled to the collegiate church of Maidstone to claim sanctuary. He subsequently escaped with the assistance of a local cleric who dressed him in priest's

---

28. Baker, *Sir John Spelman*, p. 66.
29. McSheffrey, *Seeking Sanctuary*, p. 7.
30. McSheffrey, "Sanctuary Seekers".

clothing and secretly led him out of the church, although this made the clergyman an accessory to murder.[31]

Occasionally the central authorities became actively involved in trying to prevent escapes, especially in notorious cases. For example, in August 1526, John Veer wrote to Cardinal Wolsey, noting that he had done what he could to seize William Gilbank. Gilbank had broken out of permanent sanctuary (see below) at St John's Abbey, in Colchester, where he had fled after committing a murder, and then taken refuge again with the Crossed Friars in the same town. When Veer went to the friary with Sir Geoffrey Gates, and asked the prior to hand Gilbank over so that Wolsey could examine him, the friars refused to give him up, saying that their privilege was as extensive as that of the abbey. At this point, Gilbank was openly standing in the choir, near the high altar, a holy place where Veer freely conceded he "durst not to enterprise". Before leaving, Veer ensured that a watch was set around the friary to arrest Gilbank if he tried to break out again. In the meantime, Gilbank requested a coroner, before whom he confessed his crime and asked to begin the abjuration process. (Veer advised the coroner to defer the abjuration until he had received Wolsey's reply.)[32]

In March 1527 a group of men were appointed to watch the sanctuary at Westminster after several gentlemen fled there. William Sandys (1470–1540), the Lord Chamberlain, then wrote to Cardinal Wolsey, noting that he had sent for the Archdeacon of Westminster, and told him to advise those in the sanctuary to come out of their own free will, and submit to the mercy of the King.[33]

The number of those taking 40-day sanctuary appears to have increased significantly in the years immediately after 1526 and remained near that high level between 1531 and 1535, before collapsing rapidly after 1536.[34] However, as some of the cases mentioned above suggest, as well as there being a general right to short-term (40-day) sanctuary in any church, there were also at least 22 "special" or "chartered" sanctuaries which could give permanent sanctuary; these were usually based on particular

---

31. *Ibid.*
32. Brewer, *Letters and Papers, Foreign and Domestic, Henry VIII, Vol. 4, 1524–1530*, pp. 1057–1066.
33. *Ibid*, pp. 1310–1323.
34. McSheffrey, *Seeking Sanctuary*, p. 37.

religious houses. (There were about 800 of these, of all types and sizes, in England during the 1520s.)

Confusingly, contemporary observers sometimes failed to distinguish between 40-day and permanent sanctuary. The situation was further complicated by the ability of chartered sanctuaries to provide temporary 40-day sanctuary, so that in 1513 a removed sanctuary seeker from such an establishment could be asked whether he "would claim this privilege as a church or cemetery for forty days or as a sanctuary for life".[35]

"Chartered" Sanctuaries

It was often claimed that chartered sanctuaries had been created either by historic royal or papal grants and charters, or had existed by immemorial custom. Typically, the prior of the Crossed Friars in Colchester (discussed above) produced the supposed legal transcription of a papal bull giving his institution the privilege (the house had been established in the town in the 1240s). However, in reality their roots, especially when it came to sheltering felons, were often fairly shallow in the early Tudor period.

Chartered sanctuary for criminals sometimes seems to have grown out of an older privilege accorded to debtors. For some of the latter, a spell in sanctuary was akin to modern bankruptcy protection, allowing them time to settle their affairs and then return to their trades. For example, in 1535 George Tadlowe took sanctuary at Westminster for debt, due to problems with his Bordeaux wine-importing business occasioned by several shipwrecks and bad loans. He eventually reached an agreement with his creditors, left sanctuary, and went on to sit as an MP in the middle of the century and to assist in setting up Christ's Hospital.[36]

At some point during the closing years of the fourteenth century, several religious houses started to offer permanent sanctuary within their precincts to felons, rather than just the traditional 40 days' grace. Westminster Abbey may have been the first in this regard, with St Martin's Le Grand in London following shortly afterwards, although it is possible

---

35. J. H. Baker (ed.), *The Notebook of Sir John Port* (London: Selden Society, 1986), p. 38.
36. S. T. Bindoff (ed.), *The History of Parliament: The House of Commons, 1509–1558* (Woodbridge: Boydell & Brewer, 1982), p. 417.

that a handful did so even earlier. By the middle of the fifteenth century, these establishments included, inter alia, Durham Cathedral and the abbeys of Beaulieu, Glastonbury, and Beverley, although the registers of Durham and Beverley (for example) suggest that they saw few claims until after 1475. It was partly for this relative novelty that, in the 1480s and 1490s, House of Commons petitions to regulate them sometimes referred to new "feigned" sanctuaries.[37]

More establishments purported to join them in ensuing years, although it is difficult to draw up an exhaustive list of chartered sanctuaries, as it was never certain how far the privilege extended.[38] For example, it was often argued that all houses of the Knights Hospitaller (a military-religious order) could grant permanent sanctuary. In a bizarre attempt to extend this even further, in September 1506 two felons unavailingly argued that they had managed to claim sanctuary by grasping the cloak of John Rawson, a knight of the order, and requesting the privilege, while being led away from the sessions conducted at Canterbury Castle.[39]

Some smaller monastic houses claimed that they, too, could grant permanent sanctuary in specific cases, although many others had no such pretensions. A case first heard at the Lent Assizes for Northamptonshire in 1513, and then removed to King's Bench later the same year, is indicative of the uncertainty this produced. Hugh Boswell was indicted for stealing from a church, a crime for which benefit of clergy for those who were not in holy orders had been removed. Initially, Boswell alleged that he was a friar, which would have allowed him to claim the privilege. He then changed his plea, claiming that he had been forcibly taken from permanent sanctuary at the Cluniac priory of St Andrew in Northampton. In his note of the case, Sir John Port expressly observed that Boswell claimed sanctuary for life, not just for 40-days. However, when the prior was summoned to court, he stated that he did not claim any such privilege for his monastery. As a result, Boswell was sentenced to hang.[40]

Further complicating matters, it seems that the "limbs" of some of these establishments could also afford protection. In 1514 the London

---

37. McSheffrey, *Seeking Sanctuary*, p. vi and p. 37.
38. *Ibid*, pp. 10–11.
39. McSheffrey, "Sanctuary Seekers".
40. Baker, *Sir John Port*, p. 38.

summoner (employed to call people before the ecclesiastical courts) Charles Joseph, alarmed at the possible consequences of his involvement in the murder of Richard Hunne, fled to the "sentuarie towne called good estur in essex". Good Easter was a manor owned by Westminster Abbey and, by the early sixteenth century, seems to have shared its ability to offer permanent sanctuary. Once there, Joseph acknowledged his involvement in the killing and duly "paide the dewtie of the saide regestring". That the manor had a register of sanctuary seekers suggests that he was by no means the first felon received there.[41] In a coroner's inquest held in York, in May 1521, witnesses reported that after a man named Feysche had attacked and mortally wounded another man he had fled "to the town of Crayke, which is a sanctuary". Crayke, in Yorkshire, was a manor held by the Bishop of Durham, who, it seems, claimed sanctuary rights in the dependency as well as his cathedral.[42]

By the early sixteenth century, major, undisputed, chartered sanctuaries were found at Abingdon, Armathwaite, Beaulieu, Battle Abbey, Beverley, Colchester, Derby, Durham, Dover, Hexham, Lancaster, St Mary le Bow (near London), Glastonbury, St Martin's Le Grand (London), Merton Priory, Northampton, Norwich, Ripon, Ramsey, Wells, Westminster, Winchester, and York. Some of them had a national reputation. For example, Durham, although taking the majority of its inmates from the North, also attracted men such as George Hogson from Middlesex and Thomas Coke, who arrived from as far away as Somerset.[43]

The number of felons involved in seeking long-term sanctuary was significant, but not enormous. Durham's register records the arrival of 332 people between 1464 and 1534, while Beverley admitted 493 between 1478 and 1531 (albeit that around 200 of these may have been debtors). Many felons were also found in much more urban sanctuaries. In June 1533 there were 95 residents in that for Westminster.[44] Similarly, in 1525 two royal commissioners named 12 "prisoners" as being within St Martin's

---

41. Anon, *The enquirie and verdite of the quest*, pp. 1–24.
42. William Page (ed.), *A History of the County of York North Riding: Vol. 2* (London: Victoria County History, 1923), pp. 119–124.
43. Thomson, *The Early Tudor Church*, p. 100.
44. Kesselring, *Mercy and Authority*, p. 45; S. Pope, "Sanctuary: The Legal Institution in England", *University of Puget Sound Law Review*, Vol. 10, p. 677.

sanctuary in London, eleven men and one woman; five of them were identified as felons or murderers, one a trespasser, and one a debtor (the status of the other five is unknown).[45]

As the figures for Beverley suggest, many sanctuary seekers were debtors, rather than criminals fleeing justice. A few were both; the Durham sanctuary register records that a man named Potter sought protection there in June 1508, shortly after stealing grain from a mill at Uckerby in North Yorkshire; however, he also sought immunity for the debts he owed to various people.[46] Alien craftsmen also sometimes resided in, and enjoyed the protection of, urban sanctuaries, although not formally seeking the privilege.

Asylum seekers who were felons typically entered permanent sanctuaries through a process that involved being presented before the abbot, prior, dean, or his deputy; confessing their sins and the wrong that caused them to seek sanctuary, swearing an oath of fealty to their superior; and promising to maintain good behaviour while in the refuge. Sometimes they would relinquish all (potential) weapons apart from (typically) a "poyntlese" knife to carve meat.[47] In exchange they would (in theory) be allowed to remain in the sanctuary for the remainder of their lives without having to abjure, surrender to the authorities, or escape again. However, they would have to submit to at least some forms of ecclesiastical discipline. In 1488 Archbishop Rotherham instructed the steward and bailiff at Beverley to ensure that their sanctuary men attend the annual mass of King Athelstan on pain of losing their status if they failed to do so.[48]

The grounds of permanent sanctuaries frequently extended considerably further than the abbey or cathedral precincts. This was important, as felons (and debtors) could be arrested (by officials or creditors) if they stepped outside them. At Hexham and Beverley the grounds stretched a mile from the abbey, the limits being carefully marked. This space was easily large enough to afford sanctuary men an opportunity to practise their trades, if they had them, and to live an almost normal life within any adjoining settlement or the monastic environs. For example, those

45. McSheffrey, "Sanctuary and the Legal Topography", p. 493.
46. McSheffrey, "Sanctuary Seekers".
47. *Ibid.*
48. Thomson, *The Early Tudor Church*, p. 100.

in St John's Beverley could freely work in the local village without risking their privilege.[49]

When in April 1538 the monastery at Beaulieu surrendered to the Crown following the dissolution of religious houses, it was recorded to have accommodated 32 sanctuary men for "debt, felony, and murder". These men had houses and grounds where they lived with their wives and children. They asked the King to be allowed to remain there for the rest of their lives, on the basis that no more people would be admitted to the privilege.[50] Shortly afterwards, Thomas Stepyns, the former abbot there, wrote to Thomas Wriothesley, Earl of Southampton and Clerk of the Signet, urging him to allow the men who had sought sanctuary for debt (he did not mention the felons), and who had been "very honest" while he was their governor, to stay. He pointed out that it would damage the local economy if they were to leave, as their houses would otherwise yield no rent. John Crailford, a royal official, writing to the same individual at about the same time, agreed that the debtors should be allowed to stay, although accepting that murderers and other felons ("hopeless men") should depart immediately.[51]

Other permanent sanctuaries were much more territorially confined, and long-term survival was correspondingly harder and less comfortable, especially for those who lacked money, with crowded tenements being let out at extortionately high rates. Even so, in both 1532 and 1533, lists of the "privileged" drawn up for Westminster identify a tailor named Gonne as the longest-serving sanctuary man, having been in residence since 1512. He rented a substantial property in the sanctuary in the early 1530s and was still there in 1537.[52]

It was partly because of the attendant expense that those who sought permanent sanctuary might, if given time, prepare themselves financially for their future lives. Some men did have such time. After Thomas Bennett murdered and secretly buried a man in 1516, he had several years as a free individual, during which rumours increasingly swirled around his Essex village, until he was, eventually, officially questioned about the

---

49.   Kaufman, "Henry VII and Sanctuary", p. 467.
50.   Gairdner, *Letters and Papers, Foreign and Domestic, Henry VIII, Vol. 13, Part 1*, pp. 250–260.
51.   *Ibid*, pp. 291–301.
52.   McSheffrey, "Sanctuary Seekers".

missing person. He decided to seek permanent sanctuary at Beaulieu Abbey in Hampshire for the killing. Appreciating that money would be vital he sold off all his considerable assets in advance, and arranged (unsuccessfully) to ship other goods to the sanctuary. As he travelled there, he appears to have taken a black horse from a neighbour and then sold the animal for cash. As a result, when he arrived at Beaulieu he had some £60 in money and goods worth £40. (Some of the cash was paid to the abbey.)[53]

Of course, those in chartered sanctuaries who were accused of felonies could safely leave if and when they secured a pardon. It was not unusual for men of noble and genteel status, who had become involved in lethal quarrels, to use them as temporary bolt holes while influential friends and contacts intervened on their behalf. Sanctuary provided much more security than hiding elsewhere, and it was healthier and more comfortable than being in prison. Thus, in December 1531 James Layburn wrote to Thomas Cromwell, while also sending him a gift of a hind and £6 13s 4d in cash. He begged Cromwell to speak to the King, and ask for a pardon for his brother, Robert Layburn, who was then in sanctuary at Ripon, after committing a murder at Oxford the previous year.[54] Similarly, but at a more elevated level, in 1532, after Richard Southwell and his colleagues slew Sir William Pennington, they fled to the Westminster sanctuary to await their eventual pardons.[55]

Criticism of Sanctuary

By the late medieval period there was growing criticism of the abuse of sanctuary. Even the papal curia cautioned the English Crown against showing too much deference to permanent sanctuary when pursuing criminals.[56] In 1442 Pope Eugenius IV wrote to the Bishop of Lincoln, complaining that permanent places of refuge provided a morally "detestable example" to others. The Commons petitioned the King on two occasions, early in the fifteenth century, asking that he correct abuse

---

53. Roger, *Tudor Trials: Confessions from the Star Chamber.*
54. Gairdner, *Letters and Papers, Foreign and Domestic, Henry VIII, Vol. 5*, pp. 271–288.
55. McSheffrey, "The Slaying of Sir William Pennington", p. 177.
56. Shoemaker, *Sanctuary and Crime*, p. 153.

of the privilege.[57] In 1483 another petition complained that those who sought sanctuary did not regret their offences and used permanent sanctuaries as a base for further criminal forays into the wider community.[58]

Such criticism continued unabated during the Tudor era. In 1495, Lord Chief Justice William Hussey likened a permanent sanctuary to a den of thieves, while his successor, Sir John Fyneaux, was equally hostile.[59] In 1500 a Venetian visitor to England claimed that a criminal who had been forced to take refuge in such an establishment often went out of it to "brawl in the public streets, and then, returning to it, escape with impunity for every fresh offence he may have been guilty of".[60] In 1528, the author Polydore Vergil complained that sanctuaries gave their inmates a licence to do further harm.[61] More specifically, in 1536 the mayor and aldermen of London alleged that the presence of the St Martin's sanctuary had left unpunished "all maner of enorme enymyes of god".[62]

As some of these comments suggest, there was a fear that the privilege was criminogenic, not least because some felons offended with the intention of fleeing to permanent sanctuary. For example, in July 1513 Sir John Style, the English ambassador to Spain, told his hosts that robbers who had recently attacked wagons bringing money to London for the French war had always planned to seek refuge in this manner.[63] More specifically, in August 1519 Robert Lorde wrote to Cardinal Wolsey complaining that, while he was away on business for the cleric, his servant had stolen £80 from him, and then fled to a sanctuary, where he remained "by reason whereof I, my poor wife and children, is like to fare the worse whilst we live".[64] It was because of cases like this that a statute from 1536 (27 Henry VIII c 17) expressly denied sanctuary to servants guilty of stealing goods worth 40 shillings or more from their masters.

This widespread hostility appears to have found a fairly receptive audience in Henry VIII (unlike his father), even early in his reign, especially

---

57. Kaufman, "Henry VII and Sanctuary", pp. 470–475.
58. Shoemaker, *Sanctuary and Crime*, pp. 168–169.
59. Baker, *Oxford History*, p. 547.
60. Anon, *A Relation, or Rather A True Account*, p. 35.
61. J. H. Baker, "The English Law of Sanctuary", *Ecclesiastical Law Journal*, Vol. 2, Issue 6, pp. 9–10.
62. McSheffrey, "Sanctuary and the Legal Topography", p. 494.
63. Brewer, *Letters and Papers, Foreign and Domestic, Henry VIII, Vol. 1*, pp. 952–967.
64. *Ibid, Vol. 3*, pp. 148–156.

after a JP, John Pauncefote, was shot dead (a very early firearm homicide) and mutilated while travelling to the Gloucestershire quarter sessions at Cirencester in 1516. Some of his well-connected killers, including John Savage, fled to St John's Priory in Clerkenwell. The court of Star Chamber subsequently considered the legitimacy of the protection afforded to them, hearing legal argument on the issue from canon lawyers in November 1519, in a debate that was conducted in the presence of the monarch. There was no final judgment in the case, Savage and his knighted father (also the Sheriff of Worcestershire), who had harboured the killers, eventually being pardoned, after a payment of 4,000 marks to the Crown. However, the King himself observed that it was unlikely that the Saxon Kings and clerics who had recognised sanctuary in England ever intended that it be used either for cold-blooded murder or larceny committed in the specific hope of returning to its protection: "And so I will have that reformed which is encroached by abuse".[65]

Despite this threat, the attack on sanctuary began in earnest only several years after 1529, encouraged by the anti-clericalism of the Reformation Parliament(s). Indeed, some research suggests that in the decades immediately prior to (de facto) abolition, the use of sanctuary increased rather than declined. According to this analysis, although such claims had been fairly modest for much of the fifteenth century, the number of felons seeking temporary refuge in churches started to grow after about 1480, while the number of those seeking shelter in chartered sanctuaries soared during the years from 1531 to 1535.[66]

Reform of Sanctuary

The Henrician statutes (26 & 28 H 8 c. 13 & 7) that eventually curbed sanctuary reiterated the oft-repeated grievance that special sanctuaries made malefactors "more bold and willing to offend".[67] Change was partly prompted by a case in July 1533, in which John Wolfe, his wife Alice (apparently a common prostitute), and a pair of accomplices committed

---

65. Baker, "The English Law of Sanctuary", p. 9; Gwyn, *The King's Cardinal*, p. 133.
66. McSheffrey, *Seeking Sanctuary*, p. 43.
67. William Staunford, *Les Plees Del Coron* (London, 1560), p. 119.

a particularly brutal murder. Alice enticed two foreign merchants onto a boat on the River Thames. John then leapt out of hiding and, with the aid of the other men, killed and robbed them. By the time Parliament met, the accomplices were dead, and John and Alice had taken refuge in the Abbot of Westminster's sanctuary. Shunning common law proceedings, Thomas Cromwell introduced a bill in Parliament to attaint the fugitives and to authorise their immediate arrest and execution, wherever they were. This may, in part, have been done because the murder of foreign merchants generated acute diplomatic pressure. Such an act, specifically denying sanctuary to those attainted, allowed the government to seize Wolfe and his wife despite their special place of residence. It also indicated that Cromwell would not tolerate what he saw as an increasingly anachronistic threat to public order, and established a clear precedent for future intervention.[68]

In 1535 all permanent sanctuary men were required by statute to wear badges and to forfeit their privilege if caught out at night or with weapons. It is possible that, by then, Thomas Cromwell was already resolved to abolish the whole system. In a preserved memorandum to himself, written in 1536, he put the "utter destruction of sanctuaries" on his agenda.[69] Certainly he took a robust approach to several cases involving sanctuary at about this time.

For example, late in 1539 Cromwell ordered the forcible removal of Anthony Spencer from Westminster, where he had sought sanctuary after murdering and robbing John Morris. William Webb, the sanctuary-official who had registered Spencer, cooperated with Cromwell in arranging this. At gaol delivery held at Guildford in February 1540, Spencer was indicted for the homicide, but pleaded violation of sanctuary. The case was moved to the Court of King's Bench for further consideration. The judges there did not immediately rule on this, and he was returned to prison as they considered the matter. He stayed there until May 1544, when he appeared once more at King's Bench, and again made a plea for sanctuary. On this occasion, the King's attorney acknowledged that his plea was valid, and that he had been improperly extracted from

---

68.   Stacey, "Richard Roose", pp. 7–8.
69.   TNA, SP. 1/102, fol. 5v.

protection on (the long since executed) Cromwell's orders. Spencer was formally returned to William Webb and the safety of the Westminster sanctuary. Two months later he was pardoned.[70]

More important, Cromwell initiated legislation in 1540 that would lead to the virtual abolition of sanctuary.[71] However, his role in the process may have been slightly exaggerated. By then, his political position was already parlous (he was arrested in June of that year), although he was probably involved in the early stages of the bill. Furthermore, although noting that sanctuary had been abused, the 1540 statute made it clear that the King did not wish to see the "utter abolishing [and] extinguishment" of all sanctuaries. Parliament appears to have shared this view, not least because several MPs were themselves former sanctuary inmates, and not all of them just for debt.[72] Nevertheless, change, when it came, was to be drastic.

The new Act extinguished existing chartered sanctuaries, although some inmates were allowed to retain their privilege on a personal basis and continue living inside them. It replaced them with eight secularised (but permanent) sanctuaries, located in set areas of identified cities: Wells, Manchester, Northampton, Norwich, York, Derby, Launceston, and Westminster (the city, not the religious establishment). However, Manchester petitioned against being made a sanctuary town, and Chester ("West Chester") was initially substituted, with orders that sanctuary men in the former be transferred to the latter.[73] This last choice proved unsatisfactory, because the town adjoined Wales and was close to the sea, so that malefactors could escape from it to Scotland, Ireland, and more distant parts. As a result, the King ordered the constables of Manchester to bring any sanctuary men there to Stafford and deliver them by indenture to the town bailiffs.[74] Each of these statutory sanctuaries could take up to 20 people; if it was full, a sanctuary seeker's application would be recorded, and they would then be sent on with a constable to another of the eight locations.

---

70. McSheffrey, "Sanctuary Seekers in England".
71. Stacey, "Richard Roose", pp. 7–8.
72. McSheffrey, *Seeking Sanctuary*, p. 183.
73. Gairdner and Brodie, *Letters and Papers, Foreign and Domestic, Henry VIII, Vol. 17*, pp. 10–19.
74. *Ibid*, pp. 199–218.

Even more significantly, the 1540 Act placed severe restrictions on the offences for which any form of the privilege, even the basic 40-day sanctuary, was available. It would no longer be granted to anyone who had committed wilful murder, rape, arson, burglary, or robbery on a highway or in a house or church, i.e. the majority of offences for which people had sought the privilege during the Tudor era. Nevertheless, it was still, in theory, available for grand larceny (however serious) and manslaughter, as well as a few more recondite felonies. Even so, the 1540 Act was not well thought out, and failed to function effectively. Very few felons had recourse to the eight urban sanctuaries, and some, it seems, never became fully operational.[75] However, at least two cases are known; there were probably others before the system petered out.

Although the 1540 statute did not mark the complete demise of sanctuary for felony, it quickly became largely insignificant thereafter, albeit that it seems to have had a small-scale and localised return in Westminster during the reign of the Catholic Queen Mary. The diarist Henry Machyn observed that sanctuary men there were part of the abbot's procession as late as December 1556. He noted that walking before this cleric "went all the Sanctuary men, with crosse keys upon their garments".[76] His account makes clear that they included felons rather than just debtors; amongst them were a thief and a youth who had killed another boy by "the hurling of a stone". The following year, a coroner's inquest held at St Clement Danes, Westminster, on the body of one William Stokesly, concluded that he had been murdered by a man named Kerle who had subsequently fled to the sanctuary of St Peter at Westminster, where he remained.[77]

There appear to be no extant records of sanctuary (in any form) being claimed under Queen Elizabeth. Statutes formally abolishing nearly all the surviving sanctuary privileges (other than for some debtors) were enacted under James I in 1603 (1 James I, c. 25) and 1623 (21 James I, c.28). The protection of sanctuary was abolished or severely limited in much of Europe, not merely in Protestant states, at about the same

---

75. McSheffrey, *Seeking Sanctuary*, p. 24 and p. 192.
76. Shoemaker, *Sanctuary and Crime*, p. 170.
77. McSheffrey, "Sanctuary Seekers".

time, suggesting that it was not purely a fruit of the Reformation. For example, Francis I abolished sanctuary in France in 1539, although two further statutes were needed to enforce this. In 1597 Pope Gregory XIV all but abolished the privilege at canon law, although it lingered on in a few places.[78]

Abjuration

Abjuration was closely associated with sanctuary, albeit not a specifically ecclesiastical privilege. In 1485 it had changed little since the fourteenth century, although its use declined between the late 1300s and 1450. The procedure was correspondingly well-established. An offender in a general (40-day) sanctuary who wished to abjure rather than submit to trial was required to summon a coroner to the church in which he was sheltering, or attend on such an officer who arrived of his own initiative; he then had to formally confess his crime before him, in a public ceremony held in the presence of ecclesiastical officials and local people. His confession was put into writing and had to be specific and detailed; as Ferdinando Pulton later noted, he "must confesse before him the felonie certainely, *viz.* the yeare, day, and place, where, and when hee committed the felonie".

Sanctuary seekers might follow this path if they did not feel that they could escape from the church in which they were sheltering without recapture but held out little hope of acquittal at trial. As a Venetian envoy observed in 1500, "If a thief or murderer who has taken refuge in one [a church], cannot leave it in safety during those 40 days he gives notice that he wishes to leave England". The abjuror was then assigned a port or (much more rarely) the Scottish border by the coroner, to which he was sworn to proceed forthwith for embarkation, never to return to England without the King's express permission and a special licence.

Such permission was sometimes granted. For example, in February 1529 Thomas Cheselet, a Wiltshire tailor, stole silver plate from a woman in the parish of Fisherton Anger. In July that year, he sought sanctuary there, in the church of St Mary and St Peter, where he duly confessed

---

78. Shoemaker, *Sanctuary and Crime*, p. 170 and p. 284.

the theft to William Chawsey, a local coroner, as part of the abjuration process. However, in November 1529 he was pardoned for the crime. (What Cheselet had done after beginning the abjuration process but before receiving his pardon is unclear.)[79] In early 1533, George Courtney from Romsey, in Hampshire, fled to a parish church in Lincolnshire and confessed to Thomas Goodhande, one of the county coroners, that a few weeks earlier he had broken into a house in Long Ludford (in the same county) and stolen cash, and that a considerable time earlier he had assaulted and robbed an unknown man at Wallop in his native shire. He abjured the realm, and was assigned the port of Kingston-upon-Hull for his departure point. In May of that year he received a pardon for the felonies that had led to him abjuring and also a pardon for returning to England (if he had ever left) without a licence.[80] Nevertheless, such pardons were fairly rare.

If a sanctuary seeker sought a coroner immediately, and one was readily to hand, the process could take place quite expeditiously. For example, on 23 July, 1507, a weaver named Roger Prentice struck John Bradshaw a fatal blow on the head with his staff in Newark-on-Trent. He appears to have escaped from the scene of the crime, but after a month of "lying low" claimed sanctuary in St Mary Magdalen, the parish church of Newark, and asked for a coroner to be brought to him. On the same day, Richard Skrymsher, a county coroner, came to the church, and Prentice immediately confessed to murdering Bradshaw and asked to abjure the realm. He was assigned the port of Chester, a cross was placed in his right hand, and he duly departed. However, despite his abjuration, Roger was outlawed in the county court at Nottingham in October 1511. Perhaps it was rumoured that he had not gone abroad as required. (A co-accused who had stabbed the dead man's body post mortem surrendered for trial and was acquitted).[81]

During the medieval period, coroners frequently selected Dover as the embarkation point for their abjurors, as it provided the shortest crossing to France. Many went from there across the Channel to Wissant, a

---

79.   Brewer, *Letters and Papers, Foreign and Domestic, Henry VIII, Vol. 4*, pp. 2704–2710.
80.   Gairdner, *Letters and Papers, Foreign and Domestic, Henry VIII, Vol. 6*, pp. 540–553.
81.   Hunnisett, *Transactions of the Thoroton Society of Nottinghamshire, Vol. XXV*, pp. 18–19.

French (though mainly Dutch-speaking) port near Calais, where there was an English agent. From Wissant most made their way into other parts of France or the Low Countries. However, Portsmouth, Southampton, Sandwich, and Kingston-upon-Hull were also favoured ports, and many others, from Berwick-upon-Tweed to Yarmouth, from Rochester to Ilfracombe, were used occasionally. Groups of men who had sought sanctuary and abjured together would usually be given different ports of embarkation.[82]

Once their port had been selected, abjurors were required to travel to it by the most direct route available. A time limit, even for specific stages of the journey, was usually imposed. The traditional oath included a promise not to spend more than one night at any town on the way. They were supposed to throw away their clothes before setting out, and walk bareheaded, dressed in a long white or sackcloth robe, carrying a wooden cross or crucifix in their right hand as they went. They were legally protected from attack, as long as they remained on the royal highway. Any abjurors found away from it could, in theory, be executed immediately, although, by the late medieval period, this was discouraged.[83]

Before the abjuror set out for his designated port, the coroner was also obliged to give a public warning to local people, including relatives of the victim if an abjuror had killed someone, against interfering with him while he was en route to his destination, although it was disregarded in some cases. For example, a Breton who murdered a London widow in 1431, and then sought sanctuary followed by abjuration, was stoned to death by a mob of enraged women as he made his way down Aldgate towards his port of embarkation.[84]

On arrival at the allotted port, abjurors had to seek the first passage abroad available.[85] According to Ferdinando Pulton, they would swear before the coroner that once at their designated port they would "not tarrie there but one flowing and ebbing if I may have passage: And if

82. Kesselring, "Abjuration and its Demise", *Canadian Journal of History*, Vol. 34, No. 3, p. 350.
83. Jorge L. Carro, "Sanctuary: The Resurgence of an Age-Old Right or a Dangerous". Misinterpretation of an Abandoned Ancient Privilege?", *University of Cincinnati Law Review*, Vol. 54, No. 3, p. 761.
84. Bellamy, *Strange, Inhuman Deaths*, p. 42.
85. Anon, *A Relation, or Rather A True Account*, p. 35.

I cannot have passage in this time, I will go every day up to the knees into the sea, assaying to passe over". The immersion in water signified a willingness to depart the country.

In practice, absconding en route was a regular occurrence. A large number of abjurors simply disappeared, becoming outlaws or quietly resuming their lives in remote parts of the country, where they were not known. However, some were captured and executed, especially if they failed to put sufficient space between themselves and their crimes or points of abjuration. Among them was John Bere, who "fled to church" in Lambeth, in March 1480, and confessed to a coroner that, shortly before Christmas 1476, he had murdered Richard Hylles at Sampford Peverell in Devon. He abjured the realm but does not seem to have left its shores, as he appeared at King's Bench later that year, having been found in England, and was duly sentenced to hang.[86] Similarly, in March 1486 a man named White took sanctuary in the church of All Saints on the Wall in London, and confessed to a coroner that, more than three years earlier, he had slain a man in Herefordshire. He abjured, but in October the following year was found in England and brought before the King's Bench, where he was sentenced to death. In like manner, a coroner's memorandum from October 1502, recorded that a man named Barley had fled to the Church of St Andrew in Enfield, and then abjured, after confessing that the same day he had killed a local chaplain, Thomas West, with a dagger. However, by Easter 1503, he was back in custody, having been found in the realm without licence, and was hanged.[87]

As a result, by the 1490s, some coroners were trying to prevent escapes en route by ordering that abjurors be passed from one parish constable to the next until they reached their designated port, rather than leaving them to their own devices, although such chains often broke down.[88] In other situations a single constable would be assigned to escort the abjuror all the way to the relevant port, although this was often neglected if it required an arduous journey, the officer discreetly abandoning his man on the road. A statute of 1529 (21 Henry VIII, c. 2) sought to discourage

---

86. McSheffrey, "Sanctuary Seekers".
87. McSheffrey, "Sanctuary Seekers in England".
88. St. Germain, *Doctor and Student*, p. 37.

abjurors from absconding or returning illegally from abroad by ordering that coroners brand them before they abjured, as was already done
in benefit-of-clergy cases, so that they "cause every such felon or murderer to be marked with an hot iron upon the braune of the thumbe
of the right hand, with the signe of an A to the intent he may bee the
better known among the kings subjects".[89] This requirement was being
met almost immediately it became law. In May 1530 Henry Danby, a
London baker, took sanctuary in Chichester Cathedral and abjured
before the town coroners after confessing to murdering a friar in Kent
and committing a burglary in Sussex. He was branded on the inside of
his right hand below the thumb, and then assigned Portsmouth as his
port of departure.[90]

Abjurors who returned to, or remained in, England (without licence)
could not claim the privilege a second time. They would be arraigned
upon their original abjuration, which was effectively a recorded confession to felony, and swiftly convicted and executed.[91] However, literate
abjurors who were caught in England could still plead their clergy to
escape execution, and this occurred in a few cases. In these situations it
may seem strange that they did not submit to trial *ab initio*; they may
have hoped to avoid the possibility of going to a bishop's prison if they
were clergied.

Very few excuses were accepted for failure to depart. For example, in
R. v Preston (1491) an abjuror claimed that he had unavailingly tried to
find a ship for two weeks after arrival at his designated port, but was then
so hungry that he went inland to search for food. The court concluded
that he should have begged for alms where he was.[92] In *R v Danby* (1532),
Henry Danby (see above), claimed that he had boarded a Flemish boat
at his assigned port of Portsmouth. However, it was blown back to land
at Plymouth by a storm, where the crew threw him off the vessel as they
thought he brought bad luck. The abjuror then returned to London,
where he was arrested. (It is likely that he went there immediately after

---

89. Staunford, *Les Plees Del Coron*, pp. 108–9.
90. R. F. Hunnisett, "The Last Sussex Abjurations", *Sussex Archaeological Collections,* Vol. 102,
     pp. 39–51.
91. Baker, *Oxford History,* p. 543.
92. Baker, *Sir John Spelman*, pp. 43–44.

leaving Chichester and fabricated his account of the voyage.) He apparently hoped to take advantage of the then new 1531 statute (see below) requiring that abjurors be sent to internal exile (rather than abroad) in one of nine designated permanent sanctuaries. The Court of King's Bench concluded that, even accepting his story as true, he should have stayed at Plymouth and waited for another vessel. Danby was duly hanged.[93] However, in 1440 it was held that genuinely losing his way was a defence for an abjuror who had strayed from the correct route, provided all reasonable steps were taken to regain it as quickly as possible.

Abjurors were treated as dead at law. Like convicted felons, their land was, in theory, escheated, and their goods and chattels were forfeit to the Crown, which could then alienate them. For example, in November 1529 the Crown granted the Manor of Willyngall Rokell and certain other lands in Essex to William Newdegate. They had formerly belonged to Richard Bedell, who had abjured the realm after murdering one John Vavasor.[94]

On one estimate, there were at least 75,000 cases of abjuration between 1180 and 1350 (although reliable figures are difficult to draw-up), and the system has been described as operating like a well-oiled machine. Even so, such cases declined enormously during the middle of the fourteenth century, as growing nationalism and the Hundred Years' War (1337–1453) made the Crown nervous about driving Englishmen into the arms of the country's enemies. Instead, the state preferred to offer healthy male felons royal pardons, on condition that they serve in the King's armies.[95]

Abjuration never fully recovered its former significance thereafter. According to the Venetian ambassador, writing at the start of the 1500s, the insular nature of the English made it difficult for ordinary people to imagine that life would be possible outside their homeland, discouraging recourse to the privilege.[96] Nevertheless, the system survived, and, it seems, in the late fifteenth and early sixteenth centuries its use started to expand again, especially in cases of homicide. Typically, in January 1486

---

93. Hunnisett, "Sussex Abjurations", pp. 39–51.
94. Brewer, *Letters and Papers, Foreign and Domestic, Henry VIII, Vol. 4*, pp. 2704–2710.
95. William Chester Jordan, *From England to France: Felony and Exile in the High Middle Ages* (Princeton: Princeton University Press, 2015), p. 140 and pp. 81–82.
96. Anon, *A Relation, or Rather A True Account*, p. 35.

Thomas Smallwood confessed to a coroner in the churchyard at Battle, in Sussex, that he had killed a man on the outskirts of Colchester, in Essex, the previous Whitsun. Smallwood took the abjuration oath, and the coroner assigned him the port of Winchelsea from which to begin his journey abroad.[97]

Abjuration was still being claimed by a number of felons every year in the late 1520s. For example, in 1527, after John Richardson fled to a church in Canterbury when accused of burglary, the coroners assigned him the port of Harwich in Suffolk.[98] Similarly, when Thomas Parker fled to a church in Leicester, the same year, after murdering Thomas Otfield, he abjured in front of the two city coroners who attended him. Upon swearing to leave the realm, he was sent to Boston, in Lincolnshire.[99]

Reform in 1531

Radical change to the system did not take place until 1531, when statute (22 Henry VIII, c. 14) provided that those who claimed common sanctuary and then abjured before a coroner should not leave the country. Instead, they were to be led by a constable into one of nine designated permanent sanctuaries (supposedly of their choice), usually large monasteries such as Ripon and Westminster, for internal exile. They still had to be branded with the letter A. If abjurors committed any further felony within or outside these sanctuaries, they would forfeit their right to remain, and could be forcibly removed and imprisoned.

Just 51 such abjurors are recorded as having been sent to these special sanctuaries in the surviving records for the ensuing years, although there may well have been more. Among them were three men who abjured in front of Edward Broke, one of the Essex county coroners, in 1531. The trio (from Wiltshire, Gloucestershire, and Romford) took sanctuary in the church of St Peter, at South Weald. They confessed to having broken into a house at Bicknacre, in Essex, tied up one of its occupants, and stolen money and other valuables. They chose the chartered sanctuary

---

97.   Field, "Biblical Influences", p. 224.
98.   Kesselring, *Mercy and Authority*, p. 49.
99.   Kesselring, "Abjuration and its Demise", p. 350.

at Beaulieu Abbey, in Hampshire, under the new (and recent) statute.[100] The following year, William More, a sailor from Bristol, made the same choice after taking sanctuary at the church in Lancing, in Sussex. More confessed to having killed a man at Great Yarmouth by hitting him over the head with a "botehoke" and to having broken into Simon Combes' house in Lancing during the summer and stolen a coat and knife. He took his oath, was branded, and was escorted to Beaulieu by a constable from Brightford. In September 1533 Edward Holland, a Chichester tailor, took sanctuary there after attacking William Skinner with a stone. Skinner lingered for two days before dying, following which Holland fled to a local church. (Had Skinner recovered, the case may well have been dealt with as a misdemeanour.) When Holland abjured in front of the city coroners, he also chose to go to Beaulieu (clearly a favoured destination at the time), whereupon he was branded, and passed from parish constable to parish constable until he got there. A wooden cross was put into his hand before he went. Interestingly, when one of the same coroners who presided over the abjuration conducted an inquest on the body of William Skinner, it was determined that Holland had acted in self-defence after the dead man had drunkenly threatened him with a sword. Even if a conviction had ensued in these circumstances, it would probably have led to a reprieve *de cursu*. Perhaps Holland was not willing to risk a trial. In any event, in the light of the inquest verdict, it is fairly likely that a royal pardon would subsequently have been obtained, allowing him to leave Beaulieu.[101]

The preamble to the 1531 Act suggests that the change may have been motivated by renewed concern that abjuration encouraged the emigration of militarily useful men, including skilled archers and sailors, who could assist with the "defence of this realme". Interestingly, in 1525, at a time of mounting tension with Scotland, it was noted that various sanctuary men in Durham, of "tall personage" and good demeanour, had stated that they would be glad to serve in the royal army if permitted.[102] Even so, the change applied to women as well as men. Shortly after it came

---

100. Gairdner, *Letters and Papers, Foreign and Domestic, Henry VIII, Vol. 5*, pp. 111–130.
101. Hunnisett, "The Last Sussex Abjurations", pp. 39–51.
102. Brewer, *Letters and Papers, Foreign and Domestic, Henry VIII, Vol. 4*, pp. 556–569.

into force, Alicia Walker fled to a Canterbury church and confessed to burglary. The coroners who attended ensured that she was duly branded and then had her taken directly to the sanctuary at Westminster, where she was to spend the rest of her life, also wearing a badge so that her status was readily apparent (as required by the statute).[103]

The final major attack on abjuration was an Act of 1540 (32 Henry VIII, c.12) that followed the dissolution of the monasteries and the dismantling of the surviving great abbeys, including the nine post-1531 permanent ecclesiastical sanctuaries that were used by abjurors. Nevertheless, ordinary churches retained their ability to provide 40 days' protection for a few lesser felonies and, in lieu of the nine sanctuaries, eight towns and cities, secular "places of privilege", were appointed to which coroners could direct abjurers.

However, and significantly, the Henrician statute of 1540 decreed that, as with sanctuary, abjuration no longer applied to a large number of serious crimes, mimicking the process that had gradually removed benefit of clergy from grave offences.[104] These changes almost marked its end. Records of only two subsequent abjurations into the newly specified sanctuary towns survive, although there may have been a few more. In 1541 William Cripps, a Rye fisherman, sought sanctuary at Bledlow parish church, in Buckinghamshire, and asked to abjure. When Robert Woodless, the local coroner, arrived, Cripps admitted stealing a horse, by then an unclergyable form of grand larceny, but still theft, and so not excluded from sanctuary by the 1540 Act. Woodless was branded, as required by the 1531 Act, and assigned to the new secular sanctuary in Norwich, albeit still given a cross to hold, as was the "law and custom of England". The following year, William Arthur, a weaver, sought sanctuary in a church at Culmington, in Shropshire, for the same crime. A local coroner was summoned, took his confession to horse theft, and then assigned him to Wells.[105]

Despite these cases, abjuration largely died out in the early 1540s; it was no longer an attractive option to felons who might claim benefit

---

103. Kesselring, *Mercy and Authority*, p. 49.
104. John Wilkinson, *A Treatise Collected out of the Statutes of this Kingdom, Book 1* (London, 1618), p. 24.
105. McSheffrey, *Seeking Sanctuary*, p. 24 and pp. 196–197.

of clergy, seek pardon from the King, or risk flight or trial in lieu. Nevertheless, its existence lingered in legal theory, as it was never formally abolished. In 1556 leet court tithingmen (peace officers of the parish) were still being advised to examine whether "there be any amonge you that hath taken the churchyarde and escaped withoute abjuration of the realme as the lawe wyll".[106]

Characteristics of Tudor Abjurors

A close examination indicates that the overwhelming majority of Tudor abjurors were male, with a relatively high proportion coming from the "middling" and upper social orders. This is understandable, as exiles faced numerous hardships and dangers when abroad, and many people, particularly if poor or female, would have preferred to take their chances at trial.[107] Thus the (very incomplete) surviving coroners' records from the Court of King's Bench show that, of 212 people who claimed the privilege between 1485 and 1545, four were women; 75 per cent admitted to thefts or burglaries and 34 per cent to homicides (20 cases involved both murder and theft).[108] Similarly, the historian Shannon McSheffrey has concluded that, between 1391 and 1541, only fractionally over one per cent of felons who claimed sanctuary were female.[109]

Many records reveal a significant distance between the place of an offence and that of the felon claiming sanctuary and abjuring for it, suggesting an initial escape before safety was sought. For example, in January 1515 Richard Scrivener, an Essex labourer, took sanctuary in Salehurst Church, in Sussex, and asked for the local coroner. A day later, this officer, Nicholas Tufton of Hastings, attended him. Scrivener confessed to having beaten and robbed a man in his native county, stealing a coat, sword, shield, dagger, and cash from his victim before fleeing almost 100 miles. He then asked to abjure the realm. The local port of Rye was assigned as his departure point.[110] There could also be substantial delays

---

106. Fitzherbert, *The Contentes of this Booke* (London, 1556), p. 85.
107. Carro, "Sanctuary: The Resurgence", p. 761.
108. Kesselring, "Abjuration and its Demise", pp. 350–351.
109. McSheffrey, "Sanctuary Seekers".
110. Hunnisett, "The Last Sussex Abjurations", pp. 39–51.

in time between offending and abjuring. In November 1506, the Durham sanctuary register records that a man named Myre sought sanctuary for killing one Robert Robinson with an axe 12 years earlier, while in Carlisle.[111] Another man who claimed sanctuary in 1510 did so for a homicide that he had committed seven years earlier.[112] (That they felt obliged to do so might indicate a slightly more effective early Tudor criminal justice system than is sometimes suggested.) In a more typical delay, in September 1495 Richard Barlow sought 40-day sanctuary in the church of St Ethelbert, in Hereford, for stealing a gown, socks, and cash worth a total of 8s from one Hugh Collins at Worcester the previous April.[113]

Other abjurors appear to have sought sanctuary immediately, and locally, after committing a felony. In March 1527, Thomas Goffe, a native of Chichester, ran to a church in the same city just after stabbing another man to death and promptly asked for the two coroners of the city to attend him so that he could abjure; a few days later he formally did so, and Portsmouth was assigned as his exit point. (Both coroners also presided over the inquest on the dead man's body as another part of their work.)[114]

Conclusion

It is easy to see sanctuary and abjuration as relics of the medieval era, and their demise after the 1530s as an inevitable aspect of the triumph of modernity over medievalism. This was a popular trope amongst Victorian historians, who viewed their abolition as a hallmark of progress. However, more recent work, especially that by McSheffrey, has challenged this analysis, not least because both of them enjoyed an Indian summer in their final years, shortly before (de facto) abolition, suggesting that they had proved their value by adapting to a new legal environment.[115]

The privileges had originally served important social functions. Sanctuary allowed serious legal decisions to be reached in a calmer atmosphere,

---

111. Shannon McSheffrey, "Sanctuary Seekers".
112. Thomson, *The Early Tudor Church*, p. 99.
113. McSheffrey, "Sanctuary Seekers".
114. R.F. Hunnisett, "The Last Sussex Abjurations", pp. 39–51.
115. McSheffrey, *Seeking Sanctuary*, pp. 10–11.

so helping to prevent violent revenge from taking place.[116] Abjuration rid the realm of a felon and confiscated his property for the Crown without requiring execution. However, in their final years, they also helped address the problems occasioned by a criminal justice system that was going on the offensive, and that was much more efficient than previously, yet still wedded to the death-for-felony rule.[117]

In many respects, these two privileges were no more "irrational" and can be seen as fairer (given that they extended to women and did not require literacy) than benefit of clergy, which, in a slightly reformed version, survived long beyond the Tudor era and frequently allowed serious felons to go almost scot free. The end of sanctuary and abjuration was as much linked to the emergence of new concepts of mercy and justice as it was to their inherent deficiencies, although it is unlikely that homicide could have remained within their ambit forever, and unlike the post-trial award of benefit of clergy there was no ready mechanism for distinguishing between the "quality" of killers (manslaughter or murder) who sought them.

Most important, Tudor England witnessed a growing determination on the part of the Crown, in an increasingly centralised state, to be seen to administer all justice, not least because wrongdoing increasingly came to be conceptualised as an offence against its authority. Benefit of clergy had been adapted in the medieval period so that it was normally claimed only after conviction; defendants first had to face trial in the King's courts. However, sanctuary and abjuration had been rights, not indulgences granted by a compassionate ruler, and were invoked before trial, which they often precluded. Arguably, their disappearance was a result of punishment and mitigation ceasing to be independent of state authority.[118] As the Court of King's Bench noted in the case of *R* v *Boswell* in 1513: "Having a sanctuary is the highest thing against the crown that may be; for the highest things the king has are governance and power over the bodies of his subjects, and this sanctuary discharges them from the law and the execution thereof".[119] However, and as McSheffrey has

---

116. Carro, "Sanctuary: The Resurgence", p. 769.
117. McSheffrey, *Seeking Sanctuary*, p. 19.
118. Kesselring, "Abjuration and its Demise", p. 358; Kesselring, *Mercy and Authority*, p. 54.
119. Baker, *Sir John Port*, p. 38.

pointed out, the demise of the two privileges was also, in part, a simple matter of practicality: the Reformation destroyed the infrastructure of religious houses on which permanent sanctuary and "internal abjuration" depended.

CHAPTER 14

Down-valuing and Lesser Verdicts

Introduction

The artificial down-valuing of the proceeds of a theft was a common means of avoiding the death-for-felony rule, both before and during trial, especially in the final decades of the Tudor era. Larceny was by far the most common offence indicted at assizes, always making up a majority of prosecutions conducted at this forum. It was also indicted on a regular basis at quarter sessions and, unlike many other felonies, this remained the case to the end of the Tudor era and beyond in most counties. However, only theft of a shilling or more in value (grand larceny) was capital. The normal punishment for petty theft (below this value) was flogging, followed by discharge, although genteel thieves might be fined. As a result, the down-valuing of stolen items to below 12 pence, whether by complainant or jury, was to become an important mechanism for limiting the impact of the death-for-felony rule during the sixteenth century. A few other forms of unclergyable capital crimes were also artificially found to be lesser offences, in an analogous manner, and can be considered in this chapter.

Down-valuing

Deliberate down-valuing could be performed in three ways: by a victim prosecutor, who ensured that the indictment was for petty theft *ab initio*; by the grand jury considering a bill of indictment for grand larceny (extremely rare); by a trial jury when a defendant was prosecuted for grand larceny but convicted of petty theft by the jurors' valuing the stolen items at under one shilling. Frequently ten pence was selected as the nominal value of down-valued stolen items, but other figures, such as six pence and eleven pence, were sometimes chosen.

Of course, sometimes, grand jury and trial jury down-valuing simply reflected a more realistic assessment of the value of stolen items than that placed on them by the prosecutor (also usually the victim), especially where the original valuation was only slightly over one shilling. However, in the majority of cases this was not the situation, the stolen items being artificially reduced in worth. For example, in a blatant but not unique example from the Essex Assizes in August 1594, it was alleged that John Larkin had stolen ten shillings in cash (not goods) from another man, but he was merely convicted by the trial jury to the value of ten pence, whipped, and discharged.[120]

Although down-valuing was to become an enduring feature of the English criminal justice system in the seventeenth and eighteenth centuries, it was already well-established by the end of the 1500s. In the Tudor era it was usually done because victims and jurors did not wish to have a person's death on their consciences for a simple, often relatively modest, non-violent theft, and were concerned about the ability of a woman or illiterate man to claim benefit of clergy; however, they were also persuaded of the defendant's guilt and so were not prepared to take no action at all (if a victim), or return an outright acquittal (if a jury).

Complainant Down-valuing

Many complainants artificially undervalued the goods that they had lost to less than a shilling. It is apparent that those suspected of theft who lived near their victim, had an advantage in this regard. This is unsurprising. Killing a poor neighbour by getting him or her capitally convicted for grand larceny might excite hostility among their relatives and even prompt revenge attacks. In the case of bread-winning family men, it could also risk burdening the parish with the cost of providing for their widows and offspring, something that would make the prosecutor unpopular. It might also make neighbours who had been witnesses

---

120. Cockburn, *Calendar of Assize Records: Essex Indictments: Elizabeth I*, p. 423.

to the crime, and whose evidence would be vital in the event of a not guilty plea, reluctant to testify for the prosecution. Unlike offending vagrants from out of area, local thieves appeared less threatening. For example, when Richard and William Tebbes of West Mersea (part of a small tidal island off the Essex coast) were indicted at quarter sessions for stealing a sheep, it was valued at just ten pence. The victim was also resident there, and would certainly not have wished to have such close neighbours hanged.[121]

However, doing nothing at all was also potentially dangerous. If a man or woman got a reputation for weakness among their neighbours, they were likely to be victimised again. In these circumstances, an indictment for petty larceny had numerous attractions. The victim appeared magnanimous but also someone not to be trifled with.

There seems to have been a slightly greater willingness among defendants in these situations to acknowledge their prosecutor's compassion by tendering guilty pleas. Indeed, there is also some (albeit limited) evidence for a form of plea bargaining taking place, at least during the later Elizabethan period, in which the clerk amended the valuation of stolen goods to less than a shilling, with the agreement of the complainant, on the understanding that a guilty plea would then be entered by the accused. This would have been an attractive option to the court, as it would help to clear the heavy backlog of cases to be tried at assizes or quarter sessions that was often found at this time, especially as juries were likely to down-value the matter if it did go to trial.[122] Thus, at the Epiphany Quarter Sessions for Essex in 1590, Mary Hamon appears to have been indicted for stealing a waistcoat worth two shillings and an apron costing six pence (i.e. a case of low-value grand larceny). However, she seems to have offered a plea of guilty of petty larceny to the value of ten pence that was accepted by the court.[123]

A selection of cases is indicative of the range of matters that were the subject of complainant down-valuing. For example, in March 1594

---

121. ERO Q/SR 115/120.
122. Louis A. Knafla, "'Sin of all Sorts Swarmeth': Criminal Litigation in an English County in the early Seventeenth Century", in Eric William Ives and A. H. Manchester (eds.), *Law, Litigants and the Legal Profession* (London: Royal History Society, 1983), p. 52.
123. ERO Q/SR 111/93.

Warren Whyston, a labourer from Graveley, Hertfordshire, was indicted for petty theft after stealing nine hens, implausibly valued (together) at just ten pence, from another man in the same village. He was convicted and sentenced to the standard whipping.[124] Very similarly, at the Essex Assizes held at Chelmsford in February 1597, William Lange of Walthamstow was accused of stealing nine hens valued, on this occasion, at eleven pence. He pleaded guilty ("confessed") and was whipped.[125] At the Hertfordshire Assizes in March 1596, Robert Manveild, a labourer from Wymondley, was indicted for stealing a sheep valued at ten pence, although it was probably worth at least three shillings. He, too, pleaded guilty.[126] A year later, at the same forum, Thomas Sawes of Offley was convicted of stealing two sheep that were together valued at just ten pence by their owner. The year was one of ferocious hardship, and the victim a fellow townsman, which might help explain his merciful decision.[127] In an even more extreme case, from the Essex Assizes in March 1602, Isreal Owens valued three sheep and a ram stolen by John Andrews at the ludicrously low value of ten pence rather than their likely worth of at least 16 shillings.[128]

The history of complainant down-valuing is not entirely clear. For example, although instances have been found as far back as the 1300s, it has been argued that there is little evidence for it in Kent during the early sixteenth century.[129] Instead, victims would have recourse to indicting thefts that were valued at well over a shilling as misdemeanours (trespasses) rather than felonies, a phenomenon that can be traced back to the fourteenth century and which lasted until the 1700s. As Thomas Marowe observed at the start of the sixteenth century, "Although a man has taken my goods feloniously, I can if I please treat that felony as a mere trespass, and so can the king if he pleases".[130] This would preclude a death sentence.

---

124. Cockburn, *Calendar of Assize Records. Hertfordshire Indictments: Elizabeth I*, p. 107.
125. Cockburn, *Calendar of Assize Records. Essex Indictments: Elizabeth I*, p. 455 and p. 460.
126. Cockburn, *Calendar of Assize Records. Hertfordshire Indictments: Elizabeth I*, p. 119.
127. *Ibid*, p. 129.
128. Cockburn, *Calendar of Assize Records. Essex Indictments: Elizabeth I*, p. 535.
129. Jones, *Gender and Petty Crime*, p. 34.
130. Harvey, *The Law Emprynted and Englysshed*, p. 34.

Almost no cases of petty theft that were brought as such have survived for the Essex Assizes prior to the 1570s, suggesting that they were largely being indicted at quarter sessions at this time. The only (surviving) exception is a prosecution for the (petty) theft of a blanket that was brought alongside an indictment for grand larceny. The first obvious case of complainant down-valuing that has been preserved for the county does not occur until well into the Elizabethan period.

Grand Jury Down-valuing

A grand jury had the power to revalue allegedly stolen goods before a case went to trial, although this was exercised extremely infrequently, unlike complainant and jury down-valuing. Clearly, grand jurors did not normally feel that this was part of their duty. Nevertheless, very occasionally they used this power to reduce an allegation of grand larceny to one of petty theft, and sometimes this reduction appears to have been artificial. For example, in Elizabethan Colchester, James Keller was presented for stealing herrings initially valued by the complainant at 3s 4d but the grand jury endorsed the bill "billa vera 11d".[131]

Petty Jury Down-valuing

By the end of the Tudor era, trial jury down-valuing of grand-larceny indictments to convictions for petty theft was a regular phenomenon. Trial judges usually accepted such decisions without complaint, not least because, in appropriate cases, it avoided the need to "fiddle" the benefit-of-clergy test or ask for a pardon in cases deserving of clemency.

It is difficult to say precisely when this practice developed. It has been suggested that it can be traced back to the fourteenth century.[132] However, it was probably not a regular phenomenon before the Elizabethan era, at least on the Home Circuit, and was still largely absent in the 1560s, developing only in the years after 1570. A contributory factor to

---

131. Joel B. Samaha, "Hanging for Felony: The Rule of Law in Elizabethan Colchester", *The Historical Journal*, Vol. 21, Issue 4, p. 769.
132. Jones, *Gender and Petty Crime*, pp. 34–38.

this development may have been the severe inflation that set in after the early sixteenth century. (On one assessment, goods that were worth a shilling in 1600 could have been purchased for three pence in 1510). In real terms, the theft of much less valuable items had become a capital offence.

On the Home Circuit there appears to be some variation in timings between counties in this regard. For example, at the Surrey Assizes there is no case of a lesser verdict of petty theft being returned that has been preserved before February 1586, and this was exceptional. John Rolson was indicted for grand larceny after being accused of stealing a cloak, doublet, and sword, implausibly valued by the complainant at just 12 pence (the legal minimum for the crime). He was convicted of petty theft to the value of eleven pence. In this case, it must be wondered if the prosecutor thought that a shilling was not a capital amount, as some contemporary legal observers believed was the case. Was the jury simply trying to carry out his wishes? The next case of jury down-valuing followed a year later, and was also extreme, but in the other direction. Elizabeth Stevens was prosecuted for grand larceny, accused of stealing goods worth £2, but convicted to the value of just ten pence (about two per cent of the worth placed on the items) and whipped. A year further on again, in February 1588, and much more typically of such cases, Edward Ellis was convicted of petty theft after being accused of stealing shoes worth 20 pence. Another such case does not occur (or is not preserved) before February 1592. Thereafter, instances of jury down-valuing begin to crop up more frequently. There is a case in March 1593, two cases in March 1594, and two more in February 1595, by which time this is clearly a "mainstream" verdict.[133]

By contrast, although, in Hertfordshire, county records are not preserved before 1573, two cases of jury down-valuing occur in the March Sessions for the county that year, with 9s 6d worth of shirts and shoes and four shillings' worth of clothes and napkins both being reduced to ten pence, suggesting that it was already a well-established verdict. At the next sessions that have been preserved for the county, those from July 1575, Richard Atkins and Richard Reeve both had grand larceny counts

---

133. Cockburn, *Calendar of Assize Records. Surrey indictments: Elizabeth I*, p. 298, p. 316, p. 375, p. 390, p. 396, and p. 411.

reduced to petty theft. These concerned stolen clothes worth about eight shillings and two sheep valued at ten shillings (respectively), each valuation being reduced to eleven pence.[134]

In Essex the first preserved case does not occur until June 1573, when Simon Selle was accused of stealing a sheep valued at seven shillings, but convicted only of a theft to the value of ten pence. There are no more cases until the sessions held in March 1577, when, quite dramatically, there are five. Thereafter they occur periodically.[135]

Sometimes, it is obvious why a jury down-valued the stolen goods. For example, in March 1596 Henry Elston, a labourer from Weston, in Hertfordshire, was indicted at the assizes for grand larceny after stealing two flitches of bacon valued by the complainant at just a shilling (right on the boundary of the offence). This was then down-valued to ten pence to give a verdict of petty theft for which he could be whipped.[136] The following year Robert Peeter in Standon was indicted at the same forum for the same crime, after allegedly stealing a bow worth eleven pence and a bolt valued at two pence, i.e. a total of 13 pence. He was found guilty to the value of eight pence and whipped.[137] It would have been a hard jury that failed to shave off a penny or two in these situations, even if the items were worth a shilling.

However, the process went much further. In many situations, down-valuing seems to have become almost institutionalised, just as it would be for the following two centuries, with juries methodically reducing stolen goods of small or medium value to below the 12 pence threshold. It has been suggested that on the late sixteenth century Home Circuit few people were found guilty of stealing goods worth between a shilling and ten shillings, and that those cases where juries did convict for such (capital) sums usually involved defendants who could plead benefit of clergy, or instances in which the crime had involved an aggravating feature, such as an assault.[138]

134. Cockburn, *Calendar of Assize Records. Hertfordshire Indictments: Elizabeth I*, p. 6.
135. Cockburn, *Calendar of Assize Records. Essex Indictments: Elizabeth I*, pp. 155–159.
136. Cockburn, *Calendar of Assize Records. Hertfordshire Indictments: Elizabeth I*, p. 117.
137. *Ibid*, p. 126.
138. Bellamy, *The Criminal Trial*, p. 125.

A selection of cases from Hertfordshire is indicative. For fairly standard examples, from the Summer Assizes in July 1592, can be considered the two men who were accused (in separate trials) of stealing shirts, sheets, and linen valued at three shillings and 2s 10d. Both men were convicted to the value of ten pence.[139] Similarly, in March 1597 William Dowsinge was indicted at the same forum for stealing two shirts worth 3s 4d, but found guilty to the value of ten pence. At the same sessions, Robert Heynes received an identical disposal after being accused of stealing three pecks of maslin (a mixture of different types of grain) worth three shillings.[140] At a slightly higher value, at the same forum, in March 1585 William Royle, accused of stealing five shillings worth of curtains from a house in Waltham Cross, was convicted to the value of ten pence. At the same sessions Richard Hayward received the same verdict after stealing capons valued (again) at five shillings. More dramatically, in July 1596 a pair of labourers were accused of stealing two bushels of meal worth eight shillings and a piece of sack valued at six pence but merely convicted of petty theft.[141] Jury down-valuing in these situations is probably unsurprising. Jurors would regularly see complainants down-valuing their own goods by similar amounts so that they could prosecute for petty theft.

Nevertheless, some cases were more extreme, involving thefts valued at well above ten shillings, albeit that these usually occurred when the jury thought there were mitigating factors. At the Hertford Assizes in March 1597, Edward Reyday of Wadesmill was indicted for grand larceny, having allegedly stolen a cloak and three felt hats worth a total of 16 shillings. He was found guilty to the value of eleven pence and whipped.[142] However, this degree of mercy was unusual.

Some indication of the frequency with which such down-valuing was taking place by the late sixteenth century can be seen at the Hertford Assizes held in March 1597, where 14 cases of grand larceny were indicted and prosecuted to some form of a conviction. Two of these were for horse theft, which had been a capital form of theft for several decades, irrespective of the value of the animal, and so can be disregarded. Five

---

139. Cockburn, *Calendar of Assize Records. Hertfordshire Indictments: Elizabeth I*, p. 94.
140. *Ibid*, p. 126.
141. *Ibid*, p. 55 and p. 122.
142. *Ibid*, p. 126.

of the remaining 12 cases produced guilty verdicts for the full offence. These were for ascribed values of between 33 shillings and £11. Seven cases were down-valued to petty theft. The lowest of these was reduced from 13 pence to eight pence and the highest from 16s to eleven pence. Another case involved a reduction of a valuation of 6s (a sheep) to 10d. However, four cases involved sums of between 3s and 3s 6d being reduced to ten pence.[143] Thus, six of seven down-valued cases were from an original value of less than six shillings.

Such down-valuing was certainly not confined to the assizes. For example, at the Epiphany Quarter Sessions for Essex in 1584, Nicholas Samewell was indicted for breaking into the close of William Goore and stealing three aprons valued at 18 pence, but found guilty of petty theft to the value of five pence.[144] Similarly, at the Epiphany Quarter Sessions for the same county in 1599, William Seaman, a labourer from Barking, was indicted for stealing three geese (accurately) valued at three shillings in his home parish. He was convicted of petty larceny and sentenced to the customary whipping.[145] At the Surrey Quarter Sessions held at Reigate in April 1598 Francis Constable and John Kneller from Epsom were indicted for grand larceny, accused of stealing two sheep worth ten shillings the previous February. Constable was acquitted, but Kneller was found guilty to the value of ten pence. A labourer, he was probably illiterate, so the decision saved him from a death penalty if the test was applied properly (not always the case).[146] Similarly, when a man named Read was accused of stealing a sheep in Charing, in Kent, he swiftly confessed when questioned and blamed his crime on a "wante of victuals". He was indicted for grand larceny, the sheep being valued at ten shillings (quite a lot for such an animal). He pleaded not guilty at the Epiphany Quarter Sessions held at Canterbury in 1602, and the jury down-valued the animal to just ten pence, so that he was, presumably, whipped and discharged.[147]

---

143. *Ibid*, pp. 125–131.
144. ERO Q/SR 87/101, 102.
145. ERO Q/SR 144/40.
146. Cockburn, *Calendar of Assize Records. Surrey Indictments: Elizabeth I*, p. 470.
147. Knafla, *Kent at Law 1602*, p. 116.

Furthermore, down-valuing was found throughout the country, not merely on the Home Circuit. For example, at the Chester Great Sessions in 1607, Daniel Casman, accused of stealing several cheeses, was found guilty to the value of just ten pence. At the same sessions, James Hopwood, accused of stealing a number of hats, was also found guilty to the value of ten pence.[148]

Other Forms of Jury Mitigation

Although artificial down-valuing in grand-larceny cases was the most common form of jury equity in property cases, it was not unique. The growing number of crimes put beyond the reach of benefit of clergy during the sixteenth century meant that the absence of another, essential element of a capital offence could also be vital in making it a non-capital crime — for example, that a break-in to domestic premises had occurred in daylight, rather than at night, whatever the reality. Thus, at the Essex Assizes held at Brentwood in June 1597, John Vincent, a Hornchurch labourer, was indicted for burglary. It was alleged that he had broken into a house during the night and stolen a firkin of butter worth ten shillings and a shirt valued at two shillings. He pleaded not guilty and was merely convicted of "felony", meaning simple grand larceny in this context. This was a clergyable offence, unlike burglary (after 1576); Vincent claimed the privilege, was deemed able to read, and so escaped a death sentence.[149]

At about the same time, Anne Clarke was an extremely active Colchester cutpurse. In 1565 secretly stealing goods worth a shilling or more from the person had been withdrawn from clergy (8 Eliz. I c. 4). However, picking pockets of goods below 12 pence in value remained petty theft, and thus was not capital, even if done secretly. When Clarke was finally brought to trial at Colchester Borough Sessions, on five separate counts of cutting purses in its market, despite strong prosecution evidence, she was found guilty of only one crime; the value of goods taken in this case was reduced to a mere ten pence, making it a case of petty

---

148. TNA CHES 24/109/1.
149. ERO T/A 418/64/62.

theft, for which she was whipped, rather than capital pickpocketing. Much is explained when it is appreciated that she was only 13-years-old.[150]

Similarly, when Thomas Bacon and two other men were tried for (capital) highway robbery at the Surrey Assizes in July 1578, they were merely convicted of assault (a misdemeanour), albeit committed on a public road, followed by clergyable grand larceny (theft of a cloak, dagger, and sword). All three then claimed and were granted clergy.[151]

Furthermore, where a defendant was accused of more than one count, some of which were clergyble and others not, juries could convict of the former and acquit of the latter. This occurred at the Surrey Assizes in July 1582, when a Streatham butcher named Andrew Ady was accused of stealing sheep and a horse from an unknown man. He was merely convicted for the (clergyable) sheep. Oddly, it seems that he was formally granted the privilege only when he appeared at the same forum more than 18 months later.[152]

---

150. Samaha, "Hanging for Felony", p. 769.
151. Cockburn, *Calendar of Assize Records. Surrey Indictments: Elizabeth I*, p. 177.
152. *Ibid*, p. 233 and p. 254.

CHAPTER 15

Benefit of Clergy, Pregnancy, and Pardons

Introduction

This chapter considers three mechanisms by which those who had gone to trial and been capitally convicted could avoid death. Two of them were decided at court. After a guilty plea or verdict was returned in a felony case, convicts would be asked whether they had anything to say prior to sentence being passed. This provided an opportunity for males to ask for benefit of clergy and females to "plead their bellies", i.e. claim to be pregnant. Where they applied, these two privileges might allow the convicts to escape execution, the mandatory penalty for all felonies other than petty theft. For example, at the Hertford Assizes in February 1584, four people were capitally convicted. Two of them were horse thieves (by then an unclergyable form of theft) and sentenced to hang. However, another man successfully claimed benefit of clergy, and a woman successfully pleaded her belly.[153]

Even if they were not able to rely on these two privileges, those who had been capitally convicted might still escape death, if they could secure a pardon from the Crown, following a temporary adjournment authorised by the trial judge. Thus, at the Lent Assizes for Surrey in 1530, a shoemaker named Jacob Barre was convicted of stealing an old horse worth just 12 shillings after breaking into the close of John Westbroke at Beddington. Even so, his gaol calendar later recorded that he had been pardoned.[154] All three expedients were employed at the Essex Quarter Sessions of Easter 1566, where 14 people were convicted of, or pleaded

---

153. Cockburn, *Calendar of Assize Records. Hertfordshire Indictments: Elizabeth I*, pp. 30–33 and pp. 51–52.
154. SHC LM/961/1.

guilty to, felony. Of these, six were clergied, one was pardoned, and two women successfully claimed pregnancy, so that just five were sentenced to death.[155] Similarly, at the assizes held at Hertford in March 1580, 20 people were tried, all but five of them in single-defendant hearings. Nine were acquitted outright (45 per cent of the total), and eleven (55 per cent) were found guilty. However, of the latter, only four (38 per cent of those convicted) were immediately sentenced to hang; the remainder (well over half of those found guilty) being pardoned or reprieved (two cases), found to be pregnant (one case), or successfully claiming benefit of clergy (four cases).[156]

None of these mechanisms for avoiding execution was new in Tudor England; they had been available throughout the late medieval period. For example, four of the 33 convicts whose cases have been preserved and who were tried at gaol delivery in Northumberland, Cumberland, and Westmoreland during the 1440s and 1450s avoided death using these expedients: there was one successful claim of pregnancy, one of clergy, and one of pardon (the nature of the fourth case is uncertain).[157]

However, as the above figures suggest, the number of people who escaped death by one of these three routes was fairly modest in the mid-fifteenth century, both in absolute numbers (only a small number of people were capitally convicted at this time) and, more pertinently, as a total proportion of those found guilty. Clearly these privileges were not being claimed or granted lightly. By contrast, clemency on such grounds was being extended much more readily by the latter decades of the sixteenth century. Just 41 per cent of all those found guilty of felony on the Home Circuit between 1559 and 1624 were sentenced to death, and some of these probably received late pardons that allowed them to escape the noose.[158]

To some extent, the increased use of such privileges mitigated the consequences of an increasingly efficient criminal justice system that remained wedded to the death-for-felony rule, and greatly reduced the number of convicted felons who were executed in Tudor England, very

---

155. ERO Q/SR 18/41.
156. Cockburn, *Calendar of Assize Records. Hertfordshire Indictments: Elizabeth I*, pp. 30–33.
157. Neville, "Gaol Delivery", p. 59.
158. Wood, "The Deep Roots", p. 406.

high though the figure still was. Whether it would not have been better to radically revise the criminal justice system, as was occasionally suggested, rather than having recourse to what were often fairly arbitrary and even entirely fictitious mechanisms to moderate it is, of course, open to debate. In 1500 a visiting Venetian was struck by the conservatism of the English on historic privileges such as benefit of clergy, feeling that if the King should "propose to change any old established rule, it would seem to every Englishman as if his life were taken from him". Even so, he (mistakenly) thought that if Henry VII lived long enough he would do away with many of them.[159] Nevertheless, such privileges were subjected to increased — albeit not necessarily stricter — royal control and supervision during the Tudor era, and occasional proposals for more radical reform were considered, if not acted upon.

Benefit of Clergy

The notion of clerical immunity from secular courts and punishments dated back to the Council of Nicaea in 325, when Constantine argued that, as clerics were sent to judge men, they could not be judged by them. The practice of allowing clergy their own forums spread, to various degrees, throughout much of Christendom during the Middle Ages.[160] In England benefit of clergy was largely a legacy of the church-state struggles of the medieval period and the trauma occasioned by, inter alia, the murder of Archbishop Thomas Becket after his quarrel with Henry II. The English privilege allowed criminal clerics ("criminous clerks") to escape temporal punishment if they insisted on being handed over to the ecclesiastical courts before or (after the fourteenth century) following trial and conviction for felony in a secular forum. Church courts could not shed blood, so that those accorded benefit of clergy necessarily could not be executed or mutilated.

The Reformation and its conclusion that the state is superior to the church might have occasioned the end of the privilege. Nevertheless,

---

159. Anon, *A Relation, or Rather a True Account*, p. 37.
160. Lesley Skousen, *Redefining Benefit of Clergy During the English Reformation*. University of Wisconsin MA thesis, 2008, p. 65.

many English observers, such as Christopher St Germain, who had fairly strong anti-clerical inclinations, were adamant that it had been granted not by spiritual authority but by Parliament, and was based on the "olde customes and maximes of the law of the realme". This meant that the bishops had control only over who was to be granted clergy by authority of the King's law. Although the granting of clergy and sanctuary were under the control of Parliament, this body had decided not to abolish them.[161] More correctly, Ferdinando Pulton, writing at the start of the seventeenth century, thought that, although the privilege had its "beginning from the Cannon Law, and not from the common Law of this Realme, yet it hath bin confirmed by divers parliaments". Nevertheless, St Germain's analysis, even if historically inaccurate, allowed benefit of clergy to survive and flourish throughout the Tudor era and well beyond.

By the early 1300s the King's courts were usually prepared to accept that any man able to read a biblical passage in the Latin of the Vulgate must be a clergyman.[162] This was expressly recognised by Parliament in 1351, and meant that the production of formal ordination papers, let alone appearing tonsured and in clerical garb, was not necessary to ensure protection for members of the clergy who were arrested without ready proof of their status. This conflation of literacy with ordination was almost correct in 1350, but increasingly less so in ensuing centuries, when the number of laymen who could read increased significantly, and they, too, started to claim the privilege on a regular basis. Formally accepting this situation, in 1482 the Westminster judges agreed that any man whose literacy was proven should be delivered to the ordinary (court chaplain), even if he was obviously not a clergyman employed at an ecclesiastical institution. In about 1490, after an ordinary's deputy failed to accept a member of the Middle Temple (i.e. a lawyer) who, unsurprisingly, could read as a cleric (the deputy may have been bribed), the court fined the ordinary and forced him to accept the lawyer as a cleric.[163]

As a result of these developments, by the end of the fifteenth century the privilege had become heavily secularised. Even so, some traces of its

---

161. St. Germain, *Doctor and Student*, p. 322.
162. Thomson, *The Early Tudor Church*, p. 92.
163. Baker, *Oxford History, Vol. VI*, p. 532.

origins survived. Obviously, women were still excluded, as they could not be clergymen. However, a few arcane restrictions also survived with regard to men. At the Middlesex gaol delivery held at Newgate at Michaelmas 1507, Thomas White was convicted of theft; he then claimed clergy, but the King's attorney alleged that he had married a widow, making him ineligible for the privilege. The case was referred to King's Bench, where the Bishop of Worcester provided evidence that this was indeed the case. The issue was not that he was married, per se, but that he had married a widow. A man who had been married to a woman who was not a widow remained eligible to become a priest after the death of his wife. But if the man had been married more than once, or if his wife had been a widow when they married, he was no longer eligible for ordination. As a result, the court ruled that White should be hanged.[164] The lay authorities raised this issue again after a tailor named John Vaughan was convicted at gaol delivery in Bristol in 1515. He claimed clergy but the mayor of the city asserted that he was married to a widow, and so not entitled to the privilege, writing to the Vicar General and asking him to certify this issue. (The outcome is unknown.)[165] There were several other, similar cases in the early sixteenth century, suggesting that the Crown was sometimes looking for technicalities to limit benefit of clergy.

Even as recourse to clergy expanded, there was concern that it allowed undeserving laymen to avoid punishment, and resentment in the church at its privilege being shared with those who were not genuine clerics. In 1455 the House of Commons submitted a petition to the King complaining that benefit of clergy was contributing to the emergence of career criminals and high levels of offending. Certainly the only example offered in the *Year Books* of a repeat offender around this time involved a layman. In 1484 a merchant named Richard Hains was indicted for robbery on numerous occasions and in multiple counties but always claimed clergy and escaped punishment.[166] Such abuse required reform, if the privilege was to survive. This duly took place in the fourth year of the reign of Henry VII.

---

164. McSheffrey, "Sanctuary Seekers". I am grateful for a communication on this issue from Professor McSheffrey.
165. Thomson, *The Early Tudor Church*, pp. 95–96.
166. Skousen, *Redefining Benefit*, p. 21.

In 1489 Parliament upheld the clerical privilege in full but (effectively) created a second, weaker form by limiting literate laymen (i.e. those not truly in holy orders) to claiming the privilege on just one occasion (4 Henry VII. c. 13). This was prompted by a fear that "upon Trust of the Privilege of the Church, divers persons lettered, have been the more bold to commit Murder, Rape, Robbery, Theft, and other mischievous Deeds; because they have been continually admitted to the Benefit of the Clergy as often as they did offend".[167] (In practice, this rule may have been applied on some occasions even before the statute came into force.)[168] This divergence between the two forms of the privilege would last until 1536.

To prevent the privilege being claimed more than once, the gaoler was to brand clergied laymen on the brawn of the thumb of the left hand with a hot iron before the judge(s) in open court.[169] Sir Thomas Smith noted in the 1560s that a successful claimant would be "marked with the letter T for a theefe, or M for a mansleer". Despite this observation, it seems that after 1531 many of those who were allowed clergy for the lesser charge of manslaughter would also receive a T, murder having been permanently withdrawn from the privilege. (This was later to become known as the Tyburn T).

The brand alerted the authorities to the need to search out proof of a convict's previous convictions. The "mark betrayeth them to have been arraigned of felony before, whereby they are sure at that time to have no mercy".[170] It was not a record of the earlier conviction per se. In *Snore's Case*, heard in the Court of King's Bench early in the sixteenth century, it was noted of the accused that although it "appeared plainly to the court by showing and by view of his left hand that he had previously been burned with a 'T,' yet the court would not give judgment upon him until the record was certified". In 1510, in *R* v *Malory*, an appeal of felony brought against three men in the same forum produced convictions, but the guilty trio pleaded clergy and "read well enough". However, a stranger then told the court that they had previously been convicted

---

167. Jeaffreson, *Middlesex County Records: Vol. 1*, p. xxxiv.
168. Blatcher, *The Court of King's Bench*, p. 57.
169. Jeaffreson, *Middlesex County Records: Vol. 1*, p. xxxiv.
170. Harrison, *Elizabethan England*, p. 244.

at Winchester, and pointed out the T brands on their hands. The court then adjourned until the records of their convictions at the Hampshire Assizes could be certified.[171] In 1518 the central courts began to supervise the granting of clergy to those tried in the provinces slightly more strictly. Lists of men to whom it had been given were solicited by writ, this practice being regularised by statute in 1543 (34 & 35 Henry VIII c. 14).[172] How carefully this was done is debatable.

After 1489 genuine clerics were given a day to produce documentary proof of their orders so as to avoid the need for branding after claiming clergy. If no papers were found within that period, the ordinary could also vouch for the priest, if so willing, as an alternative to use of the hot iron; presumably his decision was usually based on conversing with the convict about ecclesiastical matters. However, clerics could still use the privilege repeatedly. Prior to the Reformation, but after 1489, it was alleged that some professional criminals, in order to circumvent the one claim limitation, took up minor clerical orders, such as psalmists, lectors, cantors, exorcists, and acolytes, for which the qualifications were slender, and the duties often quite modest (lighting candles, reading biblical passages, singing in a religious house, etc.). According to Pope Leo X (1475–1521), this meant that, sometimes, the "crimes of ne'er-do-wells remain[ed] unpunished'.[173] There were a few recorded examples of this occurring. For example, in 1513, when Hugh Boswell was indicted for feloniously stealing chalices from a church, at the Lent Assizes for Northamptonshire, he claimed to be a clergyman, alleging that he had been made an acolyte at the house of the Carmelite Friars in Alnwick, in (distant) Cumberland, and then a sub-deacon by the diocese of Carlisle some years earlier.[174]

---

171. Baker, *Sir John Spelman*, pp. 43–44 and p. 67.
172. Cockburn, *Calendar of Assize Records. Home Circuit Indictments: Elizabeth and James 1: Introduction*, pp. 118–119.
173. Arthur Ogle, *The Tragedy of the Lollards' Tower* (Oxford: Pen-in-Hand, 1949), pp. 167–168.
174. Baker, *Sir John Port*, p. 39.

End of Special Status for Clergy

Until 1536, clergymen normally enjoyed a significant advantage over lay claimants who claimed the privilege, not having to "read" if they had other proof of their status, not being confined to a single claim, not being branded when clergy was granted, and being able to claim it for several offences for which it had been withdrawn from laymen.[175]

This bifurcated system of benefit of clergy changed in 1536, when the distinction between clerical and lay forms of benefit of clergy was temporarily eliminated by statute (28 Henry VIII c. 1), which effectively declared that the justice system would treat all criminals as laymen, and brand clerks and laity alike when granting offenders benefit of clergy. The final lines of the statute noted that those "within holy order shall from henceforth stand and be under the same pains and dangers for the offences contained in any of the said statutes, and be used and ordered to all intents and purposes as other persons not being within holy orders". Parliament made this condition permanent in 1540, the final paragraph of the statute reiterating that those within holy orders, would be "burnt in the hand in like manner and form as lay clerks be accustomed in such cases". The process by which benefit of clergy had become a secular legal loophole independent of any connection to ordination was complete.[176]

Multiple Claims

When it came to limiting laymen (and clerics after 1536) to a single claim of clergy the theory and practice appear to have parted company, on a fairly regular basis, well before the end of the sixteenth century, albeit not as frequently as would be the case 100 years later. By the 1590s Edward Hext could claim that branding was often being carried out in such a perfunctory manner that the mark quickly disappeared and failed to alert the courts to a previous claim.[177]

---

175. Skousen, *Redefining Benefit*, p. 79.
176. *Ibid*, p. 65 and p. 83.
177. Tawney and Power, *Tudor Economic Documents, Vol. 2*, p. 340.

Almost a quarter of a century after the end of the Tudor era, in January 1627, the Kent Quarter Sessions discussed the problems attendant on proving that someone had been clergied on an earlier occasion. It could be exceptionally difficult to establish to the satisfaction of a jury (as was required) that a man had received the privilege within the same county, let alone in another shire. The record would normally have been "entred either upon the indictment, or in some other place soe dispersed and confused, as that it is hard to finde out and almost impossible to have in a readiness the recordes thereof". As a result, the privilege was frequently claimed more than once. The JPs resolved to deal with this problem by preparing a special parchment book that would be produced at each quarter sessions in which the clerk of the peace would carefully record the names, places of abode, and offences of all those who were clergied in Kent: "And that booke shalbe the record to trye whether when any such shall crave his book againe, whether he hath beene formerlie burnte in the hand or noe."[178] Of course, this would not be of value in detecting those clergied outside the county, and, as Hext observed, such men would often "change both name and habytt and commonly go ynto other shires so as no man shall knowe them".[179]

However, despite such concerns, it seems that the courts would sometimes knowingly (rather than unwittingly) grant lay felons a second use of the privilege as a way of mitigating the death-for-felony rule. Unsurprisingly, this was particularly common at Elizabethan quarter sessions, which were increasingly reluctant to pass death sentences. Nevertheless, it sometimes appears to have occurred earlier in the century and took place at the higher jury forum as well. In 1589 an Essex JP, Sir John Smythe, complained to Lord Burghley that assizes judges on the Home Circuit were allowing clergy to convicts who had already received it on several previous occasions "under pretence of pity and mercy".[180]

Even so, earlier claims were not invariably missed, even at the lower jury court. When, at the Epiphany Quarter Sessions for Essex in 1582, Thomas Lawrence was convicted of breaking into a house at Dedham

---

178. Melling, *Crime and Punishment*, p. 185.
179. Tawney and Power, *Tudor Economic Documents, Vol. 2*, p. 340.
180. Cockburn, *A History of English Assizes*, p. 125.

and stealing clothes and cloth worth £5, it was noticed that he "hathe byn burned in hand as a Clarke."[181] On the Home Circuit, at the Old Bailey, and at King's Bench (and presumably elsewhere), periodic hearings were held to determine whether a convict who had claimed clergy had already been granted the privilege, after court officials' suspicions were aroused.

For example, in 1510 an abjuror named Richard Sandy appeared at King's Bench, apparently having failed to leave the realm. He claimed benefit of clergy (for the original offence) to avoid execution, and duly read as a clerk. However, the King's attorney then claimed that he was the same man as one Richard Saunders of Kingsclere, who had been convicted of robbery at the Winchester Assizes in Lent 1505, and had then successfully claimed benefit of clergy, and been branded with a T. Sandy denied that he was Saunders, but a jury found against him, and he was sentenced to hang.[182]

As this case suggests, throughout the Tudor era a specially empanelled jury — different from that which had convicted the claimant — would have to determine the issue of a previous claim. Otherwise, the hearing was similar to a normal trial, although in *Malory* (1510) the three appellees could not, apparently, challenge the jurors chosen to decide the matter because "such an inquest is only an inquest of office".[183] Frequently an adjournment would be granted after a suspect claim was made to allow a search of court records. For example, in July 1595 Geoffrey Smith from Headcorn, in Kent, was remanded in custody after being convicted of stealing eight oxen worth £40 in two thefts because the court was uncertain whether he had had the privilege before. His claim was allowed at the following sessions.[184]

In a strange case from November 1511, a man named Saville was found guilty at the Newgate gaol delivery of robbery and pleaded clergy, but the King's attorney claimed that he had had a previous felony conviction clergied, so he was remanded in custody while investigations were made. Nothing was found, and he pleaded and was granted clergy on

181. ERO Q/SR 79/135.
182. McSheffrey, *Seeking Sanctuary*, p. 103.
183. Baker, *Sir John Spelman*, pp. 43–44.
184. Cockburn, *Calendar of Assize Records. Kent Indictments: Elizabeth I*, p. 375.

his next appearance, and was delivered into the custody of the ordinary. However, this was not his first *claim*; he had apparently claimed the privilege unsuccessfully in 1502, although he had still escaped the gallows (probably by a pardon), and appears to have learned to read in the intervening nine years.[185]

The Crown appears to have actively challenged claimants on this issue only when it was fairly confident of success. At the Surrey Assizes just four hearings of this type, involving five men, have been preserved for the Elizabethan period. All resulted in findings that the men had received the privilege on an earlier occasion, so that they were sentenced to death. For example, at the assizes held in February 1568, John Abbott was convicted of grand larceny and claimed clergy. The matter was adjourned to the July Assizes, when Abbott was found to have made an earlier claim, and was duly refused the privilege. In another case, James Slade unsuccessfully claimed clergy after conviction for grand larceny at the Southwark Assizes in March 1574, just a year after being granted the privilege at the same forum for the same crime.[186] As this suggests, claiming clergy a second time in the same county, within a short period of time, was dangerous; recognition was much more likely, and it was far easier to secure the earlier record and other evidence to prove identity.

The situation was broadly the same in other criminal forums. For example, in May 1559, at the Old Bailey, Thomas Shaw pleaded guilty to stealing silver goblets in the parish of St Clement Danes, Middlesex. He then "asked for the book". However, the "Crown" (probably the court clerk in practice) claimed that he had been clergied on an earlier occasion, an allegation that Shaw denied. A jury subsequently concluded that he was indeed the same previously convicted "clerk", and he was sentenced to death.[187]

A letter written in early 1591 illustrates some of the workings of the clergy process. Geoffrey Nightingale wrote to Baron Robert Clarke, noting that Andrew Howe, who was about to come for trial at the Essex Quarter Sessions for stealing three of his bullocks (grand larceny), had

---

185. McSheffrey, "Sanctuary Seekers".
186. Cockburn, *Calendar of Assize Records. Surrey indictments: Elizabeth I*, p. 66 and p. 119.
187. Jeaffreson, *Middlesex County Records: Vol. 1*, pp. 34–37.

also confessed to his examining JP (Sir Thomas Lucas) to having been tried and convicted 12 months earlier at the same forum (held at Chelmsford), for stealing eight other bullocks; he had successfully claimed clergy, been burnt in the hand, and freed. Nightingale noted that the county clerk of the peace had the record of this procedure ready to show the judge should Howe attempt to claim it again. (Just to blacken the individual further, he alleged that he had learned that six years earlier Howe had raped a young woman, who could not be traced.) Nightingale finished his letter by saying that, "laying theise his often offences together, whether he deserveth to be cutt of or not, I referr the same to your worships good consideracon". It seems clear that he sought a death sentence if, as he hoped, Howe was convicted of stealing his animals, and was well aware that, in the normal course of events, clergy would readily be granted at the lower jury forum by this time.[188]

Criticism of Benefit of Clergy

Benefit of clergy was subject to much criticism throughout its post-medieval existence. It was hard to justify such an idiosyncratic, socially biased, and gender restricted privilege, and attempts to do so, such as William Harrison's suggestion that it was devised to encourage a "love of learning" among the country's inhabitants, did not ring true.[189] Many observers, both foreign and domestic, thought it absurd and its consequences malign. In 1500, before the removal of clergy from serious felonies had properly got under way, a Venetian thought that literate criminals were effectively "liberated from the power of the law".[190] At the other end of the century, Edward Hext still feared that the privilege, and the increasingly watered-down test that allowed it, undermined the deterrent effect of the criminal justice system.[191]

In the eighteenth century William Blackstone was to praise the way in which benefit of clergy had been adapted under English law so that it was converted, by gradual mutations, into a merciful mitigation of the

---

188. ERO Q/SR 115/28.
189. Harrison, *Elizabethan England,* p. 244.
190. Anon, *A Relation, or Rather A True Account,* p. 36.
191. Tawney and Power, *Tudor Economic Documents,* p. 340.

general law. (The literacy test was totally abandoned in 1706 and women had been allowed an equivalent privilege in the 1600s.) However, a more rationally thought out reform of the death-for-felony rule and its exceptions might have been better. Parliament did consider a comprehensive reform of the privilege in 1589. If passed, a bill that year would have meant that the privilege would be "denied to som who might before have it, but granted to more to whome it was before denied". This proposal may have been officially inspired, and the work of a committee of lawyers appointed before the Parliament began. Even so, it did not come to fruition.[192] As some of the criticism suggests, benefit of clergy had the potential to be very unfair.

Unfairness

Benefit of clergy could be highly indiscriminate. Even at the end of the period, those convicted of quite extreme instances of grand larceny could escape death by claiming the privilege, while fairly modest cases of theft, only slightly over the petty-larceny limit, might lead to execution for the illiterate. For example, at the Hertford Assizes in July 1592, two men, both described as labourers, were convicted, in different trials, of grand larceny and claimed clergy. George Webb had stolen sheets and towels to the value of about £1. He was unable to read and was sentenced to death. By contrast, John Higgyns had been found guilty of stealing sheep and lambs worth five times as much, but was literate and so allowed the privilege.[193] At about the same time, Robert Harding, a Sussex glover, appears to have almost been a professional animal-thief, but always steered clear of taking horses (by then an unclergyable form of grand larceny.) At the Surrey Assizes in February 1592, he was convicted of, or pleaded guilty to, five counts of stealing cattle and sheep valued at almost £9. The guilty plea to one of the counts probably reflected the fact that he was literate, and had not previously been convicted of a felony, although tried and acquitted for stealing a sheep a year earlier. He knew that he could claim

---

192. Dean, *Law-Making and Society*, pp. 56–58 and pp. 190–191.
193. Cockburn, *Calendar of Assize Records. Hertfordshire Indictments: Elizabeth I*, p. 94.

clergy when convicted, as indeed occurred.[194] In an even more extreme case, in November 1554 Henry Williams and an accomplice stole various chattels and, more significantly, foreign gold and silver coins worth almost £24 from the house of the Lord Steward at Westminster. Both men pleaded guilty, immediately asked for their book, "read like clerks", and were handed over to the ordinary.[195]

This unfairness was especially blatant in the case of co-defendants. At the Essex Assizes in March 1561, a labourer and a husbandman were jointly convicted of burglary (then still a clergyable offence). The (slightly) more prosperous husbandman was successful in his claim for clergy; the labourer was sentenced to death.[196] Similarly, in July 1589 two men were convicted of the same theft after stealing two cows and a steer from a close at Langham, in Essex. One of them was allowed his clergy, but the other could not read, and so was sentenced to hang.[197] Because literacy was closely connected to social class, on those occasions where the test was applied strictly it inevitably discriminated against the poor, even though they might often be more deserving of clemency if accused of property crimes, as a few contemporary observers noted.

State of Literacy

Given that literacy was ostensibly the test for clergy, it is pertinent to ask how many men in Tudor England could read. (Reading and writing were often seen as separate skills, the former being mastered before the latter.) The number was slowly increasing. By the end of the fifteenth century, a few of the more prominent livery companies in London required that apprentices have a basic degree of literacy before qualifying. Thomas More suggested that well over 40 per cent of men in the early sixteenth century could not read, indicating that just over half could.[198] However, most modern academics would place the functionally illiterate proportion

194. Cockburn, *Calendar of Assize Records. Surrey indictments: Elizabeth I*, p. 357 and p. 376.
195. Jeaffreson, *Middlesex County Records: Vol. 1*, pp. 17–21.
196. Cockburn, *Calendar of Assize Records. Essex Indictments: Elizabeth I*, p. 19.
197. *Ibid*, p. 336.
198. David Cressy, *Literacy and the Social Order: Reading and Writing in Tudor and Stuart England* (Cambridge: Cambridge University Press, 1980), p. 44.

of the male population at a very much higher level, especially outside London. Although the Elizabethan era experienced a significant growth in literacy, not least because of the emphasis on Bible reading contained in reformed forms of Christianity, the great majority of men below the status of yeoman (and even one or two above) were still totally illiterate at the end of the Tudor period.[199] Those lacking even the smallest ability to read and write usually signed documents with a mark instead of their name. Using this and other indications, it has been suggested that, at the start of the seventeenth century, two-thirds of Englishmen were still, effectively, illiterate.[200] Other estimates place the total even higher.

Literacy was particularly low in rural areas, i.e. most of Tudor England. By way of illustration, in January 1591 10 of the prominent inhabitants of Marks Tey in Essex petitioned the authorities on behalf of a physically challenged couple from the village. Henry Cornwall, minister of the parish, and two other men signed the document. However the other seven petitioners marked it.[201] Similarly, in the early 1600s the village of Hernhill petitioned the Kent Quarter Sessions about the allegedly excessive number of widows and fatherless children resident in their parish, asking that they might be relieved elsewhere. The letter was written and signed by the local vicar. However, eight of the remaining nine petitioners were not even able to leave a written initial (itself not conclusive evidence of the ability to read). Significantly, these included four officeholders from the village (two churchwardens and two overseers of the poor), positions that were traditionally associated with relatively high social status in the local community.[202]

Proportion of Successful Claims

Despite low levels of literacy, and the disproportionate number of criminals drawn from the "lower orders", who were more likely than the

---

199. Keith Wrightson and David Levine, *Poverty and Piety in an English Village: Terling, 1525–1700* (Oxford: Clarendon, 1995), pp. 15–16.
200. Cressy, *Literacy and the Social Order*, p. 59.
201. ERO Q/SR 115/61.
202. Linda Taylor, "Literacy and Book Ownership in Seventeenth century Faversham", *Archaeologia Cantiana*, Vol. 134, p. 217.

national average to be unable to read, a relatively large number of convicts were successful in claiming benefit of clergy, especially after the middle of the 1500s. This had not always been the case. The numbers and, more significantly, the proportion of successful claims had been much more modest at the start of the Tudor period, before increasing after the early decades of the sixteenth century, albeit that this occurred at varying rates around the country, with the extremities apparently lagging behind the centre.

On one estimate, Middlesex records suggest that 32 per cent of the felons capitally convicted in the county were successfully asking for the privilege by the late 1550s.[203] Typically, after one sessions held at Newgate in 1560, a third of them received clemency in this fashion (they "wher cast xij, and vj was bornyd in ther hand").[204] This high number might not be altogether surprising, given the partly urban background of the convicts in that county. However, fairly high totals were also found in the provinces, especially towards the close of the century. For example, in the years from 1566 to 1570, successful claims for benefit of clergy had already reached about 33 per cent at the Essex Assizes, but only about 15 per cent at the (equivalent) Court of Great Sessions in Cheshire. Even so, the Essex figure had grown to more than half by the 1580s, with Cheshire reaching almost 39 per cent in the first half of the 1590s.[205]

The (preserved) cases that were tried at the Hertford Assizes held in March 1589 can also be considered. All four capitally convicted men were described as labourers, and in three cases were convicted of very serious cases of grand larceny, each having taken oxen or cows valued at £5, £10, and £12 (beyond the realistic scope of jury down-valuing). The fourth case was more modest, involving goods worth less than 12 shillings. All four men claimed and were allowed clergy. Similarly, at the same forum in March 1590, 15 men were convicted of grand larceny in 13 trials; all successfully claimed benefit of clergy.[206]

Sometimes, even vagabonds were granted the privilege, although literacy cannot have been very high in this group. In June 1575 Thomas

203. Cressy, *Literacy and the Social Order*, p. 17.
204. Nichols, *The Diary of Henry Machyn*, pp. 221–239.
205. Sharpe, *Judicial Punishment in England*, p. 41.
206. Cockburn, *Calendar of Assize Records. Hertfordshire Indictments, Elizabeth I*, pp. 186–188.

Poynt was convicted of vagrancy in Southwark at the Surrey Assizes, held in Croydon, having been found guilty of the same offence at the March Quarter Sessions (his first such conviction, for which he had been whipped and bored through his right ear). As a repeat offender he faced a potential death sentence, but was deemed able to read.[227]

It is almost inconceivable that all these men, many from poor backgrounds, were properly literate. The explanation for the high success rate probably lies in the nature of the forensic test and the robustness with which it was applied. More men claimed clergy, and there was a greater willingness to grant it.

Administering the Test

Determining literacy (and so the award of clergy) was usually a matter for the court chaplain, or ordinary. This officer was normally a local (to the court) clergyman, appointed by the diocesan bishop to attend assizes and quarter sessions as his representative, although it seems that a trial judge could, in theory, reject his decision, at least after the Reformation. At the Old Bailey the court chaplain was the Newgate Ordinary, who held a permanent position in the prison that contained or (after 1539) was adjacent to the court.

In the absence of the chaplain, the test could not normally be conducted (at least during the late medieval and Tudor era). For example, in 1406 the convicted London thief William Hegge claimed that he was "a clerk, and that he can read etc". Because the ordinary was not present, the court could not proceed further. Hegge was committed to Newgate Prison until the test could be carried out at later sessions.[208] In the Tudor age, in August 1536 Sir Humfrey Wyngfeld wrote to Thomas Cromwell, informing him that, at the last gaol delivery held at Ipswich, three felons had been tried, found guilty, and claimed clergy. However, the See of Norwich being vacant, no ordinary had been appointed to hear them read, so that the justices temporarily reprieved and remanded them in custody pending the tests being conducted (the men subsequently

---

207. Cockburn, *Calendar of Assize Records. Surrey Indictments: Elizabeth I*, p. 136.
208. Riley, *Memorials of London*, pp. 561–566.

escaped from prison).[209] Similarly, at the Surrey Assizes held in Guildford in July 1559, Richard Smythe was convicted of grand larceny and asked for clergy. The ordinary being absent on this occasion, he had to be remanded until the following assizes, when he successfully claimed the privilege.[210]

Unexpected claims for clergy in small jurisdictions could create particular problems in this regard. In February 1541 the vicar of Much Wenlock noted that William Lowe, an 18-year-old Cheshire man, one of two people capitally convicted at the recent quarter sessions in the town, had "desired the priviledge of the Church, saying he could read". This appears to have come as a surprise, as the sessions had to be prorogued for a few days until the local dean, the ordinary for the court, could be summoned to administer the test. Lowe proved to be illiterate, however, and was sentenced to death and executed, having confessed to various robberies.[211]

The mechanism for claiming clergy was relatively straightforward. After the customary request to a convicted felon as to why death should not be passed on him, "The Criminal [would] answer, I demand the benefit of the Clergy". A bible or psalter would then be handed to him, and the chaplain would ask him to read out a passage.[212] As Sir Thomas Smith noted, the convict would then read as well as he could. The ordinary would make up his mind, and the court ask him for his decision: "The commissarie must say *legit* or *non legit*... If he say *legit*, the Judge proceedeth no further to sentence of death: if he say *non*, the Judge forthwith, or the next day proceedeth to sentence". At the Old Bailey, around 1600, the ordinary was, apparently, usually able to decide after just a few words, and this probably reflects practice elsewhere.[213]

By the latter decades of the sixteenth century (if not long before) the passage used to test for literacy was usually either a verse taken from St Matthew's Gospel or (much more commonly) the first verse of Psalm 51 (Psalm 50 according to the Vulgate and Septuagint numbering), which

209. Gairdner, *Letters and Papers, Foreign and Domestic, Henry VIII, Vol. 11*, pp. 103–114.
210. Cockburn, *Calendar of Assize Records. Surrey Indictments: Elizabeth I*, p. 5.
211. Hartshorne, *Sir Thomas Butler*, p. 7.
212. Platter and Busino, *Journals of Two Travellers*, p. 148.
213. *Ibid.*

began, appropriately, "*Miserere mei, Deus, secundum misericordiam tuam*" (Have mercy upon me, O God, according to thy loving kindness.) The latter passage was used so frequently and repetitively that it became known as the "neck verse", and was sometimes committed to memory by those who intended to claim the privilege, even if illiterate. Its use was sufficiently well-known for a character in the pre-Shakespearean *King Leir* (written about 1594) to observe: "I hope your grace will stand/ Between me and my neck-verse if I be/Called in question for opening the King's letter".

The test had not always been so predictable, although as early as 1365 a prisoner in Cumberland was able to recite certain biblical passages, but was found to be illiterate (the judge gave him the bible upside down). His attempt to anticipate the readings suggests that some passages were preferred, even then. (It transpired that two fellow prisoners in Appleby Gaol had taught him certain verses by heart.)[214]

More pertinently, an anonymous medieval morality play titled *Mankind*, written about 1470, has two references to memorising the neck verse, made by the character Newguise. In the first he declares: "Let us con well our neke-verse, that we have not a cheke [check]". In the second, he announces: "Mischief is a convict, for he could [sic] his neck-verse".[215] Nevertheless, in the late fifteenth century the passage was still sometimes chosen at random by the presiding judge, and he never lost this power, even if it was only rarely exercised. In 1616 the well-regarded Recorder of London, Thomas Coventry, personally selected the passage that the ordinary was to give a man convicted of manslaughter, so avoiding use of the neck verse.[216]

Memorising the test became increasingly feasible, even for complete illiterates, when the Great Bible, written in English, temporarily replaced the Latin Vulgate in 1539, and again following the death of Queen Mary. Committing a passage to memory is much more difficult if it is in a

---

214. P. S. King, *The Middlesex Justices, 1590–1640: The commissions of the peace, oyer and terminer and gaol delivery for Middlesex*, Durham University MA thesis, 1972, p. 85; John C. Appleby and Paul Dalton (eds.), *Outlaws in Medieval and Early Modern England: Crime, Government and Society* (Farnham: Ashgate, 2009), p. 81.

215. Act I, Scene 2.

216. Baker, "Criminal Justice at Newgate", p. 315.

foreign language. This development helps to explain (if only in part) the major increase in successful claims of clergy after the middle of the sixteenth century. On other occasions, it seems that someone in the court itself (such as the ordinary/chaplain) might prompt the reader, *sotto voce*. This was often done with the court's connivance, a blind eye being turned to their assistance, unless the presiding judge had strong feelings about the issue, as was the case in 1616, when the Recorder of London ordered that a defendant be "set apart from other the standers by, to the ende no man might prompte him".[217]

When it came to the test for those who were not truly literate, everything turned on decade, forum, offence, and the personal inclinations of the judge, attending justices, court chaplain, and (possibly) other observers. Richard Pulham was convicted at the Canterbury Quarter Sessions in September 1506 for killing John Wode the previous month. He unsuccessfully asked for clergy but was not immediately executed. In June 1507 his case was referred to King's Bench, where he again pleaded clergy. On this occasion he read successfully, and was delivered to the custody of the Archdeacon of Westminster. It is possible that he had learned to read in the meantime.[218] Interestingly, in 1560, the Westminster judges, assembled at Serjeants Inn, considered the legal implications of just such a possibility; they noted that, if a convict failed the test, but his execution was postponed, and he was literate when brought up again, he would be entitled to the privilege, although the gaoler might be punished for allowing him to be taught to read.[219] However, it is much more likely that the difference in decision reflects the rigour with which Pulham's two tests were administered.

Another intriguing case in this regard occurred just after the Tudor period. In February 1609 Thomas Saffold, a butcher from Barling, was convicted of grand larceny at the Essex Assizes after stealing a brown cow. He successfully claimed clergy and presumably was branded and discharged. Three years later, in March 1612, he was convicted before the same forum for the same type of crime (the cow was black on this

---

217. *Ibid.*
218. McSheffrey, "Sanctuary Seekers".
219. *Anon.* (1560) 2 Dyer 205, 73 E.R. 453 1560.

occasion). He claimed clergy again. In theory, of course, this was not permissible because of his earlier claim. However, he was allowed to take the test, but on this occasion was deemed to be unable to read and sentenced to death. It is highly unlikely that he had become illiterate in the meantime! Had a prompting court chaplain indulged him on the earlier occasion? Was a stricter approach taken the second time because it was suspected that he had had clergy before, but it could not conveniently be proved? It is impossible to say.[220]

By the Elizabethan period, Edward Hext was concerned that some JPs at quarter sessions were so lax about granting clergy that convicts were "havynge their books by intreatye of the Justices themselves that cannot read a word".[221] This is unsurprising, given that, by the 1590s, most quarter sessions were reluctant to pass death sentences if they could possibly avoid it. However, such leniency also seems to have occurred in the higher jury court on some occasions.

Even so, many Tudor men were not so fortunate, especially prior to the Elizabethan period. Convicts regularly failed the literacy test, particularly at assizes, and many did not even ask to take it. For example, at the Hertford Assizes in July 1590, William Button was accused of grand larceny after stealing a petticoat and blanket worth ten shillings. He claimed clergy, but was found to be unable to read, and sentenced to death.[222] Occasionally, when two or more men had been convicted of grand larceny at assizes, some would pass and others fail the test, suggesting that it was certainly not a formality.

A successful claim of clergy did not result in immediate release (at least in theory) for most of the first century of the Tudor era. Those granted the privilege did not get off scot free, even if allowed to escape death. A successful convict, whether cleric or layman, was "given as a clerk into the hands of the bishop", putting him under the control of the court chaplain (the same man who had administered the literacy test).[223] Thus in November 1555 Robert Nicholas successfully claimed clergy after pleading guilty to stealing cattle in Middlesex and was "delivered to the

---

220. Cockburn, *Calendar of Assize Records. Essex Indictments: James I*, p. 53, and p. 109.
221. Tawney and Power, *Tudor Economic Documents*, p. 340.
222. Cockburn, *Calendar of Assize Records. Hertfordshire Indictments: Elizabeth I*, p. 76.
223. Anon, *A Relation, or Rather a True Account*, p. 36.

Ordinary".[224] The cleric had no choice in the matter: "And if the ordinary will not come to receive them that be clerks, the king's justices may set a fine upon him".[225] This probably provided some encouragement to court chaplains to be slightly selective about granting the privilege, at least where the claimant was very insalubrious.

Ecclesiastical Imprisonment

Clergied convicts would normally spend some time in a bishop's prison, certainly months and often years during the early Tudor period, before going for "purgation" in front of an ecclesiastical court. For example, William Edwards, a painter, was convicted of housebreaking and clergied in 1499 but was not purged until 1502. Thomas Snaydon, a thatcher, was convicted of stealing sheep in 1505 but went for purgation in 1511.[226] In 1500, after committing a string of burglaries and robberies in Kent a couple of years earlier, George Sawyer successfully pleaded clergy in the Court of King's Bench and was put into the custody of the Archdeacon of Westminster. However, in 1510 another record indicates that he had escaped from the Westminster "convict house" (the prison for convicted clerics), suggesting that he had been there for almost a decade.[227] As these cases indicate, large numbers of lay people, who made up the majority of those being clergied by the late fifteenth century, could be found in pre-Reformation ecclesiastical prisons.

Conditions were harsh, as they were in all Tudor prisons. Once incarcerated, as Ferdinando Pulton later observed, they would have "upon the Sonday bread, ale, and pease, and vpon all the other daies, courser bread, and small drinke once in the day onely". However, and as this comment suggests, the bishop seems to have been obliged to provide a higher level of sustenance (and clothing) than was usually found in secular jails. Even so, it is probably significant that the bishop's prison at Wells was known as the "Cowehouse".[228] The unpleasantness of such

224. Jeaffreson, *Middlesex County Records: Vol. 1*, pp. 21–26.
225. St. Germain, *Doctor and Student*, p. 311.
226. Thomson, *The Early Tudor Church*, pp. 92–93.
227. McSheffrey, "Sanctuary Seekers".
228. Thomson, *The Early Tudor Church*, p. 92.

incarceration may help to explain regular escapes. (Security was as poor in ecclesiastical establishments as in other prisons.) For example, in November 1493 20 men broke out of the Bishop of London's prison at Bishop's Stortford in Hertfordshire (the see had purchased the manor there in 1060, explaining both the name and the presence of a penal establishment), for which the cleric was fined very heavily, far more so than the keepers of secular prisons in such situations, perhaps because he had the resources to cover being amerced such an amount.[229]

The generally poor conditions found in ecclesiastical prisons may also explain why in 1527 Nicholas Allott, a "scholar" (student) who stole a horse but then fled to sanctuary in a nearby church, initially abjured the realm rather than relying on benefit of clergy, despite being literate. Allott returned or (more likely) never left the country after abjuring, and was eventually arrested and indicted. On this occasion, he successfully pleaded benefit of clergy (as did several other "returnees").[230] Against this, in the late 1450s several literate men who had been imprisoned for debt appear to have deliberately had themselves falsely indicted for felony, with a view to pleading guilty and claiming clergy, being placed in the hands of the Church, going through purgation, and then being released, apparently freed from their previous debts by virtue of their convictions.[231]

Purgation

Under the process of purgation, whenever it took place, a public proclamation would be made, inviting anyone concerned to come forward and object to the clergied offender who was due to be purged; usually, this was done by asserting that he had committed the relevant crime. In most cases, no-one came forward, and the felon would then swear that he was innocent of the charge of which he had been convicted in a secular court (whether assizes, Old Bailey, or quarter sessions), in front of the bishop or his representative. He would then produce 12 compurgators to swear that they believed his declaration of innocence to be

---

229. Talk at British Legal History Conference, University College, London, July 2017.
230. Thomson, *The Early Tudor Church*, p. 92.
231. Richard Crompton, *Star Chamber Cases: Showing What Cases Properly Belong to the Cognizance of That Court* (Boston: Soule and Bugbee, 1881), p. 56.

sincere and truthful, rather than directly asserting that he was innocent of the offence(s) for which he had been clergied. (This was a standard method of trial in ecclesiastical courts.) During much of the first half of the sixteenth century, Rochester Episcopal Registers suggest that in this diocese, at least, a separate proclamation was made with regard to each felon, in the place where he committed his crime or (less commonly) resided, and each offender had to produce a separate group of 12 compurgators, drawn from the same diocese.[232]

It was very rare for a "genuine" cleric to fail in his purgation, particularly by the early Tudor era, although, if he did, he would, in theory, be punished. The church could not impose death or mutilation, so that degradation was the normal penalty for those who truly were in holy orders, although a criminous clerk might also be ritually whipped, relegated to a monastery before the Reformation, or even imprisoned for life.[233] For lay claimants, failure at compurgation was even more exceptional by the early 1500s. Nevertheless, at Chichester in 1520, after such a proclamation was made by the curate of Grinstead in the case of a man accused of buggery (not then a secular crime), one Edmond Pynfold appeared to object and offered to prove the guilt of the accused, with the aid of two witnesses. The planned purgation was consequently suspended.[234]

In the absence of such objections, everything would turn on the compurgators. By the early sixteenth century, they were often not reliable men, their presence frequently being a formality, especially in benefit of clergy cases. This situation became worse as the century advanced. Henrician statutes of the 1530s (such as 23 Henry VIII 2 c. 1) complained that "manifest thieves and murderers" were being set at large having been allowed to make their purgations "by such as nothing know of their misdeeds".[235] It was partly for this reason that the short-lived and unusual 1531 Poisoning Act, although still allowing genuine clerics (unlike laymen) to claim benefit of clergy if convicted of the crime, required that, after a guilty clergyman was handed over to the custody of the church,

---

232. Melling, *Crime and Punishment*, pp. 182–185.
233. Newman F. Baker, "Benefit of Clergy—A Legal Anomaly", *Kentucky Law Journal*, Vol. 15, Issue 2, p. 96.
234. Helmholz, "Crime, Compurgation", p. 16.
235. Beattie, *Crime and the Courts*, p. 142.

he would "remayne and be in p[er]pertuall prisone during his lyfe w[ith] out any purgacon therof in any wise to be made".[236]

Despite such criticism, this method of disposing of cases, where clergy had been claimed successfully, survived the Reformation and lasted until 1576. Even in the 1560s, after a layman or clerk was clergied he would be delivered to the ordinary "to be kept in the Bishops prison, from whence after a certaine time by an other enquest of Clarkes he is delivered and let at large".[237] Thus, at the Surrey Assizes held in July 1564, two Southwark labourers, Thomas Parker and Robert Young, were indicted for grand larceny, after stealing nine sheets and a tablecloth, together worth £2 6s 8d. Young was acquitted, but Parker was found guilty. He successfully claimed clergy and was delivered to the rector of Croydon (the bishop's representative).[238] Similarly, in March the following year, at the Essex Assizes, a Maldon glover named William Appleton was convicted of grand larceny after stealing a purse containing 12 shillings, but allowed his clergy and, eventually, delivered to Thomas Simnell, the ordinary to the Bishop of London.[239]

By the Elizabethan period, the process of purgation had become even laxer and more fraudulent than it was in the 1530s, if only because of the huge increase in the number of successful claims of clergy after the middle of the century, so that it was almost entirely a formality, its effects being virtually synonymous with outright acquittal. A case from the Rochester diocese, shortly before the requirement of purgation was abolished, is indicative. In early 1573, five clergied felons from Kent who had been convicted at the county assizes were handed over to the diocesan authorities. As required, a proclamation, asking people to come forward if they could "objecte anythinge against the purgacions" of the men, was made in three market towns; however, these were situated far from where the five convicts lived or had committed their crimes. On 17 March the five men appeared before an ecclesiastical court at Rochester Cathedral. The indictments on which they had been convicted were read out, and all

---

236. Kesselring, "A Draft of the 1531 'Acte for Poysoning,'" *The English Historical Review*, Vol. 116, No. 468, pp. 894–899.
237. Smith, *De Republica Anglorum*, p. 116.
238. Cockburn, *Calendar of Assize Records. Surrey Indictments: Elizabeth I*, p. 36.
239. *Ibid*, p. 56.

then declared on oath that they were "stainless" of the alleged crimes. At this, a single group of a dozen compurgators were called, who swore that they believed that the oaths of the five men were true according to their knowledge. The men were then delivered from the custody of the gaoler and released. Thus no-one who was likely to have objected to the purgations (given the location of the advertisements) was made aware of what was happening, and a single set of compurgators was used to clear all five men, even though they could not possibly have known them all personally, given the very varied parts of Kent they came from.[240]

Although the early Elizabethan process was a charade, it seems that even this procedure may not have been required of all men who were clergied, some of whom may have been quietly released to go home after being branded. The sheer inconvenience occasioned by the privilege may also have encouraged some jury down-valuing, perhaps at the behest of the trial judge; a whipping for petty theft was much more convenient to administer and painful for the recipient than granting clergy. It was also feared that the (often) fraudulent compurgation process encouraged perjury.

The residual link with the ecclesiastical courts was finally abolished by statute in 1576 (18 Elizabeth I, c. 7), when the requirement that clergied offenders be turned over to the ordinary to undergo purgation was abolished.[241] Under the same statute, they were liable to be jailed for up to a year, at the discretion of the secular court, although this very rarely occurred, as there was not enough space in the country's gaols. Thereafter, a successful claim of clergy was normally followed by branding and immediate discharge.[242]

Withdrawal of Clergy from Specific Offences

In 1607 John Cowell observed that anyone could be asked to "reade at the barre, being founde guilty, and convicted of *such felonie as this benefit*

---

240. Melling, *Crime and Punishment*, pp. 182–185.
241. Dean, *Law-Making and Society*, p. 190.
242. Beattie, *Crime and the Courts*, p. 142.

is still granted for. "[243] As this suggests, by the end of the Tudor period many felonies had been withdrawn from clergy or, if newly created, such as those in the 1542 and 1563 Witchcraft Acts, had expressly excluded the privilege. By contrast, in the late medieval period benefit of clergy was allowed for all serious offences except treason (withdrawn from the privilege during the reign of Edward III) and theft from churches. However, its absence from the former meant that even a cleric who was convicted of some forms of coining could be executed like any layman, as the crime, for arcane historical reasons, was classified as high treason under the 1351 statute. As a result, when in 1532 a priest was convicted at Newgate for clipping gold nobles (a high-value coin), he was drawn on a sledge to Tyburn and hanged in the same fashion as a layperson, without being defrocked ("degraded"). It was claimed that many churchmen "murmered" at this disrespectful treatment, which did not portend well.[244] As Cowell's comment also suggests, at the other end of the penal spectrum, clergy had never extended to misdemeanours or petty theft, where the penalties could not include the shedding of blood (making the protection unnecessary).[245]

However, within a few years of 1485, statute was beginning to withdraw some felonies from the privilege. During the reign of Henry VII, this was done on a modest and restricted scale. In 1492 clergy was withheld from the new statutory felony of desertion, allowing soldiers and sailors who left their ships and units without permission to be executed, even if literate (7 Henry VII, c. 1). As a result, when Thomas Smyth was convicted of desertion at the Hertford Assizes in March 1601, he was immediately sentenced to hang.[246] In 1496 another statute (12 Henry VII, c. 7), apparently prompted by the killing of a gentleman named Richard Tracy by his (literate) servant, provided that those who committed petty treason, like anyone who was guilty of high treason, should not be entitled to clergy. The servant, James Graeme, was dealt with by an Act of

---

243. John Cowell, *The interpreter: or Booke containing the signification of words wherein is set foorth the true meaning of all, or the most part of such words and termes, as are mentioned in the lawe writers* (Cambridge: John Legate, 1607).

244. Baker, *Sir John Spelman*, p. 49.

245. Thomson, *The Early Tudor Church*, p. 97.

246. Cockburn, *Calendar of Assize Records. Hertfordshire Indictments: Elizabeth I*, p. 161.

attainder (a parliamentary Act declaring a person guilty of a particular crime without a judicial trial), allowing clergy to be withdrawn in his own case (i.e. retrospectively), rather than merely denying it to those in his position in future. This meant that he could be properly punished for his "abominable and wilful" crime.[247]

The speed of change quickened slightly after Henry VIII came to the throne in 1509. Benefit of clergy was temporarily denied to murderers and those who committed highway robbery in 1512, although the statute (4 Henry VIII c. 2) preserved it for genuine clerics (rather than literate laymen) or "suche as ben within holy orders only excepte". This covered those in the major orders of deacon and above. This Act lapsed with the enacting Parliament. A bill to renew it passed the House of Commons in 1515 but did not complete its passage through the Lords in time, partly due to opposition from the bishops there, who were concerned that minor religious orders, such as pardoners and lectors, were being excluded from the privilege.[248] Even as Parliament was sitting on the issue, Richard Kidderminster, the Abbot of Winchcombe, preached a sermon at St Paul's Cross maintaining that the statute passed three years earlier was against the law of God and the liberties of the church.

After the advent of what was later termed the Reformation Parliament, in 1529, the speed of change quickened. Clergy was abolished for deliberate acts of poisoning in 1530 (22 Henry VIII, c. 9), in this case by making the crime treason (long excluded from the privilege). Murder, arson, and robbery committed on the highway or in an occupied house were (again) withdrawn from clergy in 1531.[249] However, manslaughter remained a clergyable offence throughout the period and beyond, so that in 1592 George Goodhelp, convicted for "felonious killing" at Ewell at the Surrey Assizes, was able to claim the privilege.[250]

In 1533 benefit of clergy was taken away from those who refused to enter a plea when arraigned. In the same year, it was excluded from the newly created felony of buggery, whether committed with man or beast (25 Henry VIII c. 6). In 1535 statute (27 Henry VIII c. 17) withdrew clergy

---

247. Stacey, "Richard Roose", p. 4.
248. Thomson, *The Early Tudor Church*, p. 95.
249. Baker, *Oxford History*, p. 571.
250. Cockburn, *Calendar of Assize Records. Surrey Indictments: Elizabeth I*, p. 384.

from a non-violent property offence for the first time, servants stealing goods or cash worth 40 shillings or more from their masters being denied the privilege (28 Henry VIII c. 15). In 1542 clergy were also excluded from the new, albeit short-lived (on this occasion), offence of sorcery (33 Hen. VIII c. 8). The theft of horses was withdrawn from clergy in 1547 (I Edw. VI c. 12). Pickpocketing and cutpursing — secretly stealing (rather than openly snatching) goods worth one shilling or more from the person — followed in 1565 (8 Eliz. I c. 4). The Elizabethan Witchcraft Act of 1563 (5 Eliz. I c. 16) created an unclergyable felony of using sorcery to kill. The Benefit of Clergy Act 1575 (18 Eliz. I c. 7) took clergy away from offenders in burglary and rape cases. Several more arcane offences, "divers other felonies particularized by the statutes", were withdrawn from the privilege in ensuing years.[251] Most of these changes were officially inspired, and even began their voyage through Parliament in the upper house.

As a result of these developments, by the end of the Elizabethan period, the typical clergied offender had been convicted of a first offence of simple grand larceny, involving the theft of goods, cash, materials, food, or animals (other than horses) of a shilling or more in value, without aggravating circumstances. A few more had been found guilty of manslaughter or other, more recondite, felonies. For example, at the Midsummer Quarter Sessions for Devon in July 1598, eight people were convicted (or pleaded guilty to) felonies that were unclergyable (as with four cases of horse theft and picking pockets) or were deemed unable to read and so claim the privilege, or were female. Seven men were convicted of felonies for which they could and successfully did claim clergy.[252]

Increase in Successful Claims

Despite the growing exclusion of serious offences from benefit of clergy, use of the privilege to escape the gallows showed a major increase between the late medieval period (when it was claimed and granted quite sparingly) and the final decades of the Tudor era. This growth was largely

---

251. Melling, *Crime and Punishment*, p. 47.
252. Hamilton, *Quarter Sessions from Queen Elizabeth to Queen Anne*, pp. 33–34.

made up of a substantial increase in the number of laymen successfully claiming the privilege. For example, of 36 felons known to have been convicted at gaol delivery in Cumberland between 1335 and 1457, just four (about eleven per cent) successfully claimed the privilege.[253] In the fifteenth century generally, between 13 and 17 per cent of all English convicts made successful claims. Thus, 14.7 per cent of those found guilty at gaol delivery in the East Anglian Circuit were granted clergy during the 1420s and 1430s. (Interestingly, there is no record of a claimant failing the reading test there during this time.)[254] However, by the 1560s the figure was between 41 and 47 per cent in Kent, Essex, Sussex, and Hertfordshire, while in Surrey it was about 58 per cent of all those convicted for felony.[255]

When did this change take place? A lack of preserved records occasions problems in answering this question. It seems that it was still a comparatively recent (and perhaps ongoing) development in the early years of Queen Elizabeth's reign, and that the expansion largely occurred in the years after the middle of the sixteenth century. For example, in Middlesex the incidence of successful claims increased by 250 per cent between the 1550s and the 1560s.[256]

This process may have started in the metropolitan area and then spread to the rest of the country, with more distant parts only slowly catching-up. The North appears to have preserved a fairly "medieval" approach to the privilege until late in the Tudor era. For example, in July 1545 the justices of assize kept sessions of oyer and terminer and gaol delivery at York Castle as a result of which 12 people were capitally convicted of burglary and other felonies. Of these, ten were executed and two reprieved, but no-one appears to have been clergied.[257] In March 1557 Sir Thomas Gargrave noted that he had sat with assizes judges at the same forum. Of seven people indicted for felony, six had been convicted and executed and just one committed to the ordinary (i.e. clergied).[258] In August 1565

253. Summerson, *Crime and Society*, p. 112.
254. Maddern, *Violence and Social Order*, p. 71.
255. Kesselring, *Mercy and Authority*, p. 78.
256. Bellamy, *The Criminal Trial*, pp. 136–137.
257. Gairdner and Brodie, *Letters and Papers, Foreign and Domestic, Henry VIII, Vol. 20, Part 2* (London: HMSO, 1905), pp. 45–61.
258. Green, *Calendar of State Papers Domestic: Elizabeth, 1601–3, With Addenda 1547–65*, p. 446.

the Archbishop of York and the Council of the North informed the Queen that they had held a session of oyer and terminer and gaol delivery. Twenty-four people were indicted for felonies, of whom 14 were capitally convicted. Of these, eleven were executed, one reprieved, and two received benefit of clergy (just over 14 per cent).[259]

The reasons for this change are not entirely clear. Literacy increased, but to nothing like the degree that would be needed to explain such a development. The huge growth in prosecutions and the almost doubling of the felony conviction rate in the same period might have contributed to the process, encouraging leniency in conducting the test, to limit the impact of the death-for-felony rule and the number of those executed for relatively minor offences. Even so, some research suggests that the percentage of arraigned felons executed at the end of the sixteenth century was still higher than in the late medieval period (26 per cent rather than only 14 per cent), because the increase in the use of clergy did not negate the huge growth in the proportion of convictions.[260]

Women and Clergy

Women could not be clerics, and so could not claim clergy in the Tudor era, although two seventeenth century statutes would eventually grant them an equivalent privilege. As the judge and legal author John Spelman (c.1480–1546) noted: "A woman can abjure, but she shall not have the privilege of clergy, for it is not fitting [for a woman] to be any minister in Holy Church".[261] Even allowing for pleas of pregnancy (see below), this needed to be factored into jury decisions on verdicts for female felony defendants. To some extent, gendered unfairness could be circumvented by increased jury willingness to acquit women at trial, or at least downvalue their crimes, and by greater judicial willingness to reprieve them afterwards. Most evidence does suggest that Tudor women were more likely to receive favourable verdicts. For example, at the Kent Assizes between 1559 and 1570 almost 70 per cent of women were found not

---

259. *Ibid*, pp. 570–572.
260. Bellamy, *The Criminal Trial*, pp. 155–156.
261. Baker, *Sir John Spelman*, p. 68.

guilty, while only about 30 per cent of men secured the same result.[262] Perhaps more typically, in Hertfordshire the figures for the half century after 1573 were 52 per cent and 30 per cent respectively. (This general pattern can also be identified in the fifteenth century, albeit with much lower conviction levels for both genders).[263] In part there was express legal justification for such benign verdicts. The doctrine of *feme covert* seems to have been established by the middle of the thirteenth century, at the latest.[264] It meant that many female felons who offended with their husbands were deemed to be under the latter's control and coercion, and so not culpable.

Nevertheless, as late as 1645 juror ignorance about benefit of clergy created problems, such as in the case of Susan Adams, who beat her servant, Hester Pride, who had committed some fault, "with a small stick, by way of correction". Unfortunately, Hester died from her injuries. At trial, the jurors deemed Adams guilty of manslaughter, not murder, forgetting (or not knowing) that as a woman she would not be able to plead the privilege for such a crime. They were shocked and alarmed when they realised that their mistake meant that Adams was liable to be executed, something that was never their intention. Ultimately, Parliament saved Adams with a special ordinance pardoning her for the killing.[265] Even so, use of "benefit of the belly" was particularly important in preventing excessive verdict discrimination by gender.

Pleading the Belly

A woman who had been capitally convicted of a felony, however serious, and then sentenced to death, could "postpone" her execution if pregnant by "pleading her belly". Once a female convict made such a claim the high sheriff would have to return a jury of matrons to consider whether

---

262. Jones, *Gender and Petty Crime*, p. 38.
263. Bellamy, *The Criminal Trial*, p. 124.
264. Henry Summerson, "Maitland and the Criminal Law in the Age of *Bracton*", *Proceedings of the British Academy*, Vol. 89, p. 117.
265. Kesselring, "Bodies of Evidence: Sex and Murder (or Gender and Homicide) in Early Modern England, c.1500–1680", *Gender & History*, Vol. 27, Issue 2, p. 246.

she was "quick with child".[266] Early pregnancy was not enough; as Pulton noted, it would "not availe her to be yong with childe". The baby had to be capable of moving in the womb, which was deemed to occur between the fifteenth and sixteenth week of gestation. This rule was partly founded on an older notion that an unborn child was not properly alive until such quickening occurred.[267] Many medieval theologians appear to have rejected the idea that life was present at conception, and there had been speculation since the time of Galen that a foetus might not possess a soul until the third month after conception. However, quickening was notoriously difficult to establish, at least initially, even for the women concerned, let alone observers. Colic or wind could easily be mistaken for movement in the womb.[268]

The Jury of Matrons

The Tudor jury of matrons was normally the same size as the trial jury, i.e. it was made up of a dozen women. As the case of 1332 suggests, it seems that it was sometimes smaller during the medieval period, and juries with as few as four women have been noted. Nevertheless, by the later fourteenth century, 12 women had become the norm.[269] Thus, a file from a trial held at York Castle, in the year 1433 to 1434, contains a dozen names (alongside which is written "the matrons said that she was not pregnant").[270] This continued during the Tudor period. At assizes held on the Elizabethan Home Circuit a dozen women were always appointed, with the names of prospective matrons that had been crossed out for non-attendance carefully replaced by those of other women, as occurred in March 1562 in Essex.[271] In like manner, at the Old Bailey, 12 named women were always found on such a body during the latter part

---

266. A jury of matrons might also be called in a civil case if, for e.g., a recently widowed woman claimed to be pregnant. Their decision could affect any subsequent distribution of property.
267. Sara M. Butler, "More than Mothers: Juries of Matrons and Pleas of the Belly in Medieval England", *Law and History Review*, Vol. 37, Issue 2, p. 382.
268. Cathy McClive, "The Hidden Truths of the Belly: The Uncertainties of Pregnancy in Early Modern Europe", *Social History of Medicine*, Vol. 15, Issue 2, p. 224.
269. Butler, "More than Mothers", p. 357.
270. *Ibid*, p. 366.
271. Cockburn, *Calendar of Assize Records. Essex Indictments: Elizabeth I*, p. 37.

of the Tudor period and beyond, as can be seen from those sworn in to consider Margaret Fisher's unsuccessful plea of pregnancy, after she was convicted of murder in 1612.[272]

At best the jury of matrons was made up of, or at least included, mid-wives; for example, it was reported that six "lawful and wise midwives" had determined a claim of pregnancy made by Agnes of Kent, a woman convicted of coining at Newgate in 1332.[273] More typically, during the sixteenth century at least, mature women with personal experience of childbirth, sometimes gathered from the environs of the court or drawn from the wives of court personnel (such as the goaler), would be selected. The matrons were sworn in, in open court, but received their evidence in private, where they conducted an intimate physical examination of the convicted woman, looking for signs of at least moderately advanced pregnancy (lactating breasts, etc.). They then publicly announced their verdict to the court.

Occasionally, claims of pregnancy were adjourned to a following assizes because: empanelling a jury of matrons for one case was not considered worth the trouble, there was a shortage of women readily available that day, or to allow time (almost six months) to make the convict's preg-nancy or lack of it apparent. Such deferment was also found at the Old Bailey, which had far more frequent hearings than assizes, albeit that this allowed less time for signs of pregnancy to develop. Thus, in Janu-ary 1562 the unmarried Elizabeth Cholmeley from London stole a gold ring and other valuable items from Peter Hoker. She pleaded guilty and claimed to be pregnant. The matter was adjourned to the following ses-sions, held on 20 February, where a jury of matrons examined Elizabeth and declared her not to be with child.[274]

Scrutiny of the *Year Books* and other sources suggests that female fel-ons did not routinely claim pregnancy if not with child during the late medieval period. Thus, Agnes of Kent's capitally convicted female col-league made no such claim in 1322, and she appears to have been fairly typical. Additionally, medieval matrons were reasonably discerning about

272. William Le Hardy (ed.), *County of Middlesex. Calendar To the Sessions Records: New Series, Vol. 2, 1614–15* (London: Clerk of the Peace, 1936), pp. 35–66.
273. Butler, "More than Mothers", p. 370.
274. Jeaffreson, *Middlesex County Records: Vol. 1*, pp. 44–46.

who was found to be pregnant. Furthermore, where it was claimed successfully, its effects were usually temporary. Normally, at best, women would be kept in slightly better prison conditions until they gave birth (if truly pregnant), and then, having been suitably "churched", would face execution.[275]

However, this changed during the 1500s and, by the late sixteenth century, pleading the belly was often something of a fiction, frequently claimed indiscriminately and undeservedly by convicted women to escape death. On one estimate, 224 women, or 41 per cent of those capitally convicted on the Home Circuit during the reign of Queen Elizabeth, successfully claimed pregnancy.[276] Additionally, by then, successful claims led to many (but not all) women permanently avoiding execution, for one reason or another.

Illustrative of the ubiquity of such claims by the end of the Tudor period, at the Huntingdon Assizes in 1593, considerable public amusement was occasioned after the octogenarian witch Alice Samuel insisted on pleading pregnancy. However ludicrous, this was seen as a right; the judge tried to persuade her to abandon her plea "but in no case shee would be driven from it, till at length, a Jury of women were impanelled, and sworne to search her: who gave up their verdit, that she was not with childe".[277] It is probably safe to assume that, by then, a majority of capitally convicted women who were even remotely of childbearing age, and some who were not, claimed pregnancy. Nevertheless, there were still occasional cases of single women who were too proud to admit to fornication by making such a claim, even to save their lives.

Although pleading the belly gave women some of the leeway that was available to men with benefit of clergy, the two privileges were not analogous, even in the Tudor era. Clergy did not apply to all offences, especially as the sixteenth century advanced and very serious crimes were withdrawn from its ambit; it also had permanent results. Pregnancy did apply to all offences, even murder, but was, at least in theory, only

---

275. S. M. Butler, "Pleading the belly: a sparing plea? Pregnant convicts and the courts in medieval England", in S. M. Butler and K. J. Kesselring (eds.), *Crossing Borders: Boundaries and Margins in Medieval and Early Modern England* (Leiden: Brill, 2018), pp. 147–150.
276. Kesselring, *Mercy and Authority*, p. 212.
277. Anon, *The Most Strange and Admirable Discoverie*, p. 112.

temporary in its effect. Furthermore, significantly fewer women (proportionately) escaped immediate execution by pleading their bellies than did men by benefit of clergy.[278]

Convicted women who made such a claim had always enjoyed a good chance of a positive finding, even if their numbers were quite modest in the medieval period. Most (but by no means all) of the claimants at gaol delivery in the years around 1400 were successful.[279] Even so, at assizes, the jury of matrons was still moderately discriminating about claims to pregnancy to the end of the Tudor period. For example, at those held for Essex in March 1562, only one of the four women who made such a claim was successful.[280] Similarly, Agnes Brisley was the only one of three female burglars claiming pregnancy in a case tried at the Hertford Assizes in March 1599 who was successful.[281] Nevertheless, by then, this low level of success was fairly unusual, even at the higher jury forum.

The surviving verdicts from the seven juries of matrons empanelled for the Hertfordshire Assizes in the years immediately after 1573 identify ten female convicts as pleading their bellies, of whom four were successful. At the Surrey Assizes for the years between 1559 and 1603, the records (they are largely complete) produce 18 occasions when a jury of matrons was empanelled to consider the status of 43 women who had claimed to be pregnant. The decisions in seven of the 43 cases are illegible or lost. Of the remainder, 26 women were found to be with child, including five "spinsters", convicted of four separate crimes, who were considered on one occasion, while only ten were found not to be pregnant (a success rate of 72 per cent where a verdict can be identified).

It is also apparent from these (and other) cases that the decision on pregnancy was not based solely on obvious physical signs, which are sometimes fairly modest at sixteen weeks' gestation. Much must have turned on the matrons' private questioning of the convict. This had probably always been the case. For example, on one occasion, it seems that a medieval jury of matrons became frustrated when a female convict

---

278. Jones, *Gender and Petty Crime*, p. 36.
279. Kathleen E. Garay, "Women and Crime in Later Mediaeval England: An Examination of the Courts of Gaol Delivery, 1388 to 1409", *Florilegium*, Vol. 1, p. 92.
280. Cockburn, *Calendar of Assize Records. Essex Indictments: Elizabeth I*, p. 37.
281. Cockburn, *Calendar of Assize Records. Hertfordshire Indictments: Elizabeth I*, p. 143.

refused to tell them when she had last menstruated. It is possible that other contemporary tests for pregnancy that required active cooperation by the female convict were also conducted. One recognised test of the era involved examining the colour of the woman's urine to see if it was very pale yellow to white, with a cloudy surface.

However, in borderline cases, during the second half of the Tudor era, it seems that factors other than a genuine assessment of the possibility of pregnancy came into play. For example, a slightly disproportionate number of women who received positive outcomes from the Surrey Assizes matrons were accused of cases of grand larceny, without aggravating features, in which goods worth several pounds had been stolen (too much for most juries to feel comfortable about down-valuing to petty theft), for which many men would have escaped execution via benefit of clergy. Thus all five of the Surrey spinsters mentioned above fell into this situation. By contrast, of the ten Surrey women who were unsuccessful in their claims, half had been convicted of infanticide (not calculated to encourage sympathy for a claim to pregnancy), and another had been found guilty of manslaughter after stabbing a man to death during a heated quarrel. Cases involving the minority of unsuccessful women who had been convicted of offences against property normally had aggravating features. One had committed the by then unclergyable crime of horse theft (very unusual for a woman). Another had been convicted of three counts of breaking into yards and stealing poultry and animals, spaced out over the course of a month, suggesting that she was a habitual thief.[282]

It should be stressed that these considerations were not in any way rules. Two women found to be pregnant at assizes in Elizabethan Essex had been convicted of infanticide. Similarly, at the Kent Assizes in July 1584, Emma Ashwell was convicted after cutting the throat of her newborn child while in her master's house, but remanded on a plea of pregnancy. Conversely, some women were found not to be with child despite being convicted of simple grand larceny. Nevertheless, although generalisations are difficult, it seems that the matrons considered three

---

282. See generally Cockburn, *Calendar of Assize Records. Surrey Indictments: Elizabeth I.*

factors when making their assessment of pregnancy: how plausible it was that a woman was pregnant; how grave the crime of which she had been convicted; and the forum in which the privilege was claimed.

However serious the offence, even if it was a case of murder, if a female convict was clearly or very probably with child, she would be granted a temporary reprieve. For example, Elizabeth Lowys, convicted of two cases of murder by witchcraft at the Colchester Assizes in July 1564, successfully claimed pregnancy.[283] Avice Cunny, convicted of an identical crime at the same forum in 1589, secured the same result. However, with women who were not so obviously pregnant, where the diagnosis might have been partly based on oral representations from the female convict rather than her physical appearance, it seems that the type of crime involved influenced the matrons' decision. The less serious the felony, the more likely was a positive result. Finally, at quarter sessions, which, unlike assizes, were usually reluctant towards the end of the era to inflict a death sentence, the matrons were probably actively encouraged to return a positive finding, just as it is likely that the court chaplain at this forum was prompted to find that male convicts claiming clergy could read.

For example, three women were capitally convicted at the special gaol delivery conducted by JPs at Maidstone in January 1597. They all claimed to be pregnant, were examined by the jury of matrons, and all were granted a stay of judgment because they were deemed to be quick with child. Significantly, 12 men who were convicted with them were also "read as clerks and burnt on their left hands" despite it being highly improbable that all were literate. In this situation, pleading the belly (like benefit of clergy) was a procedural device that allowed JPs to determine felonies while simultaneously avoiding the need to pass death sentences.[284] The same thing happened at Shrewsbury Quarter Sessions in November 1580. A total of 25 people were convicted of capital felonies, but only five were sent to the gallows: "The rest were saved by their book and women supposed to be with child".[285]

---

283. Cockburn, *Calendar of Assize Records. Essex Indictments: Elizabeth I*, p. 31.
284. Melling, *Crime and Punishment*, pp. 135–136.
285. Barrett and Harrison, *Crime and Punishment*, p. 65.

What cannot now be recovered, so many centuries later, are the tacit understandings between judiciary, justices, and matrons as to how to deal with lesser, and less obvious, cases in which pregnancy was claimed. Given the patterns contained in the matrons' verdicts, which cannot be explained purely by random chance, they must have existed. Just as judges hinted to trial jurors that an acquittal was appropriate, and to court chaplains that a man should be declared literate, they probably gave subtle signs to the matrons that pregnancy might be found if there was a doubt.

The "Temporary" Nature of Reprieve

If the jury of matrons gave an affirmative answer, execution would (in theory) be put back until after childbirth, or until it became apparent that the woman was not pregnant.[286] Unlike a finding of benefit of clergy, a positive result from the matrons did not permanently prevent the punishment from being inflicted. Nevertheless, after a female felon had been temporarily reprieved by pleading her belly, a warrant for her execution had to be issued before she could be hanged. By the middle of the eighteenth century this was rarely done, except for the most heinous offences, such as murder. By contrast, in the late medieval period it was commonplace to execute women who had earlier been respited for pregnancy. The Tudor period fell between the two when it came to permanent clemency.

On one assessment, more than half the women granted a temporary reprieve for pregnancy on the Home Circuit during the reign of Queen Elizabeth were eventually put to death. Furthermore, some of the fortunate 47 per cent shared in general pardons that had nothing to do with their physical condition.[287] Thus in 1549 Alice Cowland broke into a house in Tottenham, in Middlesex, and stole a worsted frock worth 30 shillings, along with several other items and some cash. Although capitally convicted of grand larceny, Alice was reprieved because she was

---

286. Anon, *The Lawes Resolutions of Womens Rights: or, the Lawes Provision for Woemen* (London: John Grove, 1632), p. 207.
287. Kesselring, *Mercy and Authority*, pp. 213–214.

pregnant, and afterwards successfully pleaded King Edward VI's general pardon.[288] Similarly, Joan Johnson of Send, in Surrey, was capitally convicted at the county assizes in March 1571, but successfully pleaded her belly. She, too, subsequently benefitted from a general pardon. At the same sessions, the case of Helen Kelley, convicted of the manslaughter ("felonious killing") of a two-year-old infant she had picked-up and thrown to the ground, had exactly the same outcome.[289]

Nevertheless, other women in this situation received personal pardons, as had been the case ever since the thirteenth century. For example, two women were recorded as receiving benefit of the belly in 1228 and two others in 1248 and 1253. The king individually and permanently pardoned at least three of them. (The fate of the fourth is not recorded.)[290] A few Tudor women received permanent clemency very quickly in this manner.

At the Summer Assizes for Essex in 1570, Susan Mason was convicted of grand larceny after stealing clothes worth about 30 shillings from a house at Great Horkesley. She was found to be pregnant by the jury of matrons and personally pardoned shortly afterwards.[291] Less speedily, but more typically, at the assizes held a few months earlier at Chelmsford, in March 1570, Alice Harvey was convicted of stealing the large sum of £18 17s in cash from Humphrey Cocke of Great Warley. She claimed pregnancy and was formally pardoned in July the same year.[292] Alice Haydon had to wait even longer. At the March Assizes for Hertfordshire in 1580, she was convicted of stealing clothes and cash worth more than £1 10s in Bishop's Stortford. She pleaded her belly, was remanded after being found to be pregnant, and pardoned the following year.[293]

Other women who had been respited for pregnancy were less fortunate. Unsurprisingly, this was especially likely if they had committed very grave crimes. Emily Pott, convicted at the Kent Assizes in April 1562 of murdering a man with an axe, successfully pleaded her belly but was sentenced to death at the same forum in July 1564. Similarly, in July

---

288. Jeaffreson, *Middlesex County Records: Vol. 1*, pp. 1–2.
289. Cockburn, *Calendar of Assize Records. Surrey Indictments: Elizabeth I*, p. 89.
290. Thomas R. Forbes, "A Jury of Matrons", *Medical History*, Vol. 32, Issue 1, pp. 23–33.
291. Cockburn, *Calendar of Assize Records. Essex Indictments: Elizabeth I*, p. 80.
292. ERO T/A 418/16/19.
293. Cockburn, *Calendar of Assize Records. Hertfordshire Indictments: Elizabeth I*, p. 31.

1576 Joan Bretton was convicted of infanticide at the Essex Assizes but found to be pregnant. Exactly a year later, she was sentenced to death.[294] In 1589 Avice Cunny, and her mother, Joan, from Stisted, in Essex, were capitally convicted of witchcraft at the county Summer Assizes held in Chelmsford. Joan was hanged immediately after the sessions, but Avice successfully pleaded her belly. Even so, she was executed the following year, after giving birth.[295]

At the very end of the Elizabethan era, Elizabeth Caldwell tried to murder her husband with poisoned cakes that, unfortunately, were eaten by others, including a frail child who subsequently died. Caldwell was examined by three JPs, quickly made full admissions, and pleaded guilty at the Chester Great Sessions. At the time that she was convicted, Caldwell was genuinely, and heavily, pregnant, and so execution was deferred. However, her husband had no wish to see her escape the noose. After she gave birth to a boy, who joined his older brother in their father's custody, it was claimed "hee made sute to the judge to precure a warrant to have his wife executed within a certain time after her deliverance". A warrant was duly granted and sent to the prison keeper to have her executed within 13 days of giving birth. Despite attempts to obtain a temporary reprieve to allow an opportunity to petition the king for a pardon (see below), the execution went ahead.[296] Similarly, at the Surrey Assizes in July 1600, Margery Mills was convicted of poisoning her husband the previous September and, although allowed to delay her execution for alleged pregnancy, was duly burned for petty treason the following year.[297]

Although these were serious cases, some Tudor women convicted of simple property offences and then found to be pregnant were also executed after giving birth or (more commonly) proving not to be with child. For example, in November 1560 Katherine Harrison stole a petticoat, a cassock, a silk hat, and various pieces of linen cloth together worth more than £3. She pleaded guilty and successfully claimed pregnancy

---

294. Cockburn, *Calendar of Assize Records. Essex Indictments: Elizabeth I*, p. 151.
295. Barbara Rosen, *Witchcraft in England 1558–1618* (Amherst: University of Massachusetts Press, 1991), p. 182.
296. Gilbert Dugdale, *A true discourse of the practises of Elizabeth Cauldwell* (London, 1604), ff. B2–B4.
297. Cockburn, *Calendar of Assize Records. Surrey Indictments: Elizabeth I*, 1980, p. 496 and p. 501.

after being examined by a jury of matrons at the Old Bailey in February the following year. However, in June (seven months after the original claim), another jury of matrons found that she was not with child, and she was sentenced to death.[298] Margaret Squire, who was one of a group of five women convicted of burglary in Sussex in May 1604, claimed pregnancy to secure a temporary reprieve. Just over two years later, on 29 July 1606, she, too, was hanged.[299] Even so, it seems likely that some women who successfully pleaded their bellies for less serious crimes, were kept in prison for a year or so and then quietly released back into the community, even if they had not been formally pardoned.[300]

Pardons/Reprieves

All crimes, however serious, that had been, or could be, prosecuted on indictment to a capital conviction, whether felonies or cases of treason, could be pardoned, so that the guilty person escaped execution or even, in some cases, trial. Some 13 per cent of pardons awarded during the Tudor era involved homicide (usually murder) convictions.[301] This power was held and exercised directly by the Crown and not devolved to the judiciary; as Sir Thomas Smith observed in the 1560s, it was "not in the Judges or the Justices power, to aggravate or mitigate the punishment of the Lawe, but in the Prince onely and his privie Counsell".

Additionally, by the Tudor period the power to pardon was no longer granted to local magnates, this change being part of the process of centralisation by which the royal government made itself the sole source of leniency in the criminal justice system. Indeed, in 1535 Parliament formally removed the power to pardon from all others (27 Hen. 8, c. 24), including the Roman Church (against which the provision was aimed), although by then this merely reflected longstanding practice. The statute provided that nobody "of what estates or degrees soever they be of, from the first day of July which shall be in the year of our Lord 1536 shall

---

298. Jeaffreson, *Middlesex County Records: Vol. 1*, pp. 37–44.
299. Hunnisett, *Sussex Coroners' Inquests*, p. 10.
300. James Sharpe, *A Fiery & Furious People: A History of Violence in England* (London: Random House, 2016), p. 199.
301. Kesselring, *Mercy and Authority*, p. 76.

have any power or authority to pardon or remit any treasons, murders, manslaughters, or any kinds of felonies".[302] Such a consolidation was found in many other European countries at this time, and can be seen as an aspect of state formation during the era. However, applications for pardons issued *de cursu* for self-defence and accidental killings (see below) did not have to be considered personally by the monarch and his council; they were often issued directly from the Chancery, a situation that seems to have been established by the early fourteenth century.[303]

Royal pardons had originated in Saxon times, but their use increased significantly after the advent of the mandatory death-for-felony rule. They could be (and sometimes were) issued up to the very moment of execution. In December 1552 William Fitzwilliam, Lieutenant of Windsor Castle and Keeper of the Great Park there, wrote to Henry Polsted and William More, sending them King Edward VI's pardon for several "poor men" who were awaiting execution. However, he urged that they keep this secret from the recipients, until they were at the gallows.[304] Similarly, five people were sentenced to death at quarter sessions held at Shrewsbury in November 1580. One of them, a young woman, was ultimately reprieved because of her pious behaviour while on the way to execution.[305] Indeed, pardons were still of benefit to those who had been capitally convicted and pleaded benefit of clergy. In February 1512 Bishop Mayhew of Hereford received a royal writ, dated the previous month, noting that a yeoman named John Williams who had been found guilty of felony the previous July, and pleaded clergy to escape execution, should be released from ecclesiastical custody, as he had now been fully pardoned by the king. He was released, slightly belatedly, in April.[306]

However, pardons could be obtained prior to trial, not just after conviction, in which case they could be presented upon arraignment, should it occur (often not the case once a pardon had been issued). This would allow the immediate release of the suspect, without any obligation to

302. William F. Duker, "The President's Power to Pardon: A Constitutional History", *William & Mary Law Review*, Vol. 18, Issue 3, p. 487.
303. Kesselring, *Mercy and Authority*, p. 210.
304. SHC LM/COR/3/235.
305. Barrett and Harrison, *Crime and Punishment*, p. 65.
306. Thomson, *The Early Tudor Church*, p. 93.

undergo a hearing.[307] Ingram Frizer, who (apparently) killed Christopher Marlowe in a brawl in a Deptford tavern on 29 May 1593, obtained a pardon from the Queen just four weeks later, although it appears he had spent some of the intervening time in prison. The pardon is unsurprising, even if the speed with which it was granted was slightly unusual. According to the coroner's inquest that enquired into Marlowe's death, the dead man had spent the day drinking with his killer and two others, but had argued with Frizer over the "Reckoning" (bill), exchanging "divers malicious words". Marlowe had then snatched Frizer's dagger and wounded him, and was stabbed to death in the ensuing struggle. The inquest jury decided that Frizer had been unable to flee and so was forced to act in self-defence. The wording of the pardon repeated their conclusion, which is unsurprising given that the record had been adduced to support the application for clemency.[308]

In 1621, after George Abbot, the Archbishop of Canterbury, accidentally shot and killed a gamekeeper, the coroner's inquest that considered the matter concluded that the keeper's death had occurred by "misfortune". Even so, to ensure that there was no risk that the cleric face trial for felony, the king pardoned him after the inquest verdict. The terms of the pardon also removed any threat of loss of property.[309] As this suggests, a pardon did not save the offender from forfeiture for a felony conviction unless it expressly included a gift of his goods.

Royal pardons freed felons from the punishment awarded for their crimes when the monarch was a party to proceedings. This meant that they did not cover an appeal of felony, which was, essentially, an entirely private (albeit criminal) matter between appellor and appellee. For example, in 1527 William Herbert fled to France after murdering the prominent merchant William Vaughan during an affray in Bristol. Two years later he secured a pardon from Henry VIII. However, he also had to deal with an appeal brought by Herbert's widow. Presumably, money

307. Powell, *Kingship, Law, and Society*, p. 84.
308. 303 Leslie Hotson, *The Death of Christopher Marlowe* (London: Nonesuch Press, 1925), p. 78.
309. Will Adam, "The Curious Incident of the Homicidal Archbishop: The Dispensation Granted to Archbishop George Abbot, 1621", *Ecclesiastical Law Journal*, Vol. 17, Issue 3, p. 312.

was paid, as records show that the "parties were agreed", a common outcome of homicide appeals (see also *Chapter 8*).[310]

General and Special Pardons

Reprieves were awarded as general pardons and special pardons. The former were extended to whole classes of offenders, or even (albeit rarely) felons generally. The latter were awarded to individual offenders, often for specific crimes. Both were important during the Tudor era and, taken together, particularly significant. In the few cases where the records allow comparison between the number of criminal trials and the number of pardons, it seems that more than ten per cent of all capitally convicted felons received royal pardons of some description. More specifically, but fairly typically, of ten cutpurses and horse thieves condemned at the Old Bailey on one Friday in 1585 (by which year both crimes were unclergyable), nine were executed the following (Saturday) morning "the tenthe [being] stayed by a meenes from the Courte".[311] Perhaps unsurprisingly, women, who could not claim clergy (for which pleading pregnancy was not an entirely satisfactory substitute), often did somewhat better than men in this regard.

Pardons were issued for several reasons. Some were political. For example, after the Battle of Bosworth many of those who had supported Richard III were pardoned for any treason committed against the new monarch's retrospectively dated reign. However, they also reflected contemporary notions of forgiveness and royal magnanimity.[312] In 1509 Edmund Dudley expressly noted that it was advisable for a king to minister justice "discretly medled with mercy, for els his Justice will be sore, that it will oftentymes appe to be crueltie rather then Justice".[313] In the medieval period, such notions had sometimes led to a rather random allocation of mercy. For example, in the late fourteenth century William Taylor killed Henry Harald and fled to the Church of St Peter, Ely, where

---

310. Moore, *Tudor Murder Files*, pp. 48–49.
311. Tawney and Power, *Tudor Economic Documents, Vol. 2*, p. 337.
312. Pat McCune, "Justice, Mercy, and Late Medieval Governance", *Michigan Law Review*, Vol. 89, p. 1672.
313. Edmund Dudley, *The Tree of Common Wealth* (Manchester: Charles Simms, 1859), pp. 1–66.

he admitted the felony before the local coroner, and abjured the realm. He then set out for his port of embarkation on the coast. By chance, the king encountered him on the road, carrying his wooden cross. On seeing him, the monarch was "moved by pity" to pardon both the abjuration and the killing.[314]

Although the granting of pardons became slightly less arbitrary during the Tudor period, the reasoning behind them remained largely the same. Typically, statutes granting a general pardon during the reign of Queen Elizabeth would note that her subjects had been deservedly sentenced to death, and could not be delivered from this penalty but by her "great mercye". This latter quality appertained to her princely estate, and could be distributed to her subjects "as occasion shall serve".[315]

However, during the Tudor era pardons also played a valuable role in reducing the number of people who went to the gallows at a time when an increasingly efficient (or less inefficient) criminal justice system was producing an unprecedented number of capital convictions. For (dramatic) example, in 1517 ill feeling towards foreign merchants in London, at a time of economic hardship, led to what was termed the Evil May Day. A mob at least a thousand strong gathered in Cheapside, attacking foreigners. They were eventually dispersed by troops summoned from the Tower of London. More than 300 people were arrested. Their supposed leader and 13 others were executed and then gibbeted. On 4 May royal officials charged another 278 people with high treason for their involvement in the riot. Numerous further executions appeared to be in the offing. However, in a piece of Tudor theatre, the Queen, Catherine of Aragon, intervened on their behalf, going on bended knee with tears in her eyes before her husband to beg for lenience. Afterwards, nearly all those charged with treason were pardoned in a mass ceremony at Westminster Hall, after filing past the monarch shouting, "Mercy!"[316] Nevertheless, as will be seen, the trade in pardons could also be highly lucrative for the Crown.

---

314. Shoemaker, *Sanctuary and Crime*, pp. 142–143.
315. Dean, *Law-Making and Society*, pp. 56–58 and p. 90.
316. Robert Bucholz and Carole Levin, *Queens and Power in Medieval and Early Modern England* (Lincoln: University of Nebraska Press, 2009), p. 33.

Once a pardon was issued, a crime was closed and could not be re-litigated on indictment, unless a flaw was found in the pardon process itself. Francis Cartwright's initial pardon for murdering a clergyman at the end of the Elizabethan era, secured using influence, wealth, and possibly corrupt practices, was subsequently questioned by the newly crowned James I, who appears to have had second thoughts about the clemency he had shown to a brutal killer. The king was, in Cartwright's words, "very willing that some defect, if possible, might have beene found in my pardon, and so should I have undergone the just stroke of the Law". Fortunately for him, the pardon proved legally "firme".[317]

A bizarre case in this regard occurred in respect of a homicide that occurred in Lancashire in 1597. Lawrence Foxe, a county bailiff, was shot and killed when trying to arrest Thomas Murrayfield at Crewkerne Fair. Murrayfield subsequently received a royal pardon. Many years later, in 1633, two men named Foxe (presumably relatives of the dead man) tendered a bill of murder against Murrayfield at the Somerset Assizes. It was thrown out when the grand jury learned of the Tudor pardon, and it was ordered that anyone troubling Murrayfield further about the matter be committed to gaol.[318] Some Elizabethan pardon acts expressly provided that if officials tried to impose penalties for offences pardoned by the statute, they themselves were to be fined, and the parties affected were to receive damages and their costs.[319]

Even as the use of pardons expanded, some observers had reservations about their effect on the wider criminal justice system. Towards the end of the era, Robert Parsons thought that they should not be awarded for highway robbery because the hope of such clemency, however misplaced, encouraged potential felons; he thought that the crime would decline markedly if it were known that the "Prince would hardly or never dispense or give pardon in that offence, but upon great, rare and extraordinary occasion".[320] His criticisms were very similar to those that would be voiced on the same subject by men such as Martin Madan almost two centuries later. Others had theological or jurisprudential objections.

---

317. Cartwright, *The life, confession, and heartie repentance*, pp. 1–36.
318. Cockburn, *Western Circuit Assize Orders*, p. 67.
319. Dean, *Law-Making and Society*, pp. 56–58 and p. 90.
320. Parsons, *The Jesuit's memorial*, pp. 210–11 and p. 253.

Philip Stubbes, like many early Jacobean and Elizabethan Puritans, did not feel that a monarch should dispense with what he termed God's law, which (presumably) included violations of the Ten Commandments. He was aware that many thought that the monarch might, by an exercise of his prerogative power, "pardon and remit the penaltie of any law, either divine or humane, but I am of opinion that if God's lawe condemne him, no prince ought to save him, but to execute judgement and justice without respect of persons to all indifferently".[321]

General Pardons

General pardons might be granted by royal proclamation or by parliamentary statute. People accused of crimes covered by the former could obtain copies from the Chancery (usually for a fee) and then present them in court. When the latter means was employed, as was increasingly the case during the Tudor era, Crown law officers would draw up the enabling Act, and little or no time would be needed to discuss its contents, which were not really open to debate, so that the bill would usually be introduced at the end of the session and quickly pass through both houses of Parliament.[322] Although such Acts were phrased in general terms, the pardons awarded were as valid as if each successful claimant had been specifically named. Moreover, it seems that any defendant could claim one, if he or she fell within its terms, without claiming an actual document, merely being required to pay a fee of 16 pence to the court clerks for recording the claim. This made them the cheapest and simplest form of pardon, at least by the end of the Tudor period.[323] Shortly afterwards, Ferdinando Pulton thought that, in practice, "Euery prisoner shall take aduantage of a generall pardon graunted by Act of Parliament, without pleading of it. And the court shall giue him the aduantage thereof, though he doth waiue and refuse the benefit of the same Act".

General pardons had been used on a regular basis during the late medieval period. For example, more than 4,800 people received mercy during

---

321. Stubbes, *The anatomie of abuses*.
322. Dean, *Law-Making and Society*, pp. 56–58 and p. 90.
323. Paul Griffiths and Simon Devereaux, *Penal Practice and Culture, 1500–1900: Punishing the English* (Basingstoke: Palgrave Macmillan, 2004), p. 128.

three years under Henry V's second general pardon of 1414 alone.[324] At this time, they often pardoned all offences committed prior to a specified date. That the authorities could (sometimes) show mercy to even the worst of sinners was still fundamental to late medieval notions of Christianity.[325] However, even medieval pardons might exclude crimes such as treason, murder, and rape, as was the case with the general pardon of 1377, granted to mark Edward III's golden jubilee.[326]

By the Tudor period, general pardons did not normally extend to the most heinous of crimes. Sometimes they expressly listed the felonies covered; at others they named the offences excluded, which might extend to robbery and coining. Many legal observers thought that murder was such a grave offence that a general pardon that was couched as extending to those that committed "all maner of fellonyes" would not cover this form of killing. It had to be specifically named, even though it was itself a felony.[327]

General pardons were normally granted to mark significant events in the life of the monarch and the nation, such as a coronation, jubilee, or marriage. Henry VII issued five of them; the first was granted just after his accession, the last as his death approached in 1509, when he granted a pardon to all offenders, "saving only thieves and murderers". At least 1,612 people benefitted from these general pardons. On his own accession in April 1509, Henry VIII went even further and granted a more "ample" pardon under the Great Seal than that recently granted by his dying father; he allowed it to all felons who had committed their crimes prior to the start of his rule who sued for it from the chancellor, including (very unusually) traitors and murderers. However, he prudently exempted from its terms a long list of named individuals. Unsurprisingly, this included those who were suspected of crimes of state, such as Edmund Dudley and Sir Richard Emson. However, it also extended to some individuals who were guilty of conventional felonies. Among

324. McCune, *Justice, Mercy*, p. 1670.
325. McSheffrey, "Sanctuary and the Legal Topography", p. 509.
326. Musson and Powell, *Crime, Law and Society*, p. 182.
327. Glazebrook, *The Boke of Justices of Peas*, p. Aiii.

them were Henry Stoughton, a London fishmonger, and Robert Porter, a murderer then in prison at Cambridge.[328]

Even so, in the first year of the reign of Henry VIII, nearly 3,000 people received clemency through this inaugural pardon, although the government still normally charged for it, viewing it as a valuable source of revenue. Within five years the king issued another one, and further general pardons followed periodically throughout the remainder of his life. Edward VI and Mary I also issued general pardons, as did Queen Elizabeth, although Elizabeth's pardon statutes gradually became more restrictive, covering fewer serious offences.[329] For example, the Pardon Acts of 1584–5, 1586–7, 1589, and 1593 normally excluded, inter alia, high treason, piracy, murder, coining, burglary, and robbery. However, arson, rape, abduction, and horse theft were also among those frequently excluded.[330]

All ranks in society, from peasants to gentlemen, and both sexes, claimed the benefit of general pardons, which were normally construed so as to favour the subject if there was any ambiguity in their terms.[331] Thus, in the last year of Queen Mary's reign, William Wickes and Elizabeth Gondye from London were accused at the Old Bailey of counterfeiting. They were found guilty of uttering, or putting the coins into circulation, but acquitted of manufacturing them. They then successfully pleaded the queen's general pardon.[332] Cases of simple grand larceny were probably the most frequently forgiven offences, not least because of the number of cases prosecuted, and because the crime was rarely excluded from the list of felonies covered by general pardons.

Typically, at the Surrey Assizes in July 1563, William Mayer, a Lambeth labourer, pleaded guilty to grand larceny after stealing more than £2 in cash from a chest. His plea was presumably entered in the knowledge that he could claim the general pardon of 1563, which was duly granted.[333] Lucy Jones of North Ockendon, in Essex, did contest her trial after

---

328. Brewer, *Letters and Papers, Foreign and Domestic, Henry VIII, Vol. 1*, pp. 1–8.
329. Kesselring, *Mercy and Authority*, pp. 56–69.
330. Dean, *Law-Making and Society*, pp. 56–58.
331. *Ibid*, p. 90.
332. Jeaffreson, *Middlesex County Records: Vol. 1*, pp. 29–33.
333. Cockburn, *Calendar of Assize Records. Surrey indictments: Elizabeth I*, p. 33.

she broke into the house of John Foster, a local gentleman, and stole a black cloak worth 50 shillings, but was convicted at the Braintree Assizes in July 1581. Even so, she was pardoned under the general pardon issued that year.[334]

It was not just those capitally convicted at assizes or the Old Bailey who could benefit from a general pardon. The much smaller numbers of people who faced death after conviction at quarter and borough sessions could also rely on them. For example, the general pardon of 1575 saved the lives of at least two condemned men who had been convicted at the Colchester Borough Sessions. James Lavering was pardoned after being found guilty of breaking into Matthew Brown's home in the town and taking cloth worth 40 shillings. Peter Field, who pleaded guilty to breaking into John Smart's house and taking money and silver worth 7s 4d, also escaped death in this manner. Lavering's case is particularly interesting in view of the terms of the general pardon from which he benefitted. It specifically excluded robberies from homes that secured goods and cash in excess of 41 shillings. He barely avoided this limit, which may raise the possibility that the valuation of the goods he stole was specifically tailored to meet the statutory provision.[335]

As these cases suggest, other than limiting the type of offender to whom they were granted, general pardons were entirely indiscriminate in their operation, not reflecting the merits (or connections) of the individuals who claimed them, or the strength of the prosecution case against them. This was not the case with special pardons.

Special Pardons

Statistically, the individual reprieves, or "special pardons", granted to "deserving" cases were probably even more important than general pardons during the Tudor era. Despite inadequate sources, the surviving patent rolls from 1485 to 1603 name nearly 14,000 individuals who obtained direct, personal grants of mercy from the Crown.[336] In a typical example, in the last two weeks of April 1531, the Crown issued separate

334. ERO T/A 418/36/27.
335. Samaha, "Hanging for Felony", pp. 763–782.
336. Kesselring, *Mercy and Authority*, p. 74.

pardons to at least four capitally convicted men. Thomas James, a yeoman from Quinton, in Northamptonshire, was pardoned for a theft committed at Edgware, in Middlesex; John Pulter, a Cambridge student, was pardoned for an unknown offence; Thomas Brown of Walden, in Essex, was pardoned for the murder of Richard ap Yevan ap Jenkyn; while Jack Musgrove, a gentleman from Bewcastle, in Cumberland, was pardoned for another unknown crime.[337] Sixty years later, in one week in September 1594, three men from different parts of England were granted special pardons by the Crown: Roger Orme of Whittington, in Staffordshire, for killing one Thomas Pudsey; Thomas Towley, for the burglary of clothes from one of the queen's servants in a house at Hampton Court, in Middlesex; and Richard Brantingham of County Durham, for another burglary.[338]

During the first 50 years of the Tudor era, it appears that between 300 and 500 special pardons were awarded each decade. Henry VII granted them to an annual average of 41 people during his reign. After about 1535 the numbers increased swiftly for the next two decades, before falling again and then stabilising in the years after 1565. As a result, during the reign of Queen Elizabeth, an average 109 people received special pardons each year. Even allowing for population growth, this was a significant increase on her father's time.[339]

It was always open to those who had been accused or convicted of a capital felony, or those acting on their behalf, to petition the sovereign for a pardon that would cover their particular crime, however grave. Illustrative of this, in October 1550 John Cheyney (c.1510–1567), a former soldier from West Woodhay, in Berkshire, led a group of men armed with swords who attacked and murdered a man named Robert Parrys in Newbury. King Edward VI was petitioned to grant letters patent pardoning Cheyney for his part in the murder.[340] Cheyney was pardoned in 1552. Although his goods would, in the normal course of events, have been seized on conviction (felony forfeiture), the Privy Council ordered

337. Gairdner, *Letters and Papers, Foreign and Domestic, Henry VIII, Vol. 5*, pp. 94–106.
338. Green, *Calendar of State Papers Domestic: Elizabeth, 1591–94*, pp. 554–559.
339. Kesselring, *Mercy and Authority*, pp. 74–75.
340. SHC LM/1739/1.

them to be retained by his wife so that she could maintain her children. Cheyney became an MP for Dover and JP for Berkshire a few years later.

It seems that, throughout the Tudor era, judges who became aware of deserving cases could also refer the matter to the Crown for consideration. During the reigns of Mary and Elizabeth this process appears to have become increasingly formalised. By the 1560s (if not well before), assizes judges might grant a temporary stay of execution after a capital conviction in these situations, then apply for a reprieve and "so declare the matter to the Prince, and obtaineth after a time for the prisoner his pardon".[341] For example, in 1561 Robert Durant was one of a group of four men convicted at the Old Bailey of highway robbery, but unlike the others he was reprieved without judgment. At the following sessions, Durant brought the Queen's special pardon of his felony (issued under the Great Seal the previous month) into court, and humbly begged that it might be allowed him.[342] Such judge-sponsored pardons eventually became a central part of the criminal justice system as more offences were withdrawn from clergy and society became increasingly reluctant to hang large numbers of capitally convicted felons. They persisted throughout the seventeenth and eighteenth centuries (when they became known as circuit pardons).

If the judge did not personally grant such a temporary reprieve at the end of sessions, for whatever reason, the convict would have to ask for short-term clemency to allow him time to make a more considered approach to the Crown for a permanent pardon. This would have to be done quite urgently, as Tudor executions were usually conducted shortly after the close of sessions, sometimes on the following day, and rarely more than a few days later. In 1538 the unfortunate Philip Witherick was convicted of murder at the Bury Assizes and executed a day or two later. Just two days after he was hanged, his alleged victim appeared, hale and hearty.[343] Unusually, when three witches were convicted at Chelmsford in July 1589, they had even less time to prepare: "After they had received their judgments, they were convayed from the Barre backe againe to

---

341. Smith, *De Republica Anglorum*, p. 120. Barnes, *Somerset Assize Orders*, p. 19.
342. Jeaffreson, *Middlesex County Records: Vol. 1*, pp. 37–44.
343. Bellamy, *Strange, Inhuman Deaths*, pp. 94–95.

Prison, where they had not stayed above two howers, but the officers prepared them-selves to conduct them to the place of execution: to which place they led them".[344]

As a result, an application for a temporary delay to allow a convict to petition for a pardon might be made in court or by a hurried letter thereafter. Thus, at the Chester Great Sessions in 1607, Richard Bradford, although convicted of murder and sentenced to death, was granted such a short-term reprieve.[345] Contacts and cash might be invaluable in these situations. It seems that, in practice, even a ten day deferral of sentence might cost the supplicant as much as £20. Other convicts might offer a few pounds to the judges' clerks or servants to encourage a short delay on their behalf. A petition would then be made to the monarch and council or Privy Council asking for mercy. If successful, the pardon might be presented at the following sessions; if not, the sentence would be carried out. However, the system lacked a formal apparatus for putting such petitions before the Crown for consideration. Frequently it relied on an applicant's having or making contacts.

After the mid-sixteenth century it became increasingly common for the Crown to refer a convict application for a special reprieve back to the assizes judge who had presided over the original trial, asking for his observations on its merits. These would be influential but not conclusive of the issue. This process would eventually become standard practice, lasting for several centuries to come. Thus, it seems that, after conviction at the Croydon Assizes in 1581, even the murderer William Sherwood "continued still obstinately denying the fact, hoping for some healpe by pardon, but a just judge prevented an ungratious hope".[346]

In a society with limited bureaucratic capacity, care had to be taken to ensure that a special pardon properly identified both its recipient and the crime(s) for which clemency was being granted. As Ferdinando Pulton noted, it ought to "agree with the Indictment, in the name, surname, and addition of the partie ... to the intent, that he may be knowne to be the same person which is indited". For example, in May 1509 a pardon was

---

344. Anon, *The Apprehension and confession of three notorious Witches*, p. 5.
345. TNA CHES 24/109/1.
346. Anon, *A true report of the late horrible murther*, pp. 1–16.

granted to a gentleman named Richard Yard of Bradleigh, in Norfolk, for all "murders, robberys, felonies, transgressions etc." It then gave all possible "aliases" for the same man by identifying other spellings for his home village, and other places associated with him or where he owned property (some of them in Devon), such as Highweek, Newton Bushel, Haccombe, and even London.[347] In January 1565 a copy of a royal pardon issued at the Middlesex Sessions of the Peace held at the Castle Inn in St John Street to one John Mathew, indicted for feloniously breaking and entering the house of the Earl of Rutland at Shoreditch and stealing silk curtains, had to be carefully compared with the allegation, with a note at the foot of the document recording that "this agreeth with the indictment".[348]

Special pardons might be granted for the most serious felonies and the most heinous offenders. This had always been the case. In 1455, Sir Thomas Courtney and his men brutally murdered and robbed Nicholas Radford, a long-serving and effective Devonshire JP and the Recorder of Exeter. Even so, they were pardoned the following year.[349] This continued during the Tudor era. In June 1507 Roger Leukenore of Fletching, in Sussex, who was described as a "gentilman", stabbed a local tailor to death with a knife. The ensuing coroner's inquest concluded that the tailor had been murdered. A week later, Leukenore feloniously killed another man with a dagger. He was eventually arrested and committed to Lewes Gaol to await trial at the next assizes. However, the case was transferred to King's Bench, and in 1508 he produced a pardon for all felonies and murders committed before 30 January that year.[350] In July 1585 Thomas Turke of Romford was convicted of three counts of highway robbery in Essex, during which almost £28 had been stolen, despite, it seems, having trained as a lawyer at the Inns of Chancery and Court (New Inn and the Inner Temple respectively). At the Essex Assizes he was sentenced to hang but appears to have had his sentence temporarily deferred while he sought a pardon, which was issued in February 1586.[351]

---

347. Devon Heritage Centre 231M/F/3.
348. SHC 6330/7/1/6.
349. Musson and Powell, *Crime, Law and Society*, pp. 86–87.
350. Hunnisett, *Sussex Coroners' Inquests*, p. 6.
351. Cockburn, *Calendar of Assize Records. Essex Indictments: Elizabeth I*, p. 288.

Special pardons were not confined to members of the upper orders, even broadly construed, although their wealth and contacts ensured that they were disproportionately the recipients of such mercy. Nevertheless, in 1555 Nicholas Palmer, a London tailor, killed another man with a sword at Bunhill in Middlesex. He pleaded guilty to murder but subsequently received a pardon by letters patent.[352] In like manner, in 1557, a yeoman named Francis Draycotte fled following a fatal stabbing in Nottingham. In 1560 he, too, was pardoned by letters patent.[353]

Factors Influencing the Grant of Special Pardons

A variety of factors appear to have influenced royal willingness to grant special pardons, and judicial preparedness to support them. Special pardons reflected such diverse matters as the merits of the offender, the circumstances and gravity of his crime, the need to set an example, and the personal contacts and financial resources of the petitioner. Most involved a combination of these factors. Many of them would be considered important mitigation today, and were to influence such decisions for centuries to come. Others would be viewed as irrelevant in the modern era, and some would be considered quite improper.

Safety of the Conviction

The safety of a conviction was always an important factor in encouraging clemency, especially (but not solely) when raised by a trial judge. There was no appeal on issues of fact or law from a jury conviction, however mistaken. As a result, judges often suggested reprieves for those who had been found guilty if they felt that a jury had convicted on unsatisfactory proofs and "upon slender evidence they have pronounced him giltie, whom the Judges and most part of the Justices thinkes by the evidence not fullie prooved guiltie".[354] (Such cases also suggest that juries did not always listen to judicial hints favouring an acquittal.) This was not a new

---

352. Jeaffreson, *Middlesex County Records: Vol. 1*, p. 24.
353. Hunnisett, *Calendar of Nottinghamshire Coroners' Inquests*, p. 155.
354. Smith, *De Republica Anglorum*, p. 120.

consideration in the Tudor era. Sir John Fortescue, a former chief justice of the King's Bench, had observed it in the 1460s.[355]

In these situations, as Sir Thomas Smith noted, at the point when a judge would normally pronounce sentence of death upon the convicted person, "he will differ it, which is called to reprive the prisoner (that is to say to send him againe to prison) and so declare the matter to the Prince, and obtaineth after a time for the prisoner his pardon". When supporting a special pardon on these grounds, assizes judges would often comment on the strength of the prosecution case and the nature of the evidence. For example, they might note that a conviction had been secured on purely circumstantial evidence (sometimes termed a "presumption of guilt"). During the 1500s, 26 men and ten women secured special pardons that expressly noted their likely innocence; in many other cases the belief of innocence may well have been present but the reasons not properly enunciated.[356]

A selection of cases is indicative of pardons granted on these grounds. In 1524 a signed bill for the pardon of Joan Burleton noted that she was now deemed innocent of poisoning her husband, after having been indicted by the "procurement, instance, and special labour of certain malicious gentlemen" (by no means the only such case during the era).[357] In 1537 Sir William Drury, the High Sheriff for Norfolk and Suffolk, wrote to Sir William Paston, noting that one Thomas Laynde had been arraigned at a recent assizes, found guilty of felony, and sentenced to death. Nevertheless, Drury had reprieved him for the King's consideration, along with another capitally convicted man. He did this at the last moment possible, without publicly announcing it in advance, looking for a reaction that was indicative of guilt or innocence from the two convicts when they arrived at the gallows and saw "other men die before them, not knowing the contrary but that they should have suffered likewise". Clearly neither man had made a gallows confession while awaiting death, and they were then temporarily respited while the Crown considered their case further. Drury had personally examined both men, and

---

355. Grigor, *Sir John Fortescue*, p. 91.
356. Kesselring, *Mercy and Authority*, pp. 93–94.
357. *Ibid*, p. 274.

concluded that Launde, at least, was not present at any of the robberies for which he had been convicted. He begged Paston to obtain a pardon, as Launde had seven children depending upon him for support.[358] In March 1584 Agnes Hughes, a spinster (possibly a servant maid) from Stepney, was tried for murdering her newborn male baby in a bedroom of the house of Mathew Stafford, a butcher from the same parish. At her arraignment at the Old Bailey, Hughes pleaded not guilty and was, it seems, convicted of suffocating the infant, but reprieved because the evidence against her was uncertain.[359]

On the occasions when quarter sessions tried felonies, the JPs present might consider who among those capitally convicted was suitable for a pardon. For example, in 1562 Robert Nigeon, a London shoemaker, was convicted of highway robbery after trial at gaol delivery in the Liberty of Havering at Bower. However, he was not executed. The justices of the peace who had presided over the tiny quarter sessions remanded him into the keeping of the town bailiff, and he appears to have been kept in custody in its small gaol for the ensuing 29 months, when the Queen pardoned him on the basis of further information supplied by the town magistrates.[360]

In other situations, new evidence came to light in the short period between conviction and execution, casting doubt on the safety of the original verdict. In 1565 Margaret Watson was convicted of poisoning her husband. Fortunately, the person who had accused her admitted fabricating the evidence shortly before she was due to be burned at the stake, allowing a reprieve. Sometimes, wrongly convicted persons were pardoned after confessions were made by those who had actually committed the crimes, and who were about to be hanged for other offences, or when statements were made by other convicted principals in the crime absolving them from involvement as accomplices.[361] In the early 1590s John Neale was found guilty of murder at the Devonshire Assizes, allegedly because of a semi-malicious prosecution and because none of his own witnesses was available at the hearing. He was sentenced to death.

---

358. Gairdner, *Letters and Papers, Foreign and Domestic, Henry VIII, Vol. 12, Part 1*, pp. 292–305.
359. Jeaffreson, *Middlesex County Records: Vol. 1*, pp. 145–155.
360. McIntosh, *A Community Transformed*, p. 329.
361. Kesselring, *Mercy and Authority*, pp. 93–94.

The true circumstances of the case were quickly submitted to the assize judges, who twice reprieved him, and then left the matter to the Queen's "merciful consideration".[362]

Of course, not all attempts to secure a reprieve on these grounds were either well-founded or successful. In 1573 a minister named Mell who had closely followed Anne Saunders' trial and conviction for murdering her husband, and spiritually counselled her while she was in Newgate Gaol awaiting execution, was so taken in by her protestations of innocence that he fell in love and "perswaded himselfe that she was utterly cléere". He asked her convicted accomplice, Anne Drury, to take the whole blame for what had occurred so that he could petition for a pardon on behalf of Saunders. Drury agreed, after Mell promised to provide a marriage portion for her daughter, and she made a statement completely absolving Saunders of any involvement in the killing. Mell then approached the Privy Council, to "sue for hir pardon, which thing he did with such outrage of doting affection, that he not only proffered summes of mony, but also offered his owne body & life for the safety of the woman". However, the members of the council quickly appreciated that Saunders truly was guilty, and, even worse for Mell, learned of his plan to marry her. They dismissed his petition and ordered that Mell be pilloried with a paper on his breast stating that he was being punished "for practising to colour the detestable factes of George Saunders wife".[363]

Degree of Culpability

Despite such cases, there were few doubts about the guilt of the great majority of people who were specially pardoned. Other factors were involved. Typically judges might recommend a pardon if they thought that the convict, although technically guilty, was not deserving of death "for some other cause".[364] One important factor was their degree of culpability. In a few cases, this was minimal or even non-existent.

---

362. Green, *Calendar of State Papers Domestic: Elizabeth, 1595–97*, pp. 121–138.

363. Arthur Golding, *A briefe discourse of the late murther of master George Saunders, a worshipfull citizen of London and of the apprehension, arreignement, and execution of the principall and accessaries of the same* (London, 1573), pp. 1–32; Joseph H. Marshburn, "'A Cruell Murder Donne in Kent' and Its Literary Manifestations", *Studies in Philology*, Vol. 46, No. 2, pp. 131–140.

364. Smith, *De Republica Anglorum*, p. 120.

De Cursu Pardons

During the Tudor period people were still being prosecuted and convicted for homicides where self-defence had been raised successfully at trial, with an express acknowledgment by the jury as to the circumstances in which they had been found guilty. This had been the medieval practice. However, by the seventeenth century, those who had killed in this manner were either not being indicted, or were being acquitted outright at trial if they were (the modern situation). In a transitional period during the late sixteenth century, a declining number of individuals were still formally convicted in such situations. Nevertheless, pardons were granted almost automatically or *de cursu* ("of course") to those found guilty in these circumstances, often being issued by the chancellor without direct royal involvement. In the early 1500s Thomas More alluded to this when noting that if a man killed for "hys owne defence, or misfortune drawe hym to that dede, a pardon serueth whic … the law graunteth of course".[365]

More specifically, in February 1520 Thomas Carew was granted a pardon for having killed Robert Bawdewyn in self-defence. According to an inquest taken before Thomas Barnwell (the London coroner), Bawdewyn had first assaulted Carew in a house in the S. Katherine's Liberty.[366] Similarly, in February 1533 William Baily, a blacksmith from Blandford, in Dorset, received a pardon for having killed Edward Calverley, a fletcher from the same village, by a blow given in self-defence, this being certified before the assize judges for Dorset sitting at Shaftesbury.[367] In 1561 a coroner's inquest held at Holborn, in Middlesex, decided that Thomas Hewys had murdered Lewis Howell with a dagger. Hewys pleaded not guilty at trial. The petty jury returned a verdict stating that he had been furiously assaulted by Howell, and had endeavoured to escape (a required feature in cases that took place outside the home), before killing him in self-defence. As a result, Hewys was committed to gaol "ad graciam domine Regine expectandam".[368] William Johnson did even better when an Essex assizes jury found him guilty of homicide in self-defence after

---

365. Thomas More, *The History of King Richard the Third* (London, 1513), pp. 47–49.
366. Brewer, *Letters and Papers, Foreign and Domestic, Henry VIII, Vol. 3*, pp. 206–217.
367. Gairdner, *Letters and Papers, Foreign and Domestic, Henry VIII, Vol. 6*, pp. 79–89.
368. Jeaffreson, *Middlesex County Records: Vol. 1*, pp. 37–44.

he mortally wounded a miller with a knife; he was bailed until he secured the requisite pardon.[369]

A case from early 1589, in which Charles Wrenne fatally stabbed Robert Ratclyff with a sword, is indicative of the mechanics of this procedure. On his arraignment at the Old Bailey, Wrenne pleaded not guilty to felonious "manslater" (he was not indicted for murder) but guilty to killing Ratclyff in self-defence. This seems to have been accepted, and the matter was put over to a later sessions. At a summer gaol delivery he produced the queen's pardon, issued under the Great Seal of England in May, and asked that it might be allowed him, which it duly was.[370]

The same clemency might be shown towards those who committed their crimes while suffering from severe mental illness (as understood by contemporary observers). As with self-defence, the sixteenth century was something of a transitional period in this regard. Insanity was slowly recognised as a simple defence to a criminal allegation, one that would entitle the accused person to an acquittal, unlike the former (medieval) approach, which suggested that its presence might be dealt with by a pardon following conviction. For example, in a case heard at King's Bench in 1535, Maud Petuous was discharged because it was found that she "did the felony when [she] was insane, i.e. mad. For in such sickness a man does not have the use of reason, and so he cannot have animum felonicum".[371] Nevertheless, the medieval procedure was often followed until late in the era. In 1563 Thomas Hughes was convicted of a murder by a jury that also found that he was insane at the time. He had attacked another man in his native Camberwell with a knife. He was subsequently granted a pardon.[372] Rather strangely, in June 1589 Henry Cheseman was tried for murder at the Surrey Assizes, convicted of manslaughter, pleaded and was granted benefit of clergy, but, because he was deemed to be insane, remanded in custody (presumably for public safety).[373]

---

369. Cockburn, *Calendar of Assize Records. Essex Indictments: Elizabeth I*, p. 279.
370. Jeaffreson, *Middlesex County Records: Vol. 1*, pp. 182–189.
371. Henry Spelman, *Archaeologus* (London: Johannem Beale, 1626), p. 58.
372. Kesselring, *Mercy and Authority*, p. 96; Cockburn, *Calendar of Assize Records. Surrey Indictments: Elizabeth I*, p. 33.
373. *Ibid*, p. 336.

Mitigating Circumstances

Mitigating factors that might justify a special pardon went much further than those that warranted *de cursu* reprieves. As Thomas More noted, the king could grant a pardon out of simple "pitie".[374] For example, such compassion might be extended to those who were very young, albeit over the technical age of legal responsibility (seven years), and not deemed able to properly understand the quality of their actions, especially for lesser capital offences. In 1544 the queen, Catherine Parr, wrote to Henry VIII, who was then in France, asking him to authorise the grant of a pardon to a servant boy who had stolen a low-value item from his mistress, on the basis that he was extremely repentant and in view of his "young years and because the fact is but hardly construed felony".[375]

Mercy might also be shown towards those people who killed in sudden anger, rather than with premeditation, particularly if they had been convicted of manslaughter but were illiterate or female (and so could not claim benefit of clergy). Such was the case with a man who had killed in an argument about who was to clean some stables, and another who attacked a person who had abused his dogs.[376]

In a strange case from 1565, John Brett, a yeoman, and two other men, described as a husbandman and labourer, all of them from Broomfield in Essex, broke into the close of Henry Welde in the same village, violently assaulted him, stole a bushel of rye worth 2s 6d, and a plough with chains attached valued at 13s 4d. They were prosecuted but subsequently discharged by pardon in early 1567. The singular nature of the items stolen and the lack of concealment for their actions, might suggest that a dispute over property or payment lay behind their behaviour, so that they acted under a sense of entitlement, perhaps explaining the decision.[377]

Nevertheless, pardons were sometimes granted for reasons that would be considered wholly inappropriate in the modern era. Most important, influential contacts and money could be vital to the process.

---

374. More, *Richard the Third*, pp. 47–49.
375. Kesselring, *Mercy and Authority*, p. 109.
376. *Ibid*, p. 105.
377. ERO Q/SR 21/29.

Contacts

During the medieval period royal pardons were often readily available to aristocratic felons, even in the most serious cases, by dint of their social status, financial resources, and contacts. As an examination of fifteenth century indictments determined in the Court of King's Bench suggests, in most circumstances, people of landed rank could rely on a pardon for any crime short of high treason. The medieval Crown often appears to have viewed the judicial execution of a member of aristocratic society for a conventional felony as an intrusion into what were essentially private matters. As a result, pardons might be granted for blatant murders conducted as part of family property disputes, as occurred after Sir John Basynge's illegitimate son, the beneficiary under his will, was hacked to death by rivals in 1446.[378]

Rank and connections continued to provide significant protection to those members of the upper orders who were guilty of serious crimes during the Tudor period. Many did not even get as far as conviction before being pardoned, especially if their victims were poor. For example, Thomas Culpepper was a favourite of Henry VIII's until executed as Catherine Howard's lover in 1541. He had an elder brother by the same name. In 1539 it seems that one of them (it is not entirely clear which) was accused of raping a park keeper's wife in a thicket while four of his attendants held her down. Local villagers seized him, but not before he had killed one of them in the attendant struggle, after which he was taken into custody. Even so, the family's influence was able to secure a pardon fairly swiftly from the king, and they continued to flourish for a while longer, although the award of clemency occasioned some concern.[379]

However, despite such cases, the Crown abandoned some of its previous high degree of tolerance for aristocratic crime during the Tudor era, whether as a result of changing social mores, an assertion of its growing power (see *Chapter 2*), or simple personal animosity towards those involved. The last of these factors may have been operating in a case from the latter part of the reign of Henry VIIII. Thomas Fiennes

---

378. S. J. Payling, "Murder, Motive and Punishment in Fifteenth century England: Two Gentry Case-Studies", *English Historical Review*, Vol. 113, Issue 450, pp. 1–20.

379. Hastings Robinson (ed.), *Original Letters Relative to the English Reformation* (Cambridge: Parker Society, 1847), pp. 226–7.

(1517–1541), the ninth (southern) Lord Dacre, was keen on hunting, and not overly concerned about doing it on other men's land. In 1537 he wrote a letter to Thomas Cromwell blaming the "frailness of my youth" for being led into such activity. Even so, late one evening in April 1541, Dacre and a party of eight "rakish" young men (mostly of good family) left his castle at Hurstmonceux to poach in the neighbouring park of Sir Nicholas Pelham, taking deer nets with them to trap bucks. On their way, the company became split into two groups. One group, which does not appear to have included Dacre, came across some of Pelham's servants (they may have been gamekeepers), one of whom, the elderly John Busebridge, was mortally wounded when an affray ensued, dying almost two weeks later. Pelham pursued the case aggressively, and Dacre's entire company (not just those present at the killing) were indicted for murder, possibly under personal pressure from the king. The coroner's inquest into the death concluded that they had bound themselves by oath, before the expedition, to kill anyone who might oppose them, facilitating such a conclusion.[380]

The matter came before a jury of 17 peers, and was held in front of the Lord Chancellor, who was "sitting that day as high steward of England" in the court of the same name, Parliament being in recess (see *Chapter 11*). Lord Dacre initially pleaded not guilty to murder, but, after (allegedly) "sufficient" evidence on the Crown's part was given in open court, he was (very unwisely) persuaded to change his plea and "cast himself on the king's mercy.[381] A capital and unclergyable conviction necessarily followed. Lord Cobham and other members of the jury of peers then attempted to use their influence to obtain a pardon, meeting the Privy Council in Westminster. The council passed on their concerns to Henry VIII, together with a personal plea from Dacre. However, the king was determined that the law should take its course, and four days after his conviction, having been given false hope when a temporary stay of execution arrived on the morning of his execution, Dacre was hanged (not even being beheaded) at Tyburn and later buried in St Sepulchre's Church on Snow Hill. Seven of his companions were also indicted for the crime.

---

380. Hunnisett, *Sussex Coroners' Inquests*, p. 33.
381. Gairdner and Brodie, *Letters and Papers, Foreign and Domestic, Henry VIII, Vol. 16*, pp. 444–465.

Three were convicted and then executed at St Thomas a Watering. Four received clemency, one of the latter was a well-born youth named John Cheyney, son of Sir Thomas Cheyney (a courtier then in favour), who was "freely pardoned" by the Crown.[382]

Dacre's case was quintessentially one that might have been expected to produce a pardon. His victim was poor and had died some time after the violent incident, in which Dacre's own involvement was quite marginal. He had been a fairly important figure at court some years earlier. The king may have sought his substantial estate (by felony forfeiture) or had a personal animus towards the young nobleman.

Arguably, the execution of Charles, Lord Stourton and four of his servants in 1557 for the murder of his steward, William Hartgill, and another man, is even more indicative of a lower tolerance for aristocratic crime by the mid-sixteenth century. It appears that Stourton thought he would be able to secure a pardon until almost the very end, and it seems that such clemency may have been in the offing when he was executed.[383]

Even so, and despite such cases, to the end of the Tudor period and well beyond, social rank continued to provide the landed felon with some immunity from the consequences of his actions, even if the victim was highly respectable, as was the case with Francis Cartwright, a gentleman who had hacked to death the Reverend William Storr, the minister of Market Rasen, in Lincolnshire, in 1603.[384] Similarly, in 1599 John Fitz, an ill-tempered, paranoid, drunken, and confrontational young man from a prominent West Country family, brutally ambushed and murdered the genteel Nicholas Slanning, his erstwhile dining companion, after a drunken quarrel. Like Cartwright, he immediately fled to France while his wife went about securing a pardon from the queen by means of the "procurement of her worthy freendes". This allowed him to return some six months later. Far from this irreversibly damaging his position, Fitz was knighted shortly afterwards, one of many gentlemen so rewarded

---

382. Robert Hutchinson, *The Last Days of Henry VIII: Conspiracy, Treason and Heresy at the Court of the Dying Tyrant* (London: Weidenfeld & Nicolson, 2006), p. 39.

383. Narasingha Prosad Sil, *Tudor Placemen and Statesmen: Select Case Histories* (Madison, N.J.: Fairleigh Dickinson University Press, 2001), p. 122.

384. Payling, "Murder, Motive and Punishment", p. 17.

by the newly crowned James I. Two years later he went on to murder a tavern keeper in Twickenham and, soon after, to commit suicide.[385]

In like manner, after cold-bloodedly murdering Henry Long with a pistol in 1594 (as an inquest later found) in Corsham, in Wiltshire, following alleged insults on an earlier occasion, the brothers Charles and Henry Danvers, both knights, were given refuge by the Earl of Southampton at his seat near Titchfield. Three days later they moved on to nearby Calshot Castle before escaping to France. There they distinguished themselves in the army of Henry IV and set about securing clemency or, as the Earl of Shrewsbury put it in October 1596, tasting the queen's "pittie and mercie". In June 1598 the brothers were pardoned, possibly after the French king petitioned Elizabeth, although the fact that their influential widowed mother had contracted a marriage to Sir Edmund Carey, the queen's cousin, was probably as important. The pair returned to England later that summer, albeit required to pay Sir Walter Long, Henry's brother £1,500.[386]

As all three of these cases suggest, the ability of the well-connected and wealthy to get to a foreign jurisdiction, so allowing a cooling-off period and time for intercession, was helpful when seeking pardons. However, clemency was especially likely if rank was combined with a substantial cash payment, and even the former was unnecessary if enough of the latter could be secured.

The Trade in Pardons

Reprieves were an important source of finance for the Crown. Such money might be paid directly in exchange for clemency. For example, in March 1533 it was suggested to Cromwell that a pardon for Robert Rice might be worth the enormous sum of 4,000 marks (more than £2,500) to the king.[387] In May the same year, the *coram rege* roll of the Court of King's Bench, which contained the murder indictment against Richard Southwell and several other men for killing Sir William Pennington a

---

385. J. Fitz, *The bloudy booke, or, The tragicall and desperate end of Sir John Fites (alias) Fitz* (London: Francys Burton, 1605), ff. B1–3 and C3.
386. Moore, *The Tudor Murder Files*, pp. 176–181.
387. Gairdner, *Letters and Papers, Foreign and Domestic, Henry VIII, Vol. 6*, pp. 89–99.

year earlier, noted that the accused men had presented to the court letters patent from the king, granting a pardon, as well as the monarch's
letters directed to the judges observing that the men had each provided
sufficient sureties for their future good behaviour. They went free. However, a note among Thomas Cromwell's memoranda also recorded that
Southwell had paid the King £1,000 for the pardons, something that
necessitated selling several manors.[388] It was not necessary to be a member
of the upper social orders to pay for clemency. In 1544, Queen Catherine
Parr and her regency council suggested to Henry VIII (who was away
on campaign) that £300 be accepted from two gypsies who had been
convicted of felony in exchange for a pardon.[389]

Alternatively, those seeking pardons could persuade someone with
connections (direct or indirect) to the king or queen to intercede on
their behalf. The monarch might then grant them a pardon as a favour
to the supplicant, which in its turn would put the latter under an obligation towards the Crown. Sometimes such intercession would be the
result of personal relationships. In February 1568 William Paulet, the
Marquess of Winchester, wrote to William More, a Surrey JP, on behalf
of the 23-year-old son of one of his tenants. The young man was accused
of stealing goods and cash to the value of 40 shillings from his master's
house (an unclergyable felony under an Act of 1535), and was likely to
face trial at the forthcoming assizes. The marquess asked that More delay
submitting the case papers (examinations, etc.) until after these sessions
had finished, so that the alleged thief was listed for the following assizes,
and to bail him in the meantime. This would "give him time to try his
friends for a pardon to the Queen's Majesty". Interestingly, the marquess
felt it necessary to stress that by encouraging such a course of action he
was not seeking to prevent justice being implemented, merely to limit
the suspect to receiving "some good warning now in his youth".[390]

However, in many other cases, those seeking pardons might have to
pay men and women with influence to intercede on their behalf, in a
blatantly financial transaction. This situation had been inherited from

---

388. McSheffrey, "The Slaying of Sir William Pennington", p. 187.
389. Kesselring, *Mercy and Authority*, p. 132.
390. SHC 6729/6/107.

the late medieval period. For example, and at a very grand, expensive, and successful level, can be considered the case of Sir John Basynges' illegitimate daughter, Alice, prosecuted for being an accessory to murder in 1446 committed as part of a property dispute following the implementation of his will (see above). She took steps to secure a pardon, apparently promising the Basynges' substantial lands in Kent to Sir James Fiennes, Lord Saye and Sele, who was influential at court, to intercede on her behalf. He duly used his influence with Queen Margaret to obtain a pardon for Alice in 1448, the Kentish lands being transferred to him just days later.[391] Such transactions continued during the Tudor era.

For example, at Christmas 1518 Thomas Bennett, an Essex park-keeper, widely (and correctly) rumoured to have murdered a local man who had disappeared, began to feel that the net was closing in on him, and decided to look for a long-term solution to his problem. A few months later, he met with an elderly man named Thomas Christmas in Colchester, who advised him to sell all his goods and lands and move away, while seeking out a "young gentleman" who would be able to get him a royal pardon for 20 marks (about £14). Such a modest sum may have been slightly optimistic for a murder. Bennett appears to have made some, if unavailing, efforts to find such an intercessor.[392]

Conditional Pardons

During the Tudor period almost all general pardons, and most special pardons, were unconditional. However, even then, some of the latter were subject to specific requirements and obligations, albeit not nearly as many as would be the case 200 years later (by which time penal transportation was a widespread condition of clemency).

Enlistment during time of war was one of the most common conditions imposed for the grant of a Tudor reprieve, as it would be for centuries to come. For example, in January 1596 the queen resolved that appropriate prisoners sentenced to death at gaol delivery could be pardoned on condition of military service. The following month the lord

391. Payling, "Murder, Motive and Punishment", p. 8.
392. Roger, *Tudor Trials: Confessions from the Star Chamber.*

mayor, recorder and sheriff of London drew up a list with the names of those so pardoned, noting that the remaining convicts were to be executed to prevent a bad example being set to other potential felons.[393] This form of pardon had already existed for several centuries. In 1284 Edward I had recruited from the prisons for his Gascon campaign. More than a century later, in 1389 Parliament had successfully petitioned for a temporary limitation on pardons being granted for violent crimes in exchange for army service, after the government had trawled the nation's gaols granting reprieves to numerous healthy convicts on this basis.[394] Concern about the excessive use of reprieves then led Parliament to pass the Statute of Pardons of 1390, which excluded treason, homicide, and rape from general pardons. However, its provisions were being disregarded by the reign of Henry V (1413–1422), and were then generally ignored.[395]

Galley service was also occasionally imposed as a condition of reprieve during the sixteenth century. Contrary to popular belief, Tudor England did experiment with such vessels, often maintaining a small force of them, especially in the second half of the era, and sometimes using reprieved convicts to man them.[396] For example, at the start of Edward VI's reign the council pardoned some condemned criminals in exchange for their becoming oarsmen, before deciding that the vessels were too expensive to maintain and taking them out of service in 1551. The idea was subsequently revived, and in 1586 the Privy Council selected six commissioners (one of them the Lord High Admiral) to reprieve able-bodied convicts (murderers, rapists, and burglars apart) on condition of galley service. In a letter to assizes judges, Queen Elizabeth observed that such service was physically very demanding and "painful", and was therefore widely used in other countries as punishment.[397]

The commissioners would reprieve suitably fit men from time-to-time, as and when needed. These individuals would then serve for at least three years, or longer if the commissioners thought fit. In April 1586 Sir

393. Harrison, *A Second Elizabethan Journal*, pp. 77–79.
394. McGlynn, "Violence and the Law", pp. 53–59.
395. Powell, *Kingship, Law, and Society*, p. 84.
396. J. E.G. Bennell, "English Oared Vessels of the Sixteenth Century, Part I", *The Mariner's Mirror*, Vol. 60, Issue 1, pp. 9–26.
397. Kesselring, *Mercy and Authority*, pp. 84–85.

Francis Walsingham wrote to the Solicitor General, noting that one galley had already been built, and expressing the hope that manning them with felons would reduce an apparently burgeoning level of crime, if only because they would "terrify ill disposed persons from offending".[398]

Galley service was mentioned again in a statute from 1598, and in June 1602 the Privy Council wrote to Judge Francis Gawdy of the Queen's Bench and serjeant-at-law John Hele, who were also assizes judges for the Home Circuit, noting that the queen had prepared galleys to protect the coast and proposed to employ as oarsmen those who were physically strong and "justly deserved death", but might otherwise receive ordinary pardons and commit further offences if set at liberty.

As previously, rapists, murderers, or burglars were stayed from execution in exchange for serving at least seven years in the galleys. Their friends were asked to contribute £3 a year; otherwise their county bore the charge. JPs were also urged to commit "incorrigible rogues" to the galleys as a deterrent. At the end of each circuit the assize judges were to prepare a list of those so punished (and those paying the £3).

Perhaps unsurprisingly, the £3-a-year subvention quickly proved problematic. In July 1603, in reply to the Privy Council's letter, Gawdy and Hele presented a list of men from the Home Circuit who were spared from execution for galley service, while Hertfordshire had even identified some suitable incorrigible rogues, but the judges also noted that few of them could procure friends to contribute towards their maintenance. The judges had encouraged county JPs to defray the cost instead, but with mixed results. Those in Sussex and Surrey agreed to furnish £3 yearly for every man reprieved in these circumstances. However, the JPs in Essex, Kent, and Hertfordshire were concerned at the potential expense.[399]

Even so, because the rough waters around the British Isles, with their shallow drafts and low level of clearance between sea and deck, were not conducive to the use of galleys, they were not widely employed, with few being fully-manned, and so such service was comparatively rarely stipulated as a punishment or condition of reprieve.

---

398. J. Payne Collier (ed.), *The Egerton Papers: A Collection of Public and Private Documents* (London: Camden Society, 1840), pp. 116–117.

399. R. A. Roberts (ed.), Calendar of the Cecil Papers in Hatfield House,: Vol. 1, 1306–1571 (London: HMSO, 1910), pp. 239–252.

PART V
CRIME

CHAPTER 16

Homicide and Violence

Introduction

In the late 1400s, the substantive law governing homicide was confused. Medieval criminal law had focussed heavily on a killer's deeds, at the expense of their state of mind when they carried them out or, to use legal parlance, on the *actus reus* rather than *mens rea* of the crime. This started to change during the Tudor era, but the process was still far from complete at its close, and was particularly significant in homicide cases.

At the end of the fifteenth century, most killings were not legally differentiated in their consequences; more particularly, a meaningful distinction was not made between murder and manslaughter, although both terms were in use. This had not always been the case. The Statute of Pardons of 1390 *had* made such a distinction, for a short period, but it had fallen into abeyance by about 1430. As a result, JPs normally adopted a standard form when drawing up homicide indictments in which it was simply alleged that the suspect assaulted and "feloniously slew and murdered" the deceased person. In this context, "murder" was merely a general descriptive term for any form of culpable killing. There was no fully formulated and articulated lesser homicide offence. At the end of the fifteenth century Serjeant Keble still believed that excessive chastisement that resulted in death, such as the beating of children or young servants with fatal consequences, would produce either a murder or a misadventure verdict; there was nothing in between, although the circumstances of such a killing might affect the grant of a royal reprieve.[1]

---

1.   J. M. Kaye, "The Early History of Murder and Manslaughter", *The Law Quarterly Review*, Vol. 83, Issue 4, p. 570.

Late-fifteenth century jurors dealing with an allegation of homicide could: convict, which led to the gallows in the absence of benefit of clergy or a pardon; acquit, which resulted in release and freedom; or produce a finding of some specially mitigating or "excusing ground", such as self-defence, insanity (in which an accused person killed while of "unsound mind"), or misadventure/misfortune (*per infortunam*), an accidental killing. This third, general category of verdicts did not (yet) lead to an acquittal, as it often did by the following century — most observers viewed such findings as convictions — but would result in the defendant's being returned to gaol, or even bailed, pending the formal issue of a pardon as a matter of course, or *de cursu* (see *Chapter 15*).[2]

This general inflexibility in the law might have occasioned considerable injustice. However, in practice, during the era of the self-informing jury, when most evidence was not given in public, it could be circumvented. Jurors were able to stretch the facts of a case to produce what they perceived to be a just result. They tended to find that deserving defendants were acting in specially exonerating circumstances, whatever the reality. For example, they might find a homicide excusable; this led to an automatic pardon. Occasionally, they might even acquit outright.

A law report written in Anglo-Norman French, from the Northamptonshire Eyre (a circuit court) of 1329, which involved the trial of men accused of feloniously killing one William atte Grene, is illustrative of this phenomenon. Grene had been caught stealing a cow and escaped while being led to gaol. His captors responded by pursuing and decapitating him. The eyre justices ordered their arrest, because they had made themselves judges by killing him, and a jury was eventually convened to try the men. The jurors concluded that the alleged victim was a notorious thief who had drawn a knife on his pursuers. They also declared that they did not suspect the defendants of any felony, and so acquitted them.[3]

However, by the start of the Tudor era, trial jurors had lost their previously high level of control over verdicts because they ceased to supply most of the facts on which convictions were based. In theory, they could

---

2. Kesselring, "No Greater Provocation? Adultery and the Mitigation of Murder in English Law", *Law and History Review*, Vol. 34, Issue 1, p. 207.

3. Elizabeth Papp Kamali, "Felonia Felonice Facta: Felony and Intentionality in Medieval England", *Criminal Law and Philosophy*, Vol. 9, No. 3, pp. 397–421.

still apply their own standards through a blank not guilty verdict, disregarding in-court evidence, but this risked judicial ire (see *Chapter 11*), as obviously at variance with the material led at trial. As a result, this became an occasional rather than regular phenomenon, especially in homicide cases. In response and, it seems, to prevent injustice being occasioned by this development, definitions of homicide necessarily underwent fairly rapid, but largely unplanned, change in the early Tudor era.[4]

By the start of the sixteenth century, common law had begun to formally differentiate between classes of homicide by distinguishing murder from manslaughter.[5] By then the law recognised that there were two types of killings, one of which was "called murder, and that is, when one man upon malice prepared, and forethought, doth feloniously kill another. And the other is called manslaughter, as Chance-Medley, and that is, when two men fight together upon a suddaine heat of blood, without an malice precedent, and one of them kill the other".[6]

As this comment suggests, and as a lawyers' reading delivered in Gray's Inn in the early 1520s expressly noted, murder required deliberation or malice aforethought (*malice prepense*).[7] The most common reason for determining that this was absent, and so reducing murder to manslaughter (a word first widely disseminated in the *Boke of Justyces of Peas* of 1506, but often termed "felonious killing" or simply "homicide" in court), was that the death occurred against a background of "chance medley".[8] Such cases normally involved a sudden, unplanned, and "hot-blooded" killing in the course of a fight engaged in by perpetrator and victim. Most such killings arose from spontaneous quarrels .[9]

Thus, and typically, a coroner's inquest held in September 1511 concluded that Henry Baskerville, a Hereford man, had been killed in a knife

---

4. Kaye, "The Early History", p. 570.
5. Kamali, "The Devil's Daughter of Hell Fire: Anger's Role in Medieval English Felony Cases", *Law and History Review*, Vol. 35, No. 1, pp. 160–163; Kesselring, "No Greater Provocation?", p. 207.
6. Pulton, *De Pace Regis,* p. 324.
7. Graham McBain, "Modernising the Law of Murder and Manslaughter: Part 1", *Journal of Politics and Law*, Vol. 8, No. 4, pp. 56–57.
8. J. H. Baker, "The Three Languages of the Common Law", *McGill Law Journal*, Vol. 43, p. 9; Glazebrook, *The Boke of Justices of Peas,* p. Aiii.
9. Kesselring, "No Greater Provocation?", p. 208.

fight with Roger Lloyd by "chaunce medley".[10] Similarly, and in more detail, one afternoon in August 1579 Robert Lenewood was drinking with Henry Farmer and another man in a tavern in St Martin-in-the-Fields when they exchanged "contumelious words". The three men went outside, and Lenewood drew his sword and advanced on Farmer, who drew his own weapon, the third man (also armed with a sword) actively encouraging him. The pair exchanged blows until Lenewood was stabbed and mortally wounded in the chest. At his trial, and as was common in such situations, Farmer was merely convicted of manslaughter (and then clergied).[11]

The legal notion of chance medley was eventually to be swallowed up by its seventeenth century replacement, the doctrine of provocation, which started to emerge after the early 1600s.[12] Notions of male honour and physiology helped shape this development, so that specially provoking behaviour began to supplement existing notions of "hot-bloodedness" when reducing homicides to manslaughter. The key legal issue then became determining precisely what constituted "sufficient" provocation.[13] However, certain forms of provocation, which were eventually recognised as sufficient to reduce the more serious form of homicide to the lesser, did not have this effect during the Tudor era.

For example, catching an unfaithful wife *in flagrante* did not excuse murder, whether of the erring spouse or her lover, something that would begin to change only during the seventeenth century. As late as 1602, Richard Cofield, the miller of Sible Hedingham, in Essex, who found his wife in another man's house at 6 am, and stabbed her through the heart with his knife, was hanged.[14] When adultery did emerge as a legitimate form of provocation, it initially mitigated only a husband's killing of the co-respondent, not of his wife.[15]

Similarly, in theory, throughout the Tudor era, purely verbal provocation, however extreme, and even very minor physical liberties, such as

10. McSheffrey, "Sanctuary Seekers".
11. Jeaffreson, *Middlesex County Records: Vol. 1*, pp. 116–119.
12. Bernard J. Brown, "The Demise of Chance Medley and the Recognition of Provocation as a Defence to Murder in English Law", *The American Journal of Legal History*, Vol. 7, No. 4, p. 311.
13. Kesselring, "No Greater Provocation?", at p. 208.
14. Emmison, *Elizabethan Life: Disorder*, p. 154.
15. Kesselring, "No Greater Provocation?", p. 199.

tweaks of the nose, were not enough to reduce a killing to manslaughter. Nevertheless, in 1603, during the first year of the reign of James I, the so-called Statute of Stabbing (1 Jac 1 c. 8), provided that anyone who stabbed another person who had not drawn a weapon or "not then first stricken the party" and died within six months as a result of their wounds (rather than the year and a day found in murder cases), had committed a felony without benefit of clergy. This put the crime in the same situation as wilful murder. Essentially, it created a form of capital manslaughter, in which the only escape from execution after conviction would be a reprieve.

As the black-letter law governing murder then stood, this was not a novel proposition. It seems that the 1603 Act was not intended to change the existing law, but to force juries to follow it. (It was often indicted as an alternative count to one for murder.) Its introduction suggests that in practice more than a few late Tudor juries had been convicting murder defendants of manslaughter, when killings committed with blades (swords, daggers, or knives) had resulted from heated quarrels in which there had been purely verbal provocation by the victim.

The notion of *malice prepense* was refined during the course of the Tudor era. For example, in 1541 the trial of Lord Dacre saw a clear enunciation of the doctrine of "constructive malice", imputing its presence to cases where a killing took place during the course of another felony (in this case, deer poaching). The notion of "transferred malice" was also established. Thus, in 1573 John Saunders poisoned an apple, which he then gave to his wife, hoping that her death would allow him to marry another woman. Unfortunately, his spouse gave the apple to their daughter, who ate it and died. The defendant was charged with the murder of his child, on the grounds that his *malice prepense* towards his wife could be transferred to the killing of his daughter.[16]

---

16. Kesselring, *Making Murder Public*, pp. 26–27; *R. v Saunders* (1573) 2 Plowd 473.

Consequences of the Murder/Manslaughter Distinction

Ultimately, the two main forms of homicide that had been distinguished by the early sixteenth century had very different legal consequences. Throughout the Tudor period, and for centuries beyond, manslaughter remained a clergyable offence, unlike murder, which was withdrawn from the privilege in many situations for three years after 1512, and then permanently, in all situations, after 1531. For example, in December 1560 Edward Bugge from Harlow assaulted Augustus Sawkyn with a "hedg-yng byll", inflicting an injury from which Sawkyn languished until early January, when he died. Bugge was indicted for murder at the Chelmsford Assizes on 20 March 1561. He was acquitted of this charge, and merely convicted of the lesser offence of "homicide" (i.e. manslaughter). Given that he was described, even if loosely, as a "gent", it is unsurprising that he then asked for and was granted clergy: literacy was normal amongst higher-status men by this time. He was duly delivered into the "custody" of Lawrence Clayton, the deputy for the Bishop of London.[17] After 1576 he would have been freed without more ado or (albeit rarely) sentenced to a year's imprisonment in lieu of this disposal.

Of course, for women and the illiterate, manslaughter remained a capital crime, like any other felony (apart from petty theft). People convicted of the lesser homicide did sometimes fail the literacy test during the sixteenth and seventeenth centuries and were executed. It may even be that as these trials involved "cases of blood", court chaplains were slightly stricter when conducting the test than they were for cases of simple grand larceny. For example, in October 1564 Ralph Houghton was indicted at the Old Bailey for murder; he pleaded not guilty, and the jury convicted him of the lesser offence of manslaughter. He failed in his attempt to claim benefit of clergy, and was sentenced to death.[18]

Even so, those convicted of manslaughter, even if illiterate, were much more likely to receive a discretionary (*de gratia*) pardon than were people found guilty of the more serious form of homicide, and also normally fell within the coverage of general pardons, unlike those convicted of

---

17. ERO, ASS 35/3/2/18.
18. Jeaffreson, *Middlesex County Records: Vol. 1*, pp. 50–52.

murder (usually expressly exempted from their terms).[19] For example, at the Hertford Assizes in March 1593, Ralph Sea was indicted for murdering Richard Symson during an argument by stabbing him in the chest with a dagger. He was merely convicted of manslaughter. It appears that he could not read, and so could not be clergied. Even so, he was remanded in custody, presumably to allow a reprieve to be considered.[20] Similarly, in February 1600 James Bell, a London yeoman, was indicted for manslaughter (not murder) *ab initio* at the Old Bailey, after throwing a dagger at William Richards and mortally wounding him. He pleaded guilty and asked for his book, but was deemed illiterate. However, the court remanded him before judgment, which suggests, again, that the trial judge would recommend a reprieve.[21]

Even so, the grant of mercy in such situations was certainly not universal. For example, John Honeywell was hanged for manslaughter in Essex in 1614, having failed in his claim for benefit of clergy. He was not subsequently pardoned, and, anticipating this, had even carried out a complicated prison yard conveyance of his property in the hope of avoiding the felony-forfeiture rule.[22] Nevertheless, numerous Tudor killers did escape the noose due to a finding of manslaughter, whether by benefit of clergy or pardon (general or discretionary).

Excusable Homicide

As previously noted, the excusable forms of homicide, for which a convict was normally guaranteed a pardon *de cursu*, were primarily limited to self-defence, enforcement of the peace, accident, and killings committed by those of "unsound mind".[23] This situation had largely been established by the fourteenth century.[24] A sample of female killers pardoned between 1200 and 1500 includes eight cases in which the homicide occurred in "self-defence", including one in which a woman killed her

19. Kesselring, *Mercy and Authority*, p. 103; Kesselring, "No Greater Provocation?", p. 206.
20. Cockburn, *Calendar of Assize Records. Hertfordshire Indictments: Elizabeth I*, p. 98.
21. Jeaffreson, *Middlesex County Records: Vol. 1*, pp. 257–266.
22. Kesselring, "Coverture and Criminal Forfeiture", p. 200.
23. Kesselring, "No Greater Provocation?", p. 206.
24. Hanawalt, "Violent Death in Fourteenth and Early Fifteenth century England", *Comparative Studies in Society and History*, Vol. 18, No. 3, p. 298.

husband while protecting her father, and the same number in which the woman acted because of "madness" or in a "fit of frenzy". Accident or "misadventure" was less common as a ground for pardoning female killers, but still present in four cases in the same sample.[25] Such near-automatic pardons could be claimed directly from the Lord Chancellor rather than going before the king and his council, in an expedited and cheaper process than the normal pardoning procedure, one that bypassed everything but the Great Seal.[26]

Eventually, during the seventeenth century, the presence of such excusing factors would produce simple not guilty verdicts. However, until the close of the Tudor period, the traditional (medieval) approach normally (though not quite invariably) prevailed. Because such a finding would, ultimately, lead to release, their legal prerequisites were strict and not easily established in a forensic environment.

Self-defence

On one analysis, it was not a crime under medieval law to kill those who had already clearly committed a felony, such as highway robbery or burglary. Such felons were no longer the "king's lawful subjects", and had forfeited the protection of the law. However, a simple "brawler", a man who physically threatened or even hit someone out of pure aggression, had not yet fallen into this category, as assault (however serious) was normally just a misdemeanour. As he had done nothing to take himself outside the protection of the law, he was still the king's lawful subject, and killing him deprived the Crown of his services, making it a crime. Furthermore, the law generally assumed that when a violent quarrel arose, both parties were at fault, at least to some degree.[27]

As a result, in theory, the pre-requisites for a finding of self-defence, whether by coroner's inquest or trial jury, required clear attempts to

---

25. Anne L. Grauer and Andrew G. Miller, "Flesh on the Bones: A Historical and Bioarchaeological Exploration of Violence, Trauma, Sex, and Gender in Medieval England", *Fragments: Interdisciplinary Approaches to the Study of Ancient and Medieval Pasts*, Vol. 6. Available at http://works.bepress.com/anne-grauer/2/
26. Griffiths and Devereaux, *Penal Practice and Culture*, p. 127.
27. Thomas Regnier, "The Law in *Hamlet*: Death, Property, and the Pursuit of Justice", *Brief Chronicles*, vol. III, p. 112.

retreat from a conflict before having recourse to force. A plea of self-defence was justified only if "someone assaults another, who flees from him and, in the last resort, in his defence and for safeguard of his life, without malice, kills the person who committed the assault".[28] For this reason, in April 1520, an inquest held at Tuxford, in Nottinghamshire, before a county coroner, concluded that Adam Hill had feloniously slain Robert Stephenson in self-defence, stressing that Hill had been chased for more than 200 feet across a cornfield but had been unable to escape, due to the speed of his pursuer, so that he was forced to hit him with a clod mallet.[29] Similarly, an inquest conducted in 1577 emphasised that John Tarlton, who fatally stabbed Richard Blunt in Smithfield, had retreated as far as physically possible before giving Blunt the mortal wound, "so killing the said Richard in no other way than that of self-defence".[30] In like manner, in 1593 a coroner's inquest, held at Goldhanger, in Essex, concluded that the dead man, Gilbert Hyndes, had furiously assaulted one Ralph Elzynge with a sword. This eventually forced Elzynge to save his own life by drawing his hanger and giving Hyndes a "thrust" from which he died later that day. Elzynge pleaded not guilty at trial; he was found to have acted in self-defence and duly pardoned *de cursu*.[31]

Accident and Insanity

Someone who killed another by accident, even if weapons were involved, might also receive a *de cursu* pardon when indicted. For example, one night in Nottingham in October 1508, two men were playing with a sword when one accidentally stabbed the other in the intestines, from which wound excrement flowed out, with death following shortly afterwards. The inquest concluded that William Hall slew Alan de Sables "by misadventure against his will". Even so, Hall had to appear in the Court of King's Bench and plead a general pardon in 1512 to avoid prosecution and conviction.[32] Towards the end of the century, in March 1594, Richard

---

28. McBain, "Modernising the Law", pp. 56–57.
29. Hunnisett, *Calendar of Nottinghamshire Coroners' Inquests*, p. 38.
30. Jeaffreson, *Middlesex County Records: Vol. 1*, pp. 103–111.
31. ERO T/A 418/57/62.
32. Hunnisett, *Calendar of Nottinghamshire Coroners' Inquests*, p. 25.

Carpenter, a 16-year-old youth, and Thomas Goldston found a pair of firearms in the hall of a house in Hackney. Unaware that the guns were loaded, the two started playing with them. Carpenter accidentally shot Goldston in the face, killing him instantly. On his arraignment, Richard Carpenter put himself "guilty by mischance", which plea was accepted, and he was presumably reprieved and then pardoned.[33]

It was thought that an insane person should not be punished for a crime, because they did not have the capacity to form the relevant guilty mind or *mens rea*. Furthermore, it was felt that draconian punishment was pointless in such cases, as mad defendants could not be deterred. Many offenders who were severely mentally-ill were probably not even indicted when caught. However, this was harder to do in cases involving homicide. Thus in 1565 Henry Pellynge from Lindfield was prosecuted at the Sussex Assizes for murdering his wife, Joan. He was apparently a "frantick man" when he attacked her with an axe, and the inquest jury considered him mad; even so, he was still tried for murder, and found guilty, but with a note that he was adjudged to be insane.[34] This would have led to a reprieve *de cursu*.

Fictitious Killers

A strange feature of contested homicide cases tried at Tudor assizes, especially those with a domestic or quasi-domestic background, was that "benign" juries would sometimes return a simple not guilty verdict and, at the same time, ascribe the killing to a patently fictitious character. These might include, inter alia, John at Noke or John a Style, who were the sixteenth century equivalents of John Doe. However, they extended to, for example, Thomas Staff (when this was the implement used to effect the killing), John at Death, John Slye, John at Love, or other similar names. This practice can be seen throughout the Elizabethan Home Circuit, although its incidence varied from county to county.[35] It was certainly not just an Elizabethan phenomenon. In 1548 a jury found that

33.   Jeaffreson, *Middlesex County Records: Vol. 1*, pp. 219–225.
34.   Cockburn, *Calendar of Assize Records. Sussex Indictments: Elizabeth I*, p. 23.
35.   Louis A. Knafla, "'John at Love Killed Her': The Assizes and Criminal Law in Early Modern England", *University of Toronto Law Journal*, Vol. 35, No. 3, p. 315.

John at Noke had killed an apparent murder victim during an affray occasioned by rabbit poaching in Sussex, even describing the fictitious killer as a labourer, late of Henfield.[36]

In some of these cases, such a verdict may have been returned because the facts would not legally justify a finding of clergyable manslaughter for the defendant, although this is what the jurors thought appropriate. In others, it seems that, even if the facts did provide potential for a manslaughter verdict, jurors were concerned that a female or illiterate perpetrator would not be able to claim the privilege, if convicted of the lesser homicide. Sometimes juries may have felt that defendants did not deserve the "corruption of blood" and forfeiture of property that would still be attendant on a manslaughter conviction, even if clergy was successfully claimed. In a few cases, jurors probably thought that the accused person did not deserve any form of conviction but that acquitting outright, without further comment, was not appropriate. The use of such verdicts may have dated back to the gradual emergence of a jury from the fourteenth century onwards that was increasingly informed by testimony in court rather than personal knowledge.

Some of these cases concerned the familial killing of children or young servants by what might be termed abuse or the imposition of excessive discipline (see *Chapter 16*). Others involved adults who were unexpectedly killed in, for example, heated quarrels or during rough horseplay. It appears that jurors sometimes viewed these deaths as merely an aspect of the rough and tumble of early modern life, for which conviction (and perhaps execution) would be wholly inappropriate. A few related to deaths occasioned by gross negligence or even, perhaps, those perceived as mercy killings.

For example, at the Essex Assizes of July 1589, Agnes Knight was indicted for feloniously killing her ten-year-old stepson. The previous May she had assaulted the boy with a "wand", striking him repeatedly across the hips and backside. Two days later, she did the same thing again, and as a result of the beatings he died the following day. The jury,

---

36. Hunnisett, *Sussex Coroners' Inquests*, p. 40.

perhaps mindful that the injuries were inflicted in a disciplinary context, acquitted her on the basis that "John Anoke" had killed the child.[37]

At the Surrey Assizes held in March 1560, John Tucker, a blacksmith from Chertsey, was indicted for murdering a six-year-old of the same name (very likely his son). The coroner's inquest had concluded that the boy, who was sick and weak, had been placed naked on hot coals so that he died shortly afterwards. (Interestingly, the inquest had not been held until more than two weeks after the child's death.) At trial the jury acquitted Tucker, finding that "John Astyle killed him".[38] They may have thought the death resulted simply from carelessness.

In 1571 Jane Turner was accused of the felonious killing (manslaughter) of a five-year-old boy, allegedly adopted by her husband, who had then (it seems) died of neglect, having been over several months deprived of adequate food and drink. At the Essex Assizes she, too, was acquitted on the basis that "John a Style killed him". At the same sessions that tried Turner, John Carbitt was also indicted for felonious killing, after fatally hitting Catherine Lee with his staff when she threw a brickbat at him during a heated argument. Again, he was acquitted (rather than being found guilty of manslaughter) on the basis that "John att Noke killed her". (It was highly unusual to have two such cases in the same sessions.)[39]

The notoriously rough and unregulated sports of the era could also occasion this type of verdict. At West Ham, Essex, in April 1582, a labourer named John Ward was playing football (*ad pilam pedalem*) with Thomas Turner. It was claimed that during the game Thomas assaulted John and threw him to the ground so that he died instantly. At the assizes held at Chelmsford in August that year, Thomas was found not guilty of murder "but John Astyle is". It seems likely that the trial jurors viewed such deaths as an intrinsic hazard of playing such a violent game.[40]

John Tidswell was indicted for manslaughter at the Hertford Assizes in March 1601. The coroner's inquest into the killing concluded that he had acted in self-defence after being attacked with a sword by the victim. The jury verdict that John Noke killed his assailant saved Tidswell the

---

37. Cockburn, *Calendar of Assize Records. Essex Indictments: Elizabeth I*, p. 337.
38. Cockburn, *Calendar of Assize Records. Surrey Indictments: Elizabeth I*, p. 12.
39. Cockburn, *Calendar of Assize Records. Essex Indictments: Elizabeth I*, p. 86.
40. ERO T/A 418/38/41.

inconvenience of waiting for a *de cursu* pardon, and is perhaps indicative of transitional attitudes to the proper effect of the defence.[41]

Exactly how petty jurors became aware of such potential verdicts is uncertain. However, they do not seem to have prompted hostility from the judiciary or (normally) to have been referred to the Star Chamber.

Duels and the Law

The formal duel, an arranged combat between two armed men, subject to certain conventions, and conducted to settle a matter of honour, emerged during the Tudor period. To some extent, duels replaced larger-scale faction fights in which retainers fought with, and on behalf of, their masters, something that has led some modern observers to view them as a civilising agent.[42] Indeed, there appears to have been an interstitial period in which the distinction between the two was quite fluid. For example, in April 1532 Richard Southwell killed Sir William Pennington in Westminster after an argument that had been engendered by litigation between the two men. Pennington challenged Southwell to meet him in Tothill Street. Both men then gathered their retinues. The two parties met on a bridge where members of each retinue unavailingly tried to dissuade them from violence. A sword fight ensued between the pair, until Sir William had Southwell on the ground and at his mercy, at which point the latter's brother Anthony intervened and fatally wounded the knight.[43]

However, in its more organized and modern manifestation, the duel appears to have originated in Italy shortly before the middle of the sixteenth century and arrived in the British Isles via France in the 1570s, its initial popularity peaking in the early seventeenth century.[44] An Italian fencing master, Rocco Bonetti, had set up a school in London by 1576, and fencing manuals and instructors from his homeland became popular with prosperous young men in the capital during the 1580s and 1590s.

41.   Cockburn, *Calendar of Assize Records. Hertfordshire Indictments: Elizabeth I*, p. 160.
42.   Kesselring, *Making Murder Public*, p. 95.
43.   McSheffrey, 'The Slaying of Sir William Pennington', p. 172.
44.   Manuel Eisner, "Interpersonal Violence on the British Isles, 1200–2016", in Alison Liebling, Shadd Maruna, and Lesley McAra (eds.), *The Oxford Handbook of Criminology* (Oxford: Oxford University Press, 2017), p. 577.

Mercutio in *Romeo and Juliet* (probably written between 1591 and 1597) uses Italian fencing terms for different kinds of rapier thrust, suggesting that these were fairly widely known amongst the London audience.

Even so, the duel was not yet the finely orchestrated contest that it would become in the eighteenth century. It often involved a greater range of weapons, fewer formalities, and, it seems, a greater social range of participants, so that it was sometimes difficult to distinguish from spontaneous fights. For example, in September 1567 the death of James Whettell, a gentleman from Lyneham, in Wiltshire, may have been the result of either type of conflict. Early one afternoon he met John Woodroff, a local yeoman, and they argued, Whettell publicly making "opprobrious and unbecoming" comments about the other man. They then parted, but later that afternoon met at a long barrow near the town. According to the coroner's jury, Whettell attacked Woodroff with both a sword and dagger and wounded him several times. However, Woodroff drew his own sword to defend himself and was (rather improbably for a "spontaneous" meeting) also carrying a buckler (small shield) at the time. After Whettell knocked Woodroff to the ground, he allegedly ran onto the point of the latter's sword and died. Very unusually, the coroner's jury did not formally report on the killing until seven months after the death, suggesting that they had had considerable difficulty agreeing a verdict. Their language included phrases often used in murder indictments to describe Whettell's attack on Woodroff. For example, it was alleged that he made it with malice aforethought. They also emphasised that Woodroff was retreating at the time, something that frequently occurred in narratives involving killing in self-defence. Somewhat bizarrely, the jury's official verdict was that Whettell had feloniously murdered himself, i.e. a suicide verdict. However, one clerk wrote a note on the report (later struck out), suggesting that the killing was a case of self-defence, another that it was due to misfortune, i.e. that it was an accident. It is impossible in these circumstances to say whether it was a chance meeting in which a quarrel was renewed or an arranged duel.[45]

---

45. Discovery of the Month—Everyday Life and Fatal Hazard in Sixteenth century England, tudoraccidents.history.ox.ac.uk/?page_id=177

If the substantive criminal law had been strictly applied, any killings that resulted from Tudor duels would have been defined as murder, because, being the result of a premeditated combat, they could not fall under the doctrine of "chance medley". A rare illustration of this actually happening may have occurred in September 1580, after a coroner's inquest sat in Stepney, Middlesex, on the body of John Sherwell, a local sailor. It decided that a week or so earlier he had exchanged opprobrious words with one John Lawrence, another mariner. At the break of day the following morning, the two men went, by mutual agreement, to a nearby field with the intention of fighting. Sherwell was armed with a sword and buckler and Lawrence with a pikestaff called a "Danske javelin". For some time between 4 am and 5 am they exchanged blows, until Lawrence gave Sherwell a mortal wound in the head with his javelin, from which he died a few days later — i.e. he was not finished off by his opponent while on the ground. Even so, the inquest concluded that Lawrence "slew and murdered" Sherwell. Perhaps rather strangely, given the circumstances, when arraigned for the murder, Lawrence pleaded guilty to the more serious homicide and was sentenced to death.[46]

However, from a very early stage in the evolution of the law of homicide, killings occasioned by duels fought over matters of honour were normally deemed to be manslaughter, and so usually treated relatively leniently.[47] This can be seen in a case from Middlesex in 1573, even though it involved two shoemakers, John Lowbery and Hugh Yenans, who would probably not have been deemed socially elevated enough to conduct such a combat under the more formal rules of the eighteenth century. The two men quarrelled while in their master's house, and harsh words were spoken. That evening, they went together to a field in St Giles with the intention of fighting. Lowbery had a sword and buckler, and Yenans carried a pikestaff in each hand. They fought for some time without producing a conclusive result, and parted. Unfortunately, the fight was renewed several hours later, after more words were exchanged between the pair. On this occasion, Yenans gave Lowbery a mortal wound

---

46.   Jeaffreson, *Middlesex County Records: Vol. 1*, pp. 119–121.
47.   Jeremy Horder, "The Duel and the English Law of Homicide", *Oxford Journal of Legal Studies*, Vol. 12, Issue 3, p. 420.

in the thigh with one of his small pikes, from which the latter died within two hours. Yenans pleaded not guilty to his murder indictment and was merely convicted of manslaughter, for which he successfully claimed benefit of clergy. (The victim's brother may have attempted to "appeal" Yenans as a way of challenging this verdict.)[48]

In a much more famous case, in 1598 the playwright Ben Jonson was merely indicted for feloniously slaying (manslaughter) rather than murdering the actor Gabriel Spencer in a duel at Hoxton, in Middlesex. This was a consensual fight, and Spencer, known for his quick temper, had killed another man in just such an argument two years earlier, though no proceedings had resulted. Jonson was tried at the Old Bailey; he pleaded guilty, claimed clergy, read the neck-verse, was branded, and discharged.[49]

Continuing Uncertainty

Nevertheless, the precise boundaries between the two main homicide offences, the effect (and definition) of defences on such crimes, and the distinction between accidental and negligent killing remained fairly confused for much of the Tudor era.[50] Illustrative of this, in 1560, after a Staffordshire man killed another who was attacking his house with a crossbow, assize jurors from the county were unable to decide if this was a case of murder, manslaughter, or self-defence. Queen Elizabeth ultimately resolved the matter by pardoning him.[51]

Conviction Rates for Homicide

The Tudor era saw an increase in conviction rates in homicide cases (murder and manslaughter verdicts taken together), as it did for many other felonies. By the late sixteenth century, at least half of those accused of killing were found guilty of some offence, at least double the rate in the medieval period. However, the percentage of homicide defendants

---

48. Jeaffreson, *Middlesex County Records: Vol. 1*, pp. 78–80.
49. Arthur Lyon Cross, "The English Criminal Law and Benefit of Clergy During the Eighteenth and Early Nineteenth Centuries", *The American Historical Review*, Vol. 22, No. 3, p. 544.
50. McBain, "Modernising the Law", pp. 56–57.
51. Kesselring, *To Pardon and To Punish*, p. 143.

actually condemned to death was much the same as it had been during the medieval era, being approximately between 20 per cent and 25 per cent, while the percentage of self-defence verdicts was significantly lower. It appears likely that juries, recognising that the expanded use of benefit of clergy provided them with a non-capital alternative when they returned manslaughter verdicts, felt free to convict of the lesser form of killing in many cases that they had formerly described (inaccurately) as acts of self-defence. As a result, it is probable that more Elizabethan recipients of pardons for self-defence were genuine claimants rather than the beneficiaries of jury stratagems. The formal legal rules on killing and their interpretation by trial jurors had come closer together.[52]

Role of the Grand Jury in Homicide Cases

In the late seventeenth century, several legal commentators, the most important being Zachary Babington, the author of *Advice to Grand Jurors in Cases of Blood* in 1677, urged grand jurors to indict for murder—rather than a lesser homicide charge such as manslaughter—in all cases in which one person had killed another. Furthermore, by then it was unusual for a homicide defendant to stand trial solely on a coroner's inquest, unless a grand jury found no case to answer for any form of killing. Instead, the latter body would normally indict for murder, irrespective of the conclusion of the inquest, and leave the issue to the trial jury to decide, even where a manslaughter finding was highly likely on the facts of a case. In these situations, a trial jury might consider a grand jury murder indictment and an inquest charge that was for manslaughter; they usually ignored the manslaughter count if they returned a verdict of guilty to the more serious homicide.

However, this was not the situation during the Tudor era. A significant number of homicides were indicted as simple manslaughter *ab initio*. Furthermore, many (but not all) defendants stood trial solely on the coroner's inquest without, apparently, the grand jury's feeling it necessary to add an indictment of its own or to consider the merits of the

---

52. Green, *Verdict According to Conscience*, p. 116; Thomas A. Green, "The Jury and the English Law of Homicide, 1200–1600", *Michigan Law Review*, Vol. 74, pp. 493–494.

allegation. Even so, some prosecutions for murder still produced convictions for the lesser type of homicide. For example, in late 1586 there were complaints about the manner in which a trial jury in the North had returned a verdict of guilty to clergyable manslaughter on three men from Alnwick and Newton, in Northumberland, who had been indicted for murdering one William Clavering.[53]

Attempted Murder

During the Tudor period, inchoate offences (attempt, conspiracy, etc.) were still not properly developed at common law, so that even assaults that would be considered to be attempted murder in the modern era were often indicted as misdemeanours, for which the available punishment was necessarily quite limited. As Sir Thomas Smith observed in the 1560s, an "attempt to impoison a man, or laying await to kill a man, though he wound him daungerously if death followe not, is no felony by the lawe of Englande, for the Prince hath lost no man, and life ought to be given we say, but for life only".

Perpetrators were well aware of this. Those who had inflicted life-threatening wounds regularly fled until it became clear that their victims would recover, when they might return, confident that the legal consequences of their crime would be relatively modest. For example, in Kent, in the early 1500s, William Peryn attacked George Bekerton with a hedge-bill, inflicting serious injuries. Shortly afterwards, Peryn left his home in Maidstone "for a long time", and stayed away until he was sure that his victim would not die. Once he knew that Bekerton had survived, he returned to his native town.[54] Others who had been involved in violent quarrels fled to sanctuary (prior to the 1540s), thinking that they had mortally wounded another person, but quickly left their shelters when they found out that their victim had survived.[55]

Conspiracy to murder was punished equally leniently. For example, in about 1590 a married woman and her lover conspired to murder the

---

53.   Green, *Calendar of State Papers Domestic: Elizabeth, Addenda 1580–1625*, pp. 196–199.
54.   Jones, *Gender and Petty Crime*, p. 32.
55.   McSheffrey, *Seeking Sanctuary*, p. 37.

former's husband, hiring one Rowland Griffith to be the "executioner". The plot came to light and was merely referred to quarter sessions. It was suggested by area JPs that Griffith, the only person in custody, be released without further action after he had admitted his role and spent several months in gaol.[56]

Accomplices

In theory, accomplices to murder were as liable as the perpetrator of the killing. As Sir Thomas Smith observed, when a man was murdered, "all be principals and shall die, even he that doth but hold the candel to give light to the murderers". For example, in September 1590 a London coroner's inquest into the death of John Wilford noted that he had been attacked and mortally wounded by Humphrey Powntney, who was armed with a sword, while walking in St Pancras. However, they also decided that Powntney's companion, Thomas Percy, who was carrying a pikestaff, had been "feloniously present", and so was also a murderer, like the principal. His mere presence had aided and abetted Powntney's fatal attack, even if he had not inflicted a wound.[57]

This aspect of the law was widely known. Many of those who sought chartered sanctuary for homicide (until its abolition in the 1530s) claimed to have had a peripheral role in the killings, sometimes merely being physically present when they were committed, but were fearful of being indicted for the crimes. Thus, in October 1500 the Durham sanctuary register records that a man named Goldthwate sought protection there because he feared that he might be considered an accessory to Richard More in the killing of one William Bradethwate at Azerley, in Yorkshire. More had struck Bradethwate on the knee with a sword, causing a wound from which he died three months later. Although Goldthwate did not inflict any injury, he had been physically present, and so he feared he would be prosecuted for the killing.[58] The same register recorded that in February 1503 Robert Middilton, William Jackson, and John Joy sought

---

56. ERO Q/SR 112/8.
57. Thomas R. Forbes, "London Coroner's Inquests for 1590", *Journal of the History of Medicine and Allied Sciences*, vol. XXVIII, Issue 4, pp. 383–384.
58. McSheffrey, "Sanctuary Seekers".

sanctuary because they, too, had been present when two other men assaulted and killed one Reginald Middilton, and feared being indicted as accessories.[59]

Nevertheless, in practice, accomplices with a relatively peripheral involvement in felonies, including murder, were often acquitted at trial, if they were prosecuted at all, if only to keep the number liable to be executed within reasonable bounds. For example, in May 1580 a coroner's inquest found that William Baker, a Thaxted barber, was responsible for killing William Cranford. He had struck Cranford on the head with a ten feet "pykestaffe", giving him a mortal wound from which he died within three hours. It appears that Baker had been hired to take possession of land in a property dispute at the behest of William Barnish, a Finchingfield gentleman who, before the killing, warned Cranford that "there are com those nowe that will kepe possession and I can tall yt will cost knockes".[60] Baker was prosecuted for murder at the Essex Assizes in July 1580, while Barnish was indicted as an accessory to the crime. Baker was merely convicted of manslaughter (homicide) and duly clergied and released. Barnish was acquitted outright.[61] Sometimes accomplices who had been very marginally involved were not even indicted.

The Nature of Tudor Killing

Homicide Rates

Compared to the present, it seems that English homicide rates were extremely high during the Tudor period, albeit probably declining, from even greater medieval levels, until fairly late in the era. Of course, the value of such comparisons as an indicator of behaviour over the centuries can be exaggerated, even if the figures are accurate (and some scholars vigorously challenge such a notion). For example, it is vital to establish whether they include cases of neonaticide, which made up a significant proportion of prosecuted killings after the 1560s (perhaps a fifth in Elizabethan England), but were largely absent beforehand and (again) after

---

59. *Ibid.*
60. ERO T/A 418/34/36.
61. Cockburn, *Calendar of Assize Records: Essex Indictments: Elizabeth I*, p. 204.

the early nineteenth century. Additionally, it should be noted that many late medieval and sixteenth century fatal injuries would be survivable in the modern era because of improvements in medical knowledge and practice. Thus, in 1438 Thomas Elam attacked Margaret Perman in an attempt to rape her. In the process he broke three of her ribs and bit off her nose. Her wound became infected, and she died a few days later. Elam was hanged for murder.[62] Margaret would probably have lived by the late nineteenth century, and would certainly have survived today.

Even the best medical treatment available in Tudor England was often not enough to prevent a lingering death from wounds. In 1602, after being attacked with a sword, the Reverend William Storre received immediate first aid in a nearby constable's house, where local people made "very good, and speedy meanes to bind up his wounds, and to staunch his bloud". The following day, he was provided with a bonesetter and "three or foure of the best surgeons thereabout". Even so, he languished for six days and then died.[63]

In some cases, a patient's prospects for recovery actually declined after treatment. In September 1515 a man assaulted William Maister in Nottinghamshire, striking him on the head with a staff. Maister went to a surgeon to have the wound healed, and, as a result of his poor treatment (rather than the wound itself), died a few weeks later.[64]

Nevertheless, Tudor homicide rates remain high, even if infanticide is ignored, while the pre-modern period did not witness a sufficiently major advance in medicine to come close to explaining their apparent fall during the centuries after 1485. Indeed, one assessment suggests that evidence of delays between wound and mortality, and their relative consistency between the fourteenth and the late nineteenth centuries, indicate that improved wound treatment is not a plausible source of major bias before about 1900.[65] (This might understate the impact of advances in the 1800s.) As a result, though the figures may be disputed,

---

62. McGlynn, "Violence and the Law", pp. 53–59. Musson and Powell, *Crime, Law and Society*, p. 96.

63. Anon, *The manner of the cruell outragious murther of William Storre*, pp. 1–10.

64. Hunnisett, *Calendar of Nottinghamshire Coroners' Inquests*, p. 33.

65. Manuel Eisner, "From Swords to Words: Does Macro-Level Change in Self-Control Predict Long-Term Variation in Levels of Homicide?", *Crime and Justice*, Vol. 43, No. 1, p. 76.

most social historians feel that apparent changes in the rate of non-infant homicide during the early modern period reflect changes in behaviour and a decline in the use of lethal violence.[66]

Some evidence suggests that, in the late thirteenth century, there was approximately one deliberate killing each year for every 20 villages in England.[67] More specifically, homicide rates for five rural counties, based on eyre rolls covering three-to-five-year periods at scattered points between 1202 and 1276, produce figures ranging from nine per 100,000 people in Norfolk to 23 per 100,000 in Kent.[68] Other assessments indicate a national average homicide level that may have been about 20 to 25 killings per 100,000 people during the thirteenth and fourteenth centuries.[69] In a few places, it was much higher. The city of Oxford, with its large number of young single males and constant town and gown tensions, was exceptionally violent, albeit not remotely typical. Between 1342 and 1348 it saw between 90 and 120 killings per 100,000 people each year, one of the highest levels recorded anywhere in medieval Europe.[70]

Death from violence in medieval London, although less likely than in Oxford, was still so common that an ordinary man ran a significantly higher risk of dying at the hands of his fellow citizens than from an accident, despite the numerous hazards of everyday life at this time. The criminologist Manuel Eisner used nine years of surviving coroners' rolls from the first four decades of the fourteenth century to consider the extent and context of London homicides. Assuming a population of 80,000 people, he concluded that medieval murder rates in the city were about 15 to 20 times higher than would be expected in a town of a similar size in modern England.[71] Although slightly more modest, the number of homicides in rural Northamptonshire at about the same time was still only ten per cent lower than that for accidental deaths in the county.[72]

---

66. Kesselring, *Making Murder Public,* p. 11.
67. McGlynn, "Violence and the Law", pp. 53–59.
68. Gerd Schwerhoff, "Criminalized Violence and the Process of Civilisation: A Reappraisal", *Crime, History & Societies*, Vol. 6, No. 2, pp. 103–126.
69. Eisner, "Interpersonal Violence", pp. 565–586.
70. Schwerhoff, "Criminalized Violence", p. 110.
71. *The Guardian,* 28 November 2018.
72. Hanawalt, "Violent Death", p. 302.

However, England then appears to have taken a leading place in the long, uneven, and periodically interrupted decline in homicide rates seen throughout North-west Europe from the late fifteenth century onwards.[73] Exactly when this set in is problematic, as reliable figures are least available for the two centuries from 1350 to 1550, during which period the process seems to have started. Nevertheless, according to one estimate, the national homicide level was down to about seven cases per 100,000 by the sixteenth century.[74] On another, it had fallen to about six cases per 100,000 by the Elizabethan period.[75] A scrutiny of assize files, quarter sessions rolls, and coroners' inquests for the decade after 1559 suggests that an average of just under two (non-infanticidal) homicides a year occurred in Essex, with a few years seeing none at all; it is probably safe, however, to assume that some have been lost or missed.[76] Even so, this might suggest a significant fall between the high medieval and Tudor eras, and, indeed, in 1983 the historian Lawrence Stone came to the conclusion that "medieval English society was twice as violence-prone as early modern English society".[77] (Some other observers are more cautious about such claims).

Determining the national homicide rate in England at the time is complicated by the considerable variation between regions. In the period from 1559 to 1625, Cheshire (in the north) and Middlesex (on the fringes of London) had comparatively high homicide rates, Sussex and Kent were middle-ranking counties in this regard, and Essex (see above), Surrey, and Hertfordshire appear to have had fairly low rates. On one analysis, Cheshire's rate may have been three times higher than those for Surrey and Hertfordshire.[78]

Although, in a specifically Tudor context, the incidence of English homicides — as reflected in indictment and inquest rates — is still a matter of considerable dispute, it seems probable that, from the advent of

---

73. Eisner, "From Swords to Words", p. 76.
74. Manuel Eisner, "Long-Term Historical Trends in Violent Crime", *Crime and Justice*, Vol. 30, p. 99.
75. Sharpe and Dickinson, "Revisiting the 'Violence We Have Lost'", p. 293.
76. Samaha, *Law and Order*, p. 20.
77. Schwerhoff, "Criminalized Violence", p. 110.
78. Randolph Roth, "Homicide in Early Modern England 1549–1800: The Need for a Quantitative Synthesis", *Crime, History & Societies*, Vol. 5, No. 2, 2001, pp. 33–67, p. 48.

Henry VII until the late 1560s, it fell, if only slowly.[79] It is widely thought that there was then an increase in homicide rates that lasted from the late sixteenth to the early seventeenth centuries, during which much of this improvement was reversed, even if the precise figures are not subject to consensus. (Some other parts of Europe also saw increases at this time.) For example, on one assessment, Sussex saw three to four killings per 100,000 people in the 1560s, 1570s, and 1580s, after which the rate rose to five or six in the 1590s, before declining again to four in the early decades of the seventeenth century.[80] According to another account, Kent experienced an average annual homicide rate of 4.6 per 100,000 people in the sixteenth century, but saw its highest rate in that period during the decade from 1581 to 1590, when it reached six per 100,000.[81] In Essex, in the decade from 1593, the entire county had just under six (non-infanticidal) killings a year (19 of them in 1602 alone).[82] This temporary upswing in the English homicide rate probably peaked in the early 1600s. On one northern-based (and so untypical) assessment, this was at a total (for all killings) of about 15 per 100,000 persons a year, after which it started to fall again.[83] Other estimates are very much more modest as to the extent of the peak, although acknowledging an increase.

Further complicating matters, it has also been argued that the spike in English homicide rates after 1580 was more apparent than real, because all inquests, not just those relating to homicide, increased in this period, so that the proportion of killings found among (for example) Sussex inquests remained the same in the decades before and after 1580, at about 25 per cent. Given that an economic, political, and social crisis is unlikely to have had a huge effect on accidental deaths and unexpected illness, it has been suggested that it is increased reporting of sudden deaths (including homicides), rather than an increase in such deaths, that is occurring in these years. According to this analysis, because it is inherently unlikely that an increase in people falling from wagons or drowning in wells could

79. L. Stone, "Interpersonal Violence in English Society, 1300–1980", p. 22.
80. James Sharpe, *A Fiery & Furious People: A History of Violence in England*, (London: Random House Books, 2016), p. 118.
81. J. S. Cockburn, "Patterns of Violence in English Society", pp. 76–78.
82. Joell Samaha, *Law and Order in Historical Perspective: The Case of Elizabethan Essex*, p. 20.
83. Randolph Roth, "Homicide in Early Modern England 1549–1800: The Need for a Quantitative Synthesis", *Crime, History & Societies*, Vol. 5, No. 2, pp. 45–46, and p. 50.

be occasioned by social and political anomie and economic stress, or a cultural change in manners (the main explanations advanced for apparent fluctuations in homicide levels at the time), it must be reporting levels that changed.[84]

Instead, it is argued that the increase in reporting was encouraged by much closer central government oversight of coroners after the 1530s. This led to better record keeping and reporting to the centre after the middle of the century, even though the requirement to send inquest details to King's Bench or file them with assizes went back to an Act of 1487. This process may have been further encouraged by the increasingly active involvement of the almoner in representing the Crown's interests at inquests during the second half of the 1500s. As a result, the number of all (preserved) inquests increased greatly.

Of course, the reporting of homicide, which is so much more serious and alarming than death by accident, could have been inherently more reliable throughout the Tudor era; an increased number of murder and manslaughter findings by inquests could reflect a real increase in killings, even as those for other (less troubling) types of sudden death, such as drowning, might reflect increased reporting. Furthermore, scholars such as Randall Roth have also questioned the statistical basis on which the "increased reporting" argument is based. As a result, other paradigms that attempt to explain a real decrease in homicide still attract considerable support, and so need to be explored further.

Explanations for the Decline in Homicide

A range of explanations has been advanced for the apparent decline in homicidal violence in post-medieval England. Some are a little eccentric. For example, it has been suggested that liberal use of the death penalty for much of the early modern period reduced "violent genes", and so helped bring down the murder rate.[85] Nevertheless, broadly speaking, and more plausibly, explanations for the fall in homicide rates, and their temporary reversal at the end of the Elizabethan era and during several

---

84. Lockwood, *The Conquest of Death*, p. 277.
85. Oliver Moody, "How the Death Penalty Killed Our Violent Genes", *The Times*, 11 March 2015.

other short-term periods in ensuing centuries have usually taken two approaches.

Some recent scholars, such as Pieter Spierenburg and Steven Pinker, have followed Norbert Elias in attributing the (uneven) post-medieval decline in non-state violence to long-term cultural changes, particularly, in manners in which self-control became increasingly important, whether manifest in public nose-blowing or levels of aggression. Whenever this went temporarily into reverse, as was the case, for example, with the youth counter-cultures of the 1960s, violent crime increased.[86] Elias linked this development to the emergence of powerful early modern states in Western Europe, political entities that possessed a hitherto unprecedented monopoly on the use of force and a novel willingness to intervene in everyday life through the administration of justice (facets of Tudor society that are considered in *Chapters 1* and *2*); as a result, external constraint became internal restraint.[87] This change encouraged popular recourse to alternative, non-violent methods of dispute adjudication, such as civil litigation, which increased significantly during the second half of the sixteenth century. By contrast, even in the modern era, violence still festers in anarchic "failed states", such as Somalia.[88]

Other observers, such as Gerd Schwerhoff and Randall Roth, have (from varying perspectives) been more sceptical of the Elias thesis. Roth has stressed the role of environmental, political, and social stress in these developments rather than any change in manners. According to this interpretation, murders among unrelated adults (i.e. most early modern killings) correlate with wider feelings towards government and society, especially the "legitimacy" of the former and its ability to redress wrongs and protect lives and property, and so inculcate trust.[89] Such scholars have emphasised a combination of, inter alia, demographic pressure, economic depression, the terrible harvests of the late sixteenth century (because of poor weather), cultural militarisation occasioned by regular

---

86.   Eisner, "From Swords to Words", p. 66.
87.   Roger Lane, Review of *The Civilization of Crime: Violence in Town and Country Since the Middle Ages*, in *Journal of Social History*, Vol. 31, No. 3, pp. 750–753; Norbert Elias, *The Civilizing Process, Vol. 2: State Formation and Civilisation* (Oxford: Basil Blackwell, 1982), p. 232.
88.   Steven Pinker, "A History of Violence", *The New Republic*, 19 March 2007.
89.   Randolph Roth, "Biology and the Deep History of Homicide", *The British Journal of Criminology*, Vol. 51, Issue 3, p. 544.

wars between 1585 and 1604, and the resultant demobilisation of veterans when peace returned, to explain early modern homicide rates and, more particularly, their (apparent) late Elizabethan increase. This concatenation of problems may have led to relationships between friends and neighbours becoming more volatile and to increased numbers of people feeling alienated from society and less bound by its "rules" in a manner that encouraged recourse to homicidal violence.[90]

Such observers sometimes argue that there was relatively little variation in the rate and level of interpersonal violence between the fourteenth and the sixteenth centuries, and that the rise in homicides at the end of the sixteenth century, and their precipitous fall over a comparatively short period during the seventeenth century are too sudden to be explained by a gradual process of cultural transformation; societies do not normally change that swiftly. For example, Cheshire saw a rising level of homicides between 1580 and the 1620s, which last was an exceptionally difficult decade in North-west England, as harvest failures followed wet summers.[91] This was followed by a dramatic fall in killings after 1630 and a more gradual decline in the decades after 1640. As a result, homicide rates, as measured by cases tried at the palatinate Court of Great Sessions, rose to between eight and 12 per 100,000 people in the 1620s, but had fallen to just two per 100,000 by the 1690s.[92] Interestingly, even Pinker accepts that there seems to have been an identifiable point in regard to the decline in violence at about the onset of the "Age of Reason" in the early seventeenth century.[93]

Of course, both approaches, along with a questioning of the statistics on which they are based, may have some value, and are not necessarily entirely incompatible. A slow underlying change in manners may have worked in tandem with the more dramatic, short-term effects of a change in perceived political legitimacy during the same period to reduce early modern homicide; the figures themselves may not be entirely reliable, exaggerating what actually occurred, even if they reflected a real (but more muted) development.

---

90.   Eisner, "Interpersonal Violence", pp. 565–586.
91.   Sharpe and Dickinson, "Revisiting the 'Violence We Have Lost'", p. 298.
92.   Eisner, "Interpersonal Violence", p. 576.
93.   Pinker, "A History Of Violence".

Whatever the causes behind a fall in homicide rates, or the precise figures for such a phenomenon, it seems that, during the sixteenth century, England was one of the least homicidal major states in Europe. Pardon papers from France, inquests from The Netherlands, and criminal examinations from Sweden and Finland suggest that homicide rates in these countries were already much higher than those in English counties for which both inquests and indictments are available.[94]

Even so, Tudor England was still far more violent than its modern successor. Perhaps because of this, there is a common perception amongst present day observers that early modern society, like its medieval predecessor, was desensitised to violence by constant exposure to assault and murder.[95] This probably contains a modicum of truth; people were less squeamish than their more sheltered modern counterparts. When pain, suffering, and premature death are routine features of everyday life, there probably is less compunction about inflicting them on others.

Nevertheless, such an impression does not fully accord with detailed studies of fifteenth century and sixteenth century England. Certainly, and despite a relatively high incidence of homicide, the law was never blasé about cold-blooded murder, and would pursue such killings long after they were committed. For example, in May 1512 the Durham sanctuary register noted that a man named Slake had sought protection because 26 years earlier (1486), he had fatally wounded a stranger with a pikestaff in Shoreditch (Middlesex).[96] Presumably, he had become concerned about being prosecuted for the crime. Similarly, William Cashell was convicted of murdering three men in a Lambeth house in November 1563, some five years after the crimes occurred. He had broken into the residence of a London haberdasher, cut the owner's throat with a knife, and then strangled his son and another man with a cord.[97]

Also revealing is the continued investigation into the murder of a wealthy widow, Alice Green, and her maid, Agnes Bear, along with the killing of Green's two small dogs and theft of goods worth a few pounds, during a burglary at her house at Poole, in Dorset, in January 1599. The

---

94. Roth, "Homicide in Early Modern England", pp. 45–46 and p. 50.
95. McGlynn, "Violence and the Law", pp. 53–59.
96. McSheffrey, "Sanctuary Seekers".
97. Cockburn, *Calendar of Assize Records. Surrey Indictments: Elizabeth I*, p. 73.

following year, it seems, a man named Robert Hill was executed for the crime. Even so, rumours lingered in the town that others had been involved. Some ten years later, interest in the murders was reignited, and the mayor and other justices from Poole conducted fresh and extensive (if unavailing) examinations of potential suspects.[98]

An even more extreme example of cold case investigation, coincidentally also dating from January 1599, involved Alice Jones, who alleged to John Grange, a Middlesex JP, that one David Jones had murdered her brother in Monmouthshire three decades earlier. Despite this huge delay, a substantial recognisance was taken from her: "That she shall preferre or cause to be preferred one bill of Inditement againste one David Johnes of Abergeynie in the county of Monmouth yeoman, for a supposed murther by him committed uppon one Thomas Johnes her brother some thirtye yeares past".[99] Tudor England may have been prone to homicidal violence, but life was not "cheap".

Background to Tudor Homicides

There has been something of a dearth in studies distinguishing between particular types of homicide during the Tudor period.[100] Very broadly (indeed, crudely) most (but not all) of them can be categorised as having occurred as a result of disputes or brawls outside the family, in a domestic environment (liberally construed), or in the course of acquisitive crimes such as robberies and burglaries. Inevitably, these categories sometimes overlap.

Brawls

Physical violence was a fairly common form of social interaction in late medieval and early modern England. As a result, a high proportion of killings, more than half, took place in a public place, such as a street or tavern. Some foreigners, like the Silesian knight Nikolaus von Popplau, who visited the country in 1484, found Englishmen to be "hot headed

---

98. Poole Record Office DC-PL/C/H/1.
99. Jeaffreson, *Middlesex County Records: Vol. 1*, pp. 251–257.
100. Roth, "Homicide in Early Modern England", pp. 33–67, p. 44.

and [of a] choleric disposition, and when they burst out in anger take no pity on anyone".[101] Andreas Franciscius, an Italian in London in 1497, shared his views. However, foreign visitors also attributed such characteristics to several other European nations at this time, and great care must be taken in relying on such subjective assessments. Even so, disputes and quarrels conducted away from the home, that suddenly turned violent, provided the most common background to Tudor killings.

Such killings were a largely male phenomenon. Although some 20 per cent of indicted killers and victims in early modern England were female, the former includes killings attributed to witches (a primarily female crime), which can be disregarded, and cases of infanticide *(sui generis* and considered in *Chapter 17).*[102] Tudor women committed less than a tenth of real, non-infant, killings. Tudor men of all social ranks, like their medieval predecessors, linked physical strength and courage to honour, and were socialised to regard violence as justified and even necessary in certain circumstances. They could not afford to be slighted, especially in public, if they were not to lose status and appear vulnerable to further victimisation. As a result, many men were decidedly prickly about the most minor affronts. This prompted the distinguished historian Lawrence Stone to compare the behaviour of both rich and poor to the "ferocity, childishness, and lack of self-control of the Homeric age". He felt that their nerves appeared to be perpetually on edge, leading to a readiness to resort to force and a general contempt for legal restraint.[103]

Certainly, quarrels about comparatively trivial matters could quickly escalate to violence among all social classes.[104] Disputes over cards, games, money owed, slights on personal honesty, and even the respective qualities of men from different counties led to serious assaults and deaths, frequently via a litany of escalating and oft-repeated (in the records) insults, such as "rascal", "knave", and "dog". For example, in August 1499 two London gentlemen went out to Hornsey, in Middlesex, to practice archery, gambling on which of them could shoot the greatest

---

101. Chris Skidmore, *Richard III: Brother, Protector, King* (London: Weidenfeld & Nicolson, 2018), p. 1.
102. Kesselring, *Making Murder Public,* p. 14.
103. Lawrence Stone, *The Crisis of the Aristocracy, 1558–1641* (New York: Galaxy. 1967), pp. 108–109.
104. Sharpe and Dickinson, "Revisiting the 'Violence We Have Lost'", p. 302.

distance. Robert Tickhill shot his arrow further than Edward Plumpton, but Plumpton thought he had cheated, claiming that he "lyed falsely lyke a knave, that he had nott wonne the shott but that he lyke a boy ha takon up his shaft and pyckyd it ferther". Plumpton then struck Tickhill on the head with his bow and, as he lay on the ground, beat his body and arms so fiercely that the bow broke. His victim got up and ran for his life, closely pursued, until he reached a large hedge and found he could not cross it to escape. At this point Tickhill turned and shot Plumpton in the neck, fatally wounding him (apparently in self-defence, given his attempt to retreat).[105]

Similarly, in April 1532, Richard Southwell killed Sir William Pennington in Westminster, after an argument involving imputations in which the latter declared: "Yf thow wyll abyde by the wordes I shall kytt thy knaves flesshe!".[106] In like manner, when, in August 1557, Francis Draycotte ran across Thomas Bristowe in a Nottingham suburb, a quarrel ensued, and opprobrious words were exchanged, both men (unoriginally) calling the other "knave". They then unsheathed their weapons, Bristowe having a dagger and Draycotte a sword; the latter was described as a gentleman, although such weapons were certainly not confined to men of that class. They fought, and the under-weaponed Bristowe was stabbed to death.[107]

It was partly because of this volatility that so much stress was placed on preventing neighbourhood tensions from arising in the first place, and why several specific criminal offences punished those who threatened community harmony. For example, when, at the Epiphany Sessions for Essex in 1568, Silvester Walden was indicted as a common barrator (one who incited quarrels and litigation among neighbours), it was argued that his behaviour meant that "murder, homicides, quarrels and disorders are likely to arise from day to day amongst the inhabitants unless some remedy be speedily provided".[108]

The courts sometimes tacitly recognised the significance of provocation by punishing those who had used abusive words rather than the

---

105. Steven Gunn, "Archery Practice in Early Tudor England", *Past & Present*, Vol. 209, Issue 1, p. 69.
106. McSheffrey, "The Slaying of Sir William Pennington", p. 172.
107. Hunnisett, *Calendar of Nottinghamshire Coroners' Inquests*, p. 155.
108. ERO Q/SR 24/7.

men who had responded to them with violence. This was the case with Hugh Charles (admittedly a servant) who was fined for "giving occasion" to another man to hit him. Non-lethal assaults that had been committed without any provocation were often treated much more seriously by the courts, as evidenced by the substantial 30 shillings fine imposed on John Gillowe of Walmer, in Kent, for striking another man with his dagger "without any occasion by him given unto the said Gillowe".[109]

Many, indeed most, of the killings that ensued in these circumstances produced manslaughter rather than murder convictions, even if indicted as the former, because of the lack of premeditation or *malice prepense* (see above). As a result of this fairly common background to such verdicts, manslaughter has been described as a male form of killing. Very few women were convicted of the lesser homicide, not least because they were less likely to participate in such hot-blooded and lethal quarrels. (Female manslaughter verdicts were also discouraged by awareness that women could not claim benefit of clergy to avoid the death penalty if convicted of the lesser form of homicide).

For example, of a selection of 713 accused female killers in the period from 1500 to 1680, for whom the trial jury verdict can be given with a degree of confidence, 49 per cent were acquitted, and 51 per cent found guilty. By contrast, of a group of 1,348 men from the same period, only 33 per cent were found not guilty or convicted of a non-culpable form of homicide, such as killing in self-defence, while just 30 per cent of the men were found guilty of murder. However, approximately 37 per cent were convicted of manslaughter.[110] Similarly, in the first half of the seventeenth century, manslaughter verdicts were reached in 63 per cent of homicide cases indicted at the Great Sessions in Cheshire. The defendants there were overwhelmingly male, in a county that saw few female homicide defendants generally (other than in cases of infanticide).[111]

This pattern of male homicide was hardly unique to England. In sixteenth century Seville, individuals of all social classes readily resorted to violence to settle disputes that were often occasioned by trivial matters,

---

109. Jones, *Gender and Petty Crime*, p. 38.
110. Kesselring, "Sex and Murder", p. 255.
111. Sharpe and Dickinson, "Revisiting the 'Violence We Have Lost'", p. 302.

creating what has been described as an atmosphere of social intranquility. Killings could (and did) result from questioning the quality of olives sold by a street vendor or the accidental soiling of a cape. As in England, even the best medical attention could not prevent death following relatively modest wounds, and a high proportion of killings took place in public spaces. However, unlike England, Seville had small groups of professional ruffians, or *rufos*, even in the late 1500s; they might be paid to kill, cut, or cudgel others, perhaps as part of a dispute over money or property.[112]

When homicide rates eventually fell, the decline was much sharper among men (the vast majority of killers) than women, largely because they brawled and fought less, something that was closely (though not solely) linked to changing attitudes towards masculinity and upholding personal honour.[113] Thus the very large fall in homicide cases tried in Cheshire during the course of the 1600s included a particularly marked decline in the sort of unpremeditated, sudden killings that normally resulted in manslaughter verdicts.[114]

Situational Factors

A variety of situational factors encouraged lethal brawling. For example, due to shorter average longevity, there were disproportionate numbers of young males in Tudor society. (Men aged from 16 to 30 are most likely to commit homicide).[115] As in most eras, alcohol could play an important role in such conflicts, although the absence of spirits reduced the speed with which it could be ingested, and so the incidence of drink-fuelled violence. Even so, a bill "against excessive and common Drunkenness", originally drafted in 1584–5 by a parliamentary committee, which reappeared in 1601, declared that intoxication, caused "Quarrelles, fyghtinges, Bloodsheddes, manslaughter".[116] Specifically, in May 1579 it was noted that one Isaac Sexton had been a habitual haunter of alehouses

---

112. Pike, "Crime and Criminals", pp. 7–8.
113. Pieter Spierenburg, *A History of Murder: Personal Violence in Europe from the Middle Ages to the Present* (Cambridge: Polity Press, 2008), p. 112.
114. Sharpe and Dickinson; "Revisiting the 'Violence We Have Lost'", p. 302.
115. Eisner, "From Swords to Words", p. 73.
116. Dean, *Law-Making and Society*, p. 177.

in Burnham, and: "being often dronken, hath sondry tymes broken the peace and comytted affrayes and bloudesheade".[117]

More important, the widespread possession of (potential) weapons greatly increased the risk of killings when violent quarrels occurred, just as it had in the medieval period. Many men, especially those of gentry and yeoman status, still carried swords, hangers (short swords), and daggers in public, whether for protection or status. Typically, in 1558, when George Foscum from Harrow, in Middlesex, was assaulted on the highway, he was robbed of a sword and a dagger, the only items of value taken during the attack, even if they did not help him.[118]

The presence of such weapons meant that heated quarrels were much more likely to have lethal consequences. For example, one August evening in 1579, Richard Gitteys and John Griffith exchanged "contumelious" words in King Street, Westminster, after which they fought. Initially, this was with hands and fists, but Griffith eventually drew his dagger and mortally wounded Gitteys over the eye, from which injury he died a week later. (At trial at the Old Bailey in October, Griffith pleaded guilty to manslaughter and successfully claimed his clergy.)[119] Similarly, in the early afternoon of a January day in 1589, Nicholas Fawcett and a gentleman named Sidrake Vere were in St John Street, in Westminster, when they exchanged insulting words; they drew their swords and daggers and fought; Fawcett was mortally wounded and died seven days later.[120]

Just as problematic was the ready availability of staffs and domestic tools of all varieties, especially knives and agricultural implements, that could be pressed into service should an argument flare into violence. Again, this had always been the case; more than a quarter of murder cases in late medieval East Anglia involved such improvised weapons.[121] However, their presence was even more marked (as a percentage of lethal implements) during the following century. Unsurprisingly, the ubiquitous work knife featured heavily in this regard. For example, late one evening in 1578, two yeomen from Heston, in Middlesex, Harmond

---

117. ERO Q/SR 71/22.
118. Jeaffreson, *Middlesex County Records: Vol. 1*, pp. 33–34.
119. *Ibid*, pp. 116–119.
120. *Ibid*, pp. 182–189.
121. McGlynn, "Violence and the Law", pp. 53–59.

Johnson and Robert Cooke, were in the stable of Sir Thomas Gresham (the famous merchant and financier) in the same parish when they quarrelled and "railed at one another with abusive speech". Johnson then struck Cooke on the face with his hand. Cooke responded by stabbing Johnson in the chest with a meat knife; he died an hour-and-a-half later. At the subsequent gaol delivery, Cooke pleaded guilty to manslaughter and successfully asked for clergy.[122]

In 1591, in a house in St Clement Danes, in Middlesex, Thomas Wright, a London tailor, and a man named Humfrey "spoke insultingly" to one another. That evening the two men ran into each other again in the street, and Wright assaulted Humfrey, beating him about the head with a thick stick. Humfrey responded by stabbing him in the groin with a knife, from which wound Wright eventually died. The coroner's inquest decided that this was a case of felonious killing, and Humfrey was duly indicted for manslaughter (not murder), admitted the crime (i.e. pleaded guilty) at the Old Bailey, and asked for, and was granted, benefit of clergy.[123]

The heavy use of both purpose-made weapons and work tools to effect sudden killings (discussed further below) was a general European phenomenon during the sixteenth century, as manifest in Spain as it was in England. Although blades (of all types) occasioned the highest number of deaths there, other tools were pressed into service. Pedro Lopez, a Seville pastry cook, even used an iron confectioner's stick to kill his victim.[124]

Domestic Killings

As with the medieval period, a far higher proportion of Tudor homicides involved relative (but not necessarily total) strangers than is the case today. Killings were more likely to involve neighbours (very broadly defined) rather than family members, even if the latter is taken to include live-in servants and apprentices. As a very general phenomenon, as the number of homicides found in a society falls, the proportion of domestic killings increases.[125] In modern Britain, about a third of all homicides take place within the family, albeit that the proportion appears to be declining. By

---

122. Jeaffreson, *Middlesex County Records: Vol. 1*, pp. 111–116.
123. *Ibid*, pp. 191–202.
124. Pike, "Crime and Criminals", p. 9.
125. Kesselring, *Making Murder Public*, pp. 14–15.

contrast, in early modern Essex, for example, only about a fifth were in that category. Some estimates, for other parts of the country, are even lower, especially if confined to relatives rather than resident domestic staff and employees. A survey of three South-eastern counties between 1558 and 1625 suggests that only 13 per cent of homicides that went to assizes were of this type.[126] It may have been particularly low in some parts of the North. The Cheshire data for the seventeenth century suggest that non-infanticidal homicide in the county was essentially a matter of male perpetrators and victims; presumably, this was a continuation of earlier patterns.[127]

This does not mean that there was not a significant number of domestic killings in Tudor England, merely that they were much less common in relative terms than they are today, and that the heavy fall in homicide rates during the early modern period was disproportionately concentrated on those that occurred outside the household. Domestic killings also fell during this period, but not at the same rate.

Such killings occurred against all manner of backgrounds. For example, Alice Neate hated her sister-in-law, believing that she had killed two of her (Neate's) children. Just after midnight in January 1577, she crept into a Colchester bedchamber and slit her throat. She then wrapped the corpse in a blanket and dragged it into a nearby yard, where it was found the next morning. Neate was committed to prison until the next gaol delivery at which she was convicted (largely on the evidence of her own daughter) and sentenced to death.[128]

Nevertheless, this sort of domestic homicide, along with parricides and matricides, was fairly unusual. Many such killings occurred against much more commonly occurring relationship and factual backgrounds. Spousal murders, along with the murder of children, especially stepchildren (relatively high mortality rates meant that remarriage was a common phenomenon) and young living-in servants, were the most common forms of familial killing in Tudor England.

---

126. Sharpe, *A Fiery & Furious People*, p. 170.
127. Sharpe and Dickinson, "Revisiting the 'Violence We Have Lost'", p. 302.
128. Samaha, "Hanging for Felony", pp. 763–782.

Spousal Murders

Spousal killing was fairly rare. Barbara Hanawalt famously observed, in a medieval context, that, with the family as the basic unit of the peasant economy, a man would no more consider killing his wife than his ox. The records for Yorkshire, which yield information on some 2,212 victims of fatal violent crime between 1333 and 1393, provide some support for this proposition. Just 52 cases involved spousal homicides, of which 41 (78.8 per cent) appear to have been uxoricides (wife killings), with the balance being mariticides (husband killings). Thus they made up only 2.5 per cent of all purported homicides in Yorkshire at this time. In the case of uxoricide, the husband was almost always suspected as the principal offender, rather than an accessory, and in 37 of the 41 cases was thought to have been acting alone. (All other domestic homicides, taken together, make up only 1.6 per cent of the alleged killings in the county, producing a combined total of 4.1 per cent of homicides).[129] The Tudor situation was broadly the same. Although spousal murder may have been slightly more common, it was still unusual, and wife killing was at least twice as common as husband killing.[130]

As today, many such killings were impulsive, being committed on the spur of the moment, albeit often after a period of deteriorating domestic relations. For example, in April 1594 a Middlesex coroner's inquest concluded that William Saxton had killed his wife, Joan. Shortly before ten o'clock one evening, Joan had been preparing to get into the bed in which her husband William was lying, when he, having earlier had a quarrel with her, threw a chamber pot at her. This struck and fatally wounded Joan.[131]

However, some other cases, especially those involving the use of poison, were more clearly planned. Romantic triangles provided classic backgrounds to such premeditated killings. For example, in 1582 Thomas Cash, unhappily married to a sickly wife at Holton, in Lincolnshire, and conducting affairs with both his maid and the wife of a neighbour, strangled his spouse with the active encouragement and support of the former.

---

129. Sara M. Butler, "Spousal Abuse in Fourteenth century Yorkshire: What Can We Learn from the Coroners' Rolls?", *Florilegium*, Vol. 18, No. 2, pp. 63–64.
130. Kesselring, *Making Murder Public*, p. 15.
131. Jeaffreson, *Middlesex County Records: Vol. 1*, pp. 219–225.

The maid was to be disappointed in her hopes of marrying Cash, whose other lover became a widow shortly afterwards, allowing the unfaithful pair to wed. In 1604, by which time Cash was on his third marriage, sheriff's officers arrived at his house in a nearby town to arrest him in connection with the murder some 22 years earlier. The long forgotten maid, by then in London, feeling herself to be "sick unto death", had confessed to a clergyman about what had occurred decades earlier to clear her conscience. The cleric passed the information on to Sir Richard Hamcotes, the Sheriff of Lincolnshire. Cash quickly confessed to examining JPs, telling them that his own conscience had troubled him for many years. He was duly convicted and executed. (The case is also indicative of the long memory of the criminal law for very serious offences and the gravity with which murder was viewed.)[132]

Petty Treason

As a result of the Statute of Treason of 1351, the notion of treason was not limited to rebellions against the Crown, but extended to those against domestic authority. Women accused of killing their husbands, servants (whether male or female) accused of killing their immediate masters or mistresses, and clerics accused of killing their superiors (such as curates who killed their priest, vicar, or rector, or any clergymen who killed their bishop), could be charged with petty treason. Thus Elizabeth Stafford, maid to Thomas Ardern, who assisted his wife in the plot to kill him, was convicted of petty treason in 1551 and burned for killing her master, as was Ardern's spouse.

In practice, mariticide (rather than master/mistress killing) was by far the most common manifestation of the crime. Originally, several defences available to the accused in other forms of homicide were not open to husband killers, because they were tried under the rules that applied to high treason. However, by the late sixteenth century, petty treason was increasingly being treated as simply another species of homicide, albeit with some unusual evidential features and a highly singular method of

---

132. John W. Weatherford, *Crime and Punishment in the England of Shakespeare and Milton, 1570–1640* (Jefferson, N.C.: McFarland, 2001), pp. 60–62.

capital punishment, especially for women (see *Chapter 12*). This was important because it allowed mitigating factors such as self-defence and provocation to be considered and so engendered a measure of gender equality in the trial (if not the punishment) of spousal homicide.[133]

Because of their scandalous nature, with its attendant reversal of the natural order, many instances of petty treason became *causes célèbres*. Among them was the notorious case of Agnes Hungerford, who was executed for the crime in 1523. During the summer of 1518, Agnes (1470–1523) and John Cotell visited the household of the Wiltshire landowner and widower Sir Edward Hungerford, whose seat was at Farleigh Castle. John subsequently disappeared, and Agnes and Edward married five months later. In January 1522 Edward died, leaving everything to Agnes, to the exclusion of a son from his first marriage. Shortly afterwards it was claimed that John had been murdered "by the procurement and abetting of Agnes". It was alleged that two of her servants had strangled John with a neckerchief and then burned his body in the kitchen furnace of Farleigh Castle. It is likely that Agnes had her first husband killed so as to marry the second, and possible that Hungerford was a participant in, or at least aware of, the murder, as it took place in his home. It may have been his considerable status and influence that prevented charges being brought against Agnes during his lifetime, and his son's resentment that ensured that they resurfaced afterwards.

In August 1522, Agnes and her two male accomplices were indicted for murder, and their hearing came on in late November. Unusually for a domestic murder, all three were confined in the Tower of London while awaiting trial, records showing that the cost of guarding and providing for Agnes came to ten shillings a week. At trial, all three were convicted and sentenced to death.[134] According to the *Grey Friars Chronicle*, in February 1523 Hungerford was led from the Tower to Holborn and once there put into a cart with her servants "and so carried unto Tyborne, and there all were hongyd, and she burryd at the Grayfreeres in the nether

---

133. Matthew Lockwood, "From Treason to Homicide: Changing Conceptions of the Law of Petty Treason in Early Modern England", *The Journal of Legal History*, Vol. 34, Issue 1, pp. 31–49.
134. Levin et al., *A Biographical Encyclopedia*, p. 29.

end of the myddes of the churche on the northe syde".[135] Strangely, Agnes escaped the normal punishment for petty treason of being burnt at the stake (perhaps a reflection of her social status).

As this case suggests, some instances of petty treason during the era involved romantic triangles, where killing was a way out of an unsatisfactory marriage for the woman concerned, and sometimes even carried out by her lover. In a widely reported case, Anne Welles was executed for such a crime in 1592. Rival London goldsmiths, John Brewen and John Parker, had courted her, the former lavishing valuable gifts on Welles, while the latter enjoyed illicit sexual relations with her. When Brewen realised he was unlikely to win Welles, he asked her to return the gifts he had given her. When she refused, he had her arrested. Meanwhile, Welles had become pregnant by Parker, who then refused to marry her. She offered to wed Brewen if he would withdraw the charges against her, and the two were duly married. Perversely, this revived Parker's interest, and he said that he would marry Anne if she killed her husband. Her first attempt to poison him was made after they'd been married only three days.[136]

Corrective Violence and Domestic Homicide

Corrective violence was an accepted (if occasionally deprecated) means by which sixteenth century heads of household could enforce their authority over wives, children, young domestic servants, and living-in apprentices. Although *The Lawes Resolutions of Womens Rights* was first published in 1632, it was probably written in the late Elizabethan period, and so reflects Tudor practice.[137] Its author, known only as TE, ruefully acknowledged that a husband could not inflict on his spouse any bodily damage "otherwise than appertains to the office of a husband for lawful and reasonable correction". When, in 1588, Simon White was brought before a London church court for abusing his wife, he freely conceded

---

135. Geoffrey Abbott, *Female Executions: Martyrs, Murderesses and Madwomen* (2006, Summersdale Publishers Ltd., Chichester), p. 130.

136. Anon, *The Murder of John Brewen* (1592, London), pp. 1–10.

137. Kesselring, 2019, *Making Murder Public: Homicide in Early Modern England, 1480–1680*, 2019, p. 88.

that he had employed such violence on earlier occasions when punishing her for "misusage and intolerable misbehaviours".[138] In their turn, wives might employ such violence against children and servants.

However, corrective violence was subject to constraints, both legal and social, although their borders were uncertain. As TE observed of spousal correction, "How far [it properly] extendeth I cannot tell". Indicative of the presence of such restraints, Simon White stressed that his discipline was imposed in accepted circumstances, on "juste occasion", and within proper limits, being conducted in "honest, reasonable and moderate sorte". Furthermore, he had never used more than a small beech wand to impose it.[139]

If such violence became extreme, or patently unreasonable, if it threatened life or limb, both neighbours and the secular and ecclesiastical courts might intervene. For example, in April 1583 the Essex JP Edward Barret took depositions about Henry Grigges' mistreatment of his wife. Isabel, the victim, testified that her husband had come home that same afternoon and "did pull her by the heire of her hedd and beats her with his fyste about her hedd". Elizabeth Brooman supported her account, while Jane Cock, another local woman, stated that Isabel had told her about her husband's attack shortly after it occurred.[140]

Similarly, in 1605 Elizabeth Head became so concerned at her husband's violence that she complained to Sir Nicholas Coote and Thomas Fanshawe, two Essex JPs. She told them that her husband had regularly beaten her, so that she was black and blue, and had also "most vilely used hir that shee vas ashamed to tell". She asked that the magistrates bind her husband over to keep the peace. Unfortunately, this merely prompted fresh threats to "thompe hir as shee was never thomped", along with a promise to cut off the head of any magistrate who committed him to a house of correction.[141] Inevitably, some official interventions came too late or were ineffective, and wives died from the effects of disciplinary action.

---

138. Sharpe, *A Fiery & Furious People*, p. 173.
139. *Ibid.*
140. ERO Q/SR 85/18.
141. ERO Q/SR 173/110.

Children and Servants

Children (especially stepchildren) and young living-in servants and apprentices were particularly vulnerable to this form of mistreatment, sometimes dying as a result. In early modern England, servants were much more likely to be killed by their masters than to kill them, just as children were much more likely to be murdered by their parents than vice-versa.[142] The authorities were not blasé about such deaths, and sometimes attempted to forestall them, just as they did with attacks on wives.

For example, in March 1579 Robert Lyvesey wrote to Sir William More asking that More and John Southcott (both of them Surrey JPs) issue a warrant to bind-over a woman in his neighbouring parish (Tooting) to good behaviour. She had, apparently, almost beaten her daughter to death and would let no-one in to see her, claiming to be affected by the plague. He also alleged that five years earlier the same woman had caused a maid's suicide by misusing her.[143]

Nevertheless (and as with wives), outside intervention was often ineffective or even absent. For example, in 1580 Amy Harrison, a "cruel unjust mistress", had a servant living with her in St Giles-in-the-Fields. She eventually killed her with an "excess of correction", after beating her from head to foot with large cudgels. Harrison was convicted and executed next to her house to set a public example.[144] Many other employers who found themselves in a similar situation were more fortunate.

At the Essex Assizes in March 1571, Joan Ive was indicted on a coroner's inquisition for murdering her servant, 18-year-old Sarah Foster, by assaulting her with a bed staff. She was merely convicted of "homicide" (manslaughter) and ultimately pardoned (as a woman, she could not claim benefit of clergy).[145] Some secured outright acquittals. At the same forum, in March 1591, Richard Collins was indicted for feloniously killing his 14-year-old servant, Joan Atkins. An inquest jury concluded that he had assaulted Joan, thrown her down on a "thresholde" in his house, then kicked and struck her, crushing and bruising her body so severely that she lingered for three days and died. Even so, he was acquitted of

---

142. Kesselring, *Making Murder Public*, p. 15.
143. SHC 6729/1/64.
144. Anthony Munday, *A View of Sundry Examples*, p. D.111.
145. Cockburn, *Calendar of Assize Records. Essex Indictments, Elizabeth I*, p. 84.

any offence, the trial jury deciding that the fictional John at Death (see above) had killed the child.[146]

Instrumental Killings

Killings committed in the course of burglaries and robberies made up a relatively modest proportion of all Tudor homicides but, unsurprisingly, a much larger percentage of killings that were defined as murder (rather than manslaughter). For contemporary observers, such homicides occasioned special concern in a way that brawling deaths did not, being viewed as the quintessential form of murder. They loomed large in the criminal chapbooks produced in the latter part of the era and were much less likely to be pardoned than other killings. For example, in 1530 the home of Lucy Lacey, a wealthy London widow, was burgled, and her maid, the sole person then at home, brutally murdered. All the perpetrators who were apprehended were executed, as they were arrested over ensuing months.[147] Similarly, when, in 1582, William Story and five other men, who had burgled several houses in various Sussex villages, were caught after clubbing a servant to death, all those convicted were hanged. Robert Russell met the same fate after he burgled a yeoman's house at Puttenham, in Hertfordshire, in December 1600. Once inside the premises, he encountered Margaret Eldredge, a maid-of-all-work, and beat her to death with a fire shovel before stealing £11 from a chest.[148]

Methods of Killing

A dataset compiled from a sample of almost 4,000 coroners' inquests and court indictments for cases of homicide (including infanticide), from between 1500 and 1680 provides an indication of the most and least common forms of killing in early modern England. Just over ten per cent of deaths were attributed to witchcraft, which needs to be removed from consideration. This being done, it seems that stabbings made up about a

---

146. *Ibid*, pp. 361–362; ERO T/A 418/54/19.
147. McSheffrey, "The Murder of Mistress Lacey's Maid", p. 334.
148. Cockburn, *Calendar of Assize Records: Hertfordshire Indictments: Elizabeth I*, p. 162.

third of all killings. Almost half of these involved the use of weapons such as swords and daggers rather than "domestic" blades. Blows inflicted by staffs or cudgels were responsible for another 17 per cent of homicides, the unarmed beating or kicking of the victim to death slightly under ten per cent, and the use of work tools (other than knives) as weapons somewhat under ten per cent. By contrast, shootings made up less than four per cent of all killings (most of these being in the Jacobean and Caroline periods), strangling or suffocation less than seven per cent (many of these would have been infanticides), while poisoning was used in fewer than two per cent of all homicides.[149]

More particular to the early Tudor period, the inquests on 24 people who were deliberately killed in Sussex have been preserved for the 30 years from 1487 (some others from this time have been permanently lost). In 23 cases the weapons used in these homicides can be identified. In five cases a domestic knife was employed. In eight of them, the only implement used was the widely carried wooden staff. In one more, both a staff and a knife were used in the same killing. Two blunt instruments, a boundary marker and a large stake, and two agricultural instruments, a pitchfork and a shovel, were employed in four more homicides. However, just four cases involved purposely manufactured bladed weapons, three daggers and a hanger, and use of the latter was combined with that of a domestic fork. One killing was carried out by two men armed with "bylls"; nevertheless, even if this referred to a military weapon rather than an agricultural tool (they went by the same name), it seems that little more than a fifth of deliberate killings involved weapons that had been manufactured as such, which is quite a modest total when compared to some other surveys.[150] In her study of violence in East Anglia during the years 1422 to 1442, Philippa Maddern calculated that almost 29 per cent of violent incidents that reached King's Bench from the six counties on the circuit involved the use of a sword alone.[151]

Firearms were still in their infancy during the early Tudor period, and their total absence from Sussex at this time is unsurprising. If anything,

---

149. Kesselring, "Bodies of Evidence", pp. 245–262.
150. Hunnisett, *Sussex Coroners' Inquests*, pp. 1–11.
151. Maddern, *Violence and Social Order*, p. 28.

it seems that England was a little slower than some continental countries in adopting such weapons. It was distant from their European centres of manufacture, and had an historic attachment to archery, which various statutes required people to practice. As late as November 1536, Robert Packington, a prominent London merchant, may have become the first recorded murder victim in England to have been killed by a pistol (rather than a shoulder-mounted firearm) when he was shot in Cheapside. (His assassin was never traced, but the murder may have been religiously motivated, and arranged by conservative Catholic elements). The state-of-the-art self-igniting wheel-lock handgun used and its relatively small size allowed the murderer to get close to his target without occasioning suspicion, as would have been the case had he employed the very much larger matchlock arquebus, with its glowing match, that was typical of most firearms at this time.[152]

However, during the 1540s and 1550s, possession of handguns (and firearms generally) spread significantly in England, and continued to do so for the remainder of the Tudor era, so that their use started to creep into criminal offences. In 1541 this prompted Parliament to enact a stat-ute (33 Hen. 8, c. 6), in part to stop "shamefull murthers". This limited gun ownership to rich people, those who had lands, rents, fees, annui-ties or offices to the yearly value of £100. Even so, such weapons rapidly moved down the social scale, the prohibitive legislation often being dis-regarded, as the weapons themselves became more reliable, sophisticated, and cheaper to produce.[153]

As a result, a handful of killings during the late Tudor era involved firearms. For example, in the 1560s, some two per cent of Kentish homi-cides were committed in this manner. Nevertheless, although Kent was a populous county, it witnessed only 14 fatal shootings after 1560, and a few of these appear to have been accidents occasioned by gross negli-gence rather than deliberate killings.[154]

Similarly, although popular as a literary device, poison occasioned only a relatively small proportion of all Tudor homicides, albeit far more than

---

152. Derek Wilson, "The Hunt for the Tudor Hitman", *BBC History Magazine*, June 2014.
153. Gunn, "Archery Practice in Early Tudor England", p. 57 and p. 76.
154. Cockburn, "Patterns of Violence in English Society: Homicide in Kent 1560–1985", *Past and Present*, Vol. 130, Issue 1, pp. 82–84.

had been the situation two centuries earlier, when it was not identified in a single case of suspected husband-killing in the entire run of Yorkshire coroners' rolls.[155] In part, this may have been because the medieval period was largely dependent on plant-based poisons, such as aconite and hellebore, rather than the more effective and freely available mineral-extracted poisons, such as arsenic, available in the sixteenth century.[156]

Cases of poisoning made up a higher percentage of homicides that were deemed to be murders, as it was an inherently planned and cold-blooded form of killing that allowed little or no scope for defining the crime as manslaughter, accident, or self-defence. It elicited special horror, not least because it was insidious and hard to prevent, even for wealthy and powerful men, such as the Archbishop of York, Christopher Bainbridge, who was fatally poisoned by his chaplain while in Italy in 1514.[157] For this reason it had been briefly subject to the statutory punishment of boiling to death, introduced after an attempt to poison the Bishop of Rochester in 1531 (see *Chapter 12*).

The increased availability and potency of poison meant that it was not simply an elite method of assassination in the Tudor era. There were regular well-publicised cases of poisoning involving ordinary people, especially when the victims were intimates. Ratsbane (white arsenic or arsenic trioxide) was, as its popular name suggests, widely used to deal with domestic pests and vermin; as a result, it featured heavily in such killings, although a few other poisons were also employed.

Tudor women were responsible for food preparation, and so particularly well placed to use poison; perhaps unsurprisingly, they made up more than half of those accused of such killings.[158] This pattern continued into the following century. In Cheshire, during the first half of the 1600s, two-thirds of those accused in poisoning cases were female, despite their particularly low numbers generally (about six per cent) in cases of non-infant homicide in the county. Even so, well under five per cent of

155. Butler, "Spousal Abuse", p. 66.
156. Fredson Thayer Bowers, "The Audience and the Poisoners of Elizabethan Tragedy", *The Journal of English and Germanic Philology*, Vol. 36, No. 4, p. 491.
157. Moore, *The Tudor Murder Files*, p. 7.
158. Kesselring, "Bodies of Evidence", p. 250.

indicted killings in Cheshire involved poison (and this figure fell swiftly in the second half of the century).[159]

Fairly typical of such cases, in July 1503 a coroner's inquest in Kent concluded that Agnes Berry had fatally poisoned her husband, Richard, the previous March by adding ratsbane to his food.[160] In 1592, when Anne Welles killed her goldsmith husband, John Brewen, by serving him poisoned sugar sops during the week before Shrovetide the death was initially put down to natural causes.[161] On a larger scale, Eleanor Swift may have been an Elizabethan serial poisoner. She was accused of three murders at the Hertford Assizes in March 1600. It was alleged that she had poisoned her husband and two other men over a nine-month period by putting ratsbane in their food. Poisoning was notoriously difficult to prove at this time, as there was no reliable medical test for its presence, and she was acquitted on all counts.[162] Even so, at the same forum, in March 1602, Elizabeth Davy was less fortunate, and convicted of poisoning Thomas Andowne the previous year by putting ratsbane in a mess of pottage that he ate, and was duly sentenced to death.[163]

Nevertheless, poisoning was certainly not a female-only form of killing; a significant number of men also had recourse to it, some even using it in a domestic context. For example, at the Chelmsford Assizes in July 1587, George Sawyer of Thundersley, in Essex, was indicted for giving his wife, Joan, ratsbane in her "broth", so that she was violently sick and died.[164] Other men used poison to dispose of troublesome lovers.

Non-lethal Violence

Homicide was at the apex of a broad pyramid of violence that started with physical threats and minor blows. For example, from 1460 to 1560 the Sandwich *Year Books* record 236 cases of non-fatal assault or affray, and just 18 cases (seven per cent of the combined total) in which assaults

---

159. Sharpe and Dickinson, "Revisiting the 'Violence We Have Lost'", p. 309.
160. McSheffrey, "Sanctuary Seekers".
161. Bellamy, *Strange, Inhuman Deaths*, p. 487 and p. 496.
162. Cockburn, *Calendar of Assize Records. Hertfordshire Indictments: Elizabeth I*, p. 150.
163. *Ibid*, pp. 170–172.
164. ERO T/A 418/47/61.

resulted in death (i.e. homicides), that were heard in local courts or by coroners in the town. (All but one of the 18 cases involved men.) However, the *Year Books* do not record all assaults, so that the proportion of cases that actually resulted in death was probably significantly smaller.[165]

Most manifestations of non-lethal violence, in even its most serious and premeditated forms, were defined as misdemeanours, if only because of the rudimentary development of inchoate offences such as attempted murder at common law (see above). However, there were a tiny number of exceptions. Cutting out a person's tongue and/or putting out their eyes, even if they were not killed, was made a felony in 1404. This statute (5 H4 c. 4) may have been introduced to discourage offenders from trying to prevent their victims from subsequently identifying them.[166]

Because they were misdemeanours, even extremely grave assaults were normally punished leniently, usually by a fine or (very much less commonly) a short custodial sentence, although it was often pure chance that separated such a crime from its fatal counterpart. For example, in April 1568, Peter Jerome, a gentleman from Woodham Mortimer, was convicted of assaulting William Coke, the local constable, while the latter was in the execution of his office, striking him with a dagger and drawing blood. Even so, he was merely fined 6s 8d.[167] Their low legal status also had major implications for bail. In April 1593, Sir John Wolley's keeper viciously assaulted a man named Davy Davis. Wolley wrote to his fellow Surrey JP Sir William More suggesting that the keeper might be given bail if Davis seemed likely to recover.[168]

As a result of this attitude to non-lethal violence, comparatively few assaults were tried at assizes, rather than quarter sessions and leets. A few (by no means all) of those that went to the upper jury court may have done so specifically because they were viewed as fairly grave examples of their kind. For example, Walter Nicholls was prosecuted at the Surrey Assizes in February 1567 after he attacked William Leas in the highway at Southwark and stabbed him in the leg with a dagger. (The verdict is

165. Jones, *Gender and Petty Crime*, p. 63.
166. Edward Coke, *The Third Part of the Institutes of the Laws of England* (London: 1644), p. 62.
167. ERO Q/SR 39/23.
168. SHC LM/COR/3/515.

unknown.)[169] Others were determined at the higher court purely for reasons of administrative convenience.

---

169. Cockburn, *Calendar of Assize Records. Surrey Indictments: Elizabeth I*, p. 67.

CHAPTER 17

Infanticide and Abortion

Introduction

Infanticide—the killing of an infant under a year in age—was not a distinct offence in Tudor England. When prosecuted in a secular court it was as simple murder. Typically, Anne Gowsworthe's indictment merely identified her offspring as *infantem feminam* (female infant) and otherwise described the crime in exactly the same terms used for other serious homicides, accusing Gowsworthe of having *felonice interfecit et murdravit* (feloniously killed and murdered) the unnamed baby.[170]

Of course, indictments for infanticide necessarily precluded legal issues such as chance medley and self defence being raised, as they often were with other forms of homicide. The jury was usually presented with a simple choice of guilty or not guilty of murder. Even so, and for reasons that are not entirely clear, Margaret Charvye, a single woman from Stanford Rivers, in Essex, who gave birth to an illegitimate baby in 1579 and then threw him violently to the ground, was merely found guilty of "homicide" (manslaughter) when tried for murder at the county assizes.[171]

In another unusual case, of 1589, Margery Hall, also apparently a spinster, was indicted for killing her male baby. The inquest found that she had drowned the infant in a pond at Mitcham, in Surrey. The baby was unnamed, so seemingly had not undergone baptism (usually carried out within a few days of birth), but was not described as newborn. Very uncommonly for infanticide cases, Hall was acquitted on the basis that John Death had killed the child. This jury fiction was usually employed where a homicide had occurred in specially mitigating circumstances

---

170. Kesselring, "Bodies of Evidence", p. 249.
171. TNA ASS 35/21/4/5.

(see *Chapter 16*). As a result, post-partum mental disturbance or eugenics issues may have prompted the killing, rather than it being a "conventional" infanticide.[172]

The vast majority of prosecuted cases of infanticide in the sixteenth century involved neonaticide, the killing of newborn babies at or just after delivery, rather than the murder of slightly older infants. Such babies were usually illegitimate. Both characteristics would be found in infanticide cases for centuries to come. They appear to reflect the real distribution and nature of such killings. Nevertheless, it is also true that coroners' inquests were much more willing to give the benefit of the doubt to women whose babies' existence had been publicly acknowledged, and who had survived for a short period after delivery, even if they were bastards. For example, in 1573, a poor woman named Joan Cheese gave birth in public to a baby girl who died six days later in Hounslow (Middlesex). The coroner's jury concluded that the infant died after her mother "fell by mischance upon the ground, by which fall the infant's head was injured, so that she died through mischance and from no other cause".[173]

The authorities were even fairly reluctant to investigate deaths among openly acknowledged babies that were occasioned by apparent neglect during nursing, although this may sometimes have been employed as an indirect method of committing infanticide.[174] In a rare exception, from shortly after the Tudor era, Alice Milles was accused of murdering her infant in Clerkenwell in 1614. It was alleged that she unwrapped its clothing and held it naked so that it was exposed to the cold, became ill, and died shortly afterwards.[175]

Even so, it seems that the relatively small number of married women prosecuted for murdering their newborn infants reflects their lower involvement in such killings rather than better concealment, although the latter probably played a role in the process, and married women were normally far better placed to hide such activity. Nevertheless, such

---

172. Cockburn, *Calendar of Assize Records. Surrey Indictments: Elizabeth I*, p. 336.
173. Jeaffreson, *Middlesex County Records: Vol. 1*, pp. 78–85.
174. Keith Wrightson, "Infanticide in Earlier Seventeenth century England", *Local Population Studies*, Vol. 15, p. 10.
175. LeHardy, *County of Middlesex. Calendar To the Sessions Records: New Series, Vol. 2*, pp. 35–66.

evidence as there is suggests that infanticide did not often occur as a form of family planning in England, at least in a sex-selective way, and from this it might be extrapolated that it did not normally happen for other reasons. (Some Mediterranean states may have been slightly different in this regard.) A survey of the baptismal registers of 13 Yorkshire parishes in the 1530s to 1660 shows a ratio among the (nearly 40,000) recorded baptisms of 105 boys to every 100 girls, which is largely the expected gender ratio at birth. (Slightly more boys than girls are born naturally to accommodate higher male infant mortality.)[176] Home Circuit records indicate that a small majority of prosecutions where the sex of a baby can be identified involved male infants.[177]

Most prosecuted cases of neonaticide, almost by definition, were the result of unwanted pregnancies. During the sixteenth century, the English normally controlled family size by marrying relatively late and practising pre-marital abstinence from full coitus—as opposed to non-penetrative forms of sexual activity—in the meantime. The average woman was into her twenties at first wedding. This was an aspect of what has been termed the European Marriage Pattern (EMP) that emerged in the late Middle Ages and became characteristic of western society during the early modern era.[178]

However, not all women could resist temptation or pressure to engage in illicit sexual intercourse prior to marriage or, for those who never wed (a not insignificant number of females in the late 1500s) refrain from full sexual relationships for their entire lives. Inevitably, some of them became pregnant, given the lack of reliable contraception, as opposed to ineffective customary practices such as anointing the penis head with onion oil (inserting wool soaked in vinegar into the vagina was slightly more effective). However, births out of wedlock were often occasioned by dishonoured promises of marriage.[179] Anne Hathaway was not unusual

---

176. Kesselring, "Bodies of Evidence", p. 250.
177. Sharpe, *A Fiery & Furious People*, p. 197.
178. Tine De Moor and Jan Luiten Van Zanden, "Girl power: The European marriage pattern and labour markets in the North Sea region in the late medieval and early modern period", *The Economic History Review*, Vol. 63, Issue 1, pp. 1–33.
179. Robert V Schnucker, "Elizabethan Birth Control and Puritan Attitudes", *Journal of Interdisciplinary History*, Vol. 5, No. 4, pp. 655–667.

in being pregnant at the time of her marriage to William Shakespeare; unfortunately, some genitors were less honourable than the bard.

An example from a couple of years after the Tudor era is the case of Rose Arnold from Scraptoft, in Leicestershire. Arnold was a domestic maid when she embarked on a secret affair with Francis Lane, her master's son, and "upon his promise made unto me, to make me his wife, I granted unto him the loss of my chastity". However, when Arnold became pregnant, her lover attempted to trip her into a well. Despite this homicidal behaviour, and following an apology from Lane, she continued as a maid in the house until her pregnancy became apparent, a few months later. Thereafter she accepted a small sum of money and a forged pass from Francis, to move away and have their child (the baby died shortly after delivery), still apparently hopeful that he would eventually honour his promise.[180]

Abortion

In some cases, unmarried pregnant women managed to escape their predicaments by procuring abortions. For example, in 1589 an inquest held at Little Bardfield, in Essex, on the body of a female baby concluded that a local widow, Eleanor Robynson, "gave birth by abortion to a certain female infant born dead". The diminutive corpse was then dumped in a haymow.[181] In the same decade, an innkeeper from Shamley in Surrey noted that, the previous Michaelmas, a woman named Joan Holt had informed the constables of Wonersh that she was pregnant by a young man from their village. However, it was thought that she had since destroyed her unborn child.[182] At about the same time, it was claimed that the unhappily married Mistress Padge in Plymouth had vowed not to have children by her much older husband, and aborted at least two pregnancies during their short marriage.[183]

---

180. David Cressy, *Travesties and Transgressions in Tudor and Stuart England* (Oxford: Oxford University Press, 1999), pp. 73–74; Schnucker, "Elizabethan Birth Control", pp. 655–667.
181. ERO Q/SR 110/68.
182. SHC LM/2038.
183. MacMillan, *Stories of True Crime*, 2015, p. 43.

Abortions might be effected by ingesting a noxious substance or (less commonly during the Tudor era) via use of an inserted implement. Typically, in 1469 a female servant from Deal, in Kent, was accused in a church court of having "killed the infant lately in her womb by means of herbs and medicines". Similarly, in 1493 George Hemery was accused before the Rochester Consistory Court of placing medicines in a drink given to a woman "in order to destroy the boy he had procreated".[184]

It appears that Tudor women usually acquired their knowledge of herbal abortifacients from other females. For example, in 1527 in Whitstable, in Kent, two single women advised Joan Colpham as to which herbs she should ingest to bring about a miscarriage.[185] However, English medical and botanical writers also provided information about certain herbs' potentially abortive powers, either unintentionally when warning pregnant women what to avoid if they wished to prevent a miscarriage, or deliberately but couched in suitably veiled terms. As women could quite legitimately take potential abortifacients for a range of other medical conditions (such as the loss of menstruation in cases of malnutrition or illness), it was difficult to be certain that they were being consumed to end pregnancy, or that this was what the authors of such tracts were suggesting.

Illustrative of these problems, in 1577, at Cuckfield in Sussex, there was a bitter dispute as to whether Mercy Gould, a pregnant maid, had been given, by her master's wife, an abortifacient or a legitimate medicine to protect against plague. The substance, which she described as a "cruel, hot, drink" and that was popularly referred to as "dragon water", was probably extracted from dragonwort. Unfortunately, this was thought to have both properties by contemporary authors. It could give protection against the plague but was also "hurtful to women newly conceived with child".[186]

---

184. R. H. Helmholz, "Infanticide in the Province of Canterbury During the Fifteenth Century", *History of Childhood Quarterly*, Vol. 2, p. 381.
185. Jones, *Gender and Petty Crime*, p. 90.
186. Cressey, *Travesties and Transgressions*, p. 67.

Among the other plants used to induce miscarriage were artemisia, pennyroyal, rue, and calamint.[187] Many women employed "savin", an extract made from the poisonous tips of the evergreen leaves of the bushy *Juniperus sabina*. In 1574 the rector of Leaden Roding, in Essex, was supposed to have made a woman pregnant and "brought her from London a rough herbe, which he called saven willing her to use it in drink for hindering the child if she should have any". After consuming it she proceeded to have a premature child, without hair or nails, which died immediately, suggesting that the herb had been effective.[188]

Again, the use of herbs for such purposes was a Europe-wide phenomenon; the same veiled language was used in medical tracts in Germany, where laurel seeds mixed with alcohol were often favoured for abortions.[189] Closer to home, it has been argued that many Irish women were familiar with the use of abortifacients during the late medieval period.[190] Some "cunning folk" (village practitioners of medicine/magic) in England may have made something of a business in arranging, or at least promising, terminations for cash, along with their occult services.[191]

Abortion and the Law

Cases of abortion only rarely came before the secular courts, even after the Reformation, not least because it was so difficult to distinguish from natural miscarriage. On the few occasions when they were prosecuted in Tudor England, it seems that abortions may often have been indicted as misdemeanours (rather than felonies), especially if they occurred prior to the foetus' "quickening" (thought to occur about three months after gestation). This was sometimes believed to be the point at which it acquired a soul, although this had been a matter of considerable debate during the medieval period, with some observers favouring 40 days, others the formation of limbs, and a few the point of conception as key times in

---

187. Alex Gradwohl, "Herbal Abortifacients and their Classical Heritage in Tudor England", *Penn History Review*, Vol. 20, Issue 1, p. 44, p. 50, and p. 62.
188. Macfarlane, "Illegitimacy and Illegitimates", p. 71.
189. Margaret Brannan Lewis, *Infanticide and Abortion in Early Modern Germany* (Abingdon: Routledge, 2016), pp. 122–123.
190. Gillian Kenny, "Ireland, Back to the Future", *History Today*, Vol. 68, Issue 6, pp. 1–4.
191. Cressy, *Travesties and Transgressions*, p. 79.

the process. As late as 1622, when Henry Eaton was accused of seeking to induce an abortion in his maid, it was claimed that he had assured her that it was "no sin to do so, except the child were already quickened within her". (This belief also had antecedents in legislation from the reign of Edward I.)[192] However, by 1600 continental jurisprudence, possibly influenced by Protestant theology, was beginning to date the infusion of the foetus with a human soul at conception. This had been a minority view in the medieval era.[193]

Despite the efforts of Gratian, the canon lawyer and jurist from Bologna, who suggested in his twelfth century *Decretum* that the abortion of a foetus should be treated in the same way as other forms of homicide, such notions had not taken root in the lay courts of medieval England. Indeed, it was slower than some other European countries in moving abortion out of the private sphere and effectively criminalising it. On one interpretation, this was because, by the middle of the fourteenth century, English common lawyers and judges had concluded that babies did not have full personhood until they had been born and were *in rerum natura*, an analysis that largely survived to the end of the Tudor era in 1603.[194]

Even so, in March 1602 Margaret Webb, a spinster from Godalming, was belatedly indicted at the Surrey Assizes for taking ratsbane some 30 months earlier to destroy her unborn child. She appears to have taken advantage of a general pardon to avoid liability.[195] Other instances may have been dealt with at quarter sessions, and, as already suggested, a few more cases of this type went before the church courts, especially prior to the Reformation. They included that of Agnes Gybbys from Folkestone, who, it was alleged in 1497 "destroyed the child with which she was pregnant".[196] However, such cases appear to have been fairly rare occurrences, even in ecclesiastical forums, and were dealt with comparatively leniently.

---

192. Caitlin Scott, "Birth Control and Conceptions of Pregnancy in Seventeenth century England", *Retrospectives*, Vol. 2, Issue 1, p. 83.
193. Wolfgang P. Muller, *The Criminalization of Abortion in the West: Its Origins in Medieval Law* (Ithaca: Cornell University Press, 2012), p. 12.
194. *Ibid.*
195. Cockburn, *Calendar of Assize Records. Surrey Indictments: Elizabeth I*, p. 512
196. Jones, *Gender and Petty Crime*, p. 89.

Dangers of Abortion

Whatever its legal status, abortion was highly dangerous and extremely uncertain, greatly reducing its attractions. Many women poisoned themselves attempting it. In 1572 in Essex, the promiscuous but married Margaret Manister appears to have feared that she might be pregnant by one of her lovers, who included her brother-in-law. She "drank Saven, and that night she fell sick and so was the whole week after".[197] Others were even less fortunate, and died. In 1504 a coroner's inquest considered the death of Jane Wynspere cf Basford, in Nottinghamshire. She was a pregnant single woman who apparently "drank various bad and [impure] potions in order to kill and destroy the child in her body … as a result of which the said Jane then and there died".[198]

Many other women simply failed to achieve a positive result. A selection of six cases in the church ccurts from the early Tudor period, involving women who had ingestec herbs to secure abortions, produces only one that was successful.[199] Numerous women shared the experience of a pregnant London spinster whc, a decade after the Tudor era, "by a divilish practise sought to consume it [the foetus] in her body before the birth, but not prevailing (as God wo.ild have it) shee was forced by nature to deliver it alive to the world".[200] Similarly, in 1605, when Elizabeth Reve found that she had been impregnated by the vicar of Wiveton, in Norfolk, her mother paid a man 12 pence to administer "physicke". It had no effect: Reve merely "toke the drink and caste it again".[201] As a result, it seems that most pregnancies outside wedlock went to term (ignoring natural miscarriage) and produced openly acknowledged bastards.

197. F. G. Emmison, *Elizabethan Life: Morals and the Church Courts* (Chelmsford: Essex Record Office, 1973) p. 41.
198. Carla Spivack, "To 'Bring Down the Flowers': The Cultural Context of Abortion Law in Early Modern England", *William & Mary Journal cf Women & the Law*, Vol. 14, No. 1, p. 117.
199. Jones, *Gender and Petty Crime,* p. 90.
200. Anon, *Deeds against nature, and monsters by kinde tryed at the goale deliverie of Newgate, at the sessions in the Old Bayly, the 18. and 19. of July last, 1614* (London, 1614), pp. 1–12.
201. Saunders, *Sir Nathaniel Bacon of Stiffkey*, p. 18.

Illegitimate Births and their Consequences

Illegitimacy increased for most of the Elizabethan period, reaching nearly four per cent in the late sixteenth century before declining during the first 60 years of the following century, although its (official) incidence varied enormously within the country. In the late 1500s, parish rates might be as low as 0.5 per cent in Puritan-dominated areas of Essex and as high as ten per cent in some parts of Lancashire.[202]

The consequences of bastard-bearing, both practical and legal, could be serious. Situational factors and sexual double standards often made them worse for women than for the men who had impregnated them. As an (apparently) female pamphlet writer, using the pseudonym Esther Sowernam, noted in 1617: "If a man abuse a Maide & get her with child, no matter is made of it, but as a trick of youth; but it is made so hainous an offence in the maide, that she is disparaged and uterly undone by it".[203] Women were, of course, also left (literally) holding the baby. Indicative of how problematic this could be, even for mature females, is that in 1600 William Freborne admitted that he had been offered £15 (£5 cash in hand and the rest as bonds for future repayment) to marry Agnes Burrow, an Essex widow, who was pregnant by another man.[204]

Female servants featured prominently among Tudor infanticide defendants, as they would for centuries to come, for several probable reasons. In part, they were not well-placed to conceal such killings. Single women who were better situated were less likely to be exposed. An extreme (and notorious) case of 1578 is illustrative of the steps that could be taken by or on behalf of rich, well-supported women in this position. That year one Mother Barnes, an experienced midwife, made a statement regarding her involvement in the murder of a newborn male baby in Wiltshire some 12 years earlier. Two men had apparently called at her home one evening and requested that she ride with them to assist a woman who was about to give birth. She rode for several hours until she arrived at a great house, where, behind bolted doors, she ministered

---

202. Richard L. Greaves, *Society and Religion in Elizabethan England* (Minneapolis: University of Minnesota Press, 1981), p. 679.
203. Gradwohl, "Herbal Abortifacients", p. 62.
204. ERO Q/SR 149/37.

to a gentlewoman whose face was partially covered. The midwife, who was promised ample rewards if she assisted in a successful delivery and threatened as to the consequences if she failed, helped the woman give birth but was then told to throw the healthy infant into a great fire in the house. She begged to be allowed to look after him as her own child instead, but, despite her protestations, the baby went into the flames. The midwife then ministered to the recovering woman for a day before being dropped-off some miles from her home.[205]

In part, the high number of maids also reflects the large number of fertile, young, single women who were in service. The employment of domestic staff was a ubiquitous feature of English society in the sixteenth century, more so than in many other European country. Once they reached around eight years-of-age, many were sent to work in the houses of other people, being bound for several years as apprentices, during which time they would perform menial tasks. Even relatively poor households might take on pauper servants. On one estimate, a majority of early modern 15-to-24-year-old females were employed in domestic service.[206]

Perhaps most important of all, maids, often far from home and parental supervision and protection, and young enough to be unworldly, were subject to the sexual attentions, predations, and temptations of employers, as well as their male family members, fellow servants, and neighbours. They were also vulnerable, as those in service normally had the most limited resources of their own. Typically, in 1567 a "poor maid" in a Canterbury court case possessed "nothing but her personal apparel and 16 shillings a year wages and no other goods". Their lives were correspondingly precarious. This could make them particularly susceptible, especially to their employers' needs and desires.[207] For example, more than a decade after the Tudor era, John Rowse, a former London fishmonger, moved to Ewell, in Surrey, with his wife; needing a maidservant, they brought into their house "a wench, whose name was Jane Blundell, who

205. NRO SP. 46/44/fo70; Douglas Walter Rice, *The Life and Achievements of Sir John Popham, 1531–1607: Leading to the Establishment of the First English Colony in New England* (Madison, N.J.: Fairleigh Dickinson University Press, 2005), pp. 85–87.
206. R. C. Richardson, "A Maidservant's Lot", *History Today*, Vol. 60, No. 2, p. 25.
207. *Ibid*, pp. 25–31.

in short time was better acquainted with her master's bed than honesty required". His first wife dying (allegedly of a broken heart due to the dalliance), Rowse remarried, but still kept on his servant paramour.[208]

Inevitably, some of these relationships resulted in pregnancies, as was the case with Bridget Hide, who in the summer of 1591 described to two Essex JPs how her employer, Robert White, had fathered an illegitimate child by her. She had served him for a year-and-a-half before he seduced her while his wife was in London, following several earlier attempts, and having made "fair promises".[209] Similarly, in December 1599, when an Essex JP examined Joan White as to the putative father of her forthcoming child, she claimed that George Nettlefold, her late master, was the genitor. Apparently, he had had the "unlawful" use of her body since the start of Lent that year.[210]

A few men in this situation publicly owned-up to what had occurred and accepted financial responsibility for their offspring. When Mary Wilson pursued Henry Sprooke through the Dean and Chapter Court of York in 1589, he admitted that he employed her as his servant and "with whome he hath had carnallye to do and as he thinketh gett hir with childe". William Eldon behaved even more honourably, despite being known to be an "adulterer & fornicatr [who] hadeth childe with one mawd Bedell sometime his Servante whyche childe he toke for his sonne and did bring it uppe".[211]

This degree of responsibility, however, was unusual. Masters who had impregnated their female servants were often fairly ruthless when they learned of their employee's condition. When Bridget Hide became pregnant and warned her employer, he urged her go to friends before it became publicly apparent. Unfortunately, given her condition, they would not help, forcing her to stay at her master's house. He initially persuaded her to blame her pregnancy on a notorious local "knave" named Thomas Chapman, promising her cash in exchange for doing

---

208. Anon, *The Unnatural Father*, pp. 1–10.
209. ERO Q/SR 118/77.
210. ERO Q/SR 148/138.
211. Melissa Hollander, *Sex in Two Cities: The Formation and Regulation of Sexual Relationships in Edinburgh and York, 1560 to 1625*, University of York PhD thesis, 2006, pp. 145–146, and p. 181.

so (a common expedient in such cases).[212] Their wives could be just as harsh. In 1600 Susan Lay, an Essex servant girl who had been pressured into having sexual relations with both her employer and his son, fell pregnant. The mistress of the house promptly packed her off to London to prevent the family being publicly shamed.[213]

Of course, not all allegations against employers were true. In 1588 Alse (Alice) Mathew became pregnant after having relations with two fellow servants. After receiving advice, she "very lewdly, untruly and ungodly charged" her master, Robert Gosvold of Pentlow, with being the father of her child, hoping thereby to secure a financial settlement from the vulnerable cleric.[214] Nevertheless, such cases were probably relatively unusual.

Whatever their attitudes to their own mistakes, employers would usually feel no obligation at all to maids who had been impregnated by co-workers or other local men, and frequently dismissed them from their positions. Benign masters might try to pressure the putative father into marrying them. This was not the case with Mary Andros, who had been employed in 1599 to teach the children of Thomas Luthkin of Ardleigh, in Essex. Luthkin, noticing that Andros was often sick, eventually guessed that she was pregnant. He forced a confession from her, in which she identified the baby's father. Luthkin then discharged Andros from her position and asked her to leave his house forthwith, although she had little more than eight weeks to go until giving birth. More positively, an elderly woman was found to accompany her to the town where her father lived.[215]

Single mothers were also likely to lose their marriage prospects and certain to face a degree of public disgrace. Even when pregnant they might be shunned, if their condition was known, as parishes would be fearful of being made responsible for any offspring born within their limits. For example, in December 1573 the Sussex JP John Apsley, of Warnham, wrote to the constable of the Singlecross half-hundred, reiterating his earlier order for the return of Alice Legat, an unlicensed beggar and pregnant

---

212. ERO Q/SR 118/77.
213. R. C. Richardson, "A Maidservant's Lot", p. 27.
214. ERO Q/SR 107/44.
215. ERO Q/SR 148/139.

single woman, to Wonersh, in Surrey.[216] In 1577 officials in Middlesex forcibly returned an unmarried woman, who was on the verge of giving birth, to her home parish. She haemorrhaged during the trip and died of internal bleeding.

Their caution is understandable, if brutal. In 1593 Essex JPs received complaints from the constables and inhabitants of Ardleigh. Although it was a poor parish, struggling to cope with many needy residents, they had received a warrant from a magistrate requiring that they care for a six-month-old infant who had been born in their small town, after a woman passing through, who had stayed just two nights, went into labour there. Local people had helped her give birth out of kindness and to prevent the baby perishing. The townspeople urged the JPs that they should not, in fairness, be burdened "with the same child nor woman who well cannot be severed from the sucking brestes".[217] In 1602, in a fiercely contested dispute between parishes, the Surrey Assizes had to decide who was responsible for illegitimate twins born to Anne Wood-herst, a servant in Leatherhead. Her own original place of settlement was Great Bookham, but the assizes decided that Leatherhead had the responsibility for maintaining them.[218]

However, male genitors might be forced to pay child support (through the parish), and could be punished if they would not do so, something that was reinforced by statute in 1576, which Act also required the mother to reveal his name. Magistrates were certainly not remiss about ordering such maintenance. After carrying out an investigation in early 1583, two Essex JPs, Edmond Pyrton and Brian Darcey, ordered John Sylke of St Osyth, the "reputed father of a base child" born to a local spinster named Jane Peacock, to pay eight pence weekly to the town collectors for the relief of the infant, unless and until he could prove that he had been wrongfully accused of fathering it.[219] In the same county in 1587, Richard Cotterell was committed to the house of correction for failing

---

216. SHC LM/1025.
217. ERO Q/SR 126/58.
218. Cockburn, *Calendar of Assize Records. Surrey Indictments: Elizabeth I*, p. 513.
219. ERO Q/SR 84/79.

to pay the towns of Rayleigh and Eastwood for keeping a child of whom he was the reputed father.[220]

Unfortunately, some men fled when they found out that they were about to become parents. Furthermore, in the case of promiscuous women, it was sometimes difficult to establish who was the true genitor. William Lambarde was defeated when Abigail Sherwood's infant was born at Chatham, in Kent; the JP left the decision on the father's identity to the ecclesiastical courts after Sherwood "confessed herself to have been carnally known of many men".[221] Even so, justices might apportion weekly maintenance for an illegitimate child between two men, if both were strong suspects, and were often fairly pragmatic about the issue of paternity. In Surrey Elizabethan JPs eventually decided that to establish the identity of the male genitor of an illegitimate child it would be "sufficient proof that the same father and the mother of the bastard have been found or seen by a credible person to be together in suspicious manner".[222]

Not everyone was willing to accept such determinations. In June 1589 Francis Clerk wrote from Doctors' Commons to Sir William More and two other Surrey JPs, setting out the evidence against one James Jence of Oxted who had been found to be the father of an illegitimate child at the Reigate Sessions by the assembled JPs (it was not a jury matter). Even so, Jence refused to acknowledge the judgment and wanted to have the case re-examined at the next quarter sessions. If this was allowed, Clerk was willing to attend with what he claimed was compelling evidence on the issue that implicated Jence.[223]

Midwives would also be encouraged to extract the names of genitors from single mothers as they gave birth. In 1588, in Essex, Elizabeth Callys testified that she had tried (very forcibly) to get such information from Ursula Cleveland while the latter was in labour. Her efforts were in vain as "ye said Ursula wold make noe aunswere".[224] Even neighbours might get involved, on their own initiative, in resolving the issue of

---

220. ERO Q/SR 101/2.
221. William Lambarde, *Ephemeris*, p. 143.
222. SHC 6729/11/54.
223. SHC LM/COR/3/449.
224. ERO Q/SR 104/59a.

paternity. In 1591 local "wives" searched and questioned a single woman in Walthamstow, demanding to know who had impregnated her, after neighbours noticed her condition.[225]

However, it was not simply the cost of maintaining a baby that occasioned concern. There could also be penal consequences for bastard bearers and genitors, especially during the late Tudor era. The Poor Law of 1576 (18 Elizabeth c. 3) gave officials new powers to punish unwed parents whose offspring were likely to become a charge on the parish (i.e. whose mother and father were poor), something that encouraged magistrates to identify and pursue cases of bastardy, and which may have contributed to an apparent upswing in neonaticide cases in the 1580s (other possible explanations for this development are discussed below). If there was no danger of public maintenance being required, as would be the case with prosperous but unmarried individuals, no offence would be committed, and prospective parents would (in theory) merely be required to do public penance in church during divine service, at the behest of an ecclesiastical court, as they might with ordinary cases of fornication.[226]

Punishments for those prosecuted under the 1576 statute included flogging and (less commonly) imprisonment. For example, in late November 1580, William Lambarde and his father-in-law and fellow Kentish JP dealt with several bastardy cases by having the women and reputed fathers (if they had not disappeared) flogged at the cart's tail. Among them was Joan Pitchford, a widow from Seal, who was scourged in Sevenoaks.[227] Similarly, in 1590, two Essex JPs ordered that Elizabeth Pechie, a widow who had given birth to an illegitimate boy, supposedly fathered by a local miller, should be stripped naked to the waist and "whipped at a cartes tayle tomorrow in the forenone within the said towne of Finchingfield and to have xx [20] stripes to be inflicted uppon her leysurelie by the constables of the said towne". (The miller was ordered to pay ten pence a week to the parish towards the boy's support until he was old enough to be put out to service.)[228] More equitably, after their illegitimate baby

---

225. ERO Q/SR 118/77.
226. Peter C. Hoffer and N. E. H. Hull, *Murdering Mothers: Infanticide in England and New England, 1558–1803* (New York: New York University Press, 1981), p. 13.
227. Conyers, "William Lambarde's 'Ephemeris'", p. 134.
228. ERO Q/SR 111/37.

was born in 1595, Alice Franke and John Smeethe were sentenced by the Essex Quarter Sessions to be tied to the back of a cart in an open place in Steeple Bumpstead, "stripped from the waist upwards and given ten lashes with a whip fit for the purpose".[229] In the North, at the West Riding (Yorkshire) Quarter Sessions in 1598, William Pollard was whipped and also committed to the stocks for bastardy.[230]

Occasionally, the threat of flogging was used to elicit the names of putative fathers from single mothers. In 1594 Margaret Brainwoode, a servant in South Fambridge, in Essex, was told that if, within 20 days, she explained why she was concealing the true father of her child, she would be discharged from any corporal punishment, but, if she failed to do this, she was to be set in the stocks for an hour, while the village constable prepared a horse and cart, to which she would then be tied and whipped.[231]

Dropping

Some unmarried but pregnant women sought to avoid these problems by giving birth secretly and then abandoning their (living) newborn babies in church porches or similar places, especially those in built-up areas, hoping that they would be found and succoured (not always the case). For example, in the summer of 1591 a married man impregnated his maid, Alice Perier, in Great Hallingbury, in Essex. The man's wife quickly noticed her condition and elicited a confession. After failing to bribe Alice to blame another local man for her pregnancy in exchange for £10, her mistress hired a man to accompany Alice to London. In the capital she was thrown out of her lodgings after a few weeks, as she was obviously about to come to term, and gave birth shortly afterwards in the church porch of St Botolph without Aldgate. A group of kindly local women then found her temporary accommodation. A few weeks later, her mistress advised her to carry the baby into the City and leave it near a door, where someone would find and look after him. As a result, Alice

---

229. Marjorie McIntosh, *Controlling Misbehaviour in England, 1370–1600*, p. 114.
230. Lister, *West Riding Sessions Rolls*, p. 76.
231. ERO Q/SR 128/68.

left the baby "upon a poye in the parishe of Queene Hyve".[232] This practice was alluded to, in more dramatic terms, in the play *A Chaste Maid in Cheapside*, written by Thomas Middleton in about 1613: two "promoters", who are stopping passers-by to search their baskets for unlicensed meat during Lent (intending to seize and eat it themselves), are tricked by a "country wench" into accepting a basket containing her unwanted illegitimate child, thinking it a large joint of mutton.[233]

However, other women sought to avoid censure and the consequences attendant on an illegitimate birth by hiding their pregnancy as best they could, giving birth in secret, then killing their babies and quietly disposing of their bodies. The sixteenth century was to witness a major change in the legal treatment of, and social attitudes towards, such killings.

Legal Attitudes Towards Neonaticide

In the early 1500s England was still dominated by what might loosely be termed a medieval approach towards neonaticide. This had eschewed the tolerance for such a practice found in many ancient societies, and slowly abandoned in the Roman Empire during the fourth century under the growing influence of Christianity, but avoided the wave of legal severity that would peak in England in the first half of the seventeenth century.

When the Roman Empire collapsed, jurisdiction over infanticide was largely left to the Church and its courts in many parts of Europe, including England. Although infanticide appears to have occurred on a fairly regular basis in the medieval period (being mentioned in some contemporary literature) it rarely troubled secular forums. For example, of 2,933 homicide cases that came before gaol delivery justices in three counties (Norfolk, Northamptonshire, and Yorkshire) from 1300 to 1348, only one involved infanticide, that of Alice Grut and Alice Grym who were accused of drowning a three-day-old (i.e. not newborn) infant.[234] Another examination of more than 4,000 homicides from medieval

---

232. ERO Q/SR 126/34–34A.
233. Act II, Scene 2.
234. Hanawalt, "Violent Death", p. 308; Hoffer and Hull, *Murdering Mothers*, p. 211.

English court records identified just three cases.[235] Some other estimates suggest a slightly higher figure.

The ecclesiastical punishment of infanticide was usually fairly lenient, as church courts could not shed blood. It was often treated like other grave moral sins. In the seventh century, the Archbishop of Canterbury had prescribed a 15-year penance for the offence but (tellingly) stipulated that it be reduced to seven years for a poor woman. This was still significantly more draconian than the Irish Penitential of Finnian, written around 591, which prescribed penance for half-a-year with an allowance of bread and water.[236] At the end of the medieval period, many church courts merely imposed penance on the mother, often carried out by penitential processions, as occurred when Joan Rose was convicted of killing her newborn son in 1470. She was ordered to process in a white robe around a variety of major towns in her native Kent, carrying a half-pound wax candle and the knife with which she had killed the baby.[237]

However, ecclesiastical punishments for infanticide varied greatly during the fifteenth and early sixteenth centuries, as local clerics were granted considerable latitude as to the penalty that should be imposed. In the early 1500s, some neonaticide cases were dealt with by penitential whippings imposed by the local Commissary Court.[238] These were regularly used in many parts of England until the Reformation and lingered on afterwards for spiritual crimes (not for infanticide), until quite late in the sixteenth century. They eventually disappeared under pressure from the common lawyers, who argued that church court penalties should not touch limb or property.[239]

In some respects, the church courts' treatment of early Tudor infanticide was not that much worse than that imposed on the genitors of an illicit pregnancy. For example, after William Cardell made Agnes Walsh

---

235. Hanawalt, *The Ties that Bound: Peasant Families in Medieval England* (Oxford: Oxford University Press, 1986), p. 102.
236. Kenny, "Ireland, Back to the Future", pp. 1–4.
237. C. Damme, "Infanticide: The Worth of an Infant under Law", *Medical History*, Vol. 22, No. 1, p. 5.
238. R. H. Helmholz, *Canon Law and the Law of England* (London: The Hambledon Press, 1987, pp. 157–168.
239. Martin Ingram, "Shame and Pain: Themes and Variations in Tudor Punishments", in Griffiths and Devereaux, *Penal Practice and Culture*, p. 39.

pregnant, he was sentenced to three floggings and ordered to process around his parish church three times on successive Sundays, in bare feet, while carrying a candle.[240] Not only was the church-appointed punishment relatively lenient, it was not administered often. The number of infanticide cases heard in the ecclesiastical courts was always fairly modest. For much of the fifteenth century only a handful were determined each year in the very large Canterbury diocese. Frequently, it was less than this. The Canterbury Consistory Court saw just 13 citations for infanticide between 1469 and 1473, involving five couples, five women, and three men (a quite different gender profile from that of the secular crime when it was prosecuted in Elizabethan England a century later).[241] The four cases that were recorded in the Commissary Court of the Bishop of London in 1487 constituted the largest number of infanticides to come before a church court in a single year.[242]

Nevertheless, although medieval society clearly had a slightly ambivalent attitude towards the crime, English pastoral manuals showed much greater concern about preventing infanticide (and abortion), whether deliberate or accidental, than their Mediterranean counterparts.[243] More important, several contemporary legal observers, such as the cleric and jurist Henry de Bracton (c.1210–1268), were adamant that, whatever happened in practice, the secular offence of murder did extend to the killing of newborn infants *in rerum natura*.[244] It would be a serious exaggeration to suggest that in medieval England infanticide was merely regarded as a sin rather than a crime or that royal officials treated it with indifference. Medieval coroners and sheriffs did not ignore the discovery of infants' corpses found drowned or abandoned in ditches and rivers and brought to their attention, even if this only rarely happened. At a minimum, there was usually a fairly thorough physical investigation of the body, albeit inquest jurors in these situations frequently failed to ascertain the identity of the perpetrators or the precise cause of death.[245] The small

240. Thomson, *The Early Tudor Church*, p. 253.
241. Jones, *Gender and Petty Crime*, p. 89.
242. Helmholz, "Infanticide in the Province of Canterbury", p. 384.
243. Jones, *Gender and Petty Crime*, p. 88.
244. Damme, "Infanticide", p. 2.
245. Sara M. Butler, "A Case of Indifference? Child Murder in Later Medieval England", *Journal of Women's History*, Vol. 19, No. 4, p. 63.

number of infanticide cases prosecuted before secular forums, and the somewhat larger number investigated, were to provide important precedents after the middle of the sixteenth century, when attitudes towards the crime changed.

Medieval prosecution patterns — the most important being a preference for using the church courts — and attitudes towards neonaticide survived until well into the Tudor period. In 1517 a clergyman impregnated Alice Ridyng, a single woman from Eton in the Diocese of Lincoln. His clerical status precluded marriage in this pre-Reformation era. She concealed her pregnancy, even from her parents. However, as often occurred in such cases, several local women suspected her condition long before she gave birth, although she always denied it, explaining her changing shape by saying (as was also common) that "something else was wrong with her belly". Typical of many women in this situation, Ridyng chose to give birth alone, without the assistance of a midwife; in this case, it was in her father's home. Within four hours of the birth, she placed her hand over her baby's mouth and suffocated him. She then buried his corpse in a dung heap in her father's orchard. Her secret was exposed two days later, when she was seized by the suspicious women and "honest wives" of Eton and forcibly examined. Her gelatinous belly and swollen, lactating breasts (allegedly) betrayed her. The women brought her before the Bishop of Lincoln's officials, before whom she confessed her sin, swearing on oath that she had "never been known carnally" by anyone other than the father of her child. She then awaited her penance.[246] It seems that she was not prosecuted in a secular forum.

No inquest involving newborn infanticide can be found among those surviving for Nottinghamshire between 1485 and 1558, while only one has been found from more than 240 coroners' cases that have survived for Sussex for the same period (although one other case is referred to obliquely). In December 1550 a county coroner sat on the body of a baby girl in West Grinstead. The coroner's jury found that Joan Bacon, a spinster, had given birth in her father's house and immediately murdered her offspring before hiding its body in the same building and

---

246. *Ibid*, pp. 59–82.

fleeing. Nevertheless, it did enter the secular justice system. (Joan was "waived", the female equivalent of being outlawed, at the Lewes Assizes 18 months later).[247]

However, surviving inquests do not include a case from May 1532, in which Clemence Smyth, a spinster from Broadwater in Sussex, sought sanctuary in the local church after she crushed her newborn girl to death with her feet in a remote spot in the parish. Under an Act of 1531 (see *Chapter 13*), she abjured (rare for a female) and was assigned the permanent sanctuary at Beaulieu, being handed over to the constable of Brightford to be escorted there.[248] Smyth's case was not unique. More than 20 years earlier, in March 1511, Elizabeth Walsowen took sanctuary in a church near Gloucester. She, too, abjured after confessing to the coroner that a few days earlier she had killed her newborn male baby by slitting his throat with a knife immediately after birth.[249] Neither woman would have taken such drastic action if they did not think that there was a real risk of going before the secular courts on a murder indictment. Nevertheless, in practice, prosecution before such forums was very rare up to the late 1550s.

The Onset of Secular Prosecution

Early in the Elizabethan period, legal attitudes changed, and fairly quickly.[250] This may have been an aspect of a Europe-wide phenomenon, one that seems to have been linked to religion and, more particularly, the effects of the Reformation and Counter-Reformation, as well as to the emergence of more "governed" states.[251] Its specific timing may well be explained by a desire to make it clear that the secular courts in newly Protestant post-Marian England took precedence over ecclesiastical forums. Interestingly, to a considerable extent, and probably for similar reasons, the advent of the active secular prosecution of infanticide in England

---

247. Hunnisett, *Sussex Coroners' Inquests*, p. 43.
248. Hunnisett, "Sussex Abjurations", pp. 39–51.
249. McSheffrey, "Sanctuary Seekers".
250. Cockburn, "Trial by the Book? Fact and Theory in the Criminal Process 1558–1625", in J. H. Baker (ed.), *Legal Records and the Historian* (London Royal Historical Society, 1978), pp. 65–68.
251. Sharpe, *A Fiery & Furious People*, p. 199.

coincides with that of witchcraft, which was re-criminalised by statute in 1563. The Canterbury church courts saw numerous witchcraft cases in the 1550s, but fewer after the early 1560s, probably because of the advent of secular prosecutions under the 1563 act.[252] Nevertheless, it has also been argued that infanticide became a growing problem during this period, i.e. that more babies were being killed than had previously been the case, which may also have contributed to the development (see below).

In some respects (and as with sodomy and witchcraft) England was a little slower than some other countries in following wider European trends for dealing with infanticide. For example, in Germany a dearth of medieval trials for the crime gave way to active secular prosecutions some years, if not decades, before this occurred in England. The *Constitutio Criminalis Carolina*, the law code of the Holy Roman Empire, had declared both infanticide and abortion to be capital crimes in 1532; it prescribed aggravated forms of capital punishment, such as burial alive and impalement or drowning preceded by "tearing with burning pincers" for the former.[253] Nearer in time to the change in England, in March 1556, Henry II of France issued a decree complaining about infanticide as a *"crime très énorme et exécrable, fréquent en notre Royaume"*. This ordinance stipulated that the offence, which denied the baby the chance of baptism, carried a mandatory death sentence. (More constructively, the state also encouraged legal adoption for unwanted children.) Of 22 women convicted of the offence in sixteenth century Rouen during the years after 1556, all but two were executed.[254]

The number of infanticide cases from Middlesex and London heard by judges at the Old Bailey, on the Home Circuit (Kent, Essex, etc.), and presumably on other circuits (where evidence is largely absent) saw a significant increase after the accession of Queen Elizabeth. It is possible that the lack of assize records before 1559 masks a change that started slightly earlier. Nevertheless, no prosecutions for infanticide have been preserved among those for Middlesex tried at the Old Bailey during the 1550s, and the change does not seem to start until after the arrival of the

---

252. Jones, *Gender and Petty Crime,* p. 198.
253. Lewis, *Infanticide and Abortion,* p. 1.
254. Dmitry Shlapentokh, *The Proto-Totalitarian State: Punishment and Control in Absolutist Regimes* (Livingston, N.J.: Transaction, 2007), p. 72.

new queen. As the crime was always, technically, a secular felony (see above), prosecuting infanticide did not require new legislation (unlike witchcraft), merely a change in practice by the authorities.

The first preserved case from Middlesex tried at the Old Bailey appears to have occurred in 1563, although some records are missing for earlier years. Several others quickly followed or were at least considered for prosecution. Thus in August that year a coroner's inquest at Clerkenwell decided that Joan Damporte, a spinster, had murdered her newborn baby boy in a widow's house (probably where she was lodging or employed as a maid).[255] In the same year, a French maid dwelling in White Friars off Fleet Street gave birth to an illegitimate baby girl and immediately "brake the neke of the child". She then carried the baby's body to Holborn Fields, where she buried it under a turf. However, a man and woman noticed her behaving suspiciously and followed her. They then forced her to recover the corpse and took the maid before an alderman's assistant, who committed her to the compter (sheriff's prison).[256]

On the Home Circuit, timings for the onset of infanticide prosecutions varied considerably between counties. The earliest that has been preserved in Kent (and on the circuit) concerned Margary Potkyn, a spinster from Bapchild, who threw her newborn baby out of a window immediately after delivery and was convicted at the Greenwich Assizes a few weeks later, in February 1559. (Ironically, she successfully pleaded pregnancy to "defer" execution.) She was followed by Agnes Barnes, an unmarried maid from Erith, who gave birth to a baby in her master's house in August 1559, and immediately killed it by throwing it into a swine yard to be eaten by the pigs. She was convicted in 1560, deferred her execution by proving to be pregnant, but was ordered for death in July 1561; it was a particularly gruesome case, discouraging mercy.[257] Margaret Yuge was tried at the same forum in July 1560; she had killed her illegitimate baby by throwing it to the ground after giving birth in a field of oats. She was convicted, but remanded because pregnant. (It is not known if she was ever ordered for execution.)[258] In Sussex, ignoring the

---

255. Jeaffreson, *Middlesex County Records: Vol. 1*, pp. 46–50.
256. Hamil, "The King's Approvers", pp. 238–258.
257. Cockburn, *Calendar of Assize Records. Kent Indictments: Elizabeth I*, p. 2 and p. 11.
258. *Ibid*, p. 1 and p. 4.

case from 1550, it seems that the first (preserved) case from the county assizes occurred in July 1559. Alice Wood from Little Horsted drowned her baby in a stream in March that year. Even so, she was bailed after a relative entered into a recognisance for her appearance at trial, where she was convicted. She unsuccessfully pleaded pregnancy, but it is not obvious that she was executed.[259] In July 1562, at the Sussex Assizes, Alice Bankes, a spinster from Berwick, was convicted of killing her baby by throwing it out of a window. Even so, she was remanded, rather than being sentenced to death, by the presiding judge, Gilbert Gerard (who was also the Attorney General), suggesting that the possibility of a pardon was being considered.[260]

In Kent and Sussex, with their early Elizabethan prosecutions, the number of infanticide convicts successfully pleading their bellies and the willingness to grant bail in Wood's case, might be indicative of a criminal justice system adjusting to a novel situation from a previous state of relative inaction. Most other counties on the Home Circuit were a little slower to prosecute neonaticide. The first two preserved cases from Essex were tried at the assizes held at Brentwood in early April 1563, when two women were separately convicted for the crime. No case has been preserved for Hertfordshire before 1577 (the county is missing almost all assizes records prior to 1573). Although the first case in Surrey occurred in 1560, it was unusual, as it involved a male defendant who killed his mistress' day-old baby. It was not until July 1568 that a more typical infanticide, the killing by a spinster of her own newborn baby in a Cobham Inn (where she may have been employed), came before the assizes (or at least has been preserved).[261]

More generally, infanticide appears to have entered the wider Elizabethan consciousness to a greater extent than had previously been the case. For example, a periodic if scurrilous rumour was that not only was the queen herself not a virgin but that, with the aid of midwives, she had given birth and then killed her offspring. Gruesome stories were told of an illegitimate daughter whose body had been destroyed "in a very

259. Cockburn, *Calendar of Assize records. Sussex Indictments: Elizabeth I*, p. 4.
260. Hunnisett, *Sussex Coroners' Inquests*, p. 43; Cockburn, *Calendar of Assize Records. Sussex Indictments: Elizabeth I*, p. 25.
261. Cockburn, *Calendar of Assize Records. Surrey Indictments: Elizabeth I*, p. 69.

great fire of coals".[262] Chapbooks suggested that infanticide had become a crime that God would reveal, as was the case with other murders. Thus, in the early 1600s a newly delivered baby was thrown into a privy in London. By chance a youth subsequently threw a dog into the same place. It barked piteously for three days until troubled local people decided to retrieve the animal, discovering the baby's corpse when they did so. It was claimed that this occurred because God would "reward shame where it is deserved, and such unnaturall deedes, let them be acted in deserts, in the cavernes of the earth, where never light of day nor Sun shines, yet will they be discovered and brought to the worlds eye".[263]

Evidential Difficulties

Prosecuting infanticide cases was difficult unless the suspected woman was willing to plead guilty. The latter situation was fairly rare, although Joan Gamble, a servant from Edmonton, appears to have done so in 1594. She secretly gave birth to a male infant in her master's house and then stove in the left part of his head; this was an obviously violent method of killing, providing little scope for a defence, and perhaps explaining her plea.[264] In June 1593 a coroner's inquest held at Hoxton, in Middlesex, concluded that Jane Little, a local spinster, had given birth to a baby daughter, and then killed her by burying her in a nearby field. She, too, pleaded guilty at trial.[265]

Stillbirths, or natural deaths immediately after delivery, were extremely common in a society with limited medical facilities, and the authorities accepted this. Very unusually (the clergy were extremely reluctant to delegate such a function), midwives were even taught to baptise babies during difficult deliveries. Fairly typically, at an inquest held in January 1561 at Billericay, in Essex, the coroner's jury viewed the body of an unbaptised child, just half-an-hour old when it died, but concluded that Rose Parker, a pregnant married woman, had given birth prematurely,

262. David Cressy, "Demotic Voices and Popular Complaint in Elizabethan and Early Stuart England", *Journal of Early Modern Studies*, Vol. 2, p. 55 and p. 58.
263. Anon, *Deeds Against Nature*, pp. 1–12.
264. Jeaffreson, *Middlesex County Records: Vol. 1*, pp. 219–225.
265. *Ibid*, pp. 211–219.

so that the child died naturally. A verdict of "Visitation of God" was duly returned.[266]

As a result, stillbirth provided a plausible explanation for women who were found with dead newborn babies, or who claimed that they had merely disposed of the corpse of an infant improperly. In the words of the preamble to the 1624 Act that altered the law on infanticide, it was common practice that if a baby was found dead, the "woman do alledge, that the said child was born dead". This defence strategy was often successful. The legal onus on the Crown to prove such cases as murder could be difficult to satisfy.

Even coroners' juries might accept such an analysis, although tendered by single women, so that a matter did not go for trial, let alone produce a conviction. For example, in 1568 an inquest held in Pattiswick, in Essex, concluded that Margaret Hilles, the pregnant servant to a local gentleman, went into labour while in his house, and gave birth to an infant that was born dead.[267] Twenty years later, at Broxted in the same county, another coroner's jury that sat on the body of a newborn male infant reached the same conclusion, and decided that Elizabeth Kemhedd, an unmarried local servant, had secretly given birth to a baby who was already dead.[268] Most generously of all, and also in Essex, an inquest held at Frinton in May 1583 decided that a servant maid named Petronella Richard had given birth to a stillborn baby, then defaced the baby's body by placing it with her master's pigs.[269]

If a matter did go to trial, petty juries regularly returned favourable verdicts based on this analysis. Thus Agnes Death, a spinster from St Osyth in Essex, was acquitted of killing her baby as "yt was not directly proved the child was in lyff".[270] Of course, such verdicts required that there be no obvious signs of violence on the baby's body. As a result, women who were aware of this, and who were capable of acting rationally, would often have recourse to smothering.

---

266. ERO T/A 423/1/5.
267. ERO T/A 413/13/30.
268. ERO T/A 413/49/46.
269. Cockburn, *Calendar of Assize Records. Essex Indictments: Elizabeth I*, p. 242.
270. *Ibid*, p. 197.

Incidence of Prosecutions

Although the Elizabethan period saw a large increase in indictments and convictions for neonaticide, their numbers were still relatively modest compared to the levels that would be seen after the 1624 legislation came into force. This statute presumed murder when a dead infant was born to an unmarried mother where the pregnancy and birth had been concealed, unless the defendant could prove the contrary.

Illustrative of the change effected by the Jacobean statute, in the 64 years between 1558 and 1624, there were 61 prosecuted cases of infanticide in Kent and Sussex combined. However, there was a 213 per cent increase in infanticide cases in the two counties during the 64 years following the implementation of the 1624 Act to 1688 (by which time the rate was in decline again).[271]

Hoffer suggests that between 1558 and 1593 there were just 23 indictments for infanticide in the whole of Essex, a county of about 80,000 people. Even if the Essex assizes and quarter sessions are taken together (a few cases seem to have gone to the latter forum), less than 30 infanticides can be identified for the entire sixteenth century after 1558.[272] The present author's analysis suggests that 28 cases of infanticide, of all types, went to (or have been preserved from) the Elizabethan assizes in Essex, of which at least one was immediately discharged without trial, while three more may not have survived the grand jury procedure. Only 24 clearly went to a hearing. Of these, 13 cases produced convictions and eleven resulted in acquittals.[273] In Sussex there were just 14 infanticide indictments at assizes between 1558 and 1593. In populous London and Middlesex, only seven instances that have been preserved were prosecuted during the same period (although others may have been lost).

Even within the Elizabethan period, indictments for infanticide seem to have increased significantly after the middle of the 1570s when compared to the first decade or so in which it was an actively prosecuted crime. Thus the rate of indictments in the years from 1576 to 1593 was

---

271. Laura Spence, *Women Who Murder In Early Modern England, 1558–1700*, University of Warwick MA dissertation, 2010, p. 26.
272. Damme, "Infanticide", p. 11.
273. See generally, Cockburn, *Calendar of Assize Records. Essex Indictments: Elizabeth I*.

225 per cent higher than in the years between 1558 and 1575, although the increase would be less dramatic if the first five years of the Elizabethan period were ignored (when it was rarely prosecuted).[274] Similarly, the distribution of 15 infanticides from the 582 inquests held by Sussex coroners during the reign of Elizabeth I (that are known to survive) can be considered. Only six, the first dating from 1565, have been preserved from the initial 30 years of the reign of Queen Elizabeth. By contrast nine have been preserved from the last 15 years of her life.[275]

Even so, infanticides quickly became a significant component, perhaps a fifth, of all homicide prosecutions. In the years from 1559 to 1603, Essex indicted 29 people for infanticide and 129 for other types of homicide, a broadly similar proportion being found in Sussex (27 and 127 respectively) and Hertfordshire (seven and 24 cases).[276]

Social and Economic Factors

It has been argued that the increase in the rate of prosecuted neonaticides during the late sixteenth century was not purely the result of a growth in prosecutorial zeal and a change in official attitudes; it is said that it also reflected a real change in incidence, this being linked to a decline in the ability of young people to establish independent households that were able to support children. According to this analysis, the birth rate in England started to drop during the 1570s. This was due to a serious decline in real wages linked to the population growing faster than its commerce and agriculture (see *Chapter 2*), albeit with a lag of 20 years, as each generation adjusted its fertility in light of its parents' economic experience and the resources it could expect to inherit. On one analysis, the proportion of women who never married increased from five per cent in the mid-sixteenth century to as much as 20 per cent in the first half of the seventeenth century, before stabilising at more than ten per cent. A substantial number of women could not have families or households of their own. In turn this placed acute pressure on young, poor, single

---

274. Hoffer and Hull, *Murdering Mothers*, p. 8.
275. See generally, Hunnisett, *Sussex Coroners' Inquests*.
276. Cockburn, "The Nature and Incidence of Crime in England 1559–1625", in J.S. Cockburn (ed.), *Crime in England 1550–1800* (London: Methuen, 1977) p. 53.

women (i.e. most neonaticide suspects) to abstain from sexual activity. The increased numbers of those in this category who, for whatever reason, became pregnant, and who could not regularise their situation by marriage, may have meant that more were likely to succumb to the temptation to commit infanticide.[277]

Certainly, the notion that infanticide (rather than prosecution) rates were not constant during the sixteenth century is supported by evidence from the German city of Nuremberg, which kept detailed records of such cases for most of the era. Until 1524 the infanticide rate did not exceed one per 100,000 a year. It fluctuated between one and two during the next half century, but then rose to around four in the 40 years after 1574.[278] More generally, careful statistical work by the historian Randolph Roth suggests that there were major fluctuations in infanticide rates in ensuing centuries, not only in the late 1500s.[279]

However, interpreting trends in late Tudor infanticide by counting assizes prosecutions is fraught with danger. An increase in indictment rates for the crime was, at least in part, undoubtedly due to a change in attitudes on the part of coroners, JPs, and grand jurors, who gradually became more willing to accept that a homicide had been committed in suspicious cases of newborn death and to sanction prosecutions for such crimes.[280] As it was an effectively newly criminalised offence, it might be expected to take some time before all officials adopted the changed approach to the crime, especially if they were older men, rooted in earlier mores, or were geographically remote from the centre of government. Although an apparent, if limited, surge in neonaticide indictments in the 1580s could have resulted from environmental factors, it might also have come about from such men dying off and being replaced, or at least adopting new values. Furthermore, Mark Lockwood's work could suggest that at least some of the apparent increase in infanticide cases might simply reflect increased reporting of suspicious deaths generally (see *Chapter 17*).

---

277. Roth, "Homicide In Early Modern England", pp. 33–67.
278. Spierenburg, *A History of Murder*, p. 147.
279. I am very grateful to Professor Roth for information on this point.
280. Hoffer and Hull, *Murdering Mothers*. p. 8.

Very possibly, both increased reporting *and* a real increase in the incidence of such crimes took place during the late sixteenth century, albeit that the latter's growth was more modest than the official figures might indicate.

Characteristics of Tudor Infanticide

Perhaps unsurprisingly, many of the characteristics that would be associated with prosecuted infanticides in England during the seventeenth and eighteenth centuries can be identified in their counterparts from the late 1500s. Indeed, it has been argued that there was little change in the socio-demographic profile of defendants from the sixteenth to the nineteenth centuries.[281] They are also similar to those found in many other early modern Western European countries, such as Denmark, Scotland, The Netherlands, and the German states.[282]

The same observation applies to the immediate backgrounds to many of these crimes. Some of their characteristics have already been noted: in Tudor England, unlike some Far Eastern and South Asian countries, gender does not seem to have been a significant factor in the decision to kill, as baby boys were victims as often as girls; many indicted cases involved relatively young servant maids, although, of course, living-in domestic staff were necessarily deprived of privacy, making it inherently more likely that the crime would come to notice, and so prosecution; most killings occurred almost immediately after birth and rarely involved men; infanticide was normally perpetrated by spinsters or (much less commonly) widows, rather than married women, who were acting alone or (much less frequently) with a female assistant (often their "lewd mother" to quote the 1624 statute); most killings were effected by strangling, smothering, or drowning the baby; a majority of the women involved were poor.

Thus, a sample of 336 infant victims taken from the decades after the de facto criminalisation of infanticide in about 1560, and prior to the passage of the 1624 Act, suggests that: 94 per cent (316) had been killed

---

281. Eisner, "Interpersonal Violence", p. 573.
282. Manon van der Heijden, *Women and Crime in Early Modern Holland* (Leiden: Brill, 2016), p. 53 and p. 56; Schnucker, "Elizabethan Birth Control", pp. 655–667; Ulinka Rublack, *The Crimes of Women in Early Modern Germany* (Oxford: Oxford University Press, 1999), pp. 163–164.

by women, 89 per cent (300) of them by their mothers. Overwhelmingly, these women were identified in indictments as spinsters or widows.[283] In Hertfordshire females committed ten of eleven prosecuted cases of infanticide in the 27 years between 1591 and 1618.[284] Similarly, on one assessment, unmarried women committed 27 of 30 prosecuted cases of neonaticide in Elizabethan Essex.[285] However, and as already noted, the gender division of victims was very different. Of the 139 cases of neonaticide prosecuted on the Home Circuit between 1560 and 1624, in which the sex of the baby is known, 77 involved boys and 62 girls.[286]

Individual cases provide more specific examples of the typical features of such killings. For example, in April 1563, Margaret Lynett, a spinster from Loughton, in Essex, was convicted of drowning her newly born baby boy in a pond, after giving birth alone in a field near the same village the previous December. Catherine Collins, an unmarried woman from Birchanger, was more fortunate, and acquitted of infanticide when tried at the Essex Assizes in July 1564. It was alleged that the previous February she had suffocated her day-old female baby with pillows and kerchiefs.[287] In March 1568 Elizabeth Colpitt put her newborn baby in a pit near the Surrey inn where she gave birth (and probably worked) and smothered him/her with sawdust.[288] In 1580 Joan Cockburn was convicted of infanticide at the Surrey Assizes for killing her newborn boy in a gentleman's house in Bletchingley by wrapping him in an apron and then squeezing and suffocating him.[289] In 1595 Bennet Davis, a spinster of Maresfield in Sussex, killed her newly born baby girl by stopping her breathing with both hands so that the infant suffocated. Although the coroner's inquest found that she had murdered the baby, Davis was acquitted at assizes, the child being said to have been stillborn.[290] More

283. Kesselring, "Bodies of Evidence", p. 250.
284. P. Lawson, "Patriarchy, Crime and the Courts: The Criminality of Women in Late Tudor and Early Stuart England", in Greg T. Smith, Allyson N. May, and Simon Devereaux (eds.), *Criminal Justice in the Old World and the New* (Toronto: University of Toronto, 1998), pp. 21–27.
285. P. E.H. Hair, "Homicide, Infanticide, and Child Assault in Late Tudor Middlesex", *Local Population Studies*, 1972, Issue 9, p. 44.
286. Sharpe, *A Fiery & Furious People*, p. 197.
287. Cockburn, *Calendar of Assize Records. Essex Indictments: Elizabeth I*, p. 26 and pp. 31–32.
288. Cockburn, *Calendar of Assize Records. Surrey indictments: Elizabeth I*, p. 69.
289. *Ibid*, p. 216.
290. Hunnisett, *Sussex Coroners' Inquests*, p. 119.

unusually, Agnes Reeve was a widow when indicted for infanticide at the Hertford Assizes in March 1596. It was alleged that she had given birth in Royston the previous October and then immediately "squashed" and killed her baby. She, too, was acquitted after the jury decided that the infant was stillborn.[291]

Strangling was more risky than smothering, as it left a tell tale mark on the baby's neck, especially if done with some form of cord. At the Essex Assizes in July 1580, Sibyl Randolfe was convicted of throttling her baby with a woollen thread, after giving birth in a gentleman's house (where she was probably a servant).[292] In July 1584 the unmarried Rose Enknepp was convicted of strangling her newborn baby with a silk lace, immediately after giving birth in her master's garden at Chiddingfold, in Surrey.[293]

That any assistance to infanticidal mothers was usually female is unsurprising. Tudor childbirth was largely a woman's business (male midwives and routine medical attendance lay in the future). In an extreme example from the Elizabethan period, four women—Alice Shepherd, her mother, grandmother, and a midwife—broke the neck of Alice's newborn boy and buried him in a Salisbury churchyard. They were subsequently convicted and sentenced to death at the Wiltshire Assizes.[294]

However, there were periodic exceptions to most of the above generalisations. As already indicated, not all cases involved unmarried women. For example, in April 1563 Anne Gowsworthe was convicted of murder at the Essex Assizes held in Brentwood for strangling her newborn baby daughter immediately after her delivery some two months earlier. The crime took place in Anne's husband's house. He was described as a "yeoman", so she was not from the poorest social background.[295]

Some women had recourse to obviously violent methods to kill their babies, although they were much more likely to be convicted if prosecuted (as would be the case for centuries), as it was almost impossible to claim that such a baby was stillborn. Thus, at the Surrey Assizes in July

---

291. Cockburn, *Calendar of Assize Records. Hertfordshire Indictments: Elizabeth I*, p. 116.
292. Cockburn, *Calendar of Assize Records. Essex Indictments: Elizabeth I*, p. 205.
293. Cockburn, *Calendar of Assize Records. Surrey Indictments: Elizabeth I*, p. 261.
294. Anon, *Sundrye strange and inhumaine murthers,* (London: 1591), p. 214.
295. Cockburn, *Calendar of Assize Records. Essex Indictments: Elizabeth I*, p. 26.

1587, Isabel Tenney, a single woman, was convicted of infanticide. She had given birth to a female baby in the garden of her master's house in Leatherhead and promptly cut the infant's throat with a knife.[296] Similarly, in Sussex, in July 1600, Joan Ambrey gave birth to a baby girl and immediately killed the infant by violently twisting her neck with both her hands until it broke. The inquest jury concluded she had murdered the baby, and she was tried and convicted at the East Grinstead Assizes the following March.[297] Five of the 13 convictions for infanticide after trials in Elizabethan Essex involved similarly direct methods of baby killing, whether stabbing or dashing the infant to the (frozen) ground or against a bedstead, although they made up a much smaller proportion of prosecuted cases.

Furthermore, infanticide was not a purely female crime. Some men became involved in it, and a few were even prosecuted, after either committing the crime or having abetted their lovers to do so. Doubtless, many other similar cases escaped detection. For example, in 1553, long before the change in attitude towards prosecution, Richard Barnerde impregnated his own daughter, who subsequently gave birth to a baby girl in her father's house in Sussex, without the assistance of other women. Shortly afterwards, he murdered the baby with a mallet. (The next day, stricken by remorse, Barnerde drowned himself in a well.)[298] In 156c James Ellys, the rector of Chiddingfold, was tried and acquitted at the Surrey Assizes of murdering the day-old baby of his mistress, Rose Bruton, in his rectory.[299] More unusually, in 1591, an inquest found that Thomas Cranley of Homestreet, in Sussex, had murdered what appears to have been his own, legitimate, newborn baby boy by crushing the child's head with his hands. His wife was bound over to give evidence against him at the county assizes the following year. However, he was acquitted, the jury using the fiction that John at Death had killed the baby. One can only speculate at the motivation behind this benign but unusual (for infanticide) decision. Had the baby been deformed or handicapped?[300] In 1601

296. Cockburn, *Calendar of Assize Records. Surrey Indictments: Elizabeth I*, p. 305.
297. Hunnisett, *Sussex Coroners' Inquests*, p. 135.
298. *Ibid*, p. 47.
299. Cockburn, *Calendar of Assize Records. Surrey Indictments: Elizabeth I*, p. 10.
300. Hunnisett, *Sussex Coroners' Inquests*, p. 104.

William Bright allegedly killed a newborn baby that he had fathered and then buried its corpse in an Essex dunghill.[301]

Quite exceptionally, the trial of Dorcas Tyndall involved a combination of unusual features that are more characteristic of modern infanticide cases than those of the Tudor era. She was a married (not single) woman, convicted of infanticide having killed her eight-week-old (not newborn) and baptised baby, Robert, by cutting his throat rather ineffectually (he survived until the following day). That she was remanded after sentence, rather than being executed immediately, suggests that this case might well have involved some form of mental disturbance or postpartum depression, something that could justify clemency and a pardon.[302]

The Hattersley Case

Some aspects of late Tudor infanticide are illustrated in more detail by an (admittedly very) unusual case from Sussex, which covered the decade from about 1596, even if some details may be slightly exaggerated or apocryphal, and the scale of the crimes quite exceptional. A married man, Adam Adamson, regularly impregnated his long-term servant Jane Hattersley, a spinster, over a period of years, any offspring being speedily murdered and then buried in an orchard. Hattersley was finally convicted of the crime in 1609 and executed, although (significantly) Adamson escaped justice.[303]

During her frequent pregnancies, Hattersley became adept at hiding her swelling belly before giving birth, as many other maids did in this situation. She wore voluminous clothes "with loose lacing, tucking, and other odde tricks that she used, that to the very instant minute of her deliverie, none could perceive she was with childe". However, on at least one occasion she was temporarily sent away to another employer, who would not be familiar with her normal (slimmer) physical appearance, to have her baby. Unfortunately, the lady of the house caught her red-handed shortly after she had smothered her newborn infant and ran to

301. ERO Q/SR 156/30.
302. Cockburn, *Calendar of Assize Records. Essex Indictments: Elizabeth I*, p. 413.
303. Thomas Brewer, *The Bloudy Mother, Or, The Most Inhumane Murthers, Committed by Iane Hattersley Upon Divers Infants, the Issue of Her Owne Bodie* (London, 1610), pp. 1–22.

fetch the constable and other neighbours. With considerable presence of mind, before they returned, Hattersley so worked on the corpse "to clense & trim it, that there was no signe of such a hand as is minister to a hell-hardned hart, to be found vppon it: so that the babe, (ignorantly) taken to be ignorantly ouer laid (for so *Jane* bouldly & deeply swore it was) was without any great adoe, there buried". There was not sufficient evidence to preclude an accidental death in this case and it seems that the local coroner was not even involved. Hattersley was then dismissed from her position.[304]

On another occasion, when Hattersley was suspected to be with child, suspicious local women forcibly examined her, as commonly occurred in such situations, using a variety of tests to search for tell-tale indications of pregnancy, such as drawing the breasts to expose lactation. However, these signs were often ambiguous, and many pregnant women employed a variety of legitimate reasons to explain their presence.[305] The women concluded that Hattersley was with child, but she vehemently denied it. She disappeared shortly afterwards for four or five days to give birth, so that "no neighbour could have a sight of her: all which time, she lay to be deliuered of the loade that made her load her soule, with periurie, in *Adamsons* house".[306]

In another case, from 1584, a pregnant servant, this time in Whitechapel (a parish next to London), was able to conceal her condition until she went into labour because of her naturally sturdy build; the "mayde béeing tall and of a reasonable proportion went so long wt childe till the time of her labour unsuspected". When this eventually occurred, she simply left the other servants she was working with and went to a back room in the house, where she swiftly gave birth. She immediately tried to smother the baby by putting her hand over its mouth, but the infant cried out loudly, so she cut the baby's throat with a knife. She then threw its body into a privy (a fairly common means of disposal in urban areas), and immediately "went about her busines, without any signe or suspicion of any such filthiness". However, a young boy in the house, who had been

---

304. *Ibid.*
305. Laura Gowing, "Secret Births and Infanticide in Seventeenth century England", *Past & Present*, Vol. 156, Issue 1, p. 90.
306. Brewer, *The Bloudy Mother*, pp. 1–22.

aware of the woman's previous lack of chastity, heard the child's cry and reported it. Eventually, she was detained and subject to "examination and [physical] search, where shée confessed the matter, and thereupon the childe was taken up". The woman was tried at the Old Bailey and executed at Tyburn.[307]

As some of these cases suggest, desperation appears to have allowed many young women to deliver their babies surprisingly quickly. In the early seventeenth century, when another London spinster was able to keep her pregnancy largely secret from others until she gave birth in private, it was noted that her "lusty body, strong nature, and feare of shame brought an easines to her deliuery, and required in her agony no help of a midwife which among women seemeth a thing very strange". Nobody in the house where she lodged had the least suspicion she had gone into labour "nor hardly was she thought to be with child, so closely demeaned she her selfe".[308]

Investigation

Just as local women might take it upon themselves to examine spinsters they suspected of being pregnant, a jury of matrons, similar to that called at trial to consider post-conviction claims of pregnancy, and made up of midwives and other women who were familiar with childbirth, might examine a woman who was suspected of infanticide at the behest of a coroner or JP. Many were successful in eliciting confessions. The case of Isabel Nicholson on the Northern Circuit is illustrative. She was suspected of having given birth to (and buried) an illegitimate infant. A midwife and ten other women examined her body and declared that she had, indeed, recently had a baby. Nicholson initially denied the charges but then admitted giving birth to a stillborn child.[309] Sometimes it appears that several likely suspects among local women were rounded-up and tested in this manner after a baby's corpse or afterbirth was found. This occurred when the body of a newborn baby was discovered

---

307. T.I., *A World of Wonders*, pp. 1–10.
308. Anon, *Deeds against nature*, pp. 1–12.
309. Loar, "Medical Knowledge", p. 475.

in the privy of a residence near Bishopsgate, in London; the master of the house immediately reported it to local magistrates, who arranged for a "certaine number of substantiall women to make search of suspected persons, and of such who were like to be the murthered Infants mother, or murtherer". This proved successful, as the true "murtheresse came to the touch, where vpon examination, she confessed the child to be borne with life, and her selfe not worthy of life, and so pleading guilty she was brought to her trial".[310]

Less obviously, in 1578 Mary (or Mercy) Gould, described as a "lewd woman" from Cuckfield, in Sussex, was physically examined by a jury of matrons who concluded that there was no fault attached to her in the death of her newborn child.[311] (How they could tell is not apparent). In February 1586 the JP William Lambarde questioned Sarah Gold for killing her newborn infant that same day. He committed her to gaol and requested that those involved in the case liaise with others who could testify and "ask of Mr Ceates the coroner for the information of the mid-wife".[312]

Conclusion

Infanticide was a singular crime in Tudor England. Almost uniquely, women dominated the felony; malefic witchcraft was the only other serious offence that shared this status. Interestingly, and in part for similar reasons, the active prosecution of both offences started at very roughly the same time (the 1542 statute on witchcraft had been largely a dead letter). Indeed, an alleged infanticide craze has been compared with the supposed witch craze of the era. Non-secular forums had normally dealt with both offences, usually quite leniently, for much of the early Tudor era. In just half a century both offences went from being discreetly downplayed, and sometimes even tacitly ignored, to being considered the most heinous of felonies.

---

310. Anon, *Deeds Against Nature*, pp. 1–12.
311. Lemon, *Calendar of State Papers Domestic: Edward VI, Mary and Elizabeth*, pp. 587–589.
312. Conyers, "William Lambarde's 'Ephemeris,'" p. 152.

Taken together, the two crimes (witchcraft and infanticide) also transform the gender profile of those accused of homicide, if considered alongside conventional non-infant murders. For example, their inclusion would mean that female killers were responsible for as many as 45 per cent of all "bodies" in the peak decades of the 1570s and 1580s.[313] Of course, this is unsatisfactory. Modern observers would discount deaths attributed to witchcraft. Whether infanticide should be considered with other crimes of lethal violence, or viewed as *sui generis*, is more problematic; the fact that it has been given its own chapter in this book is probably indicative of the present author's own (and not uncommon) view, but would not be universally shared.

---

313. Kesselring, "Bodies of Evidence", p. 251.

CHAPTER 18

Sexual Offences

Introduction

In some respects, all sexual activity that occurred outside marriage in late-fifteenth century England was a crime, whether fornication, adultery, prostitution, or homosexuality, even if it was usually prosecuted and punished in an ecclesiastical forum. Illustrative of this, in late medieval cities, such as London and Bristol, cages would publicly display prostitutes and lecherous clergymen (required to be celibate prior to the Reformation). Other offenders might be whipped or placed in the pillory, and being required to perform penance in church, often in full white garb, was a regular punishment for those who committed lesser sexual indiscretions. This response to extramarital intercourse continued throughout the Tudor period (although clergymen could marry after the break with Rome), and would fully change only during the century and more after the Restoration of 1660.

Nevertheless, in 1500, none of the offences considered above was considered a serious crime (for which life might be forfeit), and most could not be dealt with in secular forums. There was also a considerable degree of tacit acceptance of such behaviour as an inevitable facet of human existence. The "stews", or licensed brothels, of Southwark were openly tolerated until 1506, even though England appears to have been rather less accepting of these institutions than many continental countries. Although most English towns prohibited prostitution, they did not normally make serious attempts to eradicate it. The repeated fining of the same people for keeping brothels almost suggests a de facto system of licensing fees.[314] Such attitudes continued during the sixteenth century, although a more robust approach developed after the Reformation took hold, with church courts stepping up campaigns against fornication, prostitution, and adultery, and the state intervening more actively to deal with cases of bastardy if the illegitimate offspring might become a charge on the community.[315]

However, the focus in this chapter is on those sexual offences that constituted felonies, more particularly rape, sodomy, and bestiality; their inchoate forms (attempt, etc.) are also considered, even though they were usually treated as misdemeanours.

Rape

The Anglo-Saxon and medieval history of rape had seen a complicated entwinement between the sexual offence and the abduction of females, especially heiresses, for the purposes of marriage, both of which actions might be encompassed by the same word. Sometimes both were present in the same case. Appeals in ravishment cases during the fourteenth and fifteenth centuries were often ambiguous about what, precisely, they were alleging. For example, in 1400 a man named Taillour was pardoned for the ravishment (*de raptu*) of Joan, the sister of a chaplain named John Clopton. However, the case does not make clear whether this should be deemed abduction, rape, or both.[316] Nevertheless, according to one estimate, of 1,213 "ravishment" cases identified between 1100 and 1500, only 108 (nine per cent) can unequivocally be regarded as rape in the sense of forced sexual intercourse. By contrast, 556 cases allege abduction, and 527 are ambiguous (the remaining 22 allege both rape and abduction).[317]

314. Ruth Mazo Karras, "The Regulation of Brothels in Later Medieval England", *Signs*, Vol. 14, No. 2, p. 407.

315. Faramerz Dabhoiwala, *The Origins of Sex: A History of the First Sexual Revolution* (London: Penguin, 2012), pp. 10–15.

316. Caroline Dunn, "The Language of Ravishment in Medieval England", *Speculum*, Vol. 86, No. 1, p. 88 and p. 111.

317. Caroline Dunn, *Stolen Women in Medieval England: Rape, Abduction and Adultery, 1100–1500* (Cambridge: Cambridge University Press, 2013), p. 22.

Unfortunately, this sometimes meant that sexual violence against women was placed on a par with a number of other moral infringements.[318]

However, by the early decades of the sixteenth century the two offences had started to separate, and the crime had begun to acquire its modern connotation of forced intercourse without the victim's consent, although this process was far from complete. As was noted in 1544, "Rape is where a man rauyssheth or taketh a mans wyfe, wydowe, or mayde agaynst her wyll, and hath to do with her agaynst her wyll".[319] This was expressly reiterated in an Elizabethan statute. Abduction continued as an offence, and in 1557, a discreet form of this misconduct, taking unmarried females under the age of 16 out of the custody of their parents or guardians and contracting marriages or having sexual intercourse with them, was made a specific crime (4 and 5 P. & M. c. 8). Typical of such offences, at the Surrey Assizes in February 1575, Thomas Lee, a weaver from Effingham, was indicted after he contracted a marriage with 13-year-old Isabel Mace with the assistance of the local vicar and the vicar's daughter. (The verdict is not known.)[320]

In any event although rape had been made a capital felony in 1285, it was rarely indicted in medieval England. On one assessment, it made up only 0.7 per cent of all prosecuted felonies in Yorkshire during the first half of the fourteenth century.[321] When it was indicted, it was very difficult to secure a conviction, especially if laymen were accused of the crime (clerics could plead benefit of clergy to escape death, encouraging guilty verdicts for those in holy orders). The usual lack of independent witnesses to such cases, the need for penetration, and a frequent reluctance on the part of juries to see a death sentence passed on the accused man appear to have limited the effectiveness of the thirteenth century legislation, although surviving evidence is thin. Nevertheless, in the English Midlands, it seems that almost none of the 280 rape cases that have been preserved for the years between 1400 and 1430 led to a full conviction.[322]

---

318. Maddern, *Violence and Social Order*, p. 103.
319. Anon, *The boke for a justyce of peace*, pp. 9.
320. Cockburn, *Calendar of Assize Records. Surrey Indictments: Elizabeth I*, p. 131.
321. Bellamy, *The Criminal Trial*, p. 177.
322. McGlynn, "Violence and the Law", pp. 53–59.

Perhaps because of this, cases of attempted rape and even, occasionally, the substantive crime itself, were sometimes brought before the church (rather than the secular) courts. For example, in 1492, William Mulley of Canterbury succeeded in his compurgation when charged before such a forum with raping the daughter of one John Childmell.[323] This situation continued after the Reformation. The church courts heard at least 17 attempted rapes in Elizabethan Essex, although some of them did not progress very far. A case from 1583, in which the maid to Leonard Whitfield of Little Baddow accused her master of taking advantage of his wife's absence to make advances, was among them. When she rebuffed his suggestions, he allegedly pursued her down a flight of stairs, forcing her to lock herself into a milk house.[324]

Nevertheless, despite this general reluctance to convict, rape was never condoned or tacitly accepted. An indication of how seriously the crime was viewed officially, even during the late medieval period, is that rape, along with homicide and treason, was often excluded from general pardons, such as that of 1390.[325] On a popular basis, when, in 1515, Joan Clerke and her husband attacked and killed a man who had raped her on an earlier occasion, the jury convicted the defendants of killing in self-defence, to ensure *de cursu* pardons.[326] Furthermore, during the sixteenth century, the number of convictions, if not prosecutions, for rape increased significantly. Indeed, the situation was probably better than it would be in the early 1700s (see below). In part this might reflect the increased number of guilty verdicts for felony generally. It may also have occurred because, for some of the era, rape was a clergyable crime at a time when the privilege had become available to the reasonably literate, not just clerics, moderating the effects of a conviction. Thus, in August 1565, John Beamond pleaded guilty to raping Anne Sellett, a six-year-old girl, in his house in Westminster. He asked for and was granted clergy, and so was handed over to the ordinary.[327]

---

323. Jones, *Gender and Petty Crime*, p. 80.
324. Emmison, *Elizabethan Life: Morals and the Church Courts*, p. 45.
325. Musson, *Crime, Law and Society*, p. 68.
326. Kesselring, *Mercy and Authority*, pp. 101–102.
327. Jeaffreson, *Middlesex County Records: Vol. 1*, pp. 52–56.

This situation ended when the Benefit of Clergy Act 1575 (18 Eliz. I c. 7) took clergy away from rape (along with burglary). As a result, in 1580, after Henry Cherry was convicted at the Essex Assizes of raping Martha Phippes in the Catherine Wheel tavern in Shenfield (Essex), he was sentenced to hang.[328] Nicholas Cleyvele, a Southwark upholsterer, was slightly more fortunate after being convicted of rape in March 1581. He was sentenced to death but remanded to prison afterwards, so that a reprieve could be considered.[329]

Incidence of Prosecutions

Some 44 prosecutions for rape have been preserved from the Essex Assizes and (much less commonly) quarter sessions between 1559 and 1603. In 24 of the years encompassed by this period, there were no indictments at all, while in 1581 there were seven (easily the highest annual total).[330] However, and slightly complicating matters, these courts did not quite have a monopoly of such offences; the odd case still went to one of the county borough sessions and even King's Bench. As a result, and allowing for lost records, it seems safe to assume that not more than 60 rapes were prosecuted in the county during the Elizabethan period. Essex had between 80,000 and 100,000 inhabitants during this time. Thus, significantly less than one case per 100,000 people went before Essex courts each year, and there is no reason to think that this was untypical of much of the rest of England. For example, just ten such allegations came before the grand jury for (fairly populous) Middlesex between 1549 and 1603, although the records of some cases may well have been lost. On another assessment, just 12 rapes were indicted at jury courts in Sussex between 1559 and 1603.[331]

Although prospects for success for rape indictments were much better than they had been in the medieval period, they were still comparatively low in comparison to prosecutions for most other felonies. The 23

328. Cockburn, *Calendar of Assize Records. Essex Indictments: Elizabeth I*, p. 199.
329. Cockburn, *Calendar of Assize Records. Surrey Indictments: Elizabeth I*, p. 213.
330. Samaha, *Law and Order*, p. 20.
331. Arthur F. Kinney et al. (eds.), *Tudor England: An Encyclopedia* (Abingdon: Routledge, 2010), p. 170.

preserved cases of rape for which true bills were found by the grand jury for the Surrey Assizes during the 45 years of the Elizabethan period can be considered in this regard. All but one involved individual defendants, the exception being a case with a pair of co-defendants. Of these cases, two men were on bail and failed to appear for their trial. Another remained mute of malice when arraigned and was subjected to the *peine forte et dure*. This leaves 20 trials, involving 21 accused. In 15 of these, acquittals were returned. In five (including the case with the co-defendants) the accused were found guilty. Of the six men convicted, one was clergied (this being prior to the change in the law in 1576), and the remaining five were sentenced to hang. Thus, about a quarter of those accused of rape were convicted, unlike an average for felony defendants of more than half at this time.[332] This pattern, of about a quarter of indicted cases producing convictions, appears to have been reflected in the other counties of the Elizabethan Home Circuit.[333] Thus, in Elizabethan Essex, 24 per cent of those indicted for rape were convicted, although in Sussex 41.7 per cent accused of the crime were found guilty.[334]

Unsurprisingly, some complainants felt they could not go through with the embarrassment of a trial, or privately compounded the matter with their attacker. For example, in Colchester Seth Halsnoth was presented for rape at the town's borough sessions but was not ultimately indicted or tried because Katherine Pepper (his alleged victim) failed to appear in court to prosecute him, despite her earlier sworn statement to a magistrate telling in great detail of at least three sexual assaults made upon her.[335]

In 1598 the married Earth Bickley of Crediton, in Devonshire, was sent by her husband to buy yarn from Robert Aileston. She was tricked into going into the latter's bedchamber (he said that was where he kept the material); once inside, he secured the door, then seized her: "in forcible manner against her will. And did cast her down against the edge of a certain coffer and did by the means of the sudden assaulting and laying of violent hands upon her ... immediately thereupon forcibly and against her will ravish her and had carnal knowledge of her body

332. See generally, Cockburn, *Calendar of Assize Records Surrey Indictments: Elizabeth I*.
333. Sharpe, *A Fiery & Furious People*, p. 485.
334. Bellamy, *The Criminal Trial*, p. 179.
335. Samaha, "Hanging for Felony", p. 769.

without any consent yielded by her". She was severely bruised in the process, her back allegedly being black and blue. It was claimed that she also acquired a venereal disease from the crime. Even so, negotiations for a settlement took place through Aileston's brother, and her assailant offered to pay for her medical treatment and to provide compensation, with a view to avoiding prosecution. This possibility was seriously entertained, and initially embarked upon. When Bickley was later asked why she had not gone to a JP immediately, she attributed it to pressure from her husband, so that she "dared not complain to any officer". However, when she eventually told her father what had occurred, he insisted that formal action be taken, and a prosecution initiated.[336]

Although the willingness of victims to inform the authorities had probably improved slightly since the medieval period, it is almost certain that rape remained a very under-reported crime in Tudor England. By prosecuting their attackers, unmarried victims advertised the fact that they were no longer virgins, so reducing their prospects of marriage, something that may also help to explain the high proportion of child victims who went to court.[337]

Occasional accounts hint at the number of unreported rapes. Even allowing that some such allegations were false, many were probably well-founded. For example, in July 1590 Joan Somers, of Downham, in Essex, appeared before the local Archdeacon's Court accused of fornication, probably because she was, by then, obviously pregnant. She explained her condition by saying that while she was feeding her employer's cattle in a field shortly before Christmas, one Rice Evans "came unto her and told her that she mighte now crye her harte owte, before anie bodye colde here her crie, and so indeede as she saith he did violentlye abuse her bodye and committed fornication with her".[338]

Similarly, in October 1602 Christopher Beeston, an actor, impresario, and acquaintance of William Shakespeare, appeared at the Bridewell Court. Margaret White, the widow of a clothworker, had been accused

---

336. C Mansell and J Hailwood, *Court Depositions of South West England*, humanities-research. Exeter.ac.uk (accessed 26 September 2019).

337. Jones, *Gender and Petty Crime*, p. 78.

338. Elise Bennett Histed, "Mediaeval Rape: A Conceivable Defence?", *The Cambridge Law Journal*, Vol. 63, Issue 3, p. 762.

of "incontinent lyving" but submitted a written petition to the alder-men which was passed on to the court because it contained an allegation that: "Beeston a plaier at one winters house in Star alley without Bishopp had the use of her bodie but as she saithe hee did it forciblie". Even so, Beeston merely appears to have been dealt with for some form of sexual incontinence (probably adultery), and the case may have died out after his actor friends attended the court and created uproar.[339]

The bastardy depositions taken from women at quarter sessions, aimed at identifying fathers who might maintain illegitimate children, also produce evidence of such cases. For example, it was claimed that Lydia Prince's master, Francis Haddon, swore that he "would teare her in pieces if shee did not let him lye with her". Similarly, Eleanor Symonds said that she was pregnant because Ralph Brown overtook her on the road, "carried her forcibly into John Pinkes barne and had Carnal knowledge of her body against her Consent 2 or 3 times and threatened to kill her this Examinant if she made the least noise." Sadly, the Tudor era was still wedded to the medieval notion that conception could not occur with-out consent, precluding effective criminal prosecutions in such cases.[340]

Background to the Crimes

As some of these cases suggest, many rape allegations that were pros-ecuted in Tudor England arose from the abuse of power relationships, so that female servants featured prominently as victims. For example, in three cases of rape heard at the Essex Assizes in March 1560, all the victims were domestic staff. John Rypton from Chigwell was accused of raping his maid, Agnes Dowson. Nicholas Ratclyff was tried for raping his female servant, Joan Lee, in his house at Debden. Thomas Hopkyn was tried for raping Joan Hasserd in her master's house in Ilford. As the last case suggests, servants could be vulnerable not only to the attentions of their masters but also of other domestic staff or people from the local area, in which they (the servants) were often comparative strangers. All

339. Duncan Salkeld, "Literary Traces in Bridewell and Bethlem, 1602–1624", *The Review of English Studies*, Vol. 56, Issue 225, pp. 379–385.
340. Histed, "Mediaeval Rape", p. 762.

three men were acquitted.[341] It is particularly likely that only a small proportion of such cases ever came for trial.

For the same reason (abuse of power relationships), children also featured regularly amongst rape victims in prosecuted cases. Some 35 of the victims of the 88 men indicted for the crime on the Elizabethan Home Circuit (some records have been lost) were eleven-years-old or less.[342] Of course, some victims were both servants and children, and so doubly disadvantaged, as was the case with eleven-year-old Catherine Sanson, who was allegedly raped by her employer in Richmond, Surrey, in 1559.[343]

Many of the child victims were younger than Sanson (although few of these would be domestic staff). For example, in 1579, Richard Burley was acquitted at the Essex Assizes of raping a ten-year-old girl in Great Waltham, and even younger victims came before this forum, a pattern that has also been observed in sixteenth century Kent.[344] In Surrey, the predominance of children in prosecuted cases was particularly striking. Even so, some of the most extreme and brutal examples were found in London and Middlesex.

In July 1590, in the parish of St Magnus the Martyr, in London, Sara Tumor, a five-year-old, was assaulted and raped by George Bushnell in the middle of the day. She lingered for six weeks before dying of her injuries in early September. The coroner's inquest concluded that she had been "murdered" by Bushnell. Unfortunately, he had fled immediately afterwards, and his whereabouts were unknown.[345] In 1599 a true bill was found against Edward Jacob for attacking three-year-old Mary Corey in Mile End, in Middlesex *"et ipsam Mariam Corey tunc et ibidem rapuit defloravit et … carnaliter cognovits".*[346]

Cases involving very young children occasioned legal problems. Obviously there was concern about their ability to testify at trial, although this did not fully crystallise until the seventeenth century. However, there were other difficulties. The medieval statute law governing rape

341. Cockburn, *Calendar of Assize Records. Essex Indictments: Elizabeth I*, pp. 11–12.
342. Sharpe, *A Fiery & Furious People*, p. 485.
343. Cockburn, *Calendar of Assize Records. Surrey Indictments: Elizabeth I*, p. 5.
344. Cockburn, *Calendar of Assizes Records: Essex Indictments, Elizabeth I*, p. 183; Jones, *Gender and Petty Crime*, p. 80.
345. Forbes, "London Coroner's Inquests for 1590", pp. 382–383.
346. Jeaffreson, *Middlesex County Records: Vol. 1*, pp. 256–257.

required the victim to have been of full age (at least ten and possibly 12) if the offence was to be charged as a felony, rather than merely a misdemeanour, although this sometimes appears to have been overlooked. Furthermore, "consent" to intercourse by children, even if obtained through bribery, was not automatically irrelevant, and might obviate a charge of rape. Such problems were eventually brought to a head by the trial of a Scotsman at King's Bench for raping a seven-year-old girl.[347]

This prompted the creation of a new statutory offence, established by section 4 of the same Act that abolished benefit of clergy for rape (18 Eliz. c. 7); it came into force in 1576, and provided that it was a felony without clergy to "unlawfully and carnally know any woman child under the age of ten years". This effectively introduced a form of statutory rape, in which consent became irrelevant.[348] As a result, in February 1595, when John Kidd was indicted at the Old Bailey for assaulting and raping Margaret Darsye, an infant under ten years-of-age, in a house in Middlesex, her compliance to his demands was irrelevant. He pleaded guilty and was sentenced to death.[349] Similarly, Walter Fryer, a cooper from Moulsham in Essex, was convicted of raping five-year-old Alice Colman, at the Chelmsford Assizes in July 1609, and also sentenced to hang.[350] However, men could, and did, continue to use consent as a defence when a child was over ten, and their acquittal could sometimes be secured by presenting sufficient evidence of the child's acquiescence, even if it had been obtained by inducements.[351]

Sodomy

Although strongly deprecated, sodomy does not appear to have been a major secular-legal concern in much of Western Europe until quite late in the medieval period. Like witchcraft, it was usually viewed as a matter for the church courts and their attendant administration. Although

---

347. Levine, "A More than Ordinary Case", p. 163.
348. Sarah Toulalan, "'Is He a Licentious Lewd Sort of a Person?' Constructing the Child Rapist in Early Modern England", *Journal of the History of Sexuality*, Vol. 23, Issue 1, 2014, p. 31.
349. Jeaffreson, *Middlesex County Records: Vol. 1*, pp. 225–230.
350. Cockburn, *Calendar of Assize Records. Essex Indictments: Elizabeth I*, p. 64.
351. Toulalan, "'Is He a Licentious Lewd Sort of a Person?'", p. 31.

a few medieval legal writers, such as the author of the treatise known as *Fleta* in England, suggested that (like bestiality) it was a non-statutory capital offence, this was not usually evidenced in practice.

However, this situation gradually changed from the fourteenth century onwards, especially in Northern Europe and Italy. For example, in Bruges, 90 sodomites were executed between 1385 and 1515 (though this was an unusually high number).[352] More typically, by the 1400s small numbers of men were being executed for the crime in Germany and Switzerland. Thus Zurich saw five executions for sodomy during the fifteenth century. However, German speakers increasingly associated the practice with Italians, especially those from Florence. This reputation (even if entirely undeserved) may have spread further afield. In 1575 Thomas Wilson claimed that Italians were prone to "synne horribly in suche sorte as is not to be named, although [he admitted] that same haynous filthynesse is not onelye used there". After the onset of the Reformation in 1517, some Protestant Germans associated the practice with Catholicism. Several, such as Martin Luther, even used accusations of sodomy to discredit the senior ranks of the Roman Church. As a result, the level of executions for the crime on the Continent increased significantly after the early 1500s, albeit that the totals were still relatively low.[353] Interestingly, polemicists such as Simon Fish sometimes made similar accusations against English clerics during the Reformation. In February 1536, after the Visitation of the Monasteries, it was claimed that a monk from Dereham, in Norfolk, had confessed to sodomy. Two other monks also alleged that the by then statutory crime was prevalent among secular priests as well as those in religious houses.[354] Following the *Constitutio Criminalis Carolina*, the criminal code instituted by Emperor Charles V in 1532, sodomites were officially condemned to the stake throughout the Habsburg territories, including the Southern Netherlands.[355]

---

352. Marc Boone, "State Power and Illicit Sexuality: The Persecution of Sodomy in Late Medieval Bruges", *Journal of Medieval History*, Vol. 22, Issue 2, pp. 135–153.
353. Helmut Puff, *Sodomy in Reformation Germany and Switzerland, 1400–1600* (Chicago: The University of Chicago Press, 2003), p. 25.
354. Gairdner, *Letters and Papers, Foreign and Domestic, Henry VIII, Vol. 10*, pp. 135–160.
355. Jonas Roelens, "Gossip, Defamation and Sodomy in the Early Modern Southern Netherlands", *Renaissance Studies*, Vol. 32, Issue 2, p. 238.

England was comparatively late (by continental standards) in criminalising homosexual behaviour as a secular offence, as it was with several other crimes that moved centre stage in sixteenth century Europe, such as infanticide (on a de facto basis) and witchcraft. Prior to this, the ecclesiastical authorities had occasionally become involved in regulating such activity, so that, for example, in 1463 one Brother Thomas Banns was convicted before a church forum for "sodomye".[356] In 1520 a man attempted to purge himself of an accusation of buggery at an ecclesiastical court in Chichester. However, the planned purgation was abandoned when his victim offered to establish the guilt of the accused.[357]

Nevertheless, despite such cases, it seems that homosexual offences very rarely appeared in front of the church courts during the late medieval and early Tudor period. Between 1470 and 1516 it appears that only one man was accused of sodomy out of 21,000 defendants who came before the Bishop of London's Commissary Court. Although sodomy may have been denounced as an unspeakable crime against both God and nature by clerics, it seems that concrete examples of the act—which must have occurred on a fairly regular basis—were quietly ignored unless blatant, or were discreetly dealt with by confession.[358] The preamble to the 1533 Act (25 Hen. 8 c. 6), the first statute to make sodomy a felony (see below), was adamant that the crime was not being properly dealt with: "Forasmuch as there is not yet sufficient and condign punishment appointed and limited by the due course of the Laws of this Realm for the detestable and abominable Vice of Buggery committed with mankind or beast".[359]

In 1533 Thomas Cromwell guided "An Acte for the punishment of the vice of Buggerie" through Parliament. The statute was only to last until the end of the following Parliament, but was re-enacted three times, and in 1541 was made permanent. The Buggery Act made penetrative intercourse between men, anal intercourse between men and women, and any penetrative sexual congress between a man or woman and an animal

356. Ingram, *Carnal Knowledge*, pp. 35–37.
357. Helmholz, "Crime, Compurgation", p. 16.
358. Ingram, *Carnal Knowledge*, pp. 35–37.
359. H. Montgomery Hyde, *The Love That Dared Not Speak Its Name: A Candid History of Homosexuality in Britain* (Boston: Little, Brown, 1970), pp. 147–148.

a felony that was outside benefit of clergy, even for those who genuinely were clerics. (Clergymen could still claim the privilege for murder at this time.) In part this reflected the Reformation struggle between religious and secular authority, with the Crown making it clear where power lay in this regard. Indeed, while JPs and judges presided over most felonies, the clause confirming this in the 1533 statute expressly made it clear to ecclesiastical court officials that the sin of buggery would fall outside their jurisdiction.[360]

Lesbianism was not (and never became) a secular crime in England. A reluctance, or straightforward unwillingness, to prosecute such behaviour was widespread in early modern Europe. However, this was not quite universal. In the Southern Netherlands it appears that, between about 1400 and 1550, at least 25 women were charged with having sexual relations with other women. It has been suggested that this (unusual) level of repression for female same-sex acts was a result of the relatively high level of liberty enjoyed by women in this part of Holland, compared to other areas of Europe. This may have made them more visible in urban society, and so increased their risk of being penalised.[361] Even so, their lives were not sufficiently different from those of their English counterparts to make this an entirely satisfactory explanation.

In 1547 Edward VI's first Parliament repealed (I Edw. VI c. 12) all the later felony laws created by Henry VIII, including the 1533 statute, but a year later reinstated the Buggery Act with minor amendments (goods and lands were not now forfeit on conviction). When Mary Tudor came to the throne in 1553, she repealed all laws made by her brother Edward (I Mar c. 1), and did not reinstate the Buggery Act during her reign, so that it was not contrary to secular criminal law to be a practising homosexual for most of the 1550s. After her death, restoration of the statute was mooted as early as March 1559, and a bill to this effect introduced in Parliament; however, it failed to become law after a reading in the House of Lords, and Queen Elizabeth did not reinstate the 1533 version of the

---

360. Johnson, Paul, "Buggery and Parliament, 1533–2017" (3 April, 2018). SSRN: https://ssrn.com/abstract=3155522 or http://dx.doi.org/10.2139/ssrn.3155522

361. Jonas Roelens, "Visible Women: Female Sodomy in the Late Medieval and Early Modern Southern Netherlands (1400–1550)", *Low Countries Historical Review*, Vol. 130, Issue 3, pp. 3–4.

Act (not that of 1548) until 1563.[362] This time it was not to be repealed until 1828, and sodomy remained a capital crime for even longer.[363]

According to the preamble to the 1563 statute, its reintroduction was driven by the proliferation of the crime in England, since, after repeal in 1553, "divers ill disposed persons have been the more bold to commit the said most horrible and detestable Vice of Buggery aforesaid, to the high displeasure of Almighty God". In practice, and perhaps more important, and as with the original statute, its reintroduction also constituted a symbolic assertion of the supremacy of secular over ecclesiastical courts in Protestant England after Mary's Catholic years. Interestingly, and as with the unavailing attempt to introduce such an Act in 1559, the 1563 statute against buggery was initially combined with a bill against witchcraft; this passed through the Commons but was then broken into separate Acts by the upper house.[364]

Even so, it seems that older attitudes towards the crime persisted during the Tudor period between 1533 and 1553, and in the decades following 1563, so that very few people were prosecuted or punished under these statutes for specifically homosexual offences, rather than bestiality, and even indictments for the latter offence were fairly rare (see below).[365] The crime was little discussed in vade mecums for JPs and does not appear to have occasioned a huge amount of legal concern.[366]

In an early, albeit infamous, case from 1541, Nicholas Udall, a cleric and the headmaster of Eton College, became one of the first men to be charged with a violation of the 1533 act on its own (that is, without another serious charge accompanying it) after sexually abusing several of his pupils. The matter came to light after an investigation into the theft of some plate that had been perpetrated by one of the boys. Udall was capitally convicted. He wrote to his former friends from Thomas

---

362. G. R. Elton, *The Parliament of England, 1559–1581* (Cambridge: Cambridge University Press, 1986), p. 110; Simonds d'Ewes (ed.), *The Journals of All the Parliaments During the Reign of Queen Elizabeth* (Shannon: Irish University Press, 1682), pp. 53–55.

363. *Journal of the House of Commons: Vol. 1, 1547–1629* (London: HMSO, 1802), p. 57.

364. Courtney Thomas, "'Not Having God Before His Eyes': Bestiality in Early Modern England", *The Seventeenth Century*, Vol. 26, Issue 1, at p. 159; *Journal of the House of Commons: Vol. 1, 1547–1629*, p. 60 and p. 65.

365. Puff, *Sodomy in Reformation Germany*, p. 25.

366. Salvatore J. Licata and Robert P. Petersen (eds.), *The Gay Past: A Collection of Historical Essays* (Abingdon: Routledge, 1986), pp. 70–71.

Cromwell's household, including Thomas Wriothesley, pleading with them to intercede on his behalf, and his sentence was commuted to imprisonment of just under a year, which he served in the Marshalsea Prison. Despite his nefarious history, he went on to become headmaster of Westminster School.

During the reign of Henry VIII, only one execution for sodomy has been identified, that of Lord Hungerford in 1540. He was alleged to have used "detestable vice and sin of buggery" with several of his male servants. However, the nobleman was accused of, and executed for, several other serious offences as well, including treason, suggesting that the sexual allegation may have been thrown in to darken his character, and was not necessarily valid. Ironically, he was executed alongside Thomas Cromwell, who had steered the 1533 statute through Parliament.[367]

Only four cases of homosexual buggery (that have been preserved) came for trial in the five counties on the Home Circuit during the Elizabethan period (for all but the first five years of which time the 1563 statute was in force). For example, the sole case from Sussex occurred in 1580, when Matthew Heaton, a clergyman from East Grinstead, was prosecuted at the county assizes for sodomy with "Thomas Gooble, a boy" in his own parish. (The verdict is unknown.)[368] The only prosecution from Surrey during these years took place in July 1584, when Remily Clerke, a Southwark joiner, was acquitted of committing sodomy the previous April with Richard Woolly, who was also described as a "boy".[369] No homosexual offences at all were prosecuted at the Essex Assizes during the Elizabethan period, and no record of such a prosecution has been preserved from the Hertfordshire Assizes in the years after 1573. The only conviction for buggery secured on the Elizabethan Home Circuit occurred in July 1569, when Roland Dyer, from Margate, in Kent, was hanged for sodomising five-year-old Barnaby Wright.[370]

367. Stephen O. Murray, *Homosexualities* (Chicago: The University of Chicago Press, 2000), p. 152; Gairdner and Brodie, *Letters and Papers, Foreign and Domestic, Henry VIII, Volume 15*, pp. 445–481.
368. Cockburn, *Calendar of Assize Records. Sussex Indictments. Elizabeth I*, p. 156.
369. Cockburn, *Calendar of Assize Records. Surrey Indictments Elizabeth I*, p. 261
370. Cockburn, *Calendar of Assize Records. Kent Indictments: Elizabeth I*, p. 88.

Although the statute was much broader in its effect, it seems clear that in Tudor England prosecuted cases of sodomy normally involved adult men having sexual intercourse with boys or adolescents, sometimes forcibly (i.e. homosexual rape), and this profile continued until well into the early seventeenth century.[371] For example, shortly after the end of the Tudor period, in May 1607, a gentleman named Humfrey Stafford was tried at the Court of King's Bench in Westminster for sodomising two youths a year earlier. His victims, Richard Robinson and Nicholas Crosse, were aged 17 and 13 (or 14) respectively. The crimes were committed in Stafford's lodgings in Holborn. Robinson and Crosse gave evidence on oath as to the time, place, manner, and the circumstances in which they had been committed. Their parents gave corroborative evidence on some matters relating to the case, such as the physical condition of the victims' bottoms "shewing that the boyes had receiued hurt therby, & that they were forced to vse the helpe of a Surgion for their cure". Early in the seventeenth century Coke thought it axiomatic that there must be anal penetration (not merely sexual activity) for the offence to be made out, something that explains the need for such evidence, and it is safe to assume that this was also the case during the Tudor era. Even so, Stafford denied the allegations, rather equivocally protesting that he was "guiltlesse therein, excusing himselfe, that if he had offended it was in wine; but the jurie after a little deliberation returned him guiltie". He was executed.[372]

Some homosexual offences continued to be heard in the church courts, but this was rare, even for those that did not involve penetration. In 1594, a man named Cooke, the schoolmaster of Great Tey in Essex, was presented to the Archdeacon's Court on a serious but not enunciated charge. He was reported to be a man of "beastly behavior amongst his scholars, and teacheth them all manner of bawdry". He failed to appear at the court's next session and is then lost to history. It is possible that the allegations against him involved pederasty.[373]

---

371. Murray, *Homosexualities*, p. 153.

372. Anon, *The arraignement, judgement, confession, and execution of Humphrey Stafford, gentleman Who on the tenth of this present month of June, 1607 suffered, at Saint Thomas of Waterings* (London, 1607), pp. 1–22.

373. Emmison, *Elizabethan Life: Morals and the Church Courts*, p. 47.

Bestiality

During the medieval period, bestiality had been viewed as being of a broadly similar level of sinfulness to masturbation, especially when committed by an unmarried man (if the man had a wife, it was deemed a more serious matter). It was not a secular offence, being within the purview of the church courts and authorities, but examples of formal action are fairly rare, even in ecclesiastical forums. However, in 1519 the holy water clerk of Tingewick, in Buckinghamshire, was reported to the ecclesiastical authorities after a local woman saw him attempting to have intercourse with a horse. The following year, a Sussex man had to clear himself of the slander of unnatural connection with another horse in Grinstead.[374]

Various explanations have been advanced for the early modern change in attitudes towards such behaviour, such as a fear of human interaction with demons appearing in animal form, and increased concern about the possibility of monstrous offspring resulting from such unions. Edward Coke's *Institutes of the Lawes of England* relate that, just prior to the 1533 Act making bestiality a crime without benefit of clergy, a "great Lady had committed buggery with a Baboon, and conceived by it". Agnes Bowker allegedly (and famously) gave birth to a cat in Leicestershire in 1569, although the authorities and prominent London physicians eventually concluded that this was probably a hoax.[375] It should also be noted that *Leviticus* enjoined that if a man lay with a beast he should be put to death, albeit that this injunction had generally been ignored prior to the 1530s (along with several others from that part of scripture).

Whatever the causes, the 1533 Buggery Act, which was periodically abolished and reinstated during the mid-sixteenth century, treated acts of bestiality in the same way as those involving homosexuality. Indeed, much of the terminology relating to the two offences was shared, on the basis that both involved the unnatural penetration of another being.

---

374. Ingram, *Carnal Knowledge*, p. 35.
375. Thomas, "'Not Having God Before His Eyes': Bestiality in Early Modern England", *Seventeenth Century*, Vol. 26, No. 1, 2011, pp. 149–173, at p. 150 and p. 160.

Prior to this statute, and like homosexuality, bestiality was not a felony, and may not even have been a secular misdemeanour.

Instances of bestiality appear to have been a regular, though not common, feature of country life during the Tudor period. Men in rural areas were prominent amongst those accused, with mares and cows or (less frequently) ewes, sows, and bitches among the animal victims. Although the crime could be committed by females, it required that they be penetrated by an animal, nearly always a dog in practice, and was almost unheard of.[376] In an era in which men normally married when well into their twenties, bestiality provided young males, who could not secure access to willing women, with a penetrative sexual outlet; it was easy for countrymen to be tempted to emulate the animals they saw mounting each other in fields and barns.

Tudor bestiality only rarely seems to have reflected a specific fetish for sexual congress with animals (zoophilia). Nevertheless, there are occasional hints that an accused man may have had a specific penchant for animals, something that ensured that his experiences with bestial intercourse were not isolated incidents. For example, Thomas Rice of Bushey, in Hertfordshire, was indicted for committing buggery with a steer on 11 June 1596, and again, with another steer, on 19 July of the same year. Even so, he was acquitted at the county assizes in March 1597.[377]

Prosecuted cases often involved the violation of a creature owned by someone other than the defendant, the lack of privacy and the owner's anger explaining why the perpetrators were indicted. For example, all three preserved cases from Surrey involved animals (a horse, a sow, and a sheep) that were owned by someone other than the accused. Similarly, in Colchester, on Christmas Eve 1575, Francis Hunt surprised his servant William Underwood buggering Hunt's mare in a stable. Hunt duly reported the matter to the authorities, and Underwood confessed to the town's bailiffs that he had "filthily abused himself". He was prosecuted by his master at the following gaol delivery at borough sessions, convicted, and sentenced to death.[378] When in 1594 George Dawson, a Dedham

---

376. Thomas, "'Not Having God Before his Eyes,'" p. 149.
377. Cockburn, *Calendar of Assize Records: Hertfordshire Indictments: Elizabeth I*, p. 130.
378. Samaha, "Hanging for Felony", p. 763.

glazier, committed buggery with a bitch in another man's house, and presumably with this person's animal, he made his exposure much more likely.[379] William Cotemore of Lawford, in Essex, was unusual in that he committed buggery with his own red cow, foolishly choosing a publicly viewable field (rather than a barn) for his congress with the animal.[380]

Interestingly, a statute of 1548, amending the 1533 Act, added an additional clause advising, "No person be received for witness or to lay or give evidence against the said offendor ... [who] should take any profit or commodity by the death of the said offendor if he were attained or convicted of the said crime and offence".[381] This suggests that it may have become a relatively common crime for malicious accusations, as was also the case with homosexuality.

Even so, it was not a frequently prosecuted offence. There appear to be just 29 preserved cases of bestiality indictments from the Home Circuit during the Elizabethan period (several more are almost certainly missing): four in Sussex, four in Hertfordshire, eight in Essex, three in Surrey, and ten in Kent. Very unusually, two (separate) cases in the latter county were indicted at the same sessions. At the assizes held in April 1565, Thomas Downe was indicted in his absence (presumably he was on bail and had failed to appear) by a grand jury for buggering a mare belonging to George Sede of Throwley, while Andrew Calverly of Horton Kirby was tried and acquitted of buggering a cow.[382] Nevertheless, of the preserved cases, 15 (just over half) produced convictions.

As this list also suggests, during the Tudor era, the Buggery Act was used far more frequently against those who committed bestiality than it was against homosexuals. Thus, all eight of the men (separately) indicted under the (post-1563) Act at Elizabethan Assizes in Essex whose details have survived were accused of crimes against animals. Nobody was prosecuted in the county for a homosexual offence under the same statute. Despite the demanding evidential requirements (the jury normally had to be satisfied of penetration), five defendants were convicted, two were

---

379. ERO Q/SR 129/93.
380. Cockburn, *Calendar of Assize Records. Essex Indictments: Elizabeth I*, p. 142.
381. Erica Fudge, "Monstrous Acts: Bestiality in Early Modern England", *History Today*, Vol. 50, Issue 8, p. 20.
382. Cockburn, *Calendar of Assize Records. Kent Indictments: Elizabeth I*, p. 58.

acquitted, and one, Geoffrey Childe, died in prison while awaiting trial.[383] The animals used for the (alleged) sexual congress consisted of four cows, a heifer, a bitch, and two mares. The four cases of bestiality that have been preserved from the Hertfordshire Assizes during the Elizabethan period involved a cow, a steer, and two horses. These produced one conviction and two acquittals, while Thomas Rees, accused of buggering his own horse, failed to answer to his bail to stand trial.[384]

Unsurprisingly, the physical act could be difficult to commit with large animals. William Underwood (see above) had to pull up a large basket to gain access to his animal's nether quarters. Robert Cock of Rivenhall, in Essex, drove a mare into the corner of a deep pit in a marshy area to commit the crime.[385] Given this difficulty, there was a perhaps surprising absence of (more tractable) sheep amongst animal victims in Essex and Hertfordshire, although they feature prominently in such crimes at other times and places. Even so, Thomas Twyner was convicted of buggering a sheep belonging to Walter Tickner at the Surrey Assizes in February 1592.[386] Even more unusually, in July 1569, Thomas Hiccocks was convicted at the Surrey Assizes of buggering a dark black sow, a very uncommon form of the crime.[387]

As with other capital offences, bestiality was also occasionally tried at quarter and borough sessions. Thus it seems that George Dawson, a glazier from Dedham, was tried before the Essex Quarter Sessions in 1595 for buggering a bitch in another man's house in the same town. As was typical in such cases, he was described as committing bestiality when "not having God before his eyes nor considering the dignity of human nature, but seduced by diabolical instigation".[388] William Speller appeared before the same forum, accused of buggering his own heifer, while as previously noted, in 1576 William Underwood was prosecuted to conviction at the Colchester Borough Sessions for buggering his master's horse.[389]

---

383. ERO T/A 418/27/27.
384. Cockburn, *Calendar of Assize Records. Hertfordshire indictments: Elizabeth I*, p. 48.
385. Cockburn, *Calendar of Assize Records. Essex Indictments, Elizabeth I*, p. 111.
386. Cockburn, *Calendar of Assize Records. Surrey indictments: Elizabeth I*, p. 377.
387. *Ibid*, p. 79.
388. ERO Q/SR 129/93.
389. Thomas, "'Not Having God Before His Eyes'", p. 159; Samaha, "Hanging for Felony", pp. 763–764.

CHAPTER 19

Property Crime

Introduction

Although Tudor England may have seen less lethal violence than many other European countries (see *Chapter 16*), most observers, both foreign and domestic, thought that its incidence of property crime was relatively high by continental standards. In about 1500, a Venetian diplomat suggested that no other state in Europe had so many thieves and robbers, and that few people went out alone in the country except in broad daylight, and even fewer in urban areas at night, "least of all in London".[390] As this comment suggests, the situation in the capital, along with the apparently alarming level of highway robbery, seems to have influenced many foreign assessments of the crime rate in England.

However, caution must be exercised when taking such observations at face value. Almost all large European cities (there were only a handful of them) attracted concern in this regard. In 1599 Thomas Platter the Younger, a diarist and student from Basel who also visited England during his travels, warned would-be travellers to the French capital, "Crossing a deserted forest is obviously much safer than walking the streets of Paris". For many contemporary visitors, the French city embodied the corruption of morals and a concentration of criminal dangers.[391] London was certainly not unique.

Furthermore, some European states used quasi-military forces to secure their major roads, perhaps making their English counterparts appear especially dangerous by comparison. Crime rates in London and on

---

390. Anon, *A Relation, or Rather a True Account*, p. 34.
391. Diane Roussel, "A Mosaic of Controls: The Plurality of Order Maintenance Mechanisms in 16th Century Paris", *Journal on European History of Law*, Vol. 6, Issue 1, pp. 30–37.

the highways were not necessarily typical of those found in the rest of the country. Nevertheless, with this reservation, it should be noted that Thomas More, Thomas Wilson, and several other domestic observers shared foreign views about the level of instrumental crime (law-breaking for tangible gain) in England. Furthermore, the incidence of prosecutions for such offences increased dramatically in the closing decades of the sixteenth century, even allowing for the increase in population; this raises difficult questions about the relationship between the commission of a crime and its indictment in a society where most non-homicidal crimes did not go to court.

Like a high proportion of the Tudor population as a whole, many criminals were poor, often being described in the calendars as "labourers" (landless men who worked for wages), the lowest social category, apart from vagrants. Nevertheless, there were numerous exceptions to this general proposition. Many defendants were drawn from less marginal members of society. Some were even (if sometimes very loosely) identified as "gentlemen", as was the case with Thomas Sturley, at the Essex Assizes held at Braintree in July 1581. It was alleged that the previous year he had stolen £8 in cash from another man. (He was acquitted.)[392] Many more were yeomen, husbandmen, craftsmen, or tradesmen.

The occupations of the male defendants accused of property crimes at the Surrey Assizes held at Kingston in February 1567, where they are revealed (not quite always the situation), can be considered in this regard. Fourteen cases produce 15 accused men. Six of them were described as yeomen; four were termed labourers. Several were craftsmen, including a tailor and two shoemakers. There was also a bricklayer and a groom.[393] Thus a clear majority were not drawn from the lowest social strata. Essex may have been a little more proletarian, or less generous in assigning social status. At the Chelmsford Assizes in March 1582, of 18 male defendants drawn from eleven cases, 13 were described as "labourers", with three husbandmen, a yeoman, and a scrivener making up the balance. More modestly, at the Summer Assizes for the same county the previous year,

---

392. Cockburn, *Calendar of Assize Records. Essex Indictments: Elizabeth I*, p. 216.
393. Cockburn, *Calendar of Assize Records. Surrey Indictments: Elizabeth I*, pp. 54–58.

labourers made up half of the defendants in property cases.[394] As this profile suggests, although much crime occurred against a background of poverty, it was not usually prompted by absolute destitution, a few very difficult periods (such as the 1590s) possibly apart.

Property crime dominated the Tudor calendars for felony trials. Thus 87 per cent of the felonies tried at the Court of Great Sessions in Chester (the Cheshire equivalent of the assizes) between 1580 and 1519, were for property offences of all types, and just 10.5 per cent were for homicide, with 2.5 per cent being for other types of felony.[395] Furthermore, simple larceny dominated prosecuted property crimes, whether at assizes or quarter sessions. In Kent cases of clergyable grand larceny made up a clear majority of acquisitive crimes that were indicted at the county assizes at the start of the seventeenth century. Many other cases involved petty theft (the only non-capital felony).[396] Nationally, the relative proportions between the two forms of theft were often reversed at the lower jury forum.

Some 1,921 felonies were prosecuted at royal courts in Elizabethan Sussex between 1559 and 1603. Of these, 127 cases related to "ordinary" homicides, and 27 were for infanticide. A dozen rapes were indicted, as were 14 cases of witchcraft, along with a handful of other fairly rarely prosecuted, crimes. However, 1,318 cases, about two-thirds of the total, involved crimes against property. Some 654 were allegations of simple grand larceny, 26 of theft from the person or cutpursing/pickpocketing (a form of theft that had been withdrawn from clergy), 332 of theft from premises, 267 of burglary, and 39 of highway robbery. Many more people were prosecuted for petty theft, accused of stealing goods or cash under one shilling in value.[397] (Some early Tudor observers thought that the cut-off point was 13d.)[398] In Essex over the same period (1559 to 1603), 60 per cent of prosecutions at assizes were for larceny, ten per cent for

---

394. Cockburn, *Calendar of Assize Records. Essex Indictments: Elizabeth I*, pp. 221–228 and pp. 217–220.
395. Sharpe, *Judicial Punishment*, pp. 30–31.
396. Knafla, "'Sin of all Sorts Swarmeth'"), p. 58.
397. Kinney et al., *Tudor England*, p. 170.
398. Glazebrook, *The Boke of Justices of Peas*, p. Aiii.

burglary, and 3.5 per cent for highway robbery; just five per cent were for homicide, and 5.5 per cent for witchcraft.[399]

Furthermore, a not insignificant number of (usually) minor thefts were still being heard at manorial leets at this time, where these were still operative (see *Chapter 10*). For example, during the 1550s and 1560s, the leet for Stock, in Essex, dealt with almost all local charges of petty larceny. These involved, inter alia, the theft of horseshoes, chickens, pots, aprons, tools and sheepskins that were officially valued at under 12 pence.[400]

Most Tudor property crime was fairly opportunistic, with thieves and even burglars taking advantage of chances to steal unattended goods or break into unsecured premises as they presented themselves. For this reason, in the anonymous (but possibly part-Shakespearean) late-Elizabethan play *Sir John More*, Suresby, a justice sitting at the Newgate Sessions, warns a complainant about displaying extravagant sums of money in public, as it presented an acute temptation to those who might otherwise not have offended: "What makes so many pilferers and felons,/But such fond baits that foolish people lay,/To tempt the needy miserable wretch?".[401]

Many thieves of this type appropriated goods that they found lying readily to hand. For example, in March 1600 the Essex JP Henry Maynard examined ten-year-old Robert Baker, who admitted that he had seen a plough and foot chain in a field near Tiltey, and knocked its coulter off with a mallet. He then hid the coulter and chain in a neighbouring field, subsequently recovering them and selling them to a Thaxted blacksmith. When combined with another chain he had stolen from a different plough, they fetched the modest total of seven pence, making the case one of petty theft.[402]

The theft of clothes and linen left drying on hedges and fences was a particularly frequent form of opportunistic crime. So common was it that the light-fingered Autolycus in *The Winter's Tale* (written about 1610) could note that it was his speciality, not least because it was usually much safer to commit such crimes than more serious offences. As a result, he

---

399. Penry Williams, *The Later Tudors: England, 1547–1603* (Oxford: Oxford University Press, 1995), p. 213.
400. Robey, *The Village of Stock*, pp. 202–206.
401. Act I, Scene 2.
402. ERO Q/SR 149/16.

could observe, "The white sheet bleaching on the hedge/... Doth set my pugging tooth on edge".[403] Frequently the crime was merely indicted as petty theft or down-valued to that amount. For example, in June 1597 John Forde was indicted at the Surrey Assizes, for stealing a pair of sheets (worth four pence), a shirt (valued at three pence), a table napkin (set at two pence), and two aprons (also two pence), for a total of eleven pence, which may well have been the proceeds of such a theft.[404] Basic vigilance could prevent much crime of this type. For example, in the early summer of 1590, it was noted that, after three rogues arrived at Navestock, in Essex, they wandered around the parish, "where one of them wold have stolne chyckens had he not byn espyed by one of the parishyoners".[405]

However, habitual and even "professional" (i.e. highly skilled and sophisticated) criminals also committed property offences. Perhaps unsurprisingly, they were most often encountered in the metropolitan area. For example, in 1552 Henry Machyn referred to a specialist career thief named James Ellis who was tried at the Old Bailey, and considered the greatest "pykpurs and cuttpurs that ever [was ar]raynyd, for ther was never a presun and the Towr but he had byne in them".[406] The usually crowded and busy nave of St Paul's Cathedral in London was just one of many spots that became notorious haunts for such pickpockets. Ellis was a little unlucky. Many criminals of his stamp survived unscathed for decades.[407] In 1585 William Fleetwood, the recorder of London from 1571 to 1591, and also a leading Middlesex and Surrey JP, described how a gentleman merchant named Wotton, who had fallen on hard times, had anticipated Fagin by almost 300 years, and founded a 'school" that would teach cutpurses using a dummy covered with hawk's bells.[408]

Serious habitual crime was not confined to the capital. For example, Sylvester Gest, a butter maker, and John Thomson, a labourer, burgled ten houses, shops, and churches in nine Sussex villages during the autumn of 1568, stealing large quantities of cloth, clothing, and household

403. Act IV, Scene 3.
404. Cockburn, *Calendar of Assize Records. Surrey indictments: Elizabeth I*, p. 454.
405. ERO Q/SR 113/39a.
406. Nichols, *The Diary of Henry Machyn*, pp. 13–21.
407. Gilbert Walker, *A manifest detection of the moste vyle and detestable vse of Diceplay, and other practises lyke the same* (London: Abraham Vele, 1552), pp. D5r–D6r.
408. King, *The Middlesex Justices*, p. 46; Pound, *Poverty and Vagrancy*, p. 92.

furnishings. Four other men were charged with harbouring them in different places. The two burglars were hanged along with three of their abettors.[409] Similarly, Edward Parker was capitally convicted at the Hertford Assizes in March 1598 for ten burglaries and one case of grand larceny, committed between April and December the previous year. Most of his crimes had been committed in and around Chipping Barnet and St Albans.[410] The theft of large animals, especially horses and flocks of sheep, might also attract professional thieves and gangs (see below).

It was often easy to liquidate stolen goods, and hard to prove that their eventual buyers had knowingly purchased them. In the burglary suffered by the wealthy widow Lucy Lacey in the London area in 1530, large amounts of plate, cash, jewellery, and other goods were taken. Much was sent north and sold on to a number of men in Lancashire, Yorkshire, and Westmorland. They included an esquire, a barber, and a "Master Cettle" of the collegiate church of Ripon. Were these men professional fences, totally innocent purchasers or, perhaps most likely, men who had "asked no questions" about the provenance of what they were buying? Significantly, they were not indicted as accessories to the burglary. Instead, Lacey's strategy (presumably based on legal advice) seems to have been to demand the return of her goods, requesting that the men be summoned to the Star Chamber to explain how they came to be in their hands.[411]

In a world in which almost everything, however old or worn, could be (and was) resold, even stealing the most mundane items might be profitable. For example, a man and two women who broke into three houses in Essex on separate occasions during the latter part of 1598 appropriated a very catholic range of domestic goods, including a brass kettle worth ten shillings, six pieces of pewter worth five shillings, 12 pounds of butter worth 3s 4d, four capons worth seven shillings, seven cheeses worth two shillings, a tablecloth, a pair of stockings worth two shillings, a pair of shoes worth 18 pence, a wooden bowl worth the same, three more cheeses worth one shilling, and another brass kettle, worth just ten pence.[412]

---

409. Knafla, "John at Love Killed Her," p. 312.
410. Cockburn, *Calendar of Assize Records. Hertfordshire Indictments: Elizabeth I*, pp. 133–134.
411. McSheffrey, "The Murder of Mistress Lacey's Maid", p. 334.
412. ERO Q/SR 144/5,49,50.

Stolen valuables might be traded with or at goldsmiths, silversmiths, chandlers, alehouses, inns, or other businesses of doubtful probity. Many observers, like Thomas Harman in the 1560s, were inclined to blame the very existence of thieves on the large number of "typlinge Houses in all shires, where they have succour and reliefe; and what so ever they bring, they are sure to receave money for the same".[413] A bill introduced in the House of Lords in 1597 complained that the presence of pawnbrokers encouraged thieves to pursue their wicked way of life in urban areas, helping them liquidate the proceeds of crime. There were several unavailing attempts to improve their statutory regulation during the final years of the Elizabethan period.[414]

Even so, disposing of high-value and readily identifiable items was hazardous for thieves. Unfortunately, the prospective purchasers of their goods could also be endangered. In May 1571 Martin Bullock asked a merchant named Arthur Hall to come to a house in Threadneedle Street, in London, with a view to selling him plate stolen from one Dr Gardner. Unfortunately, Hall recognised Gardner's mark on the valuable items, and announced this to Bullock, who claimed that he had been authorised to sell it on behalf of the doctor. However, suspecting that Hall had detected his crime, he fetched a heavy washing beetle (a bat used for pounding laundry) from the kitchen and, coming up behind the merchant, beat him repeatedly on the head before stabbing him and then cutting his throat. Bullock considered burying the corpse in the cellar, but the narrowness of the stairs and the early onset of rigor mortis prevented this. As a result, he hacked off the dead man's limbs, placed the remains in a chest, and shipped them by boat from the River Thames to Rye as a consignment of books.[415]

Larceny and Benefit of Clergy

At the start of the Tudor era, all forms of grand larceny were subject to benefit of clergy, and most remained so at its end. However, in 1535

---

413. Thomas Harman, *A Caveat or Warning for Common Cursitors, vulgarly called vegabonds* (London: Wylliam Griffith, 1566), p. Aiv.

414. Dean, *Law-Making and Society*, p. 151.

415. T. I., *A World of Wonders*, pp. 1–10.

Parliament denied the privilege to servants who were guilty of stealing goods or cash worth 40 shillings or more from their masters, making it one of the first non-violent property crimes to be withdrawn from clergy (27 Henry VIII c. 17). This was a widespread form of theft, although most domestics restricted themselves to pilfering lower-value goods and commodities. Typical of the latter crime, in 1599, when Thomas Howard, a servant from St Osyth, in Essex, cleansed some wheat for his master, he took the opportunity to keep about half a bushel of the grain for himself.[416]

A few other specialist forms of theft, such as stealing horses, were withdrawn from clergy over the remainder of the century (see below). Even so, thieves who were illiterate still faced death if they were convicted of stealing items of any value, especially during the first half of the era, when the reading test for clergy was conducted quite strictly. This explains why some were prepared to abjure the realm while this privilege still existed, rather than face trial. For example, in October 1519, at Finedon, in Northamptonshire, a man named Maydebury abjured for a number of thefts, including that of 60 pairs of shoes that had been stolen in Northampton many years earlier.[417]

Animal Theft

As with most pre-modern societies, domestic animals were a major store of wealth, and so featured prominently amongst allegations of theft. Stealing animals worth less than one shilling, as was usually the case with individual chickens, ducks, rabbits, and even scrawny geese, would be defined as (non-capital) petty theft, like any other larceny at this value. By contrast, stealing animals worth 12 pence or more (or, some observers thought, *over* a shilling), whether from a field, yard, or barn, was grand larceny. Almost all individual large animals would satisfy this test if properly valued.

For example, sheep were normally worth from three to five shillings, although lambs would be less. Typically, at the assizes held at Brentwood

---

416. ERO Q/SR 145/50.
417. McSheffrey, "Sanctuary Seekers".

(Essex) in February 1559, William Crowche was accused of stealing 20 ewes worth 3s 4d each, and six wether (castrated male) sheep of the same individual value.[418] Similarly, in May 1564 George Marwell of Dartford, in Kent, allegedly stole five sheep that were collectively valued at 24s 6d (about five shillings each); when he stole another five sheep later the same month, they were set at 17 shillings. (Presumably, these animals were thinner.) Pigs might be valued at eight to 12 shillings each, but a few exceeded this amount. Cattle were normally worth much more. In 1569 a butcher named Edward Slyn was convicted of theft at the Dartford Assizes after stealing a large red cow the previous December; it was valued at 33s 4d. In July 1575 John Payne, a Hertfordshire farmer, was convicted of stealing six cows in Norfolk worth a total of £10. (He received benefit of clergy.)[419]

Of course, this did not preclude the complainant's down-valuing stolen animals to make the case one of non-capital petty theft; this appears to have been a little more common with regard to large beasts (especially sheep) in the late sixteenth century than during the 1700s, when JPs and court officers may have frowned on the practice. For example, in 1587 Richard Connye was indicted, convicted, and whipped for petty theft at the Hertford Assizes after John Cox valued his two stolen sheep at the absurdly low value of just ten pence.[420] In an even more extreme case, in 1597 Elizabeth Wolley valued two sheep and three lambs that had been stolen from her by Edward Fenn at Wisley, in Surrey, at a total of just eleven pence.[421] (See *Chapter 14*).

Stealing horses was normally viewed as the most socially damaging form of animal theft because of their importance in transportation and agriculture — by the early sixteenth century, they were beginning to replace ox teams for plough work due to their greater speed and agility on light soils. They were worth far more than most other animals, something that was enhanced by Tudor breeding laws aimed at improving

---

418. ERO T/A 418/1/14.
419. NRO ASSI 35/17/6 m 4.
420. Cockburn, *Calendar of Assize Records. Hertfordshire Indictments: Elizabeth I*, p. 67.
421. Cockburn, *Calendar of Assize Records. Surrey Indictments: Elizabeth I*, p. 444.

the national stock. However, they were vulnerable to theft, often being left tied-up in the streets.[422]

An example of typical equine values can be seen in a case from August 1596, in which a grand jury found a true bill against John Freeman, a horse thief from Kentish Town, in Middlesex, who was accused of stealing a grey trotting gelding worth £5, an "amblinge" gelding valued at the same amount, a bay gelding worth £3, and an inferior "black nagge" worth just 40 shillings.[423] Very bad horses might be worth less, sometimes under a pound, while good ones could be more. Henry Willard, a labourer from Dartford, was convicted after he stole a grey horse, allegedly worth £6 13s 4d. Exceptional animals might be valued at well over £10.

During the early decades of the sixteenth century, it was feared that horse theft was increasing across much of the country. In February 1518 the Marquess of Dorset wrote to Cardinal Wolsey, noting that a tailor named James Higgenson had stolen two animals from the stable of George Hynde, but been captured at Doncaster. He complained, "Such stealing of horses as is in these quarters I have not much heard of before".[424] As a result, the crime was differentiated from other grand larcenies, and withdrawn from clergy in 1545 (37 Hen. VIII, c. 8, s. 2), the horse becoming the only animal to achieve this status in the Tudor or Stuart eras; sheep and cattle did not follow suit until the eighteenth century, although there were several abortive parliamentary attempts to bring about such a change during the Elizabethan period.

As a consequence, four trials for horse theft held at the Lent Assizes at Croydon in 1569, which all produced convictions, also ended in death sentences. By contrast, William Martin, from Wimbledon in Surrey, who was convicted of stealing ten sheep worth 30 shillings at the same sessions, could read and was allowed clergy, despite the significant value of his crime.[425] Similarly, at the Epiphany Quarter Sessions for Essex in

---

422. Peter Edwards, *The Horse Trade of Tudor and Stuart England* (Cambridge: Cambridge University Press, 1988), p. 108.
423. Jeaffreson, *Middlesex County Records: Vol. 1*, pp. 230–235.
424. Brewer, *Letters and Papers, Foreign and Domestic, Henry VIII, Vol. 2*, pp. 1220–1236.
425. Cockburn, *Calendar of Assize Records. Surrey Indictments: Elizabeth I*, pp. 414–418.

1591, John Cherry of Toppesfield pleaded guilty to breaking into a close and stealing a horse worth £5. He was duly sentenced to death.[426]

Even so, concern about horse theft did not abate, so that in 1555 a law was introduced requiring that all transactions involving their sale be recorded (another Marian legal reform). It was quickly thought to be inadequate. In 1586 a further bill "for restraining of Horse-stealing" was rejected in the Commons. However, another, based on an official (rather than purely private) initiative, was successful in 1589. This statute noted that the existing regime of controls had "not wrought soe good effect for the repressing or avoydinge of Horse stealinge as was expected". It claimed that the level of horse theft throughout the country was so high that even stabled animals were not safe because of the rapidity with which stolen animals could be sold in markets and fairs that were distant from their owner's residence.

The 1589 statute ordered all those selling horses to register with market officials, and required that such a seller produce someone to vouch for his identity (name, occupation, and residence). A copy of the bill of sale was to be given to the purchaser for a fee of two pence. The Act also allowed those whose horses had been stolen to recover them from the eventual purchaser, at the price that the latter had paid for the animal, for up to six months after the sale. There was an unsuccessful attempt in 1601 to make any selling of horses without proper vouchers felony, but one experienced MP who was also a JP warned on the bill's second reading that the provision requiring two vouchers for such sales was asking too much.

In practice it seems that the provisions of both the 1555 and 1589 statutes were often circumvented or simply ignored. However, they were not entirely ineffective. In 1598 a thief from Staffordshire stole a horse and rode it to Market Drayton, in Shropshire, intending to sell it there. When he was told that he could not sell it without someone to vouch for him, he abandoned his plan and turned around, intending to return the animal. Unfortunately, on the way back, he tried to sell it again and was arrested.[427]

---

426. ERO Q/SR 115/117.
427. Edwards, *Horse Trade*, p. 110.

The Modus Operandi of Animal Theft

The theft of large animals ranged from opportunistic crimes committed by poor individuals to those perpetrated by well-organized criminal networks, stealing on a commercial scale for resale. Theft by the former would usually involve taking a single animal, often a sheep, much less commonly a pig (unlikely to be kept isolated in fields), particularly in winter, when food supplies were short. Frequently the theft would be for personal consumption. For example, on Christmas Day 1596, a JP examined Peter Danyel after the borsholder (constable) of Sennock, in Kent, searched his house and discovered a large amount of mutton "part baked in pyes and the rest hidden in his bed". Danyel quickly confessed and told the magistrate that being driven by "greate necessitie" he broke into the grounds of a widow in Otford, where he took and killed a ewe. He partially butchered it in the field, leaving its skin and head in a hedge and taking the rest home. (He subsequently pleaded guilty to grand larceny and was clergied.)[428]

Similarly, late one August night in 1601, two men who were travelling with a cart from Faversham to Great Chart (both in Kent), could not resist the temptation to steal and slaughter a sheep they passed near Maidstone. When they got home they divided the carcass. Obviously, they had to be swift and discreet when using the meat, to avoid both discovery and putrefaction. When later examined by a local JP, the daughter of one family that received half the animal noted that they had gorged on mutton: a shoulder for dinner, two pieces for supper, and another for breakfast the next day. (One of the men subsequently stood trial at quarter sessions.)[429]

At the other extreme of large-animal theft, Thomas Harman, writing in the 1560s, thought that many professional horse thieves travelled around the country looking for animals to steal. If challenged, they claimed to be lost. Christopher Phillips, who was originally from Hockley, in Essex, was one of them, being capitally convicted at the Hertford Assizes in July

---

428. Melling, *Crime and Punishment*, p. 38.
429. Knafla, *Kent at Law 1602*, pp. 171–172.

1586 for stealing more than 20 horses on 15 occasions.[430] (His accessory was not captured.) Similarly, in June 1600 Henry Bowyer was accused of stealing a "baye nagg worth forty shillings" from William Crowther, and was the subject of nine other indictments for stealing horses in and about London (mainly the parishes to the East of the city, such as Stepney and Bethnal Green), from different people, on various dates during the previous year.[431] Just before his execution, following conviction at the York Assizes in 1617, Francis Hetherington admitted to stealing more than 100 horses during his criminal career.[432]

The theft of entire herds of cattle or flocks of sheep might also be the province of professional criminals. For example, in January 1511 a man named Gye sought sanctuary in Durham Cathedral because the previous May he had stolen 20 cows near Easington, in Yorkshire, and sold them to the prior of Bridlington monastery. A few months later he had stolen four heifers from the same area and sold them in Walton on the Wolds.[433] The large-scale theft of sheep was much more common than that of cattle. For example, in November 1555 Andrew Cooke was convicted of stealing a dozen wether sheep at Edmonton, in Middlesex.[434] Henry Denman, a petty chapman (a peddler who went on foot) from Southwark, went even further, and was responsible for the theft of 49 sheep at Ewell, in Surrey, on a November day in 1584; he was aided by a butcher named William Raynolls. (Denman had several other court appearances under his belt and was thought to have been clergied on an earlier occasion). In the same county, during the autumn of 1594, Thomas Cuddington stole seven sheep on one occasion, four a week later, and two lambs a month after that.[435] At the Essex Assizes held at Brentwood in July 1585, William Brighte was convicted of stealing 37 sheep and 25 lambs in Roding. (He had been convicted and clergied at the same forum for the theft of seven sheep worth 40 shillings in July 1580.)

430. Cockburn, *Calendar of Assize Records: Hertfordshire Indictments: Elizabeth I*, p. 62.
431. Jeaffreson, *Middlesex County Records: Vol. 1*, pp. 257–266.
432. Edwards, *The Horse Trade*, pp. 119–120.
433. Shannon McSheffrey, "Sanctuary Seekers in England, 1380–1557".
434. Jeaffreson, *Middlesex County Records: Vol. 1*, p. 25.
435. Cockburn, *Calendar of Assize Records. Surrey Indictments. Elizabeth I*, p. 410.

Of course, many who stole animals did not specialise in a single species. At the start of 1591 Israel Amyce (1548–1607), an Essex JP, examined John Brown, who apparently confessed to having been tried at the previous Suffolk Assizes in Bury for stealing four sheep (presumably he was acquitted or clergied). However, he was also "vehemently suspected in these parts to be a notable horse-stealer".[436] George Osborne of Hazeleigh, who was tried at the Essex Assizes held at Chelmsford in March 1592 for stealing a boar from John Argent, had been allowed clergy for the theft of a variety of livestock in 1591.

Hiding flocks of sheep and herds of cattle was inherently difficult, and where such thefts occurred magistrates would often request that extensive and urgent searches be made for the missing animals. In March 1593 Sir Edmund Bowyer (1552–1627), a Surrey JP (and qualified but non-practising lawyer) ordered that constables in the county search all suspicious places for sheep that had been stolen from one William Sherfield in Putney.[437]

Butchers

William Raynolls' involvement in this type of crime is unsurprising. Numerous other men in the same profession also took part. For example, in January 1582 Henry Ashewell, a London butcher, was accused of stealing 17 wethers and two ewes, together worth £6, at Hoxton, in Middlesex.[438] Butchers slaughtered the meat they sold, swiftly making a stolen animal unrecognisable, and greatly reducing the prospects of detection or of a successful prosecution if they were suspected. As a result, they were heavily, and quite disproportionately, involved in stealing animals, as they would be for centuries to come. For example, in Elizabethan Essex, 46 cases of animal theft (at both jury forums) involved butchers; some other cases have probably been lost. They tended to be fairly catholic in the animals they stole (sheep, cattle, etc.), although, because the English already had something of an aversion to eating horseflesh,

---

436. ERO Q/SR 115/27.
437. SHC 643/1/58.
438. Jeaffreson, *Middlesex County Records: Vol. 1*, pp. 129–135.

and to avoid the greater risks attendant on the crime, none involved horses. This meant that all were cases of clergyable grand larceny; about a quarter of these prosecutions ended with convictions, but the butcher concerned successfully claimed his "book".[439]

Selling Stolen Animals

If valuable animals, particularly horses but also cattle and flocks of sheep, were stolen for resale, it could be dangerous for the thief to offer them at a nearby market or fair, as their true owners were likely to go there quickly to inspect any animals being sold. John Oborne discovered this to his cost in the 1580s, when he tried to sell an ox at Warwick Fair that he had stolen in a nearby village.[440] As a result, stolen animals would often be sold at fairs and markets that were distant from the crime scene.[441] For example, in December 1532 Thomas Richardson took sanctuary in the church at Grove, in Nottinghamshire, and abjured in front of a local coroner, confessing that four days earlier he had stolen two cows at Kirton in Lindsey, in Lincolnshire, before taking them to North Clay, in Nottinghamshire, and selling them.[442] Similarly, in a letter of 1574, the Surrey JP John Skinner observed that he had caught a thief a few days earlier who had stolen a horse in Hertfordshire and sold it at St James' Fair at Charlwood in his own county.[443]

The preamble to the 1589 statute that regulated the sale of horses acknowledged this problem, noting that the crime had become widespread because of the "redye buyinge of the same by Horscorses and others in some open Fayres or Markettes farr distant from the Owner, and with such speede as the Owner cannot by pursuit possible helpe the same".[444] Steps would also be taken to disguise the appearance of animals, by trimming their manes and tails, and staining over blazes and stars, or

439. Emmison, *Elizabethan Life: Disorder*, pp. 285–286.
440. Thomas Kemp (ed.), *The Book of John Fisher, Town Clerk and Deputy Recorder of Warwick 1580–1588* (Warwick: Henry Cooke & Son, 1910), p. 50.
441. Harrison, *A Description of England*, p. 230.
442. McSheffrey, "Sanctuary Seekers".
443. SHC LM/COR/3/159.
444. Edwards, *The Horse Trade*, p. 112.

even their entire skins. Gypsies quickly acquired a reputation for being adept at this type of work.

A consideration of all thefts of large animals (i.e. ignoring those involving rabbits and poultry) prosecuted in Essex for the 45 years of the Elizabethan period, whether at assizes, quarter sessions, or (very rarely) Queen's Bench, provides a valuable profile for this type of crime, at least in the South-east of the country. Gaps in county records for these years mean that the figures below can probably, and very approximately, be increased by ten per cent for the full totals indicted.

The (prosecuted) theft of pigs was rare in the county, presumably because of their relatively modest value (compared to that of horses and cattle), size, intractable nature, slow speed, and the conditions in which they were usually held (in close proximity to their owners' homes or in outbuildings). Just 12 cases, involving 75 pigs, together worth only £32, were prosecuted in Essex during this time. Perhaps unsurprisingly, sheep (including rams and lambs) were the most commonly stolen animal; 2,834 sheep, worth a total of £541, came to court in 251 cases. However, individually, horses were much more valuable. The thefts of 289 animals were tried in 122 cases, the animals stolen being worth £827 (an average of almost £3). Cattle featured much more prominently than in many other English counties at this time, due in part to the county's rich riverine pastures and its proximity to the London market; animals from elsewhere in the country were fattened up prior to being sent on to the capital. The thefts of 660 cows, oxen, calves, bullocks, etc., worth £881, were indicted in 138 cases in Elizabethan Essex.[445]

The theft of large animals, especially horses, was overwhelmingly a male crime, not least because women attempting to sell on such animals would quickly excite suspicion. For example, men committed all 23 cases that were prosecuted at the great sessions and quarter sessions in Cheshire during the 1590s.[446] However, there were very occasional exceptions in other parts of the country.

---

445. Emmison, *Elizabethan Life: Disorder*, p. 316.
446. Garthine Walker, "Women, Theft and the World of Stolen Goods", in Jenny Kermode and Garthine Walker (eds.), *Women, Crime and the Courts in Early Modern England* (London: UCL Press, 1994), p. 82.

Poultry Theft

The theft of poultry, whether the birds were hens, ducks, or geese, was usually the province of opportunist thieves, often seeking meat for personal or family consumption. Typically, in 1598 two labourers from Rickling, in Essex, stole a goose from Alice Wheatley in the same village. She charitably valued it at ten pence (petty theft), although it was probably worth slightly more, unless very scrawny.[447] In a more extreme case, in April 1599 Thomas Barnard of Bardfield, in Essex, was examined by the JP Henry Maxey, and admitted that the previous year he had killed five geese with his "piece" during the night and carried them home to his house, where, he claimed (slightly implausibly), he devoured all of them with the help of just one other man. The pair must have gorged themselves for several days.[448]

However, like butchers, those who dealt in poultry might steal fowl on a regular and largescale basis. For example, at the Hertford Assizes in March 1585, Richard Hayward, a poulterer from Much Hadham, was accused of stealing 26 cocks, hens, capons, and pullets on three occasions. Even where it was conducted on a quasi-professional basis, the theft of birds appears to have occasioned less concern than that of larger animals. Hayward was merely convicted on one count that was down-valued to ten pence; he was whipped and discharged.[449]

Far more women became involved in the theft of poultry than of large animals, although they still made up a clear minority of defendants. Thus Mary Greene stole nine hens, in two thefts, in her home village of Great Parndon, in Essex. In both cases the birds were down-valued to a penny each so that she was merely whipped when convicted.[450] In 1598 Rose Herse, a spinster from Maldon, was acquitted outright of stealing three hens worth three shillings and a chicken valued at just four pence.[451] Frequently females stole birds for the family pot, but a few took poultry to sell. For example, a pair of women from London, Elizabeth Audley

447. Cockburn, *Calendar of Assize Records. Essex Indictments, Elizabeth I*, p. 487.
448. ERO Q/SR 145/46.
449. Cockburn, *Calendar of Assize Records. Hertfordshire Indictments: Elizabeth I*, p. 55.
450. Cockburn, *Calendar of Assize Records. Essex Indictments: Elizabeth I*, p. 225.
451. ERO Q/SR 140/158.

and Margaret Clinton, stole "twelve hens" and a "turky cock and turky hen" (worth five shillings) from an unknown man in Grays, Essex, on a single occasion.[452] This cannot have been for personal consumption.

Burglary and Housebreaking

Until about the middle of the fifteenth century, breaking into a building to commit theft was usually viewed as an aggravating feature of the larceny, rather than a specific crime. However, by the 1450s burglary had appeared as a felony in its own right, although the word itself was far more ancient. Vitally, by early in the Tudor period it was generally accepted that it was committed on entry to domestic premises with intent to commit a felony, even if nothing was ultimately stolen or any occupant raped or murdered; this clearly distinguished it from theft. As was noted in 1506, for those that "breketh houses by nyght to the entent to robbe though they take no thinge awaye it is burglary".[453] For example, at the assizes held at Chelmsford in July 1559, Geoffrey Cater was indicted for burglariously breaking into a widow's house and stealing her "women's peticots". Although no value was given to this garment, so that it might have been worth less than a shilling, he was sentenced to death on conviction.[454] Even more notably, shortly before midnight in September 1600, Francis Pigott and two other men "burglariously" broke into the house of one William Fitzwilliams in St John's Street, in Middlesex, with the intention of stealing his goods and (allegedly) murdering him. They do not seem to have succeeded in either aim, but pleaded guilty and were sentenced to death.[455]

In practice, a felonious intent was often assumed from a nocturnal breaking and entering, which did have to be clearly established, although it did not require that damage be inflicted on the building concerned;

---

452. Cockburn, *Calendar of Assize Records. Essex Indictments, Elizabeth I*, p. 328.
453. Glazebrook, *The Boke of Justices of Peas*, p. Aiii.
454. Cockburn, *Calendar of Assize Records. Essex Indictments: Elizabeth I*, p. 8.
455. Jeaffreson, *Middlesex County Records: Vol. 1*, pp. 257–266.

opening an unsecured window could be enough. Nevertheless, walking in through an already open door did not constitute "breaking in".[456]

By the end of the fifteenth century, it was also well-established that the crime had to take place at night. Thomas Marowe mentioned this relatively new requirement in his reading in Inner Temple in 1503. The *Boke of Justyces of Peas* of 1506 defined night as occurring after sunset and before sunrise, although this could occasion problems during twilight on cloudy evenings, especially in built-up areas, something that eventually led to a focus on an observer's ability to make out a man's facial features; as Coke was to observe in his *Institutes*, night had fallen when it was too dark to "discerne the countenance of a man".

Early in the Tudor period, some (but by no means all) observers thought that it was necessary that someone be in the building at the time the burglary took place, and this was alluded to by statute in 1511 and 1531. Presumably, this was why, in 1560, it was expressly noted, when Benedict Ellys was indicted for burglary at Oxted, in Surrey, that John Wever, his wife, and his servant had all been in the house at the relevant time.[457] However, this requirement, insofar as it ever existed, had been long abandoned by the end of the era, and it ceased to matter that no-one was at home when premises were burgled.

Nevertheless, it was necessary that the building be a residence, whether humble or grand, even if temporarily unoccupied when a crime occurred. If a man had a house, and he and his family left it for a short period "and in the meane time one doth come, and breake the house in the night, to commit felony, this is Burglary".[458] Breaking into commercial buildings did not constitute burglary during the Tudor era, although the notion of a dwelling was eventually expanded to include outbuildings adjacent to the house that were enclosed by a common fence. As a result, in 1579, when William Stevens broke into an unoccupied shop

---

456. Helen A. Anderson, "From the Thief in the Night to the Guest Who Stayed Too Long: The Evolution of Burglary in the Shadow of the Common Law", *Indiana Law Review*, Vol. 45, p. 633.

457. Cockburn, *Calendar of Assize Records. Surrey Indictments Elizabeth I*, p. 10.

458. Pulton, *De Pace Regis*, p. 132.

in Southwark during the night, and stole £10 in cash, he was simply indicted and convicted of grand larceny.[459]

Burglary had a complicated sixteenth century history in connection with benefit of clergy. For the first 75 years of the century, most forms of the crime were clergyable. However, in 1547 the privilege was withdrawn (5 & 6 Edw. VI c. 9 s. 4) when the house was occupied and its occupants put in fear while the offence was committed. As a consequence, when, at the Southwark Assizes in March 1563, John Goddard, was convicted of burglary after breaking into an empty dwelling house in Camberwell, and stealing a blanket and linen, he was still able to claim clergy.[460] In 1576 all forms of burglary were unequivocally withdrawn from benefit of clergy (18 Eliz. I c. 7), making its legal differentiation from grand larceny vitally important. As a result, when George Greene was convicted of burglary at the Old Bailey in 1602, for breaking into Fulham Palace, the house of the Bishop of London, and stealing five carpets worth £10, he was immediately sentenced to death.[461]

Housebreaking — forcing entry to a domestic dwelling to steal during the day — remained an aggravating feature of grand larceny, rather than a discrete crime until well into the Tudor period. Nevertheless (and like burglary), under a statute from 1547, if the premises were occupied when it occurred, and those inside were put in "fear and dread", the crime became unclergyable (5 & 6 Edw. VI c. 9 s. 4).[462] In the absence of these circumstances, it remained simple theft until very late in the sixteenth century. As a result, William Hill merely committed grand larceny (and was clergied) when he broke into a house in Wimbledon during the day in May 1580, and stole a gold ring worth 14 shillings. Similarly, in 1591, when Thomas Netlingham was convicted for the same crime after daylight housebreaking and burglary of a residence at Coulsdon, in Surrey, in which he stole clothes, shoes, and £5 6s in cash, he was allowed to plead his clergy.[463]

---

459. Cockburn, *Calendar of Assize Records. Surrey indictments: Elizabeth I*, p. 184.
460. Ibid, p. 30.
461. Jeaffreson, *Middlesex County Records: Vol. 1*, pp. 276–287.
462. Baker, *Oxford History*, p. 57.
463. Cockburn, *Calendar of Assize Records. Surrey Indictments: Elizabeth I*, p. 203 and p. 376.

However, by a statute from 1597 (39. El. I c. 15), clergy was also taken away from housebreakers who stole money or goods to the value of five shillings or more from any dwelling, outhouse or warehouse, even if they were unoccupied when the crime occurred, so that, in Ferdinando Pulton's words, the offence became "as penall as Burglary".[464] Even so, many housebreakings did not meet these prerequisites (whether of occupation or value) or, even if they did, were merely indicted as simple grand larceny.

Burglary was particularly feared, as it took place at night, in the dark, and so raised at least the possibility of serious violence. As a result, it was only rarely pardoned. Householders who had been roused from their slumbers might confront dangerous intruders. For example, in October 1556 a gang of men and women used a ten-year-old to gain entry to Henry Peter's house in Essex while he was away and his wife was sleeping there alone. The boy broke a hole through part of a wall and crept into it to open a door to the adults, who then lit a candle and entered the premises. Peter's wife was held at knifepoint and warned she would be killed if she made a noise. The burglars then broke open a chest using a dagger and took cash, a coat, two petticoats, and a sheet.[465]

At least Mrs Peter survived: fatalities could easily ensue. For example, in April 1560 Henry Phillips of Ringmer, in Sussex, was capitally convicted after he broke into a house and strangled its female occupant with a towel before stealing silver ornaments.[466] In October the following year, Thomas Harte was tried for a murder and burglary committed in a house at Great Clacton, in Essex; he had (allegedly) killed the occupier with a sword (he was acquitted).[467] Medieval burglary victims had often been killed because it was easier and safer for their assailants than tying them up.[468] This continued to be the case during the Tudor era. In 1530 the home of the wealthy widow Lucy Lacey near London was "cased" by one of her own servants, who brought in assistance from outside to

---

464. Arthur Lyon Cross, "The English Criminal Law and Benefit of Clergy During the Eighteenth and Early Nineteenth Centuries", *The American Historical Review*, Vol. 22, No. 3, p. 561.
465. ERO Q/SR 173/110.
466. Cockburn, *Calendar of Assize Records. Sussex Indictments: Elizabeth I*, p. 11.
467. Cockburn, *Calendar of Assize Records. Essex Indictments: Elizabeth I*, p. 122.
468. Hanawalt, "Violent Death", pp. 297–320.

carry out the crime. One morning, while Lacey was at Mass, they struck. The widow's maid was tied up and gagged and put under a mattress in an upstairs room. However, she continued to make a noise. One of the outsiders then went upstairs and killed her, so that "crye they herde her no more".[469]

If local men perpetrated the crime, the occupants of burgled premises might have to be killed to prevent them from identifying the intruders. For example, in January 1599, a wealthy widow named Alice Green and her servant Agnes Beard were murdered, and the former's two dogs killed, when intruders broke into her home at Poole, in Dorset. More than a decade later, in 1610, the daughter of Gowin Spencer, a (by then dead) perpetrator of the crime, provided an account of the murders that she had obviously heard from her father or others who were involved. The intruders had suddenly come across Agnes and fractured her skull. They then went into the hall where Alice Green was eating her supper, where Robert Hill "with his pressing iron strake the said Alice in the head and the said Gowin Spencer and Parmiter in like manner did thrust her into the temples of the head with the said Bodkin; and also then killed the two little dogs by her". The men then made off with cash, jewels, and gold.[470]

Furthermore, burglars could be brutal about extracting information from householders. At the Essex Assizes held at Chelmsford in July 1587, three men were accused of a burglary conducted with many others whose identities were still unknown. It was alleged that, shortly after midnight the previous May, they had broken into a house in Stebbing and assaulted Henry Purkas and his wife, Agnes, as well as five other people who were in the building, putting them in fear of their lives, so that they would reveal where valuables were concealed.[471] In 1593 Robert Coall and Edward Frimley, petty constables for Chertsey, in Surrey, noted that a gang had been perpetrating burglaries in the county during which occupants were placed in fear of being tortured as well as robbed. Some had been tormented with firebrands and lit candles to make them reveal where their money was hidden.[472]

---

469. McSheffrey, "The Murder of Mistress Lacey's Maid", p. 334.
470. Poole Record Office, DC-PL/C/H/1 and DC-PL/B/1/1a/2.
471. ERO Ass 35/29/2/40.
472. SHC LM/COR/3/523.

However, juries considering a burglary indictment could, in appropriate circumstances, convict of a lesser offence—usually simple (clergyable) grand larceny or even petty theft—if they found larceny made out but one of the prerequisites for the crime indicted missing, or did not wish to return a capital conviction (see *Chapter 14*). For example, at the Essex Assizes held at Chelmsford in February 1598, it was alleged that Edward Peacock of Shenfield had broken into the house of Edward Butler while his family was inside, near midnight, and stolen flaxen cloth worth 30 shillings. He pleaded not guilty. The jury convicted of "felony" (grand larceny), but not of burglary, although it must have been dark. As a result, Peacock could claim, and was duly awarded, benefit of clergy.[473]

Robbery

Robbery involved stealing with the use or threat of violence. It was a felony, whatever the value of property or cash taken, even if far less than one shilling (unlike theft at this value), including a "peny or lesse". This was because it posed an immediate threat to life.[474] Many observers shared Sir John Fortescue's late medieval belief that this crime was particularly prevalent amongst Englishmen, especially when conducted on the roads, which were by far the most common source of indictments for it. More than a century later, Robert Parsons was still deploring the great number of "thieves that rob and steal upon the High-ways in England, more than likely in any other Country of the World". A tacit popular respect for such felons can even be identified. Fortescue thought their courage markedly superior to that of their French counterparts. In 1572 Thomas Wilson claimed that in England such men were called "tall felowe[s]".

The attractions of this form of crime were obvious. Highway robbery, whether committed by mounted men or those on foot, could be highly lucrative, provided the correct victims were targeted, in a society in which there was little alternative to carrying large amounts of cash by road, and in which some people wore valuables for display. For example, in 1594 Thomas Thoresbye pleaded guilty to a robbery committed with two other

473. ERO T/A 418/65/49.
474. Glazebrook, *The Boke of Justices of Peas*, p. Bi.

men (still at large) near the highway in Lincoln's Inn Fields. They had assaulted and beaten Thomas Sone and robbed him of £100 in money.[475]

Major arterial routes in particular, such as the highways from London to the West and North of England, attracted robbers, especially if they also had good cover close to the road. Thus, at the Southwark Assizes in January 1560, William Allen, a London yeoman, was convicted of robbing John Appowell on the road near Egham the previous July. He had stolen £4 in money and a gold signet ring. In 1563 George Vale, a labourer from Southwark, was convicted at the same forum of robbing John Hooker in much the same place in September the previous year. He had done far better than Allen, taking £26 13s in cash and his victim's horse.[476]

There were two types of highway robbers. By the end of the Tudor era, the long-lasting social distinction between the supposedly more genteel mounted highwaymen, as they would be termed by the early sixteenth century, and poorer, horseless, "padders" (footpads), was already well established. The author Samuel Rid thought, "The first sort are called gentlemen robbers, or thieves, and these ride on horses well appointed, and go in show like honest men. The other rob on foot, and have no other help but a pair of light heels and a thick wood". Rid believed that the former were often impoverished gentlemen or discharged soldiers who could not turn their hands to an honest mode of living.[477]

Well-born robbers were not a new phenomenon in the sixteenth century. There had been a medieval tradition of robber barons, albeit that this quickly waned during the late fifteenth and early sixteenth centuries. Nevertheless, although their numbers were probably exaggerated, some upper-class highwaymen can be identified to the end of the era. For example, in June 1580 the Privy Council wrote to Sir William More, the Sheriff of Surrey and Sussex, ordering him to apprehend the gang suspected of a robbery committed near the court while it was in Surrey. Apparently, Thomas Lewknor, the son or grandson of Lady Jane

---

475. Jeaffreson, *Middlesex County Records: Vol. 1*, pp. 219–225.
476. Cockburn, *Calendar of Assize Records. Surrey Indictments: Elizabeth I*, 1980, p. 29.
477. Samuel Rid, *Martin Markall, Beadle of Bridewell*, in A. V. Judges (ed.), *The Elizabethan Underworld* (London: George Routledge, 1930), pp. 415–416.

Lewknor of Trotton, in Sussex, was its leader.[478] Perhaps significantly, Sir John Falstaff, one of the main characters in *Henry IV, Part 1*, was not just a knight, but also a dissolute thief, highwayman, and robber, albeit a comical one.

At the start of the Tudor period, many such robbers necessarily worked in small bands, and this continued to be the case throughout the era.[479] For example, in 1575 five men assaulted Mathew Davy while he was on the highway in Hackney, in Middlesex. They robbed him of the valuable cloth and clothes that he was carrying for his master, as well as his own cash, cloak, sword, and dagger. Four of the men were subsequently arrested, convicted, and sentenced to death.[480]

However, improvements in firearms technology, such as the advent of the wheellock and snaplock pistols, and their increasing availability, meant that robbery by pairs of mounted highwaymen, and sometimes even single individuals, became more viable after the middle of the sixteenth century (although their "glory days" of the early 1700s still lay far in the future). In 1575 the Privy Council noted, in a letter to the Lord Keeper and the Lord Treasurer, that Queen Elizabeth had been concerned that, among highwaymen, it was becoming a "common thing for the thieves to carry pistols whereby they either murder out of hand before they rob, or else put her subjects in such fear that they dare not resist".[481]

Various stratagems were adopted to deal with this problem. Early in her reign Queen Elizabeth issued a proclamation prohibiting travellers from carrying daggers and handguns without a valid warrant or authorisation. Those who did so were to be imprisoned until they paid a fine. It was hoped that this would make it difficult to conceal weapons while on the roads. At the start of 1561 the Privy Council, sitting at Westminster, ordered sheriffs and JPs to enforce this proclamation. They were also to appoint "honest" men (not innkeepers) in towns that were situated on main roads to help arrest those who violated it, and to bind all publicans

478. SHC 6729/13/31.
479. Fortescue, *The Governance of England*, pp. 141–2.
480. Jeaffreson, *Middlesex County Records: Vol. 1*, pp. 90–96.
481. Historical Manuscripts Commission, *Calendar of the Cecil Papers at Hatfield House, Vol. 2, 1572–1582* (London: HMSO, 1888), p. 123.

and alehouse keepers to inform their local mayor or constable immediately such armed men entered their premises.[482]

Even so, the proclamation was widely disregarded. In December 1575 the Privy Council also expressed concern about the large number of "tall" men claiming to be discharged soldiers from Ireland or the Irish conflict, who went about the highways near London and other towns, begging and robbing when an opportunity to do so presented itself.[483] The Queen issued another proclamation in 1594, emphasising that the Statute of Northampton prohibited not just the "open carrying" of certain weapons, but also the secret carrying of "small Dagges [pistols], commonly called pocket Dags". Six years later, she again ordered JPs to enforce the statute according to its true meaning, which prohibited carrying "Pistols, Birding pieces, and other short pieces" that could readily be concealed.

Highwaymen would often move around the country to avoid suspicion, and some became adept at disguising themselves. In 1592 one claimed that he was a master in this regard: "For I had first for my selfe an artificiall haire, and a beard so naturally made, that I could talke, dine, and sup in it, and yet it should never bee spied". He also had a reversible cloak that he could turn inside out to change his appearance. Allegedly, he could rob a man in the morning and dine with him at an inn in the evening, without being recognised. Equal efforts were made to disguise his horse (usually as distinctive to contemporary observers as the men who rode them). He did this by use of an "artificiall taile so cunningly counterfeited, that the Ostler when hee drest him could not perceiue it".[484]

Though frequently brutal to their victims, mounted highwaymen enjoyed an (often) undeserved reputation in some quarters for gallantry. However, there was very rarely anything remotely genteel about footpads. They were usually armed with clubs and knives rather than firearms, even at the end of the period, and were normally dependent on a sudden and violent attack from cover (bushes or trees), often in lonely or isolated spots where vegetation was fairly close to a main road, although brush

---

482. SHC 6729/10/22.
483. Historical Manuscripts Commission, *Calendar of the Cecil Papers*, p. 123.
484. Arthur F. Kinney (ed.), *Rogues, Vagabonds and Sturdy Beggars: New Gallery of Tudor and Early Stuart Rogue Literature* (Amherst: University Massachusetts Press, 1990), p. 197.

was supposed to be cleared from either side of the highway to prevent this. They were more likely to be local to the places where they robbed than were mounted robbers. Typically, at the assizes held at Brentwood in July 1578, Philip Rayneberd, a labourer from Runwell, was indicted for assaulting the Reverend John Coxe with a cudgel, on a road near his village, and stealing a hat worth two shillings.[485]

Footpads would sometimes have recourse to various ruses to get close to their victims. For example, in one case a carrier who was new to his trade was on the highway near Melton Mowbray, in Leicestershire, when he heard an unseen woman crying and moaning for help from behind a hedge next to the road. His companion on the wagon warned him about the treachery that might be behind such "dissembling cryes". Nevertheless, the carrier insisted in going to the woman's assistance. He jumped over the hedge, but was grabbed by the throat, and, if his companion had not rescued him, would have "beene robbed and murthered".[486]

Fraud

The Tudor period inherited the medieval notion that trespassory taking from the owner of property was an essential element of larceny.[487] Those who legally acquired possession over chattels that they did not own (bailees) were often not subject to criminal (as opposed to civil) liability for any subsequent misappropriation. However, in 1473 limitations were placed on the ambit of this rule in *The Carrier's Case,* decided in the Star Chamber; it held that if someone transporting a "bulk" of merchandise (in this case, bundles of woad) on behalf of someone else broke it open ("breaking bulk") to convert the goods to his own use, he would commit theft.[488] Other exceptions slowly followed. Thus servants were denied immunity for items received from their employers by statute in 1529 (21 Hen. 8 c. 7). Nevertheless, wrongful acquisition of property by fraud or artifice, in which the owner voluntarily parted with possession, was not

---

485. ERO T/A 418/30/1.
486. T. I., *A World of Wonders*, pp. 1–48.
487. Anon, "Possession and Custody in the Law of Larceny", *Yale Law Journal*, Vol. 30, No. 6, pp. 613–617.
488. *The Carrier's Case* (1473), YB. Pasch. 13 Edw. IV, f. 9., pl. 5.

normally deemed to be theft until *Pear's Case* introduced the doctrine of larceny by trick (at least in some circumstances) in 1779.

Even if goods were secured by a trick, the crime might not be viewed very seriously. Many such frauds were viewed as simple misdemeanours, even where they involved high-value items or large sums of money and a sophisticated *modus operandi*, and were punished accordingly. For example, in 1577 Benjamin Dale used counterfeit letters written in the name of one Josias Meuse and addressed to James Normanton of Mile End, in Middlesex, to induce the latter to deliver into his keeping a gelding belonging to the real Mr Meuse. Having fraudulently gained possession of the animal, he quickly sold it on. On conviction, it was ordered that Dale be fined 40 shillings and pilloried in Cheapside.[489] If he had simply stolen the horse, he would have committed an unclergyable felony and necessarily been sentenced to death.

---

489. Jeaffreson, *Middlesex County Records: Vol. 1*, pp. 103–111.

CHAPTER 20

General Conclusion

Almost all eras are "transitional", and the Tudor period was no exception, covering much of the interstitial stage between the medieval and modern eras. Unsurprisingly, the English criminal justice system saw major change between 1485 and 1603. Much of this was spontaneous. The distinguished legal historian S F C Milsom famously observed that, although great legal decisions are rare, "great consequences often follow from measures taken to meet immediate problems".[490] This is particularly apposite to any consideration of the sixteenth century justice system; change was often unplanned, the result of short-term expediency and the need to address pressing problems rather than the fruit of deep reflection and consideration.

Such "organic" change was not a new phenomenon even then. When Henry VII came to the throne he inherited a system that had been in a process of gradual transition for more than a century, with the roles of, inter alia, JPs, constables, and juries (both grand and petty) already having changed significantly since the Black Death of 1348, to deal with a radically altered society, and continuing to do so during his reign. Thus trial juries became ever more reliant on in-court evidence, and grand juries largely finished their transition from presenting to scrutinising bodies. This would have happened whoever had won at Bosworth.

Nevertheless, despite such spontaneous change, much of the criminal justice system that England inherited from the medieval period survived relatively unaltered during the first quarter of a century of Tudor rule. Indeed, in some respects, the brief reign of Henry VII's predecessor, with, for example, its important changes to the law regulating bail

---

490. S. F. C. Milsom, *The Legal Framework of English Feudalism* (Cambridge: Cambridge University Press, 2010), p. 178.

may have indicated slightly greater monarchical enthusiasm for active reform, even if it was to be cut violently short. However, Henry VII's son and grandchildren witnessed much greater legal change. Some of it was introduced by legislation or decree, as with the reform of sanctuary and benefit of clergy in the 1530s, and the Marian statutes regulating bail and the pre-trial examination of suspected felons in the 1550s. Both JPs and constables acquired ever more centrally ordained duties, while the latter enhanced their position as the system's "organ grinders", swiftly eclipsing other royal officers in importance.

Yet more change reflected a difference in emphasis and resourcing, rather than in black-letter law, such as the greater significance placed on the Star Chamber by Cardinal Wolsey, and its (and his) conscious, and highly effective, promotion of efficiency within the wider criminal justice system. This was to be one of the most important legal developments of the era, something that was also encouraged by the decline in internecine fighting after 1485.

Even so, much legal change was still organic, further evidencing Milsom's aphorism. For example, during the course of the sixteenth century several historic privileges altered (more or less) spontaneously to deal with the side effects of the widening net of the criminal law. In 1485 few observers could have anticipated how prevalent claims to benefit of clergy and pregnancy would become, and the vital function they would serve in moderating the death-for-felony rule.

Even though the fifteenth century was not quite the dark age of anarchy and violence that is sometimes portrayed, and the sixteenth century was certainly not an era of unbridled peace and prosperity (the end of the Tudor era was characterised by economic hardship), law and order in the country had been transformed by 1603. Surprising though it might appear to modern observers, by the close of the Tudor era, and despite the many social and economic challenges that it faced, England was, in relative terms, a better ordered society than it had been in 1485, with a more coherent criminal justice system, operated along more consistent and uniform principles, with markedly less corruption. There were fewer exceptions and peculiars to the wider system, both legal and geographic, and more "professionalism" could be found among judges, magistrates, lawyers, and other officials. The system had become much more stand-ardised, something that was the result of both increased legal publishing and greater governance from the centre. The criminal law was also a very much more assertive, noticeable, and potent force in the day-to-day lives of Englishmen and Englishwomen than it had been in the late medieval period. The attrition rate between the commission of a serious offence and its punishment had fallen greatly, even if still huge by modern stand-ards. Far more felons were arrested, formally accused, examined, indicted, prosecuted, convicted, and sentenced than had previously been the case. The reach of the criminal courts could often intimidate powerful men, in a way that had not been the case a century earlier, even if there was still much to do in this regard.

The legal historian William Holdsworth once observed that criminal law originated in the notion that certain wrongs were not merely the business of the injured individual, but also a violation of the King's pro-tection and security. Indeed, the notion of a crime presupposes that the Crown has an independent interest in the preservation of order, above and beyond a victim's concern for personal retribution or compensation. As a result, an infraction of the criminal law becomes an assault on the sovereign, not merely those who are injured by it, and one that neces-sitates state action and punishment.[491] However, in *practice*, this notion took a very long time to become entrenched in English society, albeit that it occurred faster there than in other parts of the British Isles. It slowly emerged and developed during the medieval period, but, as the extremely low prosecution and conviction rates of the 1300s suggest, it was far from complete, and may even have gone into reverse in some places during the Wars of the Roses. By contrast, the Tudor era was to see such a notion beginning to bed down firmly in English society.

By 1603, a criminal justice system that would be only slightly modified during the ensuing 150 years is identifiable. Students of the seventeenth and eighteenth centuries swiftly recognise such diverse matters as com-plainant/jury down-valuing of stolen items, the problems occasioned by a lack of secondary punishments and the consequent emphasis on

---

491. Paul Rock, "Victims, Prosecutors and the State in Nineteenth century England and Wales", *Criminal Justice*, Vol. 4(4), pp. 331–354, p. 334.

execution, and the extensive use of reprieves in capital cases. Many changes during the 1600s would be matters of degree, and often the logical development of patterns that were discernible before the end of the Elizabethan era.

Thus, quarter sessions would become even more reluctant to hear felonies apart from grand larceny than they had been in the late sixteenth century; JPs would meet more frequently and formally in what eventually came to be termed petty sessions; and their powers of summary jurisdiction would slowly expand from those recognised in Elizabethan England, even as the jurisdiction of leet courts continued their decline. Benefit of clergy would be granted ever more freely to convicted felons, with two statutory equivalents extending it to women during the seventeenth century, and the last vestiges of the literacy test being abandoned in 1706. However, the process whereby grave offences were withdrawn from its ambit would also continue, albeit in short and widely separated bursts.

No reform of coroner's remuneration would take place until 1756, when formal payment for inquests that were not occasioned by homicide was introduced, although salaries would wait until the nineteenth century. Doubts about the abilities of trial juries would continue. Prisons would remain squalid, insecure, and ever more entrepreneurial, with no significant and effective reform until the late eighteenth century. The use of what Blackstone would later term "pious perjury" by juries would expand, to moderate the harshness of the death-for-felony rule, especially as more offences became unclergyable and so (in practice) potentially capital.

Many of the problems that exercised the Tudor magistracy, such as the division between "workhorses" and indolent or absentee JPs, would still be readily identifiable almost 200 years later, by which time the capital would be even more attractive to provincial magistrates than it had been in the age of Shakespeare. Being appointed high sheriff of a county would become even more unpopular amongst prominent gentlemen during the seventeenth and eighteenth centuries than it was in Tudor times. The metropolitan criminal justice system, already *sui generis* during the Tudor era, became ever more singular over ensuing centuries.

Even some apparently novel post-1660 developments in the penal system had, at least, been canvassed before the close of the Tudor era. For example, by the end of the sixteenth century, the possibility of transporting convicts to America had been mooted, even though the Roanoke colony there had met disaster. James I raised it again in 1615, although it was not put on an effective statutory footing until 1718.

Arguably, patterns of crime and punishment would show more significant change than did the justice system in the centuries following the Tudor era. The highly singular nature of the far North of the country, with its border raiding and reiving, would decline fairly swiftly after the union of the Crowns in 1603, although not entirely eliminated for many decades. Much more generally, homicide rates would fall greatly, but unevenly, from their late Elizabethan and early Jacobean levels. The per capita rate of prosecutions for property crimes would also fall from the high levels seen in the difficult 1590s, although the degree to which this reflected incidence is less certain.

Use of the death penalty would continue at a very high rate until the 1630s, after which it, too, would decline rapidly, with most of the fall being explained by a decline in the proportion of felons convicted of robbery, burglary, and theft being hanged. A few ameliorations, both formal and ad hoc, to the Tudor justice system during the course of the seventeenth century, such as the growing custom of strangling women before they were burned for petty treason, and the abandonment of torture warrants, would make that system very slightly less brutal.

Whether carefully planned and radical reform to the English criminal justice system would have produced a better result than organic development combined with ad hoc improvisation and tinkering is a separate question, one that occurred to several contemporary observers, domestic and foreign. As has been seen, very occasionally, things went further, and drastic proposals for reform, whether in the form of public prosecutors or abolition of the death-for-felony rule, were briefly considered by the Crown and Parliament, before petering-out in the face of vested interests, concern about their wider political implications, or an inability to command the necessary resources to implement them. They became an intriguing "road not travelled", in some cases not being reviewed again until the nineteenth century.

Frequently Used Acronyms

DRO Durham Record Office

ERO Essex Record Office

NRO Norfolk Record Office

RO Record Office

SHC Surrey History Centre

SP State Papers

TNA The National Archives

Bibliography

Abbott, Geoffrey (2006) *Female Executions: Martyrs, Murderesses and Madwomen.* Chichester: Summersdale Publishers.

Adair, E.R. (1920) "English Galleys in the Sixteenth Century", *The English Historical Review*, Vol. 35, No. 140, pp. 497–512.

Amussen, Susan Dwyer (1994) "'Being Stirred to Much Unquietness': Violence and Domestic Violence in Early Modern England", *Journal of Women's History*, Vol. 6, No. 2, pp. 70–77.

Anand, Sanjeev (2005) "The Origins, Early History and Evolution of the English Criminal Trial Jury", *Alberta Law Review*, Vol. 43, No. 2, pp. 407–432.

Anderson, Helen A. (2011) "From the Thief in the Night to the Guest Who Stayed Too Long: The Evolution of Burglary in the Shadow of the Common Law", *Indiana Law Review*, Vol. 45, pp. 629–667.

Anon. (1491) "Petition to the king against sanctuary rights of a homicide", in H. E. Salter (ed.), *Snappe's Formulary and Other Records*. Oxford: Oxford Historical Society, 1923.

Anon. (1537) *The enquirie and verdite of the quest panneld of the death of Richard Hune wich was founde hanged in Lolars tower.* London.

Anon. (1546) *The Boke for a Justyce of Peace, never so well and dylygently set forthe.* London: W. Myddleton.

Anon. (1583) *A briefe discourse of two most cruell and bloudie murthers, committed bothe in Worcestershire, and bothe happening unhappily in the yeare 1583 The first declaring, how one unnaturally murdered his neighbour, and afterward buried him in his seller. The other sheweth, how a woman unlawfully following the devillish lusts of the flesh with her seruant, caused him very cruelly to kill her owne husband.* London: Roger Warde.

Anon. (1591) *Sundrye strange and inhumaine murthers, lately committed.* London.

Anon. (1593) *The Most Strange and Admirable Discoverie of the Three Witches of Warboys.* London.

Anon. (1595) *Two notorious murders one committed by a tanner on his wives sonne nere Horne-church in Essex, the other on a grasier nere Ailsburie in Buckinghamshire: with these is intermixt another murdrous intending fellonie at Rislip in Middlesex, all done this last month.* London.

Anon. (1603) *The manner of the cruell outragious murther of William Storre Mast. of Art, minister, and preacher at Market Raisin in the county of Lincolne committed by Francis Cartwright one of his parishioners, the 30. day of August anno. 1602.* Oxford: Joseph Barnes.

Anon. (1605) *The bloudy booke, or, The tragicall and desperate end of Sir John Fites (alias) Fitz.* London: Francys Burton.

Anon. (1606) *The Horrible Murther of a young Boy of three yeres of age, whose sister had her tongue cut out.* London: William Firebrand.

Anon. (1607) *A true Report of the horrible Murther, which was committed in the house of Sir Jerome Bowes, Knight, on the 20 day of February, Anno Dom 1606.* London: Mathew Lownes.

Anon. (1608a) *The Araignement and burning of Margaret Ferne-Seede, for the murther of her late Husband.* London: Henry Gosson.

Anon. (1608b) *The Lives, Apprehension, Araignment & Execution, of Robert Throgmorton. William Porter. John Bishop. Gentlemen … Who were all executed … the 26. of Februarie, 1608 for certaine robberies, and a muther committed on Bagshot-Heath.* London: Henry Gosson.

Anon. (1609a) *A True Relation of the most inhumane and bloody murther of Master James Minister and Preacher of the word of God at Rockland in Norfolk.* London: R. Bonian and H. Walley.

Anon. (1609b) *Foure Statutes, Specially Selected and Commanded by his Majestie to be carefully put in execution by all Justices and other Officers of the Peace throughout the Realme.* London: Robert Barker.

Anon. (1612) *The Araignment of John Selman, who was executed neere Charing-Crosse the 7. of January, 1612. for a felony.* London: Thomas Archer.

Anon. (1617) *A True Relation of a most desperate Murder, committed upon the Body of Sir John Tindall.* London.

Anon. (1618) *Newes from Perin in Cornwall.* London.

Anon. (1847) *A relation, or Rather a True Account, of The Island of England … About the Year 1500.* London: Camden Society.

Anon. (1888) *Calendar of the Cecil Papers in Hatfield House: Volume 2, 1572–1582*. London: HMSO.

Anon. (1921) "Possession and Custody in the Law of Larceny", *Yale Law Journal*, Vol. 30, No. 6, pp. 613–617.

Ashley, Francis (1981) *The Casebook of Sir Francis Ashley, J.P., Recorder of Dorchester (1614–1635)*. Dorchester: Dorset Record Society.

Bacon, Francis (1612) "Of Judicature" in *Essays*. London: J.M. Dent, Everyman, 1915.

Bacon, Francis (1630)* "The Use of the Law", in Montagu, Basil (ed.), *The Works of Francis Bacon, Volume 3*, 1844. Philadelphia: Carey and Hart. *Posthumous publication; attribution doubtful.

Bacon, Francis (1641) *Cases of Treason*. London: The Assignes of John More.

Bacon, Nathaniel; Saunders, Herbert Washington (ed.) (1915) *The Official Papers of Sir Nathaniel Bacon of Stiffkey, Norfolk, as Justice of the Peace, 1580–1620*. London: Royal Historical Society.

Bailey, F. A. (1932) *The Court Leet of Prescot*. Liverpool: The Historic Society of Lancashire and Cheshire.

Baker, J. H. (1973) "Criminal Justice at Newgate 1616–1627: Some Manuscript Reports in the Harvard Law School", *The Irish Jurist*, Vol. 8, No. 2, p. 316.

Baker, J. H. (1977a) "Criminal Courts and Procedure at Common Law 1550–1800", in Cockburn, J. S. (ed.), *Crime in England 1550–1800*. London: Methuen.

Baker, John H. (ed.) (1977b), *The Reports of Sir John Spelman*. London: Selden Society.

Baker, J. H. (1984) "Le brickbat que narrowly mist", *Law Quarterly Review*, Vol. 100, pp. 544–548.

Baker, J. H. (ed.) (1986) *The Notebook of Sir John Port*. London: Selden Society.

Baker, J. H. (1990) "The English Law of Sanctuary", *Ecclesiastical Law Journal*, Vol. 2, Issue 6, pp. 8–13.

Baker, J. H. (1998) "The Three Languages of the Common Law", *McGill Law Journal*, Vol. 43, pp. 5–24.

Banner, Stuart (1998) "When Christianity Was Part of the Common Law", *Law and History Review*, Vol. 16, No. 1, pp. 27–62.

Barnes, Thomas G. (1962) "Due Process and Slow Process in the Late Elizabethan—Early Stuart Star Chamber", *American Journal of Legal History*, Vol. 6, Issue 3, pp. 221–315.

Barnes, Thomas G. (ed.) (1959) *Somerset Assize Orders, 1629–1640*. Frome: Somerset Record Society.

Barnes, Thomas G. (1955) "Examination Before a Justice in the Seventeenth Century", *Notes & Queries for Somerset and Dorset,* Vol. 27.

Barrett, Andrew and Harrison, Christopher (eds.) (1999) *Crime and Punishment in England: A Sourcebook.* Abingdon: Routledge.

Baugh, G. C. (ed.) (1998) *A History of the County of Shropshire: Volume 10, Munslow Hundred (Part), the Liberty and Borough of Wenlock.* London: Victoria County History.

Beattie, J. M. (1986) *Crime and the Courts in England, 1660–1800.* Oxford: Oxford University Press.

Beckerman, John S. (1992) "Procedural Innovation and Institutional Change in Medieval English Manorial Courts", *Law and History Review,* Vol. 10, No. 2, pp. 197–252.

Beckerman, John S. (1995) "Toward a Theory of Medieval Manorial Adjudication: The Nature of Communal Judgments in a System of Customary Law", *Law And History Review,* Vol. 13, No. 1, pp. 1–23.

Beier, A. L. (1985) *Masterless Men: The Vagrancy Problem in England, 1560–1640.* London: Methuen.

Bellamy, John G. (1973) *Crime and Public Order in England in the Later Middle Ages.* London: Routledge.

Bellamy, J. G. (1998) *The Criminal Trial in Later Medieval England: Felony Before the Courts From Edward I to the Sixteenth Century.* Toronto: University of Toronto Press.

Bentley, D. R. (ed.) (1997) *Select Cases from the Twelve Judges' Notebooks.* London: John Rees.

Bettey, J. H. (ed.) (1981) *The Casebook of Sir Francis Ashley, JP, Recorder of Dorchester: 1614–1635.* Dorchester: Dorset Record Society.

Bindoff, S. T. (ed.) (1982) *The History of Parliament: The House of Commons, 1509–1558.* Woodbridge: Boydell & Brewer.

Blatcher, Marjorie (1978) *The Court of King's Bench, 1450–1550: A Study in Self-Help.* London: Athlone Press.

Boone, Marc (1996) "State Power and Illicit Sexuality: The Persecution of Sodomy in Late Medieval Bruges", *Journal of Medieval History,* Vol. 22, Issue 2, pp. 135–153.

Braddick, Michael J (2000), *State Formation in Early Modern England C 1550–1700.* Cambridge: Cambridge University Press.

Bradford, Gladys (ed.) (1911) *Proceedings in the Court of the Star Chamber in the Reigns of Henry VII and Henry VIII.* London: Harrison and Sons.

Braham, Humfrey (1568) *The Institucion of a Gentleman*, second edition. London.

Brewer, J. S. (ed.) (1864) *Letters and Papers, Foreign and Domestic, Henry VIII, Volume 2: 1515–1518*. London: HMSO.

Brewer, J. S. (ed.) (1867) *Letters and Papers, Foreign and Domestic, Henry VIII. Volume 3: 1519–1523*. London: HMSO.

Brewer, J. S. (ed.) (1875) *Letters and Papers, Foreign and Domestic, Henry VIII. Volume 4: 1524–1530*. London: HMSO.

Brewer, Thomas (1610) *The Bloudy Mother, Or, The Most Inhumane Murthers, Committed by Jane Hattersley Upon Divers Infants, the Issue of Her Owne Bodie.* London.

Brittain, Robert P. (1965) "Cruentation: In Legal Medicine and in Literature", *Medical History*, Vol. 9, Issue 1, pp. 82–88.

Broce, Gerald and Wunderli, Richard (1989) "The Final Moment before Death in Early Modern England", *Sixteenth Century Journal*, Vol. 20, No. 2, pp. 259–276.

Broadway, Jan (2008) "Aberrant Accounts: William Dugdale's Handling of Two Tudor Murders" in *The Antiquities of Warwickshire Midland History*, Vol. 33, No. 1, pp. 2–20.

Brooks, Christopher and Lobban, Michael (eds.) (1997) *Communities and Courts in Britain 1150–1900*. London: Hambledon.

Brooks, Christopher W. (2008) *Law, Politics and Society in Early Modern England*. Cambridge: Cambridge University Press.

Brown, Bernard J. (1963) "The Demise of Chance Medley and the Recognition of Provocation as a Defence to Murder in English Law", *American Journal of Legal History*, Vol. 7, Issue 4, pp. 310–318.

Brown, Rawdon (ed.) (1873) *Calendar of State Papers Relating to English Affairs in the Archives of Venice*. London: HMSO.

Butler, Sara M. (2001) "Spousal Abuse in Fourteenth century Yorkshire: What Can We Learn from the Coroners' Rolls?", *Florilegium*, Vol. 18, No. 2, pp. 61–78.

Butler, Sara M. (2006) "Local Concerns: Suicide and Jury Behavior in Medieval England", *History Compass*, Vol. 4, No. 5, pp. 820–821.

Butler, Sara M. (2015) *Forensic Medicine and Death Investigation in Medieval England*. New York: Routledge.

Calabria, Antonio (2004) "The Cost of a Man's Life in Sixteenth century Naples: Galley Rowers on the Early Modern Mediterranean", *Essays in Economic & Business History*, Vol. 22, pp. 1–8.

Campbell, Ruth (1984) "Sentence of Death by Burning for Women", *Journal of Legal History*, Vol. 5, pp. 44–59.

Cartwright, Francis (1621) *The life, confession, and heartie repentance of Francis Cartwright, Gentleman for his bloudie sinne in killing of one Master Storr, Master of Arts, and minister of Market Rason in Lincolnshire. Written with his owne hand.* London: Nathaniel Butter.

Clavell, John (1628) *A Recantation of an Ill led Life, or, a discoverie of the high-way law.* London.

Clough, T. H. McKay (1999) *Oakham Castle: A Guide and History.* Oakham: Rutland County Council.

Cockburn, J. S. (1968) "The Northern Assize Circuit", *Northern History*, Vol. 3, Issue 1, pp. 118–130.

Cockburn, J. S. (1969) "Seventeenth century Clerks of Assize — Some Anonymous Members of the Legal Profession", *American Journal of Legal History*, Vol. 13, pp. 315–327.

Cockburn, J. S. (1972) *A History of English Assizes, 1558–1714.* Cambridge: Cambridge University Press.

Cockburn, J. S. (ed.) (1975a) *Calendar of Assize Records. Hertfordshire Indictments: Elizabeth I.* London: HMSO.

Cockburn, J. S. (ed.) (1975b) *Calendar of Assize Records. Sussex Indictments: Elizabeth I.* London: HMSO.

Cockburn, J. S. (ed.) (1977) *Crime in England 1550–1800.* London: Methuen.

Cockburn, J. S. (ed.) (1978a) *Calendar of Assize Records. Essex Indictments, Elizabeth I.* London: HMSO.

Cockburn, J. S. (1978b) "Trial by the Book? Fact and Theory in the Criminal Process 1558–1625", in Baker, J.H. (ed.), *Legal Records and the Historian.* London: Royal Historical Society.

Cockburn, J. S. (ed.) (1980) *Calendar of Assize Records. Surrey Indictments: Elizabeth I.* London: HMSO.

Cockburn, J. S. (ed.) (1985) *Calendar of Assize Records. Home Circuit Indictments: Elizabeth I and James I: Introduction.* London: HMSO.

Cockburn, J. S. (1988) "Twelve Silly Men? The Trial Jury at Assizes, 1560–1670" in Cockburn J. S. and Green, Thomas A. (eds.), *Twelve Good Men and True: The Criminal Trial Jury in England 1200–1800.* Princeton: Princeton University Press.

Cockburn, J. S. (1991) "Patterns of Violence in English Society: Homicide in Kent 1560–1985", *Past & Present*, Vol. 130, Issue 1, pp. 70–106.

Cockburn, J. S. (1994) "Punishment and Brutalization in the English Enlightenment", *Law and History Review*, Vol. 12, No. 1, pp. 155–179.

Cooper, Thomas (1620) *The cry and revenge of blood: Expressing the nature and haynousnesse of wilfull murther*. London: John Wright.

Cooper, W. D. (ed.) (1858) *The Expenses of the Judges of Assize Riding the Western and Oxford Circuits, Temp. Elizabeth, 1596–1601. From the Ms. Account Book of Thomas Walmysley, One of the Justices of the Common Pleas*. Cambridge: Camden Society.

Cornwall, Julian (1965) "The Early Tudor Gentry", *The Economic History Review*, Vol. 17, No. 3, pp. 456–475.

Cosbie, Arnold (1591) *The manner of the death and execution of Arnold Cosbie, for murthering the Lord Boorke, who was executed at Wanswoorth towne's end on the 27 of January 1591*. London: William Wright.

Coss, Graeme (1991) "'God is a righteous judge, strong and patient: and God is provoked every day.' A Brief History of the Doctrine of Provocation in England", *Sydney Law Review*, Vol. 13, No. 4, pp. 570–604.

Cressy, David (1996) "Gender Trouble and Cross-Dressing in Early Modern England", *Journal of British Studies*, Vol. 35, No. 4, pp. 438–465.

Cressy, David (2000) *Travesties and Transgressions in Tudor and Stuart England*. Oxford: Oxford University Press.

Cressy, David (2013) "Demotic Voices and Popular Complaint in Elizabethan and Early Stuart England", *Journal of Early Modern Studies*, Vol. 2, pp. 47–62.

Crofts, Thomas (2016) "The Common Law Influence over the Age of Criminal Responsibility in Australia", *Northern Ireland Legal Quarterly*, Vol. 67, No. 3, pp. 284–287.

Crompton, Richard (1594) *L'Authoritie et Jurisdiction Des Courts de la Maiestie de la Roygne: Novelment collect & compose*. London.

Crompton, Richard (1606) *L'office et auctoritie de Justices de Peace, in part collect per Sir Anthonie Fitzherbert Chivalier, iades un de les Justices del common Banke*. London: The Companie of Stationers.

Cross, Arthur Lyon (1917) "The English Criminal Law and Benefit of Clergy during the Eighteenth and Early Nineteenth Centuries", *The American Historical Review*, Vol. 22, No. 3, pp. 544–565.

Cruickshank, John L. (2017) "Courts Leet, Constables and the Township Structure in the West Riding, 1540–1842", *Northern History*, Vol. 54, Issue 1, pp. 59–78.

Curtis, Timothy and Sharpe, J. A. (1988) "Crime in Tudor and Stuart England", *History Today*, Vol. 38, Issue 2, pp. 23–33.

Cust, Richard and Lake, Peter G. (1981) "Sir Richard Grosvenor and the Rhetoric of Magistracy", *Historical Research*, 1981, Vol. 54, No. 129, pp. 40–53.

Damme, Catherine (1978) "Infanticide: The Worth of an Infant Under Law", *Medical History*, Vol. 22, No. 1, pp. 1–24.

Darr, Orna Alyagon (2011) *Marks of an Absolute Witch*. Farnham: Ashgate.

Dean, David (1996) *Law-Making and Society in Late Elizabethan England: The Parliament of England, 1584–1601*. Cambridge: Cambridge University Press.

De Moor, Tine and van Zanden, Jan Luiten (2010) "Girl power: the European marriage pattern and labour markets in the North Sea region in the late medieval and early modern period", *The Economic History Review*, Vol. 63, No. 1, pp. 1–33.

Devereaux, Simon and Griffiths, Paul (eds.) (2004) *Penal Practice and Culture, 1500–1900: Punishing the English*. Basingstoke: Palgrave Macmillan.

D'Ewes, Simonds (1682) *The Journals of All the Parliaments During the Reign of Queen Elizabeth*. Shannon: Irish University Press.

Dugdale, Gilbert (1604) *A true discourse of the practises of Elizabeth Cauldwell, Ma: Jeffrey Bownd, Isabell Hall widdow, and George Fernely, on the parson of Ma: Thomas Caldwell, in the county of Chester, to have murdered and poysoned him, with divers others*. London: John Busbie.

Duker, William F. (1977a) "The Right to Bail: A Historical Inquiry", *Albany Law Review*, Vol. 42, No. 1, pp. 33–120.

Duker, William F. (1977b) "The President's Power to Pardon: A Constitutional History", *William & Mary Law Review*, Vol. 18, Issue 3, pp. 475–538.

Dunn, Caroline (2011) "The Language of Ravishment in Medieval England", *Speculum*, Vol. 86, No. 1, pp. 79–116.

Dunn, Caroline (2013) *Stolen Women in Medieval England: Rape, Abduction and Adultery, 1100–1500*. Cambridge: Cambridge University Press.

Dunne, Derek (2015) "Re-assessing Trial by Jury in Early Modern Law and Literature", *Literature Compass*, Vol. 12, Issue 10, pp. 517–526.

Dunne, Derek (2016) *Shakespeare, Revenge Tragedy and Early Modern Law: Vindictive Justice*. Basingstoke: Palgrave Macmillan.

Edwards, G. J. (1906) *The Grand Jury: An Essay*. Philadelphia: George T. Bisel.

Edwards, Peter (1988) *The Horse Trade of Tudor and Stuart England*. Cambridge: Cambridge University Press.

Eisner, Manuel (2003) "Long-Term Historical Trends in Violent Crime", *Crime and Justice*, Vol. 30, pp. 83–142.

Eisner, Manuel (2014) "From Swords to Words: Does Macro-Level Change in Self-Control Predict Long-Term Variation in Levels of Homicide?", *Crime and Justice*, Vol. 43, No. 1, pp. 65–134.

Eisner, Manuel (2017) "Interpersonal Violence on the British Isles, 1200–2016", in Liebling, Alison et al. (eds.), *The Oxford Handbook of Criminology*. Oxford: Oxford University Press.

Elias, Norbert (1978) *The Civilizing Process, Volume 1: The History of Manners*. Oxford: Basil Blackwell.

Elias, Norbert (1982) *The Civilizing Process, Volume 2: State Formation and Civilization*. Oxford: Basil Blackwell.

Ellis, Steven G. (1992) "A Border Baron and the Tudor State: The Rise and Fall of Lord Dacre of the North", *The Historical Journal*, Vol. 35, No. 2, pp. 253–277.

Ellis, Steven (1995) "Frontiers and Power in the Early Tudor State", *History Today*, Vol. 45, Issue 4, pp. 35–42.

Elton, G. R. (1977) *Reform and Reformation: England 1509–1558*. London: Edward Arnold.

Elton, G. R. (ed.) (1982) *The Tudor Constitution: Documents and Commentary*, second edition. Cambridge: Cambridge University Press.

Elyot, Thomas; Croft, H. H. S. (ed.) (1531) *The Boke Named The Governour, Devised by Sir Thomas Elyot, Knight, 1531, Volume 1*, 1880. London: Kegan Paul, Trench.

Elyot, Thomas (1531) *The Boke named The Governour*, 1962. London: J. M. Dent.

Emmison, F. G. (1970) *Elizabethan Life: Disorder*. Chelmsford: Essex County Council.

Emmison, F. G. (1973) *Elizabethan Life: Morals and the Church Courts*. Chelmsford: Essex County Council.

Ernst, Daniel R. (1984) "The Moribund Appeal of Death: Compensating Survivors and Controlling Jurors in Early Modern England", *American Journal of Legal History*, Vol. 28, No. 2, pp. 164–188.

Evans, Hugh C. (1969) "Comic Constables — Fictional and Historical", *Shakespeare Quarterly*, Vol. 20, Issue 4, pp. 427–433.

Field, Teresa (1991) "Biblical Influences on the Medieval and Early Modern English Law of Sanctuary", *Ecclesiastical Law Journal*, Vol. 2, pp. 222–225.

Fisher, George (1997) "The Jury's Rise as Lie Detector", *Yale Law Journal*, Vol. 107, Issue 3, pp. 575–713.

Fitzgerald, P. J. (1963) "Crime, Sin and Negligence", *Law Quarterly Review*, Vol. 79, pp. 351–354.

Fitzherbert, Anthony (1523) *Diversite des courtz et leur jurisdictions*. London.

Fleming, Peter (2013) *Time, space and power in later medieval Bristol*. Working Paper. University of the West of England.

Fletcher, George P. (1976) "The Metamorphosis of Larceny", *Harvard Law Review*, Vol. 89, No. 3, pp. 469–530.

Florio, John Florio (1578) *First Fruits, which yield Familiar Speech, Merry Proverbs, Witty Sentences, and Golden Sayings*.

Forbes, Thomas R. (1973) "London Coroner's Inquests for 1590", *Journal of the History of Medicine and Allied Sciences*, Vol. 28, Issue 4, pp. 376–386.

Fortescue, John (c.1471) *The Governance of England: Otherwise Called The Difference between an absolute and a limited monarchy*, revised edition, Plummer, Charles (ed.), 1885. Oxford: Clarendon Press.

Forster, G. C. F. (1973) *The East Riding Justices of the Peace in the Seventeenth Century*. York: East Yorkshire Local History Society.

Fortescue, John; Grigor, Francis (ed.) (1917) *Sir John Fortescue's Commendation of the Laws of England: The Translation into English of De Laudibus Legum Angliae*. London: Sweet and Maxwell.

Fraser, C. M. (1988) *Durham Quarter Sessions Rolls, 1471–1625*. Durham: Surtees Society.

Friedman, Danny (2006) "Torture and the Common Law", *European Human Rights Law Review*, Issue 2, pp. 180–199.

Fudge, Erica (2000) "Monstrous Acts: Bestiality in Early Modern England", *History Today*, Vol. 50, No. 8, pp. 20–25.

Fuller, Bostock; Leveson-Gower, Granville (ed.) (1888) "Notebook of a Surrey Justice", *Surrey Archaeological Collections*, Vol. 9, pp. 161–232.

Gairdner, James (ed.) (1880) *Letters and Papers, Foreign and Domestic, Henry VIII, Volume 5, 1531–1532*. London: HMSO.

Gairdner, James (ed.) (1888) *Letters and Papers, Foreign and Domestic, Henry VIII, Volume 11, July-December 1536*. London: HMSO.

Gairdner, James and Brodie, R. H. (eds.) (1894) *Letters and Papers, Foreign and Domestic, Henry VIII, Volume 14, Part 1, January-July 1539*. London: HMSO.

Gairdner, James and Brodie, R. H. (eds.) (1907) *Letters and Papers, Foreign and Domestic, Henry VIII, Volume 20, Part 2, August-December 1545*. London: HMSO.

Garay, Kathleen E. (1979) "Women and Crime in Later Mediaeval England: An Examination of the Evidence of the Courts of Gaol Delivery, 1388 to 1409", *Florilegium*, Vol. 1, pp. 87–109.

Gaskill, Malcolm (2000) *Crime and Mentalities in Early Modern England*. Cambridge: Cambridge University Press.

Gerard, John (2012) *The Autobiography of a Hunted Priest*. San Francisco: Ignatius Press.

Gibbs, Spike (2018) Felony Forfeiture at the Manor of Worfield, c.1370–c.1600. *The Journal of Legal History*, Vol. 39, Issue 3, pp. 253–277.

Giuseppi, M. S. and Lockie, D. McN. (eds.) (1965) *Calendar of the Cecil Papers in Hatfield House: Volume 19, 1607*. London: HMSO.

Golding, Arthur (1573) *A briefe discourse of the late murther of Master George Saunders*. London: Henry Bynnemen.

Goodacre, Kenneth and Mercer, E. Doris (1965) *Guide to the Middlesex Sessions Records, 1549–1889*. London: GLRO.

Gordon, Michael D. (1980) "The Invention of a Common Law Crime: Perjury and the Elizabethan Courts", *American Journal of Legal History*, Vol. 24, Issue 2, pp. 145–170.

Gradwohl, Alex (2013) "Herbal Abortifacients and their Classical Heritage in Tudor England", *Penn History Review*, Vol. 20, Issue 1, pp. 44–71.

Grauer, Anne L. and Miller, Andrew G. (2017) "Flesh on the Bones: A Historical and Bioarchaeological Exploration of Violence, Trauma, Sex, and Gender in Medieval England", *Fragments: Interdisciplinary Approaches to the Study of Ancient and Medieval Pasts*, Vol. 6. Available at: http://works.bepress.com/anne-grauer/2/

Greaves, Richard L. (1981) *Society and Religion in Elizabethan England*. Minneapolis: University of Minnesota Press.

Green, Mary Anne Everett (ed.) (1872) *Calendar of State Papers Domestic: Elizabeth, Addenda 1580–1625*. London: HMSO.

Green, Mary Anne Everett (ed.) (1870) *Calendar of State Papers Domestic: Elizabeth, 1601–1603, with Addenda 1547–65*. London: HMSO.

Green, T. A. (1985) *Verdict According to Conscience: Perspectives on the English Criminal Trial Jury, 1200–1800*. Chicago: University of Chicago Press.

Green, Thomas Andrew (1985) "The Transformation of Jury Trial in Early Modern England", in Green, T. A., *Verdict According to Conscience: Perspectives on the English Criminal Trial Jury.* Chicago: University of Chicago Press.

Griffiths, Matthew (1980) "Kirtlington Manor Court, 1500–1650", *Oxoniensia*, Vol. 45, pp. 260–283.

Griffiths, Paul; Fox, Adam; and Hindle, Steve (eds.) (1996) *The Experience of Authority in Early Modern England.* New York: St. Martin's Press.

Gunn, Steven (2010) "Archery Practice in Early Tudor England", *Past & Present*, Vol. 209, Issue 1, pp. 53–81.

Gwyn, Peter (1990) *The King's Cardinal: The Rise and Fall of Thomas Wolsey.* London: Barrie & Jenkins.

Hair, P. E. H. (ed.) (1972) *Before the Bawdy Court: Selections from Church Court and Other Records Relating to the Correction of Moral Offences in England, Scotland and New England, 1300–1800.* London: Elek.

Hair, P. E. H. (1972) "Notes and Queries: Homicide, Infanticide, and Child Assault in Late Tudor Middlesex", *Local Population Studies,* Issue 9.

Hale, W. H. (ed.) (1847) *A Series of Precedents and Proceedings in Criminal Causes* [sic], *from 1475 to 1640; Extracted from Act-Books of Ecclesiastical Courts in the Diocese of London.* London: Francis and John Rivington.

Hall, Joseph (1608) *Characters of Vertues and Vices.* London.

Hartshorne, Charles Henry (ed.) (1861) *Extracts from the Register of Sir Thomas Butler, Vicar of Much Wenlock, in Shropshire.* Tenby: R. Mason.

Hamil, Frederick C. (1936) "The King's Approvers: A Chapter in the History of English Criminal Law", *Speculum*, Vol. 11, No. 2, pp. 238–258.

Hamilton, Alexander Henry Abercromby (1878) *Quarter Sessions from Queen Elizabeth to Queen Anne: Illustrations of Local Government and History, Drawn from Original Records.* London: Sampson Low.

Hamilton, Charles (1973) "Star Chamber and Juries: Some Observations", *Albion* [now *Journal of British Studies*], Vol. 5, Issue 3, pp. 237–242.

Hammer, Carl I., Jr. (1978) "Patterns of Homicide in a Medieval University Town: Fourteenth century Oxford", *Past & Present*, Vol. 78, Issue 1, pp. 3–23.

Hanawalt, Barbara A. (1975) "Fur Collar Crime: The Pattern of Crime among the Fourteenth century English Nobility", *Journal of Social History*, Vol. 8, No. 4, pp. 1–17.

Hanawalt, Barbara A. (1976) "Violent Death in Fourteenth and Early Fifteenth century England", *Comparative Studies in Society and History,* Vol. 18, No. 3, pp. 297–320.

Hanawalt, Barbara A. (1986) *The Ties that Bound: Peasant Families in Medieval England.* Oxford: Oxford University Press.

Hanawalt, Barbara A. (1998) "'Good Governance' in the Medieval and Early Modern Context", *Journal of British Studies,* Vol. 37, No. 3, pp. 246–257.

Hankins, Jeffery R. (2003) *Local Government and Society in Early Modern England: Hertfordshire and Essex, c.1590–1630.* PhD thesis, Louisiana State University.

Harman, Thomas (1567) *A Caveat or Warening, for Common Cursitors vulgarly called Vagabones.* London: Wylliam Gryffith.

Harris, Barbara (1976) "The Trial of the Third Duke of Buckingham — A Revisionist View", *American Journal of Legal History,* Vol. 20, No. 1, pp. 15–26.

Harris, B. E. and Clayton, Dorothy J. (1978) "Criminal Procedure in Cheshire in the Mid-Fifteenth Century", *Transactions of the Historic Society of Lancashire and Cheshire,* Vol. 128, No. 8, pp. 161–172.

Harrison, Christopher (1997) "Manor Courts and the Governance of Tudor England", in Brooks, Christopher and Lobban, Michael (eds.), *Communities and Courts in Britain 1150–1900.* London: Hambledon.

Harrison, G. B. (1974) *A Second Elizabethan Journal.* London: Routledge & Kegan Paul.

Harrison, William (1577) "A Description of England", in Holinshed, Raphael (ed.) *The Firste Volume of the Chronicles of England, Scotlande and Irelande.* London: John Harrison.

Harrison, William (1877) *Harrison's Description of England in Shakespere's Youth.* London: N. Trübner.

Harrison, William (1577) *Elizabethan England: From "A Description of England",* Withington, Lothrop (ed.), 1889. London: Walter Scott.

Hartshorne, Charles Henry (ed.) (1861) *Extracts from the Register of Sir Thomas Butler, Vicar of Much Wenlock, in Shropshire.* Tenby: R. Mason.

Harvey, David John (2015) *The Law Emprynted and Englysshed: The Printing Press as an Agent of Change in Law and Legal Culture 1475–1642.* London: Hart Publishing.

Haule, Henry; Hull, Felix (ed.) (1990) *Henry Haule's Notebook, 1590–1595.* Maidstone: Kent Archaeological Society.

Havard, J. D. J. (1960) *The Detection of Secret Homicide.* London: Macmillan.

Heal, Felicity and Holmes, Clive (1994) *The Gentry in England and Wales, 1500–1700.* Basingstoke: Palgrave.

Hearnshaw, F. J. C. and Hearnshaw, D. M. (eds.) (1907) *Court Leet Records, Volume I, Part III, 1603–1624*. Southampton: Southampton Record Society Publications.

Helmholz, R. H. (1975) "Infanticide in the Province of Canterbury During the Fifteenth Century", *History of Childhood Quarterly*, Vol. 2, pp. 379–390.

Helmholz, R. H. (1983) "Crime, Compurgation and the Courts of the Medieval Church", *Law and History Review*, Vol. 1, No. 1, pp. 1–26.

Helmholz, R. H. (1987) *Canon Law and the Law of England*. London: Hambledon.

Helmholz, R. H. (1993) "And were there children's rights in early modern England? The canon law and 'intra-family violence' in England, 1400–1640", *The International Journal of Children's Rights,* Vol. 1, No. 1, pp. 23–32.

Helmholz, R. H. (2001) *The* ius commune *in England: Four Studies*. Oxford: Oxford University Press.

Hentzner, Paul (1889) *Travels in England During the Reign of Queen Elizabeth*. London: Cassell.

Herbruggen, Hubertus Schulte (1983) "The Process against Sir Thomas More", *Law Quarterly Review*, Vol. 99, pp. 113–136.

Herrup, Cynthia B. (1987) *The Common Peace: Participation and the Common Law in Seventeenth century England*. Cambridge: Cambridge University Press.

Hext, Edward (1596) Letter from Edward Hext, a Somerset JP, to Lord Burghley, 25 September 1596, in Tawney, R. H. and Power, Eileen (eds.), *Tudor Economic Documents, Volume 2, 1924*. London: Longman.

Hill, L. M. (1968) "The Two-Witness Rule in English Treason Trials: Some Comments on the Emergence of Procedural Law", *American Journal of Legal History*, Vol. 12, No. 2, pp. 95–111.

Hindle, Steve (1999) "Hierarchy and Community in the Elizabethan Parish: The Swallowfield Articles of 1596", *Historical Journal*, Vol. 42, No. 3, pp. 835–851.

Hindle, Steve (2010) "'Bleedinge Afreshe'? The Affray and Murder at Nantwich, 19 December 1572", in McShane, Angela and Walker, Garthine (eds.), *The Extraordinary and the Everyday in Early Modern England*. Basingstoke: Palgrave Macmillan.

Histed, Elise Bennett (2004) "Mediaeval Rape: A Conceivable Defence?", *The Cambridge Law Journal*, Vol. 63, No. 3, pp. 743–769.

Hitchcock, Robert (1580) "A Politic Plat for the honour of the Prince", in Arber, Edward (ed.) (1903) *Social England Illustrated: A Collection of XVIIth Century* [sic] *Tracts*, Westminster: Archibald Constable, 1903.

Hodgkinson, R. F. B. (ed.) (1925) "Extracts from the Act Books of the Archdeacons of Nottingham", *Transactions of the Thoroton Society*, Vol. 29, pp. 19–67

Hoffer, Peter C. and Hull, N. E. H. (1981) *Murdering Mothers*. New York: New York University Press.

Hollander, Melissa (2006) *Sex in Two Cities: The Formation and Regulation of Sexual Relationships in Edinburgh and York, 1560 to 1625*. PhD thesis, University of York.

Horder, Jeremy (1992) "The Duel and the English Law of Homicide", *Oxford Journal of Legal Studies*, Vol. 12, No. 3, pp. 419–430.

Horrox, Rosemary (ed.) (1994) *Fifteenth century Attitudes: Perceptions of Society in Late Medieval England*. Cambridge: Cambridge University Press.

Howell, Ben (1995) *Law and Disorder in Tudor Monmouthshire*. Chesterfield: Merton Priory Press.

Howlin, Niamh (2014) "Irish Jurors: Passive Observers or Active Participants?", *Journal of Legal History*, Vol. 35, No. 2, pp. 143–171.

Hunnisett, R. F. (ed.) (1969) *Calendar of Nottinghamshire Coroners' Inquests 1485–1558*. Nottingham: Thoroton Society.

Hunnisett, R. F. (ed.) (1985) *Sussex Coroners' Inquests 1485–1558*. Lewes: Sussex Record Society.

Hunnisett, R. F. (1996) *Sussex Coroners' Inquests 1558–1603*. London: PRO Publications.

Hurstfield, Joel (1973) *Freedom, Corruption and Government in Elizabethan England*. London: Jonathan Cape.

Hutchinson, Robert (2006) *The Last Days of Henry VIII: Conspiracy, Treason and Heresy at the Court of the Dying Tyrant*. London: Weidenfeld & Nicolson.

Hutson, Lorna (2007) *The Invention of Suspicion: Law and Mimesis in Shakespeare and Renaissance Drama*. Oxford: Oxford University Press.

Hyde, Patricia (1996) *Thomas Ardern in Faversham: The Man Behind the Myth*. Faversham: Faversham Society.

I., T. (1595) *A World of Wonders. A Masse of Murthers. A Covie of Cosonages*. London.

Ingram, M. J. (1987) *Church Courts, Sex and Marriage in England 1570–1640*. Cambridge: Cambridge University Press.

Ives, E. W. (1983) The *Common Lawyers of Pre-Reformation England. Thomas Kebell: A Case Study*. Cambridge: Cambridge University Press.

James VI and I, King (1597) *Daemonologie in forme of a dialogue, Book 3*. Edinburgh: Robert Waldegrave.

Jeaffreson, John Cordy (ed.) (1886) *Middlesex County Records: Volume 1, 1550–1603*. London: Middlesex County Record Society.

Jenkins, Philip. (1986) "From Gallows to Prison? The Execution Rate in Early Modern England", *Criminal Justice History*, Vol. 7, pp. 51–71.

Jones, John Gwynfor (1996) *Law, Order and Government in Caernarfonshire, 1558–1640*. Cardiff: University of Wales Press.

Jones, Karen (2006) *Gender and Petty Crime in Late Medieval England: The Local Courts in Kent, 1460–1560*. Woodbridge: Boydell & Brewer.

Jordan, William Chester (2015) *From England to France: Felony and Exile in the High Middle Ages*. Princeton: Princeton University Press.

Judges, A. V. (ed.) (1930) *The Elizabethan Underworld*. Abingdon: Routledge.

Kamali, Elizabeth Papp (2015) "*Felonia Felonice Facta*: Felony and Intentionality in Medieval England", *Criminal Law and Philosophy*, Vol. 9, Issue 3, pp. 397–421.

Kamali, Elizabeth Papp (2017) "The Devil's Daughter of Hell Fire: Anger's Role in Medieval English Felony Cases", *Law and History Review*, Vol. 35, Issue 1, pp. 155–200.

Karras, Ruth Mazo (1989) "The Regulation of Brothels in Later Medieval England", *Signs*, Vol. 14, No. 2, pp. 399–433.

Kaufman, Peter Iver (1984) "Henry VII and Sanctuary", *Church History*, Vol. 53, Issue 4, pp. 465–476.

Kaufman, Peter Iver (1986) *The "Polytyque Churche": Religion and Early Tudor Political Culture, 1485–1516*. Macon, Georgia: Mercer University Press.

Kaye, J.M. (1967) "The Early History of Murder and Manslaughter, Part II", *Law Quarterly Review*, Vol. 83, Issue 4, pp. 569–601.

Keeton, George W. (1961) "Judge Jeffreys as Chief Justice of Chester, 1680–1683", *Law Quarterly Review*, Vol. 77, pp. 36–68.

Kemp, Thomas (ed.) (1909) *The Book of John Fisher, Town Clerk and Deputy Recorder of Warwick 1580–1588*. Warwick: Henry T. Cooke & Son.

Kenny, Gillian (2018) "Ireland, Back to the Future", *History Today*.

Kent, Joan R. (1973) "Attitudes of Members of the House of Commons to the Regulation of 'Personal Conduct' in Late Elizabethan and Early Stuart England", *British Institute of Historical Research*, Vol. 46, pp. 41–71.

Kent, Joan (1981) "The English Village Constable, 1580–1642: The Nature and Dilemmas of the Office", *Journal of British Studies*, Vol. 20, Issue 2, pp. 26–49.

Kent, Joan R. (1983) "'Folk Justice' and Royal Justice in Early Seventeenth century England: A 'Charivari' in the Midlands", *Midland History*, Vol. 8, Issue 1, pp. 70–85.

Kermode, Jenny and Walker, Garthine (eds.) (1994) *Women, Crime and the Courts in Early Modern England,* London: UCL Press.

Kerr, Margaret H. (1995) "Angevin Reform of the Appeal of Felony", *Law and History Review,* Vol. 13, No. 2, pp. 351–391.

Kesselring, Krista (1999) "Abjuration and its Demise: The Changing Face of Royal Justice in the Tudor Period", *Canadian Journal of History*, Vol. 34, No. 3, pp. 345–358.

Kesselring, K .J. (2001) "A Draft for the 1531 'Acte for Poysoning'" in *English Historical Review*, Vol. 116, Issue 468, pp. 894–899.

Kesselring, K. J. (2003) *Mercy and Authority in the Tudor State.* Cambridge: Cambridge University Press.

Kesselring, K. J. (2007) *The Northern Rebellion of 1569: Faith, Politics and Protest in Elizabethan England.* Basingstoke: Palgrave Macmillan.

Kesselring, K. J. (2009) "Felony Forfeiture in England, c.1170–1870", *The Journal of Legal History,* Vol. 30, Issue 3, pp. 201–226.

Kesselring, K. J. (2015) "Bodies of Evidence: Sex and Murder (or Gender and Homicide) in Early Modern England, c.1500–1680", *Gender & History*, Vol. 27, Issue 2, pp. 245–262.

Kesselring, K. J. (2016) "No Greater Provocation? Adultery and the Mitigation of Murder in English Law", *Law and History Review*, Vol. 34, No. 1, pp. 199–225.

Kesselring, K. J. (2019) *Making Murder Public: Homicide in Early Modern England, 1480–1680.* Oxford: Oxford University Press.

King, P. S. (1972) *The Middlesex Justices 1590–1640: The Commissions of the Peace, Oyer and Terminer and Gaol Delivery for Middlesex.* MA thesis, Durham University.

King, Walter J. (1980) "Leet Jurors and the Search for Law and Order in Seventeenth century England: 'Galling Persecution' or Reasonable Justice?", *Histoire sociale/Social History*, Vol. 13, No. 26, pp. 305–323.

King, Walter (1990) "Early Stuart Courts Leet: Still Needful and Useful", *Histoire sociale/Social History,* Vol. 23, No. 46, pp. 271–299.

Kinney, Arthur F. and Swain, David W. (eds.) (2000) *Tudor England: An Encyclopedia.* Abingdon: Routledge.

Kleineke, Hannes and Ross, James (2017) "Just Another Day in Chancery Lane: Disorder and the Law in London's Legal Quarter in the Fifteenth Century", *Law and History Review*, Vol. 35, Issue 4, pp. 1017–1047.

Klerman, Daniel (2001) "Settlement and the Decline of Private Prosecution in Thirteenth century England", *Law and History Review*, Vol. 19, Issue 1, pp. 1–66.

Klerman, Daniel (2003) "Was the Jury Ever Self-Informing?", *Southern California Law Review*, Vol. 77, No. 1, pp. 123–150.

Knafla, Louis A. (ed.) (1981) *Crime and Criminal Justice in Europe and Canada*. Waterloo, Ontario: Wilfred Laurier University Press.

Knafla, Louis A. (1983) "'Sin of all Sorts Swarmeth': Criminal Litigation in an English County in the early Seventeenth Century", in Ives, E. W. and Manchester, A. H. (eds.), *Law, Litigants and the Legal Profession*. London: Royal Historical Society.

Knafla, Louis A. (1985) "'John at Love Killed Her': The Assizes and Criminal Law in Early Modern England", *The University of Toronto Law Journal*, Vol. 35, No. 3, pp. 305–320.

Knafla, Louis A. (1994) *Kent at Law, 1602. The County Jurisdiction: Assizes and Sessions of the Peace,* London: HMSO.

Kopel, David B. (1995) "It Isn't About Duck Hunting: The British Origins of the Right to Arms", *Michigan Law Review*, Vol. 93, Issue 6, pp. 1333–1362.

Lambarde, William (1576) *A Perambulation of Kent, conteining the description, hystorie, and customes of that Shire*, 1826. London: Baldwin, Cradock and Joy.

Lambarde, William (1582) *The Duties of Constables, Borsholders, Tythingmen, and Such Other Lowe Ministers of the Peace*. London: Roger Warde.

Lambarde, William (1635) *Archeion, or, A Discourse upon the High Courts of Justice in England*. London.

Lander, J. R. (1989) *English Justices of the Peace, 1461–1509*. Gloucester: Sutton.

Langbein, John (1973) "The Origins of Public Prosecution at Common Law", *American Journal of Legal History*, Vol. 17, Issue 4, pp. 313–335.

Langbein, John H. (1974) *Prosecuting Crime in the Renaissance: England, Germany, France*. Cambridge, Massachusetts: Harvard University Press.

Langbein, John H. (1994) "The Historical Origins of the Privilege against Self-Incrimination at Common Law", *Michigan Law Review*, Vol. 92, Issue 5, pp. 1047–1085.

Langbein, John H.; Lerner, Renée Lettow; and Smith, Bruce P. (eds.) (2009) *History of the Common Law: The Development of Anglo-American Legal Institutions*. New York: Aspen Publishers.

Laslett, Peter; Oosterveen, Karla; and Smith, Richard M. (eds.) (1980) *Bastardy and Its Comparative History*. London: Edward Arnold.

Lawson, Peter C. (1986) "Property Crime and Hard Times in England, 1559–1624", *Law and History Review*, Vol. 4, Issue 1, pp. 95–127.

Lawson, Peter C. (1988) "Lawless Juries? The Composition and Behaviour of Hertfordshire Juries, 1573–1624", in Cockburn J. S. and Green, Thomas A. (eds.), *Twelve Good Men and True: The Criminal Trial Jury in England 1200–1800*. Princeton: Princeton University Press.

Lawson, Peter (1998) "Patriarchy, Crime and the Courts: The Criminality of Women in Late Tudor and Early Stuart England", in Smith, Greg T. et al. (eds.), *Criminal Justice in the Old World and the New*. Toronto: Centre of Criminology, University of Toronto.

Lenman, Bruce and Parker, Geoffrey (1980) "The State, the Community and the Criminal Law in Early Modern Europe", in Gatrell, V. A. C. et al. (eds.), *Crime & The Law: The Social History of Crime in Western Europe Since 1500*. London: Europa.

Levack, Brian P. (1995) "Possession, Witchcraft, and the Law in Jacobean England", *Washington & Lee Law Review*, Vol. 52, Issue 5, pp. 1613–1640.

Levin, Carole; Bertolet, Anna Riehl; and Carney, Jo Eldridge (eds.) (2017) *A Biographical Encyclopedia of Early Modern Englishwomen*. Abingdon: Routledge.

Lewis, Margaret Brannan (2016) *Infanticide and Abortion in Early Modern Germany*. Abingdon: Routledge.

Lister, John (ed.) (2013) *West Riding Sessions Rolls, 1597/8–1602*. Cambridge: Cambridge University Press.

Litzenberger, Caroline (1997) *The English Reformation and the Laity: Gloucestershire, 1540–1580*. Cambridge: Cambridge University Press.

Loar, Carol (2010a) "Medical Knowledge and the Early Modern English Coroner's Inquest", *Social History of Medicine*, Vol. 23, Issue 3, pp. 475–491.

Loar, Carol (2010b) "'Under Felt Hats and Worsted Stockings': The Uses of Conscience in Early Modern English Coroners' Inquests", *The Sixteenth Century Journal*, Vol. 41, No. 2, pp. 393–414.

Lockwood, Matthew (2013) "From Treason to Homicide: Changing Conceptions of the Law of Petty Treason in Early Modern England", *The Journal of Legal History*, Vol. 34, Issue 1, pp. 31–49.

Lockwood, Matthew (2017) *The Conquest of Death: Violence and the Birth of the Modern English State*. New Haven: Yale University Press.

Longley, Katharine M. (1970) "The 'Trial' Of Margaret Clitherow", *Ampleforth Journal*, Vol. 75, pp. 334–364.

Lynch, Margaret et al. (eds.) (2006) *Life, Love and Death in North-East Lancashire, 1510 to 1537: A Translation of the Act Book of the Ecclesiastical Court of Whalley*. Manchester: Chetham Society.

Macfarlane, Alan (1980) "Review: *Calendar of Assize Records. Essex Indictments, Elizabeth I.*" *American Journal of Legal History*, Vol. 24, Issue 2, pp. 171–177.

Macfarlane, Alan (1981) *The Justice and the Mare's Ale: Law and Disorder in Seventeenth century England*. Oxford: Basil Blackwell.

Machyn, Henry; Nichols, J. G. (ed.) (1848) *The Diary of Henry Machyn, Citizen and Merchant-Taylor of London, 1550–1563*. London: Camden Society.

MacMillan, Ken (ed.) (2015) *Stories of True Crime in Tudor and Stuart England*. Abingdon: Routledge.

Macnair, Mike (1999) "Vicinage and the Antecedents of the Jury", *Law and History Review*, Vol. 17, No. 3, pp. 537–590.

Maddern, Philippa C. (1992) *Violence and Social Order: East Anglia 1422–1442*. Oxford: Oxford University Press.

Marcus, Richard L. (1984) "English Common Law: Studies in the Sources: The Tudor Treason Trials: Some Observations on the Emergence of Forensic Themes", *University of Illinois Law Review*, pp. 675–704.

Marshburn, J.H. (1949) "'A Cruell Murder Donne in Kent' and Its Literary Manifestations", *Studies in Philology*, Vol. 46, No. 2, pp. 131–140.

Masschaele, James (2008) *Jury, State, and Society in Medieval England*. New York: Palgrave Macmillan.

Maus, Katharine Eisaman (1991) "Proof and Consequences: Inwardness and Its Exposure in the English Renaissance", *Representations*, Vol. 34, pp. 29–52.

McBain, Graham (2015) "Modernising the Law of Murder and Manslaughter: Part I", *Journal of Politics and Law*, Vol. 8, No. 4, pp. 56–57.

McCune, Pat (1991) "Justice, Mercy, and Late Medieval Governance", *Michigan Law Review*, Vol. 89, Issue 6, pp. 1661–1678.

McGlynn, Sean (2008) "Violence and the Law in Medieval England", *History Today*, Vol. 58, Issue 4, pp. 53–59.

McIntosh, Marjorie Keniston (1984) "Social Change and Tudor Manorial Leets", in Guy, J. A. and Beale, H. G. (eds.), *Law and Social Change in British History*. London: Royal Historical Society.

McIntosh, Marjorie Keniston (1991) *A Community Transformed: The Manor and Liberty of Havering-atte-Bower, 1500–1620*. Cambridge: Cambridge University Press.

McIntosh, Marjorie Keniston (1998) *Controlling Misbehavior in England, 1370–1600*. Cambridge: Cambridge University Press.

McMullan, John L. (1984) *The Canting Crew: London's Criminal Underworld 1550–1700*. New Brunswick, New Jersey: Rutgers University Press.

McMullan, John L. (1987) "Crime, Law and Order in Early Modern England", *British Journal of Criminology*. Vol. 27, No. 3, pp. 252–274.

McSheffrey, Shannon (2009) "Sanctuary and the Legal Topography of Pre-Reformation London", *Law & History Review*, Vol. 27, No. 3, pp. 483–514.

McSheffrey, Shannon (2011) "The Slaying of Sir William Pennington: Legal Narrative and the Late Medieval English Archive", *Florilegium*, Vol. 28, pp. 169–203.

McSheffrey, Shannon (2016) "The Murder of Mistress Lacey's Maid: Ad Hockery and the Law in England circa 1530", in Witte, John, Jr. et al. (eds.), *Texts and Contexts in Legal History: Essays in Honor of Charles Donahue*. Berkeley: Robbins Collection.

McSheffrey, Shannon (2017a) "Sanctuary Seekers in England, 1380–1557", https://shannonmcsheffrey.wordpress.com/research/. Last accessed 10/3/2019.

McSheffrey, Shannon (2017b) *Seeking Sanctuary: Crime, Mercy, and Politics in English Courts, 1400–1550*. Oxford: Oxford University Press.

Melling, Elizabeth (ed.) (1969) *Kentish Sources VI: Crime and Punishment*. Maidstone: Kent County Council.

Moore, James (2016) *The Tudor Murder Files*. Barnsley: Pen & Sword.

More, Thomas (1516) *Utopia*, 1997. Ware: Wordsworth Classics.

More, Thomas (1557a) *The History of King Richard the Third*, Richard Bear (ed.), 1997. Eugene, Oregon: University of Oregon.

More, Thomas (1557b) *The Workes of Sir Thomas More, Knyght*, 1978. London: Scolar Press.

More, Thomas (1557c); Reed, A. W. et al. (eds.) *The English Works of Sir Thomas More*, 1931. London: Eyre and Spottiswoode.

Moreton, Charles (1993) "Mid-Tudor Trespass: A Break-In at Norwich, 1549", *The English Historical Review*, Vol. 108, No. 427, pp. 387–398.

Morris, John (ed.) (1872) *The Troubles of Our Catholic Forefathers Related by Themselves*. London: Burns and Oates.

Morris, Norval and Rothman, David J. (eds.) (1995) *The Oxford History of the Prison: The Practice of Punishment in Western Society*. Oxford: Oxford University Press.

Morris, T. A. (1999) *Tudor Government*. London: Routledge.

Mortimer, Levine (1963) "A More than Ordinary Case of 'Rape,' 13 and 14 Elizabeth I", *American Journal of Legal History*, Vol. 7, No. 2, pp. 159–164.

Mulholland, Maureen (2003) "Trials in manorial courts in late medieval England", in Mulholland, Maureen et al. (eds.), *Judicial Tribunals in England and Europe, 1200–1700*. Manchester: Manchester University Press.

Müller, Wolfgang P. (2012) *The Criminalization of Abortion in the West: Its Origins in Medieval Law*. Ithaca: Cornell University Press.

Munday, Anthony (1580) *A view of sundry examples Reporting many straunge murthers, sundry persons perjured, signes and tokens of Gods anger towards us. What straunge and monstrous children haue of late beene borne: and all memorable murthers since the murther of Maister Saunders by George Browne, to this present and bloody murther of Abell Bourne Hosyer, who dwelled in Newgate Market*. London: William Wright.

Murray, Stephen O. (2000) *Homosexualities*. Chicago: Chicago University Press.

Musson, A. J. (1999) "Turning King's Evidence: The Prosecution of Crime in Late Medieval England", *Oxford Journal of Legal Studies*, Vol. 19, Issue 3, pp. 467–480.

Musson, Anthony (2001) *Medieval Law in Context: The Growth of Legal Consciousness from Magna Carta to the Peasants' Revolt*. Manchester: Manchester University Press.

Musson, Anthony and Powell, Edward (eds.) (2009) *Crime, Law and Society in the Later Middle Ages*. Manchester: Manchester University Press.

Neville, Cynthia J. (1983) "Gaol Delivery in the Border Counties, 1439–1459: Some Preliminary Observations", *Northern History*, Vol. 19, pp. 45–60.

Neville, Cynthia J. (1994) "Keeping the Peace on the Northern Marches in the Later Middle Ages", *The English Historical Review*, Vol. 109, pp. 1–25.

Newton, Kenneth C. Newton and Marjorie K. McIntosh (1981) "Leet Jurisdiction in Essex Manor Courts during the Elizabethan Period", *Essex Archaeology and History*, Vol. 13, pp. 3–14.

Ogle, Arthur (1949) *The Tragedy of the Lollards' Tower: The Case of Richard Hunne with Its Aftermath in the Reformation Parliament, 1529–1533*. Oxford: Pen-in-Hand.

Oldham, James C. (1983) "The Origins of the Special Jury", *The University of Chicago Law Review*, Vol. 50, Issue 1, pp. 137–221.

O'Malley, Gregory (2005) *The Knights Hospitaller of the English Langue 1460–1565*. Oxford: Oxford University Press.

Page, William (ed.) (1923) *A History of the County of York, North Riding: Volume 2*. London: Victoria County History.

Pattenden, Rosemary (1999) "The Exclusion of the Clergy from Criminal Trial Juries: An Historical Perspective", *Ecclesiastical Law Journal*, Vol. 5, Issue 24, pp. 151–163.

Payling, S.J. (1998) "Murder, Motive and Punishment in Fifteenth century England: Two Gentry Case-Studies", *The English Historical Review*, Vol. 113, No. 450, p. 1–17.

Pearl, Jonathan L. (1999) *The Crime of Crimes: Demonology and Politics in France, 1560–1620*. Waterloo, Canada: Wilfrid Laurier University Press.

Pennington, Kenneth (2003) "Innocent Until Proven Guilty: The Origins of a Legal Maxim", *The Jurist*, Vol. 63, pp. 106–124.

Petty, William (1967) *The Petty Papers: Some Unpublished Writings of Sir William Petty*. New York: Augustus M. Kelley.

Pickthorn, Kenneth (1934) *Early Tudor Government: Henry VII*. Cambridge: Cambridge University Press.

Pihlajamäki, Heikki (2007) "The Painful Question: The Fate of Judicial Torture in Early Modern Sweden", *Law and History Review*, Vol. 25, Issue 3, pp. 557–592.

Platter, Thomas (1599) and Busino, Horatio (1618); Razzell, Peter (ed.) *The Journals of Two Travellers in Elizabethan and Early Stuart England*, 1995. London: Caliban.

Plucknett, T. F. T. (1936) "Some Proposed Legislation of Henry VIII", *Transactions of the Royal Historical Society*, Vol. 19, pp. 119–144.

Post, J. B. (1983) "Local Jurisdictions and Judgment of Death in Later Medieval England", *Criminal Justice History*, Vol. 4, pp. 1–21.

Potter, David (1997) "'Rigueur de Justice': Crime, Murder and the Law in Picardy, Fifteenth to Sixteenth Centuries", *French History*. Vol. 11, No. 3, pp. 265–309.

Pound, John (1971) *Poverty and Vagrancy in Tudor England*. London: Routledge, 1986.

Pound, J. F. (1976) "Vagrants and the Social Order in Elizabethan England", *Past & Present*, No. 71, Issue 1, pp. 126–129.

Powell, Edward (1988) "Jury Trial at Gaol Delivery in the Late Middle Ages: The Midland Circuit, 1400–1429", in *Twelve Good Men and True: The Criminal Trial Jury in England 1200–1800*, Cockburn, J. S. and Green, Thomas A. (eds.). Princeton: Princeton University Press.

Powell, Edward (1989) *Kingship, Law, and Society: Criminal Justice in the Reign of Henry V*. Oxford: Oxford University Press.

Prest, Wilfrid (1967) "Legal Education of the Gentry at the Inns of Court, 1560–1640", *Past & Present*, Vol. 38, Issue 1, pp. 20–39.

Prest, Wilfrid R. (1986) *The Rise of the Barristers: A Social History of the English Bar 1590–1640*. Oxford: Clarendon Press.

Pugh, Ralph B. (1968) *Imprisonment in Medieval England*. Cambridge: Cambridge University Press.

Pugh, R. B. and Crittall, Elizabeth (eds.) (1957) *A History of the County of Wiltshire: Volume 5*. London: Victoria County History.

Pulton, Ferdinando (1623) *De Pace Regis et Regni; Viz. A Treatise Declaring Which Be The Great And General Offences of the Realme*, London: Lincoln's Inn.

Quintrell, B. W. (ed.) (1981) *Proceedings of the Lancashire Justices of the Peace at the Sheriff's Table 1578–1694*. Liverpool: The Record Society of Lancashire and Cheshire.

Raber, Karen and Tucker, Treva J. (eds.) (2005) *The Culture of the Horse: Status, Discipline, and Identity in the Early Modern World*. Basingstoke: Palgrave Macmillan.

Read, Conyers (ed.) (1962) *William Lambarde and Local Government*. Ithaca: Cornell University Press.

Redwood, B. C. (ed.) (1954) *Quarter Sessions Order Book: Volume 54, 1642–1649*. Lewes: Sussex Record Society.

Redworth, Glyn (2008) *The She-Apostle: The Extraordinary Life and Death of Luisa de Carvajal*. Oxford: Oxford University Press.

Regnier, Thomas (2011) "The Law in *Hamlet*: Death, Property, and the Pursuit of Justice", *Brief Chronicles*, Vol. 3, pp. 107–132.

Rice, James D. (1996) "The Criminal Trial Before and After the Lawyers: Authority, Law, and Culture in Maryland Jury Trials, 1681–1837", *American Journal of Legal History*, Vol. 40, No. 4, pp. 455–475.

Richardson, R. C. (2010) "A Maidservant's Lot", *History Today*, Vol. 60, Issue 2, pp. 25–31.

Rid, Samuel (1610a) *Martin Mark-All, Beadle of Bridewell; His Defence and Answere to the Belman of London*. London: John Budge and Richard Bonian.

Rid, Samuel (1610b) "Martin Markall, Beadle of Bridewell", in Judges, A. V. (ed.), *The Elizabethan Underworld*, 1930. London: Routledge.

Ridley, Jasper (2002) *Henry VIII*. London: Penguin.

Riley, H. T. (ed.) (1868) *Memorials of London and London Life in the 13th, 14th and 15th Centuries*. London: Longmans, Green.

Roberts, Stephen (1982b) "Jury Vetting in the 17th Century", *History Today*, Vol. 32, Issue 2, pp. 25–29.

Robey, Ann Catherine (1991) *The Village of Stock, Essex, 1550–1610: A Social And Economic Survey*. PhD thesis, London School of Economics.

Robinson, Hastings (ed.) (1847) *Original Letters Relative to the English Reformation*. Cambridge: Cambridge University Press.

Robison, William B. (1988) "Murder at Crowhurst: A Case Study in Early Tudor Law Enforcement", *Criminal Justice History*, Vol. 9, pp. 31–62.

Roper, William (1556) *The Life of Sir Thomas More*, in E. E. Reynolds (ed.), *Lives of Saint Thomas More*, 1963. London: J. M. Dent.

Roth, Randolph (2001) "Homicide in Early Modern England 1549–1800: The Need for a Quantitative Synthesis", *Crime, History & Societies*, Vol. 5, No. 2, pp. 33–67.

Roth, Randolph (2011) "Biology and the Deep History of Homicide", *British Journal of Criminology*, Vol. 51, No. 3, pp. 535–555.

Roussel, Diane (2015) "A Mosaic of Controls: The Plurality of Order Maintenance Mechanisms in 16th Century Paris", *Journal on European History of Law*, Vol. 6, No. 1, pp. 30–37.

Rowse, A. L. (1950) *The England of Elizabeth*. London: Macmillan.

Rublack, Ulinka (1999) *The Crimes of Women in Early Modern Germany*. Oxford: Oxford University Press.

Ruff, Julius R. (2001) *Violence in Early Modern Europe 1500–1800*. Cambridge: Cambridge University Press.

Russell, M.J. (1980) "II Trial by Battle and the Appeals of Felony", *Journal of Legal History*, Vol. 1, No. 2, pp. 135–164.

St Germain, Christopher (1528) *St Germain's Doctor and Student*. Plucknett, T. F. T. and Barton, J. L. (eds.), 1974. London: Selden Society.

Samaha, Joel (1974) *Law and Order in Historical Perspective: The Case of Elizabethan Essex*. New York: Academic Press.

Samaha, Joel (1975) "Gleanings from Local Criminal-Court Records: Sedition Amongst the 'Inarticulate' in Elizabethan Essex", *Journal of Social History*, Vol. 8, Issue 4, pp. 61–79.

Samaha, Joel (1978) "Hanging for Felony: The Rule of Law in Elizabethan Colchester", *The Historical Journal*, Vol. 21, No. 4, pp. 763–782.

Samaha, Joel (1981) "The Recognizance in Elizabethan Law Enforcement", *American Journal of Legal History*, Vol. 25, No. 3, pp. 189–204.

Sayles, G. O. (1959) *The Court of King's Bench in Law and History.* London: B. Quaritch.

Sayre, Francis Bowes (1928) "Criminal Attempts", *Harvard Law Review*, Vol. 41, No. 7, pp. 821–859.

Schauer, Margery S. and Schauer, Frederick (1980) "Law as the Engine of State: The Trial of Anne Boleyn", *William & Mary Law Review*, Vol. 22, Issue 1, pp. 49–84.

Schnucker, R. V. (1975) "Elizabethan Birth Control and Puritan Attitudes", *Journal of Interdisciplinary History*, Vol. 5, No. 4, pp. 655–667.

Schwerhoff, Gerd (2002) "Criminalized Violence and the Process of Civilisation: A Reappraisal", *Crime, History & Societies*, Vol. 6, No. 2, pp. 103–126.

Seipp, David (2002) "Jurors, Evidences and the Tempest of 1499", in Cairns, John W. and McLeod, Grant (eds.), *"The Dearest Birth Right of the People of England": The Jury in the History of the Common Law.*, Oxford: Oxford University Press.

Selden, John (1640) *A Briefe Discourse Concerning the Powers of the Peeres and Comons of Parliament*, London.

Selig, Robert, A. (1998) "Eye for an Eye? Crime and Punishment in Early Modern Germany", *German Life: Culture, History, Travel*, December, pp. 23–27.

Sevier, Justin (2016) "Popularizing Hearsay", *Georgetown Law Journal*, Vol. 104, pp. 643–692.

Shapiro, Barbara J. (1987) "To a Moral Certainty: Theories of Knowledge and Anglo-American Juries 1600–1850", *Hastings Law Journal*, Vol. 38, Issue 1, pp. 153–193.

Shapiro, Barbara J. (2000) *A Culture of Fact: England, 1550–1720.* Ithaca: Cornell University Press.

Sharpe, J. A. (1980) "Enforcing the Law in the Seventeenth century English Village", in Gatrell, V. A. C. et al. (eds.), *Crime and the Law: The Social History of Crime in Western Europe Since 1500.* London: Europa.

Sharpe, J. A. (1981) "Domestic Homicide in Early Modern England", *Historical Journal*, Vol. 24, Issue 1, pp. 29–48.

Sharpe J. A. (1983) *Crime in Seventeenth century England.* Cambridge: Cambridge University Press.

Sharpe, J. A. (1985) "The History of Violence in England: Some Observations", *Past & Present*, Vol. 108, Issue 1, pp. 206–215.

Sharpe, J. A. (1999a) *Crime in Early Modern England 1550–1750.* London: Longman.

Sharpe, James (1999b) *The Bewitching of Anne Gunter: A Horrible and True Story of Deception, Witchcraft, Murder and the King of England*. London: Profile Books.

Sharpe, J. A. and Dickinson, J. R. (2016) "Revisiting the 'Violence We Have Lost': Homicide in Seventeenth century Cheshire", *The English Historical Review*, Vol. 131, Issue 549, pp. 293–323.

Sharpe, James (2016) *A Fiery and Furious People: A History of Violence in England*. London: Random House Books.

Shepard, Alexandra (2015) *Accounting for Oneself: Worth, Status, and the Social Order in Early Modern England*. Oxford: Oxford University Press.

Shoemaker, Karl (2011) *Sanctuary and Crime in the Middle Ages, 400–1500*. New York: Fordham University Press.

Shoemaker, Robert B. (1991) *Prosecution and Punishment: Petty Crime and the Law in London and Rural Middlesex, c.1660–1725*. Cambridge: Cambridge University Press.

Sil, Narasingha P. (2001) *Tudor Placemen and Statesmen: Select Case Histories*. Madison, New Jersey: Fairleigh Dickinson University Press.

Sil, Narasingha P. (2007) "'My Bitter Comedie': The Treason Trial of Sir Nicholas Throckmorton and the Rule of Law in Tudor England", in Ocker, Christopher et al. (eds.), *Politics and Reformations: Communities, Polities, Nations and Empires*. Leiden: Brill.

Silver, George (1599) *Paradoxes of Defence*. London: Edward Blount.

Skidmore, Chris (2017) *Richard III: Brother, Protector, King*. London: Weidenfeld & Nicolson.

Skousen, Lesley (2008) *Redefining Benefit of Clergy During the English Reformation*. MA thesis, University of Wisconsin.

Slobogin, Christopher (2000) "An End to Insanity: Recasting the Role of Mental Disability in Criminal Cases", *Virginia Law Review*, Vol. 86, No. 6, pp. 1199–1247.

Smalbroke, Richard (1728) *Reformation necessary to prevent Our Ruine: A Sermon Preached to the Societies for Reformation of Manners, at St. Mary-le-Bow, on Wednesday, January 10th, 1727*. London: Joseph Downing.

Smith, M. G. (1982) *Pastoral Discipline and the Church Courts: The Hexham Court 1680–1730*. York: University of York, Borthwick Papers No. 62.

Smith, Thomas (1583) *De Republica Anglorum. The maner of Gouvernement or policie of the Realme of England*. London: Gregorie Seton.

Spelman, Henry (1626) *Archaeologus*. London: John Beale.

Spence, Laura (2010) *Women Who Murder In Early Modern England, 1558–1700*. MA dissertation, University of Warwick.

Spenser, Edmund (1596) "A View of the Present State of Irelande", in Grosart, Alexander Balloch (ed.), *The Complete Works in Verse and Prose of Edmund Spenser*, 1884. London: Spenser Society.

Spierenburg, Peter (1991) *The Prison Experience: Disciplinary Institutions and Their Inmates in Early Modern Europe*. New Brunswick, New Jersey: Rutgers University Press.

Spierenburg, Peter (2008) *A History of Murder: Personal Violence in Europe from the Middle Ages to the Present*. Cambridge: Polity.

Spivack, Carla (2007) "To 'Bring Down the Flowers': The Cultural Context of Abortion Law in Early Modern England", *William & Mary Journal of Women and the Law*, Vol. 14, No. 1, pp. 107–152.

Spraggs, Gillian (2001) *Outlaws and Highwaymen*. London: Pimlico.

Stacy, William R. (1986) "Richard Roose and the Use of Parliamentary Attainder in the Reign of Henry VIII", *The Historical Journal*, Vol. 29, Issue 1, pp. 1–15.

Starkey, Thomas (1533–1536) *A Dialogue Between Reginald Pole and Thomas Lupset*, Burton, K. M. (ed.), 1948. London: Chatto and Windus.

Staunford, William (1560) *Les Plees Del Coron: Divisee in Plusiours Titles & Common Lieux*. London: Richard Tottell.

Staunford, William (1607) *Les Plees Del Coron: Divisee in Plusiours Titles & Common Lieux*. London: Societatis Stationariorum.

Stephen, James Fitzjames (1883) *A History of the Criminal Law of England*. London: Macmillan.

Stevenson, S. J. (1987) "The Rise of Suicide Verdicts in South-East England, 1530–1590: The Legal Process", *Continuity and Change,* Vol. 2, No. 1, pp. 37–75.

Stone, Lawrence (1967) *The Crisis of the Aristocracy 1558–1641*, abridged edition. Oxford: Galaxy Books.

Stone, Lawrence (1983) "Interpersonal Violence in English Society, 1300–1980", *Past & Present*, Vol. 101, Issue 1, pp. 22–33.

Stone, Lawrence (1985) "The History of Violence in England: A Rejoinder", *Past & Present*, No. 108, pp. 206–215.

Stow, John (1592) *The Annales of England, faithfully collected out of the most autenticall Authors, Records, and other Monuments of Antiquitie, from the first inhabitation untill this present yeere 1592*. London: Ralfe Newbery.

Stoyle, Mark (2011) "'It Is But an Olde Wytche Gonne': Prosecution and Execution for Witchcraft in Exeter, 1558–1610", *History*, Vol. 96, Issue 322, pp. 129–151.

Syme, Holger Schott (2012) "(Mis)representing Justice on the Early Modern Stage", *Studies in Philology*, Vol. 109, No. 1, pp. 63–85.

Tawney, R. H. and Power, Eileen (eds.) (1951) *Tudor Economic Documents*. London: Longmans.

Terrill, Richard J. (1985) "William Lambarde: Elizabethan Humanist and Legal Historian", *The Journal of Legal History*, Vol. 6, Issue 2, pp. 157–178.

Thayer, Ezra Ripley (1913) "A Sixteenth Century Jury", *The Green Bag*, Vol. 25, No. 296.

Thomas, Courtney (2011) "'Not Having God Before His Eyes': Bestiality in Early Modern England", *Seventeenth Century*, Vol. 26, Issue 1, pp. 149–173.

Thomson, John A. F. (2014) *The Early Tudor Church and Society 1485–1529*. Abingdon: Routledge.

Tittler, Robert (1988) "The Sequestration of Juries in Early Modern England", *Historical Research*, Vol. 61, Issue 146, pp. 301–305.

Underdown, David (1985) *Revel, Riot & Rebellion: Popular Politics and Culture in England, 1603–1660*. Oxford: Oxford University Press.

Underwood, Richard H. (1993) "False Witness: A Lawyer's History of the Law of Perjury", *Arizona Journal of International and Comparative Law*, Vol. 10, No. 2, pp. 215–252.

Uribe-Uran, Victor M. (2007) "'*Iglesia me llamo?*': Church Asylum and the Law in Spain and Colonial Spanish America" *Comparative Studies in Society and History*, Vol. 49, No. 1, pp. 446–472.

Van Caenegam, R. C. (1987) *Judges, Legislators & Professors: Chapters in European Legal History*. Cambridge: Cambridge University Press.

van der Heijden, Manon (2016) *Women and Crime in Early Modern Holland*. Leiden: Brill.

Virgoe, Roger (1980) "The Murder of James Andrew: Suffolk Faction in the 1430s", *Proceedings of the Suffolk Institute of Archaeology and History*, Vol. 34, part 4, pp. 263–268.

von Friedenburg, Robert (1990) "Reformation of Manners and the Social Composition of Offenders in an East Anglian Cloth Village: Earls Colne, Essex, 1531–1642", *Journal of British Studies*, Vol. 29, No. 4, pp. 347–385.

von Wedel, Lupold; von Bülow, Gottfried (trans.) (1585) "Journey through England and Scotland Made by Lupold von Wedel in the Years 1584 and 1585", *Transactions of the Royal Historical Society, New Series, Vol. 9*, 1895, pp. 223–270.

Waddell, Brodie (2012) "Governing England through the Manor Courts, 1550–1850", *The Historical Journal*, Vol. 55, Issue 2, pp. 279–315.

Walker, Gilbert (1552) *A Manifest detection of the moste vyle and detestable vse of Diceplay.* London: Abraham Vele.

Walker, Simon (1993) "Yorkshire Justices of the Peace, 1389–1413", *The English Historical Review*, Vol. 108, Issue 427, pp. 281–313.

Wall, Alison (2004) "'The Greatest Disgrace : The Making and Unmaking of JPs in Elizabethan and Jacobean England", *The English Historical Review*, Vol. 119, No. 481, pp. 312–332.

Walter, John (1980) "Grain Riots and Popular Attitudes to the Law: Maldon and the Crisis of 1629", in Brewer, John and Styles, John (eds.), *An Ungovernable People: The English and Their Law in the 17th and 18th Centuries.* London: Hutchinson.

Ward Richard (ed.) (2015) *A Global History of Execution and the Criminal Corpse.* Basingstoke: Palgrave Macmillan.

Warrington, John (ed.) (1956) *The Paston Letters, Volume 1.* London: J. M. Dent.

Watkin, Thomas Glyn (1984) "Hamlet and the Law of Homicide", *The Law Quarterly Review*, Vol. 100, pp. 282–310.

Watson, Godfrey (1974) *The Border Reivers.* London: Robert Hale.

Weaver, John and Wright, David (eds.) (2009) *Histories of Suicide: International Perspectives on Self-Destruction in the Modern World.* Toronto: University of Toronto Press.

Westerman, William (1600) *Two Sermons Of Assise: The one intituled; A prohibition of Revenge: the other, A Sword of Maintenance.* London: W. Westerman.

Whitman, James Q. (2005) "The Origins of 'Reasonable Doubt'", Yale Law School Legal Scholarship Repository, Faculty Scholarship Series, FS Paper 1.

Wilkinson, John (1618) *A Treatise Collected out of the Statutes of this Kingdom, and according to common experience of the lawes, concerning the Office and Authorities of Coroners and Sherifes*, London: Companie of Stationers.

Wilkinson, D. J. (1982) "The Commission of the Peace in Lancashire, 1603–1642", *Transactions of the Historic Society of Lancashire and Cheshire*, Vol. 132, pp. 41–66.

Williams, C. (ed.) (1967) *English Historical Documents, Volume V: 1485–1588.* London: Eyre and Spottiswoode.

Williams, Ian (2010) "'He Creditted More the Printed Booke': Common Lawyers' Receptivity to Print, c.1550–1640", *Law and History Review*, Vol. 23, No. 1, pp. 39–70.

Wilson, Ralph (1722) *A Full and Impartial Account of All the Robberies Committed by John Hawkins*, third edition. London: J. Peele.

Winter, Christine (2012) *Prisons and Punishments in Late Medieval London*. PhD thesis, University of London, Royal Holloway College.

Wood, Andy (2014) "The Deep Roots of Albion's Fatal Tree: The Tudor State and the Monopoly of Violence", *History*, Vol. 99, Issue 336, pp. 403–417.

Wormald, Jenny (1980) "Bloodfeud [*sic*], Kindred and Government in Early Modern Scotland", *Past & Present*, Vol. 87, Issue 1, pp. 54–97.

Wrightson, Keith and Walter, John (1976) "Dearth and the Social Order in Early Modern England", *Past & Present*, No. 71, Issue 1, pp. 22–42.

Wrightson, Keith (1980) "Two Concepts of Order: Justices Constables and Jurymen in Seventeenth century England", in Brewer, John and Styles, John (eds.), *An Ungovernable People: The English and Their Law in the 17th and 18th Centuries*. London: Hutchinson.

Wrightson, Keith (1982) "Infanticide in European History", *Criminal Justice History*, Vol. 3, pp. 1–20.

Wrightson, Keith (1983) *English Society 1580–1680*. London: Routledge.

Wrightson, Keith and Levine, David (1995) *Poverty and Piety in an English Village: Terling, 1525–1700*. Oxford: Clarendon.

Wrightson, Keith (1996) "The Politics of the Parish in Early Modern England", in Griffiths, Paul et al. (eds.), *The Experience of Authority in Early Modern England*. Basingstoke: Palgrave Macmillan.

Youngs, Deborah (2008) *Humphrey Newton (1466–1536): An Early Tudor Gentleman*. Woodbridge: Boydell & Brewer.

Zmarzly, Rebecca J. (2007) *Justices of the Peace in Mid-Tudor Devon circa 1538–1570*. MA thesis, Texas State University, San Marcos.

Zell, M. L. (1977) "Early Tudor JPs at Work", *Archaeologia Cantiana*, Vol. 93, pp. 125–144.

Zell, Michael L. (1999) "Kent's Elizabethan JPs at Work", *Archaeologia Cantiana*, Vol. 119, pp. 1–44.

Zell, Michael and Hyde, Patricia (2000) "Governing the County", in Zell, Michael (ed.), *Early Modern Kent, 1540–1640*. Woodbridge: Boydell & Brewer.

Index

A

abduction *12, 636*

Abergavenny *378*

Abingdon *159, 444*

  execution of a child *403*

abjuration *26, 139, 227, 453–462*

abortion *597, 600–602*

abuse

  domestic abuse *329*

  of charity *88*

  of neighbours *324*

  of the Sabbath *328*

  power relationships

    abuse of appointment *294*

    rape, etc. *642*

accident *159, 549, 556*

accomplices *224–225, 449, 534, 566, 628*

acquittal *373, 390*

  alternative steps *385*

  bar to other proceedings *236*

adjournment *369*

Admiralty Sessions *401*

admission *105, 171, 198, 207*

adultery *11, 54, 328, 635*

  as provocation *551*

alcohol *68, 580*

alehouses *12, 68, 94, 103, 241, 302, 580*

  trading stolen goods *661*

alibi *208, 377*

alienation *574*

aliens *362*

almoners *161, 572*

amateurism *70, 103*

amputation *408*

Anabaptists *404*

anatomy *412*

anger *577*

  sudden anger *538*

animals. See *bestiality; theft*

anti-social conduct *315*

appeal *23, 139, 225*

  appeal against conviction *393*

approvement *224*

aristocracy *48, 115, 405, 539*

arraignment *347*

arrest *100, 171–173*

arsenic *165, 593*

arson *231*

artifice *681*

assizes *263*

  Assize of Bread and Ale *318*

  Assize of Clarendon *239*

  Black Assizes *277*

  clerk of assizes *278*

asylum *445*

attainder *33, 239, 331, 504*

Attorney General *269*

attrition rate *22*, *685*

autopsy *164*

B

Babington, Anthony *404*

Babington, Zachary *564*

Bacon, Sir Francis *34*, *339*

"badgers" *67*

bail *100*, *170*, *186*, *212–216*, *537*, *683*

  bailees *681*

bailiffs *137*, *146*, *316*, *414*

  jury bailiff *379*

banditry *311*

banishment *254*, *324*, *396*

barber surgeons *164*, *412*

Barnes, Roger *167*

barrators *318*, *578*

barristers *260*, *316*

  barristers' monopoly *278*

bastardy *605*, *636*, *642*

  bastard-bearing *420*

battle *225*

beadle *65*

Beaulieu *617*

  Beaulieu Abbey *188*, *447*

  chartered sanctuary *443*, *460*

Becket, Archbishop Thomas *479*

beer *54*

begging *43*, *55*, *65*

beheading *404*

belly

  pleading the belly *237*

benefit of clergy. See *clerics*

Bennett, Thomas *188–192*

Berwick-on-Tweed *310*

bestiality *647*, *651–654*

Beverley *443*

bias *152*, *274*, *389*

bigamy

  Germany *397*

binding-over *97*, *385*, *589*

  of witnesses *199*

  to keep the peace *210*

Black Death *9*, *36*, *100*, *365*

blackmail *250*, *251*

Blackstone, William *488*

Bocardo Prison *439*

boiling to death *406*, *523*

Boleyn, Anne *332*

Borders *134*, *309*, *687*

boring the gristle *64*

borsholders *77*

Bracton, Henry de *615*

branding *64*, *457*, *482*

brawling *576*

breaking-in

  during daylight *475*

breaking on the wheel *404*

bribery *59*, *113*, *145*, *162*, *358*, *359*

bridewell

  London Bridewell *65*, *221*, *423*

    Bridewell Palace *423*

  spread of bridewells *424*

Bristol *221*, *635*

brothels *635*

brutality *222*

Buckingham, Duke of *33*, *332*, *372*

Buckinghamshire *125*

buggery *28*, *500*, *646*

Buggery Act *646, 651*

burglary *505, 657, 672*

of palaces *308*

burning to death *9, 124*

burying alive *404*

Busino, Horatio *396, 411*

butchers *668*

bye-laws *313–314, 318*

C

cages

to display miscreants *635*

Cambridge *39, 59, 416*

Black Assize *277*

Cannock *176*

Canterbury *124, 615*

diocesan court *329*

capital punishment *11, 64, 296, 396, 687*

death-for-felony rule *24–26, 466*

death-for-felony-rule

avoidance of *432–546*

summary execution *23*

William Hastings (without trial) *32*

#Carrier's Case# *681*

case

case-hardening *361*

case management *100*

Catholicism *38, 53, 123, 432*

harboring Catholic priests *350*

sodomy *645*

Cecil, Sir Robert *160*

centralisation *102, 258, 518, 572, 684*

resistance to *290*

#certiorari# *345*

chance medley *550*

chapbooks *15, 52, 182*

character

good character *208, 398*

Chelmsford *200, 553, 594*

Cheshire *26, 170, 304*

Cheshire County Court *304*

Chester *14, 657*

children *402*

sexual assaults, etc. *643*

circuits *265*

administration *278*

civil matters *264*

class *151, 357, 490*

clemency *432*

clerics *107*

benefit of clergy *26, 295, 355, 477*

Benefit of Clergy Act *505, 639*

bishops *331*

"criminous clerks" *479*

"genuine" cleric *500*

lecherous clergymen *635*

clerk of the peace *281*

Clink Prison *423*

"clipping". See *coining*

Clitherow, Margaret *349*

Cobham *74*

coining *12, 290, 405*

"clipping" *12*

Coke, Sir Edward *32, 651, 673*

Colchester *113*

cold cases *576*

combat *225*

common law *28*

compassion *464, 538*

compensation *318*

for rape *641*

compounding *60,* *238.* See also *under felony; misdemeanour*

compurgation *499, 638*

confession *184, 374, 632*

sanctuary and *453*

confiscation *41*

conflict of interest *152*

con men *203, 206*

consent *644*

conspiracy to murder *565*

contacts *539*

"contracting-out" *315*

conviction. See *appeal*

conviction rates *390*

safety of *532*

wrongful conviction *534*

Cornwall *126*

coroners *139–168*

remuneration *686*

#corpus delicti# *254*

corroboration *211*

corruption *21, 35, 58, 82, 113, 155*

concerning forfeiture *419*

"corrupt victuals" *318*

inquest juries *161*

reduced *684*

counterfeiting *12, 228, 405*

courtiers

forfeiture grants *418*

Courtney, Sir Thomas *531*

courts

assizes. See *assizes*

"bawdy court" *328*

borough sessions *288*

court baron *314*

Court of the Lord High Steward *331*

criminal courts *258–277*

ecclesiastical courts *327, 444*

leet courts *313*

lesser courts *313*

quarter sessions. See *quarter sessions*

Coventry *93, 316*

cozening *43, 174*

Cranbrook *37*

crime

acquisitive crimes *657*

crime prevention *51*

crimes of status *65*

explanations for crime *50*

habitual crime *659*

opportunistic crime *658*

political crimes *400*

property crime *655–664*

leet courts *322*

criminal justice system *69–222*

efficiency *56*

"show of justice" *33*

Cromwell, Thomas *41, 48, 55, 101, 121, 191, 259, 384, 459, 646*

crops *12*

Crown *258, 685*

Crown privilege *224*

cruentation *181*

cucking stool *324*

Culpepper, Thomas *539*

Cumberland *125, 309, 315*

cunning individuals *180*

#Custos Rotulorum# *282, 285*

cutpurses *475, 505, 657*

D

Dacre, Lord *540, 552*

dearth *52*

death

death penalty. See *capital punishment*

deaths in custody *139, 166, 425*

Richard Hunne *151*

sudden, etc. deaths *139*

suspicious deaths *146*

debtors

sanctuary *444*

deception *174*

degradation *500*

deodands *161*

depositions *196, 256*

Deptford *148*

desertion *503*

desperation *227, 632*

detection *100, 183–202*

detective work *97*

supernatural methods *180*

deterrence *415, 546*

Devon *106, 116, 191*

discretion

jury discretion *383–385*

magistrates' discretion *199*

parish officials *66*

royal discretion *416*

sick jurors *380*

discrimination *489*

dishonesty *324, 422*

dismemberment *404*

dissection *412*

dissenters *272*

dissolution of the monasteries *461*

divine intervention *180*

dock *277*

domestic violence. See *violence*

Doncaster *136, 166*

Dover *454*

down-valuing *26, 255, 322, 354, 392, 466–495, 659*

institutionalised *472*

drowning *404, 627*

drunkenness *422*

Duchy of Lancaster *141*

Chancellor of *108*

ducking *300*

Dudley, Edmund *525*

Dudley, Lord Robert *151, 162*

duelling *201, 225, 560*

dungeons *430*

Durham *148, 667*

Durham Cathedral *443*

dwellings *673*

dying declaration *375*

E

East Anglia *225*

East Riding *72, 143, 287*

eavesdroppers *318*

ecclesiastical courts *11, 313, 614, 635*

economic aspects *624*

Edinburgh *404*

Edward III *100*

Edward IV *212, 288*

efficiency *21, 56, 684*

Elizabeth I *8, 124, 151, 387*

forfeiture grants *418*

Ely (Isle of) *303, 306–308*

Emson, Sir Richard *525*

enlistment *544*

entrapment *206*

epidemics *426*

escape *218*, *226*, *238*

from prison *430*

from sanctuary *440*

Statute of Escapes *430*

Essex *46*, *79*, *96*, *174*, *241*

rape *639*

Eton College

sodomy *648*

Europe *356*, *432*, *577*, *617*, *645*

homicide rates *570*

property crime *655*

eviction *324*

evidence *194*, *198–199*, *370–372*, *683*. See
also *hearsay*

circumstantial evidence *375*, *533*

infanticide *621*

King's/Queen's evidence *229*

new evidence *534*

weight of evidence *372*

written evidence *201*

examination *100*

example *532*

excommunication *328*, *438*

execution *239*, *529*

death-for-felony rule *398*

Execution Dock *401*

incidence of *398*

mass executions *400*

exemplary punishment, etc. *397*, *408*,
412

Exeter *37*, *92*

Black Assizes *278*, *283*

Exeter Castle *422*

exile

internal exile *459*

extortion *21*, *310*

F

facts

stretching facts *549*

fairness *204*, *333*, *489*

gendered unfairness *527*

false imprisonment *71*, *231*

favouritism *31*

felony *12*, *171*, *194*

appeal of felony *230*

compounding felonies *247–250*

felonious killing *157*

misprision of felony *242*

prosecution of *224*

#feme covert# *508*

fence breaking *12*

fences (stolen goods) *660*

fictions *597*, *629*

fictitious offenders *557*

fines *318*, *422*

Finland *575*

firearms *250*, *592*

Fleet Prison *58*, *60*, *423*

flogging *64*, *299*, *420–422*, *466*

Flowerdew, Edward *307*

food *67*

football *54*, *159*

death from playing *559*

footpads *678*

foreigners *362*

forensics *163*

forestalling, etc. *67*

forfeiture *11, 51, 351, 413–416, 520*

"corruption of blood" *558*

following suicide *161*

hardship and *416*

redemption of *419*

forgiveness *521*

fornication *54, 328, 611, 635*

Fortescue, Sir John *218*

France *218, 396, 575, 655*

appeal system *393*

franchises *303, 439*

frankpledge *76*

"view of frankpledge" *315*

fraud *376, 681–683*

frivolous allegations *202*

G

galleys *397, 545, 546*

gallows *10, 101*

temporary gallows. See *Tyburn*

gambling *54*

gangs *298*

gaol *422*

gaol delivery *212, 259, 271*

gaol fever *277*

Gawdy, Sir Francis *269, 301*

gender *488, 507, 586, 599, 634*

infanticide *626*

General Eyre *258*

gentry *48, 109, 259, 277, 309*

inter-gentry feuding *61*

Germany *397, 618, 645*

gibbet *411*

Glastonbury *443*

Gloucestershire *126, 389*

Gloucester *617*

gossip *364*

grain *67*

grand jury

homicide cases *564*

Great Yarmouth *302*

forfeiture franchise *419*

Greenwich *619*

Guildford *138*

Guildhall *309*

gypsies *40, 363, 426, 543*

Egyptians Act *41*

horse theft *670*

H

Hackney *314*

Hales, John *32*

Hampshire *110, 131, 411*

hanging *25, 396*

hanging in chains *412*

suicide and hanging *167*

harbouring offenders *660*

hard labour *423*

Hattersley, Jane *630*

headboroughs *77*

hearings *368*

hearsay *201, 254–256, 372–374*

hedge-breaking *320*

Henry II *239*

Henry III *259*

Henry V *525*

Henry VII *8, 47, 213, 224*

Henry VIII *16, 52, 107, 123, 245, 539*

executions under *399*

"merciless prince" *399*

heresy *54, 123, 151, 307, 404*

Hertfordshire *473*

Hexham *436*

hierarchy *51*

high constable *70, 72–74*

high sheriff *101*

Hitcham, Sir Robert *307*

"Holy Maid of Kent" *33*

homicide *236, 385, 518, 548–557, 687*

excusable homicide *554*

homicide rates *567*

homosexuality *635*

honour *106, 560, 577*

"hot-bloodedness" *550*

housebreaking *672*

house of correction *71, 217, 385, 423, 609*

House of Lords

trial by *201, 331*

Howard, Catherine *418*

hue and cry *54, 87, 174–179*

humiliation *58, 352, 422*

Hungerford, Lord *649*

Hunne, Richard *166, 444*

hunting *197*

in the dark *187*

Hussey, Lord Chief Justice *245*

I

identification *377*

idleness *54, 63*

ignoramus *338*

illegitimacy. See *bastardy*

imprisonment. See *prison*

impulsiveness *584*

indictment *23, 170, 343–345*

bill of indictment *281*

"true bill" *336*

trial on indictment *239*

infanticide *253, 328, 568, 597*

Europe *626*

Germany *625*

"infanticide craze" *632*

influence *649*

informers *246, 250*

innocence

presumption of *382*

Inns of Court *18, 128*

inquest *139, 686*

inquest verdict *156–158*

inquisitorial method *57*

insanity *537, 549, 556*

interrogation *57*

interrogatories *204*

intimidation *22, 62, 113*

intoxication *580*

intranquility *580*

investigation *183*

Italy *219, 560*

sodomy *645*

J

James I *120, 361, 552*

Jonson, Ben *563*

judges *260*

assize judges *268*

summing-up *377*

judiciary *268*

jurisdiction *290, 302, 317*

special jurisdiction *303*

jury

coroner's jury *149, 150–152*

grand jury *9, 170, 239, 335–337*

"hung" jury *381*

imprisonment of jurors *370*

in leet courts *316*

jury activism *155*

jury box *277*

jury "equity" *354, 391*

jury mitigation *475*

jury of matrons *508*

jury punishment *31, 386*

jury sequestration *379*

peremptory challenges *361*

perverse verdict *374*

petty jury *240*

presenting jury *239*

Proclamation for Jurors *361, 384*

property qualification *357*

sanctuary decisions *438*

self-informing jury *364*

"silly men" *359*

justices of the peace *9, 29, 54, 100–107*

attendance at quarter sessions *287*

clerical JPs *107*

detection by *183*

dismissal *121*

JPs and policing *97–99*

"judicial" JPs *262*

justice's clerk *196*

lawyer JPs *130–132*

misconduct *112–114*

selection *108–111*

"trading justices" *105*

K

Kent *116*

King's Bench *149, 157, 312, 437*

King's Lynn *302*

Kirtlington *313*

Knights Hospitaller *443*

L

Lancashire *108, 120, 285*

Lancaster *282*

leet courts in *321*

larceny *254, 466, 657*

benefit of clergy re *661*

larceny by trick *682*

petty larceny

leet courts *322*

law

law and order *52*

points of law *394*

lawyers *31, 260, 316, 368*

legal representation *334*

leg-irons *430*

lesbianism *647*

"lewd" behaviour *70*

licensing *54, 103*

literacy *16, 52, 355, 490, 507*

Little Ice Age *38*

localism *70*

lock-up *185*

Lollard's Tower *166*

London *635*

City of London *92*

London Bridewell. See *bridewell*

property crime *655*

St Paul's *659*

Lord Chancellor *108*, *121*, *555*

lord lieutenant *282*

lunatics *371*

M

Magna Carta *34*, *232*

magnanimity *521*

magnates *47*, *61–68*, *105*, *309*, *518*

  magnate immunity *52*

Maidstone *37*

mainprise *439*

malice *550*

  "constructive malice" *552*

  malicious accusations *208*, *250*, *533*, *653*

  "mute of malice" *348*

  "transferred malice" *552*

manacles *221*

Manchester *84*, *451*

manners *53*

manorial system *313*

manslaughter *145*, *152*, *296*, *553*

march law *311*

Marian statutes *194*, *684*

  Marian bail statute *214*

Marlowe, Christopher *148*, *520*

marshals *280*

Marshalsea Prison *228*, *312*, *423*, *649*

martial law. See *military*

Mary (Queen Mary) *18*, *41*, *53*, *297*, *404*

mayhem *234*

medical matters *163*

medieval period *21*

memory

  refreshing memory *201*

#mens rea# *548*

mental illness *537*

mercy *521*

  mercy killing *558*

Middlesex *308*

military *49*

  cultural militarisation *309*, *573*

  martial law *10*

  military conflict *399*

  military law *311*

  military operations

    acting under orders *390*

  military service

    pardons and *544*

  private armies *50*

  quasi-military forces *655*

misadventure/misfortune *549*, *556*

mischance *163*, *557*

misdemeanour *12*

  bail for *216*

  compounding a misdemeanour *247*

  serious misdemeanours *203*

mitigation *246*, *475*, *538*

mobility *38*, *55*, *133*, *240*, *365*

morality *53*, *637*

  #Custos Morum# *312*

  moral offences *11*

  sexual immorality *328*

More, Thomas *334*, *369*, *536*

Morley, Lord *201*

Much Wenlock *289*, *423*

  execution of child *403*

murder *21*, *145*, *174*, *181*, *231*, *553*. See also *infanticide; neonaticide*

  attempted murder *565*

mute *348*, *351*

mute of malice *353, 640*

standing mute *27*

mutilation *58*

N

Naples *397*

"neck verse" *495*

need *292*

neonaticide *28, 567, 598, 613*

Netherlands *575*

Newcastle *310*

forfeiture entitlements *417*

Newgate Gaol *140, 255, 307, 401, 423, 535*

night-time *673*

nightwalkers *94*

#nisi prius# *271*

Norfolk *14, 79*

Norfolk Circuit *306*

Northampton

Statute of Northampton *680*

Northamptonshire *569*

Northern Circuit *389*

North Riding *116*

Northumberland *309*

Norwich *286*

notebooks *15*

Nottingham Gaol *147*

nullification *383*

O

oath *196, 207, 239*

offences

administrative offences *10*

inchoate offences *565*

moral offences *11*

offences against the person *321*

regulatory offences *10, 313*

repeat offending *481*

offenders

professional criminals *667*

serial offenders *659*

officeholder misdeeds *12*

Old Bailey *14, 64, 265, 278, 308, 563, 618, 659*

ordeal *230, 356*

outlawry *22, 23, 139*

Oxfordshire *77, 142, 313*

Oxford *168, 388, 401*

Black Assizes *278*

Earl of Oxford *61*

homicide rates *569*

oyer and terminer *271, 298*

P

"padders". See *footpads*

paedophilia *643*

palatine counties *303*

pamphlets *16*

pardon *22, 26, 238, 477, 518*

circuit pardons *529*

conditional pardons *544*

following malicious prosecution *415*

Pardon Acts *526*

royal pardons *519*

Statute of Pardons *545, 548*

trade in pardons *522, 542*

parish *313*

parish officers *253*

partiality *316*

passport *40, 55*

patronage *35*

pawnbrokers *661*

#Pear's Case# *682*

peculiars *280*

peddlers *667*

#peine forte et dure# *220, 349*

penal reform *429*

penance *328, 614, 635*

   Irish Penitential of Finnian *614*

Percy, Earl Henry *151*

perjury *12, 370, 422*

   jury by *388*

   "pious perjury" *686*

petitions *57, 528*

petty constable *70, 76*

petty sessions *326, 686*

physicians *163*

pickpockets *505, 657*

Pilgrimage of Grace *400*

pillory *44, 47, 58, 248, 422*

pistols *679*

pity *538*

plague *267, 278*

   false claims of plague *182*

Plankney, John *168*

plea *354*

   "plea bargaining" *468*

poaching *319*

poisoning *163–165, 219, 353, 376, 517,*
     591–593

   Poisoning Act *500*

   punishment for *406*

   ratsbane *593*

   transferred malice *552*

police *70*

police powers *65*

politics *151, 521*

Poole *676*

poor law *63*

   Poor Law Act *79*

   poor relief *44*

Popham, Sir John *34, 307*

post-mortem

   following an execution *411*

poverty *36, 51, 66–68, 292, 656*

   "impotent poor" *62*

   Poor Law *66, 611*

   poor relief *66*

pregnancy *26, 295, 355, 477*

   pleading the belly *508*

premeditation *538, 579*

prerogative *56, 222*

printing *16–18*

prison *422*

   ecclesiastical imprisonment *498*

   imprisonment *422*

   prison security *429*

prisoners

   malnutrition *428*

   overload *294*

privilege *432*

Privy Council *43, 61, 64, 97, 102, 298, 679*

   mercy *530*

   suspects and *191–194*

proclamation *236, 524, 679*

profanity *12*

professional ruffians *580*

prosecution

   malicious prosecution *251–253*

   private prosecution *242*

prostitution *54, 65, 420, 424, 635*

Protestantism *8, 123*

  burning at the stake *404*

  sodomy *645*

prothonotaries *279*

provocation *551, 578*

provost marshals *40*

punishments *396–425*

  benign punishments *23*

purgation *498–500*

Puritanism *9, 53, 605*

pursuit *172*

  hot pursuit *179*

Q

quartering *404*

quarter sessions *280, 686*

quorum *214*

R

rack *219*

raiding *309, 687*

Raleigh, Sir Walter *373, 376*

rank *539*

rape *234, 248, 296, 505, 636–640*

  benefit of clergy re *313*

  homosexual rape *650*

  of unknown victim *256*

  wording of indictment *344*

Ratsey, Gamaliel *177, 230*

ravishment *636*

rebellion *10, 91, 436*

  East Anglia *45*

  Jack Cade's rebellion *31*

  Kett's rebellion *133*

  Northern Rebellion *89*

  Oxfordshire Rising *46*

recidivism *245, 436*

recognisance *14, 60, 97*

  trial and *209*

recompense *248*

records *13*

  parish registers *55*

red-handed capture *171, 354*

Reformation *8, 38, 108, 276, 465, 479, 617, 647*

religion *8, 276*

  religious strife *123*

  ungodly customs *55*

remand *212*

Renaissance *8*

repentance *409*

reprieve *385, 514, 518*

  temporary reprieve *515*

reputation *197*

resentment *45*

revenge *251, 276, 467*

reward *250*

Rice, Robert *542*

Richard I *139*

Richard III *19, 32, 212, 521*

riding at a horse's tail *58*

riot *46*

robbery *208, 231, 296, 417, 677–679*

  "gentlemen robbers" *678*

  highway robbery *174, 256, 476, 657*

Rochester *501*

Rochford, Lord *332*

rogues *40, 43, 63, 71*

  "incorrigible rogues"

galleys and *546*

wandering rogues *65*

Roman law *28*

Roose, Richard *407*

rootlessness *43*

royal. See also *pardon: royal pardons*

royal courts *24, 31*

royal favour *418*

Ruislip *207*

rule of law *30–32*

Rutland *286*

S

Sabbath *55, 327*

Salisbury *207, 259*

sanctuary *26, 113, 139, 188, 432–441, 565*

breaking sanctuary *436*

chartered sanctuaries *442*

treason, etc. and *436*

violation *435*

scaffold *408*

scolds *300, 318*

Scotland *309*

breaking on the wheel *404*

"**searchers**" *253*

sedition *46, 435*

seditious libel *201*

seizure *250, 413*

self-defence *520, 536, 549, 555–557*

serjeants *246*

serjeants-at-law *259*

Serjeants' Inn *271*

servants *662*

service *64*

servicemen *39*

Sevenoaks *37*

Seville *579, 582*

sexual offences *635*. See also *rape;*
ravishment

shackles *430*

Shakespeare, William *80, 95, 129, 137,*
181, 600, 658

sheriff *274*

high sheriff *357*

sheriff's tourn *101, 314*

Short, Thomasine *299*

silence *350*

smuggling *113*

sodomy *11, 644–647*

sorcery *505*

Southampton *92*

Southwark *14*

Spain *397*

Spencer, Gabriel *563*

spiritual lapses *313*

spite *251*

stabbing *590*

Statute of Stabbing *552*

Staffordshire *665*

Star Chamber *56, 114, 142, 202, 258, 334,*
374, 382, 660, 681

jury misconduct *386*

starvation *426*

in sanctuary *440*

status *65, 109, 214, 331, 358, 539, 553, 595*

statutes *19*

Statute of Additions *343*

Statute of Proclamations *32*

Stephen, James Fitzjames *333*

stewards *316*

"stews" *635*

stocks *63, 71, 185, 323, 422, 612*

Stourton, Lord Charles *350, 541*

strangulation *409, 591, 628*

Stratford-upon-Avon *137*

stress *573*

suicide *161, 166, 351, 417*

 "self-murder" *561*

summary justice *325*

sureties *98*

 for bail *210*

 surety for good behaviour *243*

surgeons *163*

Surrey *14, 43, 54*

surveillance *55–58, 95*

suspects *139–222*

 examination of *186, 200*

Sussex *106*

swearing *12, 422*

Sweden *575*

Switzerland *396, 645*

T

taking wood *320*

talesmen *360*

tearing with pincers *404*

technicalities *343, 393*

"tennis" *291*

testimony *199*

theft *231, 322, 466, 657*

 animals *662*

 career thief *659*

 horses *663*

 of animals *666–669*

 "petty theft" *24*

poultry theft *671*

"throttling" *166*

thumbscrews *228*

Tooke, John *123*

torture *218*

 torture warrants *687*

Tower of London *151, 252, 332*

 as a prison *423*

 burglary at *308*

transients *39, 53, 88, 216*

treason *46, 290, 312*

 Duke of Buckingham *332*

 Great Treason Act of 1351 *12*

 high treason *12*

 petty treason *154, 585*

 punishment for *404*

 Statute of Treason *585*

trespass *12, 469*

trial *331*

 committal for trial *100, 194*

  test for *208*

 political trials *387*

 trial by jury *356*

 trial by peers *350*

 trial on indictment *239, 331*

Tudor era *8*

tumbrel *324*

"turning-off" *409*

Tyburn *401, 410*

 "Tyburn T" *482*

typhus *277, 426*

tyranny *30*

tythings *76*

U

Udall, John *201*

V

vagabonds *43, 62–64, 327*

Vagabonds Act *65, 420*

Vagabonds and Beggars Act *62*

vagrancy *39, 265, 327*

vengeance *251*

Venice *397*

verdict *378–380*

perverse verdict *387*

special verdict *395*

victims *195, 231, 242, 245, 467*

servants as *642*

violence *47, 320, 548–557, 677*

corrective violence *587*

domestic violence *329, 582*

upper-class violence *62*

W

wages *103, 624*

Wales *266*

Walsingham, Sir Francis *138*

wapentake *72*

Wapping *401*

Warbeck, Perkin *437*

Warwick *669*

watch *64, 91*

watchmen *70, 91*

"watchword" *94*

wealth *36, 215, 238, 532*

hiding wealth *419*

weapons *39, 581*

weights and measures *318, 326*

Westminster *102, 259*

Statute of Westminster *349*

Westminster Abbey

violation of sanctuary *435*

Westminster courts *394*

Westmorland *311*

West Riding *73, 77, 90, 285, 300, 421, 612*

whipping *24, 63, 64, 322, 423*

"Whipping Act" *420*

whipping post *421*

Whitechapel *631*

White Lion Prison *423, 426*

wickedness *50*

widows *627*

felon's widow *351*

Wiltshire *106, 141*

Winchester *55, 84, 136, 214, 226, 373*

borough sessions *289*

Statute of Winchester *91, 174*

hue and cry *177*

Wiseman, Jane *352*

witchcraft *9, 28, 200, 299, 618*

malefic witchcraft *633*

murder using *264, 300, 514*

Warboys witches *369*

Witchcraft Act *393, 525*

witness

competence *371*

defence witness *369*

expert witness *164*

eyewitness *164*

false witness *366*

infant witness *371*

Woking *74, 102*

Wolsey, Cardinal Thomas *57, 60, 111, 387, 399, 684*

women *9, 22, 207, 236, 324, 402, 460, 507–518, 577, 633*

Worcestershire *93*

writ of error *393*

Y

yearbooks *19*

Yorkshire *73, 114, 130, 234, 248, 261, 285*

  leet courts *321*

rape in *637*

violence in *584*

York *350*

Z

zeal *206*

zoophilia *652*

More from Gregory Durston's *Crime History Series*

  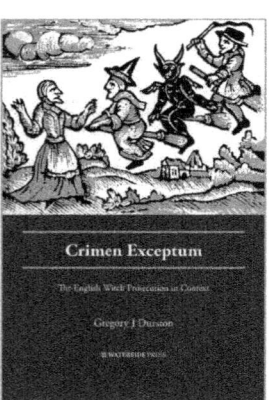

Whores and Highwaymen: Crime and Justice in the Eighteenth-Century Metropolis

Fields, Fens and Felonies: Crime and Justice in Eighteenth-Century East Anglia

Crimen Exceptum: The English Witch Prosecution in Context

For details see

www.WatersidePress.co.uk